THE
HISTORY OF CHINA.

[*Frontispiece, Vol. II.*

Sir Halliday Macartney, K.C.M.G.

history and give their statistics with the view of impressing the outside world. It is much more probable that the idea of such an audience never presents itself to their mind. Although the natural character of the people is not marked by truthfulness, the pride of the literary official class makes accuracy, or at least the attempt to be accurate, a cardinal virtue in dealing with the archives of the State. The execution of Hokwan was the penalty exacted from the most prominent citizen of the realm for indulging in systematic peculation, in which he was imitated with alacrity by his subordinates; and there is little doubt that this strong step was needed to check, if only for a time, one of the worst tendencies in the civil organization of the Chinese Empire.

Had Kiaking devoted this large amount of money to the public service, and resolutely striven to supply with it the exigencies of government, he might have left a name honoured in the annals of his country. He appears, however, to have squandered the treasure seized from Hokwan on personal amusement, and, relieved by the death of his father from an irksome restraint, he hastened to indulge in all kinds of excesses. The vast sum he had acquired by Hokwan's exposure was soon dissipated, without benefiting the State, or greatly contributing to the happiness of the man. At the same time, the moral declamations of his Government were not affected by his own conduct, and the very same year (1800) that beheld the commencement of extravagant display at Pekin was marked by the first edict passed on the subject of foreign opium. This important historical document was issued by the Hoppo, or Farmer of the Customs, at Canton, the one port open to foreign trade. The loftiness of its moral tone, in striking contrast with the conduct of the Emperor and his courtiers, only partially conceals the fact that the antipathy of the Chinese officials was directed against foreign trade as a whole, and not against the opium traffic as a part. Moreover, it must be remembered that whereas the Hoppo himself and the majority of the Canton mandarins were favourable to intercourse with the foreigner for personal reasons, and so long as they derived a pecuniary advantage from it, the Censors at the capital were consistently opposed jarring elements; and Kiaking, without his capacity, could not expect to escape the troubles that had beset his father. What wonder, then, that the accession of the new sovereign was followed by outbreaks of disturbance and sedition; although we must refuse to attribute them to any process of natural decay in the Empire, but rather incline to the supposition that they had no distinct meaning, or at the most that they were tentative schemes to test the real power of the executive? The objects at which these disturbers of the general peace aimed were as diverse as the motives of their conduct; and the following incident, which was the originating cause of much of Kiaking's misfortune, will serve to show that the apprehension of personal loss and indignity was not the least important factor in introducing the distractions of civil strife within the borders of his dominions.

Among the ministers of Keen Lung's later years, none had enjoyed the same pre-eminence as Hokwan, or Ho Chung Tong. The favour of his master secured for him a position of such importance that he was not merely the dispenser of his bounty and the director of his political affairs, but he also held the key of his exchequer. The esteem of this Emperor was so great that his confidence in his minister knew no bounds; while the age of the monarch prevented the close supervision of Hokwan's doings that might have been beneficial in his own interests. So long as Keen Lung lived Hokwan was above suspicion and secure against the animadversions of his enemies. But when that monarch died in the last year of the eighteenth century, Hokwan fell upon evil days, and had to bear without support the attack of his numerous enemies. He succumbed to the onset made upon him; but his fall has been too lightly attributed to the greed of Kiaking. If the statement is true that he had amassed eighty millions of taels or twenty-five millions sterling, there scarcely needed clearer testimony of his guilt; and Kiaking, in signing the order for his execution, did nothing more than his duty for so signal a breach of trust. It is true that the Emperor, sorely pressed for money, benefited by this prize; but there seems no reason to question the substantial truth of the official account. There is too general a fancy that the Chinese write their that he has the finest country within an Imperial ring-fence in the world."

The transfer of sovereign power from the hands of one ruler to those of another is always a matter of moment to the tranquillity of the realm as well as to the sentiment of the people. Its importance is immeasurably enhanced when the reign has been one of the exceptional length of the Emperor Keen Lung's; and men who had grown up accustomed to the ways of a staid and virtuous court feared lest his successor might depart from the search of wisdom and pursue that of folly. It is impossible to say how far the new Emperor had shown tastes or habits to give weight to the apprehension, but it does appear as if Keen Lung's favourable opinion of his chosen heir was not shared by some of his most trusted advisers. The prospect of a change in the practices of the court, and in the mode of administration, awakened some mistrust throughout the country, while it excited open dread at the capital. Even under the iron rule of Keen Lung the ambition of individuals, the aggressiveness of neighbours, and the disaffection of subject peoples had not been altogether repressed, and each in its turn had proved a source of trouble and anxiety. The appearance of a new and untried man in the place of power seemed to many to furnish the opportunity of renewing enterprises that had failed under different auspices. The mutable decrees of Fortune might well be expected to show some sign of wavering after a complete cycle of consistent favour.

To these causes, rather than to any gross incapacity on the part of the new Emperor, or to the progress of decay in the system, must be attributed the various disturbances which broke out among the people shortly after Keen Lung's death, and which were aggravated by the dissensions within the reigning house itself. None of these attained any large dimensions or threatened very serious danger, but in China the incentives to insurrection inevitable in any vast country are indefinitely increased by the difficulty of moving troops at any distance from the postal roads and water routes, as well as by the little value placed upon human life. The most prosperous and glorious reigns have not been free from these

THE HISTORY OF CHINA.

CHAPTER I.

THE REIGN OF KIAKING.

WHEN the aged Keen Lung passed from the hall of audience into the inner chamber of the palace, there were no symptoms that the power of the executive was on the wane, or that his successor would fail to maintain intact the legacy of Manchu authority which he had inherited from three vigorous predecessors. So far as external appearances went, China at the commencement of the present century was at the very height of her prosperity and renown. Never before had her Empire been recognized over a wider surface or by a greater number of subjects; and at no previous period had her Exchequer been so well replenished, or her commerce in a more flourishing condition. The dangers of national prejudice and hostility, which had long threatened to hurl the Tartar dynasty from its seat, were obliterated, or at least thrust out of sight; and to the most critical examination the Celestial Empire presented the appearance of complete unanimity between the ruler and the ruled. Never before, and certainly never since, did the Chinese appear a greater and more powerful people in the eyes of the European traveller than they did when the present century, big with the destiny of mighty things, began to dawn. As Mr. Henry Ellis, one of the commissioners sent under Lord Amherst to China in the year 1816, wrote: "However absurd the pretensions of the Emperor of China may be to universal supremacy, it is impossible to travel through his dominions without feeling

CONTENTS OF VOL. II.

CHAPTER		PAGE
I.	THE REIGN OF KIAKING	1
II.	THE EMPEROR TAOUKWANG	37
III.	INTERNAL DISSENSIONS	49
IV.	THE GROWTH OF FOREIGN INTERCOURSE	64
V.	THE BEGINNING OF FOREIGN COMPLICATIONS	78
VI.	THE FIRST FOREIGN WAR	90
VII.	THE TREATY OF NANKIN	134
VIII.	THE LAST YEARS OF TAOUKWANG'S REIGN	161
IX.	THE EARLY YEARS OF HIENFUNG'S REIGN	199
X.	THE BEGINNING OF THE TAEPING REBELLION	211
XI.	COMPLICATIONS WITH ENGLAND	247
XII.	THE SECOND ENGLISH WAR	276
XIII.	THE PEKIN CAMPAIGN	311
XIV.	THE PROGRESS OF THE TAEPING REBELLION	353
XV.	CHINESE GORDON'S CAMPAIGNS	383
XVI.	THE DEATH OF HIENFUNG AND THE ACCESSION OF TUNGCHE	415
XVII.	THE TWO MAHOMEDAN REBELLIONS	431
XVIII.	THE REIGN OF TUNGCHE	451
XIX.	THE REGENCY	468
XX.	THE WAR BETWEEN FRANCE AND CHINA	492
XXI.	THE REIGN OF KWANGSU	504
XXII.	THE WAR WITH JAPAN	515
XXIII.	THE CONSEQUENCES OF DEFEAT	530
XXIV.	THE PARTING OF THE WAYS	540
	CHRONOLOGICAL TABLE	549
	APPENDIX (Treaties of Nankin, Tientsin, St. Petersburg, Shimonoseki, Chefoo Convention, etc.)	555
	INDEX OF SUBJECTS	611

First Published 1898
Reprinted 1972

Library of Congress Cataloging in Publication Data

Boulger, Demetrius Charles de Kavanagh, 1853-1928.
　　The history of China.

　　(BCL/select bibliographies index reprint series)
　　Reprint of the 1898 ed.
　　1. China--History.　I. Title.
DS735.B77　1972　　　　951　　　　77-39406
ISBN 0-8369-9902-9

PRINTED IN THE UNITED STATES OF AMERICA
BY
NEW WORLD BOOK MANUFACTURING CO., INC.
HALLANDALE, FLORIDA 33009

THE
HISTORY OF CHINA.

BY

DEMETRIUS CHARLES BOULGER

NEW AND REVISED EDITION, WITH PORTRAITS
AND MAPS.

IN TWO VOLUMES.

VOL. II.

BOOKS FOR LIBRARIES PRESS
FREEPORT, NEW YORK

to it as a bad thing in itself, and as likely to bring many evils in its train upon the Middle Kingdom. The edict in question, although signed in the name of the Hoppo, was really drawn up by the pens, and issued by the express command, of the Board of Censors at Pekin.

Circumstances intervened, moreover, very shortly after the publication of this edict to give weight to the remonstrances of those who declared that it was intolerable that the people of the Celestial Empire should be compelled, against the inclination of their leaders, to hold communication with strangers who appeared, in the eyes of a true follower of Confucius, as little better than barbarians. The laws of war are arbitrary, and even on the China coast, during the intensity of the great European contest with France, each combatant strove to snatch an advantage from the other. The manner in which the Portuguese had come into occupation of Macao has been previously explained; but when the nineteenth century commenced the descendants of Da Gama had lost their national enterprise, and were in very deed as in name no more there than the tenants of the Chinese. Yet the position of Macao was so advantageous that it presented a standing temptation to all interested in the commerce of the Chinese seas to wrest it from the feeble hands of those who held it. Immunity from danger, so far as the Chinese were concerned, seemed to be certain from the weakness and inefficiency of their fleet; but it was different with those other Europeans who felt the inducement and possessed the power. While the French conceived the undertaking, the English had executed it; and, as it had proved in other parts of Asia between these two rival peoples, the victory was to the swift as well as to the strong. During the year 1802 Macao was occupied by an English force and squadron; and it was only evacuated as one of the minor details of the Treaty of Amiens. Macao was thus treated as if it were a European possession, and probably not the least thought was given to the breach its occupation by an armed force involved of the sovereign rights of China. The brief time that the English squadron remained there in 1802 prevented an angry discussion; but when the operation was repeated six years later, the wrath of the Chinese, as will be seen, could no longer be controlled.

The pretensions of the Chinese are only to be supported by a mighty and efficient power. Without that they must invite many difficulties, and bring down upon the country a multitude of calamities. It was only in the natural course of things that when first a sense of weakness was felt, the arrogance of the Emperor should become more apparent. To Kiaking the presence of Europeans on his coasts in increasing numbers appeared in the light of a danger, in consequence of the ill-concealed disaffection among large sections of his own subjects. Had his Government felt strong in its own resources, it could have afforded to regard the foreign traders at Canton with unaffected indifference; but the Tartars, goaded into irritation by their own fears at the aversion of the Chinese, resorted to a policy of petty provocation in their dealings with the races of Europe. The course they adopted was one well-defined and clearly arranged, for the express purpose of heightening the glory of the rulers of China, and of hindering all relations with the "outer barbarians." In so far as it succeeded it served the purpose for which it was framed, and obtained that sort of popular approval which is never refused to measures that have the tendency to show that a nation is the superior of any other. But when it proved impossible, it became the cause of much national misery and misfortune.

The antipathy to the inhabitants of a strange and unknown world, natural to the human mind, was in China fomented for its own purposes by all the means at the disposal of the ruling caste. The ill-will of Kiaking increased with his personal embarrassments. It was bad enough in his eyes that the peoples of the West should be permitted to plant their feet at any time within the borders of the Empire, but it was intolerable that they should be witnesses of the disunion spreading within the realm, and of the scanty respect paid to even the person of the sovereign. For the popular discontent had reached such a pass that Kiaking could no longer consider himself safe in his own capital. In 1803, when his illustrious father had not been dead more than four years, the Emperor was attacked in open day, while being carried in his chair of state through the streets of Pekin. The attack was evidently well-planned, and the plotters almost succeeded in attaining their object. Kiaking stood in imminent danger of murder, when the striking devotion of a few of his eunuch attendants foiled his assailants, and saved his life at the price of their own. This outrage produced a great sensation, and the public mind was much affected by so flagrant an insult upon the person of the chosen Son of Heaven. Chinese Emperors, indeed, had before that fallen victims to the assassin; but if so, it had been in the interior of their palaces, and not in the open way of the people. The national sense of decorum then incurred a grave shock.

The discovery was soon made that this attempted assassination formed part of an extensive plot with ramifications among the Imperial family itself. A series of inquisitorial investigations took place, which had as their outcome the disgrace and punishment of many of the Emperor's relatives; but even this summary proceeding failed to restore confidence to the heart of Kiaking. He never allowed himself to forget the narrow escape he had had; and while he often expressed surprise at their turpitude, he never afterwards permitted his kinsmen to pass out of the range of his suspicion.

The peculiar feature of this conspiracy was its originating, perhaps, and certainly its extensively developing, under the auspices of one of those secret societies, which, in the form of fraternal confederacies and associations, have always been a feature in Chinese life, but which have acquired during the present century an importance they could never previously claim, both in China itself, and among Chinese colonies abroad. Of these the first to attract notoriety, and to be marked out for disapproval by the Government, was the society known as the sect of the White Water-lily, or the Pe-lëen-keaou. Whether because it was as a matter of fact incriminated in the plot of 1803, or whether, and more probably, the Government availed itself of that event as an excuse to denounce and punish the members of a society which it both disapproved of and feared, the fact is certain that the members of the Water-lily association were accused of holding unorthodox opinions, and of meditating treasonable practices. The province of Shantung was the immediate scene of their appearance and outbreak; but although the Water-lilies threatened to be dangerous, they very soon lost their significance, and disappeared in the more formidable and extensive confederacy known as the Society of Celestial Reason, which at a still later period was merged into that of the Triads.

Although the designations were frequently changed, and sometimes with the express object of misleading the authorities no name was taken or at least publicly revealed, there seems little doubt that the Water-lily * sect was the originating society, and that all the subsequent orders sprang from its members. The escape of the Emperor, and the summary punishment of those leaders of the conspiracy who were captured, did not lead to the collapse of the Water-lily band, and, although proscribed by name, their operations continued, and their daring was remarkable. We have seen the financial embarrassments of Kiaking, and that the escheated property of Hokwan served but to minister to his personal pleasure, and not to the alleviation of the difficulties of government. The dissatisfaction of the seditiously inclined grew rapidly, and before the Emperor's advisers had realized the extent of the discontent, many of the inhabitants of Shantung, and of three other provinces, had joined the society of the Water-lily, and had formed themselves into a common band, no longer for the attainment of secret ends, but from open hostility to the ruling powers. In China the machinery resorted to for the redress of public grievances may assume a character of secrecy; but if the objects are based on palpable facts, such as popular suffering, the spirit of insubordination very speedily reveals itself. So it was in the case of the

* The name Water-lily was chosen on account of the popularity of that plant. M. Huc says, "The poets have celebrated it in their verses, on account of the beauty of its flowers; the doctors of reason have placed it among the ingredients for the elixir of immortality; and the economists have extolled it for its utility."—" Chinese Empire," vol. ii. pp. 309-10.

Peleen brotherhood, which, far from being crushed by Imperial edicts, and by the failure in the streets of Pekin, declared itself openly inimical to the constituted authorities, and did its best to meet force by force.

The details of this strife, if what probably partook more of the character of rioting than of open warfare can be designated by that name, elude the most careful inquiry; but Kiaking took a later occasion to inform us that he ordered his generals to proceed against the rebels, and that he was employed for eight years in unceasing operations for their chastisement. But although the particulars have not been preserved, there is no doubt that the realm was distracted by the seditious movement of the Water-lily sect, until it gave place to the more formidable association known as the Theen Te. Not, however, for the suffering of his people, nor for the rude blows inflicted on the reputation of his Government, would Kiaking abandon the life of indulgence passed in his residence at Pekin.

Even the recurrence of the personal danger from which he had had the good fortune to once escape, failed to arouse him from the torpor, or the indifference to external things, which from force of habit had become part of his nature. In the year 1813 the popular discontent had again reached so great a pass that the secret societies found it possible to organize a fresh attempt on the person of the ruler, more audacious in its scope, and more nearly successful in its object, than that which preceded it. At Pekin the Imperial residence forms almost a city to itself, and entrance to it is only permitted to privileged persons. The vigilance of the garrison insures the safety of the Emperor, for whose protection no precaution has been overlooked. The greater the discord in the country, the wider the hostility of the people, all the closer are drawn the guards round the Emperor's residence, and the more rigorously are the regulations enforced. A sense of temporary security is purchased at the cost of not merely forfeiting popular esteem, but also of losing that touch with the wants of a people which it is most necessary should be kept up between the ruler and those he rules. Such was the state of things, we can feel very sure, during the reign of Kiaking, when suspected persons were rigorously excluded from the Palace and inner fortress of the capital, and with them all heed for national necessities and expectations.

Kiaking was to learn that such protection is delusive, even in its main purpose, and that difficulties are not overcome by a refusal to recognize them. In the year 1813, when some satisfactory progress had been made towards the pacification of Shantung, the Chinese world was astonished and startled by the announcement that a band of conspirators had made a daring attack on the Palace itself, and that they had almost succeeded in their attempt to kill the Son of Heaven. A body of rebels, some two hundred in number, succeeded in making their way into the inner city, by one of the gates according to some, by climbing over the wall according to others; and, taking the guards by surprise, made straight for the presence of the Emperor. Some of them fell, or were engaged in a struggle with such of the soldiers and officials as possessed the presence of mind or the courage to bar their way; but several overcame or evaded all opposition, and reached Kiaking's chamber. It is certain that, but for the appearance and promptitude of Prince Meenning, Kiaking's days were then numbered. Meenning, fortunately for him, showed a courage and decision in action that were not expected from one of so peaceful and retiring a disposition. Snatching up a gun, he shot two of the intruders, while a nephew of the Emperor despatched a third. Kiaking was thus for a second time saved from the steel of his own subjects; but his narrow escape seems to have had the effect of heightening the worst features in his character. To Meenning his gratitude, however, was unbounded; and that prince, afterwards the Emperor Taoukwang, was at once proclaimed heir-apparent with every attendant ceremony of solemnity.

After these manifestations of vigour and resolution, the observer may feel more disposed to believe that the secret societies of China, which caused even the Emperor to feel insecure in his palace, were a formidable and well-organized association of either well-meaning or desperate men. The conditions inseparable from either a despotic sway, or a foreign domination, compel those who aspire to effect the cure or removal of public evils to have recourse to secrecy as some substitute for strength. In Europe we have some instances of this alternative having been both successfully and honourably employed. The mind will recur to the Vehmgericht and the Vespers of Palermo, to days when to belong to secret associations meant devotion to patriotic obligations, and not an inclination to criminal pursuits. China had nothing to learn from Europe, either as to the objects to be attained in this way, or as to how men are to be bound to one another by solemn oaths for the attainment of illegal ends, although they may be perfectly justifiable on some other ground.

In China, where the ordinary affairs of life are always wrapped up in some high moral sentiment, or in some axiom of accepted wisdom enunciated by one of the early sages, the objects of a political association borrow their form from this national peculiarity. Men are brought together, not with the ostensible object of ousting the Manchu, or of reforming society, but with that of "uniting heaven and earth," of propagating "celestial reason," or of spreading the worship of "the queen of heaven, the mother and nurse of all things." In China the precaution has even been taken of further masking the proposed scope of its operations by the assumption of a title of not merely inappropriate meaning, but occasionally of absolutely no meaning at all. By this device not only has the suspicion of the executive been often allayed, but the curiosity—that powerful agent and frequently very useful ally—of the public has been enlisted in behalf of its objects, without knowing whither they tended.

The first principle of a secret association is equality. Each assumes the same risk, and fidelity to the common bond can only be ensured by all being pledged to mutual support in both danger and necessity. Such conditions formed the basis of membership in those political clubs which became so numerous during the reign of Kiaking. In a couplet, wherein was supposed to be expressed the guiding maxim of one of the most important of these societies, it was said that "the blessing and the woe should be reciprocally borne and shared." In the machinery of government, drawn up for the guidance of its members, the ingenuity of the people revealed itself, and the Nihilistic associations of Russia could not find much to improve upon in the regulations of these Chinese confederacies which, after thirty years of silent intrigue, succeeded in plunging the Empire into a state of insurrection from the effects of which it is only now recovering. A similar state of things may well lead to a similar result.

The principle of Freemasonry was adopted, and all the members were called Brothers. The chosen leaders were styled in addition Elders, but this superior title was awarded to a very small number, and those only of the most trusted and experienced. Bound together by laws of which the full nature has never been revealed or discovered, treachery, or want of the necessary zeal in carrying out the behests of the order, was punished by death, inflicted by a chosen delegate, or more than one, as representative of the injured brotherhood. Various ceremonies of as impressive a character as the human mind can conceive had been assigned to mark the entrance of a new member. The night-time was selected as the appropriate hour for so grave an undertaking, and the members assembled from far and near to take part in an office which enhanced their individual importance while it added to their collective strength. When thirty-six oaths had been sworn to advance the cause and to stand by his colleagues to the last extremity, and when a present of money had been made to show that the novice placed his worldly goods at the service of the common fund, the most important part of the ceremony was next performed. This was called "crossing the bridge." The novice stood underneath two drawn swords held over his head by two members, while the Elder Brother heard him affirm his undeviating fidelity to the cause; and when this was finished the new member cut off the head of a cock with the exclamation, "Thus may I perish if the secret I divulge!" To meetings such as these, held in retired woods, lonely houses, or in the deserted burial-places of the ancient kings, did Kiaking's enemies flock, and they returned from them to their daily

ANNAM.   13

avocations with thoughts in their minds and pledges on their consciences that could not but bode ill for the tranquillity of the realm. By signs known only to themselves, and by pass-words, these sworn brothers could recognize their members in the crowded streets, and could communicate with each other without exciting suspicion as to their being conspirators at heart, with a common object in view.

In its endeavour to cope with this formidable and widespread organization under different names, Kiaking's Government found itself placed at a serious disadvantage. Without an exact knowledge of the intentions or resources of its secret enemies, it failed to grapple with them; and, as its sole remedy, could only decree that proof of membership carried the penalty of death.

Although all these disturbing elements, which seemed to require a monopoly of the ruler's attention, were at work, yet Kiaking did not abate any of his pretensions as a great ruler, and, indeed, in some ways he carried his head higher and behaved more arrogantly than any of his predecessors. In 1803 a long-standing insurrection in Annam threatened to alter the condition of affairs in that State, and to derange, in consequence, its dependence on Pekin. An ambitious minister defied his master, and raised a powerful faction against him. He defeated the ruler's troops in several encounters, and when he drew up his forces outside Hué, the capital, success seemed within his grasp. But the fortunate arrival of a Chinese expedition, although the French claim the greater credit from the presence of a few of their officers, baffled his designs and saved the dynasty. A victory gained outside Hue decided the pretensions of the rebel, who fell on the field; and, while it left Annam under the tranquil control of its sovereign, it also gave fresh significance to the claims of China over another of its remoter feudatories. Tranquillity was little more than restored in this southern kingdom, when a benefit of a different if undoubted kind was conferred on the Chinese themselves by the introduction into Canton of the practice of vaccination. To an Englishman, Dr. Pearson, belongs the credit of this real service to suffering humanity; and it only remains to be said that the Chinese betook themselves so readily to the practice that they soon spread it far and wide.

Kiaking had shown himself ill-disposed towards foreigners from the first days of his reign. Père Amiot, to whose literary efforts we owe so deep a debt of gratitude, and who rendered good service to the Chinese themselves in his official position at Pekin, was expelled, after a residence of thirty years, from the country; and the Portuguese Padre Serra owed rather to his good fortune than to any other circumstance the permission to remain at the capital. The representatives of the Church of Rome had, it is true, sunk by this time into utter insignificance, and the question of China's relations with the foreign Powers had entered upon the much larger phase of her dealings with the great conquering and commercial races of Europe. The scene of interest had also been shifted from the capital to the great city of Canton, the one port where trade was allowed with the outer races, if only on onerous conditions and subject to frequent interruptions. Hither, however, came French and American traders in their ships as well as those of England, with the view of tapping the wealth of the Celestial Empire; and the keen competition of commerce was further embittered by the progress of the great wars in Europe, which were reflected in their course on the shores of China and in the Indian seas.

It must not be supposed, although the totals appear small in comparison with the dimensions they have subsequently reached, that the China trade was considered a matter of small importance by the Directors of the East India Company, whose charter conferred on them the monopoly of the trade with that country as well as with the Indies. It was always deemed a matter of the very highest importance, on which not merely the future development, but the annual dividend of the greatest trading and administering company of all time depended. The profit of the China trade enabled Warren Hastings and the Marquis Wellesley to carry out their schemes of empire at the same time that they satisfied the wants and expectations of the Directors in Leadenhall Street. Each year was consequently marked by a steady increase in the quantity of goods sent from Calcutta and

Bombay; and as these vessels sailed during many years both unarmed and without a convoy, it is clear that the Company preserved in its dealings with the Celestials its natural character of a purely commercial venture. In this particular the old motive, which in Madras had turned our merchants into soldiers, jealousy and dread of France at last compelled the arming of these vessels, which then formed in turn the nucleus of the old Indian marine.

The advantages drawn from the trade being so great, and the available force for coercing the Chinese so insignificant, it followed as a matter of course that the English had to put up with many exactions, and to purchase the right to trade by complying with the whims of the local authorities, often couched in a dictatorial and arrogant spirit. The Emperor, whether it was Keen Lung or any of his successors, did not, in plain truth, want them to come at all. They made their way in as a thief in the dark by the back door of the Empire; and it was only the corruptness of the mandarins that supplied them with the opportunity of evading the strict injunctions of the central executive. The traffic was as profitable to these officials as to the Europeans, and they had, consequently, equal reasons for its maintenance. They grew rich upon it, and to be appointed hoppo, or farmer of the customs, was considered the way to certain fortune. Latterly it was reserved as a privilege for a member of the Imperial family. The office had always to be purchased at a high price, and the holder could only retire on his gains by making the Government a present, voluntary or enforced, of the better half of his fortune. Despite the heavy taxes and dues, and the objectionable contributions to the Consoo Fund, the English came every year in increasing numbers, and with their ships carrying larger cargoes. The Chinese remained masters of the situation, and the mere threat of suspending the trade sufficed to bring the stoutest captains and the most independent merchants to their knees.

The Chinese might have been able to have continued relations on this footing for a very much longer period than they did but for two circumstances, of which one only was within their control. They were not content with imposing taxes and custom dues; they claimed authority over the persons of foreigners, and the right to try those who transgressed their laws as interpreted by themselves. The principle, for the application of which the Chinese showed themselves singularly unanimous, is one that has often been discussed in connection with the trial of Christians by an Eastern race and code both in Europe and in Asia. But whatever may be advanced theoretically against it, the sentiment of Europeans is strongly against the admission of any such right; and after many warm debates and some hostile encounters the grand privilege of ex-territoriality has been conceded by China, imitating in this the example of Turkey and the other Mahomedan States of the West. But in the days of which we are speaking no such right had been conceded. The Chinese authority was supposed to be supreme in the Bocca Tigris; and if foreigners chose to come there, it was contended that it should be on the condition of subordination to the laws of China. Unfortunately, as the result must make us think, events showed that this was to be no empty boast, and that the Chinese really required its exact fulfilment.

As early as 1784, when the Emperor Keen Lung was at the height of his fame, an accident occurred on the crowded river. A shot from one of the trading vessels, whilst firing a salute, happened to strike and kill a Chinese sailor. The affair was really accidental, but the Chinese mandarins at once demanded the surrender of the culprit. A lengthy and heated discussion ensued; but the Chinese were persistent, and would entertain no compromise short of the actual surrender of the man. The old threat of suspending the trade was renewed, and it proved only too successful. The sailor was given up, and was forthwith strangled. Some promise seems to have been required that he would not be killed; but, of course, there was no reason to suppose, under the circumstances, that it would be kept. The Chinese were thus allowed to assert in a very effective way their sovereign rights; and, of course, such a strong proceeding as this could not fail to produce a considerable effect.

But in one sense the Chinese had over-reached themselves. The punishment of this poor gunner was so monstrously unjust, and so quite disproportionate with his unwitting offence, that it at once put an end to all idea of making a similar surrender in the future, so far, at least, as British subjects were concerned. The maintenance of a profitable trade can be purchased at too dear a price, if the return has to consist in part of national dishonour. Several cases of a like character occurred, but none of the offenders were surrendered. Sailors would show that they were free from the forbearing spirit of their officers and Government, and, on provocation, resort to a display of national vigour. In the result these outbreaks had sometimes a termination fatal for the Chinese of Canton and Whampoa. And when these brawlers were punished, it was by English law and in just proportion to the nature of their offence.

The second circumstance which threatened to complicate the question, and which did actually disturb the arrangements existing between the Hong merchants and their European visitors, was the more frequent appearance of English men-of-war in Chinese waters as the necessary consequence of the contest with France. These came not merely in the character of guards for Indian commerce, but also on a roving mission to clear the seas of the tri-colour. Wherever a French vessel appeared in those days it was not long before an English frigate followed, and the Chinese found it impossible to distinguish between these perfectly independent representatives of the same people and kingdom. The captains of these vessels thought more of enhancing the dignity of their sovereign than of the worldly interests of their fellow-countrymen; and the necessary consequence was an unceasing conflict between them and the Chinese mandarins, who were only kept in any sort of good humour by the profitable business of supplying them with provisions at extortionate charges.

The question was still further complicated by the condition of things in the Canton river and on the coast of the Kwantung province. The Chinese have never been distinguished for naval prowess as a nation, but at this period they had no navy at all worthy of the name. But the natural disposition of the people of the South prompted them to a life of adventure on the sea, and it found relief in the formation of piratical bands, with their head-quarters among the numerous islands at the mouth of the Pearl River. These bands had to a certain extent combined, and formed at the beginning of the century a powerful confederacy, which was absolutely independent of control. They mustered a force of several hundred junks, and levied black-mail with impunity on all Chinese boats and trading-vessels. The sphere of their operations was only confined by their sense of power; and when themselves in sufficient force, and their prey appeared sufficiently weak and tempting, they never hesitated to attack European merchantmen, although their discretion led them to choose those of the weaker powers, such as Spain and Portugal.

The authority of the Ladrones, as these pirates were called, from the Portuguese word, extended along the whole of the coast, from Tonquin to Foochow, the important and prosperous seaport in the province of Fuhkien. There was good reason to believe that they were in active communication, if not in direct alliance, with the leaders of the secret societies, and their chief, Apotsye, seems to have considered himself more of a patriot than a pirate. These claims were not strengthened by the more intimate knowledge we obtained of their mode of life and arrangements through the experience of two Englishmen who fell into their hands. From their narratives it is clear that these corsairs were composed of the scum of the inhabitants of Canton, reinforced by many of the fishing and boating population of the coast. Their sole object was plunder, and one of their principal sources of wealth consisted in the ransoming of such prisoners as they thought worth their while to spare from the death which was the usual fate of those who refused to join their ranks. From the experience of Mr. Turner and other Europeans, they treated their prisoners harshly, but at the same time they themselves passed a miserable and half-starved existence. Nothing but the inefficiency and apathy of the Imperial officials enabled these pirates to achieve the success they did; and whether they were made participators in the booty, or were really afraid of these depredators, the fact was clear that they attempted nothing against them, and that the authority of the Emperor was completely ignored and set on one side.

The only rebuffs with which these pirates met were inflicted by the boats of English men-of-war. Their anxiety to make prizes sometimes led them to mistake these war-vessels for peaceful traders, when they were unpleasantly undeceived; but although these reverses caused them some loss of life, they were too few to check their depredations in the China seas. Their successes over every other opponent were so decisive that they were inspired with the greatest confidence, and declared that one of their junks was a match for four of the vessels occasionally fitted out against them by the mandarins. That this belief was not without foundation may be judged from the fact that when, by a great effort, a large fleet was despatched against them, under a mandarin of reputation from Pekin, they still gained a signal victory. Nor did a joint expedition of Chinese war-junks and six Portuguese vessels, sent in the same year (1809), fare any better. The Ladrones were left masters of the sea, and the stronger from being attacked by the vessels captured during these engagements.

Although poor in their resources, and without differing in their mode of life from the lower classes of Chinese, the Ladrones showed the possession of a capacity for organization in the strict regulations which alone rendered their confederacy possible or likely to endure. How much of this was due to the instinct of self-preservation, or to the capacity of their chief, will never be known. The latter has been described as "a man of dignified presence and manner, of sound discretion, temperate habits, and bold and successful in all his enterprises." One proof of his remarkable energy was furnished when, on engaging an English ship and discovering the size of the shot fired from it, he expressed surprise, but at the same time declared that it would not be long before he would use the same. What the Chinese authorities could not obtain by force they resolved to secure by other means. The enormity of the Ladrones' offence was brought home to them by their endeavouring to seize the four vessels bearing the tribute embassy from Siam, and the attempt would undoubtedly have succeeded but for the promptitude with which the Canton officials induced some English merchants to fit out one of their vessels to proceed against the marauders.

The cruise of the *Mercury* was remarkable in a small way, and recalls the naval adventures of an earlier era. The Ladrones were severely dealt with, the Siamese tribute was rescued from the robbers of the sea, and the credit of the Middle Kingdom was saved from a damaging admission of national weakness. The bribes of the Chinese then promoted discord in their ranks, and promises proved more effectual arguments than the swords of the Emperor's lieutenants. Internal dissension broke out. The chief of the Red division quarrelled with his comrade at the head of the Black, and, in a community addicted to violence, force was the only and simple remedy. The two divisions met in mortal combat. The waters of the Bogue were strewn with the wrecks of their war-junks, and the great power of the Ladrones, which had endured during the better part of ten years, was overthrown by their own acts. The Canton mandarins, cautious if not apathetic in attempting to crush a warlike association, were prompt in availing themselves of its disintegration to complete its overthrow. Two chiefs were received into the official service, and with them eight thousand of their followers were pardoned and returned to civil life. The junks were disarmed, the old rendezvous near Lantao was dominated by a Chinese fort, and there disappeared from the China coast a most formidable band of piratical rovers who, in the picturesque official language of a literary people, were designated "the foam of the sea."

The excitement raised in the Chinese mind by the military occupation in 1802 of Macao—the settlement which they had rented to the Portuguese—has been mentioned. It was allayed by the shortness of the stay of the English troops, but peremptory orders had been sent from Pekin to demand the instant withdrawal of the force. Six years later, the whole subject was again opened by the fresh occupation of Macao as a measure of protection against the French, and the correspondence assumed at once an angry tone. In the interval some communications had passed between the Governments of London and Pekin. A present had been sent to the minister Sung Tajin, one of the most enlightened men in the country, as a remembrance of his kindness to Lord Macartney's embassy, and a letter from Kiaking to George the Third had been duly received in England. The fate of Sung Tajin's present was not merely unfortunate; it proved disastrous for that minister himself. It was haughtily returned to Canton, with a notification that a minister of the Emperor dare not so much as see a present from a foreigner. There can be no doubt that in this the Chinese were perfectly in the right, and only pursuing the same course as was the better tradition in Europe. The letter of Kiaking also was couched in terms of the most lofty condescension, not wholly out of place on the part of a potentate who ignored the whole universe outside his sphere, and who asked no favour of any foreign prince or people.

The nature of the position of the Portuguese at Macao had been made plain by the events of 1802. Although in their possession, the Chinese had established the fact that the Portuguese were only their tenants, and that Macao was an integral part of the Chinese Empire. Yet, notwithstanding this undoubted fact, the authorities in India resolved to repeat the mistake by sending another expedition to Macao, at the same time that Goa was occupied by an English force in order to defend them against any attack on the part of the French. Ill-judged as the step was as a measure of general policy, it was still more unfortunate in the way that it was carried out. A squadron was duly sent, under the command of Admiral Drury, and a small force landed to garrison Macao. But the Chinese were furious at this fresh interference with their rights. They withheld all supplies, ordered the suspension of trade, and refused to hold any communication whatever with the commander. Unfortunately, Admiral Drury entertained the opinion that a display of force would suffice to bring the Chinese to reason, and, in the persuasion that there was "nothing in his instructions to prevent his going to war with the Emperor of China," he resolved to obtain by force an interview with the Viceroy of Kwantung With this end in view, after much useless discussion, he proceeded up the river to Canton, escorted by all the boats of the squadron. The Chinese had made every preparation in their power to resist this unwarrantable proceeding, and they had placed a line of junks across the river to bar further progress. On perceiving these signs of hostility, Admiral Drury sent a fresh request to the mandarin's yamen for an interview, with a threat that unless it was conceded within half an hour he would force his way into Canton. Whether the Chinese detected some infirmity of purpose in the language of the commander, or whether they were resolved to brave the worst, they did not deign to send a reply. The fated half-hour passed; but instead of Admiral Drury ordering his boats to attack, he adopted the safer course of retiring. A similarly ignominious method of proceeding was adopted on several later occasions; but, towards inducing the Chinese to alter their manners, neither Admiral Drury's threats nor his concessions availed anything. A pagoda was erected at Canton to celebrate the repulse of the English, and after a three months' unnecessary and inglorious occupation of Macao that port was evacuated, and Admiral Drury returned with his ships to India. The Chinese were satisfied with having carried their point, and thereupon allowed the reopening of the trade. Their national self-esteem and their confidence in their ruler rose immensely when they could feel that the Edict of their Emperor on this very subject had been realized to the letter by the course of events.

It must not be supposed that there was on this occasion, or, indeed, at any time, a disposition on the part of the Chinese or their Government to show favour to one European nation more than another, or to refuse to the English at Canton what was conceded to other people at different places. The policy of the Empire has always been consistent, and it was then the same at all points, to exclude foreign trade and to keep away from the Emperor's presence the pretensions of those rulers who claimed to rank on an equality with him.

REBUFF TO RUSSIA.

Had Kiaking possessed incorrupt officials, and shown himself something of the indomitable vigour of his predecessor, China might have remained to this day as forbidden a land to European inquisitiveness as some of her tributary States still are. But the self-seeking mandarins at Canton opened the door to the outer peoples, and although many rebuffs were experienced in their attempt to gain a footing in the country, the ultimate success of their project was ensured by the political weakness and disunion of China herself.

During the interval between the first and second occupations of Macao, the Russians despatched an embassy to Pekin: but it did not succeed in accomplishing its object. It left Russia in the year 1805, and it appears to have been arranged on a scale of unusual magnificence. Count Goloyken, one of the highest dignitaries of the Russian Court, was specially selected as ambassador, and a large number of costly presents were entrusted to him for the Chinese Emperor. After encountering weather of exceptional severity, he reached the vicinity of the Great Wall, where the objections of the Chinese officials took the place of the obstacles of Nature; and of the two they speedily proved themselves the more formidable. The delays for reference to Pekin soon resulted in a refusal to allow the embassy to pass within the Wall unless the Russian envoy pledged himself to perform the prostration ceremony. This Count Goloyken, encouraged by the indulgence shown to Lord Macartney, strenuously refused to do, whereupon he was curtly informed that it would be well for him to return as quickly as possible to his own country, for his journey had already been over-prolonged.

Disappointed at this ending of a mission that had been prepared with much care and at considerable outlay, the Russian Government turned an ear to the representations of their naval officer, Krusenstern, that it would be wise to open a trade with Canton like other European countries. The attempt was made with two ships, which found no difficulty in disposing of their cargoes; but the appearance of a new foreign people at Canton raised fresh apprehensions in the mind of the Pekin Government. An edict was at once issued, ordering that "all vessels belonging to any other nation than those which have been in the habit of visiting this port shall on no account whatever be permitted to trade, but merely suffered to remain in port until every circumstance is reported to us and our pleasure made known." The course of events under Kiaking's guidance was, therefore, equally unfavourable for all Europeans. But for the corruption at Canton we do not doubt that there would then have been an end of the intercourse, until, at least, the Chinese should have come to see of their own accord its advantage to themselves.

The triumph of the Chinese in the matter of the Macao occupation did not tend to promote a feeling of confidence among the English community at Canton. Yet, strange and almost contradictory as it may be, there was, after that event, which might have been expected to increase the arrogance of the Chinese, greater harmony than there had been before. So far as trade was concerned, a period of more than twenty years passed away without any grave disagreement arising between the European merchants and the agents of the Hoppo. But, on the other hand, the political difficulties and complications between the naval representatives of the English Government and the provincial mandarins continually increased. Several collisions actually occurred, and the captains of English men-of-war could only obtain by force the supplies and water they might urgently require. Under these circumstances, it was hoped that the despatch of an embassy to Pekin from the King would have a good effect, and that the demonstration that England was a great country, and not a mere trading company, might tend to secure some fresh privileges for her subjects and some greater consideration for the King's representatives. In coming to this decision, the Home Government was guided not merely by the precedent of Lord Macartney, but by the experience it had acquired in the cases of Persia and other Asiatic States, whose rulers considered it derogatory to treat with any of lower rank than the ambassador of a sovereign. But in China the reasoning should have been exactly the opposite. The Pekin Government would much rather have dealt with the East India Company's agents at Canton alone; them it could treat as mere traders. But it was very different when it had to deal with the spokesmen of another powerful and independent Empire. Their rights and prejudices were expected to be so far considered, that the strict and never-varying ceremonial of the Son of Heaven should be waived in favour of the claims of their ruler to rank on an equality with the sovereign of the Middle Kingdom. Such a pretension was both inconvenient for the present and dangerous for the future. Embassies from kingdoms of undoubted inferiority were welcome enough at Pekin, but those from States claiming a position of equality were quite beyond the comprehension of the Celestials, and, as such, to be deprecated, and if necessary prevented.

Great expectations were naturally formed by those who saw only their own interests, and thought nothing of the practice and dignity of China, as to the probable benefits that would accrue to England both politically and commercially from such a mission. The untoward fate of the present to Sung Tajin, the lofty tone assumed by the Emperor in his letters, and the vigilance shown in asserting the sovereign rights of China at Macao, all pointed, indeed, to a different conclusion, but they were ignored as irrelevant to the subject. It mattered not also that the treatment of those Europeans who came to China on any different errand than the buying of tea or the selling of opium did not support the sanguine views prevalent in both London and Calcutta as to the reception that awaited Lord Macartney's successor at Pekin. One traveller, among the most courageous and successful of all explorers of unknown lands, Mr. Thomas Manning, came to Canton with every circumstance in his favour that could recommend him to the Chinese. He was an excellent Chinese scholar, well-versed in their history and politics, and thoroughly enthusiastic in his desire to acquire a close knowledge of their character in order to bring the great people of the East prominently before the eyes of his countrymen. All his efforts failed, however, and he turned in despair from the sea-coast in the hope of realizing from India his object of entering the Chinese Empire.* Yet where the individual failed it

* Mr. Thomas Manning succeeded in this design to a certain extent. Although the Indian Government refused to have anything to do with

was confidently anticipated that the Government would succeed.

By a singular coincidence the second British embassy to Pekin was, like the first, contemporaneous with a disturbed state of things in the Himalayan country of Nepaul. Lord Macartney, it will be remembered, reached the capital at a time when the Chinese, having concluded a brilliant campaign, were congratulating themselves on the addition of one feudatory the more to their Empire, at the same time that they felt genuine gratification in having afforded timely protection to their unoffending and ill-provided subjects of Tibet. When Lord Amherst was on his journey to the China coast, an English general was on the point of bringing to a victorious termination operations that had been in progress during three years for the chastisement of the same offenders, the Goorkhas of Nepaul. That war had been, in more than one respect, singular in the military annals of British India. It began in the year 1814, and, whether the cause was the difficulty of the country, or the incapacity of their commander, the English troops met with several slight reverses, and were constrained to admit the valour of their opponents and the first inconstancy of fortune in India. A new commander and fresh troops promptly asserted the natural superiority of English power; but another year, and one memorable in the records of English victory, had to pass away before the result was rendered assured. Sir David Ochterlony's brilliant tactics formed no unworthy counterpart of those triumphant at Waterloo. But the Goorkhas were not finally brought to their knees until the year 1816, when a force of nearly 50,000 men in all, assembled under the Company's flag, had arrived within three days' march of the capital, Khatmandoo. The aid of the Chinese had been implored, but neither from the Amban at Lhasa, nor from the Viceroy of Szchuen, nor from the Emperor in Pekin, did the Nepaulese get the smallest grain of comfort. They were told that they were a race of

his undertaking, he managed, at great personal risk, to make his way across the Himalayas into Tibet. He resided at the capital of the Dalai Lama during the greater part of the year 1812, and remains to the present time the only Englishman who has ever visited Lhasa.

THE EARL AMHERST.

robbers, who richly deserved any punishment inflicted upon them.

An embassy having been decided upon, the next important point was to select the ambassador, and the choice fell upon Lord Amherst, a diplomatist of experience and a nobleman of distinguished parts. The embassy left England early in the year 1816, and reached the mouth of the Peiho in the month of August. The principles by which Lord Amherst intended to guide his action were those of " conciliation and compliment," but it was clear to the experienced mind of Sir George Staunton that the embassy had arrived at a wrong moment to have much chance of effecting its object. The arrival at Tientsin was immediately followed by the commencement of the difficulties which, throughout the whole of the time Lord Amherst resided in China, continually presented themselves. It is certain that, but for some curiosity on the part of the Emperor to see these strange visitors, and a much stronger desire among some of the officials to receive the presents brought from Europe, the embassy would not have been allowed to land. It is not certain, also, how far the sentiment of vanity entered into their calculations; and, no doubt, if the British ambassador had consented to perform the prostration ceremony, he would have been received in audience, and the fact would have been duly chronicled to the glorification of the Middle Kingdom.

Lord Amherst and his companions were, after many altercations, permitted to proceed to Pekin on the understanding that the prostration ceremony would be dispensed with. The circumstances of the journey were little calculated to inspire much confidence as to the good results likely to accrue from an interview with the Emperor. The embassy was hurried along at a rapid rate without being allowed time for rest or refreshment; and when Lord Amherst had been led outside the city walls, and by a roundabout way to the Palace of Yuen-min-yuen, he was told that the Emperor awaited him in immediate audience. The plain truth, as was afterwards discovered, was that Kiaking had not been apprised of the approach of the English ambassador; and when he learnt that he had actually arrived in his palace, he could not repress the curiosity to see him without delay. Hence the sudden summons to the envoy to proceed into his presence. It is impossible to say with any confidence whether Lord Amherst was right or wrong in begging to be excused, under the circumstances, from this precipitate interview. He was undoubtedly exhausted by the hardships of the hurried journey from Tientsin, the uniforms of his suite and the presents for the Emperor had not arrived, and it might even be that the tired and travel-stained appearance of the former would have thrown some stigma on the fame and greatness of the English sovereign. Moreover, the proposal was in violation of every diplomatic punctilio; and Lord Amherst was supported in his refusal by both of the Assistant Commissioners, Sir George Staunton and Mr. Henry Ellis.

And yet there is scarcely any doubt that Kiaking's proposal was meant in a friendly spirit, and as a mark of honour. It was so disinterested that it absolutely disconcerted all the schemes formed by his principal minister and brother-in-law, Ho Koong Yay, who was resolved on compelling the English ambassador to perform the kotow. One refusal, a single pleading of the ancient excuse of indisposition, did not suffice to put off an irresponsible ruler from the gratification of a wish; and Ho Koong Yay came himself to use every argument to induce Lord Amherst to consent to the immediate interview. His final assurance that it should be strictly in accordance with English ceremony—*ne-muntihlee*, "your own ceremony"—failed to induce the English representative to modify his decision. Whether Lord Amherst was right or wrong, there can be no question of Kiaking's having gone very far out of his way indeed, for a Chinese sovereign, towards acquiescing with the requirements of his visitors. After the events of that night, it should, however, have been clear that the embassy would not be received at all, and that, after having overcome many difficulties and reached the capital, it would be barren of result. The circumstances attending its dismissal and return journey* were such as to

---

* These cannot be better given than in the words of Mr. Henry Ellis. "We returned by the same road to Haiteen. ... The house of Sung Tajin, selected for our residence, was extremely commodious and

A DISGRACED MINISTER.   29

leave a very unpleasant impression on the minds of those who were the victims; and the Amherst embassy, far from having improved the relations between the two Governments, placed matters in rather a worse position than they had been in before. Among the English there was a feeling of indignation at the indecorous treatment of their representative, while Kiaking undoubtedly thought that his condescension had not been appreciated, and that his favour had been spurned. The views of the Emperor found expression in a letter to the Prince Regent and in a Vermilion Edict. These official notifications closed the negotiations, and Kiaking suggested to the Regent of England that, as his country was so remote, it would not be necessary for him to send another embassy.

The Amherst embassy served one useful purpose in throwing a great deal of fresh light on the Chinese Court, and on several of the leading men in the country. Foremost among these was Ho Koong Yay, to one of whose sisters Kiaking was married. His influence with the Emperor was supreme at the time of the English mission, and he was reported to have shown great bravery and sound judgment in operating against the insurgents. If they were as striking as his pride and haughty bearing throughout his interviews with Lord Amherst were conspicuous, then they must have been great indeed. The uncertainty of Imperial favour was well demonstrated by the disgrace of Ho Koong Yay, which fell upon him when apparently his influence was at its height. The Imperial Edict in the *Pekin Gazette* dismissing Ho from all his posts expressly states that he was disgraced for

pleasantly situated, with flowers and trees near the principal apartments. Its aspect was so agreeable that we could not but look forward with some satisfaction to remaining there a few days. Such, however, was not to be our fate; before two hours had elapsed a report was brought, that opposition was made by the Chinese to unloading the carts; and soon after the mandarins announced that the Emperor, incensed by the ambassador's refusal to attend him according to his commands, had given orders for our immediate departure. The order was so peremptory that no alteration was proposed; in vain was the fatigue of every individual of the embassy pleaded; no consideration was allowed to weigh against the positive commands of the Emperor" (p. 181).

having concealed the truth from his master in connection with the English embassy, and for having generally mismanaged the whole affair. He was fined to the extent of his pay as Duke for five years, and deprived of his yellow silk riding-jacket—one of the highest honours in China, and only conferred on successful soldiers outside the reigning family. But as a special favour he was allowed to retain the title of Duke, and he may have regained his place in the esteem of his sovereign before he died.

Another of the leading men at Kiaking's Court, and one of whose prudence and moderation early proof had been afforded, was Sung Tajin, who, at the time of Lord Macartney's visit, had been a trusted mandarin under Keen Lung. Reference has already been made to the unfortunate present sent in 1805 by the English Government, which had been returned without his being so much as allowed to see it. Its evil consequences, unluckily, did not stop there. Sung Tajin was one of the most remarkable of the ministers who contributed in the later days of Keen Lung to the maintenance of his widespread administration; and had his successor only known how to utilize his services, and to follow his advice, the condition of China during the early years of the present century would have been very different from what it was. Sung Tajin was a man of neither birth nor fortune. He owed his introduction to official life to the fact that he was a descendant of those Mongols who had joined the Manchu Taitsong when he began the invasion of China, and who had thereby acquired for their descendants the privilege of an entry into the official service. Sung Tajin began his career in the modest but useful post of interpreter. From that office he was soon raised to the confidential position of secretary to Keen Lung's Council, in which capacity he acquired an intimate acquaintance with the external relations of the Empire. When the Emperor wanted an experienced and trustworthy man to send to the Russian frontier, where difficulties had arisen, his choice fell upon the secretary Sung, who justified his master's favour by the arrangement he very shortly effected with the Russian Governor of Irkutsk, Major-General Nagel.

This was not the only service that he was able to render the Emperor in the capacity of Amban at Ourga. He showed great tact and resolution in arresting an impostor who, claiming to be a connection of the Emperor, was endeavouring to form a party of his own, and to create disturbances among the Mongol tribes. In reward for this vigorous proceeding Keen Lung selected him to be his representative to meet the English ambassador, and to conduct him to Jehol. He was subsequently employed as Governor-General at Canton, but on Kiaking's accession he returned to Pekin to fill the post of chief minister to the new Emperor. Here, however, he was out of his element, as the new ruler gave himself up to amusement, and showed very little desire to follow in the footsteps of his father. Kiaking was particularly addicted to the play, and loved the society of actors. He even requested them to accompany him on his visits to the temples where he offered up sacrifice. This indifference to appearances excited the disapproval of the minister Sung, and in a memorial to the throne he called marked attention to the delinquencies of the sovereign. Such a measure, although true to the best traditions of the Chinese service, was, of course, the inevitable prelude to the disgrace of the audacious minister. Unable to profit by his wisdom, or to put up with his reproofs, Kiaking banished his faithful adviser to the Central Asian province of Ili, although with the title of its Governor.* He was recalled in 1816, as the Emperor thought his former experience would be useful in dealing with Lord Amherst, but the English embassy had departed before he reached Pekin. He was then employed as Amban at Kalgan, and also in a similar capacity at Moukden. But although his administration was always attended with good results, he was more feared by Kiaking than liked. An

* Padre Serra, in "Asiatic Transactions," vol. iii., says, "On being asked if he was the author of this admonition, he firmly acknowledged that he was. He was then asked what punishment he deserved? and he answered 'Quartering.' They told him to choose some other; whereupon he said, 'Let me be beheaded;' and on a third command he chose to be strangled. After these three answers he was told to retire, and on the following day they appointed him Governor of Ele (the country of the banished)."

excuse was made for dismissing him from the service, and he had to wait until Kiaking's death before he emerged from the obscurity of an official out of favour and without a post.

The last four years of Kiaking's reign were not made noteworthy by any remarkable occurrence. The Emperor had no hold on the respect of his subjects, and it followed of necessity that they could not be very warmly attached to his person. But for the moment secret societies had been crushed into inaction, and the remotest quarters of the Empire continued to enjoy tranquillity. The capital, or, indeed, the palace, alone revealed practical evidence of disunion and internal dissension. The princes of the Manchu family had increased to such proportions that they numbered several thousand persons, each of whom was entitled by right of birth to a certain allowance and free quarters. They purchased the possession of the right to an easy and unlaborious existence at the heavy price of exclusion from the public service. They were the objects of the secret dread of the Emperor, and they were only tolerated in the palace so long as they appeared to be insignificant. No matter how great their ambition or natural capacity may have been, they had no prospect of emancipating themselves from the dull sphere of inaction to which custom hopelessly consigned them. It is only in the present day that a different practice is coming into vogue, and that only through there having been two long minorities.

Whether Kiaking's fears got the better of his reason, or whether there were among his relatives some men of more than average ability, certain it is that an outbreak was organized among the Manchu princes, and that it very nearly met with success. The details remain a palace secret, but the broad fact is known that a rising among the Hwang-taitsou, or Yellow Girdles, as they are called, was repressed with great severity. Several were executed, and many hundreds were removed from Pekin to Moukden and other places in Manchuria, where they were allowed to employ themselves in taking care of the ancestral tombs and other offices of a similar character. About this time the country, or a large part of it, was visited by a severe famine; and the

PUBLIC SPIRIT.

river Hoangho proved another source of trouble by overflowing, as it had often done before, its banks, and breaking through the dams constructed to confine its waters. The most interesting circumstance in connection with this visitation of a periodical calamity was the fact of voluntary contributions being invited towards defraying the expenses of the necessary works. The Emperor bestowed honorary rewards and titles on those who showed any public spirit in this way; and the impulses of benevolence were developed by the conferring of titles in a country where rank in our sense has no meaning. It would be instructive to know what measure of success this experiment in the sale of unmeaning titles had; but the archives are silent, and the promptings of curiosity have to rest satisfied with the knowledge that it has not been repeated. There is consolation in the reflection, that even in the stress of pecuniary embarrassment a Chinese ruler refused to put up public offices for sale, or to vitiate the system of public education by affording to wealth a golden key of admission.

Under such circumstances the reign of Kiaking drew to its close, and, bowing to the decree to which all men must equally submit, the Emperor made his will, and nominated as his successor his second son Taoukwang, the Prince Meenning who was the hero of the conspiracy attack in the palace. Kiaking died on the 2nd of September, 1820, in the sixty-first year of his age, leaving to his successor a diminished authority, an enfeebled power, and a discontented people. There is generally some mitigating circumstance to be pleaded against the adverse verdict of history in its estimation of a public character. The difficulties with which the individual had to contend may have been exceptional and unexpected, the measures which he adopted may have had untoward and unnatural results, and the crisis of the hour may have demanded genius of a transcendent order. But in the case of Kiaking not one of these extenuating facts can be pleaded. His path had been smoothed for him by his predecessor, his difficulties were raised by his own indifference, and the consequences of his spasmodic and ill-directed energy were scarcely less unfortunate than those of his habitual apathy. So much easier is the work of destruction than the task of construction, that Kiaking in twenty-five years had done almost as much harm to the constitution of his country, and to the fortunes of his dynasty, as his father had conferred solid advantages upon the State in the course of a reign of sixty years of unexampled brilliance.

It must not be supposed that, because the available records of Kiaking's reign are few, and refer to detached events rather than to the daily life and continuous political existence of the country, the Chinese people had no other thoughts save for the foibles of their ruler, and for the numerous efforts made by the outside peoples to establish with them relations of intimacy and equality. Although we have not the means of describing it, the great life of the nation went on less disturbed than would commonly be supposed by the disquieting events of Kiaking's tenure of power, and the people, as ever, were resolutely bent on performing their mundane duties after the fashion and precepts of their forefathers. The effect of the secret societies on public opinion was unquestionably great, and the people, fond of the mysterious, and ingrained with superstition, turned with as much eagerness to the latest propagandum as they did to the predictions of the village soothsayer. Had these societies remained secret, and consequently peaceful, there is no saying whither their limits might not have stretched; but the instant the Water-lily sect threw off the mask, and resorted to acts of violence, a different condition of things came into force, and the majority of the people held aloof from open rebellion.

In no country in Asia, and perhaps in the world, do the people themselves form the national strength more incontestably than in China. It is not a question of one class, or of one race, but of the whole body of the inhabitants. The administering orders are recruited from and composed of men who, in the strictest sense of the phrase, owe everything to themselves and nothing to birth. They gain admission into the public service by passing a series of examinations of more or less difficulty, and, having entered the venerable portals of the most ancient Civil Service in the world, there is no office

A HAPPY PEOPLE. 35

beyond the reach of the humblest—even though it be to wield almost despotic power in a great province, or to stand among the chosen ministers round the Dragon Throne. The interest of every family in the government of the kingdom is a matter of personal concern. There is a sure element of stability in such an arrangement as this. A people does not quarrel with its institutions when the best brains in the land form the pillars by which they are supported. Kiaking's errors of judgment were a source of grief and anxiety to experienced ministers like Sung, who knew how easily the provincial officials neglected their duties when they perceived apathy at the centre; but they interfered in a very slight degree with the daily life of the nation at large. The people were not contented, but they were still able to obtain their own subsistence; and thus occupied they felt no inclination to disturb the tranquillity of the country by denouncing the shortcomings of the executive.

Although causes of coming trouble were beginning to reveal themselves, the material prosperity of the people * was probably higher during the first fifteen years of Kiaking's reign than it had ever been before or since in modern times. A greater portion of the country was undisturbed, and consequently a larger extent was under cultivation. The Chinese have never neglected any means of developing their agricultural resources, and, if left in security to themselves, they till every kind of land, and raise on it one crop or another. They drain the valleys, which become rich pastures, and on the slopes of the mountains they grow in successive terraces rice and opium, alternating the crop with the period of the year. Nor are they less skilful and energetic as traders. The deficiencies of one province are supplied by the abundance of another; and the necessities and luxuries of the capital are provided for by the numerous productions of a country which, in size and varied features, might rank with a continent. The great rivers connect the Western provinces with the Eastern; and the omission of Providence is supplied by the magnificent

* A census held by order of the Emperor Kiaking in the year 1812, gave the population at 362,447,183.

canal that should, if kept in repair, afford a highway for all between the South and the North. Nature was bountiful; its one oversight has been repaired by the enterprise and sagacity of man.

Revolts among the savage tribes of the remote frontier, an unsuccessful campaign in the interior, disturbed the daily life of the bulk of this fortunate people as little as the impact of a pebble thrown into a stream checks its course. Kiaking's misfortunes had only a small effect on the existence of his subjects, who, engrossed in the struggle of life, paid no heed to the mishaps or the blunders of the sovereign. A dearth in Shansi, an overflow of the Hoangho, or a block in the passage of the Grand Canal, these came home to the people with the force of a real affliction. It mattered nothing to the inhabitants of seventeen provinces and many tributary kingdoms that an insurrection should have broken out in the eighteenth province —only, as they felt fully persuaded, to be repressed with severity. In estimating the significance of Kiaking's misfortunes, and of the greater disasters that were to follow, too much importance must not be attached to their supposed effects. They tended to show the incapacity of the ruler, the weakness and corruption of the Government. But the great mass of the people were almost unaffected by them. Not until the Taeping rebellion, which with its imitators had for its sphere the greater portion of the Empire, were these seditions felt by the people as a grievous calamity; and, although the origin of that revolt may be discovered in the secret societies and other organizations of disaffected persons in the reign of Kiaking, it must not be supposed that either the country or the people felt or thought themselves to be suffering from any irreparable malady during the life of that ruler.

CHAPTER II.

THE EMPEROR TAOUKWANG.

IMMEDIATELY after his father's death, Prince Meenning was placed upon the throne and recognized as Emperor by the functionaries of the Court as well as by the people at large. There were not wanting those who thought that he was not the best fitted for the dignity to which a mere accident had raised him; and his brother Hwuy Wang, as son of the living Empress-mother, was strongly impressed with a sense of the superiority of his own claim. For a moment it seemed as if these rival pretensions might lead to a conflict; but the good sense of the Empress-mother fortunately averted what might have proved a national calamity. There had been passages of arms in earlier days between the two branches of the family, and Meenning's mother had died, as it was reported, through the machinations of this Empress. But, in face of a dynastic crisis, public spirit displaced personal animosity, and Meenning's position was assured by his prompt recognition as Emperor by the Empress-mother. Having thus made good the tranquil possession of the throne, there remained the next and highly important step to be taken of declaring what should be the name of the first year of the new reign. Momentous consequences depend on the selection made, and the records of the Hanlin are searched, and the positions of the starry heavens are scanned, to discover what may be the most suitable name and the most auspicious characters. In the case of Meenning the search seems to have been one of exceptional difficulty; but at last the official announcement was made that the name of the first year of the new reign would be Taoukwang, which signifies Reason's Light, and by that name this ruler has become generally known.

The personal appearance of Taoukwang was not calculated to inspire respect or to strike the stranger with awe. He was in his thirty-eighth year when he mounted the throne, and one writer speaks of him in rather contemptuous terms as being, at that time, "thin and toothless." The description of a more sympathetic writer is hardly more flattering to him, but it formed a true index to the character of the man. This writer calls him "lank in figure and low of stature, with a haggard face, a reserved look, and quiet exterior." The early life and training of Taoukwang had not been of a nature to bring out his good points, or to quicken whatever warm sympathies and natural talent he may have possessed. Brought up in a licentious court, and surrounded by ministers of pleasure with whom unquestionably he had not the least fellow-feeling, he had always lived a retired life, as far aloof from the pursuits of the palace as possible. He had thus obtained a reputation for reserve, if not for stupidity, that secured him against the antipathy of many, if it prevented his obtaining the friendship of more than a few chosen companions. Taoukwang's life had been neither a very happy nor a very pleasant one. It had been one of great self-restraint, and while he had passed his leisure in reflection it seems to have increased his natural irresolution, and to have rendered him still more unfitted to assume that active part in the guidance of affairs which the condition of China at the time of his coming to the throne absolutely demanded.

Taoukwang's first acts were marked by singular moderation, and afforded an appropriate commencement for his reign. While professing the greatest esteem and veneration for the person of his predecessor, he devoted his early attention to reversing his policy, and to undoing the mischief he had caused. The usual acts of clemency were granted and carried out in a spirit of wide-reaching generosity, and the prisons, which Kiaking had filled with the victims of his suspicion, were emptied by the clemency of the new sovereign. Injured merit found a vindicator, as well as those who had fallen under the ban of the laws through their nearness in blood

SUNG TAJIN AGAIN.

to the Emperor, or through their having refused to gratify the whims of a tyrant. The minister Sung was recalled to office, and many of the exiled Manchu princes were reinstated in the privileges of their rank. The strict ceremonial of the Chinese Court leaves little for the most original intelligence to devise in the way of demonstrating how completely the ruler claims to be the father of his people, or how strongly he aspires to the possession of the great virtues. The sincerity of his protestations is frequently shown by his subsequent acts to be hollow; it was Taoukwang's distinction to prove by his conduct that with him they were not empty expressions, and that they really came from the heart.

The restoration of Sung Tajin to power was a practical proof of good intentions, and meant much more than the moral platitudes enunciated in Vermilion Edicts. Sung had gained a popularity with the people that far exceeded that of the Emperor, through the lavish manner in which he had distributed his wealth—consistently refusing to accumulate treasures for the benefit of himself or his family. But his independence of mind rendered him an unpleasant monitor to those princes who see in the truth a constant reflection on their own conduct, and even Taoukwang appears to have dreaded in anticipation the impartial criticism of this minister. However, Sung returned to official life, and in a little time was appointed to the elevated dignity of President of the Board of Censors, after he had for a brief period exercised great administrative power as Viceroy of Pechihli. The edict placing Sung at the head of the Censorate is expressive of the Emperor's respect, mingled with a certain amount of fear of the greatest of his ministers. "Let Sung carefully attend to the established routine of his office instead of wildly confusing and puzzling himself with a multiplicity of extraneous matters. If he treads in his former track, he will involve himself in criminality." Even the strictures of the sovereign could not detract from the popularity of this minister, and although he was not admitted to the same responsible positions he had held at previous periods, he remained until his death unquestionably the most popular man in his country.

The release of prisoners, the restoration of Sung Tajin,

did not stand alone as acts calculated to give the Chinese people a favourable impression of their new prince's character. Kiaking had filled his harem with great numbers of women; and crowds of players, buffoons, and idlers had been attracted to the palace, where they found a welcome and free quarters as long as they made themselves agreeable and pandered to the wishes of the Emperor. Taoukwang, when prince, had always held aloof from these companions of his father's leisure, and one of his first acts on coming to the throne was to take vigorous measures and clear the palace of their presence. All who could not show some good reason for their being retained in the public service were summarily dismissed, and the atmosphere of the Court was purified by the banishment of the influences likely to prove injurious to its tone and to the integrity, if not the efficiency, of the public service. The members of the harem were sent home to their relations, where possible, and Taoukwang proclaimed his one wife by the title of Empress. Whatever else the new ruler might prove to be, the whole tenour of his conduct went to show that he was resolved to observe the most laudable customs of his nation, and to thus make himself appear, if not a capable administrator, at least worthy of the respect of his subjects, and of the favourable regard of posterity.

The misfortunes left by Kiaking to his successor were not confined to the discontent among some classes of the people. Malversations among the officials and natural disasters in the provinces, completed the effect of manifest incompetence and indifference. These further calamities seem to have commenced with inundations in the province of Pechihli, which were followed by a period of drought, and they formed the subject of edicts in the *Pekin Gazette* without any remedy being provided. Taoukwang's Government did the best it could to alleviate the prevailing distress, and a fixed allowance was made to those who were in a destitute condition. But the suffering was so intense that the Emperor gave up his annual visit to Jehol, the hunting palace and park beyond the Wall, whither the Tartar rulers had been in the habit of proceeding during the summer heats. While these events of general interest and importance were in progress, the doctors of the Hanlin had been busily employed in collecting the materials for the history of Kiaking's reign, and in the year 1824 this was completed and placed in the mausoleum of the Manchu family at Moukden.

The intensity of the general suffering was amply proved during the famine by the increase of crime in the capital and throughout the country. Robbery became rife, and cases are frequently mentioned in the official publication of the theft of bread and other provisions from the shops or stalls. Special Acts were passed for the punishment of this crime; but the only effectual remedy was found in providing gratuitously those in absolute want with the means of subsistence, thus adding greatly to the embarrassments of a straitened Government. Another form of crime revealed itself in the increased number of forgers and issuers of counterfeit coin, who attracted much attention about this time, and who were summarily punished on detection in accordance with the fears of an executive which felt that it had few means of defending itself against those who sought to foist false coin upon the public. For the principal coin of China consists of a clumsy piece of money called "cash," which requires little ingenuity to imitate, and which, when spurious, may escape detection for a long time.

During this period of popular suffering and discontent, although it hardly amounted to absolute disaffection, Taoukwang gained a name for clemency and moderation which never subsequently deserted him. The laws were harsh, and, in face of new crimes and fresh dangers, had been made more rigorous; but Taoukwang always sought to moderate them, and to give his decision on the side of mercy. He also endeavoured to avert danger by anticipating it, and he was fully impressed with the truth of the saying that it is better to prevent than to cure a malady. In this spirit an edict was passed in 1824 forbidding private persons to possess arms, and authorizing the officials to search for them in any houses where they might suspect them to be concealed, and to confiscate all they should find. So far, therefore, as Taoukwang's personal influence was felt or exerted in the work of government, it was undoubtedly beneficial; but while Taoukwang's desire for personal rule was keen, he lacked either the will, the application, or the method to accomplish his desires, and to give the bark of State the direction he might wish it to take. Taoukwang had the inclination to play the part of an independent sovereign, and even persuaded himself that he did so with effect; but in reality he was, more than most rulers, swayed by the counsels of powerful and self-seeking ministers, who sometimes made him the victim of their machinations.

Several of these ministers were men of note and ability, of whom much will be heard during the later stages of the reign; but at this point only the four principal need be named, Hengan and Elepoo, Keying and Keshen. While Hengan was the most reckless and ambitious of them all, his influence was exerted rather in private affairs and matters of the Court than in public business. Elepoo, on the other hand, was neither an intriguer nor ambitious. Without any special gift, he might have remained in the obscurity of incapacity, but for his one great quality of honesty, the rarest of all possessions at the Manchu Court. But both Keying and Keshen were men of more striking ability and influence. Keying was a Manchu in blood, and a member of a family famous among the ruling race both for wealth and for its descent and connections. He had passed all the examinations, and before his appearance at Court had amassed considerable wealth in the capacity of Superintendent of the Customs at Shanhaikwan, the important town at the eastern extremity of the Great Wall. As Taoukwang's most capable minister, he was able for many years to exercise a salutary influence over the councils of the Empire, although his advice was not always heeded as it deserved.

But of all Taoukwang's advisers, Keshen was the most remarkable for address and natural capacity. He came of Mongol race, being a member of one of the tribes which had joined the Manchus at an early period of their career, and which in return had been allowed certain privileges. In all his characteristics, as well as in the trained intelligence which made him pre-eminent, the genius of Keshen was that of a pure Chinese rather than of a Tartar. No emperor brought into contact with him failed to feel the fascination of his bearing, or to pass a compliment on the clearness of his understanding and the subtlety of his resources. There were many other ministers of note besides these four at the Court of Taoukwang, but the ability of those named may suffice to show that the new ruler had no lack of men capable of giving him sound advice; nor must it be supposed that, because they were unable to avert many national calamities they were necessarily incompetent or unpatriotic. The affairs of foreign countries attracted the larger amount of the Chinese Government's attention during Taoukwang's reign, and we must therefore be prepared to perceive some deficiency in method through want of practice in the way of dealing with strange and better equipped peoples. Excuses may fairly be made for a people claiming, and exercising the rights of, a position of pre-eminence, when suddenly called upon to encounter other States that not only disregarded its pretensions, but that undoubtedly possessed greater power. The illusions which had been successfully maintained against a body of missionaries and a few traders were destined to be hopelessly shattered when brought into contact with a Government that thought only of its dignity and of supporting the just rights of its subjects. If allowance be made for the critical turn events took during the first twenty years of Taoukwang's reign, it will be seen that his ministers were not personally to blame for the unpleasant results that followed, however unpleasant they were, if the old ideas of the Chinese can be considered as having been in any way worthy of perpetuation.

The theory that the country is happy which has no history has been converted to the use of showing that the early years of Taoukwang's reign must have been prosperous because they have left no record. The fact seems to have been, on the contrary, that they were marked by numerous disasters and by much public suffering, all the deeper and more serious because they did not admit of mention. On one point alone was it possible to feel that times had improved, but even in this matter the sense of satisfaction required large qualification. The secret societies were dormant, if not extinct; on the other hand, the discontent of a large section of the people had been substituted for the machinations of a small clique. The scarcity of work and want of food entailed still wider dissatisfaction, and a people accustomed to regard the Government as the agent and representative of Heaven had little hesitation in arriving at the conclusion that its own wants reflected the shortcomings of the ruler.

The first year of Taoukwang's reign beheld the arrival at Pekin of a Russian mission, which, if it did not partake of the formal character and importance of an embassy, was rendered remarkable by the character of its chief, and by the considerable addition it furnished to Western knowledge about the Chinese Empire. Although the Russians had been treated on terms of inferiority by the Chinese, who assumed in their official correspondence the tone, as they expressed it, "of an elder brother," they had succeeded in establishing a not inconsiderable trade from Kiachta, and also in obtaining one great concession in the right to possess a college at Pekin. Periodically, once in ten years, the residents are changed; and the students, having acquired a knowledge of the Manchu and Chinese tongues, return to Russia to be utilized as interpreters on the frontier, and their places are taken by fresh scholars. The vastness of the distance from Siberia to Pekin, and the occasionally strained nature of the relations between the two Governments, frequently resulted in the prolonged stay of this small foreign colony in the Chinese capital; but, if allowance is made for all the attendant circumstances, it may be said that the stipulations of the arrangement were fairly, if not rigidly observed. In 1820 a relieving mission, under the guidance of Mr. Timkowski, crossed the Chinese frontier, and proceeded in due course to Pekin. The exact character of the relation between the two Empires may be gathered from the fact that while the conductor of the mission was allowed to reside in the city and to go about the streets in comparative liberty, and when he had completed his task to return in safety to his own country, he held no official position, and had consequently no dealings with the Government. His principal charge, indeed, was to place at the disposal of the descendants of the garrison of Albazin, which had surrendered as prisoners of war to Kanghi in the seventeenth century, the sum allotted by the Czar for their support.

It might have been thought that in this institution lay a sure and excellent means of obtaining information concerning the progress of affairs in China, or at least at the capital. Such has not proved, unfortunately, to be the case, and knowledge lies under no obligation to the Russian college at Pekin. Whether because its members have been unlettered, or afraid to imperil their position by making inquiries, or by revealing what they knew, the result is clear that the world is none the wiser or the better for the exceptional privilege the Russians have enjoyed during two hundred years.

Although Taoukwang's attention was at this early period of his rule directed to these strange nations, who were every day obtruding themselves more and more on the attention of his Government, he sought during the first years of his reign to banish the subject from his mind; and the better to effect his object he ordered the dismissal of the Portuguese officials employed in the astronomical department and in the rectification of the Calendar, whom even the distrustful Kiaking had spared from the general penalty of expulsion which he had passed against the Christian missionaries. The question had, however, by this time got beyond any such remedy as attempting to ignore the foreign traders who came in increasing numbers to the one port of Canton; and all Taoukwang's studied indifference, and resolve to exclude them from his presence, could not avail to arrest the course of events, or to prevent the approach of that complication which he had most desire to avert.

Affairs at Canton fortunately continued to progress in a favourable manner, although the arrogance of the Chinese officials had been greatly increased by their successes in the encounters with the representatives of the English Government, both in the matter of the Macao occupation and in the general regulations of trade. Yet the existence of a good understanding did not prevent the occurrence of some difficulties or the outbreak of disputes which easily assumed an angry tone. In 1821 trade was suspended, if but for a few hours, and only the firmness of the Company's representative, Mr. Urmston, succeeded in thus promptly bringing the mandarins to reason. But no satisfaction was ever given for an attack on a boat of the man-of-war *Topaze*, wherein fourteen Englishmen were wounded. This was not the only instance of open attack on English vessels, and in no case was it found possible to exact reparation.

Nor were the English alone in their naval complications with the Chinese. The relations of the French with China, which had once promised to be of a most friendly and intimate character, had dwindled away to nominal proportions and utter insignificance. In 1802 the flag of the Republic was hoisted at Canton, but was very soon hauled down, and for nearly thirty years French intercourse with China absolutely ceased. In the year 1828 the French merchantman, *Le Navigateur*, was compelled by stress of weather to seek shelter on the coast of Cochin-China, and the crew were obliged in their distress, and on account of the unfriendly attitude of the native authorities, to sell both their cargo and ship, and to take passage in a Chinese junk for Macao. On the journey the Chinese formed a plot for their murder, and the design was carried out. The massacre was accomplished within sight of the haven whither they were bound, and only one sailor escaped by jumping overboard. His evidence served to bring the criminals to justice, and in the following year seventeen of the murderers were executed. The tragedy served one useful purpose. It enabled the French Government to establish a right to place a commercial representative at Canton.

The grievances of the merchants consisted principally in the heavy dues exacted from them, by the Hoppo and his agents, for the right to trade. Among the most deeply felt of these was the cost of the permit to proceed from Canton to Macao, without which the journey could not be undertaken. This passport, or chop, as it was called, cost in all between seventy and one hundred pounds; and seeing that in these days no ladies or children ever visited Canton, but that the merchants always left their families at Macao, this costly and rigorous imposition was felt very keenly by the European merchants. Exceptionally heavy taxes on articles of commerce were hard enough to bear without murmur; but they sank into insignificance beside those that fettered the liberty of movement, and interfered with the relations of families.

When the dissatisfaction caused by this state of things was at its height, an English merchant, Mr.—long afterwards Sir—James Matheson, the principal representative of one of the chief houses in the China trade, took upon himself to demand an interview with the mandarins, and succeeded in bringing the hardship of the regulation so clearly before their minds that its rigour was at once abated, and some of the most objectionable features were removed.* It was not until four years later that the further privilege was granted of allowing the English merchants to bring their wives and families up to Canton. The failure of some Chinese trading firms, or hongs, was the immediate cause of this further concession to the foreigner. The Hoppo and his agents were most anxious that the trade should not be in consequence suspended, and, while they were constrained to publish the Edicts of Pekin, they were fully resolved not to put an end to their own source of profit.

Although Taoukwang was in reality less disposed to cultivate relations with the outside peoples than any of his immediate predecessors, and notwithstanding that the anti-foreign party had never been more active than it was at this period, still the first ten years of Taoukwang's reign witnessed a remarkable development in the trade of Canton, and a not less striking improvement in the relations between Chinese officials and the English merchants. There was a corresponding disadvantage to be taken into account as a set-off against this agreeable progress. The more the trade increased, the firmer the foot-hold of the foreigner on the soil became, the more did the transaction present a mark to and attract the indignation of the old-fashioned party at Court, which

* The interview was not without a dramatic side. One of the mandarins present, catching hold of Matheson, passed his hand round his neck, signifying by this action that he deserved to be beheaded. Mr. Matheson was equal to the occasion, and, seizing the official, repeated the process on him, with the difference that he performed the operation twice!

regarded this growing outside intercourse in the light of an unmitigated misfortune, and which foresaw only the evils that its continuance might entail.

Even in this matter Taoukwang appears to have had no decided conviction and no settled views of his own. Personally he was too much given to reflect not to see that there were merit and strength in European knowledge; yet he was so swayed by his fears, and by the representations of his most intimate counsellors, that he banished all foreigners from the capital. Irresolute even in his new decision, he allowed the trade at Canton to go on assuming larger proportions, and, although the ultimate consequence of that course of proceeding was plain, he took no measures towards checking the development of or abolishing external commerce. Each year made the exclusion of the foreigner and the cessation of trade a matter of greater difficulty, but Taoukwang preferred to wait on the course of events rather than to take a bold initiative. He was at a later period of his life to find a counsellor whose boldness was equal to his ability; but at the period which we have been describing the Emperor had no adviser of the courage and capacity of Commissioner Lin. Had he possessed one, and struck as boldly in defence of China's right to remain a secluded country as he did in 1842, there is no saying but that the object might have been attained. If the Chinese had been as clear of vision in any of the years between the departure of the Amherst embassy and the close of Taoukwang's first decade on the throne, as they were resolute in action and unyielding in their lofty pretensions, they might have put a stop to the foreign commerce; whether they could have prevented smuggling on the very largest scale or not is quite an independent matter. The opportunity was not utilized, and, although the attempt was subsequently made, the attendant circumstances were never equally propitious. Never again was China as strong relatively as she was then, and never afterwards did the China trade appear of as little importance to the English people and Government as it did for a short time during this period, which witnessed the withdrawal of the East India Company's monopoly.

CHAPTER III.

INTERNAL DISSENSIONS.

THE overthrow of the Eleuths and the conquest of Central Asia had been among the most remarkable of the military exploits of the great Keen Lung. During fifty years and more there was after that triumph complete tranquillity from the Kansuh borders across the great desert of Gobi to the plateau of Pamir. The people had not the power to revolt, and with the loss of vigour they seemed to have forfeited the inclination; and even the nomad tribes of Kokonor on the one side and of Kobdo on the other, forgot to pursue their accustomed avocations at the expense of their neighbours. The Chinese had, therefore, every reason to feel gratified with the results of their most extensive conquest, and, so far as there was any indication of popular feeling, the great mass of the subject people appeared to appreciate the benefits conferred on them by their rulers, and to have no desire for change.

The Chinese, none the less for these satisfactory results, had undertaken a most difficult task, and one in which success becomes more difficult as the method of performing it approaches a higher ideal of perfection. They had accepted the responsibility of providing a people more numerous by far than their garrison, of a different religion, and of military habits, with a wise and provident administration, having as its foremost objects the promotion of trade and the maintenance of order. They made it their object, as it might have been their boast, to associate the natives with themselves in the work of government. The civil administration, the dispensation of justice, and even the collection of taxes, were left to the Mahomedan peoples; and the Celestials trusted to the presence of a small army to preserve their rights, and to keep the conquered pacified. When will Governments learn that there is no way of popularizing a foreign dominion, and that the search for a model method of giving the law to subject peoples by raising them to a position of equality and independence can only end in making their own overthrow easier and more simple?

The reputation of China—which seemed to the States of Asia, who are here to-day and gone to-morrow, and whose stability is no more certain than that of mounds of sand on a seashore, to be a thing past comprehension among Empires, and built on the rocks of enduring Time—served her lieutenants in Ili and Altyshahr in such good stead that they were able to maintain their master's authority undisputed throughout all the dark hours of Kiaking's reign. During that period the Chinese, who had placed their ambans, or military governors, in all the chief towns, and who had constructed outside them forts, or gulbaghs, were left in undisputed possession of the vast region lying on both sides of the Tian Shan range, and their relations with their neighbours were conducted on the basis of conscious power and undoubted superiority. The people prospered, trade increased, the population multiplied, and no sign was perceptible of any popular dissatisfaction until outside ambition interfered to make an opportunity of aggrandizing itself.

Even then the machinations of a jealous neighbour, and the personal motives of a ruling family, would not have availed to produce any result, but that the Chinese had abated somewhat of the vigour necessary to the effectual maintenance of their dominion. For the preservation of an Empire it is incumbent that the vigilance of the ruler shall never be relaxed, and that the infallible and unchanging law should never be forgotten or lost sight of, which tells us in the clearest characters that a foreign dominion can never be popular, and that to overthrow it is the first and bounden duty of every child of the soil. The Chinese were well aware of the fact; they had only allowed themselves to forget some of its attendant circumstances. Their military power had been suffered to fall to a low ebb, and a momentary sense of weakness, or a diplomatic blunder, had allowed the introduction of an alien element into the southern portion at least of their Central Asian jurisdiction.

The former circumstance arose from the natural tendency of Empires which, having overcome every adversary and enjoyed a long period of good fortune, acquire a habit of believing that success is for them assured, and that the violent principles of superior might may be safely discarded, although in no case have they any better sanction for their position than the law of the stronger. But the origin of the latter cause of weakness claims more careful consideration and elaborate elucidation. The nearest neighbour of the Chinese was the Khanate of Khokand, a State with which, from olden times, the Kashgarians had been intimately connected both in commerce and in politics. Khokand had felt the force of Chinese valour when Fouta led the Celestial armies over the Pamir, and when Keen Lung's troops withdrew from Tashkent it was on the understanding that the Khan would acknowledge himself the dependent of China, and send tribute to the Emperor of Pekin. For fifty-two years that arrangement was strictly observed in the letter and the spirit; and during that period the intercourse between the two neighbouring States increased in proportion as commerce was fostered by the Chinese governors. Although the peoples were Mahomedans, and consequently antipathetic to the Confucian or Buddhistic Chinese, no restrictions were placed upon trade or travellers, and in all essential matters no difference could be detected to show whether the country was ruled by a Celestial Viceroy or by a Khan of its own.

This state of things continued uninterrupted until 1812, when Mahomed Ali, the Khan of Khokand, a man of capacity and ambition, came to the resolution to pay tribute no longer; and the Chinese, seeing that they had not the force to compel his obedience, acquiesced in his refusal. A first concession has soon to be followed by others. The Khokandian prince next obtained the right to levy a tax on all Mahomedan merchandise sold in the bazaars of Kashgar and Yarkand,

and deputed consuls, or aksakals, for the purpose of collecting the duties. These aksakals naturally became the centre of all the intrigue and disaffection prevailing in the State against the Celestials, and they counted it as much their duty to provoke political discontent as to supervise the customs placed under their charge. Before the aksakals appeared the Chinese ruled a peaceful territory, but on the advent of those foreign officials symptoms of trouble soon revealed themselves.

Nor did the Khokandian ruler want a pretext for undertaking hostile action against his neighbours. He had long been the supporter of the Khoja family, which, expelled from its native kingdom by the generals of Keen Lung, lived, in the person of Sarimsak, on the bounty of Khokand; and when he wished to proceed to extremities he had only to proclaim his intention to restore the rightful ruler to his possessions in Altyshahr. Sarimsak had escaped the pursuit of Fouta when a mere child, and he grew up to manhood and passed into old age without having the inclination, or finding the opportunity, of asserting his pretensions. He left to his sons the duty and the privilege of expelling the Chinese, and of giving the people of Kashgaria a native rule. Those sons were named in the order of their age, Yusuf, Barhanuddin, and Jehangir; and each of them at different times proved a source of serious trouble to the Chinese.

Of these princelets Jehangir was the most active, as for a time he seemed destined to be the most fortunate. It was he who struck the first blow in the cause of liberty, or, it would be more correct to say, of tyranny. As early as the year 1822 he had quitted his retreat in Khokand, and, while his elder brothers remained in security at the capital of that State, he resolved to make an attempt to regain what his grandfather had lost sixty years before. The nomad Kirghiz of the Kizil Yart, who refused obedience to the authority of any of their settled neighbours, and who only needed the incentive of plunder to attach themselves for the nonce to any cause that offered, supplied him with the followers necessary for the adventure. With a band of these, rendered more formidable than they would otherwise have been by the

THE KHOJAS.

presence of their chief, Suranchi Beg, Jehangir advanced on Kashgar. The distance was short, and his advance rapid; but the Chinese garrison proved to be on its guard, and his motley gathering was repulsed with some loss. Such was the ignominious ending of the first expedition to disturb the Chinese in Kashgaria, and to restore the Khojas to their throne.

Jehangir, although beaten, did not lose heart. The Khan of Khokand, seeing that he had failed, repudiated all responsibility for his action, and, instead of returning to his former refuge, Jehangir fled to the region south of Lake Issik Kul, where the Syr Darya or Jaxartes takes its rise, and is long known by the name of Narym. Neither his pretensions nor his personal necessities allowed him to remain inactive, and it suited both his own purpose and the ideas of his Kirghiz hosts for him to lead forays across the Tian Shan into Chinese territory. The Chinese, mindful of their own dignity, and not regardless of their subjects' welfare, resolved to punish the robber, even at the risk of pursuing him to his hiding-place. An expedition was fitted out, and advanced through the Kirghiz camping-places to as far as Fort Kurtka. The objects of the force were ostensibly obtained, and the Chinese were retiring in good order, and with every right to feel satisfied, when their active adversary fell upon them in a difficult defile, and almost annihilated them. This disaster, the first which had befallen the conquering race, was magnified by rumour, and Jehangir at a bound became a formidable opponent and a dangerous competitor for ruling honours.

The fortitude of Jehangir had confirmed the attachment of his friends, and the Chinese reverse rallied many supporters to his side. The Khokandian ruler again threw aside the mask, and lent his troops and a general—instructed, no doubt, to advance his master's interests as much as the cause of the Pretender. Encouraged by the sight of so many fresh followers, Jehangir left his mountain fastness in the year 1826, and marched for a second time on Kashgar. The Chinese garrison quitted the citadel and attacked the invading force. The combat was fiercely contested; but, although the details have not been remembered, the result was the overthrow of the Chinese. This further defeat was the signal to the people of Kashgaria for a general rising, and the discomfiture of the Chinese was made complete by an insurrection throughout the country. Their garrisons were, after more or less resistance, overwhelmed, and those Chinese who had the misfortune to become captive experienced the cruelty of a vindictive and fanatical adversary.

Successful in the field, Jehangir was proclaimed at the capital by the title of the Seyyid Jehangir Sultan, and his authority was soon recognized at Yarkand also. His personal satisfaction certainly was not abated from his being able to check the excessive pretensions and demands of his friend Mahomed Ali; but his gratification at the departure of the Khokandian contingent must have been short-lived when he heard that the Chinese were returning in force. Reinforcements had been sent from Kansuh on the news of Jehangir's rising, and fresh levies had been raised among the Tungan colonies at Hami and Turfan, so that in the course of a few months a large army was collected at Ili for the purpose of reconquering the southern province and driving out the Khoja. A mandarin with a reputation for military capacity was sent from Pekin to take the supreme command, and some nine months after the fall of Kashgar a Chinese army of nearly a hundred thousand men was assembled on the Tian Shan. It was thought for a time that the Emperor would himself take the command; but in the end he deemed it better to leave the supervision of the arrangements to the mandarin Chang, from whose capacity much was expected thirteen years later, on the occasion of the first war with Europeans.

Jehangir was not disposed to surrender all he had won without making a fight for it, and he took up a position near the town of Yangabad, a little distance east of Kashgar. There the Chinese attacked him, and, after a fierce but brief engagement, completely defeated him.* He attempted to

* The following incident of this battle claims preservation: "When the armies sighted each other they pitched their camps in preparation for the decisive contest that was at hand. In accordance with immemorial custom each side put forward on the following day its champion.

make a second stand at Kashgar, but his troops were too disheartened for further resistance. Nor was he more fortunate when he sought to provide for his personal safety by flight. The passes were snowed up, and the Chinese, closely pursuing, succeeded in capturing him. Jehangir was sent to Pekin to show in person the thoroughness with which Taoukwang's lieutenants had carried out their commission. The Emperor or his advisers did not temper their victory with clemency; for the unfortunate Jehangir, after being subjected to various indignities, was executed and quartered as a traitor.

The defeat of the Khoja pretender was followed by various repressive measures against the peoples of Kashgaria. Not content with punishing all caught in the act of rebellion, the Chinese removed a large number of the Mahomedan population from Kashgar to Ili, on the northern side of the Tian Shan. Twelve thousand families were thus forcibly compelled to emigrate, and in their new home they became known as the Tarantchis or toilers. The energy shown in punishing refractory subjects was for a moment imparted to the policy adopted towards their neighbours, and trade and other intercourse was broken off and forbidden with Khokand. It would have been well for China if this resolve had been rigidly adhered to, for all her later misfortunes were due to the hostile influence of that State and its ruler. But the Khan was resolved not to lose so valuable a perquisite as the custom dues of Kashgar, and he accordingly proceeded to invade that State as soon as he learnt that the greater number of the Chinese troops had been withdrawn. For a second time he put himself forward as the champion of the Khojas, and employed the name and person of Jehangir's eldest brother, Yusuf, to conceal his own designs and ambitious motives. Suffice it to say that his operations

---

On the part of the Chinese a gigantic Calmuck archer opposed, on the part of Jehangir, an equally formidable Khokandian. The former was armed with his proper weapons, the latter with a gun of some clumsy and ancient design; and while the Khokandian was busily engaged with his intricate apparatus, the Chinese archer shot him dead with an arrow through the breast."

were so far successful that the Chinese agreed to revert to the previous arrangement, and Mahomed Ali, on his part, promised to restrain the Khojas. Of Yusuf and his brothers we hear no more, and fourteen years of peace and prosperity followed for the subject peoples under the auspices of the Chinese Government.

Misfortunes rarely come singly, and while the Mahomedans in Central Asia were causing much trouble, there occurred at the opposite extremity of the Empire another insurrection in the island of Formosa, where the untamed tribes of the interior fell in ferocity and hostility little short of those of Turkestan. It is impossible to say with any confidence what was the origin of the rising that took place in Formosa in the month of October, 1832, and that continued with scarcely abated force until the following summer. In 1833 tranquillity was finally restored, or, as the official edict put it, "all are now again quiet, and the mind of His Majesty is filled with consolation." But before that desirable consummation was attained many Chinese soldiers were killed and the resources of the maritime province of Fuhkien were severely strained in the task of restoring the Imperial authority. The divisions between the insurgent leaders seem to have rendered the task of Taoukwang's officers more easy than at first it appeared that it would be. In this case, however, the end was effected; the result justified the conduct of the Imperial commissioners.

The very same year was marked by another rebellion in the island of Hainan, where the Chinese, surrounded by a region of the most remarkable natural wealth and fertility, have long been content to exercise little more than a nominal authority, and to pursue the unremunerative and restricted career of fishermen. The interior of that island consists of a mountain range, whither the aboriginal inhabitants, the Black Li of an earlier period, had retired before the encroachments of the Chinese settlers. Some time before the year 1830 they broke loose from all control, and, profiting by the weakness or apathy of the Celestials, descended into the plains and committed many depredations. This onslaught by a savage people on the unprepared and peaceful settlers drew attention to the weakness of the tenure of Chinese authority, and many petitions were forwarded to Canton for aid. At last the entreaties of the settlers could be no longer ignored, and troops were sent to attack the aborigines. The Viceroy even went in person, and his measures were completely successful. Security was obtained for the people, and Hainan reverted to its natural position as a Chinese island. By right both of its resources and situation this is an island of which the outer world is certain before long to hear more.

The Emperor had many causes of anxiety in his own domestic affairs and in the condition of the country. Famine in the North, and inundations from the overflow of the great rivers, entailed an amount of suffering and a loss of human life that would appear almost incredible if stated in the bald language of figures. But in a country in parts not merely over-populated, but with a population rapidly increasing to excess, such sweeping calamities seemed to be the providential remedy of a permanent evil. Yet under a combination of difficulties the Government never showed itself supine, or allowed itself to be suspected of indifference to popular suffering. Taoukwang's energy was laudably conspicuous, and no means were spared by him to mitigate suffering and to prevent the recurrence of national catastrophes.

In his domestic life, also, Taoukwang was not free from disquietude. In the year 1831, his only son, who had been selected as his successor, and who was then twenty years of age, gave him some cause of offence. The Emperor, enraged at the prince's conduct, is said to have inflicted personal chastisement with his own hand. The blow may have hastened the end of this prince, a weak youth addicted to debauchery in every form. He certainly died soon afterwards, leaving Taoukwang without a son. The grief at this occurrence was, however, soon appeased by the news that two of his favourite concubines had been delivered of sons, one of whom became, many years afterwards, the Emperor Hienfung. At this critical moment the Emperor was seized with a severe illness, which seemed likely to prove mortal;

and his brother Hwuy Wang took steps to secure the succession for himself. Taoukwang fortunately recovered, and those who had hoped to profit by his disappearance became the objects of his suspicion, and felt the force of his righteous indignation. His troubles, however, were not yet over; the death of the Empress, his favourite wife, cast a still greater gloom over the year 1831, and made a permanent impression on the mind of the ruler, which, always disposed to brooding, became tinged with a deeper shade of melancholy.

These troubles in the palace and in the bosom of the reigning family were the fitting prelude to the far more serious perils which suddenly revealed themselves in the interior of the country. Taoukwang had had minor insurrections and popular disturbances to deal with, like all his predecessors; but they had not presented themselves in any grave form, and they had been confined to remote quarters of his dominions. Even the secret societies which had disturbed his father gave no symptoms of life, and were apparently deprived of the importance which they once possessed. These anticipations received, however, a shock not less severe than sudden in the year 1832, that following the deaths of the heir-apparent and the Empress.

The Miaotze have been mentioned on many previous occasions as a source of trouble to the governors in the southern provinces of the Empire. They had been kept in order of late years by the fear as much of losing their supply of salt as of active reprisals on the part of the Imperial authorities. But there was always a sense of strained relationship between these independent hillmen and the local mandarins, who interpreted their inaction as a testimony to their own power and vigilance, and who were disposed to be arrogant in proportion as their neighbours were humble. In 1832, tired of a life of inaction, or irritated by some more than usually dictatorial act on the part of the officials, they broke out into rebellion, and one of their chiefs was said to have taken the extreme step of proclaiming himself Emperor. However false that may have been, the conduct of the Miaotze could not have been more pronounced in its hostility than it was, and a small body of Chinese troops was ordered to proceed against the insurgents and pursue them even into their fastnesses.

The Miaotze of the district round Lienchow, in the north-west of the province of Kwantung, were the most turbulent on this occasion. Their chief took the distinctive title of Wang, with the appellation of "the Golden Dragon." But perhaps the strongest proof that in this outbreak they were prompted by some deeper motive than an instinct of marauding was furnished by the marked forbearance they evinced towards the people. Four towns passed into their possession, but the inhabitants were spared and treated with consideration. The military alone were put to the sword. Were it conceivable that the Chinese could have accepted liberty and emancipation from a foreign yoke at the hands of a semi-barbarous tribe, then the Miaotze might have been joined by large numbers of the Chinese people, discontented with their lot and not over-well disposed to the authority of Pekin. But the national dislike to the Miaotze as an alien and inferior race was not to be removed by any considerations of a temporary identity of interest, and although the Miaotze chief's proclamation and line of conduct showed political sagacity and a statesman-like instinct, it could not convert the ebullition of warlike fervour among his own people into a patriotic movement on a large scale.

Yet the valour of the Miaotze secures the movement from being consigned to the limbo of oblivion on account of its insignificance. A small detachment under the command of a Manchu officer was attacked in an ambuscade and exterminated. The arms of those who fell increased the scanty stock of weapons in the possession of the Miaotze. On the approach of a stronger force they retired to the security of their hills, covered with snow during the winter. Peremptory orders were sent from Pekin to suppress the insurrection, and Le, the Viceroy at Canton, took the field in person, with all the troops he could collect. These were not very efficient, and when Le came into contact with the rebels he found himself compelled to remain on the defensive. Other measures were resorted to in order to effect the pacification of the country, and the services of some of the Miaotze were utilized for the purpose of bringing their kinsmen to their knees. But for a long time neither manner of proceeding effected much to any purpose. The traitors were discovered and executed, and Taoukwang's levies were repulsed, although some successful skirmishes were magnified by the process common to all embarrassed administrations into great victories. Even the despatch to the scene of Hengan, one of the great functionaries of the Court, failed to produce any speedy improvement.

While the Canton troops were making this slow progress, those of Hoonan had been more fortunate. In May, 1832, they gained a decided success over the rebels at the town of Pingtseuen, and drove the Miaotze back into their hills. The blow was made still more severe by the death of the chief, Golden Dragon. So far as that portion of the country was concerned the rebels were completely overthrown, and the lieutenants of Taoukwang could conscientiously report that they had maintained and vindicated his power. This victory was, however, heavily compensated for by the signal defeat of the Viceroy Le and the Canton army in the following month. Encouraged by the success of his Northern colleague, Le attacked the main body of the Miaotze in their mountain fastness; but the result was not flattering to his skill and courage. The Chinese army was driven back in confusion, and eighty officers and many hundreds of soldiers were slain. Le endeavoured to conceal the extent of his discomfiture, and in his official report omitted to give the names of the men who had fallen. This produced great dissatisfaction in the army, and a mutiny was only averted by the prompt addition of the names of those who had deserved well of their country. For, as the soldiers said, "there is no use in our sacrificing our lives in secret; if our toils are concealed from the Emperor, neither we nor our posterity will be rewarded!"

Le was severely reprimanded for his incompetence or misfortune, and, under the goad of Imperial displeasure, raised his army in the field to an effective strength of 15,000 men, with which he prepared to exact a summary revenge.

He was not destined to effect the solution of the difficulty. The credit rested with the military of Hoonan, and with the resolute acts of the Imperial commissioner Hengan. Le was removed from his high post and recalled to Pekin, when he was banished to Urumsti. His lieutenants were punished in different ways, and the successful Hoonan officer was appointed viceroy in Le's place. Whatever may have been the causes that contributed to the speedy pacification of the Miaotze region, Hengan was able to report, "ten days after his arrival," that the principal offenders had been brought to justice, that the Miaotze had given pledges of improved behaviour, and that some of them had become so submissive as even to shave their heads and adopt the Tartar tail. Although there were subsequent rumours of fresh risings and renewed disorders, the Miaotze never after that day disturbed the Emperor's peace of mind.

Some were disposed to think that Hengan's arrangement was a farce, and that the Miaotze remained as turbulent in their practices as ever. The lapse of time served to show that such scepticism was not justified by the facts, and that the fierce Yaoujin, or Wolfmen, as they were called, had indeed consented to abstain from violence. With the death of their chief, the Golden Dragon, at Pingtseuen, the tribe lost the man who had given a motive to their uprising, and who seemed to supply, in political capacity, the main deficiencies of a semi-barbarous people. The Miaotze have ever since been quiescent, if not altogether as dutiful in their allegiance as other Chinese subjects. But they are still independent, and their mountain homes constitute a region apart from the rest of the Empire. A later generation may witness some fresh ebullition of martial ardour or of predatory instinct. But when that time comes, the Pekin Government will be able, by the aid of European weapons, to accomplish the task of correction with greater ease than at any previous period. The Miaotze have been magnified by Western writers into a source of national danger. They were never that, and even as the pest of certain localities their days of power are already numbered.

These insurrections, and the military operations which

they entailed, resulted in a great increase in the expenditure of the Government, and in 1834 the admission was made that there was a considerable deficit. The two Mahomedan risings and "the ugly monkey tricks," as they were officially termed, of the Miaotze, resulted in an excess of expenditure over revenue of not less than thirty million taels, or nearly ten millions sterling. Natural calamities had caused the decline of the revenue at the very moment that a full exchequer was most needed to meet the requirements of warlike operations in several distinct regions.

During these first fifteen years of Taoukwang's reign, the pretensions of the Emperor of China as the great sovereign of the world were preserved intact. During that period all diplomatic intercourse with the Western peoples was broken off; while the frequent embassies from the States of Asia confirmed the appearance of supremacy, and contributed to swell the pride of Taoukwang. Envoys from the tributary States of Burmah, Nepaul, Siam, and Cochin-China arrived in due succession, and resided for the stated period at the capital. The neighbouring potentates carried their grievances for settlement to the foot of the Dragon Throne, and the increasing intercourse with foreigners at Canton was a cause of anxiety within the Imperial Cabinet, rather than the sign of any waning power among the feudatory States. Riots in Szchuen and Kansuh, the revival of piratical efforts on the Canton river, were no more than ordinary occurrences in the life of a vast Empire; and although the introduction of high-priced and greatly prized European articles into the country had entailed the increase of smuggling, the evil was long nothing more than a local nuisance. Up to this point, China had remained undisturbed in a world of her own. The sense of superiority will remain much longer, but the time is now at hand when the Government and the people must be rudely awakened from several of their most cherished opinions. The great foreign question had long been approaching that crisis which has now to be described and considered, and on the settlement of which depended the right of foreign nations to trade and to hold diplomatic intercourse with the Chinese. Up to the year 1834 there was no sign that the end of the old order of things was approaching, and when Taoukwang chose, at the close of the year, a new wife to succeed the deceased Empress in her high station, there was no reason to suppose that he was not as lofty and as unapproachable a sovereign as the greatest of his predecessors.

CHAPTER IV.

THE GROWTH OF FOREIGN INTERCOURSE.

THE monopoly of the trade with China had been granted by royal charter to the East India Company, but the term (it expired in April, 1834) of its rights and privileges was approaching at the period which we have now reached, and the question of its renewal, in whole or in part, was the one matter under consideration in Leadenhall Street, as well as with the authorities of Calcutta and the merchants at Canton. But if the subject was of the greatest interest to the English community, it neither concerned nor received much attention from the Chinese; and were it not that the change in the manner of the relations between the two countries which ensued from it was followed by results of the greatest importance, the topic would not claim much notice here.

The views of Chinese officials were extremely simple. They had no objection to foreigners coming to Canton, and buying or selling articles of commerce, so long as they derived personal profit from the trade, and so long also as the laws of the Empire were not disputed or violated. The merchants of the East India Company were content to adapt themselves to this view, and they might have carried on relations with the Hong merchants for an indefinite period, and without any more serious collision than occasional interruptions. The renewal of the monopoly would have left things in exactly the same position as when intercourse was first established; and, although the English merchants were on a distinctly inferior footing, they would have been able to continue the trade in its actual restricted limits at Canton.

THE EAST INDIA COMPANY.

If the Chinese thought very little in a political sense of the Company and its representatives, they thought a very great deal about the English sovereign, and they regarded with indignation, not unmixed with alarm, the pretensions of the latter to equal rights, and to a rank of dignity in no way short of that of the Celestial ruler himself. Their opinions on this point were strengthened by the proceedings in connection with the two embassies from the King of England, and by every visit of a British man-of-war to their ports. It became clear to the most obtuse mandarin mind that, although these foreigners might not be placed in the same scale of power and civilization as the favoured people of the Middle Kingdom, they did possess in their formidable warships a power of inflicting damage with which China had nothing to cope. The cardinal point in the foreign policy of the Pekin Government thus turned on the exclusion of the representatives of the English sovereign. The officials were not unwilling to hold intercourse with a body of traders; they would willingly have nothing whatever to do with an independent and exacting sovereign. The former could be kept at a respectful distance, and in a mood thankful for the smallest favours. The latter would have to be treated after a different fashion, and one for which the records of the Empire, at any period of its existence, afforded no precedent.

The surprise and the indignation of the Chinese authorities were great, therefore, when in the year 1834 they learnt that by the decree of a remote potentate the conditions of the barely tolerated intercourse with the principal of the outer peoples had undergone a complete and radical alteration. So far as Chinese affairs were concerned, the East India Company passed out of history, and the merchants of Canton became entitled to and received the direct protection of the English Government. The Chinese neither understood nor cared to understand the causes or the precise meaning of this change. They would have thought it rather an aggravation than a mitigation of the offence, that a foreign prince should make trade with China free instead of the monopoly of certain persons. They saw clearly enough that the alteration could not possibly redound to their national honour and security, and that it must be followed by the more frequent appearance of the formidable foreign war-vessels, and of officials intent on maintaining the dignity of their sovereign. The abolition of the Company's monopoly, and what is called the opening of the trade, were followed by a sharp revulsion of sentiment among Chinese officials. Their policy towards foreigners then became one of intensified and unqualified hostility.

In the animated discussions which were carried on in the Houses of Parliament during the years 1833-34, great stress was laid upon the probable increase that would take place in the trade with China, if free intercourse were proclaimed. In this speculation hope was allowed to get the better of reason, and these favourable anticipations were only to be realized after considerable delay, and when other and violent agencies had been enlisted in the work. High authority, however, was ranged in support of these opinions; but, speaking with all the advantage of later experience, it is only possible to have the opinion that, however necessary in itself, however beneficial to English commerce, and indirectly to China as quickening her political growth, the opening of the trade may have been, it at the same time not unreasonably irritated the Chinese, and inflamed their Government against Europeans.

The transfer of authority was demonstrated by an act which left the Chinese in no doubt as to what had happened. On the 10th of December, 1833, a Royal Commission appointed Lord Napier chief superintendent of trade with China, and two other officials as assistant-superintendents, of whom one was Sir John Davis. The arrival of Lord Napier in July of the following year brought matters to a head, and his instructions left him no choice in the execution of his duties save to perform them at Canton, or at such other place as the English sovereign might appoint. His arrival at Canton was promptly followed by difficulties with the Viceroy of the province, while the European merchants were threatened with the stoppage of the trade. Lord Napier's first act was to address a letter of courtesy announcing his appointment and safe arrival to the Viceroy. But the Chinese officials, perceiving that its tone was different from the petitions of the Company, refused to so much as receive it, and returned the document to the writer. Such a commencement did not promise well for the success of the new relationship.

The arrival of the Chief Superintendent excited great attention among the Chinese, and official requests were sent to the merchants of the guild, or hong, to ascertain exactly what were the objects and intentions of this new functionary. Their views were tersely summed up and expressed in the name by which they designated the representative of the English king. He was a "barbarian eye," come to take stock of the mysteries and resources of the Flowery Land. The Viceroy was not content with instituting inquiries; he issued an order. The foreigners had, by the laws of the Empire, the right to reside only at Macao, but as an act of special grace they had been permitted, on receiving and paying for a passport, to proceed to Canton. A special order was made that the new "barbarian eye" was not to be allowed to visit Canton, except after request made in compliance with established regulations. Lord Napier asked neither permit nor favour. He hardly deigned to touch at the so-called Portuguese possession of Macao, and went straight to Canton as the representative of his sovereign to the Chinese ruler. The mandarins were not merely furious at the audacity of the English official, but full of apprehension at the consequences that might follow to themselves when it became known at Pekin that a foreign ambassador had forced his way through one of the gates of the Empire. There was, under the circumstances, little to wonder at in the Viceroy curtly returning Lord Napier his letters of announcement, and refusing to hold any intercourse with one who came uninvited, and who established himself of his own accord in the position of a welcome guest.

The Hong merchants and the Hoppo, or Superintendent of Trade, being responsible for the good behaviour and prompt obedience of the foreigners, who were only allowed to come to Canton on their guarantee, it was always a very easy matter for the Viceroy to assert his official authority. On this occasion he brought all the pressure he could to bear on the native merchants in order that the mission of Lord

Napier might be rendered abortive, and that the foreign traders should be subjected to the most complete subservience under the laws of China. He succeeded as well as he could have possibly desired. The Hoppo and his subordinates were all devotion, for "the national dignity was at stake," and presented a memorial for the suspension of the trade. Lord Napier was confined to the factories. All business transactions were discontinued. The native servants left the employ of the Europeans; even their boatmen refused to perform their duties, and they became virtually prisoners. The trade was suspended in the most practical and pronounced manner, and the Europeans were confined to their small settlement. Such were the immediate consequences and the attendant features of the transfer of the supervision of English trade from the Company to the Crown.*

In addition to the national dislike of the foreigners, and to the official desire to maintain intact the dignity of the Empire, another circumstance contributed to increase the Chinese indignation against Lord Napier, and to make them regard with more or less indifference the prospect of a cessation of the foreign trade. This was the steady decrease through exportation in the amount of silver coin in the country. A report to the throne in 1833 stated that during the previous eleven years nearly sixty million taels of silver had been sent out of the realm, and that the Empire was

---

* It may be parenthetically observed at this point that comment on these facts is reserved to the end of this chapter. It must not be supposed that, while giving this summary of events in the most favourable light for China from her point of view, we are able to see any ground for acquiescing in the lightly formed and easily adopted view that England was "forcing a trade on China"—a phrase first used during the debates of 1833. In one form or another the change was inevitable. Respect for Chinese pride, admiration for an undeviating and historic policy, will not blind the eyes of the thoughtful to the truth that the attitude of the Chinese was one that could not be maintained save by superior force. There will be agreement also that it was well for the world at large, well probably for China herself, that pre-eminence in war was wanting to leave the Celestial Empire an unsolved mystery—the inscrutable embodiment, as a Government, of the most intense selfishness—to the end of time.

consequently poorer by this amount. Various edicts were passed prohibiting the export of silver, and ordaining severe punishments for the infringement of the law. But as the people continued to purchase opium and other articles from the foreigners, they were compelled to give in return their silver. In all sincerity the Chinese authorities most ardently desired the stopping of the trade.

Lord Napier had a very difficult task to perform, and one in which it was, perhaps, impossible to attain complete success with honour. He presented to the personal abuse and violent attacks of the mandarins a courteous firmness which almost repelled their efforts. But he did not confine his action to defensive measures; he assumed a vigorous offensive by giving expression to several home-truths. His first document, which was of the character of a public notice to the Chinese merchants, closed with the following sentence: "The merchants of Great Britain wish to trade with all China, on principles of mutual benefit; they will never relax in their exertions till they gain a point of equal importance to both countries, and the Viceroy will find it as easy to stop the current of the Canton river as to carry into effect the insane determinations of the Hong." There is not much reason to feel surprise if the Chinese officials construed this proclamation into an open defiance of their power, and viewed it as an arrogant claim to prosecute a trade with China by or against their will. They retorted with an edict absolutely and unconditionally prohibiting all intercourse whatever with the English people.

That the Chinese were quite in earnest and fully prepared to brave the worst was clearly shown when their military appeared at the factories and forcibly removed all Chinese servants, and when the batteries of the Bogue forts fired on two English men-of-war. Lord Napier's difficulties were aggravated by his ill-health, and, in deference to the requests of the English merchants, he consented to leave Canton and to retire to Macao. The Chinese thus obtained another diplomatic victory, and they reasserted in this way, and with undiminished vigour, the principle that no foreigner, merchant or envoy, should be allowed to come to Canton, save by their permit, granted only to the petition and on the guarantee of the Hong merchants. Lord Napier published a formal protest against "this act of unprecedented tyranny and injustice." But it had no effect, and, allowing for the views of the Chinese Government, it cannot be disputed that, not only were they fully in the right, but that their fortitude and fearlessness may not unjustly attract some admiration.

A correspondence which, at this early stage, assumed so acrimonious a tone, could hardly have proved beneficial to either country by being continued. It was suddenly interrupted by the death of Lord Napier, who had been taken ill before leaving Canton, and who suffered many privations on his journey to Macao, where he died less than three months after his first arrival in China. Although Lord Napier's method of dealing with the Chinese officials was blunt, if not dictatorial, he saw clearly enough that there was nothing to be gained by truckling to them, and his position as a representative of England forbade his resorting to those concessions which the mercantile community had previously been in the habit of offering as the price for the toleration of their presence.

The departure of Lord Napier from Canton was followed by the opening of the ships' holds, and by the resumption of trade. But the trade superintendents were ignored, even after his death, which shortly followed, and a petition was sent home to the King praying for his protection and effectual intervention in the interests of English commerce in China. Trade with foreigners was placed under certain provisions, which received the express sanction of Taoukwang himself, and became the recognized law. These provisions were divided under eight heads as Regulations, of which the principal were the prohibition of the entry of men-of-war into the inner seas, and the compulsion on Europeans to make all their requests through the Hong merchants in the form of a petition. The powers conferred on the superintendents of trade by the Commission of William IV. were completely ignored, and so far as it lay in mandarin power to decree the manner in which the foreign intercourse should be carried on, the position reverted to the conditions under which it was managed during the days of the Company. For a short space of time it seemed as if the appointment of Lord Napier were to be only a passing episode, and that the Chinese had effectually attained their one object, " to prevent the English establishing themselves permanently at Canton."

While the English officials were busy reporting their opinions on the new system, the Chinese, flattering themselves that they had carried their points, did not further interfere with the dealings between the Hong merchants and the Europeans. There was the usual amount of opium smuggled into the country, followed on rare occasions by the detection of those engaged in it, and by their punishment and the forfeiting of their goods. Sometimes the opium was publicly destroyed, but more often only a portion was burnt for the benefit of public morals, while by far the larger part was reserved for the gratification of the mandarins in their privacy. More serious cause of disturbance arose out of the piratical attacks on merchant vessels becalmed off the coast, or in distress. One vessel, the *Troughton*, was attacked in the Canton estuary by two junks filled with armed natives. The ship was plundered, and the captain and several of the crew seriously injured and maltreated. It was a matter of surprise how, under the circumstances, they escaped with their lives. Some attempt was made to discover the assailants, and several arrests were made, probably of innocent persons. But, although the subject was long under discussion, no one was ever punished for this daring outrage in Chinese waters.

The death of the Canton viceroy, named Loo, who had conducted affairs during this period of change, was attended by a certain modification in the relations between the two peoples. After long discussion and many threats to put an end to the trade altogether, the new superintendent, Captain Elliot, was granted permission, in March, 1837, to come to Canton; but the privilege was only conceded in the usual way on the petition of the foreign merchants through those of the Hong. During the interval of more than two years since Lord Napier's death the matter had been several times referred to Pekin, and it was only by special Imperial decree that Captain Elliot's arrival was sanctioned in order that he might fulfil his official duties of "controlling the merchants and seamen." The value of this concession was very greatly reduced by the stipulation that he was to strictly observe the old regulations, and not to rank in any way above the supercargoes. The conditions which the Chinese sought to, and did for a time, impose on these English officials, were those that a proud and arrogant Government might seek to inflict on a body of traders. They could not possibly have proved enduring in the case of a Government not less proud and solicitous of its dignity than any other.

A new element of discord revealed itself with steadily increasing force during these years. The foreign trade, regarded in the abstract, had always been distasteful to the Government of Pekin and to the old school of ministers, but it had become a means of livelihood to a considerable class in the population of Canton and the maritime provinces of the South; it was also a source of profit to a large number of the active officials. Its abolition would, therefore, excite as much disapproval as approbation, and the Pekin authorities felt constrained to allow matters to progress in the natural way, consoling themselves with the reflection that so long as the trade was confined to Canton, the influence of the "outer barbarians" could not do much mischief. But if it was just endurable that foreign races should come to traffic with the Celestial people for the purpose of enriching them, and in order to place at their service articles unknown in the Flowery Land, it was simply intolerable that these strange traders should carry off with them much of the national wealth, and in the form of all others the most disagreeable, its money—the silver bullion of the realm. The Doctors of the Hanlin, the most prejudiced of the students of Confucius, availed themselves of the fact to stir up the prejudices of the people, and to arouse the Emperor's mind to the terrible dangers that would accrue from the impoverishment of the State.

The facts, too, were startling enough, and would have excited apprehension in the minds of any thoughtful Government. The Chinese were neither unreasonable nor exercising any questionable right in attributing this extraordinary drain of public treasure to the foreign intercourse, and in denouncing it accordingly. It was officially stated—and the figures do not appear much exaggerated—that ten million taels of silver were annually taken out of China; and it was not difficult to draw from this the conclusion that, if it were allowed to proceed unchecked, the country would be reduced to a state of bankruptcy. The Chinese did not attempt to analyze the matter, and they could not lay any consolation to their hearts about the balance of trade being against them. They saw the plain fact of the depletion of the national treasure, and they angrily denounced the trade with foreigners as its sole cause. The mind of the Government being cleared up on this point, it only remained to decide how best to put a stop to, or at least to reduce to its smallest possible limits, the cause of this glaring evil.

Never at any period of their history had the ruling powers in China been more desirous of curtailing and arresting the growth of intercourse with foreigners than in the years immediately following the expiry of the monopoly, and the transfer of authority from the Company to the Crown. But with the will the power of doing so did not come. The difficulty of summarily ending the matter had been indefinitely increased by the fact that the foreign trade had become an integral part of the national life in the great emporium of the south, and that it could only be discontinued at the cost of some popular suffering and discontent. Dislike of the whole connection with foreign countries screened itself behind the opposition to one item in particular, and the immutable principles of morality were invoked to cast a stigma on those who supplied the people, in defiance of the law, with the means of gratifying their passions.

There had been references at an earlier period to the import of foreign opium, and the Emperor Kiaking had begun a reign of misfortune with an edict denouncing its use as the indulgence of a hopeless sin. But the lesson he strove to inculcate had never been learnt. A new generation had grown up, which only knew that the life of Kiaking and his courtiers had been in flat contradiction with these fine moral theories, and who continued to follow their inclination in the matter of opium-smoking. When attention was officially drawn to the same subject under Taoukwang, it was not as a question of morality, but of finance. The annual drain of the silver coin, not the deterioration in the moral or physical qualities of the Chinese, was the motive which stirred Taoukwang's Government into action. The proof of this is furnished by numerous edicts and decrees issued by both the Emperor and the Viceroy at Canton. If further proof were needed, it would be found in the simple fact that the first official utterance on the subject was a proposal to legalize the importation of opium, and for the simple reason that the greater the penalties passed upon its use, the wider had the practice spread.

The views of this memorialist, although stated in clear language, were not such as to commend themselves to the minds of Chinese officials. At Pekin it seemed that to legalize the importation of opium would have exactly the opposite effect from what was contemplated. By increasing the opportunity of purchasing opium, it was said that the quantity consumed would increase in the like proportion. An angry discussion followed in the pages of the *Pekin Gazette*, and the memorialist was roughly handled, although his arguments remained unanswered. The one remedy received with any favour was to expel the foreigner, and to destroy all the stores of opium on which the authorities could lay their hands. Many threats were made to execute the former project, and some attempts to carry out the latter; but although a little opium was burnt, and a great deal more appropriated for the personal use of the mandarins, the Pekin Government long hesitated, not so much from fear of foreign reprisals as from a not unnatural dread of the consequences of disturbing the existing order of things, to give effect to its own wishes and decrees.

Increased significance was given to this controversy by the interruption of official communications between Captain Elliot and the Chinese authorities at the end of 1837, less than six months after he had been permitted to proceed to Canton. He sent home a letter of complaint, in general terms, as to the difficulty of conducting any sort of amicable relations with the local mandarins, and endorsed the growing demand for the right of dealing with the Pekin Government direct. So far as official intercourse was concerned, this rupture proved complete. Captain Elliot hauled down his flag at Canton and removed to Macao—thus showing, for a second time, that the attempt to conduct diplomatic relations on a basis of trade involved circumstances that were incompatible with one another, and that could not be reconciled.

Twelve months later, when a small squadron had been sent to the Bogue from India, Captain Elliot returned to Canton and re-hoisted his flag. A conflict seemed likely to ensue when the Chinese forts fired on an English ship and compelled her to undergo a search. The English fleet proceeded to Canton, and the Chinese mustered their forces, both on the river and on shore, for the purpose of making such resistance as they could. When the affair looked at its worst, and seemed to hardly admit of a peaceful ending, a friendly understanding was happily effected. The admirals met and exchanged cards; and the mandarins, being assured of the general good-will of England, seemed disposed to relax their hostile regulations towards her subjects. But the import of opium and the steady outflow of silver continued to excite their feelings; and the antipathy arising from these causes, after a very brief interval, regained the upper hand in their councils.

It will be appropriate to close this chapter at a point when the growing dimensions of the trade, and the extraordinary conditions under which it was conducted, were beginning to raise grave doubts as to the possibility of placing it, until the Chinese had been compelled to recognize in foreign countries nations with rights equal to their own, on any basis likely to endure, but before the hope had been abandoned of discovering a solution save by force. Chinese policy was of a double kind, and it was hampered in its action by two rival influences, urging it in opposite directions. Neither the knowledge nor the traditions of the Pekin Government allowed it to look with a favourable eye on the possibility of close intercourse with foreign nations. The admission of equality with outside peoples could not but exercise a corrosive effect on the ideas and political existence of the Celestials. On the other hand, the people themselves, particularly those in the great commercial capital of the South, were most strongly disposed to trade, and in the indulgence of these natural instincts it mattered comparatively little with whom they carried on commercial relations. The one condition, from their point of view, was that the trade should be profitable to them. It became the chief object of the Government, in its endeavour to arrest its development, to show that the profits were secured by the foreigner; and in this, as later events will reveal, it met with more than partial success.

An event had occurred which, although having apparently no direct connection with the further progress and development of China's external relations, was destined to prove the precursor of many circumstances calculated to bring the minds of two great peoples to an inclination of greater friendship, and to make the policies of their respective Governments more harmonious and compatible with each other. It so happened that, at the most critical point of the question of English intercourse with China, a new sovereign, young and accomplished, succeeded to the discharge of the difficult duties of ruler of the British Empire—a circumstance which, if in itself not calculated to ensure conviction as to a satisfactory issue from a tedious and intricate controversy, raised a hope in at least some loyal breasts * that the yet unwritten pages of Queen Victoria's reign would record the settlement of the relations between England and China, not on a footing of distrust and latent hostility, but on one of confidence and mutual consideration. Glancing back in the full light of our present knowledge to the events of a reign which with each year has gathered new glory, and in which each achievement, whether in peace or in war, has seemed to

* "'A new reign is fertile in brilliant projects,' and one might argue from probabilities that the plans that are to fill one day with their details the yet unwritten history of Queen Victoria, will be distinguished by no common lustre. From such a series of noble attempts one, at least, should not be wanting—a sincere and persevering endeavour to improve the British relations with China."—"Chinese Repository," vol. vii. p. 149.

prepare the way for some still more remarkable triumph, it is clear that even in this particular the reign of Queen Victoria has been illustrious, for the acts of her successive Governments have gone far to improve the character of English relations with China. If it was reserved for Queen Victoria to be the English sovereign to twice draw the sword in anger on China, it remains to the glory of her reign, and as demonstrating her sincere and effectual efforts to promote the interests of her subjects and the cause of peace, that her present relations with the Celestial Empire are such as promise a durable and friendly understanding, and a peace which nothing but some untoward event or ill-timed accident can prevent being permanent.

CHAPTER V.

THE BEGINNING OF FOREIGN COMPLICATIONS.

THE Chinese character has always been marked by a certain astuteness in seizing upon the most convenient and plausible argument to support their contentions, whether it be in politics or in commerce; and, as time went on, they fastened in their foreign relations more and more on the question of the opium traffic, about the merits of which they found opinion to be divided among the Europeans themselves. This detail seemed to offer more vulnerable points of attack on moral grounds than the whole question of foreign intercourse. Not merely were edicts drawn up and published, forbidding, in the most peremptory language, the use of the drug, but severe punishments were threatened and sometimes inflicted on the unhappy individuals who yielded to the temptation. In one province it was even said that the singular punishment of cutting out a portion of the upper lip was resorted to; but those who suffered always belonged to the poorer classes of the community. The officials, more addicted to the practice than any others, screened their delinquencies behind the zeal with which they prosecuted those who had neither the means nor the influence to protect themselves. Without going so far as to directly question the sincerity of the Chinese Government's abhorrence of the use of opium, the fact remains that those who suffered for its offended majesty were the poor, or those only who could not defend themselves. The most inveterate opium-smokers continued their practice, amused perhaps at the credulity or the ignorance of the Pekin authorities.

The question might have gone on for a long time in this way—enthusiastic fervour among the theoretical statesmen and doctors at Pekin, and self-seeking and systematic apathy and indifference among the practical officials at Canton—but for the despatch to the South, in the character of Special Commissioner, of one of the most remarkable men China has produced, to our knowledge, within this century. It need hardly be said that we mean the Commissioner Lin. In January, 1839, when the trade had been twice suspended and timidly resumed, the Emperor commissioned Lin Tsihseu, an official of good reputation, and governor of the double province of Houkwang, to proceed to Canton to report on the exact position of affairs, and to propound the best remedy for the evil.

Before Lin's arrival affairs had become extremely critical. The Hong merchants, who were held responsible by the Viceroy for the good conduct of the foreigners, had been compelled by the officials to go so far as to threaten to pull down the house and factory of one English merchant who was assumed to be an opium trader. The officials themselves caused the execution of criminal delinquents, for the use of opium or of some different offence mattered little for their purpose, to be held in the square outside the very doors of the foreign houses. Increased significance was given to this latter event by the collision it entailed between the mob and the foreign residents, who, under great provocation, took the law into their own hands, and cleared the square of spectators and executioners alike. The consequences of this riot might have been most serious, but the timely arrival of a magistrate and a small body of soldiers restored order before dangerous passions had been given full play. None the less this riot is worthy of record as the first symptom of the latent antipathy smouldering on both sides. A public notice was then issued by the English superintendent, Captain Elliot, warning all English subjects to discontinue the illicit opium trade, and stating that "Her Majesty's Government will in no way interfere if the Chinese Government shall think fit to seize and confiscate the same."

After this formal repudiation of all sympathy and

connection with the illicit opium traffic on the part of the representative of the English Government, it became essentially a question for the Chinese authorities to deal with as they felt able and thought fit. Protection had been officially withdrawn from those engaged in this trade, and thus one of the first consequences of the cessation of the monopoly was that the Crown declined to sanction the most important branch of the Indian trade which the Company had done everything in its power to foster and extend. This important decision naturally increased the energy of the Canton mandarins, who issued numerous proclamations to the people, calling upon them to follow the path of virtue and to abstain from vice—exhortations, it may be added, that were very much needed then and at all times. The announcement of Lin's forthcoming visit still further fired their zeal; and, not satisfied with denouncing the traffic in one condemned article, official notices were circulated to the effect that the true remedy lay in the cessation of all foreign intercourse, and that the presence of strangers and their ships on the Canton river detracted from the dignity of the Middle Kingdom. Commissioner Lin made his formal entry into Canton on the 10th of March, 1839, and with his arrival the question at once entered upon a more acute—and, as it proved, its final—stage.

The zeal of the High Commissioner was matched by his energy. He had not been a week in his new post when he drew up an edict of remarkable literary power, and one also, it must be allowed, breathing the noblest moral sentiments. But the only terms in which he condescended to address the foreigners were those of superiority, and he called upon them to listen to, and to obey with trembling, "his commands." Those who had no sympathy with the opium traffic saw in Lin's declarations clear evidence that no trade could long be compatible with the natural arrogance of the Chinese official who regarded commerce as beneath his notice, and Europeans as a barbarian but dangerous people, living in hopeless ignorance. Lin did not confine himself to words; he resorted to action. He peremptorily forbade any foreigner to leave Canton for Macao, or elsewhere, until the matter about which he came had been satisfactorily settled. Within a few days

SURRENDER OF OPIUM.

of his appearance it was evident that what he wanted to achieve was the complete humiliation of the foreigners.

But by far the most important of Lin's earlier proclamations was that demanding the surrender of all stores of opium within the space of three days. This naturally produced great excitement among the European community; but after a little delay, and mainly by the action of individuals and not by the collective decision of the Chamber of Commerce, more than a thousand chests were surrendered to the Chinese to be destroyed. Almost simultaneously with this act of subservience on the part of the merchants, Captain Elliot issued a proclamation announcing that, as Her Majesty's subjects were detained against their will at Canton, all English ships should assemble at Hongkong and prepare to resist with force any act of aggression. The inevitable collision was thus at length approaching with rapid strides, for the Chinese mandarins could neither understand nor tolerate the foreigners in any other capacity than as traders; and Captain Elliot spoke, and expected to be treated, as the representative of a ruler as proud and as powerful as the Emperor of China himself. The English Superintendent publicly declared that he had lost all confidence in the justice and moderation of the provincial Government. Nor did the matter stop at this point. Captain Elliot hastened to Canton, where an apparent attempt had been made, under cover of an invitation, to get possession of the person of one of the foremost and most influential merchants, Mr. Dent; but on the hoisting of his flag the excitement among the Chinese knew no bounds, and the settlement was not merely abandoned by all its native servants, but forthwith surrounded by a vast concourse of armed men, half coolies, half soldiers. For a moment the apprehension spread that the settlement at Canton might prove a second Black Hole.

The next move in this intricate question was in seeming contradiction with the steps that had immediately preceded it. While the whole British community, official and commercial alike, remained cut off from the outer world in the settlement at Canton, Captain Elliot, in response to a special edict or address from Lin, called upon the English merchants

VOL. II.   G to surrender to him, for paramount considerations of the lives and liberties of themselves and their countrymen, all the stores of opium in their possession. More than twenty thousand chests, of an estimated value of over two millions sterling, were at once placed at the disposal of the superintendent. These were duly handed over to the Chinese at Whampoa, and other places in the Bogue; and the process of destroying the drug was commenced with all due ceremony, and under the direct auspices of Lin, at Chuenpee.

But the surrender of these stores did not satisfy the ends of the Commissioner, who wished to crown his work by the complete stoppage of all further supplies. With that object in view he addressed a letter to the sovereign of the English nation, calling upon her to interdict the traffic in opium for ever. Even in this letter the arrogance of the Chinese revealed itself, and the arguments employed were weakened by minatory language as to the penalties that would follow refusal or procrastination. However, the friendly attitude of the English superintendent and merchants during this critical period was not without some effect. The cordon established round the foreign settlement was gradually withdrawn, and after six weeks' incarceration the Europeans were allowed to leave the factories, and the passenger ships resumed their trips to Macao.

But a still more serious complication sprang out of what in its most interesting aspect was a literary controversy. The law of China made the sale of opium a penal offence, and the Chinese officials claimed the power to execute their law on the persons of Europeans. Not merely did they claim it, but they announced their intention to carry it out in the cases of sixteen Englishmen, whose names were published. Some of these had notoriously never had any connection with opium at all, and they were every one of them honourable merchants, innocent of any culpable wish to injure the Chinese. Not only did Commissioner Lin and the Canton authorities claim the right to condemn and punish English subjects, but they showed in the clearest possible manner that they would take away their liberty and lives on the flimsiest and falsest testimony. Captain Elliot felt bound to declare that "this law is incompatible with safe or honourable continuance at Canton."

The Chinese authorities seemingly acted also on the assumption that so long as there remained even one offending European, the mass of his countrymen were to be hindered in their avocations; and consequently a number of petty restrictions were placed upon the transaction of all business relations between the native and English merchants. One of these possessed more than a usual degree of importance as furnishing some clue to the real considerations guiding the policy of China on the foreign question. The withdrawal of silver had excited the keenest alarm among the Celestials, and as some means of putting a stop to it, a rule was passed to the effect that each foreign ship should take away as much bulk of exported Chinese goods as it brought of English articles. By this device it was hoped to ensure the equalisation of the trade. By their acts the mandarins proclaimed that much more than the opium of the foreigners was objected to; and the English superintendent issued a further notice warning all of Her Majesty's subjects to leave Canton with him, or to remain at their own personal peril.*

The very next day after Captain Elliot's notice, a memorial, signed by all the principal English and Indian merchants, was sent home to Lord Palmerston, then Secretary for Foreign

---

* This was dated the 22nd of May, 1839, and in it occurs the following important paragraph with reference to the opium that had been surrendered. "Acting on the behalf of Her Majesty's Government in a momentous emergency, he has, in the first place, to signify that the demand he recently made to Her Majesty's subjects for the surrender of British-owned opium under their control had no special reference to the circumstances of that property; but (beyond the actual pressure of necessity) that demand was founded on the principle that these violent compulsory measures being utterly unjust *per se*, and of general application for the forced surrender of any other property, or of human life, or for the constraint of any unsuitable terms or concessions, it became highly necessary to vest and leave the right of exacting effectual security, and full indemnity for every loss directly in the Queen." Unfortunately, Captain Elliot's earlier statements had conveyed the impression, and certainly bore the construction, that the English Government was disposed to agree with Commissioner Lin and the Chinese authorities as to the moral iniquity of the practice of smoking opium.

Affairs; and in this document support and protection against "a capricious and corrupt Government" were demanded, as well as early compensation for the two millions' worth of opium surrendered to China at the urgent request of the English superintendent. For the moment Commissioner Lin had triumphed, and his gratified sovereign forthwith rewarded him by raising him to the very dignified post of Viceroy of the Two Kiang, which includes in its jurisdiction the three important provinces of Kiangsi, Kiangsu, and Anhwei, and of which the principal city is Nankin, one of the former capitals of the Empire. The confidence and self-congratulations of the Chinese were certainly not weakened by the fact that, in this critical state of affairs, there was not a single English man-of-war in any part of the Chinese waters. The English residents were at the mercy of the Chinese, and without either sure means of escape or efficient sources of defence. The second anniversary of the Queen's birthday after her accession to the throne found the Chinese question portending the gravest danger, and an accident was nearly producing an immediate conflict; for one of the merchant vessels, whilst firing a salute on this auspicious occasion, discharged a shot in the direction of a Chinese war-junk. No damage, fortunately, was done, but a less event than that might have provoked a hostile collision at such a time. A catastrophe might indeed have ensued but for the simple fact that only two or three Englishmen had remained in Canton.

Up to this point the English merchants and subjects had endured with meekness all that the ill-will and reforming enthusiasm of the Chinese could do them; but the indignation and resentment felt at their treatment were naturally extreme, and needed only an occasion to display themselves in acts. No class of the community is as sensitive of a slight on the national honour as the English sailor, and none is more prone to resent it in the simple and effectual way of his forefathers. The merits of diplomacy are concealed from a nature that sees only the object before it, and takes no count of the attendant circumstances. The caution and circumspection which seemed prudent to the English superintendent were beyond the understanding and beneath the notice of the numerous sailors who, by the stagnation of the trade, were kept in a state of idleness in the Bogue. Collisions necessarily occurred when parties went on shore from the ships, but no serious mishap took place until the 7th of July, 1839. On that occasion a large party of sailors were drawn into a quarrel with the inhabitants of a village near the anchorage at Hongkong, and a villager named Lin Weihe was so much injured that he died the next day of his wounds. A demand was at once made for the surrender of the murderers, as the law of China demanded a life for a life; but, as such a surrender meant handing over the sailor accused to a certain and cruel death, the demand was, of course, refused. There was also no evidence to incriminate any one in particular of this act of manslaughter; but five sailors were sentenced to various terms of imprisonment for rioting on shore.

The Chinese authorities could not, perhaps, be expected to regard this affair with the same discriminating power as is presumably vested in an English jury. As soon as the circumstances were reported in the Canton Yamen, the Commissioner Lin seized his pencil, and proceeded to pour forth his wrath, and to demonstrate over again his literary skill in an edict on the occurrence, which he characterized as "going to the extreme of disobedience to the laws." If an Englishman had been killed, the Commissioner argued that he would at once have ordered the execution of his murderer, therefore it was only right that the slayer of a Chinese subject should be handed over to justice. That a man may not be a murderer intentionally, is beyond Chinese comprehension—in short, all, or almost all the circumstances that we term extenuating are unknown to the Chinese Statute Book. Lin's final commands were that the murderer must be surrendered, and that, until he was, supplies were to be withheld from the foreign ships. Nor was this an empty threat. Although the English had removed to Macao, where it is right to say that, old jealousies forgotten, they received a most hospitable welcome from the Portuguese, the power of the Commissioner reached them even there; and both supplies and servants vanished on the publication of Lin's decree. With the view of not compromising the Portuguese, Captain Elliot, a few days later, removed his quarters to Hongkong.

The death of the Chinese villager did not long remain without an outrage on the side of the Europeans to in some sense counterbalance it. A small schooner was boarded on its way from Macao to Hongkong by a band of pirates. The crew were all killed, the single English passenger was grievously wounded, and the miscreants escaped with the plunder of the vessel. It was thought, at the time, that this attack was committed by order of the Chinese officials; but later discoveries showed, what ought never to have been doubted, as the capture of a living Englishman would have entitled the taker to Lin's gratitude and highest reward, that it was one of those piratical outrages which, unfortunately, fill a great place in the annals of the Canton river and the Bogue. At this critical moment the opportune arrival of an English ship-of-war restored confidence among the residents, by showing that, although distant, they were still under the protection of the Queen's Government.

At this point the gravity of the complication was still further increased by an official proclamation, signed by Lin and the Viceroy of Kwangtung, calling upon the people to arm themselves, and to oppose with force any attempt on the part of the foreigners to land. Despite the surrender of a vast quantity of opium, the departure of the greater number of the Europeans from Canton, and the practical stoppage of the foreign trade, the Chinese officials were not disposed to rest satisfied with what they had accomplished, and, trusting to their overwhelming numbers, on which their official notices never tired of dwelling, they sought to complete the humiliation of the "outer barbarians." The appeal to force was an act of indiscretion that betrayed the height of confidence, or a strange depth of ignorance; and when the mandarins sanctioned the withholding of water and other necessary supplies, they voluntarily surrendered the advantage which the definiteness of their plans and their diplomatic capacity gave them over the English. The English naval officers at once denounced the withholding of provisions as an act of hostility, and declared a blockade, which was raised in a few days, only, however, to give place to vigorous measures for the seizure of supplies whenever necessary.

Several encounters took place between the two English men-of-war at last placed on the station, and the small forts situated at Hongkong and on the adjoining peninsula. But nothing serious happened until the 3rd of November, 1839, when a naval engagement was fought off Chuenpee. A Chinese fleet of twenty-nine junks, under the command of a high admiral named Kwang, ventured to menace the two English frigates, when they were attacked and dispersed with the loss of four of their number. Although this encounter arrested the hostile measures of the Chinese, it further embittered the conflict, and it was no longer doubtful that the solution of the question would have to be accomplished by force of arms. The capture and imprisonment of an English subject, Mr. Gribble, in the last days of the year 1839, showed that no improvement was likely to take place by means of an amicable agreement; and the arrival of the English warships outside the Bogue, to demand the surrender of the English captive, brought the one effectual remedy still more clearly into view.

When Taoukwang received news of the fight at Chuenpee, described to him as an engagement reflecting the highest credit on the valour of his sailors, if not as an absolute victory, he issued a special edict rewarding the admiral with a high Tartar title for his courage, and commanding his officers at Canton "to put a stop at once to the trade of the English nation." In consequence of this decree from the Vermilion pencil, the Canton authorities published an edict calling upon all English subjects to quit Chinese territory for ever. They were peremptorily commanded to leave even Macao. At this juncture the news that an expedition was about to be despatched with the view of asserting the dignity of the English crown, and of affording protection to English commerce, exercised a tranquillising effect. A lull ensued, and although the English were placed outside the pale of the law, and although the whole motive of their presence was removed by the suspension of the trade, Mr. Gribble was released from his confinement, and the merchants with their families continued to reside partly at Macao, and partly on board ship at the anchorage of Tungkoo near Hongkong.

Considering the events of this troubled period—the seven years following the removal of the monopoly—it cannot be contended from an impartial review of the facts, and divesting our minds as far as possible from the prejudice of accepted political opinion, and of conviction as to the hurtful or innocent character of opium in the mixture smoked, that the course pursued by Captain Elliot was either prudent in itself, or calculated to promote the advantage and reputation of England. Captain Elliot's proceedings were marked by the inconsistency that springs from ignorance. The more influential English merchants, touched by the appeal to their moral sentiment, or impressed by the depravity of large classes of the Canton population, of which the practice of opium-smoking was rather the mark than the cause, set their faces against the traffic in this article, and repudiated all sympathy and participation in it. The various foreign publications, whether they received their inspiration from M. Gutzlaff or not, matters little, differed on most points, but were agreed on this, that the trade in opium was morally indefensible, and that we were bound not only by our own interests, but in virtue of the common obligations of humanity, to cease to hold all connection with it. Those who had surrendered their stores of opium, at the request of Captain Elliot, held that their claim for compensation was valid in the first place against the English Government alone. They had given them up for the service of the country at the request of the Queen's representative, and, considering the line which Captain Elliot had taken, many believed that it would be quite impossible for the English Government to put forward any demand upon the Government of China. The two millions sterling, according to these large-hearted and unreflecting moralists, would have to be sacrificed by the people of England in the cause of humanity, to which they had already given so much, and the revenue of India should for the future be poorer by the amount that used to pay the dividend of the great Company!

The Chinese authorities could not help being encouraged

in their opinions and course of proceeding by the attitude of the English. Their most sweeping denunciations of the iniquity of the opium traffic elicited a murmur of approval from the most influential among the foreigners. No European stood up to say that their allegations as to the evil of using opium were baseless and absurd. What is more, no one then thought it. Had the Chinese made sufficient use of this identity of views, and showed a desire to facilitate trade in the so-called innocent and legitimate articles, there is little doubt that the opium traffic would have been reduced to very small dimensions, because there would have been no rupture. But the action of Commissioner Lin revealed the truth that the Chinese were not to be satisfied with a single triumph. The more easily they obtained their objects in the opium matter, the more anxious did they become to impress the foreigners with a sense of their inferiority, and to force them to accept the most onerous and unjust conditions for the sake of a continuance of the trade. None the less, Captain Elliot went out of his way to tie his own hands, and to bind his Government, so far as he could, to co-operate with the Emperor's officials in the suppression of the opium traffic.*

* That this is no random assertion may be judged from the following official notice issued several months after the surrender of the stores of opium. Captain Elliot announced, " Her Majesty's flag does not fly in the protection of a traffic declared illegal by the Emperor ; and, therefore, whenever a vessel is suspected of having opium on board, Captain Elliot will take care that the officers of his establishment shall accompany the Chinese officers in their search, and that if, after strict investigation, opium shall be found, he will offer no objection to the seizure and confiscation of the cargo."—" Chinese Repository," vol. viii. p. 322.

CHAPTER VI.

THE FIRST FOREIGN WAR.

THE inevitable crisis long foreseen, had, therefore, at last arrived, and the English Government, forced to send an armed expedition as the only way of preventing the expulsion of its subjects, could not expect to overawe a proud and powerful empire such as China was, without using the means which it had been reluctantly compelled to invoke for the occasion. The humility of the representatives of the East India Company, and the absence of that naval and military power upon which the Europeans placed implicit reliance, had encouraged the Chinese to proceed to extreme lengths in their attacks upon foreigners, and, although there is not room to doubt the sincerity of the opposition to the opium traffic on fiscal grounds, the main object with Taoukwang and his ministers became to limit the extent of the intercourse with foreigners, if not to put a stop to it altogether. More than one cause contributed to the result, but in 1840 the question had been reduced to the simplest proportions. The Chinese did not wish the foreigners to remain even at Canton, except in the most subservient capacity. Did the English possess the power and the resolution to compel what the stronger race ever calls proper treatment, and, as it was a contest of wits as well as of armaments, would they show themselves sufficiently diplomatic to obtain from the astutest people in Asia some valid guarantee for the security of their persons and property, and for respect towards their Government, when the naval and military forces that obtained these concessions had been withdrawn? Those were the two questions that had to be decided.

From the outset it was plain that no mere demonstration would suffice. The presence of a few men-of-war carried no sense of terror to the hearts of the mandarins. The arrival of English soldiers, after many months' delay, seemed only to prove, from the smallness of their numbers, that the Chinese had little to fear from an invasion, and that the victory must incline to the countless myriads of the Celestial armies. Nor are these opinions to be wondered at. The Chinese have never admitted the vaunted superiority of the European. At this time they had had no experience of the advantages he possessed from better weapons and an improved system of warfare. The prestige of the Empire was undiminished, and not a Chinese patriot doubted that, as he inherited from his forefathers a position of pre-eminence among the nations, so did the great Emperor wield the power and dispose of the resources necessary to support and maintain this indefeasible birthright of a son of the Middle Kingdom. It is nothing to the point that these assumptions were untenable, and, it may be, absurd. They must be realized as constituting the public opinion of China at the time, if the events of a critical period are to be followed and appreciated. Not even now do the Chinese, with all their increased experience, not free, as it has been, from bitter and painful incidents, see in our persons and civilization the proofs of the superiority that is the first article of our faith. In 1840, without their subsequent knowledge, they believed implicitly in themselves, and reposed unshaken faith in the majesty of the great Emperor.

Yet if the precedent of other Asiatic countries might be applied to China, the English expedition was sufficiently formidable to make Taoukwang tremble on the Dragon Throne. A less formidable force than that Sir Gordon Bremer disposed of had before decided the fate of famous dynasties and effected the conquest of flourishing kingdoms on the plains of India. Fifteen ships-of-war, four steam-vessels, and twenty-five transports with 4000 soldiers on board arrived at the mouth of the river in June 1840, and with such a force on the spot it seemed scarcely probable that the Chinese would long hold out against the reasonable demands of the English representative.* Such an anticipation was destined to be soon dispelled, as the reply of Commissioner Lin to this display of force was to place a reward, not merely on the persons of English officers and men, but also on their ships.† The establishment of a blockade was a not ineffectual mode of replying to the empty threats of the Emperor's officials, but it was becoming clear that the most energetic action at Canton alone would not avail to obtain a settlement of the question. The difficulty could only be satisfactorily arranged by direct communication with the Pekin Government; and consequently Sir Gordon Bremer proceeded northwards after the arrival of the whole of his troops. For a time the destination of the fleet remained obscure, but it was soon made known that its object was to effect the occupation of the island of Chusan, which had been praised by more than one English captain for the salubrity of its climate and the convenience of its harbours, and on which as far back as the middle of the seventeenth century the East India Company had established stations.

* The Queen's Speech for the year 1840 contains the following passage relating to the Chinese imbroglio :—" Events have happened in China which have occasioned an interruption of the commercial intercourse of my subjects with that country. I have given, and shall continue to give, the most serious attention to a matter so deeply affecting the interests of my subjects and the dignity of my crown." Lord John Russell summed up the whole policy of England, not only on this particular occasion, but generally, towards China in the following words :—" The expedition was authorised for the purpose of obtaining reparation for the insults and injuries offered to Her Majesty's Superintendent and Her Majesty's subjects by the Chinese Government; and in the second place they were to obtain for the merchants trading with China an indemnification for the loss of their property incurred by threats of violence offered by persons under the direction of the Chinese Government; and, in the last place, they were to obtain a certain security that persons and property in future trading with China shall be protected from insult or injury, and that their trade and commerce be maintained upon a proper footing." Macaulay called the war "a most rightful quarrel," and Sir George Staunton thought it was "a just and fitting war."

† One hundred dollars were to be paid for an English prisoner, and twenty for each killed. Twenty thousand dollars for an English man-of-war of eighty guns ; others in proportion.—*Canton Register.*

The operations of the English expedition commenced, therefore, in a way calculated to impress the Chinese authorities at Canton with the idea that the foreigners were so far in earnest that they would treat the integrity of China with scant respect. The occupation of Chusan was intended to convey this lesson to the Celestials quite as much as to supply our force with a convenient base. Its prompt execution left no room to doubt that the English possessed the power to execute what was necessary. The capture of Chusan presented no difficulties to well-trained troops and a formidable navy; yet the fidelity of the inhabitants to their charge afforded a touching, and by no means isolated, instance of patriotism and courage. To the summons to surrender, the officials at Tinghai replied that they could not yield, although they admitted resistance to be useless. Their duty to the Emperor, and their military pride, would not allow of their acquiescing in the loss of one of their master's possessions. It was their duty to fight, and the enemy must overcome them by force. The English commander resorted with reluctance to extreme measures against so insignificant, if gallant, a foe; but the obstinacy of the Chinese left him no choice. Tinghai was subjected to a brief but destructive bombardment; the troops were landed, and the island of Chusan passed into the possession, for a time, of the Queen of England.

The first act in the drama was promptly followed by another, not less important in itself, and still more striking in its attendant features. An English subject, Mr. Vincent Stanton, had been carried off from Macao as a prisoner to Canton, and the reiterated demands for his surrender had failed to obtain any satisfactory answer. At the same time the Chinese forces were more than doubled in the permanent camp outside Macao, the junks were collected for the defence of the barrier, and all the able-bodied men of the coast were summoned to wage war by sea and land against the barbarians. There was no alternative save to assume the offensive and to arrest the hostile preparations of the Chinese before they had attained a more advanced stage of strength and efficiency. The first action with the barrier forts was carried out by two English war-ships and two smaller vessels. The bombardment was for a time heavy, and 400 blue-jackets and sepoys were landed to complete its effect. The objects of the attack were obtained with trifling loss, and the dismantled forts and ruined barracks brought home to the minds of the Chinese that the hour of foreign moderation had passed by, and that it only remained for them to prove themselves the stronger, or to accept, with as much resignation as they could muster, the portion of the weaker. As it was said at the time, " China must either bend or break."

But the main difficulty was still to obtain some means of direct communication with Pekin, and to place Lord Palmerston's official letter in the hands of Taoukwang's ministers. The first attempt to effect this object at Amoy had failed, and almost resulted in the massacre of the officer and boat's crew sent under the white flag to establish communications with the local mandarins. Amoy itself was bombarded in retaliation by an English man-of-war, but the incident did not bring our authorities any nearer to the realization of their object. Nor did the occupation of Chusan facilitate the matter, for the authorities at Ningpo stood upon their dignity, and refused to forward to the capital any document from a people in hostile possession of a part of Chinese soil. No other course remaining, the fleet sailed northward for the mouth of the Peiho, where Lord Palmerston's communication was at once delivered to Keshen, one of Taoukwang's principal ministers, and forwarded to Pekin.

Taoukwang's indignation was aroused by Keshen's representations, although he could no longer deny the necessity of making some concession in form to the English. The English fleet was supplied with everything it required by his order, and payment was for a time emphatically declined, while the main object of the expedition seemed to be obtained by the nomination of Keshen as High Commissioner to treat with the English for a satisfactory adjustment of the difficulty. But the suppleness of the Tartar official secured an honourable issue from his dilemma, and Captain Elliot, whose work at Canton has been described, proved to be no match for the wily Keshen. Even at Peiho there were delays; yet the

English representative was weak enough to allow himself to be persuaded that the despatch of business would be more expeditious, and attended with greater advantage, if the scene were shifted to Canton. After a short negotiation, it was decided that the fleet would withdraw from the Peiho, and that Keshen should proceed to Canton to conduct the negotiations for some definite arrangement.

Meantime the operations in Chusan, and the blockading of Canton, Amoy, and Ningpo, had spread confusion along the coast, and even disturbed the equanimity of the Imperial ruler. The first contact with the Europeans had exposed the defencelessness of the kingdom. It brought to light also the corrupt state of the public service, whose members had grown rich on the treasure that should have been expended on the administration; and the indignation of the Emperor found expression in several edicts from his own pencil. The first burst of the Imperial wrath fell upon the man who had seemed the most fortunate individual in China, because allowed to be the favoured executioner of the high morality of the Boards and Cabinet of Pekin. Lin had been entrusted with a task of extreme difficulty, and he had proceeded towards its effectual performance with zeal and devotion. The most exacting master could not have complained of his being lukewarm or negligent in the carrying out of his commission. Honours had been showered upon him, in the belief that the whole question was settled, that the supplies of "the flowing poison," opium, had ceased, and that the foreigners were possessed with a due sense of their subordination. For a few months Lin was the object of official envy; but the arrival of the English fleet dispelled these expectations, and showed that Lin's action, far from reducing the foreigners to submission, had roused their resentment and opposition. Lin had stirred up a hornet's nest, and Taoukwang's indignation was in proportion with the annoyance he felt at having to deal direct with the foreigners, and to make his own arrangements for the future. Lin was removed from all his posts, and ordered to proceed with "the speed of flames" to Pekin, there to meet with his deserts.

But even Lin's disgrace and the arrival of Keshen at

Canton did not produce that satisfactory arrangement which had been too confidently expected. Keshen's first official act was to send the Emperor a memorandum approving, if not of the method, at least of the objects which his predecessor had pursued; and the Pekin Cabinet, relieved of its most pressing fears, resumed the arrogant tone which was its habit. The days of delay outside the Taku barriers lengthened into weeks of inaction before the river forts of Canton, and, although Mr. Stanton was released from imprisonment, the question was not much advanced towards settlement at the close of the year 1840. Sir Gordon Bremer had again succeeded to the command, through the enforced departure of Admiral Elliot* on account of ill-health, but, although six months had elapsed since the arrival of the expedition, the results accomplished by it remained invisible. Keshen's tactics were the same at Canton as they had been at Taku. Procrastination in the north had saved the dignity of the Emperor; in the south it would give time for all the levies to be raised, and for the maritime provinces to be placed in a condition of defence. It might be harsh, under all the circumstances, to apply to this policy the term of treacherous; but certainly, in the eyes of those who were to suffer by it, none would be more appropriate. In the alternations of negotiation and violence which constituted English action at the time, Keshen's wilful neglect to carry out the conditions of his appointment made it again evident that the moment had arrived for resorting to that force which had been fitfully but vainly applied before.

The first week of the year 1841 witnessed, therefore, the preparations for the attack on the Bogue forts, which had been strongly and skilfully constructed on the many islands that dot the intricate channels leading to Canton. Those who regarded them with the unprejudiced eyes of scientific knowledge saw that they were formidable obstacles, and that, if defended by brave and capable troops, they could not be forced without heavy loss to the assailant. Fortunately for

---

* Rear-admiral the Honourable George Elliot, son of 1st Earl of Minto, not to be confounded with the superintendent, Captain Charles Elliot.

the English, the Chinese troops, although always evincing a sort of courage, were quite ignorant of modern warfare, and incapable of directing with any precision even the artillery which they possessed. The 7th of January was the day selected for the attack, and early in the morning the troops were landed on the coast to operate on the flank and rear of the forts at Chuenpee. The advance squadron, under Captain, afterwards Sir Thomas, Herbert, was to engage the same forts in front, while the remainder of the fleet proceeded to attack the stockades on the adjoining island of Taikok. The land force, consisting of some 1400 men and 3 guns, had not proceeded far along the coast before it came across a strongly entrenched camp, in addition to the forts of Chuenpee, having in all several thousand soldiers and many field-pieces in position. The forts were, after a sharp cannonade, carried at a rush, and a formidable Chinese army was driven ignominiously out of its entrenchments, with hardly any loss to the assailants. The forts of Taikok were destroyed by the fire of the ships, and their guns were spiked and garrisons routed by storming parties. A large number of war-junks were also captured or blown up. The Chinese lost at the least 500 killed, including their commander, besides an untold number of wounded. Yet, although the loss of the English was only 38 wounded, it was generally allowed that the Chinese defence was "obstinate and honourable." A considerable proportion of the Chinese were slain in consequence of a treacherous attack on the English troops after they had given every token of surrender.

The consequences of the capture of the outer forts in the Bogue were immediate and important. The Chinese begged for a cessation of hostilities, and Keshen, although his reports to the Emperor were still full of his plans for circumventing and driving off the barbarians, accepted, as the preliminaries of a treaty, terms which conceded them everything they had demanded. A large indemnity, the cession of Hongkong, and direct official intercourse between the two Governments, seemed to cover every point on which the English Crown had either the right or the wish to make a claim. The one stipulation which was carried into immediate effect, was that relating to Hongkong. While the other provisoes remained the subject of future discussion, and, as it proved, disagreement, the troops were withdrawn from Chusan in order to occupy Hongkong, and Captain Elliot issued a proclamation, dated 29th January, 1841, announcing the fact that this island had henceforth become part of Her Majesty's dominions. The prevalent opinion at the time attached but little value to the acquisition, and most persons believed that Hongkong would never prove a possession of any great importance. Certainly no one was sufficiently far-seeing to realize the material prosperity and political importance that lay before that barren island.

That the concessions made by Keshen at Canton were due solely to his own embarrassments, and not to any intention on the part of the Imperial Government to admit the equal rights of foreign nations, was shown by an edict issued in Taoukwang's name two days before Captain Elliot's notice. In this order from the Vermilion pencil, it was said that no other course was left save "to destroy and wash the foreigners away without remorse;" and with the intention of carrying this bold decision into execution, troops were ordered from the interior, and even from Szchuen, to proceed with all despatch to Canton. Although Hongkong had been annexed to the possessions of the English Crown, the attitude of Taoukwang himself showed that the hope of a durable amicable settlement must still remain remote. The Chinese Emperor denounced the English by name as "staying themselves upon their pride of power and fierce strength," and called upon his officers to proceed with courage and energy, so that "the rebellious foreigners might give up their ringleaders to be sent encaged to Pekin to receive the utmost retribution of the laws." So long as the sovereign was swayed by such opinions as these, it was evident that no arrangement could endure. The Chinese did not admit the principle of equality in their dealings with the English, and this was the main point in contention between them, far more than any difference of opinion as to the evil of opium-smoking. So long as Taoukwang and his ministers held the opinions which they did not hesitate to express, a friendly intercourse was quite impossible. There remained no practical alternative between withdrawing from the country altogether, leaving the Celestials to their own exclusiveness, and forcing their Government to recognize a common humanity, and an equality in national privileges.

Hostilities were, therefore, suspended only to be resumed. Fresh proclamations were issued offering an increased reward for the heads or persons of Englishmen, and, the period fixed for the ratification having expired, Sir Gordon Bremer felt compelled to resume the offensive, and to re-occupy those places from which he had retired. Keshen, who, with all his faults, saw from the commencement the impossibility of opposing the English forces, and who had had the courage to state his opinion in plain language to the Emperor, no longer possessed the direction of affairs even at Canton, where the Governor Eleang, another of Taoukwang's ministers, and for the time an ardent admirer of Lin, had assumed the chief power. On the 25th of February, therefore, five days after the date when the treaty should have been ratified, Sir Gordon Bremer made his arrangements for attacking on the following day the forts which guarded the inner approaches to Canton. Three howitzers and a small body of troops were landed at a spot which the Chinese had neglected to fortify, and whence the British were able to shell some of the principal batteries and forts on the adjacent islands and mainland. The Chinese position was not only strong, but exceedingly well arranged, the defences being covered with sand-bags, and, had their artillery been well served, they must have offered a protracted if unsuccessful resistance.

As it was, however, neither the advantages of position, nor the tardy advance of our men-of-war on a slack tide, enabled them to defend their forts. The English ships approached to within less than a quarter of a mile of the batteries with impunity, and then delivered their broadsides with terrible effect. In a short time the Chinese showed that they had had enough of this unequal cannonade, by abandoning their positions. This they did with comparatively little loss, as not more than 20 Chinese were killed, but they left the formidable lines of Anunghoy, with 200 pieces of artillery, in the hands of the victors. Similar encounters, with like results, took place at the other forts on North Wangtong; and Captain Herbert, on the following day, attacked with great gallantry a force of 2000 men in an entrenched camp with 100 guns, and compelled them to flee ignominiously. The Chinese had erected masked batteries, and made other preparations for defence, the whole way up to Whampoa (the port of Canton eleven miles below the city), but none of these offered any strenuous defence. On the 1st of March the whole of the forts had been carried, and the English squadron drew up off Howqua's Folly in Whampoa Reach, at the very gateway of Canton. The day after this signal success the new English commander arrived at Hongkong. Sir Hugh Gough landed there on March 2, 1841.

In consequence of the entreaties of the local officers at Canton an armistice was granted for a few days, but this fact was not sufficient in itself to provide a remedy for the evil. The Emperor and the high ministers were still pronounced in their resolution to resist and exterminate the foreigners, and there was no official at Canton who would dare to take upon himself the responsibility of negotiating for a durable understanding with the English. The fears of the commercial community obtained a brief respite, but, that period having expired, the advance of the English to Canton was resumed. When there was every reason to no longer defer decisive measures, Sir Hugh Gough was certainly not the man to favour delay. The outer defences of Canton having been carried, it only remained to capture and occupy those which guarded the approach from Whampoa to the city. A proclamation was issued to the people of Canton informing them that their town would be spared, while the English expedition resolutely attacked and speedily captured the fort known as the Dutch Folly. Here again the official documents admit the constancy of the Chinese, although they were unable to inflict any serious loss on their opponents. The defences of Canton were carried with as much ease as those of the Bocca Tigris had been, and the navigation of the river from that city to the sea was at last under the complete control of the English.

The first English successes had cost Lin his offices and

reputation; the later effected the ruin of Keshen. Taouk-wang, in his indignation, not merely ordered Keshen to return to Pekin forthwith, in order to suffer the extreme penalty of the law, but he sent a Tartar official with the strictest injunctions to drag him into his presence. In his misfortunes his colleagues turned upon him, and he was made responsible for the incompetence or ill-luck of the time. An indictment of eight charges was drawn up against him, and not the least grave of the offences laid to his fault was that he had held interviews and carried on a correspondence with Captain Elliot on terms of equality. Everything went to show that the Celestial Government had not learnt a single lesson from its latest experience, and that it still based its claims on an intolerant and unapproachable superiority. Keshen's trial was held at Pekin a few months later, when the court of inquiry decided that his policy was very bad, which signified that it had not been successful. His large property * was sequestrated to the Crown, and he was himself sentenced to decapitation. It may be interesting to state that by an act of special favour this sentence was commuted, some months later, to one of banishment to Tibet, where he was appointed the Emperor's Resident at Lhasa.† His career was not yet run, if the result showed that he could not escape his allotted end.

But the settlement of the question of the hour was passing

* The list of his treasures recalls his predecessor Hokwan, and shows that if he did not abuse he certainly did not neglect his opportunities. The inventory of his possessions reads as follows :—" Gold, 270,000 taels weight; sycee silver, 3,400,000 taels weight; foreign money, 2,000,000 taels weight; land cultivated, 39 *king* (a *king* equals about 30 acres); 4 pawnshops in the province of Pechihli; 2 pawnshops at Moukden; 84 banking-shops; large pearls, 94; strings of pearls, 14; pearl lamps, 8; arrow thumb-rings, made of the feathers of the *fei tsuy* bird, 34; deer horns, catties, 25; lengths of silk, 420; broad cloth and English camlet, 30 pieces; striking clocks, 18 in number; gold watches, 10; fur garments, 24; images of horses, made of precious stones, 2; images of lions, made of precious stones, 2; crystal wash-hand basins, 28; tortoise-shell bedstead, 1; chariots, 4; female slaves 168."

† In this capacity he amassed considerable wealth, and succeeded in making such powerful friends at Court that he was subsequently appointed Governor-General of Szchuen.

out of the hands of Taoukwang, and the indignant astonishment of the Emperor at the uselessness of his threats and commands contributed as little towards victory as the disgrace and punishment of his lieutenants. The foreign factories were re-occupied on the 18th of March, two years, it was observed at the time, after Commissioner Lin's first edict demanding the surrender of the opium; and several merchant vessels proceeded up the river as far as Whampoa. While the central Government maintained its attitude of hostility the resumption of commercial intercourse had, therefore, been partially attained by force in the one place of trade open to foreigners. Even Eleang signified his acquiescence in what he was unable to prevent, and both the native and the English merchants renewed with ardour those commercial relations which had been so long and reluctantly suspended. Captain Elliot returned to Canton, and received visits of ceremony from some of the authorities of the town. Unfortunately, the State policy had not changed in the least. The arrival of three new Commissioners, and of a Governor, expressly appointed for the purpose of informing the Emperor of the exact state of affairs, was the first indication that the feeling of China had undergone no change. Their careful avoidance of all contact with our officers made the suspicion more or less a certainty.

If the month of April, 1841, gave much promise of things settling down on a satisfactory basis, the following month as rapidly dispelled the expectation. The merchants of Canton were willing enough to trade, and the inhabitants of a city which felt itself to be under the command of the guns of the English fleet, were naturally reluctant to do anything to provoke an enemy whose power they could no longer deny. But if what may be termed the local opinion was averse to sanctioning the desperate chance of a fresh encounter, the views of the capital and the central authorities were formed in a happy sense of security. Taoukwang did not so much as know that the English had practically gained their points when he despatched his Commissioners to drive them out, and to succeed where Lin and Keshen had failed. And they, not so much with the fear of death as the certainty of disgrace before them, were fully resolved that, whether they succeeded in getting rid of the English or not, they would do nothing to recognize the position they had acquired, or to admit that there was a possibility of its enduring. The confidence of the Commissioners was increased by the fact that there were still large bodies of troops, nearly 50,000 men, in the neighbourhood of Canton, and that reinforcements had been summoned from the extremities of the Empire. Such being the position of the case, it was very evident that the apparent settlement rested on an insecure foundation, and that the tranquillity was only the lull that precedes the storm.

The Emperor's resolution to hold no relations with the foreigners found expression in acts as well as words. He summoned to his private cabinet the most narrow-minded Manchu ministers of his court, believing that their counsels would be inspired by the same fears and prejudices as played so strong a part in moulding his own policy. At the same time he ordered strenuous efforts to be made for the effectual defence of Chusan and Ningpo, should the English attempt to take them a second time. At the very moment that trade was being renewed with spirit, and under circumstances that seemed to promise for it a satisfactory continuance, the Emperor decreed that the leaders of the barbarians should be captured and sent in cages to Pekin, in order to suffer the extreme penalty that could be inflicted upon them. The strong and the brave were especially invited to take up arms, and their patriotism was encouraged by the promise of reward. Commissioner Lin was restored to some portion of his former favour, and sent to Chekiang to levy forces, and to provide for the defences of the coast. The greater quickness of the foreigners, it was said, had given them a momentary advantage, which would speedily vanish when the forces of the Empire had been rallied. The war-spirit * was excited on all sides, and the hope of a better

---

* It was said of Taoukwang at this time he threatened to punish with death any one who suggested making peace with the barbarians. The order of the day was to exterminate them as rebels. The contrast between this implacable hostility and the pacific desires of Queen Victoria was

issue from the conflict emboldened the official and governing classes to appeal to national instincts that had long been dormant, because consistently discouraged.

While the foreign merchants were actively engaged in their commercial operations, and the English plenipotentiaries in conducting abortive negotiations with a functionary who, far from representing the views of his Government, was only put forward to amuse the barbarians, and to keep them occupied, the Chinese authorities were busily engaged raising and drilling troops, casting new guns at Fatshan to replace those lost in the Bogue forts, and at the same time in lulling the foreigners into a false sense of security, so that when all was ready they might be taken at a disadvantage. The plot was kept secret for a few weeks; but such extensive preparations could not be wholly concealed, even in a city of the size of Canton. On the 11th of May, Captain Elliot paid the Prefect of Canton a visit of ceremony, and, the better to show the friendliness of his intentions, he was accompanied by his wife. The hollowness of the Chinese professions for a friendly agreement was at once exposed in the military preparations visible on all sides, and in the discourteous demeanour of the mandarins. Captain Elliot was so astonished and alarmed at the change that had taken place, that he hastened back with all speed to Hongkong * to concert with Sir Hugh Gough as to the best measures to be adopted in the face of a new danger.

The prefect, Yu, was instructed to make one further attempt to allay the rising apprehension of the foreigners; and, while his militant colleagues were punishing in a summary manner those who ventured to declare that the

---

striking, and requires noting. In the speech from the throne for the Session of 1841 it was said, "My plenipotentiaries were by the last accounts in negotiation with the Government of China, and it will be a source of much gratification to me if that Government shall be induced by its own sense of justice to bring these matters to a speedy settlement by an amicable arrangement."

* Hongkong was already growing apace. Sixteen thousand Chinese had taken up their residence there. On the 7th of June, 1841, it was declared a free port, and about the same time the first sale of land was held. An acting governor was also appointed in the same month.

maintenance of peace was in every way desirable, he issued an edict calling upon all nations, and the Chinese also, to remain quietly at home, to pursue their usual avocations, and to fear nothing. The most expressive commentary as to the soundness of his views and the accuracy of his information was supplied by the effect of this proclamation. The respectable Chinese quitted the city in thousands, and Captain Elliot felt compelled, the day after Yu's edict reached him, to publish a notice recommending all foreigners to leave Canton before sunset on the same day, 21st May, 1841.

The necessity for this precaution was promptly demonstrated, as well as the accuracy of Captain Elliot's information. That very night the Chinese made a desperate attempt to carry out the plot they had so patiently laid. The batteries which they had erected at various points in the city and along the river banks began to bombard the factories and the ships, at the same time that many fire-rafts were sent against the latter in the hope of creating a conflagration, and of thereby effecting their destruction. These designs were fortunately baffled, and the first attempt of the Chinese was repulsed with loss to themselves, and without injury to either the English or their vessels. The combat was resumed on the following day, the English this time taking the offensive for the purpose of silencing the land batteries. They accomplished their purpose, destroyed the fortifications erected on Shameen, now the site of the foreign concession, and burnt a fleet of nearly forty war-vessels. It was only a poor equivalent, and a sorry sop for even Chinese military ardour to feed upon, that when the day closed the Emperor's Commissioners could only count as a set-off to this loss of life, ships, and guns, that the Cantonese mob had sacked and gutted the foreign factories. Nor had the similar attempts made lower down the river any better fortune. They were all baffled without loss to the English, save in one instance, when a raft blew up and injured a boat's crew, of whom four ultimately died. All the Chinese Emperor had gained by his continued and arrogant defiance was to bring home to the English a sense of the depths of his animosity, as well as of the treachery to which he would not hesitate to have recourse in order to free his land from their presence.

These events made it clearer than ever that the views of the contending parties were quite incompatible with each other. The Chinese wished to be rid of the outer barbarians at any price; the foreigners, and among them the English prominently, were as resolved to remain in the country, and, still more than that, not on the old conditions of subordination, but on terms of absolute equality. The sword alone could decide such antagonism, and the hostilities which had been carried on spasmodically during more than twelve months were now resumed with fresh vigour and bitterness, and assumed the dimensions of open war.

The main body of the English force was summoned from Hongkong, and Sir Hugh Gough made the final dispositions for an attack on Canton. The preliminary arrangements were completed on the 24th of May to the sound of the volleys which celebrated the Queen's birthday, and which informed the people of Canton of the near approach of the English. On the following morning the attack commenced with the advance of the fleet up the Macao passage, and the landing of bodies of troops at different points which appeared well suited for turning the enemy's position and attacking the gates of Canton. The landing of the military portion of the expedition presented exceptional difficulties, and could not have been accomplished without very heavy loss had the Chinese only shown ordinary activity. More than 2500 fighting men were, however, conveyed, on the evening of the 24th, to the shore, without the loss of a single man either by the enemy or from accident; and during the next night the artillery, the remainder of the troops, and the necessary stores and ammunition were landed in perfect safety, and without encountering the least opposition. Although this very considerable force was placed in a position not more than two miles distant from Canton, the Chinese did not seem to be aware of its presence, or, if they were, they thought it most prudent to affect ignorance. Yet no thought of surrender had entered the minds of Yihshan, or of any other of the great officials sent to Canton to uphold the Emperor's dignity.

The Chinese commanders had selected a position along the hills which lie north of the city, and this they had fortified with no mean skill, and had connected their lines with several forts. Their position resembled a series of fortified camps, and in these were gathered many thousands of the picked soldiers of the southern provinces. Little fault could be found with the judgment they had shown in the selection of their position, and, although the result of every previous encounter had been unfortunate, there is no doubt that both the Chinese leaders and their men were sanguine that the fortune of war was about to delare itself in their favour. Their anticipations were not without some reason, as their more strenuous resistance sufficiently testified.

The English force* was divided into two columns, which advanced in parallel lines upon the Chinese entrenchments. The advance was slow, for the difficulties of marching through the paddy-fields, which were rendered harder of passage from being frequently occupied as burial-grounds, effectually restrained the ardour of the men ; and here again the military incapacity of the Chinese was made very apparent by their allowing the English force to cross this tract without opposition. When they did attempt to hinder their advance, it was only by firing from their forts at too great a distance to do any harm. As soon as the troops had made their way through the rice-fields, the artillery began to play with effect on the Chinese positions. After an hour's bombardment the Chinese made a movement which may have been misunderstood by the spectators, but which certainly appeared to signify an inclination to take to flight ; but if such was their intention, it was promptly abandoned on the advance of the

* The force comprised two line regiments, the 18th, 26th, two native regiments, 37th and 49th Madras Infantry, a large number of Royal Marines, 460 blue-jackets, a detachment of Bengal Volunteers, artillery, engineers, etc. etc. The guns included 4 howitzers, 5 mortars, 52 rockets, and 4 9-pounders and 3 6-pounders. Lieut.-Colonel Morris commanded one column, Major-General Burrell the other—the whole of the arrangements being under the immediate supervision of Sir Hugh Gough in person.

English troops to attack their positions. It will never be known whether they feared the artillery more than the foreigners personally; but certainly when the English advanced to storm their forts, they stood to their guns with no small degree of fortitude.

The task of carrying this line of entrenchments and the detached forts was by no means easy or without danger, especially as the walls of the city, which at one place were not more than 100 yards distant, were lined with gingall * men who kept up a sustained fire upon the English troops both while marching to, and while engaged in the attack. The four principal forts, which had nearly fifty pieces of artillery in position, were attacked simultaneously. Three of these forts were hurriedly evacuated by the Chinese; but in the fourth the garrison refused to retire, and, continuing an ill-directed resistance, were cut down to a man by the sailors to whom the capture of this fort had been entrusted. It was in this particular assault that the English suffered most severely, principally from the cross-fire kept up from the walls, but also in the hand-to-hand fighting that took place in the interior. The capture of the forts closed the first part of the battle, but more remained to be accomplished before the operations of the day could be considered at an end. The Chinese forces had retired to and rallied upon an entrenched camp situated about a mile from the scene of this contest, and acquiring fresh courage from their numbers they seemed disposed to make a resolute defence, and bade loud and prolonged defiance to the barbarians of the West. Their new-found confidence failed to supply the deficiencies of discipline and arms; and a vigorous attack by one English regiment—the Royal Irish, who have distinguished themselves on more memorable fields, although never more conspicuously—led to their speedy discomfiture and the capture of their camp. With this incident, the battle † of the 25th of

---

* The gingall is a long heavy gun, something like a duck gun. It is fixed on a tripod, and carries a 2-lb. ball about 1000 yards.

† The English loss amounted to seventy killed and wounded; that of the Chinese was never ascertained. Sir Hugh Gough had "a narrow escape, having been at one time completely covered with dust from a

SURRENDER OF CANTON.

May closed, and the English army bivouacked in its position as comfortably as the galling fire maintained from the city ramparts during the night would permit.

The following day, which was to have witnessed the storming and destruction of Canton, beheld instead the warring of the elements; and the deluge of rain, by delaying the arrival of the needed ammunition and ladders, saved in probability the city from the horrors of being carried by storm. In place, therefore, of any further operations against Canton, the 26th of May was marked by inaction within the lines of the English force, and by the precipitate withdrawal of all those among the Chinese who possessed the means of retiring to a place of safety. The suspension of military operations was utilized for another purpose—that of negotiating a pacific arrangement. The main object with the Chinese had become to save the city; and in order to effect that they were quite prepared to make every concession, if they only attached to their pledges a temporary significance. These negotiations only served to while away the wet day on the land-side, where Sir Hugh Gough saw the city at his complete mercy, and was very loth to provide Chinese tergiversation with fresh opportunities. On the 27th of May every preparation had been made for delivering the assault, but at the very moment of the signal for the attack a special messenger arrived from Captain Elliot to announce that he had come to terms with the Chinese, and that all hostilities were to be immediately suspended.

The Chinese authorities, and particularly those responsible to the people of Canton for their homes and property, entered into negotiations with Captain Elliot in person, and, in striking contrast with their usual dilatoriness, complied within a few hours with all the terms demanded of them. These terms were that the Imperial Commissioners and all the troops should leave the city within six days, and withdraw to a distance of not less than sixty miles, and that six millions of dollars should be paid over "for the use of the English Crown." The promptitude with which these conditions were

shot that struck the ground close by his side."—'Chinese Repository,' vol. x. p. 393.

acceded to and complied with brought into stronger relief the delay and deception previously practised by the Celestials; but it remained far from certain that they were moved to this decision by any more sincere desire for peace than their temporary difficulties imposed upon them as a matter of imperative necessity. To the military authorities * the conditions appeared totally inadequate, and a fresh proof of the precipitancy of Captain Elliot.

If there was ever any doubt as to the action of the Chinese being directed by opposite counsels, it was removed by the extraordinary contradiction that was revealed in their subsequent action on this very occasion. Five million dollars, more than one million sterling, had been actually paid over to Captain Elliot; and, so far as the attitude of the Canton population went, nothing could appear more remote than the idea of their resuming a hopeless struggle. Yet even at this eleventh hour Yihshan, and his fellow-Commissioners, had not abandoned all hope of reversing the decision of war; and impelled by alarm at the penalties that their failure entailed, or possibly encouraged to believe in the chances of success by the English confidence in their security, they made a sudden attempt to surprise Sir Hugh Gough's camp, and to retrieve many disasters at a single blow. The plan was not without some hope of success, although it demanded very prompt execution, and no hesitation in coming to close quarters. And the latter was precisely the point which the Chinese never seemed to understand. They could remain to be shot down without revealing the least symptoms of fear, or they could die with a certain phlegmatic desperation when driven into a corner. They could even, and this was more conspicuous among the Manchus than the native Chinese, turn their weapons against their own persons to escape the military dishonour of acknowledging their discomfiture. But when it came to making an assault, the whole success of which depended on its being delivered with vigour and rapidity,

---

* Sir Le Fleming Senhouse, who had greatly distinguished himself throughout the whole of the operations, and who died a few weeks later at Hongkong on the 13th of July, declared his objections in emphatic language: " I protest against the terms of the treaty *in toto*."

their ignorance and hesitation became plainly visible. So it was on this occasion. A large body of troops and armed men, between ten and fifteen thousand strong, suddenly appeared on the hills about two miles distant from the English camp; but instead of seizing the opportunity created by the surprise at their sudden appearance, and at the breach of the armistice, they contented themselves with waving their banners and uttering vain threats of hatred and defiance. As an expression of national scorn and antipathy this demonstration was not without character; as a mode of delivering the land from a foreign invader it can only be described as ineffectual.

The probability seems to be that the great majority of these men were armed villagers who had been incited to take up arms by the warlike proclamations of Taoukwang, and by the lavish rewards promised to approved valour. There must also have been a strong leaven of "braves" from the garrisons of the southern provinces, for they stood well under fire, and only dreaded coming into close contact with the foreigners. The English pursued them for three miles, without, however, succeeding in bringing them to a regular engagement, and further pursuit was rendered impossible by the outbreak of another tremendous storm which flooded the country and rendered the muskets of the English soldiers useless.

That the Chinese could not have suffered very heavily was clearly shown by the vigour with which they in turn harassed the line of retirement. In a novel form of combat they succeeded in pulling over several English and native Indian soldiers by means of a crook fastened to the end of a long bamboo stick, when they despatched them with their swords. Such success as they obtained was due to the fury of the storm, not to their own valour; but they very nearly obtained a more striking advantage than the cutting off of a few stragglers. A company of native infantry lost its way, and became detached from the main body. Its absence was not discovered until the force had regained its original position, and then the men were so saturated and exhausted that it was out of the question for them to attempt to discover and bring in the missing company. Fortunately, there remained the marines in reserve, and these were at once sent out to find traces of the missing sepoys. The marines had been lately armed with the new percussion gun, which rendered them to some extent independent of the weather. After some search they were attracted by the sound of firing to a spot where they found the sepoys * drawn up in square, and surrounded by a large number of Chinese, who at once broke and fled on the approach of the relieving force. This terminated the contests of an eventful day. On the resumption of somewhat similar demonstrations on the following morning, Sir Hugh Gough, instead of exhausting his men in a vain pursuit, sent a notification to the city authorities that, unless these hostile attempts were discontinued, he would reply to them by bombarding Canton. It is almost unnecessary to add that this threat proved sufficient; but when the stipulated ransom had been received the English forces were withdrawn, leaving Canton for a second time, as it was said, "a record of British magnanimity and forbearance."

Once more, therefore, a certain degree of tranquillity was attained in the south, and the people and merchants of Canton, relieved by the departure of Taoukwang's Commissioners from expressing a patriotism which they did not feel, turned from martial pursuits to the practice of commercial affairs, for which they were better suited. The foreign merchants were nothing loth to follow their example, although their well-founded doubts as to the sincerity of the Chinese protestations of good-will, and the remembrance of many unatoned-for outrages on the persons of their friends and

* The steadiness of this company of native infantry (37th Madras), deserves special record. Lieutenant Hadfield and Mr. Berkeley were the English officers. Out of sixty men one was killed, fourteen were severely wounded, and Mr. Berkeley received a bullet in the arm. During the retirement it had to form square three times, but, although their guns were useless, they never wavered in face of several thousands of assailants. "Many of the sepoys, after extracting the wet cartridge, very deliberately tore their pocket-handkerchiefs or lining from their turbans (the only dry thing about them), and bailing water with their hands into the barrel of their pieces, washed and dried them;" they were thus able to fire a few volleys. The conduct of this company reflected the highest credit on the sepoy army, and deserves to be remembered with the earlier and more memorable achievements of the soldiers of Madras.

countrymen, impressed the necessity of caution upon them, if the conviction of superiority left room no longer for any sense of insecurity. We may turn from the review of the local position to briefly consider the report of Taoukwang's Commissioners to their sovereign. They had been charged, in the most emphatic manner, to free the Empire from the presence of "the rebel barbarians," and their instructions left them no choice save to succeed in their mission, whether by force or by fraud mattered nothing to Taoukwang's conscience. The failure of their predecessors increased the incentive and the necessity for their faring better in the great enterprise entrusted to them; and, to do them justice, neither Yihshan nor any of his "rebel-quelling" colleagues, as they were termed, doubted for an instant their ability to bring the matter to a successful issue and to dispose of any number of the inferior races of the West. And now they had to tell a tale of failure and discomfiture. Within the space of a few short weeks their hopes of success were dashed to the ground, and they could not deny that all their measures had been in vain, and that they were no better than Lin and Keshen— only weak creatures for an arrogant potentate to lean upon in an hour of blindness and adversity.

For a Chinese officer to fail in any mission entrusted to him is a capital offence. In the case of Yihshan the offence was the greater because the peril was the more grave, and because his very nearness to the throne rendered success more of a personal obligation. Yet his memorial to the Emperor, describing the course of events and the position of affairs, was an unqualified confession of failure, and, although it naturally sought to place in the most favourable light everything Yihshan had done, there remained the undoubted facts that he had failed in his commission, and that he had come to terms with the English authorities. The one distinct misrepresentation of fact contained in this document was so characteristic of Chinese diplomacy, which aimed at preserving the dignity of the Empire much more than at promoting the material interests of the Chinese people, as to call for notice. The six million dollars paid in compensation for the losses inflicted on English merchants by Commissioner Lin's destruction of the opium were represented as the private debts of the Hong merchants, and the contribution from the Imperial exchequer was stated to be a loan to these native traders, granted at their urgent petition, and on the promise of speedy repayment from "the consoo fund." Yihshan did not, of course, deny the greatness of his blundering, and prayed in the stereotyped form to be sent before the Board of Punishments for trial. The one fact that was revealed by the tone of this document was that with the barbarians there should be no permanent arrangement of amity, while Europeans could only see in it further proof of the untamed arrogance of the Chinese. The Canton convention was essentially a truce, not a treaty.

The operations before Canton had terminated about six weeks, and the trade had been resumed for half that period, when the arrival of Sir Henry Pottinger,* as sole Plenipotentiary to the Court of Pekin, and of Sir William Parker to assume the command of the fleet, brought new characters on the scene, and signified that the English Government was resolved to accept no prevarication on the part of the Chinese, and also to bring the question of their relations to a speedy and satisfactory issue. Yet when the new representatives of English policy and power came, they found what purported to be a friendly relationship in existence, and, so far as it was possible to identify the situation at Canton with the Emperor's policy, that most of the objects of their mission had been attained before their arrival. There were not wanting many reasons to justify a certain scepticism as to the durability of the arrangement, but still for the time being there was peace at the spot of most immediate importance to the foreign trade.

Sir Henry Pottinger's principal object was to conclude a treaty with the Imperial Government. A commercial agreement for the conduct of trade at Canton could not be

---

* Sir Henry Pottinger was an Anglo-Indian officer of long experience and distinguished service. He had travelled through Beloochistan with Christie, and he had been Political Resident with the Ameers of Scinde. He was afterwards Governor of Madras, and died in 1856. His younger brother was Eldred Pottinger, the heroic defender of Herat.

SIR HENRY POTTINGER, BART., G.C.B.

considered an equivalent for the trouble and expense of fitting out and despatching large expeditions to the Far East. Moreover, there was no guarantee for its durability. Taoukwang had not taken the least step towards meeting foreign Governments on a common footing, and it was an open secret that he would repudiate all sympathy with, and responsibility for, Yihshan's personal engagement. The English plenipotentiary resolved, therefore, to follow up the recent successes without delay, and by moving the scene of action one stage nearer the capital he hoped to effect his object, and to bring home to the Celestial Government the necessity of conceding the just demands of the English Crown and people. Before the end of August, therefore, the English expedition sailed from Hongkong, and on the 26th of that month Amoy, which had for a time been a port open to foreign trade, fell into the hands of the invaders. The defence made by the Chinese was described as "short but animated," and with only trifling loss to the assailants a strong position, with 500 cannon mounted in its batteries, and defending vast supplies of munitions of war, was lost to the Emperor of China.

The Chinese authorities had neglected no means in their power of making Amoy capable of standing a siege ; and in their hearts they trusted for a time to a belief in its impregnability. The town of Amoy is situated on an island, the largest of a group lying at the entrance to the estuary of Lungkiang, and it has long been famous not only as a convenient port, but also as a place of opulence. Nearly 200,000 persons dwelt in the city at this time, and about half as many more inhabited the prosperous villages that covered the island. On the eastern side of the harbour is the large but flat island of Quemoy, with abundant rice-fields and a toiling population ; and on the western is the elevated but barren islet of Kulangsu. On the chief island, and facing the sea, the Chinese had raised a rampart of 1100 yards in length, and this they had armed with ninety guns of different sizes. The flank of this fortification was defended by another battery of forty-two guns, while on the island of Kulangsu were many other guns in position which may be designated by the convenient term of batteries. No lack of energy or caution could be laid to the charge of the Chinese authorities. The town of Amoy was one of the principal places in the province of Fuhkien. Those entrusted with its custody were prepared to perform their duty.

When the English fleet appeared off the entrance of the harbour, the Chinese sent a merchant ship with a flag of truce—the use of which, when convenient to themselves, they had thoroughly learnt—to inquire what they wanted. The reply was the surrender of the town. It would be difficult to justify the necessity of this proceeding, for the people of Amoy had inflicted no injury upon our persons or our trade, and their chastisement might not bring our envoys any nearer to Pekin; nor can the action be approved of on the theory that to have passed on without touching Amoy would have been to have left a strong hostile position in the rear of our expedition. Amoy was strong only for itself. It threatened nothing; its capture had no important consequences, and to have left it unharmed would not have interfered with the grand result.

The summons to surrender meeting very naturally with no response, the English fleet approached the batteries for the purpose of engaging them. The first shot was fired from an English vessel, and the batteries replied briskly from all sides. The Chinese stood to their guns "right manfully," to use the phrase of an English tar who was present in the action, and were only induced to abandon their position when a landing party, having gained the rear, opened a destructive fire upon them. Then, after a faint resistance in hand-to-hand encounter, the Chinese were worsted, and sought safety in flight. Some of the officers, preferring death to military dishonour, committed suicide, and one of them was seen to walk calmly into the water and drown himself sooner than yield to the hated foreigner. The defence of Amoy was creditable to the Chinese; and had the direction of the defence been as skilful as the construction of the lines, it is not improbable that Sir William Parker's attack on Amoy would have failed.*

* The fortifications and sand batteries were excellently built. "The

CHUSAN OCCUPIED.

After a few days Amoy itself was evacuated, without any definite arrangement being made with the Fuhkien authorities, who had disappeared and did not present themselves to the victor. Three war-vessels were left at the anchorage, however, and a small garrison of 400 men was stationed on the island of Kulangsu; but the main force of the expedition sailed northwards to bring the occupant of the Dragon Throne to his knees, or to what is called reason by the stronger power. The fleet was dispersed during a severe hurricane, after passing through the Formosa channel, and only reassembled off Ningpo after a week's delay and waste of time. But Ningpo was not the first object of attack, and the fleet, leaving that place behind, proceeded to again seize and occupy the island of Chusan, which, despite many proofs of insalubrity and the undoubted heavy loss which English soldiers had experienced from a fluctuating or inclement atmosphere, presented such inducements from its position that the English commanders held it to be necessary in the first place to make sure of its possession.

The chief town of this island is known as Tinghai, and great preparations had been made there to avert the fate which had befallen it in the previous year. Here, again, the defences were admirably constructed, the artillery far from inefficient, and many of the soldiers animated by a fierce spirit of hostility and by a laudable anxiety to do their duty. Moreover, in the artillery-duel that ensued the Chinese artillerists held their own, for neither side succeeded in inflicting any serious damage on the other. But when the English batteries were never completely silenced by the ships' guns, and it is believed they never would have been." The stolid courage of the Chinese against Europeans and superior arms first attracted attention during this period, and it was prophesied about this time, " Let the Chinese be trained and well found with European implements and munitions of war, and depend on it they will prove themselves no contemptible foe "—a prophecy to be realized, perhaps, in a future generation. Another spectator describing the scene wrote as follows :—" An officer of low rank was the bearer of a paper demanding to know what our ships wanted, and directing us 'to make sail for the outer waters ere the Celestial wrath should be kindled against us and the guns from the batteries annihilate us!' The batteries were admirably constructed, and manned by Europeans no force could have stood before them."—"Chinese Repository," vol. x. p. 621.

troops landed and advanced to carry the batteries by storm, the superiority of Western discipline was asserted; and although the Chinese fought valiantly, and did not retreat until the line of bayonets was at spear's length, the batteries fell in rapid succession. Yet, to those who were not prejudiced against the Chinese as mere Asiatics, their valour on this and many other occasions had something in it noble and worthy of respect in the highest degree.*

Chusan having been thus speedily reoccupied, for the fall of Tinghai † signified the capture of the island, as no subsequent attempt was made at resistance, a garrison of 400 men was placed in charge of the island, similar to that left in occupation of the island of Kulangsu off Amoy. From Tinghai the main force still under the joint command of Sir Hugh Gough and Sir William Parker, with the plenipotentiary Sir Henry Pottinger accompanying it, sailed for Chinhai, a seaport of some importance on the coast of Chekiang. With the futility of bombardments impressed upon them by their late experience at Amoy and Tinghai, the arrangements to attack this town were made almost independent of an useless cannonade. A force of rather more than 2000 men was landed, and Sir Hugh Gough made his dispositions for an immediate attack. Dividing his small army into three columns, of which he assumed the command of the centre in person, he moved his two flank columns towards the sides of the enemy's position. Thanks to some inequalities in the ground their approach was not observed, and when the

* "Many of the Chinese," wrote an officer in the attack, "seeing our men advance into the battery, quickly turned, and a very smart affair followed. They assembled in great numbers close to some brass guns, and there fought like Turks; in their haste, however, they fired too high to do much injury, and some of the advance saved their lives by making good use of their pistols. At this place General Keo, the chief naval and military commander, was killed, and all his officers sticking to him to the last also fell with him. Their conduct, in fact, was noble: nothing could have surpassed it."—"Chinese Repository," vol. x. p. 624.

† In Sir Henry Pottinger's proclamation to the people it was said that "years may probably elapse before the said city will be restored to the Emperor's authority," as it was to be held until the demands of the English Government "were not only acceded to, but carried into full effect."

Chinese saw only the few men that composed the centre body advancing to the attack they boldly left their lines, and, drawing up in battle array, hastened to engage the foreigners whom in their imagination they had already exterminated. The opposing lines had come within short musket-distance before the presence of the two flanking columns was revealed, and the rapidity of their fire left the Chinese not even the time for flight. Astonished by the sudden revelation of so many foes, those of the Chinese soldiers who escaped the murderous fire to which they were exposed, broke into panic-stricken flight; but many of the braver preferred, even in the midst of this disorder, an honourable death to a cowardly safety. Some fell by their own act. Hundreds perished at the point of the bayonet, hundreds more were drowned in the swift-flowing stream of the Tatsieh. Chinhai shared the fate of Tinghai, and its occupation left the English commanders free to devote their attention to the capture of Ningpo.

Apparently the Chinese had trusted so implicitly to the defences of Chinhai that they thought it was unnecessary to make any further preparations at Ningpo. When Sir Hugh Gough reached this important city, he found no one to resist him, and the townsfolk in their anxiety to allay the wrath of the victors had gone so far as to shut themselves up in their houses, and to mark their doors with the phrase "submissive people." The occupation of Ningpo, although effected without any military operation of consequence, was of the greatest importance, for it completed the effect produced by the successes at Amoy, Tinghai, and Chinhai; and showed a large number of the coast population of China that the foreigners possessed the military superiority, and were resolved to assert it without the least compunction. Ningpo was garrisoned, and a public notice was issued by Sir Henry Pottinger, informing the mandarins and other authorities that he held Ningpo to ransom, and that unless the amount were forthcoming within a stated time he would hand over the town to pillage and destruction. This threat, which struck even those on the spot as unduly harsh, was probably never meant to be put into execution, and was only employed with a view of showing that the English were in earnest and were no longer to be put off with specious promises. The growing importance of the question was shown on the one hand by the steady arrival of reinforcements for the English army and navy, and on the other by the advent of a French commercial mission under Colonel de Jancigny who reached Macao in the last month of the year 1841.

But neither the swift recurring visitation of disaster, nor the waning resources of the Imperial Government both in men and treasure, could shake the fixed hostility of Taoukwang,* or induce him to abate the proud pretensions which imperatively demanded that he should triumph in some decisive fashion over the arrogant and hitherto too successful Europeans. Minister passed after minister into disgrace and exile.† Misfortune shared the same lot as incompetence, and the more the embarrassments of the State increased the heavier fell the hand of the ruler and the verdict of the Board of Punishments upon beaten generals and unsuccessful ministers. Preparations for defending the approach to the capital were made at Tientsin and along the Peiho; and in every other part of the Empire measures were taken to resume at the earliest possible date a vigorous offensive against the invaders. Long before the necessary levies had been made, the Imperial will which decreed the prolongation

---

* At this point in the struggle an interesting event occurred which merits attention. In 1839 the Dalai Lama of Tibet wrote to Lord Auckland (see Gleig's "Life") offering "to invade and conquer China" on the receipt of a sum of money and some horse artillery. This correspondence, of which nothing came, was in the possession of the East India Company; but, in reply to inquiries we have made as to its present existence, all we can ascertain is that it is not now in the Indian Office. Almost at the same moment the Goorkhas had come to a precisely opposite decision. Meng Pao, the Chinese Resident at Lhasa, wrote that an envoy came to him from Nepaul, offering aid against the Li-ti, who had often molested the Goorkhas, and who were then at war with China. The Amban did not know that the English were the Li-ti, and proudly replied that "China should not trouble herself with the quarrels of such petty states."—See M. Imbault Huart's translation of "A Chinese Account of their Conquest of Nepaul," 1879.

† Lin was appointed Commissioner of the Yellow River in consequence of great floods—an elevation. Elepoo, once one of the foremost ministers, was banished to Ili.

of the struggle was reflected in the acts of some of the more fanatical or desperate among his subjects, who lost no opportunity of attacking solitary individuals or weather-bound vessels. Outrages upon the Canton river again became frequent ; and more than one ship's crew, after having experienced the treachery of the China seas, felt that also of the Chinese people.

There ensued a lull also on the English side, partly because the trade went on smoothly enough at Canton, and because it was thought that the continued occupation of Amoy, Chusan, and Ningpo must eventually bring the Celestial Court to reason, but also and principally because the disaster in Afghanistan, which lent so sombre a colour to British history during the winter of 1841-2, monopolized the attention of the Indian executive and prevented the vigorous prosecution of the Chinese question until the Cabul catastrophe had been retrieved and avenged. Therefore the early months of the year 1842 proved uneventful, although a foreign army was in possession of several of the strongest and most important places along the coast south of the great river Yangtsekiang. This inaction greatly encouraged Taoukwang to adhere to his warlike resolutions, and invested with an appearance of increased credibility the official reports from the Chinese commanders, who alleged that, although defeated, they had inflicted heavy losses on the foreigners.

The month of February 1842 brought many rumours to the English head-quarters at Ningpo of the contemplated resumption of hostilities on the part of the Chinese, and small detachments sent out from that city to various places from ten to thirty miles distant never failed to come into contact with parties of braves. Nothing serious occurred until the following month, when the Chinese, having suddenly collected a number of men, made a vigorous attack upon Ningpo itself. It is not unlikely that the delay was caused by some disturbances which broke out in the province of Hupeh, probably in connection with the raising of recruits and revenue for the purposes of the war. The reconnoitring of the country beyond Ningpo had shown, indeed, that there were still armed parties of Chinese in the province, but it also seemed to prove that the rumours current as to their numbers and military efficiency were exaggerated. Both Sir Hugh Gough and Sir William Parker were absent at Chusan when these suppositions were suddenly and rudely dispelled by the appearance of a large body of Chinese troops on the 10th of March at daybreak, outside the south and west gates of Ningpo. Not fewer than ten thousand men, and by some as many as twelve thousand, were computed to have taken part in this attack, which fulfilled all the conditions of a surprise. The Chinese got over the walls and reached the very heart of the city; but, instead of being the way to victory, this early success proved only a trap for their more complete discomfiture. Attacked in the market-place by artillery and foot, they suffered very heavy loss, and were only too glad to beat a hasty retreat from their meditated prize. During this contest at close quarters and the subsequent pursuit, which was kept up with great vigour, the Chinese suffered very heavily, and 250 killed alone were found within the city walls. At the same time an attack was made on Chinhai, at the mouth of the river, but it was comparatively feeble and was repulsed without difficulty. Similar attempts were made from the islands neighbouring to Chusan, but all were defeated. The Chinese lost a large number of men; they suffered more seriously and irreparably in war material of every kind.

The Chinese, no doubt encouraged by the absence of the English commanders, had played a bold card, and they had lost. They were approaching the end of their resources; for the Imperial Exchequer was exhausted, and the task of defraying the expenses had been cast on those provinces which were near the sea, and which were consequently the scene of operations. The prolongation of the war promised to become most unpopular, for it affected the people in their purses, and they really did not know what they were to fight for. But while these sentiments were acquiring further force from the failure of the attack on Ningpo, the English had determined to assume the offensive and to strike a decisive blow against the Chinese army reported to be assembled in some strength in the neighbourhood of the important city of Hangchow, the Kincsay of the mediæval travellers.

A STRIKING ATTACK.

The first blow was struck at the small town of Tszeki, where the men who had attacked Ningpo, reinforced from Hangchow, had taken up a strong position in a fortified camp on a hill. A picked force, some 1100 strong, was conveyed by water to attack this position. The town of Tszeki offered only a nominal resistance, and was evacuated by the Chinese on the near approach of the English; but they had resolved to make a more vigorous stand in the fortified camps which they had constructed, with great pains and skill, on two hills of some altitude immediately outside the town. The operations of the day were carried out under the direct supervision of Sir Hugh Gough, who was accompanied by the admiral, Sir William Parker, and they were marked by all the dash and impetuosity for which the former was so well known. Although the Chinese position at first appeared imposing, it proved, on examination, to be extremely faulty. Large as the Chinese army was, it could only occupy a small part of the long range of hills which surround this place on three of its sides; and the Segaou hills, on which they had pitched their camps, were commanded by some loftier altitudes in the same or the adjoining range. So it happened that, while they were confident in their fancied security, the English commander had detected the fact that their left was commanded from some hills on his right, and that their left again commanded their own right. It was, evident, therefore, that the capture of the left portion of the Chinese encampment would entail the surrender of the rest, and the attack of the key of the position was attended by such facilities that it left little or no doubt as to the result. The difficulties of the ground caused a greater delay in the advance than had been expected, and the assault had to be delivered along the whole line, as it was becoming obvious that the Chinese were growing more confident, and, consequently, more to be feared from the delay in attacking them. The assault was made with the striking impetuosity with which good troops always attack an inferior enemy, no matter how great the disparity of numbers may be; and, notwithstanding that the Chinese stood their ground in a very creditable manner, they were driven out of their encampments over the range of hills to the fields below, and pursued for a considerable distance. The Chinese, it afterwards appeared, were picked troops selected from the Imperial Guard * and the garrisons of the frontier provinces of Kansuh and Shensi. They lost not fewer than one thousand men killed—a tremendous loss relatively to the number of men engaged and the shortness of the engagement. The English loss was only six men killed and thirty-seven wounded, of whom a large proportion were officers. As a consequence of this victory, the strongly-situated Changki pass fell into the hands of the English, and all the Chinese forces retired to Hangchow.

For a time it was thought that the next step would be to make a direct attack upon that city, where a new High Commissioner, Chulahang, had arrived with fresh warlike instructions, and with the Emperor's authority to freely confer decorations for valour and enterprise, but, above all things, for success. The arrival of large reinforcements from India for the English army more than compensated for the fresh forces Taoukwang had succeeded in putting in the field; but the change in the plans of operation caused by the fresh instructions received from the new Governor-General, Lord Ellenborough, produced a still greater effect so far as the final result was concerned. Lord Ellenborough has been charged with committing some acts of doubtful policy, and with overlooking the practical side in the affairs with which he had to deal; but it should be remembered to his credit, that he was the first to detect the futility of operations along the coast as a means of bringing the Chinese Government to reason, and to suggest that the great water-way of the Yangtsekiang, completely navigable for war-ships up to the immediate neighbourhood of Nankin, afforded conveniences for effecting the objects which the English Cabinet wished to secure. The opinion among the older English residents was altogether in favour of a direct attack on the capital itself; but this presented too many risks, and, indeed, was hardly feasible, considering the smallness of the English force, and

---

* Five hundred of these were present, and Sir Hugh Gough described them as being "remarkably fine men."

BATTLE OF CHAPOO.

the fact that the large naval squadron would be of practically little value in the Yellow Sea. On the Yangtsekiang the naval superiority of England could be both conveniently and effectually demonstrated.

Before the importance of this change of plan had been realized at head-quarters at Ningpo, there had been considerable debate as to whether it would be prudent to deliver an immediate attack on Hangchow or not. That proposal was finally overruled, and the English expedition sailed northwards from Ningpo, evacuating both that city and Chinhai in quest of fresh adventures. It had not to proceed far. On the opposite shore of the Han estuary, and near the northern limits of the province of Chekiang, is situated the seaport of Chapoo, well known in old days as the only authorized landing-place for Japanese vessels. At this port not only had many measures of defence been carried out, but a considerable number of troops had been assembled for purposes obviously the reverse of friendly. The heights were crowned with numerous defensive works, and batteries had been erected on several advantageous sites commanding the approaches from the sea. It was determined to attack and carry these positions without delay. The troops selected for the attack, some 2000 in number, were landed at a few miles distant from the town; and while the principal column, under the command of Sir Hugh Gough in person, attacked the position on the heights, his left wing effectually cut off the line of retreat which the Chinese meditated following into the city of Chapoo. The main body of the Celestials was routed without much difficulty, but 300 desperate men shut themselves up in a walled enclosure, and made an obstinate resistance. The survivors refused to surrender until more than three-fourths of them had fallen, when some fifty wounded men accepted the quarter which the English officers had from the beginning requested them to accept. The loss[*] of the assailants was severe, not so much in proportion to that of the defeated as to their own numbers

---

[*] Two officers killed and six wounded; eight privates, &c., killed and forty-nine wounded. The Chinese lost over a thousand.

and the expectations of their commander before the engagement; but the capture of a place of the importance of Chapoo was, on the whole, cheaply purchased, especially as the Manchu element was very strong there and suffered very heavily. The dispersion of the levies in Chekiang was thus carried to a further point, and might be considered as so far complete that there was no longer any reason to dread a descent on or attempt to surprise the garrison left in charge of the island of Chusan.

In pursuance of the new plans, the expedition then proceeded round the southern headland of the province of Kiangsu towards the entrance of the Yangtsekiang. Woosung, the port of Shanghai, was the first obstacle that presented itself, and here the resources and levies of a new province had been employed to oppose any attempt to land on the part of the invader, or to attack the important inland cities of Shanghai and Soochow. The entrance to the small river Woosung had been strongly guarded with batteries on both sides, and as many as 175 guns had been placed in position. The difficulties of attack consisted to a great extent in the difficulties of approach; for the channel had first to be sounded, and then the sailing vessels had to be towed into position by the steamers of the fleet. Twelve vessels were thus placed broadside to the batteries on land, a position which obviously they could not have maintained against a force of anything like equal strength. However, the naval attack was completely successful, and, notwithstanding that several of the English vessels went aground, the batteries were cleared one after the other, and the principal forts demolished. The Chinese were admitted to have stood their ground in a very creditable manner, but they were really helpless before the superior fire of the English artillery. The army was landed immediately after the cessation of the bombardment, and took possession of the batteries and camps in and around the small towns of Woosung and Paushau. Preparations were at once made for an advance on Shanghai.

The town of Shanghai, which has since become so well known as one of the principal foreign settlements in the country, lies sixteen miles up the Woosung river, of which the English expedition had secured the entrance by the action of the 16th of June just described. While one column proceeded by a forced march across land to Shanghai, the main force was conveyed by the fleet up the river, but so well-timed or so fortunate were their movements that they arrived almost simultaneously at the desired object. The Chinese had for the moment no inclination to renew an encounter, the inequality of which it was no longer in their power to deny. They withdrew from the city after firing a few shots from the walls. Large quantities of warlike stores and many pieces of artillery were captured, while the people showed a more amicable spirit than in other places. Shanghai was taken only to be evacuated, and the expedition returned to Woosung for the purpose of resuming the journey up the Yangtsekiang, while orders were sent to the very considerable reinforcements * which had reached Chusan to proceed to the same destination, and form a junction with Sir Hugh Gough.

The next operation was to be the capture of Chankiang, or Chinkiang-foo, a town situated on the southern bank of the Yangtsekiang, and at the northern entrance of the southern branch of the Great Canal. At all times this had been a place of great celebrity, both strategically and commercially; for not merely does it hold a very strong position with regard to that important artery—the Imperial canal—but it forms, with the Golden and Silver Islands, the principal barrier in the path of those wishing to approach Nankin. The movements of the fleet were delayed by contrary winds, as well as by the necessity for extreme care in navigating an unknown channel, so that the month of July had run most of its course before the English fleet of some seventy vessels in all appeared off the town of Chinkiangfoo. The first

* Prominent among these were the 98th under the command of Colonel Colin Campbell, afterwards Lord Clyde. They left England on the 20th of December 1841, with detachments for the regiments serving in China, and arrived at Hongkong on the 2nd of June, 1842. They joined Sir Hugh on the 21st of June at Woosung. For an excellent soldier's narrative of an excellent soldier the reader can refer on this point to General Shadwell's "Life of Colin Campbell."

matter of surprise was that there was no appearance of any military preparations either in the town itself or outside the city walls. The curious townspeople assembled on the ramparts to look at the foreign fleet as at some strange show or interesting spectacle. But a more careful reconnaissance revealed the presence of three strong encampments at some distance to the south-west of the town, and the principal operation of the day became to carry them, and to prevent their garrisons joining such forces as might still be stationed in the city. The execution of this portion of the attack was entrusted to Lord Saltoun's brigade, which included two Scotch regiments,* and portions of two native regiments. Three guns, all that were obtainable through some accident in landing the artillery, were sent with this force. The opposition they had to encounter was insignificant. The fire of the gingalls was promptly silenced and overcome by that of the guns, but a flank attack made by the Bengal troops led to some hand-to-hand fighting, in which the Chinese showed considerable gallantry.

While this engagement was in progress on the right, the attack on the city itself was being executed with spirit, but the strength of the walls, which were in excellent repair, and the difficulty of crossing the canal, which was too deep to be forded, prevented the success being as rapidly attained as was expected. The attack was chiefly directed against the western gate, which was blown in by the engineer officer, Captain Pears; and almost at the same point of time the walls were escaladed at two separate places, at one by the marines under Captain Richards, and at another by the 2nd Brigade under Major-general Schoedde. Taken thus in flank, front, and rear, the Tartar soldiers found themselves

* The 26th Cameronians and the 98th. Lord Clyde's biographer thus describes his part in this day's operations :—" The 98th had little or no opposition to contend with. A feeble fire from gingalls was opened by the Chinese. A few discharges from the guns quickly dispersed them. But a foe of far more formidable character had now to be encountered. The heat soon told on the 98th. Unprovided by the authorities with an equipment suitable to the climate, this regiment landed in its ordinary European clothing—a costume ill-adapted for the fierce summer heat of China. Thirteen men perished on the spot."

unable even to retreat, and a considerable number retired into a detached outwork which they held to the bitter death. These soldiers perished to the last man, either from the fire of the English or in the flames of the houses, which were ignited partly by their own act, and partly by the shot of the troops. The inner or Tartar city was stoutly defended, and the intense heat, having greatly exhausted the Europeans, favoured the Chinese renewal of the combat. Sir Hugh Gough had wished to postpone further operations until the evening, but the resolute stand made by the Manchus, who galled the English troops from their enclosure with a harassing fire, compelled the continuance of the engagement. The Tartars were driven back at all points, but the men were so distressed that it was found impossible to push home the advantage. The interval thus obtained by the Tartar citizens was employed not in seeking safety in flight, but in massacring their women and children, and in committing suicide. Their hatred of the enemy and their military honour were conspicuously shown in that, being unable to conquer, they would not grace the triumph of the victor, or experience either his clemency or vindictiveness. As soldiers of the Great Emperor, as representatives of the dominant race, they had no right to exist unless they were capable of commanding victory.*

* Sir Hugh Gough described the scene in the Tartar city in the following sentences:—" The Tartar general's house was burnt; that of the lieutenant-general, Hailing, it appears, had been set on fire by his own orders, and he was destroyed in it; his secretary, who was found the next morning by Mr. Morrison, principal Chinese interpreter, related this event and pointed out the body of the unfortunate chief. Finding dead bodies of Tartars in every house we entered—principally women and children—thrown into wells or otherwise murdered by their own people, I was glad to withdraw the troops from this frightful scene of destruction. A great number of those who escaped our fire committed suicide after destroying their families; the loss of life has been, therefore, appalling, and it may be said that the Manchu race in this city is extinct." An interesting summary is given of this engagement, from the Chinese point of view, in a translation by Mr. Morrison, the son of Dr. Morrison and chief interpreter to the Plenipotentiary, of the General Hailing's own account of it. From this document it appears that he was shamefully abandoned by his superiors, and that he had made various suggestions for the proper defence of Chinkiang, all of which had been disregarded and

The battle of Chinkiang was chiefly remarkable for the stubborn resistance of the Chinese soldiers, who were composed to a larger extent than had previously been the case, of Manchus. The casualties on the English side were heavy, more than thirty being killed and over one hundred wounded. When to these were added the many deaths that occurred during the following week from the exposure to the sun, it will be apparent that this battle was not cheaply purchased, and that their gallant resistance was highly creditable to the Tartar soldiers and their commander Hailing. It showed that the time may come when Chinese soldiers, with proper weapons in their hands, and led with such spirit as Hailing exhibited on this occasion, will be able to render a good account of themselves against even European soldiers. But although we may admire the Spartan resolution which would not recognize the possibility of having any intercourse with a victorious enemy, yet we cannot close our eyes to the fact that China lost some of her bravest and most competent officers by this blind devotion to duty, or this infatuation of a warrior caste. The Manchus of Chapoo and Chinkiang, had they only thought a little more of their lives, might have remained to render sterling service to their sovereign when his authority came to be challenged from within as well as assailed from without. Brave men are not so common in any state that their voluntary destruction, when no object is served by it, can be regarded as anything less than an irreparable loss.

Some delay at Chinkiang was rendered necessary by the

neglected. Among these was a proposal for staking the river. " Now the whole fleet of the rebellious barbarians is approaching, ship quickly following ship. Your slave is under the banner of the Tartars, an hereditary servant of the Crown. He, then, can do no otherwise than exert his whole heart and strength in endeavouring to repay a small fraction of the favours he has enjoyed from his Government." The day after this he fought bravely for many hours, and when he found his troops all routed, and the city committed to his charge fallen into the enemy's hands, he sat down in one of the public courts of his official house, and, ordering fire to be set to it, remained there and perished in the flames. "And what else could he do?" is each Chinaman's remark, "he never could again see the Emperor."—" Chinese Repository," vol. xi. pp. 470–79.

exhaustion of the troops, and by the number of sick and wounded; but a week after the capture of that place in the manner described, the arrangements for the further advance on Nankin were completed. A small garrison was to be left, not in possession of the town, but in camp on the heights commanding the entrance to the canal; but there was really little reason to apprehend any fresh movement on the part of the Celestials in this quarter, for the lesson of Chinkiangfoo had been a terrible one. That city lay beneath the English camp as a vast charnel-house, its half-burnt buildings filled with the self-immolated Tartars who had preferred honour to life; and so thickly strewn were these, and so intense the heat, that days passed away without the ability to give them burial, until at last it became absolutely impossible to attempt the last kind office to a gallant foe. Even as it was, Chinkiangfoo became the cause of a pestilence, and the utmost precaution of the English authorities failed to keep the ravages of cholera from their camp. Many a brave soldier and gallant officer who had led the charge up to the very line of Tartar spears in safety, and escaped the gingal fire without a scratch, succumbed to the fell disease which originated from the slaughtered defenders of their hearths and homes; so that the garrison at Chinkiang remained exposed to more serious danger in its state of inaction than awaited the larger part of the expedition, which proceeded to lay siege to the great city and once famous capital of the Mings.

Contrary winds imposed a further delay on the movements of the English expedition, and it was the 4th of August, or a fortnight after the battle of Chinkiangfoo, before the transports were able to proceed. On the 5th the fleet reached Nankin, a large city of about a million inhabitants, surrounded by walls and with a garrison of nearly 15,000 men, of whom two-fifths were Manchus. The vastness of the city—the walls of which exceeded twenty miles in length—hindered more than it promoted an effectual defence, and even the difficulties of approach from the surrounding country operated as much in favour of the assailants as of those who were assailed. The prospect of a pacific settlement was in view when the expedition had assembled in front of Nankin, but

Sir Hugh Gough made all the preparations for attack with his force of rather less than 5000 men, by way of demonstration for the purpose of driving, as it were, the last nail into the coffin of Chinese resistance. The details of these are preserved in his official report; but although they exhibit the tactical skill of the commander, and no officer was more skilful than Sir Hugh Gough in drawing up a plan of action, their interest and importance have long departed. Suffice it to say that the battle of Nankin, admirably as it was arranged for us as a complete English victory, was never fought, and, although the great demonstration before this second city of the Empire had much to do with the promptitude with which the terms of peace were agreed upon and ratified, the last operation of the war of 1841-42 was performed without the shedding of blood on the one side or the other.

The war which had continued during the greater part of two years was at last over. At first conducted without any system, and in a desultory manner, and prosecuted in its larger phases almost with reluctance, the military operations had gone to prove that neither the courage nor the ingenuity of the Celestials could compensate them for the want of proper weapons, and of the discipline and experience in war which made the armies of Europe victorious. Although the English did not enjoy the same superiority in scientific and mechanical engines and instruments as they enjoyed in the second war, seventeen years later, yet they possessed so many advantages over Taoukwang's levies that the result of an encounter was never in doubt, even although the latter possessed a strong position and an overwhelming preponderance in numbers. The war of 1842 demonstrated that the English soldier who had vanquished the most warlike races of Hindostan was the superior of the Chinese also on such conditions as they met under sixty years ago. But it showed to the intelligent another lesson. The Chinese soldiers were the worst equipped, and the most innocent of military lore among a long list of foes with whom in the course of a conquering career the sons of these islands had crossed weapons. Often and often they were no better than a badly-armed mob; and even the Manchus had no more formidable weapons than the bows and spears suitable to an earlier age. Yet on no single occasion did these badly-armed and ignorant men evince cowardice. The English commanders always testified to their gallantry even when helpless, and to their devotion to duty when most other peoples would have thought that the time demanded thought only of safety. Their defeat was under all the circumstances inevitable; they knew how to save their reputation for courage, and to prove beyond the shadow of dispute that men who could fight so manfully when victory was practically impossible could never be permanently conquered, and only needed the proper arms and knowledge to hold their own against good troops. Such seemed the moral of these encounters at this time to the most competent observers, and if the experience of the last Japanese war has seemed to falsify them, the future may show that the natural deduction from what happened in 1841-42 was not unjustifiable or misleading.

CHAPTER VII.

THE TREATY OF NANKIN.

NEGOTIATIONS of an informal character had been begun several months before they were brought to a satisfactory and conclusive issue at Nankin. The minister Elepoo, who had once enjoyed the closest intimacy with Taoukwang, and who represented, better than any other of the chief officials, what might be called the Peace Party—which, without any particular regard for Europeans, desired the termination of an unequal struggle—had neglected no opportunity of learning what were the views of the English officers, and what was the minimum of concession on which peace could be procured. Elepoo alone had striven also to give something of a generous character to the struggle, and he had proved himself, on more than one occasion, a courteous as well as a gallant adversary. After the capture of Chapoo and Woosung, he had sent back several officers and men who, at various times and places, had fallen into the hands of the Chinese, and he had availed himself of the opportunity to address the English commanders on the subject of the misfortunes entailed by a continuance of the strife, and also upon the desirability of coming to as speedy an amicable arrangement as possible. At the time when he first gave expression to these laudable sentiments, it is clear that Elepoo spoke only on his own authority, and that the hard lesson of submission had not been fully learnt at Pekin; for although his representations could scarcely have failed to impress the Emperor Taoukwang, seeing that the urgent appeals for help in men and money received from every quarter lent irresistible force to his arguments, this minister was for a time disgraced and deprived of his office.*

The reply of the English commanders to Elepoo's letter had been clear and to the point. They reciprocated the desire of the Chinese officer for the cessation of hostilities; but Her Majesty's Plenipotentiary could only treat with some high official directly empowered by the Emperor to conclude a treaty. Had Elepoo received that authority? If he had not, it was impossible to discuss affairs with him, or to suspend the progress of the expedition. And at that moment he had not the requisite authority, so the English forces proceeded, as we have seen, up the Yangtsekiang, fought the battle of Chinkiangfoo, and appeared in due course beneath the walls of Nankin,† before the happy moment arrived for

* The closing paragraph of Elepoo's letter to Sir Hugh Gough deserves quotation :—" Our two Empires have now for three years been at war; the soldiers and people who have been killed are innumerable, and the misery entailed is unspeakable and grievous to recount. It is therefore requisite, in accordance with the Celestial rule, to feel regret at those evils, and to put down the war; but if one proves disobedient to the dictates of Heaven it is to be feared that Heaven will visit us with punishment, and who will be able to endure this? Your honourable country has hitherto laid strong stress upon commerce, and considered war as nefarious, with the hope of putting a stop to the misery of war, and enjoying the advantages of an open market. Now if this takes place, the people of your honourable country may all return home and enjoy their property, and the men of our own nation could also every one of them go back to their families and gain a livelihood, enjoying the blessings of peace. Is not this far better than to fight for successive years and fill the land with the bodies of the slain!" This letter was written about the first of June.—(Translated by Gutzlaff) "Chinese Repository," vol. xii. p. 345.

† It will be appropriate at this point to give a brief description of Nankin, for a time the capital of China under the Ming dynasty, and which as Kiangning (see *ante*, vol. i. p. 157) was the chief town of some of the smaller dynasties of the fourth and fifth centuries. The walls, originally erected by Hungwoo, exceeded thirty miles, but the city never grew to the extent of its walls. The Tartar city again was walled off from the rest of the town, but the vast extent of the place rendered it practically incapable of defence. Much of the city was in ruins—a fact which induced Sir John Davis to compare it to Rome. There are some fine streets, with good shops and well-paved roads. The principal architectural remains are the Tombs of the Mings and the Porcelain Tower. Dr. Wells Williams describes the former as follows in his

the realization of the pacific wishes to which Elepoo had given expression three months earlier. The next point in the process of conciliation was reached when, immediately after the capture of Chinkiang, the mandarin who had been employed as an intermediary on the previous occasion, arrived in the English camp as the bearer of a despatch signed by Keying and Elepoo, as accredited representatives of Taoukwang, and the direct consequence of this step was that, although the English fleet and army were moved up to Nankin, no further hostilities occurred. In the interests of both sides it was only necessary to give the Chinese no reason to believe that the English could be put off by any deviation from the terms of peace as originally presented; and this end was thoroughly attained by the military demonstrations made outside the city of Nankin while the Commissioners on both sides were employed in the act of negotiating and almost of signing a treaty of peace.

The great minister Keying, who, as the Emperor's maternal uncle, had sometimes enjoyed an ascendency in the Imperial Council, had been ordered, in the month of March, when warlike views were supreme at Taoukwang's Court, to Canton, where he was to assume the command of the Manchu troops, but the greater danger in which the province of Chekiang was placed had led to his immediate transfer to that quarter.

"Middle Kingdom":—"Several guardian statues are situated not far from the walls. These statues form an avenue leading up to the sepulchre where the Emperor Hungwoo was buried about 1398. They consist of gigantic figures, like warriors cased in armour, standing on either side of the road, across which, at intervals, large stone tablets are extended, supported by great blocks of stone instead of pillars. Situated at some distance are a number of rude colossal figures of horses, elephants, and other animals, all intended to represent the guardians of the mighty dead." The celebrated Porcelain Tower, which was at this period in a perfect state, was destroyed at a later period by the Taeping rebels. It was built by the Ming Emperor Yunglo in the fifteenth century, and took nineteen years to build. The tower was made of bricks of fine porcelain, and the ornamentation was extremely brilliant. The population of Nankin was about one million, but it suffered greatly under the Taepings, and is only now beginning to regain the ground it had lost. General (Chinese) Gordon considered that this is the natural and safest capital for the Chinese Empire.

In March, therefore, he proceeded, not to Canton, but to Hangchow, where he was to put everything in a proper state of defence, and to leave nothing undone for the vigorous continuance of the war; and the disgraced official, Elepoo, was so far forgiven that he was handed over to Keying, probably at his request, as a lieutenant. At first their instructions were simply to make a stout defence, but the gravity of the situation was soon brought home to them by the capture of Chapoo. Then it was that they resolved to conclude an arrangement with the English, and to justify their claims to the title of High Commissioners, to which they had just been raised, by bringing a disastrous war to a conclusion.

In response to the first pacific expressions of Elepoo, Sir Henry Pottinger had felt bound to make a clear exposition of the wants and requirements of the English Government; and accordingly, after the capture of Woosung, he drew up in Chinese a proclamation for the information of the people of the country. In this document the equality of all nations as members of the same human family was pointed out, and the right to hold friendly intercourse insisted upon as matter of duty and common obligation. "England coming from the utmost west has held intercourse with China in this utmost east for more than two centuries past, and during this time the English have suffered ill-treatment from the Chinese officers, who, regarding themselves as powerful and us as weak, have thus dared to commit injustice." Then followed a list of the many acts of high-handed authority which had marked the term of office of Commissioner Lin, and from which the record of his successors had not been free. The Chinese, plainly speaking, had sought to maintain their rights of exclusiveness and to live outside the comity of nations, and they had not the power to attain their wish; therefore they were now compelled to listen to the terms dictated by the English Plenipotentiary at the end of a victorious campaign, and not merely to listen, but to accept.

And those terms were as follows: The Emperor was first of all to appoint a high officer with full powers to negotiate and conclude arrangements on his own responsibility, when hostilities would be suspended. The three principal points on which these negotiations would be based were compensation for losses and expenses, a friendly and becoming intercourse on terms of equality between officers of the two countries, and the cession of insular territory for commerce and for the residence of merchants, and as a security and guarantee against the future renewal of offensive acts. The first step towards the acceptance of these terms was taken when an Imperial Commission was formed of the three members, Keying, Elepoo, and Niu Kien, Viceroy of the Two Kiang. Yihshan retained the rank and name of Principal Commissioner, but he remained at Canton and took no part in the peace arrangements on the Yangtsekiang.

Niu Kien, the junior member of the Commission, made the first definite statement in reply to Sir Henry Pottinger's public notification. On the 29th of July a messenger arrived at the English camp outside Chinkiang with a highly important and not less conciliatory letter from the Governor of the Two Kiang. The letter was important in more than one sense. It held out to a certain extent a hand of friendship, but it also sought to assign an origin to the conflict; and Niu Kien could find no more convenient object on which to cast the odium of the war than opium. There was also the admission that "as the central nation had enjoyed peace for a long time, the Chinese were not prepared for attacking and fighting, which has led to this accumulation of insult and disgrace." The letter concluded with the expression in general terms of a desire for a prompt adjustment of the difficulty. The arrangement of the details for the necessary interviews was left in Niu Kien's hands, owing to Elepoo's absence, and a temple on the bank of the river was denoted as a suitable place for the meeting between the diplomatists of the two countries. In a later communication on the 14th of August Niu Kien wrote that he was fully aware that foreigners residing at Canton had been exposed to "insults and extortions for a series of years," and that the High Commissioners would take steps to ensure that "in future the people of your honourable nation might carry on their commerce to advantage, and not receive injury thereby."

This letter showed a great concession of principle on the part of the Chinese rulers, and made it evident that negotiations could at last be commenced on a fair basis and with good prospect of attaining a satisfactory result.

On the 12th of August both Keying and Elepoo had arrived at Nankin, and during the following week several meetings were held between subordinate officials for the purpose of arranging preliminaries, and also with the view of allowing time for a reply to be received from Taoukwang to a memorial drawn up and presented by the Commissioners, stating the demands of the English, and also the advisability, and even the absolute necessity, of complying with them. This important document was of considerable length, and entered into the details of the matters in dispute; and although a Chinese minister was bound in addressing his sovereign to eliminate the harsh language most suitable to the actual position of affairs, the facts were stated plainly enough, and no one supposed that the Emperor had any other choice in the matter than to yield with as good a grace and as promptly as he might. Keying and his colleagues put the two alternatives with great cogency. Which will be the heavier calamity, they said in brief, to pay the English the sum of money they demand (21,000,000 dollars), large as it is, or that they should continue those military manœuvres which seemed irresistible, and from which China had already so grievously suffered? Even if the war were continued, the evil day could only be put off. The army expenses would be very great, the indemnity would be increased in amount, and after all there would be only "the name of fighting without the hope of victory."

Similar arguments were used as to the wisdom of compliance with the demands for the surrender of Hongkong, and of the right to trade with five of the principal ports. The English demanded a great deal more than they had any right to expect, but as they were the masters of the situation, what was the use of arguing the matter with them? Moreover, there was some solace to be gathered in the midst of affliction from the fact that the English were willing to pay duties on their commerce, which would in course of time enable the Imperial Government to recover the money it was now surrendering, and which would contribute at a still later period to "the expenditure of the Imperial family." And, lastly, with regard to the question of ceremonial intercourse, on a footing of equality, the Chinese Commissioners, well knowing that that was a question to be arranged in its details, calmly stated that it might be "unreservedly granted." The reply to this memorial was an endorsement of its recommendations on the assumption that each point would be vigorously contested, and that the minimum of concession would be allowed. But Taoukwang and his councillors talked no longer of sending "rebel-quelling generals" to drive out the English. They would feel well satisfied if their departure could be secured by the payment of a sum of money, and the surrender of some trade privileges and even of national rights.

The delay in discussing preliminaries before Nankin while Sir Hugh Gough was energetically engaged in bringing up his troops, had not, therefore, been without its use. The Commissioners felt that they were pursuing the best course for China, and that their sovereign, however reluctantly, shared their opinions and endorsed their counsel. There was no longer any reason to doubt that peace was assured and that a disastrous war was on the eve of terminating. The terms of peace had been virtually agreed to, when the Chinese Commissioners accepted the invitation to visit the English Plenipotentiary on board the *Cornwallis* man-of-war on the 20th of August. The scene was sufficiently interesting, if not imposing. The long line of English war-vessels and transports drawn up opposite, and within short range of, the lofty walls of Nankin ; the land-forces so disposed on the raised causeways on shore as to give them every facility of approach to the city-gates, and yet so as to leave it doubtful to the last which gate was the real object of their attack ; and, lastly, the six small Chinese boats, gaily decorated with flags, bearing the Imperial Commissioners and their attendants to sign for the first time in history a treaty of defeat with a foreign power. It was noted at the time that the Commissioners were dressed in their plainest clothes, and the circumstance was set down in explanation to the fact that Imperial Commissioners are supposed to proceed in haste about their business, and have no time to waste upon their persons; but it is at least as reasonable to assume that their costume reflected their sense of the inauspicious character of the occasion.

The reception passed off in a very satisfactory manner, and the Chinese officials were received by the General and Admiral, in addition to the Plenipotentiary. They were shown over the man-of-war, which they examined with great curiosity, and remained on board two hours. As they were shrewd and enlightened men, their surprise at the discomfiture of their country probably vanished after their inspection. It was arranged that this visit should be returned two days later, but bad weather necessitated its postponement until the 24th. The interview was held in a temple outside the walls, and on the approach of the English officers a salute of three guns was fired. The Chinese Commissioners behaved in a most courteous manner, and after an hour's stay the English took their departure, to the strains of the National Anthem. A still more interesting ceremony took place when, on the 26th of August, Sir Henry Pottinger rode into Nankin for the purpose of arranging several matters of business with the Commissioners. He and his suite of some twenty officers, with an escort of native cavalry, and accompanied by an equal number of Chinese mandarins of every grade of official rank, rode through the streets to the College Hall, where a chamber of audience had been prepared for their reception. It was noted that the many thousands of people through whom the English passed, and who had never seen a foreigner before, refrained from making any audible observations. They were content to gaze at the strange foreigners who had brought with them a new method of war, and who only a few days before had threatened their ancient city with more complete destruction than had fallen upon it during the Manchu conquest. The interview was not less cordial or satisfactory than its predecessors had been. Sir Henry Pottinger was seated in the centre, with Keying on his left and Elepoo on his right. This interview suggested reflections as to the past, for it so happened that the 26th of August had been marked by an event of importance in each of the three previous years. In 1839 Commissioner Lin had expelled the English from Macao; in 1840 the English representatives appeared off the mouth of the Peiho; and in 1841 the English troops drove the Chinese from Amoy;—and these events, which showed the state of the question at different phases of its progress and development, had all occurred on the same day as that of the formal meeting in the College Hall at Nankin.

The signature of the treaty was performed three days later on board the *Cornwallis*, when the Commissioners arrived in a similar manner to their previous visit. Elepoo came by himself some little time afterwards, but it was thought that he would be unable to come at all through ill-health. He had been seriously indisposed for several days, but he evidently wished to have his share in the last act of the treaty which he had done so much to bring to pass. He was helped on board by the English officers in person, and supported, for he could not walk, to a couch in the cabin where the treaty was to be signed. The proceedings were hastened rather than retarded by his malady, for out of consideration to the sufferer all the ceremonial part was curtailed. The treaty was signed first by the three Chinese Commissioners, and then by Sir Henry Pottinger. They next partook of refreshments, and to the salute of twenty-one guns the flags of China and England were run up on the mast of the *Cornwallis*. The treaty of Nankin was concluded, and the war was finally over. Taoukwang ratified it in the promptest manner possible, although the extreme party at the capital made another effort to obtain the renewal of the war by rejecting the terms of this peace. It was noted as a remarkable fact at the time that the Manchus were altogether in favour of the treaty. They had already seen symptoms that the prolongation of the war, which could not be advantageous to the country, must prove fatal to their supremacy and to the existence of their dynasty.

On payment of the first instalment of the indemnity the troops were withdrawn to Chusan, but not, unfortunately, before a most regrettable occurrence had happened to cast a stigma on the honour and good conduct of English officers and men. A party of these soldiers went five days after the treaty was signed to the Porcelain Tower, from which they broke or cut off numerous fragments, thus committing a wanton and irreparable injury to one of the finest architectural monuments in China. Sir Henry Pottinger ordered the payment of a sum of money as compensation, an inadequate if the only reparation in his power. It was truly said of this outrage at the time that this party of Englishmen acted "the barbarian" in right good earnest.

When the fleet withdrew from before Nankin, all the places occupied on land were abandoned; but 2000 troops were left at Chusan, and 1000 at Kulangsu near Amoy, while the garrison of Hongkong was fixed at 1700 strong. At the same time Sir Henry Pottinger published a notification that no trade would be allowed with the four additional ports until the tariff had been agreed upon with the Chinese. Canton remained open as heretofore, and Tinghai so long as the English forces were in occupation; but Shanghai, Ningpo, Foochow, and Amoy were to be considered closed until the tariff had been drawn up and consular officers duly appointed.

Two vessels had been wrecked on the coast of Formosa, and their crews made prisoners. On the conclusion of peace a man-of-war was sent to Taiwan to ascertain their fate, and demand their surrender in accordance with the promises of the Emperor. It appeared that the local authorities had taken the law into their own hands, and inflicted the punishment of death on these shipwrecked mariners as "invaders of their country." When, therefore, they found that a treaty had been concluded with the foreigners, and that ample reparation was to be made for every injury inflicted, they were naturally afraid, and declined to reveal anything that had occurred. On the frigate returning from Taiwan without any more definite news than the report that these crews, to the number of more than a hundred persons, had been massacred in cold blood, Sir Henry Pottinger at once had an interview with Eleang, the Governor of Chekiang, and issued a proclamation expressing his "extreme horror and astonishment," and demanding the degradation and condign punishment of the local authorities. The correspondence in connection with this matter went on for some time, but at no point did the Emperor's officials show a desire to approve of or screen the acts of the Formosan mandarins. Eleang was sent as Imperial Commissioner to investigate the matter, and on the receipt of his report, in April, 1843, the Emperor issued an edict, degrading the principal officials inculpated, and ordering them to proceed to Pekin for punishment by the Criminal Board. In this edict occurred the important pledge that "we will not allow that because the representation comes from outside foreigners, it should be carelessly cast aside without investigation. Our own subjects and foreigners, ministers and people, should all alike understand that it is our high desire to act with even-handed and perfect justice."

If the great obstacle to foreign intercourse with China was overcome by the signature of the Treaty of Nankin, there still remained much to be done towards placing the relations of English merchants with those of the country on a footing calculated to promote trade and harmony. Sir Henry Pottinger's work was only half performed until he had arranged the tariff, and installed Consular officers in the new ports * opened by the treaty. Chinese movements are always deliberate, and a new year had begun before any progress was made towards the settlement of the tariff. In December, 1842, Sir Henry Pottinger, having returned to Macao, where he awaited the arrival of the Chinese Commissioners at Canton, addressed the English merchants with the view of obtaining the expression of their sentiments about the coming commercial treaty. This appeal failed to elicit any reply at the time, beyond a bare acknowledgment; but a committee was formed for the purpose of collecting opinions and information, to be laid before the Plenipotentiary at a later period.† The most important points which called for adjust-

---

* These were Amoy, Ningpo, Foochow, and Shanghai, making with Canton the Five Treaty Ports.

† Sir Henry's letter contained the following important paragraph on the subject of the opium traffic: "You will observe that no allusion is

ment, after the concession of the principles involved, were the adoption of a common tariff for all the ports, and the right of permanent residence in the factories and settlements for which land was to be allotted. The Emperor's representatives readily conceded the demand of the Europeans to bring their families with them as "a natural compliance with the constant principles of human nature;" but the accompanying statement that, when their commercial affairs were over, they should return to their vessels and go home, suggested the idea that the favour was not heartily granted, and that it would be attended with as many restrictions as the Chinese could devise or dared to enforce.

It was not to be expected that a people accustomed to regard their external relations from so exclusive a national point of view as the Chinese were, could become all at once reconciled to treat on a footing of equality with races and Governments considered, from a remote period, to be on a distinctly inferior basis. From the earliest period of history, and the testimony is not less applicable to European states than to China, it has been observed that the classes which make the noisiest protestations of patriotism are those which contribute least to sustain and ennoble national effort. The mob of Canton represented the most dangerous and degraded section of the population of a great Chinese city. They had contributed nothing towards the defence of their country, neither had they incurred any loss by its discomfiture. Yet there was little surprising in their constituting themselves the champions of their country. Riots disturbed the harmony of the closing year, and placards were posted up in prominent places to protest against the Fanquai, or foreign devils, being allowed to enjoy the rights conceded to them by the great Emperor. The prompt action of the local authorities did

---

made in any of these documents to the subject of the trade in opium. It is only necessary that I should at present tell you that the subject has not been overlooked by me, and that I indulge a hope, a very faint one, I admit, that it will be in my power to get the traffic in opium, *by barter*, legalized by the Emperor." The italics are ours; and the phrase shows that Sir Henry had grasped the fact that the real objection of the Chinese Government was to the export of silver, and not to the import of opium, except as the cause of the depletion of the currency.

something towards nipping the danger in the bud; but it was not until the arrival of Elepoo, in his character of Imperial Commissioner for the arrangement of the tariff, that the Cantonese were convinced that their Government was in earnest in allowing foreigners to acquire land for their factories, and to carry on trade-relations with whom they liked. The emphatic language used in Elepoo's proclamation had the effect of arresting the progress of the agitation, and of preventing the infection seizing the higher classes, who had already shown some symptoms of forming themselves into "a society of spirit and loyalty."

The arrival of Elepoo was the most hopeful sign for the speedy adjustment of the tariff question, as he was unquestionably sincere in his desire to arrange matters with the English on a friendly footing, and as he saw very clearly the necessity of peace to his own country. The preliminary discussions had been carried on with courtesy and good feeling. Sir Henry Pottinger, although without the support of the merchants' opinion, which he asked for more than once, and which was consistently withheld for fear of incurring responsibility, or, more probably, of making some greater concession in the matter of dues than the Chinese would stipulate for, saw, within two months of Elepoo's arrival, a near prospect of realizing the goal of his wishes. At this moment the death of the Chinese Commissioner arrested the progress of negotiations, and, as it was impossible for his successor to be equally well disposed, the possibility arose that he might be inclined to procrastinate, to raise objections, and to curtail, in such ways as he could, the usefulness of recent diplomacy.

Elepoo died on the 4th of March, 1843, in the seventy-second year of his age. He was remarkable in his origin, as well as for his talents. He sprang from the Imperial family of the Manchus, and enjoyed the privilege of wearing the "red girdle," which the Tartars had preserved among themselves as the mark of their supremacy. Elepoo was the grandson, or great grandson, of one of those brothers of the Emperor Yungching, who, in the plots of the beginning of his reign, were banished from the capital, and consigned to the retirement of the provinces. Elepoo entered the service at an early age, without enjoying any apparent advantage over those of lower birth. He filled several minor offices in the administration of Yunnan, and in time rose to be Governor of Kweichow, and afterwards Governor-General of the united provinces of Yunnan and Kweichow. In 1839 he was summoned to the capital and appointed Governor-General of the Two Kiang. Subsequently, in that post, and as Imperial Commissioner at Ningpo, he was outspoken in his recommendation of peace, which brought down upon his head the spite and vengeance of the extreme party. At the instance of Yukien, who came for a moment to the front at Pekin, he was degraded, and reduced to a state verging on servitude, from which he was only rescued when Keying asked that he should be placed at his dispcsal for the conduct of peace negotiations. His later services have been dwelt upon, but the admiration felt for his energy and devotion must be largely increased from the knowledge that during the last months of his life he was in constant suffering from ill-health. Yet he never slackened in his efforts to conclude the settlement of China's foreign relations, and in his attention to the business of his office, up to the last he was never remiss. The finger of reproach has been pointed at the probity and efficiency of the Chinese civil service; but there have been many honourable exceptions, and Elepoo should be remembered as one of the most favourable specimens of what a high official of the Celestial Empire ought to be.

The appointment of Keying to carry on the work of his former colleague furnished satisfactory proof that there was no real change of views in the Emperor's Cabinet, and the delay proved in the result to be no more serious than of the time needed for the receipt of the news of the death of the old, and for the despatch of the new, Commissioner. Meanwhile the ratification of the Treaty of Nankin had been performed by the English Government. On the last day of the year 1842 the Great Seal had been affixed in the office of the Lord Chancellor, and on the 16th of March, 1843, the officer entrusted with the important document accompanying a very handsome silver box containing the seal arrived at Hongkong, after a very rapid journey. The death of Elepoo was not followed by the untoward consequences that at one time seemed only too likely to ensue, and on both sides an unqualified desire was manifested to hasten the conclusion of the pacific arrangements.

That the final settlement of the question was eminently desirable, for more than one reason, was shown by the large increase of smuggling, particularly of opium, that took place along the coast. Several communications passed on the subject between the representatives of the two Governments, and Sir Henry Pottinger took the unusual course of repudiating all sympathy with those foreigners who were engaged in the illicit trade. But at the same time that he repudiated all participation in these acts of some among his countrymen, he distinctly stated that the responsibility of putting an end to the smuggling rested with the Chinese themselves. The utmost he could do, he pointed out, was to refuse them the protection of the English flag. But the Chinese officials were not so well versed in the precepts of international law as they should have been, and it seemed to them that the duty lay rather with the English than upon them to prevent the commission of acts which were both illegal and a violation of the first principles of goodwill and amicable relations. The Chinese view of the position was not concealed in their reply, for it was said, with some quaintness, that if the supervision of the English representatives was not perfect, "there will be less or more of smuggling." The matter was not at this time of the first importance, although it could not fail to indicate that, if the tariff were fixed at too high a rate, its objects would be defeated by the extension of the practice of smuggling, which already attracted no inconsiderable amount of attention. The official relations were undoubtedly more cordial, or at least more courteous, than those in commercial circles; and the visit of several high officials to Hongkong, where they were received in the most flattering manner, served to show that there was no insuperable obstacle to prevent the gradual disappearance of the prejudices which kept the two nations apart.

Keying reached Canton on the 4th of June. Three weeks

later he visited Sir Henry Pottinger at Hongkong, where on the 26th of the month the exchange of ratifications was made in the most formal manner. The Chinese Commissioner took his departure with every appearance of gratification at the reception he had met with, and more practical evidence was furnished in the same direction by the conclusion of the commercial treaty within less than a month of his visit. On the 22nd of July Sir Henry Pottinger was able to announce that he had signed the arrangements for the conduct of trade which were to be the most important provisions under the treaty of Nankin. The announcement of this fact was made in a proclamation* well calculated to show that the English

* " Her Britannic Majesty's Plenipotentiary trusts that the provisions of the Commercial Treaty will be found in practice mutually advantageous, beneficial, and just, as regards the interests, the honour, and the future augmented prosperity of the Governments of the two mighty contracting Empires and their subjects ; and His Excellency most solemnly and urgently calls upon all subjects of the British Crown, individually and collectively, by their allegiance to their Sovereign, by their duty to their country, by their own personal reputation, respect, and good name, and by the integrity and honesty which is due from them as men to the Imperial rights of the Emperor of China, not only to strictly conform and act up to the said provisions of the Commercial Treaty, but to spurn, decry, and make known to the world any base, unprincipled, and traitorous overtures which they or their agents may receive from, or which may be in any shape made to them by any subject of China—whether officially connected with the Government or not—towards entering into any collusion or scheme for the purpose of evading or acting in the contravention to the said provisions of the Commercial Treaty. The Plenipotentiary will not allow himself to anticipate or suppose that the appeal which he now makes to all Her Majesty's subjects will be unheeded, or overlooked, by even a single individual; but, at the same time, it is his duty, in the responsible and unprecedented situation in which he has been placed by the course of events, to distinctly intimate that he is determined, by every means at his disposal, to see the provisions of the Commercial Treaty fulfilled by all who choose to engage in future in commerce with China ; and that in any case where he may receive well-grounded representations from Her Majesty's Consuls, or from the Chinese authorities, that such provisions of the Commercial Treaty have been evaded (or have attempted to be so), he will adopt the most stringent and decided measures against the offending parties ; and where his present powers may not fully authorise and sanction such measures as may seem to him fitting, he will respectfully trust that the Legislature of Great Britain will hold him indemnified for adopting them in an emergency distinctly compromising the national honour, dignity,

Plenipotentiary was resolved to sanction no measure derogatory to the dignity of China, and that he was anxious to impress on his countrymen a sense of their own obligations so long as the Chinese did not hinder the progress of trade on the fair and supportable conditions which were now laid down in the most formal manner possible.

That the Chinese Government having once resolved to acquiesce in the extension of its trade relations should offer to the other nations of the outside world the privileges which had been snatched by the English, was only in accordance with the dictates of sound policy, as well as being under all the circumstances unavoidable. Keying accordingly issued a proclamation informing the public that henceforth trade at the five ports named in the treaty was open to "the men from afar" without distinction, and "the weapons of war being for ever laid aside, joy and profit shall be the perpetual lot of all." This result must not be attributed to the success of the English expedition exclusively, as the French Government had established official relations with the Canton authorities, and even deputed a Consul to that city; while the Government of the United States had been represented in the Bogue during the whole crisis by men-of-war. All that can be said is that had the English forces been defeated instead of being victorious, these concessions would not have been made to the general body of foreigners.

One point alone, but that unfortunately of the first importance, remained unsettled. Sir Henry Pottinger had not succeeded in obtaining the assent of the Chinese Government to the legalization of opium; and no reference is made to that article in the tariff or any part of the commercial treaty. The settlement which left undecided the principal point of all in controversy could not be considered completely satisfactory. The old sores might be re-opened at any moment. Yet Sir Henry Pottinger, notwithstanding that he had previously encouraged the expectation that the opium trade might be legalized, was sincere in his wish to uphold the stipulations of the treaty; and when, therefore, it was

and good faith in the estimation of the Government of China, and in the eyes of all other nations." 22nd of July, 1843.

suggested that opium should be held to come under the final clause of the tariff, which provided that all other articles of commerce not expressly named should be admitted at an *ad valorem* duty of five per cent., the Plenipotentiary, in his double capacity of diplomatist and Governor of Hongkong, issued a strongly-worded proclamation stating that such a construction was untenable, as "the traffic in opium was illegal and contraband by the laws and imperial edicts of China."

So far, therefore, as the opium trade could ever be said to have existed under the countenance of the English Government, that element of support was now withdrawn in the most complete and formal manner. But the Chinese were not able to comprehend the nice distinctions which, in international law, separate repudiation of participation in a stated proceeding from active prevention. The English Government withdrew its protection from those who pursued a forbidden traffic; but it rested with the Chinese to devise measures for the prevention of smuggling. This was strictly in accordance with international law, but the Chinese may be forgiven for failing to comprehend that the Government which denounced the opium traffic in language that seemed to borrow its moral fervour from some of the writers of the Hanlin, need take no steps towards stopping the arrival of the drug or cutting off the supply. The explanation of this difference was simple, but it was to prove the precursor of a long series of troubles which have not even in the present day reached a settlement or exhausted their power for mischief. Far better would it have been if Sir Henry Pottinger had openly declared that the settlement of the question did not lie in his hands, and that as the East India Company would continue to grow opium, so would it be exported from India to China, whether as contraband or not. The Government of Queen Victoria could do little or nothing in the matter. If the Chinese did not feel strong enough to guard their coasts, to enforce the laws both on their own people and on treaty-breaking foreigners, then the wisest and the most dignified policy to pursue was to legalize the import of opium. But Sir Henry Pottinger did not take this course, and the Chinese were left to unravel for themselves as best they might the mystery of how the action of the Company, and of English and Indian merchants, was compatible with the solemn pledges and the sometimes indignant language of the representative of the English Queen.

With this important question left in doubt and unsettled it followed that there was a weak point in the arrangements made under the Treaty of Nankin. The continuance of friendly relations depended obviously on the exercise of forbearance on both sides, as well as on the continued belief of the Chinese authorities in their military inferiority and their consequent inability to reverse the decision of war. For a time the Chinese believed in the sincerity of the large promises conveyed by the official language of the English officers; but as they never realized the fact that English action was directed from two different sources, and controlled on this question by two opposite and antipathetic opinions, those of Leadenhall Street, and Whitehall, so did it never occur to them as being worthy of a moment's credence that the English Plenipotentiary did not possess the power to carry out his promises, and that his threats were in the eyes of English merchants devoid of terror. So long as opium was manufactured at Patna or Benares, so long as the poppy flowered on the plains of Malwa, so long could no human power, save the strong arm of Chinese authority itself, prevent its finding a way to the most profitable market in Canton or the other parts of China. The war and treaty of 1842 failed to provide a remedy of the evil, and the opium question was left unsettled to disturb the harmony of later relations.

One unqualified good had resulted from the war, for there will be none to deny that the study of the Chinese language and literature received an immense impetus from the events which have just been recorded. The missionaries of the Church of Rome had long enjoyed and utilized opportunities denied to other foreigners, of learning the Chinese tongue, and of becoming conversant with its peculiarities as well as with much of the accumulated mass of its literature. Yet although they fully and freely placed their knowledge at the service of the world by narrating the history, describing the customs and the geography of the Chinese people and nation, they did nothing towards the increase of the knowledge of the Chinese tongue itself. Without accusing them of having any settled policy on the subject, the fact remains that they possessed, and did nothing to lose, the exclusive knowledge of the Chinese language. So, when the mission of Lord Macartney to Pekin was determined upon and despatched, there was for a moment complete uncertainty on the important point as to who should be the interpreter. As has been said, there was no man eligible for that employment then existing in the British dominions.

The difficulty was fortunately averted on that occasion by the appointment of Mr., afterwards Sir George, Staunton, then at Canton, who, perhaps, of all English sinologues, best deserves the grateful remembrance of his countrymen for the services he rendered not merely as a diplomatist, but as an illustrator and expositor of the laws of China. Staunton had a greater incentive and a more practical object in taking up the language of the country than had Stanislas Julien, who was the first among Continentals to prosecute the research from motives apart from religious zeal, and who must always be remembered for both the work he did and the difficulties he overcame as one of the foremost and most brilliant of Chinese scholars. Four secretaries possessing a knowledge of Chinese accompanied the mission of Lord Amherst, and of these two became well known in their respective spheres—Sir John Davis and Dr. Morrison. Both did excellent service in their way, the former in work that will endure longer perhaps than the more laborious and erudite productions of his colleague. These early seekers in a new field left more than an example to the generation then growing up. They helped by their teaching and guidance the studies of those who in name, as well as in a common pursuit, continued their labour and made it more familiar. Dr. Morrison left a son,[*] who was chief interpreter to Sir Henry Pottinger, and who was thought by some to possess a more finished style of Chinese conversation than his father. To him Mr. Charles Gutzlaff could hardly be considered inferior, for they had

[*] Mr. John Robert Morrison, who died prematurely in 1843.

both been trained at the same school, and had derived inspiration from a common source. But there were others too numerous to name, the opportunity of whose service did not afford them the same occasion of distinction as their predecessors in an age when Chinese scholarship was the privilege of a few individuals. Two alone need be named—the missionary Dr. Medhurst, and Professor James Legge, who began more than forty years ago those studies which gained for him no fleeting reputation as an erudite and conscientious investigator of a language presenting unusual difficulties to the inquirer and student. It will be sufficient, and the present purpose will be served, if in recalling the incidents and results of the first foreign war some small allowance be made for the undoubted impetus which it gave to the study of the Chinese language.

Nor must it be supposed that viewed in its larger aspect the war of 1840–42 was only disastrous in its incidents and unfortunate in its consequences. Those who never fail to apply to the action of the English Government the test of a standard not yet attained, and perhaps unattainable, in international relations, have not refrained from denouncing this war as iniquitous. They have sought to give it, as an opprobrious title, the name of "The Opium War." Never was a title given with less pretence of a justification. On the same principle many wars in this continent might have been termed wars of brandy or whisky—articles much more injurious in their effects when abused or taken to excess, than opium used in the only form known among the Chinese. But although one of the early incidents in the struggle had been the destruction of the stock of opium by Commissioner Lin, the subject of opium sank into the background, and was hardly mentioned after the fervour of the literary class had been checked by the failure of their schemes, and the disgrace of their foremost representative. True it is that compensation had been demanded and obtained; but this was not because it was opium, but because it was the merchandise of English subjects. Had it been wheat or cotton the demand would still have been made.

But while there is not room to doubt that the war was not

waged for the purposes of continuing the trade in opium, with which the English Government distinctly repudiated all sympathy and connivance—not because a few enthusiasts denounced its use as the indulgence of a hopeless sin, but because the Imperial Government of China had on more than one occasion expressed a belief that it was corrupting its people, and impoverishing the country—it may be urged, with some show of fairness, that the English Government would have shown greater prescience and statesmanship, that the English Plenipotentiary would have revealed a more perfect grasp of the subject, had they insisted, not on the prohibition, but on the legalization of opium. Of course this would have provided the self-appointed champions of morality with a fresh ground of complaint; but then this might have been tolerated for the sake of the advantages that would have accrued to the Governments of China and of England. The Chinese Government alone could put a stop to the import of opium. No arbitrary act of the Indian authorities could prevent the Chinese supplying themselves with a luxury which hosts of producers would be only too eager to supply, whether from Persia or from Yunnan mattered little. But the Chinese Government did not possess the power to prevent smuggling. It would have been wiser and more profitable to have recognized this. The second foreign war might have been averted, and the dignity of China would have been preserved from some of the rude shocks which it has since had to incur, if the candid statement had been made, and admitted that the responsibility of crushing smuggling remained on the Chinese alone.

It is taking a very narrow view of this struggle, however, to suppose that the question of opium was the principal matter at stake. The real point at issue was whether the Chinese Government could be allowed the possession of rights which rendered the continuance of intercourse with foreigners an impossibility. Those claims were unrecognized in the law of nations. They were based on the pretension of a superiority, and of a right to isolation, which the inhabitants of the same earth have never tolerated, and will never allow to any single branch of the human family. What China sought to retain was a possession that no other State attempted to hold, and one which superior might alone could establish, if it could no more justify selfishness in the case of a country than in that of an individual. There was never any good reason to suppose that China possessed the sufficient strength, and the war clearly exposed the military weakness of the Celestial Empire.

When people talk, therefore, of the injustice of this war as another instance of the triumph of might over right, they should recollect that it was China which in the first place was in the wrong, as claiming an impossible position in the family of nations. The initial stages of the making of that claim were accompanied by an amount of arrogance on the part of the Chinese officials towards foreigners, which was the fitting prelude to the destruction of their property. We cannot doubt that had these acts been condoned there would have been no delay in enforcing the right to treat the persons of foreigners with as scant consideration as had been shown for their belongings. The lives of Europeans would have been at the mercy of a system which recognizes no gradation in crime, which affords many facilities for the manufacture of false evidence, and which inflicts punishment altogether in excess, according to Western ideas, of the fault. Commissioner Lin was filled with an enthusiasm in exalting the majesty of his sovereign and the superiority of his nation that left him no room to consider the feelings or claims of the outside peoples. They ought, in his mind, to have been well-satisfied at being allowed to come within even "the outer portals" of the Middle Kingdom, and in return for this favour they should have been willing to show due subordination, and humility in face of insult, danger, and tyrannical interference.

All this was of course intolerable, and not to be acquiesced in by the meekest of people; and the English, despite all their lip-zeal about equal rights and the virtue of timely concessions, are not at heart a meek people at all. The inevitable result followed with rather more delay than might have been expected, a fact which may be attributed to the distance between Canton and London and the imperfection in the existing means of communication; but it may be confidently said that were any Chinese official to now attempt the acts of high-handed authority which made the name of Commissioner Lin historical, the redress would have to be far more promptly rendered than it was years ago. Yet we cannot hope to have heard the last of the cuckoo-cry that the war of 1842 was unjust.

There were some, however, at the time to see the injustice of these allegations, and to point out with much clear and cogent argument that not only was England in the right morally, but that she was conferring a benefit on all foreigners alike by her decided and spirited action. Prominent among these was John Quincy Adams, the famous American professor on International Law, who, at an earlier period, had filled with lustre the highest place in the community of the United States. The question of the relations between China and foreign countries was passed by him in able and detailed review, and the conclusion to which he came was that England was in the right—he said "Britain has the righteous cause." The conclusion forced itself on his mind, as we fain believe it will on those who read the events we have detailed, that the opium dispute was an incident, and not the true cause of the war. There is the more reason to accept his opinion as he thought that the opium traffic was an evil in the suppression of which the English Government might have taken a much greater part; yet, notwithstanding his accord with the opponents of opium, he could not deceive himself as to the fact that England was fully justified in her policy, and that she being in the right, China necessarily must be in the wrong.*

---

* Professor Adams's lecture will be found in full in vol. xi. of the "Chinese Repository," pp. 274-89. The following may be quoted as his concluding opinion: "Which has the righteous cause? You have perhaps been surprised to hear me answer Britain—Britain has the righteous cause. But to prove it, I have been obliged to show that the opium question is not the cause of the war. My demonstration is not yet complete. The cause of the war is the kotow!—the arrogant and insupportable pretensions of China that she will hold commercial intercourse with the rest of mankind not upon terms of equal reciprocity, but upon the insulting and degrading forms of the relation between lord and vassal.

When, too, the justice of this war is impugned, let it not be forgotten that the arrogance of the Chinese authorities was of no fleeting character. It even survived the rude shock of a period of open defeat and unqualified disaster. The confidential utterances of Chinese ministers showed that they never ceased to contemplate the return of the time when they would be in a position to advance their old claims to supremacy, and to withdraw the concessions which had been wrung from them by the necessities of the day. They gave way in order to gain the time needed to collect their resources, and they fancied that by military reforms, and by punishing their unfortunate generals, they might in the course of a little while create a new army, and obtain fresh commanders to show the way to victory and to undo the many concessions which they held had been made to Europeans. How far their hopes were thought even by themselves to be practical it is not necessary for us to inquire. The persistence of their pretensions after discomfiture shows how deep-rooted must have been the sentiment to regard all foreigners as inferiors, rigidly to be excluded from the benefits and privileges of their own nation.

The melancholy catastrophe with which I am obliged to close, the death of the gallant Napier, was the first bitter fruit of the struggle against that insulting and senseless pretension of China. Might I, in the flight of time, be permitted again to address you, I should pursue the course of the inquiry through the four questions with which I have begun. But the solution of them is involved in the germinating element of the first, the justice of the cause. This I have sought in the natural rights of man. Whether it may ever be my good fortune to address you again, is in the disposal of a Higher Power; but with reference to the last of my four questions, "What are the duties of the Government and the people of the United States, resulting from the existing war between Great Britain and China?" I leave to your meditations the last event of that war, which the winds have brought to our ears—the ransom of Canton. When we remember the scornful refusal from the gates of Canton in July, 1834, of Mr. Astell, bearing the letter of peace and friendship from Lord Napier to the Governor of the two provinces, and the contemptuous refusal to receive the letter itself, and compare it with the ransom of that same city in June, 1841, we trace the whole line of connection between cause and effect. May we not draw from it a monitory lesson, written with a beam of phosphoric light—of preparation for war and preservation of peace?"

No circumstance revealed this feeling of pride and suspicion more clearly than the tone adopted by the enlightened Elepoo, in one of his last despatches to Sir Henry Pottinger with regard to the English Sovereign, and which evoked from the English Plenipotentiary the indignant sentence that "his royal mistress, the Queen of England, acknowledges no superior or governor but God; and that the dignity, the power, and the universal benevolence of Her Majesty are known to be second to none on earth, and are only equalled by Her Majesty's good faith and studious anxiety to fulfil her royal promises and engagements." There can, therefore, be no kind of doubt, and the evidence lies before us in accumulated piles from both sides, from those engaged in the fray, as well as from the critical and disinterested spectator, that not one questionable branch of trade brought England and China into hostile collision, but the grand incompatibility of Chinese pretensions with universal right. Unless we are prepared to cancel all the obligations of international relations, to deny the claims of a common humanity, to maintain that the deficiencies of one region are not to be supplied by the abundance of another, and to hand down to future generations a legacy of closed frontiers, public suspicion, and interminable strife—unless we are to agree in denying every common principle of probity since the founders of nations went forth in all directions from the Tower of Babel, then we must come to the conclusion that the Chinese brought the humiliations of the first foreign war upon themselves, and that they, however blindly, were the erring side in what was, regarded by its consequences, a momentous struggle.

It is more gratifying to be able to leave the scene of contest, to turn from the record of an unequal and inglorious war, with the reflection that the results of this struggle were to be good. However inadequately the work of far-seeing statesmanship may have been performed in 1842, enough was done to make present friendship possible, and a better understanding between two great governing peoples a matter of hope, and not desponding expectancy. The Treaty of Nankin did not place the English representatives on that footing of dignity which the equality of their sovereign with the Chinese Emperor demanded. The commercial arrangements at Canton ignored the opium trade—according to some, the *teterrima causa belli*. The Chinese Government made not the smallest overture, and showed no desire to establish relations with the European capitals, even with the view of learning something about the kingdoms which had sent strong fleets and brave armies to the seas and lands of the Far East. So long as this was the case, it was impossible to feel any belief in the cordiality of the friendship established in name. The English Government had obtained a material guarantee in the cession of Hongkong; the English merchant fresh opportunities of trade by the opening of four additional ports, and by the abolition of the Hong monopoly; and Englishmen generally increased security, if not perfect safety, by the vindication of the majesty of British law and citizenship. That was all. If it was not everything, if it was not even enough to stifle the pride and dissipate all the pretensions of China, it was still no small result for an expedition which had not approached the capital, and which could only be conducted under extreme difficulties, from considerations of distance, pre-occupation, and, it must be added, of ignorance of Chinese matters. That the war accomplished what it did is sufficiently creditable to its conductors, and explains the reason why English residents in China have always held dear, as one of the principal charters of their presence in that country, the memory of the Treaty of Nankin.

CHAPTER VIII.

THE LAST YEARS OF TAOUKWANG'S REIGN.

THE years immediately following the signature of the Treaty of Nankin were occupied with the adjustment of the numerous matters that claimed attention from those employed in the difficult task of harmonizing the relations of two lately conflicting races. Consuls had to be appointed at the treaty ports, and a staff of interpreters provided. The undue expectations of the foreign merchants had to be checked at the same time that the mandarins were not encouraged to believe that the Queen's representatives were disposed to look down upon trade and thought merely of cultivating relations on a kind of philosophical basis with the Celestial Government. The difficulties of enforcing the right of residence in the new towns opened to foreigners were not few; and time, as well as tact, was needed to bring the matter to a satisfactory conclusion. The solution of these questions with England alone was certainly not simplified by the appearance of diplomatic agents from other countries, for it brought the fact home with greater clearness to the Chinese Government that they were making a great concession of principle not merely to a victorious opponent, but to all foreigners alike. They were, in short, taking a new departure in their practice of conducting their outside relations, and it could not but seem the more unpalatable the greater the points conceded, and the longer the time occupied in their discussion. Yet, although the effort of wresting these concessions, in which all foreigners equally shared, from the Chinese had been made by England herself, there were not wanting those at the time to suggest that England was the one European Power that thought only of trade, that the rest were influenced by noble and disinterested motives, and sympathized with the grandeur and antiquity of China, apart from matters of tea, silk, or opium. Chinese diplomacy, trusting to the natural antipathy of nations towards each other, was not slow to avail itself of the chance of creating occasions of embarrassment; but the advantages it expected to derive from this discord have yet to be realized when clashing interests and individual ambitions have become more clearly revealed.

The Consulates were established and opened at Shanghai and Amoy in November, 1843; and with this formal recognition trade could at once be legally carried on. The consulate had already begun its work at Canton, and sometime afterwards that at Ningpo was also opened. The island of Chusan being still in English occupation, trade at Tinghai was conducted without the aid of a consul.* At Amoy the difficulty of acquiring land for residence was increased by the fact that for some reason or other Kulangsu had not been mentioned to the Emperor; and although by the consular reports included within the limits of Amoy waters, objections were raised to the settlement of Europeans upon it. So long as the English garrison remained in occupation the question was left undecided, but on its withdrawal in 1845 the Europeans also took their departure, and a hospital which had done much good was necessarily closed. That matter was therefore arranged by concessions to the Chinese.

* It will be useful to state here briefly who the respective Consuls were, and also something as to their staff. Mr. G. T. Lay was Consul at Canton; Captain George Balfour at Shanghai; Mr. Henry Gribble at Amoy, and Mr. Robert Thom at Ningpo. The respective interpreters, taking the ports in the same order, were Mr. Thomas Meadows, Mr. W. H. Medhurst, Jun., Lieutenant—the late Sir Thomas—Wade, and Mr. Charles Sinclair. Mr. G. T. Lay was also Interpreter-in-Chief to the Plenipotentiary, while the Rev. Charles Gutzlaff was Chinese Secretary and Interpreter. The latter's assistant was Mr.—afterwards Sir—Harry S. Parkes. It is worthy of notice that in this small body of men there were two destined to represent the English Government at Pekin, Sir Thomas Wade and Sir Harry Parkes.

SIR HENRY'S DEPARTURE.

Some delay also had occurred at Canton in building the necessary residences for the foreign merchants, but in this case the Chinese pleaded a variety of excuses; and the delay might be attributed to the confusion caused by an extensive and very destructive fire, not an altogether insufficient excuse in itself, and one of which those having other intelligible grounds of objection would naturally make the most. The Chinese had some reason for vigilance, it will be admitted, as the English merchants endeavoured to extend the limits of their settlement by building on a portion of the ground occupied by the Chinese houses that were then burnt down. The Chinese proved, however, too quick for their opponents, and baffled their attempt by constructing their new houses in a night. All this was not very dignified, and may explain some of those hidden reasons which defy description, but which afford the true explanation why the progress of the settlement proved so slow.

Almost simultaneously with the arrival of the American representative, Mr. Caleb Cushing, and with the announcement that the French plenipotentiary, M. de Lagrenée, had left Europe, the departure of Sir Henry Pottinger had to be recorded. With the final adjustment of the provisions for commerce and consular representation his work was done, and the long services which he had rendered to his country, both in India and the further East, entitled him to return home as soon as his labours for the settlement of the Chinese question had been brought to a satisfactory termination. Taking up the thread of negotiations from Captain Elliot at a time when the Chinese entertained little doubt of their capacity to hold their own, he was soon compelled to suspend the action of diplomacy until the sword had decided the simple question of superior strength. But once the Chinese authorities became sincerely disposed to negotiate, they found in the English representative not merely courtesy but an anxious desire to be as little exacting as the terms which he was instructed to demand, and which were really necessary for the continuance of the intercourse if it were to go on at all, would allow. If the policy he was entrusted to execute failed in any point, it was in demanding too little direct concession on the part of the Pekin Government. Much was obtained in the principal sea-ports; but so long as the capital could claim immunity from the presence of foreigners it was impossible to say when or how soon the mood of reasonable concession might not pass off. But the impression left by Sir Henry Pottinger could not have been other than favourable, and his attitude did something to disabuse the Chinese mandarins of the impression that the English were only traders, and neither very honest nor very considerate in the attainment of their objects. Had Lord Napier succeeded in coming into the same close communication with the Chinese, his amiable character would not have failed to impress them favourably; but his premature death left his chief successor the opportunity of enjoying the principal credit in improving the character of the official relations between the two countries.

Sir Henry Pottinger left Hongkong in June, 1844, after a residence of nearly three years, and after arranging the transfer of his post to the gentleman appointed to succeed him, Mr., soon to be created Sir, John Francis Davis. The appointment was in some degree a surprise, as no one had anticipated the selection for the Chief Superintendentship of Trade and Governorship of Hongkong of an official who had been connected with the East India Company; but there was little room to dispute the excellence of the choice. Mr. Davis* possessed the long experience of the Chinese which was the first essential towards dealing with them, and his literary pursuits had brought home to him the more attractive and respectable side of the Chinese character. In him also the Chinese were to deal with one who was far indeed from

* The following is a brief sketch of his career: "He arrived in China at the early age of 18. In 1816 he accompanied Lord Amherst to Pekin. In 1832 he became President of the East India Company's factory in China. In 1834, October 11th, on the demise of Lord Napier, he was placed at the head of H.B.M. Commission as his lordship's successor. On the 21st of January, in the following year, having delivered over to Sir G. B. Robinson the seals of office, he embarked for England, whence he now, in 1844, returned. Sir John Davis will be best remembered by the numerous works of value and interest which he wrote on Chinese matters. He died at a great age a few years ago.

being void of sympathy with them. There came with him also, as Colonial Secretary, Mr. Frederick Bruce, long afterwards to be the first to fill the high post of resident minister at Pekin. With the departure of Sir Henry Pottinger, and the installation of Mr. Davis, we shall be able to turn a little attention to those internal affairs of the Chinese Empire which not less than the development of its external relations affected its welfare.

Judged by the favourite standard of a Chinese ruler, the Emperor Taoukwang came up to the requirements of his exalted office in his sense of how much the people required of him, and also in his manner of giving expression to their wishes. But Taoukwang wanted the energy or the method of supervising the execution of his own orders, or of inspiring his officials with the conviction that they must be carried out without subterfuge. A period of confusion and misfortune always brings the elements of disunion to the surface, and in China, where things are kept quiet among the masses only for want of an opposite example, it has always happened that the smallest symptoms of rebellion are followed by frequent ebullitions of national discontent, which would produce formidable consequences were they better directed or more unanimous in their expression. On this occasion it was thought that China had passed through the crisis without any very untoward mishap, and many were the congratulations on the ground that with a tranquil China paying heed to the Emperor's mandates a profitable trade might be carried on. But although the internal dangers which had presented themselves with such force to the Imperial Cabinet before the signing of the Nankin Treaty, did not reveal themselves as promptly as had at one time appeared probable, the public discontent was deep-rooted and not to be permanently repressed.

To a defeated Government people pay only a reluctant obedience. If that government be an alien one there is a strong temptation to revolt. The authority of Taoukwang was exposed to the double peril. The corruption of the official class, combined with the need for an increased revenue, not merely to provide for the amount of the indemnity, but also to meet the increased charges on the administration in the way of providing for the greater naval and military expenditure, aggravated the popular discontent, and left no room to hope that it could be allayed save by the removal of grievances which pressed most heavily on the industrious and the toilers. Taoukwang himself was not unaware of the evils existing in the state, nor was he disposed to press with undue harshness on subjects whom he was bound to regard in the light of children. But his officials had to reconcile the two conflicting recommendations in their instructions. They were to supply an increased revenue at the same time that they prolonged the period of paying the land-tax. Under such circumstances it is easy enough to understand the mode they adopted. They sent the stipulated amounts of revenue to the capital, and they praised the sovereign's desire for the welfare of his people; but of practical alleviation they accomplished none.

The Yellow River, despite the ex-Commissioner Lin's special personal attention, continued a source of misfortune to the people dwelling on its banks, and frequent inundations not merely thinned the population, but cut off the means of sustenance of the survivors. Of all forms of misrule and misfortune which affected the welfare of the people none pressed more heavily upon them than the increase in the robber-bands which haunted the country in many directions. The official "Gazette" contains frequent references to outrages by these desperadoes, and sometimes states the rewards conferred on those who distinguished themselves in their pursuit or capture. To such a pass had their depredations gone that it was asserted that a band of these marauders had even made their homes within the limits of the Imperial city itself; but it is not certain whether this language is to be accepted literally or as a figurative expression of the fact that those who supported these iniquities were harboured within the Imperial palace.

The inability of the executive to ensure order and to enforce respect was fully exemplified in Canton as well as at the capital. In the months of May and June a riot was got up by the mob on the excuse that a vane erected on the top of the flag-staff over the American Consulate interfered with the Fung Shui, or spirits of earth and air; and although it was promptly removed in deference to the clamour of the superstitious, the disturbance continued, and assumed the proportions of absolute riot. Personal encounters took place between Europeans and Chinese, and in one of these a native was killed. The circumstances were such as justified in every way the act of the European; but the Chinese authorities, led by a weak and vacillating governor, demanded the surrender of the man who fired the shot as a self-convicted murderer. That the Chinese authorities should make such a demand after they had formally accepted and recognized the jurisdiction of consular courts, must be set down as very strong proof that they had not mastered the lessons of the late war in the way that had been hoped and believed. The fortunate coincidence of the arrival of Keying* to treat with the representative of the United States did more than anything else to allay the agitation; but the malice of the Canton mob required very little inducement to break forth, and all Keying's vigilance was needed in his capacity of Viceroy of the Two Kwang to effect his object of "amicably regulating the commerce with foreign countries."

One of Keying's first engagements was to arrange the treaty with the special envoy sent by Louis Philippe and M. Guizot to extend French commerce and influence in the Far East; and the arrival of M. de Lagrenée and his brilliant suite at Macao followed almost immediately the departure of Mr. Caleb Cushing. A whole month was given up to the discussion in that town of an equitable arrangement; and Keying being now thoroughly sincere in his wish to arrange matters with the foreigners, and the French having no further concessions to demand beyond those obtained by the English for all, it naturally followed

* Keying was appointed at this time both Governor-General of the Two Kwang, and also a High Commissioner for Foreign Affairs—in itself a fact of the greatest importance, as showing that those affairs had already become so important as to constitute the work of a special department.

that the negotiations proceeded briskly and without a hitch. The treaty between France and China was signed on the 23rd of October, 1844, and Keying is reported to have told M. de Lagrenée that France was a great nation which did not think of questions of trade. The capacity of being ironical is not denied even to the Chinese.

The Chinese Government showed a spirit of concession and moderation in more than one point; but perhaps none was more striking or noteworthy in itself than the tolerant views which suddenly began to prevail in Taoukwang's cabinet on the subject of the Christian religion. There is no doubt that the credit of this change of opinion was largely due to the representations of M. de Lagrenée, who obtained the marked concession of an Imperial edict ordaining the toleration of the Christian religion as being one that inculcated principles of virtue. The practical value of this concession was much enhanced by the right conceded at a later period to religious bodies of holding land.

Meanwhile, the day for the evacuation of Chusan and Kulangsu was approaching. An instalment of the indemnity was paid in July, 1845, leaving only one more to be received; and when that fell due, some appeared to think that what was held a short delay invalidated the terms of the treaty, and afforded an opening for the retention of Chusan. But it was soon discovered that the Chinese had not left themselves open to any adverse criticism on the score of not being up to time. By the terms of the treaty the last instalment was to be paid in the twelfth month of the Chinese year, which corresponds to the month of January, not December, and it was paid in the most punctual manner. The English Government personally expressed its admiration at the honourable way in which the Chinese had complied with all the stipulations of the treaty. But the local officials at Canton seemed unable to enforce the clause giving foreigners right of entry into that city, and for several months after the payment in full of the indemnity English troops remained in occupation of both Chusan and Kulangsu.

There was another reason for this hesitation in abandoning the former place, which many thought preferable to

Hongkong as the permanent site of British power, and that was the current belief that the French would have hastened to appropriate the island for themselves on the withdrawal of the English troops. Probably this had no better foundation than the fact of the French navy being strongly represented at the time in Chinese waters, but that circumstance sufficed to give point to international jealousy. It was not until the spring of 1846, several months after the English troops should all have been withdrawn, that an arrangement was come to for the evacuation of Chusan and for the concession of the right for foreigners to enter Canton; but the execution of the latter right was to be postponed until "the population of Canton shall be more under the control of the local government." This was considered as almost a surrender on our part by those who did not believe that the Chinese could be too much humbled, and who would have allowed them the exercise of their independence only on sufferance; but a consideration of the following summary of events which had occurred at Canton before this arrangement will at once show that there was really no other course to be pursued save that of facilitating instead of hindering the assertion of Taoukwang's authority.

The Cantonese needed but little excuse to break out into disorder, and all Keying's tact and authority did not avail to make peace a matter of assurance. When affairs seemed likely to settle down, the whole progress of the relations was complicated and thrown back by the violent death of a native at the hands of an American, and the details of the occurrence went to show that the act was scarcely to be justified on the ground of adequate aggravation. The death of another Chinaman at the hands of a foreigner stirred up the popular passion to a dangerous pitch, and even the moderate Keying was obliged to bend before the wave of national indignation, and to make a forcible remonstrance and an explicit demand for reparation on the American representative. What Keying demanded was that "the law be executed on the proper person by a forfeiture of his life." But after a long and heated correspondence which continued to the end of the year, the matter was hushed up on payment of compensation to the wife of the slain Chinaman. The American President laid down in the most emphatic manner the ex-territorial rights of the citizens of the United States, and it was pronounced that "all Americans in China are to be deemed subject only to the jurisdiction of their own Government both in criminal matters and in questions of civil right."

It was long before the popular agitation caused by this and other incidents of a similar kind settled down, and the Chinese authorities found themselves compelled to adopt a tone towards their own people that was not quite compatible with their dignity; for, not possessing the material force to support their declarations, they were unable to employ the language of menace and authority that would alone have overawed the mob of Canton. Designing persons, therefore, seized the occasion afforded by the outbreak of the populace to express their hatred of the foreigners, and of the English in particular. The walls were covered with placards declaring that "the injuries, the deceits, the cruel deeds, the evil and wicked acts of the English resident barbarians are like the hairs of the head, innumerable." There was much more to the same effect, showing that there was a dangerous spirit abroad, and that the people had lost respect for their authorities at the same time that their foreign antipathies were revealed with increased bitterness. The torch was applied to this magazine of popular ferment by an act of tyranny on the part of the city prefect, but it fortunately exhausted its force upon an officer of Taoukwang instead of upon the Europeans. The mob attacked the prefecture and set fire to it. The prefect escaped with difficulty; but after the rioters had expended their force, the turmoil gradually settled down on the formal repudiation of the prefect's acts by the Governor-General. It was not until February of the following year that Keying felt able to adopt firmer language, and to command the Cantonese to abstain from posting placards, and from interfering with those of the foreigners who, by the Emperor's express wish and permission, entered their city. If impartial allowance is made for these circumstances, it will not be denied that the

CHUSAN EVACUATED.

Chinese authorities had good reasons for deprecating a precipitate decision in reference to the right of entry into Canton.

There remained, therefore, no longer any objection to the surrender of Chusan, and, indeed, no further excuse for prolonging an occupation which had benefited the people of the island, and which had also reflected great credit on the English troops and commander entrusted with its charge. In July, 1846, Sir John Davis arrived at Tinghai for the express purpose of handing over the island to the Imperial Commissioners appointed to receive it. The ceremony was marked by an exchange of friendly compliments. The kindness and liberality towards the people of the English commander were frankly admitted, and it was also stated that "the European soldiers never ill-treated or annoyed the inhabitants." These statements deserve to be remembered, if only because they form an agreeable and honourable exception to the usual tale of foreign occupation. A public notification from Sir John Davis, stating that Chusan was no longer to be considered as one of the ports or places of trade, brought the English occupation of that island to a final termination. The withdrawal of the small garrison on the island of Kulangsu near Amoy completed the military evacuation, leaving Hongkong alone permanently in the possession of the English Crown.

Even before the official relations had reached this final phase the foreign trade had shown signs of great increase, and it was already evident that a busy future was in store for Shanghai. There had been changes in the various consulates owing to deaths and retirements. Mr. Rutherford Alcock, whose long connection with China and Japan then commenced, reached China during this period. For a short time he was consul at Amoy, and then he was transferred to Foochow; and in both offices Mr. Harry Parkes accompanied him as interpreter. Of Mr., afterwards Sir Rutherford, Alcock there will be so much to be heard and said in the development of the Chinese question, that it is only a matter of interest to mark here the exact date at which he arrived in China. Before the end of the year 1846 he was transferred to the Consulate at Shanghai. It will therefore be seen that the honour and dignity of the British Government were appropriately sustained in the persons of the new consular service, as well as by the Chief Superintendent of Trade at Hongkong.

Before the evacuation of Chusan * was completed the internal confusion of China had become worse. We have described what it was like at Canton, where the presence of foreigners may have complicated the question at the same time that the European war-ships prevented its becoming as acute as in other places at which the Emperor was alone dependent on his own authority. Yet already had Taoukwang declared that "his servants did not know what truth was," and the habit of concealing what was happening in the Empire until the matter had become too grave to admit of further concealment was one that could only be fatal in the end. The extent to which the secret societies were ramified throughout the Chinese nation may be inferred from the fact that a proclamation against the Triads enacting severe penalties for belonging to that association was made at Hongkong itself. Members of the same society broke out in open revolt at Chowchow, in the northern part of the province of Kwantung, and a large body of troops had to be sent against them from Canton. Nearly one thousand of the insurgents either perished in the fight that ensued, or were executed after it. The survivors escaped into the eastern districts of the province, and, joining other members of the same society, proved a constant source of alarm and anxiety. The remission of all arrears of taxes previous to the year 1840, granted by the Emperor in February, 1846, was a boon scarcely appreciated by the people at large, and did little or nothing to alleviate distress or to allay popular sedition.

If the Triads were troublesome in Kwantung, a new sect or association, called the "Green Water-lily," was not less an element of disturbance in the central provinces. The

---

* In connection with this act it ought to be added that Sir John Davis had claimed and retained for England the exclusive right to re-occupy it and to defend it against other foreigners.

INTERNAL AGITATION. 173

scene of their activity was the vast provinces of Hoonan and Hupeh, covering the greater portion of middle China. The coast provinces, too, were not without their troubles. Pirates or water-thieves were numerous along the coasts of Formosa, Fuhkien, and Chekiang. Several cases of piracy occurred on the Canton river, and more than one European lost his life. In Yunnan the Mahomedans were reported to be stirring and to be leaguing with the wild men of the border. But here the measures of the Viceroy were prompt and vigorous; and the authority of the Emperor was fully asserted. The island of Amoy, small as it was, was not so small as to be able to avoid the conflict of opinion prevalent throughout the state. Village was arrayed in arms against village; and an official notice was given by the English Consul that foreigners could not visit any of them except at serious personal peril. In the district of Tunkwan, in Central China, more than 20,000 robbers were affirmed to have banded themselves together and set the constituted authorities at defiance. To the least inquisitive observer this internal agitation presented all the symptoms of decay.

If there be trouble and weakness at the core, it is an old saw that the extremities must suffer. The report of the Chinese defeat in a foreign war took several years to penetrate to the heart of Asia; but its reverberation at last echoed on the Pamir, and roused the hopes of the Khoja adventurers of Khokand and Altyshahr. The ill-fortune of Jehangir, who had at an earlier period of his reign openly challenged the authority of Taoukwang, had deterred for a time the many enemies who hated the Chinese not less for the order which they brought in their train than for the sake of race and religious antagonism. When Jehangir was captured and sent to Pekin—and his brother Yusuf fared little better than he did, for if his life was saved by a precipitate flight his hopes were blighted—the Chinese authorities, who had ruled the cities of Eastern Turkestan with justice and prudence for three parts of a century, changed their method of government in more than one particular by importing into it that sternness and cruelty which some would have us believe are most in accordance with their character.

We need not dwell on those summary executions, on that confiscation of property, on the banishment of suspected persons, which must follow the suppression of revolt, whether the offended authority be a despot or the most immaculate of Republics. Those repellent features could not be absent from the Kashgar risings of 1829–31, with all the darker hues of Asiatic thoroughness and indifference to reproach.

One act detaches itself from the rest, and preserves its place in history, if only because it carried with it the penalty that generally finds out human transgression. The large Mahomedan population of Kashgaria presented the ready means of providing needy adventurers with the materials of an army. The name of the Prophet, the incitement to a jehad, were sufficient to draw the toiling people of the plains from their occupations to attempt the imprudent, or dare the impossible. The Khoja adventurers escaped for the most part over the mountains to vaunt their deeds of valour in the bazaars of Ferghana; the duped and unfortunate people of Kashgaria remained to lament their folly and expiate their crime. The Chinese were never wholly cruel. The quality of their intellect prevented their feeling any satisfaction in the wholesale slaughter of a people whose worst fault was that they had been too easily deceived. Other Asiatic conquerors would have offered up a holocaust of the Mussulman population. The Chinese contented themselves with removing 12,000 families from Kashgar and Yarkand to the Ili. The balance between the Chinese and the native populations south of the Tian Shan was thus more equally apportioned; but the children of these immigrants were the Tarantchi* rebels who placed the seal on Chinese discomfiture in 1864.

The Chinese succeeded in vanquishing all their enemies in the field; and this measure was in itself one that well comported with the idea of strength. But they were oppressed with a sense of embarrassment from the many new matters that imperatively demanded the attention and seriously taxed the strength of the central Government; and the Executive in Central Asia felt that it would most please the Emperor by appealing to him as seldom as possible for assistance.

* The Tarantchi means, as already stated, the toilers.

Therefore it was that while, on the one hand, they took measures to weaken the Mahomedan population, they agreed, on the other, to make concessions in matters of trade to the neighbouring Khan of Khokand, in return for which he gave the easy promise to discourage and to keep inactive the Khoja chiefs who lived within his borders.

Concessions to the unscrupulous ruler of Khokand could only purchase a brief and uncertain truce. Concessions are always the sign of weakness, and of a self-distrusting mind. When made by a foreign conqueror in a state held to subjection by the sword alone, they can have but one significance; they herald the victor's downfall. In Kashgar the merit of an individual, the rare tenacity of the Chinese, served to postpone the inevitable day of evil; and the great overshadowing reputation of the Empire availed for many years to repel the fatal attack. It was strange that the main credit of this respite should have been due to a Mahomedan and a son of the soil; but so it was, although it should be remembered that when the subjected are held worthy of the highest seat in the administration the basis of an alien rule is destroyed. Zuhuruddin gave peace to the Kashgarians for many years, and a new sense of security to the Chinese by the construction of fresh forts at the principal cities; yet there is no doubt that Zuhuruddin's example was the most powerful inducement to his co-religionists and fellow-countrymen to believe that they could displace the Chinese authority.

It was not until the year 1846, when the result of the foreign war was well known, and when the embarrassments of the Pekin Government were patent to all beholders, that any fresh attempt was made to molest the Chinese. In the previous year a change had taken place in the chiefship of Khokand. Mahomed Ali, a Khan of some character, was murdered by his neighbour, the ruler of Bokhara, in 1842, and after an interval of a few years his authority passed to his relative, Khudayar; but this prince proved unable to retain the possessions which his predecessor had drawn together. Mahomed Ali had given plenty of employment to the turbulent spirits of his state, as well as to those numerous adventurers who made their home in his dominions. It was evident to all that Khudayar, with less capacity, had a greater desire for the tranquillity that, in unsettled countries, is only to be won by constant vigilance and the proof of effective valour. The loss of employment raised an effervescence among these adventurers, and the opportunity of distinction seemed most encouraging to them in the direction of Kashgar. Therefore they went to the sons of Jehangir, and appealing to them, both by the necessity of avenging their father's death and by the prospect of gaining much fame and advantage through the expulsion of the Chinese from Central Asia, laid their plans of action before them. These Khoja princes were young, and seven in number. They were impelled to make the attempt by the temper of their age, as well as by the knowledge that if many of them refused there would surely be one to accept the adventure, the more readily, perhaps, in the hope of enjoying the fruits of victory alone.

The seven Khoja princes, who gave their joint name to the invasion, issued their proclamation in the winter months of 1845–46, rallied their adherents to their side, made allies of the Kirghiz tribes, and summoned recruits from far and near. They hung on the frontier during the winter months, and Zuhuruddin seems to have thought that they and their forces would melt away with the snows. Truly they and their nondescript following were not a very formidable body, and seemed ill able to conquer kingdoms and dictate the fate of nations. But, on the other hand, the Chinese garrison was very weak, and was distributed over a wide surface; the people of Kashgar might be easily won over, and Zuhuruddin had been so inactive as to raise a suspicion, probably unfounded, of his treachery. The chances, therefore, were not as unequal as they seemed, and only the miserable incapacity and tyrannical injustice of the Khojas prevented their achieving a greater success than they did.

The Khojas at last quitted the hills, and marched upon Kashgar, to which they laid siege. The fort successfully defied their efforts, and so might the town have done, but that one of its gates was opened by a traitor thirteen days after the Khojas appeared before the walls. They then attempted to raise the country, but their misbehaviour at

THE SEVEN KHOJAS.

Kashgar disgusted their sympathizers, and, after a two months' occupation, they were defeated in a fight at Kok Robat by the garrison of Yarkand, and driven out of the country. The invasion of the Seven Khojas, which at one time threatened to assume serious proportions, thus terminated in what was practically a collapse. The Chinese had not to bring up any fresh forces, their attenuated garrison sufficing to hold the citadels of the various towns, and in the end to inflict a decisive defeat on the Mahomedan army. The sympathy of the people was alienated by the excesses of the Kirghiz and Khokandians, who found a bad example in the Khoja princes; and they were, fortunately, not induced to betray any wish for their success before it had become evident that the Chinese were certain to crush the invading foe without any serious difficulty. This campaign was only fatal to Zuhuruddin. His conduct was open to the charge of over-confidence, and he was removed from his high office. The remembrance of what he had previously done ensured him his life.

The famous Commissioner Lin was indirectly connected with the suppression of this movement. After his disgrace at Canton in the winter of 1840, he was summoned before the Board of Punishment, and sentenced to banishment in Ili. The sentence was not carried out, for before he had completed the arrangements for his departure the Yellow river broke its banks, and he was called upon to proceed to the scene of disaster. The choice naturally fell upon him, as the greater portion of his early official career had been passed as commissioner of rivers in different quarters of the Empire. At the end of 1845 he was rewarded for such services as he had been able to render in this post with the viceroyalty of the two north-west provinces, Shensi and Kansuh, and of these Ili was, in a certain sense, the outlying dependency. But although we know this fact in connection with his career, the details of his government are wanting, and we only obtain some idea of the disturbance in Central Asia from the fact that in the spring of 1846 he requested that rewards might be bestowed upon the worthy soldiers of Kansuh.

The progress of intercourse with the peoples of Europe did not bring that better understanding with it which was generally expected, and the last four years of Taoukwang's reign witnessed an unceasing struggle on the part of the Chief Superintendent and the Consuls to obtain the fulfilment of all the Treaty stipulations, and, on the other hand, of the Chinese officials to retard their realisation and to limit their application. Great allowance should be made, and, generally speaking, was made, for the embarrassment of the Central executive of China in having suddenly to violate and fly in the face of every principle of government which it had sought to impress on its subjects. The greatest peril in the whole situation was that the authority of the Emperor might be set on one side and fall into contempt. Therefore, while the English representatives had to afford protection to the Queen's subjects, and to secure the execution of the terms of the Treaty, they had also to make every allowance for the weakness of the mandarins, and to remember that their acts were not to entail, above all things, the collapse of the Chinese administration in the treaty ports. It is satisfactory to be able to feel, on looking back to this period, that the action of the English consuls came up to this standard, and that no charge can be made against the agents of the British Crown of having abused their superiority during a most critical period.

The production of opium in India during these years was greatly increasing, not because the East India Company was oblivious of moral considerations, and thought only of increasing its revenue, but simply in obedience to the irresistible law of supply and demand. The Chinese would have opium, just as the English during the Napoleonic wars would have French brandy, and it was supplied. The dangers of the contraband trade in this article could not obscure its profitable nature, and the coasts of China were visited each year by a steadily increasing number of opium vessels. To be correct, the perils of the adventure were not excessive. The Chinese navy had been reduced to the lowest point, and among no class were the merits of opium better appreciated than by the officials. Such danger as there was arose chiefly from the attacks of pirates, who wished to obtain the source of pleasure

OPIUM SMOKING.

without paying for it, or who captured the rich plunder for sale. These piratical gangs were well armed, and composed of desperate men. Generally they were baffled in their attempts, but sometimes they succeeded in their purpose.*

But for the time being there were many more urgent matters than the opium trade; and of these none was so pressing as the question of the right of foreigners to proceed beyond the limits of their factories and compounds. The Chinese wished for many reasons, perhaps even for the safety of the foreigners, to confine them to their settlements; and it might be plausibly contended that the Treaty bore no other construction. Of course this confinement was intolerable, and with the examples before them of M. Huc and his companion, M. Gabet, who had just traversed the whole extent of the

---

* A reaction was beginning to set in against the sweeping denunciations of the missionaries as to the evils of opium-smoking—charges which had been rendered more plausible to the public mind by the brilliant Confessions of De Quincey as to the effect of opium-eating, between which there is an immense difference. Christison had made scientific investigations, which minimized the evil consequences, but the first authoritative statement in contradiction to these views was made by Sir Henry Pottinger on his return to England. The following is his expression of opinion: "I take this opportunity to advert to one important topic on which I have hitherto considered it right to preserve a rigid silence—I allude to the trade in opium; and I now unhesitatingly declare, in this public manner, that after the most unbiassed and careful observations, I have become convinced, during my stay in China, that the alleged demoralizing and debasing evils of opium have been, and are, vastly exaggerated. Like all other indulgences, excesses in its use are bad and reprehensible; but I have neither myself seen such vicious consequences as are frequently ascribed to it, nor have I been able to obtain authentic proofs or information of their existence. The great, and perhaps I may say sole, objection to the trade, looking at it morally and abstractedly, that I have discovered or heard of, is that it is at present contraband, and prohibited by the laws of China, and therefore to be regretted and disavowed; but I have striven—and I hope with some prospect of eventual success—to bring about its legalization; and were that point once effected, I am of opinion that its most objectionable feature would be altogether removed. Even as it now exists, it appears to me to be unattended with a hundredth part of the debasement and misery which may be seen in our native country from the lamentable abuse of ardent spirits; and those who so sweepingly condemn the opium trade on that principle need not, I think, leave the shores of England to find a far greater and besetting evil."

country from Tibet to Canton, and of Mr. Robert Fortune, who had explored the botanical mysteries of much of southeast China, it was not to be supposed that English merchants on the Pearl river would be prevented from taking boating or shooting excursions in the neighbourhood of their place of residence. These excursions were inevitable and only in the natural course of things, but they were opposed by the Chinese authorities, and it necessarily followed that a period of hostility and doubt had to be passed through before they could become the rule. A cause of collision was not long presenting itself.

In March, 1847, a small party of Englishmen proceeded up the river in a boat to the large manufacturing town of Fatshan. On reaching the place symptoms of hostility were promptly manifested, and the Europeans, thinking that they would be safest with the authorities, hastened to the yamen or residence of the prefect, in the heart of the town. The magistrate, unfortunately, was not at home, and the strange appearance of the foreigners, who had never been seen before, and some of whom carried guns, was well calculated to excite the popular mind to a dangerous pitch. The return of the magistrate and his prompt assistance fortunately averted the most serious consequences; and the party of foreigners were escorted in safety back to their boat. Here, however, a new danger presented itself. The people lined the banks, and pelted them with stones as they hurried past in their boat as rapidly as the tide and hard rowing would carry them. That they succeeded in escaping with their lives was little short of marvellous, and was largely due to the chief mandarin, who courageously * escorted them from the

* One of the party wrote : "The chief officer who was with us conducted himself with great dignity and a most noble magnanimity, standing outside in the midst of the flying missiles without fear or trepidation. His subordinate also was not deficient in generosity and energy of character, behaving in a very undaunted manner. Receiving a gash upon his head from a stone, he made light of it, and once he was nearly up to his waist in water helping the boat forward." A French account of this affair stated that the mandarin said to the English, "Follow me closely; my body shall serve you as a shield."—"Chinese Repository," vol. xvi. pp. 142-47, and p. 512.

beginning of the riot until they had reached a place of safety. This occurrence was destined to have important consequences.

Now there can be no question that this expedition to Fatshan was a most reprehensible and inexcusable proceeding. All the attendant circumstances were such as aggravated the original offence; and those who participated in the escapade were deserving of the most severe condemnation on the part of the English representatives. The only person to come out of the affair with any credit was the mandarin, whose conduct proved that some of the Chinese Government's agents were anxious to treat foreigners with consideration and to afford them all possible protection. The hostility of the people of Fatshan was to be attributed to their want of knowledge of foreigners, and to the fact that none of the many precautions taken at the Treaty Ports had been enforced to secure the safety of English visitors. Fatshan was the Birmingham of Southern China. Was it to be supposed that the white faces which dared not venture into the main streets of Canton would be safe among a manufacturing population which had never gazed on them before? Had the matter been decided on its merits the Chinese Government would have been complimented on possessing one courageous and honourable official, and the participators in a foolish freak would have been severely admonished.

But the authorities at Hongkong did not reason on the matter. The Fatshan affair was treated as an outrage instead of as an accident, the cause of which was the stupidity of a few Englishmen and others tired of the confinement of their ships or the settlement. Sir John Davis resolved to bring the Canton authorities to reason. He proclaimed that he would "exact and require from the Chinese Government that British subjects should be as free from molestation and insult in China as they could be in England," a demand which was not only in distinct violation of the Treaty of Nankin, but which was in itself impossible. Neither Sir John Davis nor anybody else had the right to substitute for the treaty ports the whole of China; and the line of argument taken by the Chinese throughout the negotiations had been that they could not guarantee the safety of foreigners outside a few special and fixed places. In plain language, the English had no business at Fatshan, and might think themselves lucky in escaping with their lives. Yet the principal English official resolved to take the matter up and to resort to force. Never was a more unjust or unreasonable excuse seized for forcing events.

On the 1st of April all available troops at Hongkong were warned for immediate service. On the following morning they left in three steamers and one ship-of-war. They landed at the Bogue forts, seized the batteries without opposition, and spiked the guns. The Chinese troops, whether surprised or acting under orders from Keying, made no attempt at resistance. Not a shot was fired ; not a man injured on the part of the assailants. The forts near Canton, the very batteries on the islands opposite the great city, were served in the same way ; although at the Whampoa forts the Chinese gunners, having partially recovered from their surprise, discharged their guns. Here the good fortune of the assailants stood them in excellent stead, for the fire of the Chinese batteries was well directed, and it was considered to be little short of miraculous how the boats conveying the landing parties to the shore escaped complete destruction. On the 3rd of April Canton was again at the mercy of the guns of an English squadron. The Superintendent issued a proclamation in which he said that he felt "that the moderation and justice of all his former dealings with the Government of China lend a perfect sanction to measures which he has been reluctantly compelled to adopt after a long course of misinterpreted forbearance." Moderation and justice seemed strange terms in the mouth of a man who, without warning, like a thief in the night, seized the defences of a friendly Government, and sought to acquire at the cannon's mouth concessions which had not been demanded after a protracted war by the accredited representative of the English sovereign. Sir John Davis was, no doubt, actuated by the best intentions. He saw the advantage of free and unrestricted intercourse, and he knew that the time must come when it would be a fact. He thought only to accomplish the object

OPENING CANTON GATES.

himself at one stroke, and to anticipate events by a whole generation.*

The appearance of the English forces, far from cowing them, roused the populace of Canton to a height of animosity never exhibited before. Keying was denounced as the friend of the English and as being worthy of death; and placards were placed in the most prominent spots calling on the people to attack the barbarians. But the authorities distrusted their strength, and, although the English force was small, the counsels of Keying and his more pacific colleagues prevailed. It was resolved that the demands † of the English should be granted. A special proclamation was issued by the local magistrates enjoining the people not to interfere with or rudely gaze at those of the foreigners who happened to roam about the open country. The cause of doubt continued to be whether the people would obey the undoubtedly sincere orders of Keying, and those who had little or nothing to lose were, of course, loudest in their advocacy of violent measures, and of driving the handful of foreigners into the sea. The officials presented a united front to the demands of the fanatical and lawless. Proclamations from Keying the Viceroy, Chow Changling the General, and Yeh the Financial Commissioner, all impressed upon the people the necessity of remaining in their houses and of attending to their personal duties.

If some advantage was gained by these summary proceedings, it is none the less impossible to discover their justification. As Keying truly said, "if a mutual tranquillity is to subsist between the Chinese and foreigners, the common

---

* Commissioner Yeh, at this time Territorial Commissioner of the Provinces, makes his first appearance at this date as the author of an official proclamation to calm the public mind.

† These demands may be summarized as follows: The city of Canton to be opened at two years' date from the 6th of April, 1847. Englishmen to be at liberty "to roam for exercise or amusement" in the neighbourhood of the city, the one condition being that they should return the same day. The other stipulations, for the erection of a church, the granting of a site at Honan for buildings, the clearing of the river in front of the factories from boats, were not only reasonable, but calculated to promote good feeling and to remove causes of collision.

feelings of mankind, as well as the just principles of Heaven, must be considered and conformed with." It would be hard to show that Sir John Davis was swayed by any similar considerations. The success of the operations concealed their illegality and injustice; but we do not impugn his proceedings because they were accompanied by successful violence. Having decided to use his small force for the purpose of a military demonstration in front of Canton, he was bound to supply the place of numbers by unusual celerity and daring. Indeed, the military officer, Major-General D'Aguilar, made this the condition of his moving at all. And it is, of course, perfectly obvious that the necessity of ensuring a safe retreat left no choice except to occupy the river-forts and to disable their guns. The execution of the plan was creditable to English pluck and enterprise; but the plan itself was not merely without valid excuse, it was also singularly imprudent and deserved to fail. It was disapproved of at the time, and, as soon as the facts became known, was strongly condemned by the Home Government. Lord Grey wrote in November, 1847, in reference to an application made by the Major-General for a reinforcement, peremptorily forbidding him to undertake any further offensive measures against the Chinese,* and the general opinion was and remains that the adventure of April, 1847, was both unnecessary and imprudent. There is generally some defence, and very often a valid one, for the past proceedings of English officials and negotiators in China against the charge of being high-handed and unjust; but Sir John Davis's Canton expedition is the exception to the rule.

The distinction between necessary force and unnecessary

* Lord Grey went on to say that "Her Majesty's Government are satisfied that, although the late operations in the Canton river were attended with immediate success, the risk of a second attempt of the same kind would far overbalance any advantages to be derived from such a step. If the conduct of the Chinese authorities should unfortunately render another appeal to arms inevitable, it will be necessary that it should be made after due preparation, and with the employment of such an amount of force as may afford just grounds for expecting that the objects which may be proposed by such a measure will be effectually accomplished without unnecessary loss."—Correspondence (presented to Parliament in 1857).

violence, which Sir John Davis showed himself unable to appreciate in 1847, was well realized by Mr. Rutherford Alcock at Shanghai, where precisely the same questions presented themselves and similar difficulties arose to those that created anxiety at Canton. There the impatience of an European community to enjoy at once all the advantages that might accrue in the course of time from the change in the historic policy of China, had threatened to entail that rupture which the Consuls had been appointed specially to prevent; and a claim was laid to the privilege of travelling in the interior as a matter of course, while it was in reality a concession dependent on a variety of circumstances that could not be said to have yet come into action. The impulse of curiosity and the promptings of religious zeal combined to carry the Europeans from the security of Shanghai into the dangers of the neighbouring country. Those dangers would not have been insignificant at any time. They were rendered the more grave at this period by the fact that a large number of the boatmen, employed on the Grand Canal in conveying the grain tribute to the capital, had been thrown out of work in consequence of the Emperor's orders to send a large portion of the rice round by sea. These men to the number of 15,000 were thrown upon their own resources in the province of Chekiang. They were nearly all natives of Shantung, and in their desperation they showed no scruple in resorting to acts of violence and oppression. They were perfectly beyond the control of the local mandarins, and were virtually masters of their portion of the province.

The stipulation effected at Canton in 1847, that the English settlers might travel so far from a treaty port as they could return in the course of twenty-four hours, was given a general application. It was considered to be as valid at Shanghai as at Canton. Therefore there was no obvious reason to object to a party of missionaries proceeding in the month of March, 1848, to Tsingpu, a town some thirty miles west of Shanghai, as it was possible to perform the double journey within the specified time. Although the facts in connection with the Shantung navigators were generally known, the people at Shanghai were not aware that they had broken loose from all restraint. When, therefore, these missionaries * reached Tsingpu and began to distribute their tracts, they were soon molested by a party of these boatmen. At first their interference partook more of the character of boisterous fun than malicious attack; but the accidents which never fail to occur on such occasions aggravated the situation, and made matters extremely grave. In a very little time the attack became one in earnest. The missionaries attempted to escape by flight; they were pursued and captured. They were roughly treated, seriously injured, and plundered of all their possessions. The nature of their wounds made their escape appear a matter of marvel. They were led back to the town, where the officials and respectable people did everything in their power to show that they did not sympathize with the acts of these ruffians. The victims themselves were most generous in exonerating the townspeople from all complicity in the outrage.

The circumstances of the Tsingpu outrage and the Fatshan incident were radically different. Not only were the missionaries unarmed, but they were acting in accordance with a right which had been formally conceded and enforced on more than one previous occasion. There was no possible reason or necessity to overlook what was an inexcusable outrage. Yet Mr. Alcock did not proceed to an act of overt war by despatching a force to Tsingpu or by the seizure of Woosung. He resorted to the most efficacious proceeding within what were his legal rights. He sent one of his two ships-of-war, with the Vice-Consul on board and Mr. Harry Parkes as interpreter, to Nankin, to deal with the Viceroy of the Two Kiang face to face, while he prohibited the sailing of the rice-boats. The plan was an admirable one to secure prompt redress, at the same time that it avoided creating any additional bad feeling or compromising the position of the English Government. An interview was held with Li, the Governor-General, on the 31st of March, and the greatest anxiety was shown to grant redress and to capture the criminals for condign punishment. The first step in the measure of reparation was the removal of Hienling, the

* The missionaries were Dr. Lockhart, Dr. Medhurst, and Mr. Muirhead.

intendant of Soochow, and another official was assigned to his place, charged with the special duty of detecting the guilty in the Tsingpu outrage, and of arranging matters with the foreigners generally on a satisfactory basis. Ten of the ringleaders were recognized and punished with flogging, placing in the cangue, and banishment. The course adopted by Mr. Alcock, in what might have proved an embarrassing situation, was thus completely vindicated by the result, and the incident closed with deserved encomiums on Mr. Harry Parkes for the skilful manner in which he had conducted the interviews with the Viceroy Li at Nankin.

The connivance of the Chinese authorities in the Tsingpu outrage was never matter of suspicion. Their subsequent acts clearly showed that they had not the least sympathy with the lawless proceedings of the canal boatmen, and that they were prepared to acquiesce in the practice of daily excursions on the part of the English residents. It remained, therefore, for the English representative to show on his part an intention to uphold the Treaty regulations, and to see that the Queen's subjects abided by them. Nor was this an obligation that he had only to meet as a matter of form. The English merchants were never satisfied. The addition of four new ports, the removal of an infinity of trade-exactions, and the relief from official tyranny—all accomplished by a single war over a proud and powerful State whose weakness arose from military unpreparedness—were not enough. They next claimed the concession of the right to travel a day's journey into the country, and to this privilege rapidity of movement gave a significance that was never contemplated. The merchants and missionaries soon showed that they were resolved to treat even this qualification in a very elastic manner. One day meant, in their eyes, two; and in the execution of their plans it very often meant much more. Against this violation of faith Mr. Alcock firmly set his face; and in a statesman-like notification he showed that the proceeding was both indefensible and calculated in the long run to defeat its own object.*

* "Such proceedings on the part of British subjects, were they not otherwise as aimless as they are unlawful, can only tend to place Her

Before the occurrence of the Tsingpu outrage Sir John Davis had left Hongkong and returned to Europe. His successor, Mr. S. G. Bonham, was destined to enjoy a more tranquil tenure of office than those who preceded him. The extension of China's relations with Europe was shown by the arrival of an Embassy from Spain, under the charge of Don Sinibaldo de Mas, who recorded his experiences of China, under exceptional circumstances, in one of the most interesting works on the country. He was among the first critical

Majesty's Government in a false position with the Chinese authorities, and deprive the former of the protection claimed for them on the faith of Treaties. It is for the British to set the example of scrupulous respect for the Treaties, under which they claim advantages often repugnant to the Chinese. If Her Majesty's Government and their authorities in this country cannot secure this result, and keep within lawful limits and control one or two hundred individuals, the Chinese local authorities may well plead reasonable excuse when they fail in the same duty with millions under their jurisdiction. It cannot be concealed that acts such as those reported are an open reproach to Her Majesty's Government; and it is a subject of deep regret to the Consul that any just cause of complaint should be afforded to the Chinese authorities or people, more especially at the present moment, while the rigorous enforcement of British treaty-rights at this port is still fresh in their memory. Nothing could be better calculated to weaken their respect for British honour and nationality, or more effectually serve to diminish the security which is based upon good faith. Her Majesty's Consul must hold such bootless infractions the more indefensible, that the tendency of affairs at this port is gradually to enlarge the limits and remove restrictions by legitimate means—these have indeed been already relaxed by authority on several occasions, upon good and sufficient reason shown as exceptional cases. Whatever may be the advantages anticipated from a freer access into the interior, they are not to be won by acts proving to both Governments that British subjects are not to be restrained by any regard to the obligations of Treaties, or the authority of their own Sovereign; nor can any argument more unanswerable be adduced to prove the impolicy of the one Government granting, or the other claiming, larger privileges than facts showing the deliberate and habitual abuse of those already conceded. Her Majesty's Consul would appeal to the good sense and good feeling of the British community generally to prevent the recurrence of acts so mischievous in their tendency and objectionable in every sense. But it is his duty also publicly to notify to all British subjects that he will take the most effective means to exonerate Her Majesty's Government from all suspicion of tacitly sanctioning or conniving at similar violations of the provisions of the Treaty, and spare no exertion to ensure the conviction of any parties who may be found wilfully offending."

observers who failed to detect the alleged evils of opium-smoking, and to point out that even if they existed they were a matter for the police of China to deal with. Taken on the whole, the year 1848 * was the least eventful of those that followed the Treaty of Nankin. The year 1847 had seen the enforcement of the important concession of the right to make expeditions into the neighbourhood of the ports, and there was a lull until the date arrived for the formal opening of the gates of Canton.

The question of the opening of the gates of Canton was not to be settled in the easy and straightforward way that had been anticipated. The Chinese had agreed that the gates of the great city of the South were to be opened on the 6th of April, 1849, and doubts were felt, the nearer that date approached, whether the promise would be complied with, and whether, in the event of refusal, it would be wise to have recourse to compulsion. The prospect of fresh complications arising from this cause produced a disturbing effect on the minds of the community; trade was reported to be greatly depressed in consequence; and the well-to-do classes of Canton were discouraged in proportion as the lower orders saw fresh opportunity of riot and outbreak. The one satisfactory circumstance connected with the situation was that a collision was deprecated on both sides. The principal European residents gave counsels of moderation; the Chinese invoked the intervention of their gods in the interests of peace. †

At the same time there was never any room to doubt what the almost unanimous opinion among the Cantonese was on the subject. The opening of the city gates could only

---

* The year 1848 witnessed a remarkable increase in the importation of opium. It was also noteworthy as containing the first mention of the Chinese Minister of the present day, Li Hung Chang. Li was then Financial Commissioner at Soochow; and in that capacity he issued a proclamation against coiners and those who debased the current coin of the Government.

† See, for instance of this, vol. xviii. of "Chinese Repository." Others breathed nothing but hostility and war. One literary student exhorted the people of Canton to prepare kettles of boiling water to pour on the heads of the barbarians when they should enter the city.

be effected by the forcible assertion of the central authority in face of the expressed opposition of the populace; and in order to be effectual there would have to be the sustained effort which could alone bend the people to the Emperor's will. The commotion among the militant Chinese had been great; and it was only suspended in order to await the arrival of the Emperor's commands. Taoukwang's reply, if ambiguous, was favourable to the pronounced wishes of the more patriotic of the Cantonese. "That," he wrote, "to which the hearts of the people incline is that on which the decree of Heaven rests. Now the people of Kwantung are unanimous and determined that they will not have foreigners enter the city, and how can I post up everywhere my Imperial order and force an opposite course upon the people?" There was much benevolent expression towards the foreigners, and of a desire that the two nations should be at peace and in harmony with each other. But for the time it was clear that Taoukwang's declaration settled the question, and the settlement was in direct opposition to the arrangement concluded between Keying and Sir John Davis two years before. The English Government had realized that the growth of foreign rights must be slow, and that a good case would only be injured by precipitation. It refrained from opposing, or indeed from challenging, Taoukwang's decision, and the matter was allowed to drop for the time. But although waived for the moment, the right acquired by treaty and the Keying Convention was not surrendered.

The moderation which the people of Canton showed over what might have been considered a great national triumph, did much towards its being tacitly acquiesced in by both the official and commercial sections of the foreign community. Every one felt that the special circumstances at Canton justified the reluctance of the Chinese officials to open its gates, while the after knowledge acquired, that Taoukwang had never formally ratified Keying's promise in 1847, left a loop-hole for regarding the matter as involving no distinct breach of faith. To press the matter home was to provoke fresh disagreement, perhaps hostilities. It could only embitter diplomatic relations and hamper trade. Convenience as well as a sense of justice suggested that the question of the Canton gates was one that could be dropped with dignity and advantage. The Cantonese were able to give tokens of their grateful feeling to their gods at the same time that they erected tablets of honour to Viceroy Su, whose name was identified with what seemed to the popular mind the first successful stand made against the encroachments of the Western peoples.

These causes of possible disagreement being thus satisfactorily settled or removed, it seemed probable that the progress of friendly relations would continue unchecked, and that the defences of Chinese exclusiveness would one by one be removed or beaten down. Much of the energy which had been devoted to the single purpose of coercing the Canton Government was turned, after this incident, to the attainment of an object which was beneficial to all alike. Several causes had combined to make the career of piracy more attractive and profitable to the maritime population. A time of war induces all to think more flatteringly of pursuits in which the sword counts of most service. The fire of patriotism was kindled to a fiercer glow by the prospect of the rich prizes to be landed in the capture of opium vessels. The Bogue was never completely free from those capable and willing to commit a profitable outrage; and periodically they rallied under some more than usually successful leader. As they had done under Apotsai in 1810, and under many of his predecessors at earlier periods, so did they in the year 1849 under a leader whose name may be given as Shapuntsai. Unwonted success made him unusually daring, and from the Tonquin Gulf to the coast of Fuhkien his junks levied black-mail on the coast, and plundered every trading vessel, Chinese or European, that did not seem able to defend the rich cargo in its hold.

Had Shapuntsai and his chief lieutenant, Tsu Apoo, left European vessels alone, they might have continued to plunder with impunity the villages and junks of their fellow-countrymen, for the Canton officials had no force with which they could bring them to reason. But English vessels fell to their prey, and the murder of English officers called for summary redress and active measures of punishment. In September of the year 1849 one war-ship began the pursuit of these marauders as the preliminary of still more active proceedings. Her commander, Captain Hay, had in a short time the satisfaction of bringing fourteen junks of the pirate fleet to action in circumstances especially favourable to their chances of escape, but this did not prevent his inflicting some merited chastisement upon them. Four junks were destroyed, and the remaining ten, much injured, were obliged to seek shelter and a place of refitment in a small bay, which was guarded by Captain Hay until the arrival of reinforcements should enable him to attack. In the course of six months fifty-seven piratical vessels were captured and destroyed by English men-of-war, and more than a thousand of their crews were either killed, drowned, or taken prisoners. Captain Hay resumed his operations on being joined by another vessel, and had the satisfaction of destroying the remaining junks, the buildings which had been erected on shore, and of dispersing the followers of Tsu Apoo.

There remained the more arduous task of dealing with the pirate chief Shapuntsai, who had established his headquarters in the neighbourhood of Hainan and the Gulf of Tonquin. As he had captured and plundered an English vessel, there was the greater necessity to deal with him, and Captain Hay was commissioned to proceed against him. At Hainan it was ascertained that Shapuntsai had recently retired to the Gulf of Tonquin after a successful raid along the coast. The mandarins in that island were in extreme fear of the marauder, and gladly co-operated with the English when they found them able and anxious to inflict punishment on the common enemy. The piratical fleet succeeded in baffling pursuit for several days, and want of fuel was nearly compelling the return of the squadron when the pirates were discovered at anchor in a bay. In the engagement which followed, nearly sixty junks were destroyed, and Shapuntsai only succeeded in escaping with four vessels. The victory was complete, and Shapuntsai's band ceased to be formidable. In its distress it found neither allies nor sympathizers, and the mandarins were stirred to

MURDER OF MACAO GOVERNOR.

activity to compass the complete overthrow of the man they had feared so long. The Cochin-Chinese troops, that is to say, the forces of the late King Tuduc, combined in chasing the remnants of a band that had been the terror of the land and seas.

In the year 1850 there was a revival of piratical violence, chiefly remarkable for the fact that the Chinese authorities invited the assistance of an English steamer, which was readily granted. Another band of pirates was then broken up without loss, and the Chinese authorities were informed that the English Government would be happy at all times to afford such aid.

To those who believed that the prevailing calm was delusive, and that the Chinese were only biding their time to revert to a policy more in accordance with their convictions than was possible by strict compliance with the terms of the Nankin Treaty, the murder in open daylight of the Portuguese Governor of Macao seemed to come as the most expressive and unqualified confirmation. Governor Amaral was taking his usual ride with an aide-de-camp when a man struck him in the face with a long bamboo stick, and on his remonstrating with him, six men armed with swords, concealed in their sleeves, rushed out upon him, and, as he had lost his right arm, easily dragged him from his horse and murdered him on the high-road. The event naturally produced the greatest excitement, and led to a hostile encounter between the Portuguese garrison and the Chinese troops quartered in the fort beyond the barrier. The fort was carried by a vigorous charge, and the Chinese hastily evacuated their position, leaving ten or twelve dead behind. This operation of open war fortunately did not produce the serious consequences that might have been expected. The murder of Governor Amaral gave rise to a lengthened correspondence, and reinforcements were sent from Lisbon to China, but in the end matters reverted to their original position. One man who accused himself of the crime, but who was not confronted by any witness of the deed, was publicly executed at Canton. There was every reason to believe that he was not one of the criminals, and that he either voluntarily accepted death, in return for a sum of money to his family, or, being under sentence for some other crime, was made use of by Viceroy Su for the purpose of allaying the indignation of the Portuguese. These explanations were not held to be sufficient, and after several months' litigation the question was settled in a more satisfactory manner than at one time seemed possible, by the discovery of the real culprits, and by their being handed over to the hands of justice. Some had subsequently fallen in a piratical fray with the English, but the survivors were publicly executed.

At Foochow, Shanghai, and Formosa, events of happier augury occurred throughout this year. At the first-named place the most amicable relations were preserved with not merely the Government, but also with the people of the province. More than one trip into the interior was accomplished in safety. The scenery of the river Min, among the most picturesque in China, was surveyed with a sense of agreeable security by English residents, and here the rule as to a twenty-four hours' absence was relaxed without inconvenience or untoward circumstances. Nor were matters less auspicious at Shanghai. While the allotment of a piece of ground as a site for the French Consulate signified the extension of the foreign relations of China, the superior advantages of that town as a place of trade were obtaining ready recognition. Here, too, the day rule was frequently relaxed or ignored, and the Chinese officials began to regard with growing indifference the more frequent violation of it by the Europeans during their visits to the hills some thirty miles west of Shanghai. The attitude of the people was on these occasions noticed to be friendly, and the worst tourists had to fear was from their importunate curiosity. The visit of an American war-vessel to Formosa, whence the report of its vast coal-fields was broughtback, and the residence of a missionary in the islands of Loo Choo, showed that the foreigners were all agreed as to the necessity of breaking down the barrier of Chinese exclusiveness, and of throwing fresh light on the dark places of an Empire of such untold wealth and unlimited resources.*

* Dr. John Bowring arrived at Canton, to fill the vacant post of

AN ECLIPSE.

The year 1850 had not long begun when the capital was agitated by the news that the Empress Mother had died. Only a short time before there had been rejoicings at her having attained the venerable age of eighty years, and the Emperor had expressed the hope that she might survive until her hundredth birthday. As the consort and widow of Kiaking, she had been a spectator of the gradual decadence of the Empire during the first half of the present century, but her influence on the progress of public events was probably not very great. It is said that she only once actively interfered in public affairs, and that was when she counselled the vigorous prosecution of the foreign war. There is no doubt, however, that she and Taoukwang were on affectionate terms; and although Chinese public men always write with a view to effect, his protestation was probably sincere that he had tenderly cared for her during the twenty-nine years that he had occupied the throne. But the hope that she might attain the felicity of her hundredth year was soon dispelled, and after a brief illness the Empress Mother, as the Emperor poetically expressed it, "drove the fairy chariot and went the long journey." Daily libations were ordered to be poured out in the Palace of Contentment, a long term of mourning was ordained, during which the courtiers wore white, and laid aside their jewels and seals of office, and Taoukwang only consented, at the urgent prayer of his ministers, to dismiss his grief and devote his attention to the brief period of authority that still remained for him to enjoy.

Taoukwang only survived his adopted mother by a few weeks. One of his last acts showed to what a depth of miserable mental hesitation he had sunk. It happened that the day on which the Chinese new year commenced, 12th of February, 1850, was to be marked by an eclipse of the sun, an inauspicious omen for the introduction of a new year, especially under the circumstances which had but recently occurred within the Imperial family. Taoukwang was at the time doubly

Consul, on the 19th of March, 1849; and in the following January, Dr. George Smith was consecrated first Bishop of Victoria—the name given to the see and island of Hongkong.

susceptible to the superstitious influences of his country and position, and he thought to avoid the evil consequences of the coincidence by a proclamation ordering the first day of the new year—the thirtieth of his reign—to be celebrated on the previous day. It speaks well for the good sense underlying the peculiarities of the Chinese character, that this alteration was disregarded and treated with marks of derision. At Shanghai the people even went so far as to pull down the placards officially announcing the fact. Even a Celestial Emperor had not the power to avert the course of time, or to avoid its natural and ordered consequences. This confession of superstitious dread and of Imperial impotence appropriately heralded the end of a reign marked by many disasters, and without a glimmer of success.

The new year of the Chinese calendar had not run its first fortnight when the inmates of the palace perceived that the Emperor's end was near at hand. The recognition of the dread truth which ultimately comes home to all the sons of man was not denied to Taoukwang, although those who have enjoyed absolute power on earth are naturally more slow than others to admit the presence of a master. But although the closing scenes of a Chinese Emperor are religiously shielded from the profane gaze of an inquisitive public, the greatest publicity was given to the fact that on the 25th of February a great council was held in the bed-chamber of the Emperor, at the very bedside of the dying Taoukwang. There may have been much discussion, and some conflict of opinion. To us it is only given to know the result, which was that Yihchoo, the fourth son, was proclaimed Heir Apparent, and his father's chosen successor.*

Taoukwang survived this important act a very short time, although the precise date is matter of uncertainty; but there

* The Vermilion Edict, signed with the pencil of that colour, reads as follows:—"Let Yihchoo, the Imperial fourth son, be set forth as the Imperial Heir Apparent. You princes and high officers, why wait for our words? Assist and support him with united hearts, and do you all regard whatever pertains to the concerns of the country and the public as of high importance, without sympathy for aught else." Yihchoo became the Emperor Hienfung.

is reason to believe that his death was hastened by the alarm caused by the outbreak of a fire within the Imperial city, and that it happened a few hours after the bedside council. The notification of his death was conveyed in an Imperial order issued by his successor, in which there is expressed the stereotyped hope that he had wished his father to attain his hundredth year. Taoukwang was in the 69th year of his age, having been born on the 12th of September, 1781. He was a young man while the power of his grandfather, Keen Lung, was at its pinnacle, and as a child he had listened to the tales of victorious campaigns and extensive conquests. But the misfortunes of his father's reign proved to be the precursors of the greater misfortunes of his own, and the school of adversity in which he had passed the better years of his manhood only imbued him with the disposition to put up with misfortune rather than with the vigour to grapple with it. The panegyric in which his son and successor extolled the paternal virtues is composed of generalities, which do not assist the reader in arriving at any certain view as to Taoukwang's character. If we do not deny to Yihchoo's periods the honourable and natural motive of personal affection, we must regret the absence of any attempt to sum up the events of his father's reign, or to convey some idea as to his character.

If an opinion may be formed on the latter point from the terms of his will, in which he might be expected to reveal the true tenor of his thoughts, it would seem that he was averse to all unnecessary display, and it is natural to suppose that this moderation may have been due to a sense of the difficulties of his people as well to his habitual reluctance to waste treasure on personal matters. As a young man he had been much attached to active pursuits, and it will not have been forgotten that his skill in military exercises was once usefully shown in saving his father's life. Even after ascending the throne, he preserved his old partiality for archery and riding ; and it was even said of him that he took "strengthening pills" to develop his muscular power. Whatever the effect of this medicine in other ways, it destroyed his teeth, and detracted greatly from his personal appearance.

He was described in not very attractive language as being "lank, tall, hollow-cheeked, black-visaged, toothless, and consequently with a pointed chin."

Although Taoukwang's reign of thirty years was one of unredeemed failure, that monarch had some satisfaction in the belief that his authority had to all appearance survived the rude shocks to which it had been so constantly exposed. The foreign war, with all its penalty of increased intercourse with foreigners and lowered dignity on the part of the Celestial Emperor, had come and gone without those grave consequences to the Chinese constitution which at one time it seemed must inevitably follow. The symptoms of internal rebellion which had revealed themselves in more than one quarter of the Empire had not attained any formidable dimensions. The great tributaries were passive and obedient. Yet it is possible that Taoukwang distrusted this calm as deceptive, and if he could not have realized the depth of popular discontent, he yet perceived that there was a resentful national feeling in the hearts of the Chinese which all the wiles and wisdom of Manchu statecraft had failed to reach. Taoukwang left to his successor the example of much fortitude. If he had been unable to vanquish his most formidable enemies, he at least showed how evils might be borne with patience and dignity. If there was not much to admire in Taoukwang's action, all sympathy will not be denied to him for the sake of his misfortunes.

CHAPTER IX.

THE EARLY YEARS OF HIENFUNG'S REIGN.

THE selection of Yihchoo for the throne threatened to disturb even the perfect arrangements of the Chinese system, which seldom fails to stifle all opposition before incurring the responsibility of making a decision. The principal ministers, Muchangah, the premier, who shared the indecision of the master he had just lost, and Keying, who was so smitten with grief at the death of the prince whose favourite companion he had been from an early period of his life, remained inactive while they should have been stirring in order to establish the authority of their new sovereign. Their inaction seems for a moment to have inspired the eldest prince, Hwuy Wang, the brother of the deceased man, with the idea of disputing the claim of his young nephew; but happily the impulse of revolt was resisted, and Hienfung's accession was generally recognized. Hwuy Wang, who had lost the favour of the Emperor and been an object of suspicion at Court through his over-eagerness to acquire possession of the throne on the occasion of Taoukwang's serious illness in the early part of his reign, was now content to become the friend and principal courtier of his nephew; but there was no reason for overlooking the hesitation of Muchangah and Keying, who were quietly removed from their places in the administration.

Hienfung was still a very young man * when he ascended

---

* Born in August, 1831; he was, therefore, in his nineteenth year. The name of Hienfung means "great abundance" or "complete prosperity."

the throne, and in the auspicious proclamation issued on the commencement of his reign, he dwelt on the difficulty of his task, expressing the hope that he would be able to continue what was admirable in the conduct of his predecessors, while an appeal for assistance concluded in the following terms: "Then do ye, O princes and ministers, civil and military, aid us in the service we have undertaken, that we may add stability to the mighty line, the succession of which has devolved upon us. Let each one give evidence of his fidelity, aiding us by his counsels to the attainment of perfection, that boundless blessings may be manifested to this realm for a thousand million of years." This call for general support was followed by the bestowal of titles upon his younger brothers, men who, in their way, were destined to exercise a profound influence on the policy of China during the thirty years that followed the death of Taoukwang. His next brother, Yih-su, was made Prince Kung; the next, Yih-tah, Prince Shun; the third, Yih-hoh, Prince Chun; and the youngest, Yih-hwui, Prince Fu. They were also distinguished by their numerical order as the sons of Taoukwang, so that Prince Kung ranked and was sometimes known as the Fifth Prince; while Prince Chun, father of the Emperor Kwangsu, was often called the Seventh.

Vigorous measures were taken against those who ventured to circulate false news as to the events which had happened at Pekin, and the hawking about of baseless rumours for the purpose of disturbing the public mind was to be punished at once with decapitation. The very strong measures thus adopted against those who discussed or described the fire in the apartment of the Sixth Prince showed that there was something in the reports, although it was soon made evident that the struggle for power was over, and that Hienfung's rivals and enemies had been silenced. Among the first acts of the new ruler, Su, the viceroy, was ordered to remain at his post in Canton, in order to " manage the important concerns of the frontier," while the arrival of a British steamer off the Peiho, with a letter of congratulation from Governor Bonham, afforded additional proof that the new reign would see no lull in the foreign question, rendered more complicated by the sudden emigration of several thousands of Chinese subjects to the newly-discovered goldfields of California. There was not as much reason to entertain surprise at this movement as people seemed to think, seeing that the Chinese had shown, by their going to the Straits Settlements, the Philippines, and Siam, that they had no objection to seek profitable employment abroad.

Hienfung came to the throne at the time of great dearth and public suffering; but his administration energetically strove to alleviate the general distress, and by means of voluntary subscriptions—a very common mode of raising money in China—succeeded in supplying the more pressing wants of the population. The spring of 1850 proved to be exceedingly fine and propitious, so that abundant crops contributed to rapid recovery from the depressing condition to which a large part of the country had been reduced. The obituary ceremonies of the late Emperor shared with ministerial changes the attention of the capital. Muchangah and Keying were removed from their offices, the former because, as it was proclaimed, "his overthrow of those of a different policy from himself when the barbarian question was first raised is matter of the deepest indignation." Nor was Keying's crime less heinous in the eyes of his new prince. "The unpatriotic tendency of Keying, his cowardice and incapacity, are very greatly to be wondered at." Both were only saved from death out of regard for their long services; but while Muchangah* was deprived of all his rank and offices, and forbidden to expect any future employment, Keying was reduced to the lowest grade, it is true, but left

---

* Muchangah had been for a great many years employed in the public service. He was considered the oldest civilian in the service. As far back as the year 1818 he was a junior vice-president of the Board of Trade and General of the Manchu White Banner. In 1823 he became senior vice-president, and was then employed on several special commissions to different parts of the Empire. In 1836 he was appointed honorary tutor to the Heir Apparent, and in the same year he was rewarded with a seat in the Cabinet. He was soon made the Governor-General of Pechihli—an office not so important then as it has appeared to be since the time of Li Hung Chang. On the death of Changling, in 1838, Muchangah became premier, or, more correctly, first Grand Secretary.

with the hope that he might regain his former position as well as the confidence of his sovereign. The fall of these two ministers, who had enjoyed a longer tenure of office than usually falls to the lot of Chinese officials, showed the instability of rank and reputation among the ministers of the Dragon Throne. Their policy had fallen out of favour, and as their views had become unpalatable, neither their age nor their services could avert their complete ruin and disgrace. The most powerful official in China can never feel certain as to where he will be to-morrow. One day he is the supposed arbiter of the Empire's destiny; the next he has often been reduced to a lower rank than the least important of his secretaries, and he may esteem himself fortunate if he manages to save his life.

The removal of Muchangah and Keying, who were the ministers principally identified with the pacific settlement of the foreign question, could not fail to be generally interpreted as signifying a change of view on the part of the new Emperor as to the mode of dealing with what he designated the affair of the outer barbarians. And whether Hienfung really meant his act to have that effect or not, it gave a fresh impulse to the sentiments hostile to Europeans, and encouraged those who hoped that the day of concessions had gone by. Among no class did Hienfung's early proceedings produce greater excitement than among those literati who, having passed the necessary examinations, become aspirants to office and fame. These saw in the disgrace of Keying, and the exaltation of the Viceroy Su, the certain precursors of a return to that policy of superiority which not merely flattered their vanity, but was perhaps really necessary to the maintenance of their position among their own people.

The effects of this change were first revealed at Foochow, where in the summer of 1850 an attempt was suddenly made to prevent foreigners residing in that town. It was said that the foreigners had the right to come only to trade, and that, therefore, they could not claim to reside within the limits of the city. That privilege had been conceded with much reluctance to the consul, but the merchants were to reside at the mouth of the river. The immediate cause of disagreement was the acquisition by purchase of some land on the part of the missionaries who intended building a place of residence and a chapel. The matter had received the sanction of the local magistrate, when the mob, incited by literati of the town, and encouraged, it was more than suspected, by the exhortation of Commissioner Lin, who chanced to be living close to it, made a hostile demonstration in front of the missionaries' new residence. The officials of Foochow were fortunately actuated by more friendly feelings than the people, and in their hands the matter passed out of the sphere of mob violence into the more satisfactory region of regular discussion. It became clear that the Chinese had the best of the controversy. Reference to the treaty showed that the place of residence had been specified as the *kiang-kan*, or mart, at the mouth of the river, and not at the *ching*, or town, itself. The Chinese were, therefore, shown to be within their right; and the question had to be left for future settlement as one of convenience and good-will.

The mention of Lin's name will serve to introduce the last passage of his eventful career. He had lived down the loss of office which had followed the failure of his plans at Canton, and it really looked as if the wheel of fortune were again turning in his favour. Certainly Hienfung was well disposed towards both the man and his policy, and when the rebels in Kwangsi grew more daring it was on Lin that his choice fell to bring them into subjection. It is far from clear that Lin was the best man for this kind of work, as his experience was altogether of a peaceful character; but the result of the experiment could never be known, as he died on the 22nd of November, 1850, on his way to the scene of the struggle. Although Commissioner Lin failed to achieve any of the objects which he placed before himself, he was thoroughly convinced of the wisdom and necessity of the policy, despite the fact that he never made it successful. His sincerity was above challenge, but he was always more of a moralist than of a statesman. He has been called a statesman, but the claim will not be allowed at the bar of history. He was rather a typical representative of the order of literary officials to which he belonged. Statesmanship is in their eyes the carrying out of political plans in strict obedience to a groove of action laid down in antiquity, and the able man is he who can most eloquently enunciate great moral truths which he probably does not carry out in his own life, and which without practice and the demonstration of vigour will avail but little to keep an empire together, or to impose obedience to the laws upon a vast population. Nothing, perhaps, showed more clearly the direction in which the young Emperor was drifting than the fact that he conferred on this man, the High Commissioner Lin, the enemy of the English, the posthumous title of the Faithful Duke.

About the same time six portals of honour were erected at Canton to the Viceroy Su for his victory over the English, in having successfully resisted their attempt to force their claims of admission into the city. There was nothing in this to excite any surprise. The authorities felt that their hold upon the respect of the people rested on far too insecure a foundation to allow them to neglect so favourable an occasion of showing that the Government still retained some of its strength. The simple country-folk expressed their admiration for their rulers by attacking and maltreating two American gentlemen in the neighbourhood of Canton. The Viceroy replied that the Americans had brought their misfortune upon themselves by going into the country without a guard, but that he would do everything in his power to capture and rigorously punish those who were guilty.

The first years of Hienfung's reign witnessed what was an entirely novel event in Chinese history—the exodus on a large scale of the Chinese people to lands across the sea. There had in earlier stages of their history been emigrations to Siam, Malacca, and the islands of the Eastern Archipelago. The Philippines had owed no fleeting prosperity to their toil. Their trading-junks had passed the Sunda straits, and many of the Emperor's subjects enjoyed wealth and prosperity in lands then and now subject to the sway of England. The Chinaman only requires a sufficient inducement to attract him from his own country, and in 1852 that inducement had been supplied in a way that it had never before been by the discovery of the gold-fields in California and Australia.

THE GOLD FIELDS.

Once the example was set, the people flocked across the Pacific in their thousands. Each emigrant vessel carried from 500 passengers to as many as 1000; and for a time it seemed as if the supply of these persistently industrious and never-desponding labourers was inexhaustible. Within a few months of the first arrival nearly 20,000 Chinese had landed at San Francisco. Nor were they unable to take care of themselves, or to do justice to their own interests. They were bound together not only by their common race in a strange land, but by the terms of a labour association which afforded them a much more effectual protection than any possessed by their white fellow-labourers. Their chiefs, such as the great and prosperous Atti, no doubt took care to draw more than their share of the spoil; but there were very efficient safeguards against any gross abuses. Nor was Australia a less attractive spot to the adventurous sons of the southern provinces; and much of the prosperity of Queensland may be traced to the work done half a century back by the cheapest labourers in the world.

These emigrants were not lost to their own country. A certain number, possibly a high percentage, of them died; but even then their bodies were conveyed to their homes for burial. But a very large number returned carrying back with them their savings, which represented for their wants a sum by no means inconsiderable. China was so much the richer by the wealth they imported; she could hardly be said to have suffered from their absence. It is difficult, perhaps impossible, to say what were the true views of the Chinese Government on the subject. They certainly did not interfere to check the emigration as they could easily have done. They seemed rather disposed to take the view that those who were willing to leave their country could not be of much use to her if they remained. When the movement attained its largest proportions the Pekin authorities were too much occupied with other matters to give it the heed that the fact in itself deserved; but the regular return of the emigrants, after a more or less brief absence, with the results of their labour, gradually reconciled their rulers to the annual migration. It was satisfactory for them to perceive that they felt none the less Chinese because they had sojourned for a period in a foreign land, and among races regarded as having views of very doubtful friendship towards the Celestial Empire.

While, therefore, the foreigners were learning something about China, a portion of the Chinese people was also becoming acquainted in a way with the foreigners. Neither California nor Australia afforded a good school for teaching the Celestials that the white men possessed those high qualities on which they prided themselves, and for the want of which they were so prompt to blame others. It is to be feared that they returned home with a worse opinion of "the outer barbarian" than any they would have formed of him in their own country as seen through the influences of national prejudice and hatred. In this sense, therefore, the increasing knowledge of foreigners and foreign countries by the Chinese, far from leading to improved relations and increased harmony, rather intensified the existing sentiments of dislike and suspicion. Thus the Chinese continued to proceed in search of the place where their labours would be best remunerated; but even to our own day the Chinaman has returned home rather with the remembrance of grievances unredressed and injury patiently endured, than with any feeling of gratitude for favours received, and for hearty recognition of his services.

This period was remarkable for its natural as well as political calamities. A severe famine at Pekin compelled Hienfung's Cabinet to devote large sums of money to the aid of the indigent. This evil had hardly been properly met when an earthquake in Szchuen caused immense loss and widespread consternation. Canton was ravaged by a fire in October, 1851, when 200 of the best shops were burnt down. The recuperative faculty of the Chinese was well demonstrated by their being all rebuilt, and in better style than before, within three months of their destruction. The day before there had been a terrible accident at Foochow. A crowd had collected on the bridge across the river Min, and the balustrade had given way and several hundred people were precipitated into the river, and it was computed that 230 of these were drowned. A few weeks later the Chinese part of Victoria or Hongkong was burnt down, and not a vestige was left of what had been a large and flourishing settlement.

The warring of the elements proved the precursor of discord in the realm. Neither Hienfung nor the foreign community was able to long devote all attention to events of such comparatively small importance as the visitation of natural calamities, or to the ordinary daily affairs of an industrious community. The changes which had taken place among his principal advisers showed that the new Emperor was disposed to pursue a more aggressive policy than his predecessor had adopted during the last few years of his reign. The curt dismissal of Keying and Muchangah had been followed up by the elevation of Saichangah to the post of premier, and by the recall of Keshen. But the Emperor soon found that the latter's views differed in no material degree from those of Keying, and after a brief tenure of office he was again dismissed into private life. His disgrace was nominally in consequence of his having failed to check the advance of the insurgents, but it was really because his general policy was distasteful to the young prince who swayed the destinies of China. The weak and incompetent Saichangah better suited a master who preferred the execution of his own wishes to conducting public affairs in accordance with the dictates of experience and necessity. Not until the full extent of his folly and incompetence was revealed, when sent as Commissioner to Kweiling, did he too share the disgrace which had fallen upon his able but unlucky colleague.

The attention of foreign observers, as well as of the Government, became engrossed in the progress of the internal rebellion, which, having extended from one end of the Empire to the other, threatened to involve the whole Manchu race in a common overthrow. No matters that did not directly bear on the issue of that struggle were thought worthy of notice, and general attention was strained to discern both its significance and the probable manner in which it would end. Neither Hienfung nor those who were around him were wholly blind to the peril. The popular discontent had found such forcible expression, as to render it impossible for the most confirmed indifference to feign ignorance of it any longer. With the recognition of the malady there could not help but be some admission from the Ruler that his acts must have fallen short in effect of the obligations of his high position. As the father of his people he could no longer overlook their necessities and sufferings, of which their insubordination might be held to be the expression. If Hienfung himself, with the careless confidence of youth, had wished to treat the general manifestation of discontent with indifference, there were those near him who could not allow so wide a departure, not merely from the path of policy, but from the less yielding principles of Chinese precedent. Therefore, while Hienfung himself continued to enjoy the ease and luxury of his palace life, the Censors and the Hanlin doctors prepared a notice to the people in his name. In this, not only did the sovereign take upon himself all the blame for his numerous shortcomings, but he charged the officials of his Government at their peril to attend more strictly to their different duties, to find out the cause of the people's discontent, and to spare no pains to effect its cure and removal.*

* The following is the text of this remarkable proclamation:—"My exalted parent, the Emperor Taoukwang, was profoundly benevolent and exceedingly gracious, enriching with his favours the whole of his vast dominions; but I, being entrusted with the important charge of the Empire, have found it difficult to provide for the interests of his extensive territory, and have thus been filled with the intensest anxiety for the last three years. I reflect on the day when my exalted parent departed this life, how impressively he inculcated on me the important duty of consulting the interests of the country and preserving the lives of the people; as all the officers who witnessed the solemn scene well know. We think again of the present period, when the interests of the country are by no means in a favourable state, and the people are brought into the most afflictive circumstances; which leads us to reproach and blame ourselves, and to exert our utmost energies in scheming and calculating, but to little effect; does not this involve us in a most serious dereliction of duty and constitute us the principal criminal in the whole empire? Throughout the court and the country there are not wanting civil and military officers who, manifesting fidelity and exerting their strength, look upon the interests of the country as those of their own family; but, at the same time, there are not a few of the easy and self-indulgent, slothful and remiss, who think much of their rank and emolument, but pay no attention to the welfare of the State. We, although not laying claim to the title of an

But the crisis had gone far beyond a remedy of words. The corruption of the public service had gradually alienated the sympathies of the people. Justice, honour, and probity had been banished from the civil service of China. The example of the few men of honour and capacity served but to bring into more prominent relief the faults of the rest. Justice was not to be found; to the rich it was sold even to the highest bidder. The guilty, if well provided in worldly means, escaped scot free; the poor suffered for their own frailties and the crimes of higher offenders. Offices were sold to men who had never passed an examination, and who were wholly illiterate. The value of office was as the means to extortion. The nation was heavily taxed. The taxes to the State were but the smaller portion of the sums wrung from the traders and peasantry of the Middle Kingdom. How was honour or a sense of duty to be expected from men who knew that their term of office must be short, and who had to regain their purchase money and the anticipated fortune before their post was sold again to some fresh competitor? The officials waxed rich in ill-gotten wealth; a few

intelligent ruler, will at the same time not lay the blame unnecessarily upon our ministers and officers; but we just ask them in the silent hour of the night to lay their hands upon their hearts, and see if they can allow themselves to rest satisfied with such a state of things; if they do not now reproach themselves most bitterly for their remissness, they will, at some future period, be involved in evils which they will not be able to remedy. We, therefore, publicly announce to all you officers, great and small, that if from henceforth you do not change your old habits, and if you pay no regard to this our decree, we are determined severely to punish you according to the utmost rigour of the law, without allowing the least indulgence or permitting rigour to be tempered by clemency; for the necessity of the present crisis demands it. Let us for a moment reason the matter with you. If the interests of the country and the lives of the people have no connection with your personal or family affairs, do you not regard your own name and fame in thus willingly becoming the faithless servants of the Manchu dynasty? Is not this very stupid? After all, the influence of reasoning may have little or no force with you; you officers great and small may deem it too much trouble to acknowledge right principles, thinking that to deceive us, a single individual at the head of the State, is comparatively an easy matter; but pray lift up your heads on high, and think of High Heaven, intelligently inspecting all below, and see if there is not something to be dreaded there. A special proclamation. Respect this."

individuals accumulated enormous fortunes, and the government of the country sank lower and lower in the estimation of the millions of people who were supposed to regard their sovereign with unspeakable awe as the embodiment of Celestial wisdom and power, and their form of political existence as the most perfect administration ever devised by man.

The Government lost also in efficiency. A corrupt and effeminate body of officers and administrators can serve but as poor defenders for an embarrassed prince and an assailed Government against even enemies who are in themselves insignificant, and not free from the vices of a corrupt society and a decaying age; and it was on such that Hienfung had in the first place alone to lean. Even his own Manchus, the warlike Tartars who, despite the smallness of their numbers, had conquered the whole of China, and given its Empire such grandeur and military fame as it had not known for more than one thousand years—for the Mongol Empire was a thing distinct from that of China—had lost their primitive virtue and warlike efficiency in the southern land which they had made their home. To them the opulent cities of the Chinese had proved as fatal as Capua to the army of the Carthaginian; and when the peril came suddenly upon them they showed themselves unworthy of the Empire won by their ancestors. So far as they individually were concerned, they lost it. Other Tartars, worthier of their earlier fame, had to come from the cold and vigorous regions of the north to help the embarrassed Hienfung and his successor out of their difficulties, and to re-assert the claims of Manchu supremacy. For the first time since the revolt of Wou Sankwei the Manchus are brought face to face with a danger threatening their right of conquest. It is evidently not a danger to be overcome by fine words or lavish promises. Yet on the eve of the Taeping revolt that is all that Hienfung or his advisers can suggest or produce in order to avert a crisis and to crush the incipient rebellion in its birth.

CHAPTER X.

THE BEGINNING OF THE TAEPING REBELLION.

DURING fifty years the provinces of China had now witnessed many disturbances, and the officers of the Government found that they had not the power to enforce their orders, and that the people would pay no heed to them except under compulsion. Yet, up to the present, these disorders had scarcely partaken of the character of rebellion, and might even have been considered the natural accompaniments of an administration so easily satisfied, both as to the behaviour of the people and also as to the execution of its own orders, as that of Pekin has generally been. We have now reached a time when, after the tranquillity of nearly two centuries, sedition was to wear a bolder front, and when it was becoming impossible for the Government of the Emperor Hienfung to pretend that the disorder in the province of Kwangsi* was anything short of an open rebellion for the purpose of driving him and the Manchu dynasty from the throne.

As far back as the year 1830 there had been symptoms of disturbed popular feeling in Kwangsi. The difficulty of operating in a region which possessed few roads, and which was only rendered at all accessible by the West river or Sikiang, had led the Chinese authorities, much engaged as they were about the foreign question, to postpone those

---

* The province of Kwangsi lies west of Kwantung, and forms with it the southern border towards Tonquin. Further west still is Yunnan. Kwantung and Kwangsi constitute the vice-royalty of the Two Kwang, with its seat of government at Canton.

vigorous measures which if taken at the outset might have speedily restored peace and stamped out the first promptings of revolt. But it was considered a purely local question, and although the people of Canton were disposed to see signs of danger and an omen of coming change in the most insignificant natural phenomena, their rulers thought it safe to ignore the popular temperament, and to treat the rebels in Kwangsi with as much indifference as they bestowed on the language of the skies. Events moved very slowly, and for twenty years it seemed as if the authorities would have no cause to repent their apathy.

The authorities were more concerned at the proceedings of the formidable secret association known as the Triads than at the occurrences in Kwangsi, probably because the Triads made no secret that their object was the expulsion of the Manchus, and the restoration of the Mings.* Their oaths were framed so as to appeal to the patriotism and personal pride of the native-born Chinese, who were instigated to resist and cast off the yoke of the Tartars contemptuously designated as an inferior race little better than barbarians. The extraordinary fact in their proceedings was not that they should plot rebellion, or that they should feel a deep antipathy to their conquerors, who monopolized as far as they could the best posts in the service, but that they should base their plans on a proposed restoration of the Ming dynasty, which was not merely forgotten, but which, practically speaking, had expired two centuries before. It was obvious to the most ordinary intelligence that to fight for the Ming dynasty was struggling for an impossible idea; and the great mass of the Chinese long held aloof from a connection which could mean nothing more in the end than furthering the personal schemes of some unknown and probably unscrupulous adventurer.

The true origin of the Triads is not to be assigned. The

* "We combine everywhere to recall the Ming and exterminate the barbarians, cut off the Tsing and await the right prince." See, for a very interesting account of the Triads, of whose oath these lines formed the opening sentence, an article in vol. xviii. of "Chinese Repository," pp. 281–95.

popular account gives a very figurative description of how the inmates of a monastery near Foochow came to the aid of a Manchu Emperor in one of his foreign wars. As their reward they were to, and did for several generations, enjoy great privileges, but their descendants at last became the victims of official tyranny. Their monastery was either destroyed or taken from them, and they went through the land in search of their revenge. Then it was that they came to the decision to put forward the Ming pretension; and members of the brotherhood went to the different provinces to stir up disaffection and to point popular aspiration towards a desirable end. We cannot accept, if we may not deny the truth of, this fanciful story. Perhaps we shall have gleaned the modicum of fact in it by saying that this tradition invests with additional probability the suspicion that the Taeping revolt was originally conceived in a Buddhist monastery. The agents of such a band would naturally be attracted to the disturbed parts of the Empire; and although there was no dearth of places to choose from, no province offered so favourable a ground for the action of conspirators as that of Kwangsi.

The summer of 1850 witnessed a great accession of energy on the part of the rebels in that province, which may perhaps be attributed to the death of the Emperor. The important town of Wuchow on the Sikiang, close to the western border of Kwantung, was besieged by a force which rumour placed as high as 50,000 men. The Governor was afraid to report the occurrence, knowing that it would carry his own condemnation and probable disgrace; and it was left for a minor official to reveal the extent to which the insurgents had carried their depredations. Two leaders named Chang had assumed the style of royalty. Other bands had appeared in the province of Hoonan, as well as in the southern parts of Kwantung; but they all collected by degrees on the Sikiang, where they placed an embargo on merchandise, and gradually crushed out such trade as there had been by that stream best known to-day as the West river. But their proceedings were not restricted to the fair operations of war. They plundered and massacred wherever they went. They claimed to act in the name of the Chinese people; yet they slew all they could lay hands upon, without discrimination of age or sex. Such of the women as suited their purposes were allowed to live a life of degradation and shame.

The confidence of the insurgents was raised by frequent success, and by the manifest inability of the Canton Viceroy to take any effectual military measures against them. A body of rebels from either the eastern parts of Kwantung or from Hoonan decoyed a party of the Imperial troops into a defile between Sinyuen and Yingtin, two places on the northern high road from Canton, and killed 200 of them.* This reverse naturally aroused considerable alarm in Canton, and the gates were barricaded and a vigilant look-out was kept to prevent any large bodies of men approaching the city. An open attack having been thus committed so near Canton, Governor Yeh was sent out with 2000 soldiers to engage them. That official was never conspicuous for his valour, and he was content to employ his force in such a manner as to impress upon the insurgents a belief as to its overwhelming strength. This object must have been attained, for they quickly retired into Kwangsi. In their retreat they were assailed by the armed inhabitants and local militia, and suffered considerable loss. Not unnaturally this success excited great enthusiasm, and the most was made of the details of the struggle. Governor Yeh took all the credit of the success to himself; and if vaunting proclamations ensure

About this time the following proclamation was discovered:—" The present dynasty are only Manchus, people of a small nation, but the power of their troops enabled them to usurp possession of China and take its revenues, from which it is plain that any one may get money from China if they are only powerful in warfare. There is, therefore, no difference between one taking money from the villagers and the local authorities taking the revenues. Whoever can take keeps. Why then are troops causelessly sent against us? It is most unjust! The Manchus get the revenues of the provinces and appoint officers who oppress the people, and why should we, natives of China, be excluded from levying money? The universal sovereignty does not belong to any particular individual; and a dynasty of a hundred generations of emperors has not been seen. All, therefore, depends on obtaining the possession" ("Chinese Repository," vol. xix. p. 568).

fame, he would then have won the reputation of a good soldier.

An outbreak at Lienchow, near the small port called Pakhoi, recalled the Canton mandarins from the pleasing dream that their efforts were crowned with complete success, and that the rebels were on the eve of returning to their duty. The importance of this movement consisted in the soldiers sent to restore order joining the rioters, and when a fresh force came from Hainan they combined and succeeded in inflicting a defeat upon it. It was said that not a single Imperialist soldier escaped alive from the fray. Some of the insurgents made overtures to the mandarins, and signified a desire to return to their duty if only the Government would give them some certain employment and a small official rank. This was no doubt a feeler or a blind; for almost at the very same time the main body of the insurgents had agreed upon the choice of a single leader, to whom they gave the royal title of Tien Wang, or the "Heavenly King."* With this act their political significance greatly increased, and it became impossible to treat them any longer as being destitute of real importance.

The strongest of monarchs cannot afford to ignore the presence of a competitor to his throne. To Hienfung, whose embarrassments were from every point of view grave as well as numerous, the elevation of Tien Wang was a direct menace as well as a warning. It was only safe to treat him as an audacious adventurer on the assumption that no time was to be lost and no effort spared in crushing his hostile movement, and in putting an end to his personal pretensions. Tien Wang was, after all, only one of the principal chiefs of the Kwangsi rebels. The people followed him with steady faith because they believed in his miraculous powers and in his capacity to earn success; but his colleagues chose him as their ostensible leader in order that they might have one, and thus derive all the strength to be acquired from

* For a long time this chief was thought to be styled Tienteh, or "Heaven's virtue"; but subsequent inquiries showed that such was not the case, and that his true title was Tien-kwoh. We use that by which he was best known.

placing before the people a man alleged to be capable of redressing wrongs, and of attaining undefinable ambitions.

There was nothing in the person of the individual selected to lead the disaffected that entitled him to seek the suffrages of the Chinese people, or to assume the responsibilities of governing the Empire. The missionaries, over-anxious to secure the long-anticipated prize of their individual labours and exertions—the conversion of the Chinese people to Christianity—were led at an early point to see in Tien Wang a possible regenerator of his country, and the certain recipient of the true religion. For ten years the hope was indulged that the Taepings were to prove the agents of the Cross, and that Tien Wang was to be to the Celestials what Ethelbert had been to the Saxons. There was nothing in Tien Wang's character or surroundings to justify these hopes and speculations. The Taeping leader was little better than a brigand. The talked of regeneration of his country was only the excuse for pillaging its villages and depopulating its provinces. Who then was Tien Wang, stripped of his celestial title?

Hung-tsiuen was the son of a small farmer who lived in a village near the North river, about thirty miles from Canton. If he was not a Hakka* himself, he lived in a district which was considered to be their almost exclusive property. He belonged to, or was closely associated with, a degraded race, therefore, and it was held that he was not entitled to that free entrance into the body of the civil service which is the natural privilege of every native of China. His friends declared that he came out high at each of the periodical examinations, but their statements may have been false in this as in much else. The fact is clear that he failed to obtain his degrees, and that he was denied admission into the public service. Hung was, therefore, a

* The term *hakka* means "a guest." They are tramps who roam over the country, settling in vacant places and then encroaching on their neighbours. Never heartily addicted to sedentary pursuits, they generally took to marauding after a brief spell of settled life. (Wells Williams.) A large colony of the Hakkas were sent from Canton to Formosa, where they were established in the hills between the Chinese and the aboriginal tribes. The Hakkas have also been called the squatters.

disappointed candidate, the more deeply disappointed, perhaps, as his sense of injured merit, and the ill-judging flattery of his friends, made his chagrin the keener.*

Hung was a shrewd observer of the weakness of the Government, and of the popular discontent. He perceived the opportunity of making the Manchu dynasty the scapegoat of national weakness and apathy. He could not be the servant of the Government. Class contempt, the prejudice of his examiners, or it may even have been his own haughty presumption and self-sufficiency, effectually debarred him from the enjoyment of the wealth and privileges that fall to the lot of those in executive power in all countries, but in Asiatic above every other. To his revengeful but astute mind it was clear that if he could not be an official he might be the enemy of the Government, the declared subverter of order and the law.

The details of his early career have been mainly recorded by those who sympathized with the supposed objects of his operations, and while they have been very anxious to discover his virtues, they were always blind to his failings. The steps of his imposture have therefore been described with an amount of implicit belief, which reflected little credit on the judgment of those who were anxious to give their sanction to the miracles which preceded the appearance of this adventurer in the field. Absurd stories as to his dreams, allegorical coincidences showing how he was summoned by a just and all-powerful God to the supreme seat of power, were repeated with a degree of faith so emphatic in its expression as to make the challenge of its sincerity appear extremely harsh. Hung, the defeated official candidate, the long deaf listener to the entreaties of Christian missionaries, was thus in a brief time metamorphosed into Heaven's elect for the Dragon Throne. Whether Hung was merely an intriguer, or a fanatic, he could not help feeling some gratitude to those who so conveniently echoed his pretensions to the throne, at the same time that they pleaded extenuating

* Mr. Meadows, in his "Chinese and their Rebellions," says that he was born in 1813, and that his failure must not be attributed to his fault, but to the excessive number of candidates competing.

circumstances for acts of cruelty and brigandage often unsurpassed in their infamy.

If he found the foreigners thus willing to accept him at his own estimate, it would have been very strange if he had not experienced still greater success in imposing upon the credulity of his own countrymen. To declare that he had dreamt dreams which left little room to doubt that he was selected by a heavenly mandate for Royal honours was sufficient to gain a small body of adherents, provided only that he was prepared to accept the certain punishment of detection and failure. If Hung's audacity was shown by nothing else, it was demonstrated by the lengths to which he carried the supernatural agency that urged him to quit the ignominious life of a Kwantung peasant for the career of a pretender to Imperial honours. The course of training to which he subjected himself, the ascetic deprivations, the loud prayers and invocations, the supernatural counsels and meetings, was that adopted by every other religious devotee or fanatic as the proper novitiate for those honours based on the superstitious reverence of mankind which are sometimes no inadequate substitute for temporal power and influence, even when they fail to pave the way to their attainment.

Yet when Hung proceeded to Kwangsi there was no room left to hope that the seditious movement would dissolve of its own accord, for the extent and character of his pretensions at once invested the rising with all the importance of open and unveiled rebellion. After the proclamation of Hung as Tien Wang the success of the Kwangsi rebels increased. The whole of the country south of the Sikiang, with the strong military station of Nanning, fell into their hands, and they prepared in the early part of the year 1851 to attack the provincial capital Kweiling, which commanded one of the principal high roads into the interior of China. So urgent did the peril at this place appear, that three Imperial Commissioners were sent there direct by land from Pekin, and the significance of their appointment was increased by the fact that they were all Manchus. Their names were Saichangah, Tatungah, and Hingteh. They were instructed to collect as many troops as they could *en route;* and, whether owing to this fact or to reluctance to meet the enemy, they did not reach Kweiling until some weeks after they were expected and sorely needed. Indeed, they would have arrived much too late to protect the small remaining portion of Kwangsi had it not been for the valour and military capacity exhibited by Wurantai, chief of the Bannermen at Canton, to whom in their distress Viceroy Su and Governor Yeh consigned the defence of the western limits of the province. Yet even he had to admit that he could devise no adequate plan for the danger, and that "the outlaws were neither exterminated nor made prisoners."*

The growth of the rebellion proved steady, but slow. Reinforcements were sent constantly to the Imperial army without producing any decisive result. Fresh levies were hard to obtain and harder still to keep in the field, although volunteers for the war were well paid and promised generous treatment. The expenses of the war were enormous. The resources of the Canton exchequer were strained to the uttermost to provide the bare expenses of the army in the field; and although 30,000 troops were stated to be concentrated opposite the positions of the Taepings, fear or inexperience prevented action, and the numbers and courage of the Imperialists melted away. Had the Chinese authorities only pressed on they must have swept the rebels into Tonquin, and there would have been an end of Tien Wang and his aspirations. They lacked the nerve, and their vacillation gave confidence and reputation to an enemy that need never have been allowed to become formidable.

While the Imperial authorities had been either discouraged or at the least lethargic, the pretender Tien Wang had been busily engaged in establishing his authority on a sound basis, and in assigning their ranks to his principal followers, who saw in the conference of titles and posts the recognition of their past zeal and the promise of reward for future service. The men who rallied round Hung-tsiuen were schoolmasters and

---

* His official report to the Emperor is chiefly remarkable for containing a direct reference to the Europeans. "The outer barbarians say," he wrote, "that of literature China has more than enough, of the art of war not sufficient."

labourers. To these some brigands of the mountain-frontier supplied rude military knowledge, while the leaders of the Triads brought as their share to the realization of what they would fain represent to be a great cause skill in intrigue and some habitude in organization. Neither enthusiasm nor the energy of desperation was wanting; but for those qualities which claim respect if they cannot command success we must look in vain.* Yet the peasants of Kwangsi and the artisans of Kwantung assumed the title of Wang or prince, and divided in anticipation the prizes that should follow the establishment of some dynasty of their own making.

The operations in the province of Kwangsi proved exceedingly monotonous. The Imperialists feared to come to blows, and the rebels adopted the most prudent tactics, shutting themselves up in entrenched camps, and only venturing out when the pressure of hunger compelled them to cut their way through the forces of the pusillanimous generals of Hienfung. The war thus dragged on in the Sikiang valley during two years, but the tide of success had certainly set in the main against the Imperialists, as was shown by the scene of operations being transferred to the northern side of that river.† The campaign might have continued indefinitely, until one side or the other was exhausted, had not the state of the province warned Tien Wang that he could not hope to be able to feed much longer the numerous followers who from one motive or another had attached themselves to his cause. He saw that there would very soon remain for him no choice except to retire into Tonquin, and to settle down into the

---

* In the confession or autobiography of Chung Wang (the Faithful King or Prince), translated by W. T. Lay, will be found statements fully bearing out this view. Even the trusted follower of Tien Wang was less enthusiastic in his belief than those who had seen in Hung-tsiuen the Chinese St. Paul.

† I am chiefly indebted to the manuscript history of the Taeping rebellion, generously lent to me by the late General C. G. Gordon, for these facts; and I have followed in the main its description of the rise and progress of the rebellion. It does not appear that General Gordon actually wrote this history, but he caused some one to prepare it during the campaign. He told me, however, that I might trust its accuracy.

ignominious life of a border brigand. Nothing can be more irksome to the man who has attained a certain notoriety, and who hopes to acquire a still higher fame, than to be suddenly consigned to a position of inferiority and self-effacement. To Tien Wang the thought was intolerable.

In sheer despair he came to the resolve to march northwards into the interior of China. The idea was suggested by the difficult plight to which he had been brought for the simplest and most necessary supplies for his army. He could not sustain himself in Kwangsi; and the skill of Wurantai, added to the large military contingent and pecuniary resources of Canton, did not make an invasion of Kwantung appear a very hopeful enterprise. It was not the inspiration of genius, but the pressure of dire need, that urged the Taeping leader * to issue his order for the invasion of Hoonan. At this point of his career he published a royal proclamation announcing that he had received "the Divine Commission to exterminate the Manchus, and to possess the Empire as its true Sovereign."

At this particular juncture the rebels were in the heart of Kwangsi at the district of Woosuen. In May, 1851, they moved to Siang, a district north of that place. They captured the villages and they ravaged the adjoining country, making no long stay anywhere. In August they were at Yungan, when 16,000 men were ranged under the banner of the Heavenly King, and for a moment Tien Wang may have thought of making a dash upon Canton. If he did entertain the thought, he promptly gave it up when he heard how well Wurantai was holding his ground at Wuchow on the Sikiang. It was at Yungan, where he remained until April, 1852, that

---

* Henceforth we shall speak of the rebels as Taepings. Various meanings are given of this word. Some say its origin is taken from the small town of that name in the south-west of Kwangsi, where the insurrection began; others that it means "universal peace," and was the style assumed by the new dynasty. In seeming contradiction with this is the fact that some of the Taepings themselves repudiated all knowledge of the name. Like the term Panthays, which we are now told is devoid of meaning, it will not pass out of use, although its origin may remain a matter of some uncertainty. See Meadows's work and Dr. Williams's "Middle Kingdom."

the Taeping leader made his final dispositions and called in all his outlying detachments.*

At Yungan a circumstance occurred which first promised to strengthen the party of the Taepings and then to lead to its disruption. Tien Wang was joined there by five influential chiefs and many members of the Triads. For a time it seemed as if these allies would necessarily bring with them a great accession of popular strength; but whether they disapproved of Tien Wang's plans, or were offended by the arrogant bearing of the Wangs, who, but the other day little better than the dregs of the people, had suddenly assumed the yellow dress and insignia of Chinese royalty, the Triad leaders took a secret and hurried departure from his camp, and hastened to make their peace with the Imperialists. The principal of these members of the most formidable secret society in China, Chang Kwoliang by name, was given a military command of some importance.

In April, 1852, the Taeping army left its quarters at Yungan and marched direct on Kweiling, the principal city of the province, where it will be remembered that the Imperial Commissioners sent from Pekin had been long stationary. Tien Wang attacked them there at the end of April or the beginning of May; but he was repulsed with some slight loss. Afraid of breaking his force against the walls of so strong a place, he abandoned the attack and marched into Hoonan. Had the Imperial generals only been as energetic in offensive tactics as they had shown themselves to be in measures of defence, they might have harassed his rear, delayed his progress, and eventually brought him to a decisive engagement under many disadvantages. But the Imperial Commissioners at Kweiling did nothing, being apparently well satisfied with having rid themselves of the presence of such troublesome neighbours.

On 12th of June the Taepings attacked the small town of

* The names of his lieutenants were Fung Yun San, granted title of Nang Wang, or "Southern King"; Seaou Chow, his brother-in-law, Shih Wang, or "Western King"; Wei Ching, Pei Wang, or "Northern King"; Yang seu Tsing, Tung Wang, or "Eastern King"; and Shih Takai, E Wang, or "Assistant King." These titles will be frequently used as their holders are referred to.

Taou in Hoonan with better success. Some resistance was offered, as may be safely assumed from the death of Fung Yun San, or Nan Wang, the southern king, during the operations which led to its capture. This individual was the best educated and most literate of all the confederates. He had taken so prominent a part in the early organization of the party, that many thought that it was he who really promoted the insurrection, and gave it the more important character which it assumed. His death was a rude blow to the Taepings. Their confidence in themselves and their cause was equally shaken, but for them to have then turned back would only have been to fall into the hands of the Kweiling garrison, while to halt would allow the Imperialists to recover from the ill-timed hesitation which paralyzed their action. They, therefore, pressed on, and the month of August beheld the capture of the three towns of Kiaho, Ching, and Kweyang. Their next march was both long and forced. Overrunning the whole adjacent country, they appeared, early in the month of September, before the strong and important town of Changsha, situated on the river Seang, and only fifty miles south of the great lake Tungting.

At this town, the capital of Hoonan, some vigorous preparations had been made to withstand them. Not merely was the usual garrison stationed there, but it so happened that Tseng Kwofan, a man of great ability and some resolution, was residing near the town at the time. Tseng Kwofan had held several offices in the service, and as a member of the Hanlin enjoyed a high position and reputation; but he was absent from the capital on one of those frequent periods of retirement which the officials of China have to make on the occasion of the death of their near relations. When the tidings of the approach of the Taepings reached him, he threw himself with all the forces his influence or resources enabled him to collect into Changsha. At the same time he ordered the local militia to assemble as rapidly as possible in the neighbourhood, in order to harass the movements of the enemy. He called upon all those who had the means to show their duty to the state and sovereign by raising recruits, or by promising rewards to those volunteers who would serve in the army against the rebels. Had the example of Tseng Kwofan been followed generally, it is not too much to say that the Taepings would never have got to Nankin. As it was, he set the first example of true patriotism, and he had the immediate satisfaction of saving Changsha.

When the Taepings reached Changsha, they found the gates closed and the walls manned. They proceeded to lay siege to it, they cut off its supplies, and they threatened the garrison with extermination. They even attempted to carry it by storm on three separate occasions. During eighty days the siege went on, but the Taepings were then compelled to admit that they were as far from success as ever. They had suffered very considerable losses, including Shih Wang, or the western king; and although it was said, and believed perhaps too readily, that the Imperialist loss was greater, they could better afford it. To have remained much longer would have been to allow themselves to be hemmed in. Therefore the Taepings as suddenly quitted their positions as they had left those before Kweiling, and on the first day of December resumed that northward march which, if communications had only been better, must have been very soon ended by their destruction.

They succeeded in seizing a sufficient number of junks and boats to enable them to cross the Tungting lake, and when they gained the Yangtse river at Yochow they found that the Emperor's garrison had fled panic-stricken at their approach. At Yochow they had the satisfaction of acquiring the war material, including a large quantity of powder, of the great Chinese leader, Wou Sankwei, of the 17th century, and these weapons served them in good stead when they came to attack Hankow. Their movements were extremely rapid. From Yochow they hastened down the Yangtsekiang. The important city of Hankow surrendered without a blow. The not less important town of Wouchang, on the opposite or southern bank of the river, was then attacked, and carried by storm after the walls had been undermined. The third town of Hanyang, which completes this busy hive of two millions of persons in the province of Hupeh, had also yielded. Up to this point the success of the Taepings had been extremely doubtful. They had overrun a long strip of country, but the strong places had baffled them. They had lost several of their leaders, and more of their followers. Their advance had borne some resemblance to a flight. The soldiers of the new Heavenly Ruler were beginning to ask what was to be the reward of their labours, and where they were to repair their losses and recover from their weariness.

The capture of the wealthy towns of Wouchang and Hankow at once removed all these causes of doubt and discouragement. The Taepings were able to repay themselves for the losses of hardships they had undergone, and they saw in the rich prize in their power the surest proof that the enterprise which they had in hand was not likely to be unprofitable. During one month they remained at Hankow, not only collecting their spoil and a vast quantity of provisions in the numerous junks on the river, but also in organizing and subjecting to the oath of allegiance to Tien Wang the many thousand recruits who from all parts now hastened to join a leader whose cause and pretensions had received the ratification of success. But even now it was no part of their mission to stand still. The possibility of pursuit by Tseng Kwofan with the levies of Hoonan was never absent from their minds.

The Imperialist commanders were hampered by their want of authority and concord. Tseng had been joined by the ex-Triad chief Chang Kwoliang, but he had neither name nor authority outside Hoonan. He had performed his duty in his own province; he could only hope that his fellow-countrymen in other provinces would do theirs. Tseng and his colleagues re-established the Emperor's authority throughout Hoonan. Unfortunately the report of the success they had achieved blinded people to the danger nearer home, and the Taepings swept like an irresistible wave or torrent down the valley of the Yangtsekiang.

The capture of Kiukiang, a town situated on the river near the northern extremity of the lake Poyang, and of Ganking followed in quick succession; and on the 8th of March they sat down before Nankin, the old capital of the Mings. The siege went on until the 24th of the same month; but notwithstanding that there was a large Manchu force in the Tartar city, which might easily have been defended apart from the Chinese and much larger city, the resistance offered was singularly and unexpectedly faint-hearted. The Taepings succeeded in blowing in one of the gates, the townspeople fraternized with the assailants, and the very Manchus, who had looked so valiant in the face of Sir Hugh Gough's force, ten years before, now surrendered their lives and their honour after a mere show of resistance to a force which was nothing better than an armed rabble. The Manchu colony of Nankin, to the number of some four thousand families, had evidently fallen off from their high renown, and had lost the military courage and discipline which could alone enable them to maintain their position in China. Instead of dying at their posts, they threw themselves on the mercy of the national leader, imploring him for pity and for their lives when the gate was blown in by the Taeping soldiery. Their cowardice helped them not; of twenty thousand Manchus not one hundred escaped. The tale rests on irrefragable evidence. "We killed them all, to the infant in arms; we left not a root to sprout from; and the bodies of the slain we cast into the Yangtse."

The capture of Nankin and this sweeping massacre of the dominant race seemed to point the inevitable finger of fate at the Tatsing dynasty. It was no longer possible to regard Tien Wang and his miscellaneous gathering as an enemy beneath contempt. Without achieving any remarkable success, having indeed been defeated whenever they were opposed with the least resolution, the Taepings found themselves in possession of the second city in the Empire. With that city they had acquired the complete control of the navigation of the Yangtse, and had cut off a part of the communications between the north and the south. They definitely abandoned Hankow, and contented themselves with holding the country from Kiukiang to Nankin. But they continued their progress down the great river with the object of securing the passage of the Grand Canal, and on the 1st of April, 1853, they occupied Chinkiangfoo, where the principal battle had been fought in the war of 1842. Chinkiang is on the southern side of the Yangtse, and to this they resolved for the present to strictly confine themselves. Yangchow, on the northern side and some miles up the canal, was indeed occupied, but it was evacuated in a few days. It was stated that here they captured a long succession of batteries covering three miles and full of guns, not one of which had been fired upon them. Everywhere the garrisons fled without attempting resistance, or waiting to incur the implacable vengeance of the Taepings.

The rebels, even after these successes, seemed less dreadful to those in their rear, who had some reason to believe them not invincible, than they did to the garrisons in their front. Tseng Kwofan had gathered up his forces, and after some hesitation had entered the province of Kiangsi and advanced to attack the Taepings at Kiukiang. He made his attack, but fortune did not smile on his effort. He was repulsed with some loss, and compelled to draw off his defeated army, which he established in quarters at Kanchang, where he placed himself in communication with the authorities at Hangchow. Another Imperialist army, under General Heang Yung, had been moved forward from Kiangsu, and had taken up a position ten miles south of Nankin. So far as further action on the part of the Imperialists went, it was confined to observation, while urgent appeals for aid were repeatedly sent to the capital.

To that summons no heed could be paid in consequence of the peril which beset Pekin itself. By extraordinary rapidity, and by a rare combination of fortunate circumstances, the Taeping leader had transferred his operations from remote Kwangsi to the very centre of the country, and by seizing the great river and one outlet of the Grand Canal he had, figuratively speaking, cut the Empire into two parts. But it was obvious to him and his advisers that, their success being little short of miraculous, there was no certainty about its continuing, unless it could be followed up by some decisive victory over the Manchus in the capital itself. At a council of war held at Nankin it was decided to send a force against Pekin as soon as Nankin had been placed in a proper state to withstand a siege. In that portion of their task they succeeded admirably. The old fortifications were repaired, new ramparts and batteries were erected, and, above all, provisions were stored to enable them to hold out for, as it was said, six or eight years.*

In the month of May these defensive measures were sufficiently far advanced to justify the despatch of a considerable portion of the Taeping army on an offensive campaign against Pekin. At this time it was computed that the total number of the Taepings did not fall short of 80,000 trustworthy fighting men, and without the adjective the number does not appear excessive, while there were perhaps more than 100,000 Chinese pressed into their service as the hewers of wood and drawers of water. The lines of Nankin and the batteries along the Yangtse were the creation of the forced labour of the population which had not fled before the Taepings. On the 12th of May an army stated to consist of 200,000 men, but probably not half that number, crossed the Yangtse and marched northwards.

The movements of this body borrowed their rapidity from Tien Wang's first advance beyond Kweiling. They captured several places on the way, and overthrew more than one detachment; and on the 19th of June they appeared before Kaifong, the chief town of Honan, and once the capital of China. They had thus transferred their advanced posts in a few weeks from the Yangtse to the Hoangho. They attacked Kaifong, but were defeated with loss. Resuming their former tactics, they abandoned their attack on Kaifong, and hastened to cross the Yellow river. That they were able to do this without opposition says very little for the enterprise of the commandant of Kaifong. They then marched westwards against the important prefectural town of Hwaiking, where they met with a valiant and unexpected resistance. After a siege of two months they were compelled

* On the occupation of Nankin it was given the title of Heavenly Capital, and the city was consecrated. The Tung Wang, or "Eastern King," was made Minister of State, and strict laws were passed to maintain order and discipline. We shall see that the irregular levies chafed at these restrictions. The families of the non-combatant Chinese employed in the works were detained as hostages for the fidelity of the males.

to admit that they had been baffled for a second time, and that they must resort to some other plan.

Alarmed as to their position, which was rendered extremely precarious by the gradual recovery of the Imperial troops from their state of panic, the Taepings quitted their camp at Hwaiking, and marched westwards along the northern bank of the Yellow river as far as the small town of Yuenking; then they turned suddenly north to Pingyang, whence, reversing their line of march, they hastened eastwards towards the metropolitan province of Pechihli. The whole of the autumn of 1853 was taken up with these manœuvres; but having defeated a Manchu force at the Lin Limming pass, the Taepings appeared in Pechihli for the first time on the 30th of September. The object of their march was plain. Not only did they mystify the Emperor's generals as to their plan, for it was thought much more likely that the Taepings, repulsed at Hwaiking, were in search of an easy crossing over the Yellow river, or at the worst intended an attack on Singanfoo, than that they meditated a descent upon the capital. But the Taepings had yet another object to serve by this detour. They passed through an agricultural country which had been untouched by the operations of war, and as they avoided the main high road, it was as difficult to ascertain what their movements were as it was to pursue them.

Their march was unopposed. The few towns lying along this route were unfortified and without a garrison, The population was unwarlike, and the Taepings had only to overrun the country and to drain it of its resources. Having forced the Limming pass, the Taepings found no difficulty in occupying the towns on the south-west border of Pechihli. The defeat of the Manchu garrison in the pass that was considered almost impregnable gave the Taepings the prestige of victory, and the towns opened their gates one after the other. They crossed the Hootoo river on a bridge of boats which they constructed themselves, and then occupied the town of Shinchow. On the 21st of October they reached Tsing, not much more than twenty miles south of Tientsin, which, again, is only eighty miles from the capital; but beyond this point neither then nor at any other time did the rebels succeed in getting.

The forcing of the Limming pass produced great confusion at Pekin. It was no longer a question of suffering subjects and disturbed provinces; nor was the danger one only affecting the privileges of the Manchus as a ruling caste. The capital of the Empire, the very person of the Emperor, was in imminent peril of destruction at the hands of a foe sworn to exact a ruthless vengeance. The city was denuded of troops. The levies were hastily summoned from Mongolia in order to defend the line of the Peiho and the other approaches to the capital. Had the Taepings shown better generalship, there is no saying that they would not have captured the capital. Had they seized Chingting, and marched as rapidly through Powting and Tso as they had shown that they could march, they might have obtained a decisive success, for the Imperial preparations had been made in the scare and hurry of the moment to defend Tientsin and the line of the Peiho; and by the other advance all these arrangements would have been outflanked.

But the Taepings themselves were far from being in the best of spirits. Their march from the Yangtse had been remarkable for the great distance covered; it had also been remarkable for the absence of any striking success on the part of an army which was credited with carrying terror in its train and with holding the fate of the Empire in its hands. On the 28th of October they were attacked by the Tientsin militia, defeated, and compelled to retire into their camp, which they hastened to fortify, at Tsinghai and Tuhlow. Here they were invested by the Tartar troops under the great Mongol chief, Sankolinsin, who was soon reinforced by the Chinese troops from Honan, that had followed the march of the Taepings. From October, 1853, until March of the next year, they were shut up in this position; but the timidity or prudence of the Imperial commanders induced them to believe that the sure and safest course was to starve them out. And so it might have been had not Tien Wang, hearing of the dilemma of his army, sent another to relieve it. This second body marched direct through Shantung, and in March, 1854, succeeded in effecting a junction at the city of Lintsing, with the original force, which had already begun its retreat from Tsing.

The army under Sankolinsin had closely pursued them, and several keenly-contested encounters had taken place in the hundred miles between the two towns named. The Taepings had suffered very severe losses, but cheered by the sudden appearance of the new force they succeeded in carrying Lintsing by storm. At Lintsing the Taepings made a further stand, establishing their quarters there, and occupying several towns in the neighbourhood. But their successes were few and unimportant. They were vigilantly watched by the Imperial army, and, if they did not suffer any great defeat, the range of their activity was circumscribed. Gradually their numbers were thinned by disease as well as by the losses in constant action. The exact nature of their collapse cannot be accurately described, though it may be easily imagined. In March, 1855, they had finally abandoned all their possessions in Shantung, and the Imperial authorities could truthfully declare that the whole of the country north of the Yellow river was free of the presence of the Taepings. Long before that they ceased to be formidable; and it may confidently be declared that only a very small number of the two armies sent to effect the capture of Pekin ever returned to the head-quarters of the Heavenly leader at Nankin.

Having described the course of the principal offensive movement made by the Taeping forces up to the point when it terminated, two years after the occupation of Nankin, it is necessary to return and describe the other military operations which were directed by Tien Wang and his principal military officers. Encouraged by the repulse of Tseng Kwofan's attempt on Kiukiang as already described, the Taepings fitted out a naval expedition, and, crossing Lake Poyang, attacked the important city of Kanchang. The siege began in June, 1853, but their ill-directed efforts were all repulsed; and in September, after one defeat in the field, the Taepings embarked on their junks and hastily retreated to the Yangtse. But after the departure of the main body the whole of the northern portion of Kiangsi was constantly subjected to raids on the part of Taeping detachments, who levied black-mail in the region round Poyang and along the valley of the Kan.

They also spread themselves in a different direction over the plains of Hoonan, and up the valley of the Seang river, pillaging the villages and capturing all the towns with the exception of Changsha, where Tseng had left a strong garrison. They made their way, too, for some distance up the Great River itself. They failed in their attempt on Kingchow, where a Manchu force valiantly held its ground; but they succeeded in reaching Ichang, now a treaty port, but then only remarkable as denoting the entrance to those great gorges which defend the approaches to the magnificent province of Szchuen. Just as the Taeping movement exhausted its forces at Tsing in the north, so had it at a still earlier date reached on the west the limit of its influence at Ichang.

During these operations the Taepings recaptured the cities of Wouchang and Hankow at the close of a siege of eighty days; but after three months' occupation they were again abandoned. Once again the need of increasing the area of the region whence they drew their supplies compelled them to retake these important places. This last occupation occurred in the early part of the year 1855. Perhaps the most important event in connection with the former attack was that the Governor of the province was beheaded for failing to defend his charge—the first recognition of the fact that the situation was desperate, and that the officials must no longer evince apathy in their measures for the restoration of order. Without some act impressing upon the mandarins at large that the old day of robbing had passed away and must give place to one of decisive action, the great body of the Chinese service would even in the extreme hour of the crisis have continued to think only of making personal profit, without entering into any larger considerations of the danger to the State and of their duty to their sovereign.

The progress of the Taeping revolt had been watched by the European community with close attention, but with feelings of an opposite character. While the missionaries, whose influence was the greater and more obtrusive because they possessed the almost complete control of the literature dealing with China, were disposed to hail the Taepings as the regenerators of China and as the champions of Christianity; the merchants saw in them the disturbers of trade, and men who threatened to destroy the prosperity of the country, and with it eventually their own. While on the one hand confident declarations were made that the last hour of the Manchu dynasty had arrived, that the knell of fate had sounded for the descendants of Noorhachu, the murmurs on the other hand were not less emphatic that the Taepings had ruined trade, and that the only way to continue it under any equal conditions was by the cessation of the payment of the stipulated customs to the Chinese authorities. It is difficult to understand how the Shanghai merchants brought themselves to the frame of mind to think that the English Government could shape its action and suspend the provisions of the Treaty of Nankin in accordance with the condition of their ledgers. But Mr. Rutherford Alcock pointed out in emphatic language that he had no choice save to abide by the Treaty of Peace and to preserve a strict neutrality. It was much more difficult for either Mr. Alcock or the Vice-Consul, Mr. Thomas Wade, to check the impulsive tendencies of those who believed in the mission of the Taepings, and who as strongly disbelieved in the vigour and resources of the Manchus. The armoury of criticism has not yet forged the weapon that shall pierce the self-sufficiency of prophets, who are little amenable to facts.

With the occupation of Nankin by Tien Wang it was thought necessary to acquaint the Taepings with the position which the English Government wished to occupy during the progress of the struggle. That position was to be one of strict neutrality coupled with the proviso that the Taepings were to observe, or at all events not to violate, the principal stipulations of the Treaty of Nankin. It is impossible to doubt that there must have been a strong feeling of curiosity at work when Sir George Bonham himself proceeded to Nankin in order to acquaint the Taepings with the existence of the English and of what they expected to be done. Several of the more experienced English officials were extremely sceptical of the good faith of the Taepings, and of their chances of permanent success; but Sir George Bonham was not equally cautious. By going out of his way to hold relations of a formal character with Tien Wang, he proclaimed that he as the representative of the English Government recognized in him something more than an insurgent leader, while the people of the great ports saw in the action of the English Government further reason to believe that Tien Wang was destined to be a great national monarch. The visit of Sir George Bonham to Nankin was not intended to be so, but it was none the less a distinctly unfriendly act to the Government of Pekin.

The decision of Sir George Bonham to proceed to Nankin was hastened by the fact that Wou the Taotai of Shanghai, an energetic official who had been a merchant at Canton and who had purchased his way to power, was endeavouring to obtain assistance from the foreign Governments at the same time that he spread abroad the report that they were anxious and prepared to support the cause of the Imperialists. He purchased several European vessels, and he sent in a request for the loan of an English warship then at Shanghai. The response to this application was not only the verbal reply that the English intended to remain neutral, but the open deed, as we have said, that the English representative hastened to Nankin to acquaint the rebel leaders with the fact.

In April, 1853, Sir George Bonham left for Nankin in the war-steamer *Hermes*. Mr. Interpreter Meadows had been previously sent to collect information about the rebels; but navigation by the canal being found impossible, he returned to Shanghai without having established any relations with the Taepings. The *Hermes* was fired upon by the batteries at Chinkiang and Kwachow; but as she did not return the fire, she succeeded in running the gauntlet and making her way without any damage or accident to Nankin. The Taepings subsequently explained that they had only fired upon the *Hermes* because they believed her to be the advance-guard of Wou's squadron. On the 27th of April the *Hermes* anchored off Nankin, and Mr. Meadows proceeded on shore to hold an interview with the Northern King, or Pei Wang. The *Hermes* remained nearly a week off the city, during which there were daily interviews and active correspondence between the English authorities and the Taepings. It is impossible to peruse these documents without feeling that the proselytizing spirit had obtained the mastery of our diplomacy, and that the Taeping leaders were fully as good adepts in the art of asserting the supreme pretensions of China as any doctor of the Hanlin. If there is any who thinks that the exclusiveness of Chinese policy is due to Manchu fear or arrogance, he will be speedily undeceived on reference to the grandiloquent proclamations of the Taeping leaders and of Pei Wang in particular.* The *Hermes* left Nankin on the 2nd of May, returning from an unwise and unnecessary expedition; but from the beginning of international relations the most difficult of all policies to follow has been that of doing nothing and of waiting upon the course of events.

Whilst these events had been happening the causes of disintegration, which must always produce the break-up of such a confederacy of lawless and unscrupulous men as formed the Taeping party, were already beginning to reveal themselves. The Tien Wang himself, after the capture of Nankin, retired into the interior of his palace and was never again seen in public. It was given out that he was constantly engaged in writing books, but the truth was that he had abandoned himself to the indulgences of the harem. He had chosen thirty of the women who had accompanied him from Kwangsi, and of those who had fallen to his spoil as a conqueror, to be his wives; but not content with this arrangement, he only allowed females to attend upon his august person. As the necessary consequence Tien Wang lost his

---

* One passage may be quoted as illustrating the rest. "Since you English have not held distances too far, but have come to acknowledge allegiance here, not only are the armies of our Heavenly Dynasty in great delight and joy, but in the high Heavens even the Heavenly Father will also regard with pleasure this evidence of your loyalty (more correctly subjection) and sincerity."

hold upon his followers; and his suspicions grew to such a height, that he exerted all the privileges of tyranny in its most savage form.

The failings of Tien Wang seemed to provide the more ambitious of his lieutenants with the opportunity of superseding him in the principal place of power. Of these none was possessed with a higher idea of his own dignity and importance than Tung Wang, the Eastern King, who had been raised to the office of Principal Minister of State. Tung Wang thought that the best way to procure the execution of his wishes was to give utterance to them whilst under a trance, during which he pretended to have communion with the Heavenly Father. In this manner he succeeded in getting rid of a large number of rivals by denouncing them as the objects of the Celestial wrath, and he seemed to be disposed to carry on this method of proceeding until he had freed himself from the presence of all likely to interfere with the realization of his ambitious plans. But either his scheme was revealed prematurely, or Tien Wang was personally threatened during the imprecations of his subordinate. The story went that during one of these trances Tung Wang summoned Tien Wang from his palace, publicly reproved him, and ordered him to receive forty blows.

Although their obedience to religious regulations was too strict to admit of any open opposition to the transmitted commands of the Heavenly Father, temporal sovereigns always submitting with a bad grace to personal chastisement even when it has the appearance of Celestial sanction, Tien Wang treasured up a grievance against his Minister both for the rebuke and for the personal injury thus publicly administered. Tien Wang was so fully employed in his own domestic matters, that he might have remained unwilling to bring his dispute with the Tung Wang to an open decision; but the same consideration did not restrain the other Wangs, who thought they had had as large a share in the Taeping success as Tung Wang, and who consequently resented his arrogance and assumption of superiority. The Northern King and the Assistant King with others of the original leaders of the revolt plotted together, and they came to the decision that the only way to get rid of their dreaded colleague was, notwithstanding his Heavenly conferences, to assassinate him.

The progress of this plot was arrested by the development of military events; for the Imperialists, long inactive, were on the point of resuming their attack on the Taeping positions at the very moment that the rivalry between the Wangs was beginning to prove dangerous to the concord of the rebels. Two Imperialist armies had with much difficulty been collected for the purpose of watching the movement of the Taepings both at Chinkiang and at Nankin. The former was closely invested by a Manchu general named Chi, and being in great danger, Tung Wang determined to send a force to its relief, although Nankin itself was vigilantly watched by another army of about 40,000 men under the joint command of Hochun and Chang Kwoliang. The conduct of this operation was entrusted to a young officer named Li, who had attracted Tung Wang's favourable notice by his energy, and who is best known by his later name of Chung Wang, or the Faithful King. The manner in which he conducted the operation amply justified his selection for the duty. He arranged with the ex-Triad leader Lotakang to make a sortie at the same time as he attacked the lines of the Imperialists. The result was a complete victory. Sixteen stockades were carried, General Chi's force was driven off, that general committed suicide, and the pressure on the Chinkiang garrison was relieved.

But this success was only half the victory, for the Imperialists closed in on the Taepings, and barred the return road to Nankin. At the same time the army under Hochun drew closer to the walls of that city. An express order was sent off to Li, ordering him to hasten back without delay. He endeavoured to make his way along the northern bank, but was checked at Loohoo by Chang Kwoliang, who had crossed the river. Not to be outdone in this kind of manœuvring, the future Chung Wang also hastened back to the southern side of the river, and defeated the weakened Imperialists there. He inflicted a second defeat on Chang Kwoliang in person, and thus cleared for himself a road back to Nankin. He was then ordered to attack and drive away the main Chinese army from before Nankin, at the head of which the Emperor's chief general, Heang Yung, had by this time placed himself. The orders of Tung Wang were so peremptory that there was no choice except to obey, for he even went so far as to say that his victorious lieutenant should not be admitted into the city until he had driven away the enemy. The Taeping leader met with more success than he believed possible with his wearied troops. He expelled the Tartars from their entrenchments, and compelled them to retire into Tanyang, where they successfully resisted all his further efforts. But Heang Yung took his reverse so deeply to heart that he would not survive his disgrace, and accordingly he committed suicide by strangling himself. Thus the Emperor not merely lost several battles, but also the services of two men who, whatever their faults, had shown that they were possessed of physical courage.

The greatness of this Taeping success carried, it seemed, its own punishment. The death of Heang Yung excited the fury of Chang Kwoliang, who had regarded him with the warmest affection. He inspired his troops with his own rage and led them out to attack the Taepings. It was now the turn of the latter to give way. Most of the positions lost were regained, and, on the admission of the Taeping leader himself, six or seven hundred of his best men, together with a brave leader named Chow, were killed. This victory fully compensated for the late discomfiture; but it was exceedingly unfortunate for Hienfung's cause that, at the very moment when the inevitable disintegration of the rebels was first beginning to be apparent, his arms should have sustained such reverses, and his commanders been compelled to abandon their advantageous positions outside Nankin. Had Heang Yung remained in undisturbed possession of the Yashua gate, which he had seized during the absence of Chung Wang, and which was regained by that officer, he would have been able to have asserted the Imperial authority during the confusion caused by the plots and counterplots which have now to be narrated.

Pei Wang personally assumed the conduct of the plot hatched for the destruction of the Eastern King. With his followers he attacked Tung Wang in the presence of Tien

Wang, and slew him and his three brothers with his own hands. Not content with this success, or perhaps carried away by the impulse of slaughter, Pei Wang massacred every man, woman, and child, to the number of 20,000, who had had the least connection with the person or fortunes of the deceased leader. And then with the distrust bred of criminal purpose he turned upon his confederate, the E Wang. That prince succeeded in escaping, but he had to leave his family and belongings at the mercy of his pursuer, who wreaked his vengeance with all the fury of baffled spite and fear. Pei Wang's excesses disgusted even the lenient Nankin populace; and he too fell by the assassin's knife. Of the five leaders who had originally assisted Tien Wang in promoting the Taeping rebellion, one alone was left, Yi Wang, the Assistant King; and the intrigues of Nankin became so distasteful to him, that he devoted himself to the prosecution of operations in other parts of the Empire.

Considering the large unsettled element in all the seaport towns, it was inevitable that the Taepings should find many imitators. Their appeal to Chinese patriotism and race feeling was far less effectual than the incentive which their success offered to those who had no regular mode of living, and who were habitual law-breakers. Amoy, Canton, Foochow, and Shanghai were in turn the scene of disturbances and active rebellion, which, if not the absolute work of the Taepings, would certainly not have happened but for the encouragement of their example. For their example had in a double sense tended to these outbreaks. While it had emboldened the turbulent, it had also spread a feeling of panic among those who were the natural supporters of the law.

The instinct of self-preservation warned the foreign residents that it behoved them to take timely measures for the protection of their lives and property. As early as April, 1853, Mr. Rutherford Alcock had convened a meeting for the purpose of devising a plan of defence at Shanghai, which, from being the nearest treaty port to the scene of the Taeping operations, was supposed to stand in the greatest danger. The principal decision arrived at was that the British residents were to form themselves into a volunteer corps; and Captain Tronson, an officer who had seen service in the Bengal Fusiliers, undertook to drill the small force, and to superintend the measures for holding the settlement if attacked. Captain Fishbourne, the senior naval officer in charge of the war-ships at the station, assumed the supreme command and direction of these military preparations. At a subsequent meeting the other foreigners agreed to combine with the English Consul and community, and thus the whole of the foreign settlement at Shanghai presented a united front to whatever danger might betide from either the weakness of the Imperialists or the hostility of the insurgents.*

The first symptom of popular excitement on the sea-coast was manifested at Amoy, where there had been a disturbed feeling for some time. In May, 1853, a strong body of the lower orders, incited, as it was believed, by the members of the Triad society, rose under the command of one Magay, who styled himself an admiral, but who had gained all his experience of war and seamanship from serving the English garrison at Kulangsu with spirits, and from a brief cruise with a renegade Neapolitan in a lorcha. The rebels, or, more correctly, the marauders, remained in possession of the town until the following November, when the Imperial forces, having collected from the neighbouring garrisons, appeared in such overwhelming strength that the insurgents hastily put off to sea, and many of them succeeded in escaping to Singapore or Formosa. Magay was among those who fled, but he was accidentally shot whilst off Macao. The assertion of the Emperor's authority at Amoy was unfortunately followed by terrible scenes of official cruelty and bloodthirstiness. The guilty had escaped, but Hienfung's officials

* Even the missionaries were not blind at last to the personal danger from the Taepings. Dr. Medhurst, in a report which puts forward prominently their alleged virtues and laudable objects, wrote that "foreigners should be prepared to resist with a sufficient force any attack which the insurgents may be induced to make on them." He had said in an earlier passage, "It would be sad to see Christian nations engage in putting down the movement, as the insurgents possess an energy and a tendency to improvement and general reform which the Imperialists never have exhibited and never can be expected to display."—Parliamentary Papers for 1853.

wreaked their rage on the helpless and unoffending townspeople. Thousands of both sexes were slaughtered in cold blood, and on more than one occasion English officers and seamen interfered to protect the weak, and to arrest the progress of an undiscriminating and insensate massacre.

Mr. Alcock's precautions at Shanghai had not been taken a day too soon; for of all the subsidiary rebellions, none attained such a dangerous height or endured so long as that which broke out there in the month of September, 1853. There had been mutterings of coming trouble for some time, and the Taotai Wou had implored the English authorities to announce their intention to co-operate with him in maintaining order in the great Chinese city under his charge. Had Mr. Alcock been at liberty to give this promise there would have been no disturbance at Shanghai; but he was not free to even so much as consider the possibility of such a breach of the strict neutrality to which his Government had pledged itself. The disaffected were restrained for a time by a doubt as to the part which the Europeans intended to play, for as a matter of course Wou had confidently declared that they were on the side of the Government; but as soon as they saw that their neutrality was assured, and it was shown as clearly by the preparations to defend only the settlement, and not the whole of the town, as by the protestations of the English Consul, the last barrier to their breaking out was removed.

The rising at Shanghai was the work of the Triads. They seized the Taotai's quarters without resistance, as Wou's body-guard deserted him, and that official barely escaped with his life. Other officials, not so fortunate, were slain by the rebels, but on the whole the seizure of Shanghai was accomplished with little bloodshed. The rebels numbered about fifteen hundred Triads, who were joined by two or three thousand of the townspeople. On the 7th of September, 1853, Shanghai had passed out of the hands of the Imperial Government into those of an independent and lawless body of men who lived upon the plunder of the city. The foreign settlement was placed in a state of siege. The broadsides of the men-of-war covered the approaches to the factories, and Captain Tronson's volunteers diligently patrolled the quarters of the European residents.

This state of affairs continued up to and after the arrival of an Imperialist force sent to recover the city. While the batteries were constructed at a very short distance from the walls, and the bombardment went on all day, the foreign merchants were the spectators of a siege which of its kind was unsurpassed in absurdity. Never were ignorance of the military art and the possession of that discreet valour in which Sir John Falstaff excelled, more conspicuously revealed. And yet some evidence of a possible higher skill was afforded, and a few acts of valour might have been recorded. The Imperialists carried their mines to the wall and under the deep moat surrounding the town; and a body of Cantonese braves stormed the breach in gallant style. But the former was a slow and costly proceeding; and in the latter act the courage of the handful of brave men was thrown uselessly away by the treachery or the folly of their more craven comrades who removed the bridge by which they had crossed the moat. The siege dragged its slow length along. The Imperialists were unable to direct with any skill their superior resources and numbers; and the insurgents made up by their vigilance and desperation for their natural deficiencies and inferiority.

It soon became obvious to the representatives of the Foreign States that the rebels at Shanghai were not fighting for any definite purpose; and that being the case, it was clear that in the interests of everybody the sooner the Imperial authorities were reinstated the better it would be for all. While the influence of several English residents was exerted to induce the rebels to surrender by throwing themselves on the consideration of the European Consulates, that of the French admiral was more openly asserted with a view to ensuring the military triumph of the Imperialists. The French settlement, which consisted of the consulate, one house, and a cathedral, was nearest the walls. There was no great difficulty, under the circumstances, in showing that it stood in danger from the bombardment; and in December, 1854, Admiral Laguerre, impatient at the prolongation of a siege which gave no indication of closing, availed himself of

FRENCH ACTION.

the excuse afforded by several shots passing over or near the French position to turn his broadsides on the city. The rebels were, therefore, cannonaded on one side by the French and on the other by the Imperialists, who were naturally elated at having obtained that foreign assistance which they had previously entreated so often and without avail.

The Shanghai insurgents, to do them justice, presented a bold front to this accumulation of dangers. The bombardment did much damage to the walls, but inflicted hardly any loss on the garrison, which kept well under the cover of an inner earthwork. While the other Europeans were pitying them for their useless devotion and fortitude, the Triad leaders were making their preparations to defend the city against assault, and their followers were eagerly asking the question when the French intended to come on. They were not merely boasters. A breach was at last declared to be practicable, and 400 French sailors and marines were landed. On their side the Imperialists, wearing blue sashes to distinguish them from the rebels, advanced in serried bodies to attack the north gate. The French made their way through the breach, the Celestial soldiers over the walls at another point. But although they gained the inside of the fortification, they could not advance. The insurgents fought desperately in the streets, and after four hours' fighting they compelled the Imperialists to take to flight. The French were carried along by their disheartened allies, who even fired upon them, and when Admiral Laguerre counted up the cost of that day's adventure he found that he had lost four officers and sixty men killed and wounded. Such was the French attack on Shanghai, and it left the lesson that even good European troops cannot ignore the recognized rules and precautions of war, and that a number of desperate men may sometimes be more than a match for the picked soldiers of a great Power.

After this the siege languished. The French abstained from any further direct participation in it, but the Imperialists pressed the attack with greater vigour than before. At last the insurgents, having failed in some attempts to surrender on terms, made a desperate sortie. Some cut their way through, and a few found safety in the foreign settlement, but by far the greater number perished by the sword of the Imperialists. The fugitives were pursued along the country roads, and in a few days more than fifteen hundred rebels had fallen by the knife of the executioner. The two leaders, Lew and Chin-ah-Lin, escaped, strange to say, for the large price of £3000 was placed upon each of their heads. The latter turned up at a later period at Hongkong, where he offered assistance against Commissioner Yeh; but on his offer being refused he left for Siam, where he acquired in worldly prosperity the position he had failed to gain as a political personage at Shanghai. At Shanghai as at Amoy the Imperialists sullied victory by their excesses; and the unfortunate townspeople, impoverished by supplying the rebels with their wants during more than a year and a half, were reduced to the brink of ruin by their belongings being given over to the Emperor's soldiers to pillage. These painful occurrences, over which we hasten to pass as briefly as we may, should serve as a warning to those who have so lightly encouraged rebellion in a country constituted like China for the sake of trade advantages and the propagation of Christianity; for however much we may identify those objects with the name of civilization, the cost has had to be paid by the Chinese people in suffering which would surpass all powers of description.

What had happened at Amoy and Shanghai had occurred on a somewhat different scale near Canton, where in June, 1854, the Triads, who it must be remembered were strongest of all in the province of Kwantung, seized the manufacturing town of Fatshan, and from that place threatened to oust the Viceroy from Canton itself. They approached the city walls on several occasions, and as they numbered some twenty or thirty thousand men, it may even be said that they held Canton in siege. But the merchants and shopkeepers of Canton had too much at stake to remain apathetic in face of a danger that threatened their lives and property. They took braves into their pay who made most efficient soldiers, and gradually their numbers increased so much that the city walls were well and efficiently guarded. There was

WHOLESALE EXECUTIONS.

much skirmishing in the neighbourhood of the city, but not of a serious character. The rebels remained in possession of Fatshan long after all danger from them to Canton itself had disappeared; and when one of their chiefs, named Ho Aluk, who had assumed the title of the Avenger of Sorrow, was defeated near Whampoa, the movement gradually lost its importance and the rebels retreated into either Kwangsi or Hoonan. The recovery of authority by the Imperialists was completed by the month of February, 1855; and it was marked by wholesale executions which went on during several months later. One hundred thousand men, most of whom had never taken up arms at all, were credibly reported to have suffered under the sword of the executioner. Governor Yeh is best known in England from his subsequent opposition to this country; but it should be recorded and remembered that it was he who instigated these barbarous holocausts of an unoffending, or, at the worst, of a deluded population.

We have now passed in review the events which marked the beginning and growth of the Taeping Rebellion from the time of its being a local rising in the southern province of Kwangsi to the hour when its chief was installed as a ruling prince in the ancient city of Nankin. The success was more striking than thorough. The Taepings had gained some victories; they had incurred almost as many defeats. They had captured the towns on the Yangtse; every other walled city had repulsed and defied them. They had sent two armies to the north, their standards had been flaunted within a hundred miles of the capital; but of those armies a mere fragment ever regained the main body. They had proclaimed their chief King not merely of China, but of the Earth, under a Celestial mandate; and the reputed sanctity of their mission, the proclaimed purity of their purpose, had not availed to keep out the dissension of worldly objects and individual ambition. Prince had murdered prince; the streets of Nankin had been flooded with the blood of thousands of their followers. The presence of a common peril could not avail to preserve union and fellow-devotion among a band of uneducated and unprincipled adventurers drawn from the lowest orders of the people, and from the most profligate temples and monasteries of the Buddhist religion.

The evil example of futile rebellion had been followed by those who had nothing to lose in the great sea-ports and places of trade. For that hour the teaching of the Triad Society, active since the beginning of the century, and drawing to itself the association of the once popular Waterlily sect, had long been preparing the way. When the successes of the Taepings showed that the authorities could be defeated, and when the charm of the Emperor's majesty, already undermined by a disastrous foreign war, was fully dissipated, it was no longer reasonable to hope that the lawless and disaffected would not make their effort to share in the plunder of the rich; to have held back would to their minds have only been to lose their share of the spoil. Therefore, there were the risings that have been described, having the one grand object of the Taepings, and the only one that they attained, viz. that their wealthier countrymen formed a fit object of plunder. We have seen how painfully slow was the reassertion of Imperial authority in the case of the rioters in or near the Treaty Ports; it could not but prove still more protracted over the bolder and more numerous Taepings. But the events at Amoy, Shanghai, and Canton helped to strip the Taeping movement of its delusive character as being an aid to Christianity; although the barbarous cruelty of some of the Imperial officers unfortunately stifled the sympathy that was beginning to rise towards their cause among Europeans.

CHAPTER XI.

COMPLICATIONS WITH ENGLAND.

THE home difficulties of the Chinese Government could not avert the perils that necessarily accrued from the many unsettled points in connection with the foreign intercourse. The Pekin authorities still disdained to hold any direct communication with the European Powers. The Canton viceroy was deputed both to control the trade at Canton and to direct such official intercourse as could not be avoided with the Chief Superintendent at Hongkong. His voice decided all questions at the other Treaty Ports with the exception of Shanghai, where the Intendant of the Susungtai district was invested with plenary powers. But even at Canton the English representative was not admitted within the city walls. Such interviews as were granted and were in themselves unavoidable were held at some spot outside the limits of the city of Canton, which was matter of arrangement on each occasion. When it is remembered that as far back as the year 1840 it had been laid down as absolutely necessary to the harmony of relations between the two peoples that there should be some channel of direct communication with the Pekin Government, and that in the year of Hienfung's accession to the throne the matter had not advanced in any appreciable degree towards solution, it will be difficult to maintain that the question was in a satisfactory condition, or that there was any better guarantee for the continuation of peace than the forbearance of the Europeans, disappointed in their expectations by the results of the last war and exasperated by the persistent finesse and ever-ready literary skill of the mandarins to thwart their views, and to continually remind them that in the eyes of their great and all-powerful sovereign these matters of trade and of diplomatic intercourse were not worthy of a moment's consideration.

There were many reasons for objecting to an arrangement which prevented England and the other chief States of Europe from being diplomatically represented at the Chinese capital besides the fact that it argued a position of inferiority. In the interests of China herself it was matter of regret that the Emperor and his responsible advisers should have no real knowledge of the wishes, power, and intentions of the great trading nations of the West. Had there been greater knowledge there must have been fewer mistakes, and many unpleasant passages in Anglo-Chinese history would not have had to be written. For not only were Hienfung and his ministers, when neither Keying nor Keshen succeeded in finding the way to their master's favour, completely ignorant of the character and capacity of Europeans, but they were dependent for their information upon men who had every motive to conceal the truth and to report what was most flattering to themselves. The Viceroy at Canton, so long as he avoided an absolute rupture, might pursue the most dictatorial course he pleased; the more dictatorial it was, the greater emphasis with which he dwelt on the inferiority of the outer barbarians, the nearer would it accord with the traditional claims of the Chinese ruler. There was grave danger in such an arrangement, no matter who the Viceroy might be, but it became perceptibly greater when the wielder of that authority happened to be a zealot such as Lin, a truculent minister like Su, or a boaster as in the case of Yeh.

The coming difficulty had been long foreseen. From the first there had been a want of cordiality on the part of the Chinese officials that augured ill for either the harmony or the durability of the relations. In 1848 Mr. Bonham's proposition that the Viceroy should place some of his subordinates in communication with the secretaries at Hongkong had been curtly declined. It was followed in a few months by the shelving of the question of opening the gates of Canton; and to postpone the settlement of a question with the Chinese has been shown over and over again to mean its abandonment, or at least the resumption of the discussion at the very beginning. The English Government in 1849, out of consideration for the strong statement of the Chinese authorities that they were unable to restrain the turbulent Cantonese, had consented to put off the execution of Keying's agreement until a more favourable opportunity. The Chinese officials placed but one interpretation on this proceeding, and that was that the right had been finally waived and withdrawn.*

The position of the English Government on the question was diametrically opposed to that taken up by the Canton Yamen. With the former the question of the right entrance into Canton was only in abeyance until the favourable moment arrived to enforce it, and Lord Palmerston laid down this view very clearly in his despatches to the Governor of Hongkong. But if it was a question of right, it was also

---

* Viceroy Su completely ignored the whole affair of Keying's promise even in 1848: "As to entrance into the city—Since the various nations have traded in Canton, none of the officers or merchants of their respective countries had ever any business requiring their going into the city. When our Government concluded a Treaty of Peace with your honourable nation, no entrance into the city was stipulated. Natives and foreigners lived previously peacefully together, and the commerce was in a flourishing condition. When, however, the entrance into the city became subsequently a subject of discussion, all the inhabitants entertained fears and suspicion; the merchants were, on this account, hampered, and their trade gradually dwindled away. The late Imperial Commissioner Keying, therefore, ordered some deputed officers and the local authorities to take proper steps for quieting the populace, and fortunately no disturbance ensued. If we now again enter upon the previous consultations about it, the public will, as before, feel fear and annoyance, goods will become unsaleable, and very great obstacles accrue to the trade. The British merchants have traversed a wide ocean, and should they have come here in order to enter the city? The entrance into the city is moreover in reality injurious, and no way advantageous to English merchants. Why should, then, by the useless entrance into the city, the commerce, their original object, be lost?"—China Papers, 1857, p. 150. It will be observed that in this document there is not a single word of reference to the pledge given by Keying that the gates should be opened in April, 1849.

one in hardly a less degree of convenience. And it was admitted that, although there was no doubt as to the concession having been made by the Chinese Government, it remained a matter of questionable policy whether it was advisable to insist on the compliance with a diplomatic stipulation if it was clear that compliance could only be secured by resorting to violence and at the cost of constant friction. The question had to be discussed, therefore, not so much on its merits as with regard to its practical consequences,* for already it was becoming clear that to yield to the Chinese on one point meant to set a precedent of concession that could not fail to be very inconvenient and in the end attended with many dangers.

No other conclusion can be drawn from the despatches of Lord Palmerston and Sir George Bonham than that they were both most anxious to avoid all occasion of serious disagreement with China. In the interest of peace itself they were desirous to obtain the fulfilment of the pledges made by the responsible Chinese officials, and they never failed to realize that the objections of the Canton Viceroy to execute

* Mr. Bonham wrote as follows to Lord Palmerston on October 23rd, 1848: "If the gates of Canton can only be opened by the force of arms, the consequences of such a step become a matter for deep consideration. I am thoroughly persuaded that the populace and the 'braves' of the adjacent country will join heartily in resisting our approach, and the result will be that we should require a very respectable force to gain our point, for the opposition will be infinitely greater than it was in 1841, when the troops and mandarins were in the first instance its only defenders. A military operation of this nature would, under the most favourable circumstances, not only for a time put a stop to all trade, but it would furthermore require a very long period to elapse before confidence would be restored. This would cause much loss to the native as well as to our own merchants, and operate most detrimentally on our revenues at home." Lord Palmerston stated in reply to this letter that the entrance into Canton was "a privilege which we have indeed a right to demand, but which we could scarcely enjoy with security or advantage if we were to succeed in enforcing it by arms. It may be true that the Chinese might be encouraged, by their success in evading compliance with their engagements in this matter, to attempt to violate other engagements; but this consideration does not seem to me to be sufficient to determine Her Majesty's Government to put the issue of peace and war upon this particular point."

what he was bound to perform, arose from a dislike to the whole transaction, and not from inability to coerce the populace and to afford protection to foreigners. In his dilemma Su had appealed to the Emperor himself, and the Imperial Council presided over by Muchangah had sent him but cold words of comfort, if he thought that there was only fear at the capital of admitting the foreigners into a provincial city. At that price the Emperor and his ministers would have been very glad to have got rid of the foreign question once and for all. When the central administration and the highest executive in the realm stated that it was a matter of right, and beyond that, moreover, one of comparative unimportance, that the barbarians should insist on the privilege, conceded by Keying, of entering the city of Canton, it can no longer be contended that either the English Cabinet or the Chief Superintendent of Trade in China was mistaken in maintaining that only a little firmness was needed to carry the point. A mistaken consideration of the difficulties of the Chinese led to the postponement of the enforcement of a right ceded in the most formal manner, and, so far as official intercourse was concerned, one that was absolutely necessary to tranquillity.*

The consideration of these early disputes is not to be avoided if the true meaning of the grave difficulties which broke out, shortly after Hienfung's accession, between his officers and the representatives of the English Government,

* The decision of the Chinese Council was conveyed in a remarkable State paper, which should alone suffice to preserve the name of Muchangah from oblivion. In it he said: "It may be said that these barbarians are of an insatiable nature, and that after being admitted into the city they will again give rise to disturbance and cause the commencement of hostilities. But you do not consider that the outside of the city is the same as the inside of the city. If they may give rise to disturbance inside the city, may they not also give rise to disturbance outside the city? . . . We therefore conclude that the repugnance to this proceeds from the ignorant populace, which relies on mere animal courage, and is deluded by false reports. . . . We now look up to your Sacred Majesty to issue orders to the Governor of that province to persuade and guide the people, and impress upon them the great principles of justice. Let them not act wantonly, and cause war upon our frontiers."—Blue Book, pp. 177-78.

is to be mastered. Those disputes did not arise out of any single occurrence, but entirely from a chain of events, of antagonistic views and of opposite readings of accepted obligations, which followed the refusal in 1849 of the Viceroy Su to carry out the promise of Keying to open the gates of Canton. The populace were noisy in their expression of the resolve to make no surrender, and the policy of the English Government was never expressed in that emphatic language which foreshadowed the employment of force. The Chinese were very shrewd in detecting that the hands of the English Superintendent of Trade were tied, and the tokens of success already rested with them when the accession of Hienfung strengthened the influence of those whose sympathies were adverse to Europeans. The long delay in enforcing the right, and the appearance of a new and less pacifically disposed sovereign on the throne, put an end to all hopes of obtaining the surrender of the principal stipulation with Keying * in 1847, of course unless force was to be employed.

The question had progressed in this manner when in 1852 Sir George Bonham returned to Europe on leave, and was temporarily succeeded by Dr. John Bowring, who had officiated for a short period as Consul at Canton. In his first instructions received from Lord Granville, at that moment beginning a very long career at the Foreign Office, he was informed that it was "the anxious desire of Her Majesty's Government to avoid all irritating discussions with that of China." The new representative of the English Government in that country, who was regarded as no more than a temporary official, was also directed to avoid pushing arguments on doubtful points in a manner to fetter the free action of his Government, but he was at the same time to recollect that it was his duty to carefully watch over and insist upon the performance by the Chinese authorities of their engagements. It will be admitted that the proper

* It may be interesting to state that Keying, applied to by Su for his advice, had replied that the opinion of the people was greatly to be considered, but that the will of the Emperor overruled all. He was careful to point out that what he had done had been sanctioned by a special Edict of the Vermilion Pencil.

fulfilment of the latter necessarily involved some infringement of the former recommendation; and while the paramount consideration with the Government in London was to keep things quiet, it was inevitable that the agent on the spot should think a great deal, if not mostly, of how best to obtain compliance to the fullest extent with the pledges given in the treaty and subsequent conventions. The emphatic manner in which the Foreign Office impressed on the acting Governor the necessity of abstaining from all decisive measures in his dealings with the Chinese was partly explained by his being a new man, and one moreover who might naturally be thought not to possess the same perfect agreement with official views as Sir George Bonham had held.*

A change of Government having taken place at home, and a Conservative Administration having been installed in office, it is necessary to state that Lord Malmesbury repeated, in language more emphatic if possible than Lord Granville's, that "all irritating discussions with the Chinese should be avoided," and that the existing good understanding was to be in no way imperilled.

The first communication from Dr. Bowring to the Chinese was dated in April, 1852, and contained the expression of a desire for an opportunity of paying his personal respects to the high Chinese officials at Canton, with a view to arranging such matters as remained unsettled. The reply of the Viceroy Su was to compliment him upon his appointment, but at the same time to express the wish that the interview should be postponed until the hostilities against the rebels had been triumphantly concluded. Dr. Bowring accepted the excuse, and more than two years passed by before the question of an interview was resumed. By that time Dr.

---

* In his reply, Dr. Bowring said: "The Pottinger Treaties inflicted a deep wound upon the pride, but by no means altered the policy, of the Chinese Government. . . . Their purpose is now, as it ever was, not to invite, not to facilitate, but to impede and resist the access of foreigners. . . . It must then ever be borne in mind, in considering the state of our relations with these regions, that the two Governments have objects at heart which are diametrically opposed except in so far that both earnestly desire to avoid all hostile action, and to make its own policy as far as possible subordinate to that desire."

Bowring had been knighted, and had received full powers as Governor of Hongkong in succession to Sir George Bonham; and the Viceroy Su had experienced the opposite extreme of fortune, and, having fallen from the position of popular champion to that of a disgraced official, his place had been taken at Canton by his former subordinate, Yeh.

Up to this point all Sir John Bowring's suggestions with regard to the settlement of the questions pending with the Chinese had been received in London with the official reply, expressed indeed in peremptory terms, that he was to abstain from all action, and that he was not to press himself on the Canton officials. But in the early part of the year 1854 there was a modification in the rigidity of this policy of doing nothing; and Lord Clarendon admitted that it was desirable to secure certain points, of which the two principal were "free and unrestricted intercourse with the Chinese officials," and "admission into some of the cities of China, especially Canton." Encouraged by this statement, Sir John Bowring felt justified in detailing his views on the points at issue, and in seizing the opportunities that presented themselves for obtaining what had been formally granted.

Sir John Bowring's first step after his definitive appointment was to notify the fact to Yeh; but the reply to this notification was so long delayed, that he had written, before any answer to the first communication had reached him, a second letter inviting the Chinese Commissioner to an early interview, but at the same time stating that there could only be one mode of reception, viz. within the city of Canton at the official yamen or residence of the Viceroy. The question which had long lain dormant was thus brought to a clear issue, and it only remained to be seen what would be the outcome of it. But while Sir John Bowring, with commendable frankness, at the very commencement of the controversy stated the conditions on which he would alone proceed to Canton, it must be observed that he was demanding less than Keying's arrangement had provided for. That convention had opened the gates of Canton, after an interval long expired, to all Englishmen. The English Government and Sir John Bowring would have been perfectly satisfied had the concession been confirmed in favour of the official representatives of England alone.

The reply of the chief Chinese official was not encouraging. While saying that he would be gratified if it were possible to hold an early interview, he stated that the management of the military arrangements in different parts of the province occupied the whole of his time, and left him no opportunity to name a day. By replying in this general way to the request of the English representative, Yeh thought that he avoided the necessity of stating his objections to the presence of Sir John Bowring in Canton. Sir John Bowring was not to be so easily balked, and encouraged by Lord Clarendon's approval of his propositions, he sent his official secretary, Mr. Medhurst, to Canton, for the purpose of overcoming the repugnance of the Viceroy Yeh to the proposed interview. This preliminary mission was not successful, and failed to provide an easy issue from the complication. Mr. Medhurst was unable to execute his charge, as the mandarins sent to meet him were of very inferior rank, and he returned to Hongkong with the report that the Viceroy stood firmly to his text of denying that Keying's arrangement possessed any validity. The Chinese contended that it had been allowed to drop on both sides, was practically extinct, and, moreover, the attitude of the Canton populace rendered it quite impossible for any attempt to be made to give it effect. The utmost that Yeh could be induced to concede was to appoint a day for an interview at the Jinsin Packhouse on the Canton river, but outside the walls of the city.*

This proposal was declared to be inadmissible, and no sign of yielding being manifested by Yeh, who at length told Sir John Bowring that he supposed he "did not wish for an interview," the English representative left for

* Mr. Medhurst wrote, on his return: "Our failure has been altogether owing to the pertinacious endeavours of the Commissioner to oblige us, against our better judgment, to meet low officials whom we could not have received without prejudice to our position as your Excellency's delegates, and whom we therefore obstinately declined to see." It should be added that Lord Clarendon conveyed the approval of these proceedings on the part of Her Majesty's Government.

Shanghai, where he hoped to be able to place himself in communication with the central authorities. On the 10th of July, 1854, he addressed Eleang, then Viceroy of the Two Kiang, complaining of the want of courtesy evinced by Yeh throughout his correspondence with him, and expressing a desire to negotiate either with him or with some other high official of the Empire. Eleang's reply did not tend to advance matters. He had no authority, he said, on the subject, and he could not interfere in what was not his concern. Commissioner Yeh was a high official specially appointed by the Emperor to conduct the relations with foreigners, and it was impossible for any one except the Emperor himself to assume or withdraw his functions.*

The insurrectionary movement, which has been already described, by threatening to result in the subversion of the Emperor's authority at Canton, seemed likely to give a more satisfactory turn to the question, as it compelled Yeh in the extremity of his distress to apply to the English representative, if not for assistance, at least for co-operation against the rebels. Sir John Bowring thereupon proceeded to Canton, where his acts made it clear that his only intention was to restrict himself to the performance of his duty, which was to protect English interests. From him, therefore, Yeh could expect no direct support. The Consuls issued a joint notice proclaiming their strict neutrality, and their firm intention to protect the lives and property of their subjects against all attacks whether from the one side or from the

* Eleang will be remembered as the Commissioner to Formosa at an earlier period. His letter concluded as follows: "I have no means of knowing what kind of treatment your Excellency or your predecessors received at the hands of the Commissioner at Canton. It is, to my mind, a matter of more consequence that we of the central and outer nations have made fair dealing and good faith our rule of conduct, and thus for a length of time preserved entire our amicable relations. Familiarity or otherwise in social intercourse, and all such trifles, are, in my opinion, to be decided by the laws of conventionality. As your Excellency cherishes such a dislike to discourteous treatment, you must doubtless be a most courteous man yourself—an inference which gives me sincere pleasure, for we shall both be able to maintain Treaty stipulations, and continue in the practice of mutual good-will to your Excellency's everlasting honour."

other. Immediately after his arrival Sir John Bowring went over the settlement with the naval officer in order to arrange for its defence, and several alterations were notified to the Canton mandarins as military precautions that were absolutely necessary. Some of these changes had been mentioned in the arrangement with Keying, others were completely new. Yeh could not be expected to receive these manifestations of self-interest with any deep sense of obligation to the English people, and when he discovered that the only result of his overtures was to induce the Europeans to encroach on Chinese rights for the purpose of guarding their own, he assumed the tone that the rebellion was on the eve of being put down, and that the foreigners had consequently nothing to fear, as he was quite able to afford them protection.

The suppression of the rebellion left matters, therefore, very much where they were; but his success over the insurgents inspired Yeh with increased confidence, and rendered him less than ever disposed to make the smallest concession to the English. Mr. Alcock, who had been temporarily transferred from Shanghai to Canton, reported many acts of obstruction on the part of the mandarins, and called attention to the many difficulties he experienced in officially communicating with them. In June, 1855, Sir John Bowring returned to the subject of official interviews, and made an explicit demand for the reception, if not of himself, then at the least of the new Consul, Mr. Rutherford Alcock. After a month's delay Commissioner Yeh replied that there was no precedent for an interview with a Consul, and that Sir John having refused his former appointment to meet him outside the city, there was an end of the matter. He went on to say that, although tranquillity was restored, the movements of the troops occupied the whole of his time and left him no leisure for "unnecessary" interviews and discussions. It was then that Sir John Bowring wrote that "until the city question at Canton is settled there is little hope of our relations being placed on anything like a satisfactory foundation."

That the difficulty of the situation was enhanced by the personal pride and character of Yeh does not admit of question; and had not the operations of the Crimean War intervened, there is little room to doubt that the year 1855 would not have passed away without another naval demonstration at Canton. But the extreme remedy of all was several times thrust on one side, and events progressed after their usual fashion. Canton remained a closed city, the Viceroy's yamen was not to be polluted by the step of a European, and the consuls had to transact their business as best they could under the difficulties of their position. Mr. Alcock returned to Shanghai as Consul, and his place at Canton was taken by Mr. Harry Parkes, and if there was continued tranquillity it may be attributed to the tact and good judgment of these officials, and to that combination of fortunate circumstances which can never be sufficiently allowed for in discussing human affairs. But the evil day could not be finally averted, and the antagonism caused by clashing views and interests at last broke forth, with the accentuated force of long restraint, on a point which would have been promptly settled had there been direct intercourse between the English consulate and the Viceroy's yamen.

On the 8th of October, 1856, Mr. Parkes reported to his superior, Sir John Bowring, at Hongkong, the facts in connection with an outrage which had been committed on a British-owned lorcha at Canton.* The lorcha *Arrow*, employed in the river trade between Canton and the mouth of the river, commanded by an English captain and flying the English flag, had been boarded by a party of mandarins and their escort while at anchor near the Dutch Folly. It had been duly registered in the office at Hongkong, and although, as was subsequently discovered, not entitled at that precise moment to British protection through failure to renew the license, no one was aware of the fact. The gravity of the outrage was increased by the circumstance that the English ensign was conspicuously displayed, while the absence of the captain gave the Chinese descent all the advantages

---

* "Lorcha" is the Portuguese name given to a special kind of fast-sailing boat used on the Canton river. Although the name is foreign, there were numerous English lorchas, and the name is specially used in the Nankin Treaty.

of a surprise. The crew, with the exception of two men left at their request to take care of the boat, were carried off by the Chinese, and the English flag was hauled down. To the remonstrances of the master, who returned during the altercation, the Chinese officials turned a deaf ear. In describing this event, which has been made the subject of much heated discussion, it is necessary to make use of the calmest language; but even in the heat of the moment the only epithet used by Mr. Parkes was to style it "a significant insult," a fact not to be disputed. Mr. Parkes also addressed Yeh on the subject of this "very grave insult," and presented a request that the captured crew of the *Arrow* should be returned to that vessel without delay, and that any charges made against them or the owner should be then examined into at the English consulate.

The reply of Commissioner Yeh was to justify and uphold the act of his subordinates. Of the twelve men seized he returned nine, but with regard to the rest he stated that one was a criminal and the two others were important witnesses. Not merely would he not return them, but he proceeded to justify their apprehension. Of outrage to the English flag, of his violation of treaty stipulations in not having first requested the English Consul to arrest the accused and investigate the charges against him, he appeared to be supremely indifferent. A Chinese official had far more serious matters to attend to than to consider the silly pride of a barbarian people. Commissioner Yeh had triumphed when he refused to fulfil the pledges contained in Keying's Convention. Why should be he less successful in ignoring the stipulations of the Nankin Treaty of fourteen years before? It would be a laudable patriotism, he thought, to make the attempt, and the consequences of failure did not enter into his calculations.

Yeh's reply to Mr. Parkes was not meant as an explanation of his proceedings, much less as an excuse for them. It consisted of the assertion of certain facts which in his opinion it was sufficient for him to accept in order that they should pass current. The evidence on which they were based was not sufficient to command credence in the laxest court of justice; but even if it had been conclusive, it could not have justified the breach of international law and right in the forcible removal of the crew from the lorcha *Arrow** when the British flag was flying conspicuously at her mast.

What in effect was the Chinese reply? It was that one of the crew had been recognized by a man passing in a boat as one of a band of pirates who had attacked, ill-used, and plundered him several weeks before. He had forthwith gone to the Taotai of Canton, laid the information before him, and presented a demand for redress. It was then that the Chinese officials had proceeded to the lorcha, and committed the acts of which complaint was made. The charge bore on the face of it the appearance of truth. It was highly probable that the man recognized the face one of his assailants, and that the perpetrator of the crime should endeavour to hide himself by taking service on one of the numerous boats trading under a foreign flag on the Canton river was only in the natural course of things. But this did not warrant the proceedings of the Chinese, which were at distinct variance with the terms of the Treaty of Nankin, and the ex-territorial rights of preliminary consular investigation before trial granted to all those who were under the protection of the English flag. They could not even plead the necessity of despatch and the delay that would have been involved by acting in the proper way through the English Consul. The accused, once the case had been legally established, could have been as easily secured at Hongkong, or any other point on the river, as he was at Canton on the 8th of October.

But Commissioner Yeh attempted no excuses. He did not plead the necessity of haste, and he did not blame the over-zeal of his assistants. So far as the matter was worthy of his notice it appeared in his eyes to be a very ordinary affair, and one at which all men should naturally rejoice as involving the capture of a criminal who seemed likely to elude the grasp of justice. Moreover, he declared "the *Arrow* is not a foreign lorcha, and therefore there is no use

---

* The lorcha *Arrow* had been registered at Hongkong, Sir John Bowring stated, in the name of a Chinese resident. The boat, moreover, was well known in the river. The registration period expired during the last cruise.

to enter any discussion about her." The Commissioner thus plainly proclaimed his intention to consider the statements of Chinese witnesses about the nationality of any lorcha as far outweighing the undoubted facts of a foreign flag flying at the masthead, and of its name being registered on the books at Hongkong.* Had his view been accepted, there

* The question of the nationality of the lorcha *Arrow* was complicated by the fact that its registry had expired ten days before the outrage. The master explained that this was due to the vessel having been at sea, and that the omission was to have been rectified as soon as he returned to Hongkong. As Lord Clarendon pointed out, this was not merely unknown to the Chinese, but it was also "a matter of British regulation which would not justify seizure by the Chinese." Lord Clarendon expressed his full approval of everything that had been done, and considered that the demands made upon the Chinese were very moderate. "No British lorcha would be safe if her crew were liable to seizure on these grounds." The following are the true facts in connection with the personal history of the *Arrow*, taken from the "China Mail," and officially certified as correct :—" The lorcha *Arrow* was heretofore employed in trading on the coast, and while so employed was taken by pirates. By them she was fitted out and employed in the Canton river during the disturbances between the Imperialists and the Insurgents. While on this service, she was captured by the 'braves' of the Soo-tsoi-che-tong Company or Guild, one of the loyalist associations organized by the mandarins for the support of the Imperial Government. By this guild she was publicly sold, and was purchased by a Chin-chew Hong, a respectable firm at Canton, who also laid out a considerable sum in repairing and otherwise fitting her out. She arrived in this harbour about the month of June, 1855, at which time a treaty (which ended in a bargain) was on foot between Fong Aming, Messrs. John Burd & Co.'s comprador, and Lei-yeong-heen, one of the partners in the Chin-chew Hong, for the purchase of the lorcha by the former. Shortly after the arrival of the vessel here, she was claimed by one Quan-tai of Macao, who asserted that she had been his property before she was seized by the pirates. Of course, the then owner disputed his claim; upon which he commenced a suit in the Vice-Admiralty Court. After a short time, by consent of the parties, the question was referred to arbitration; and the arbitrators appointed were Mr. Edward Pereira, on behalf of Quan-tai, and the Hon. Mr. J. F. Edger on behalf of Lee-yeong-heen, as representing the parties who opposed the claims of Quan-tai. These arbitrators could not agree; and Mr. George Lyall was appointed umpire, who awarded that the possession or ownership of the lorcha should continue undisturbed; but as he was not satisfied that Quan-tai had sufficient opportunities afforded him of regaining what he asserted to have been originally his property, he also awarded that the sum of 2100 dollars should be paid to him, being the sum at which the lorcha had been sold

would have been an end to the security of English subjects—under the English flag* and to the special rights accorded by the Treaty of Nankin.

The immediate act of reprisal decided upon was to capture an Imperial war-junk, with the view of showing that the British Government was in earnest in its demand for reparation. Within less than a week of the seizure of the

by the Soo-tsio-che-tong Guild, and which appeared to be the value of the lorcha at the time of such sale. Upon this award, a question rose between Fong Aming, of Messrs. John Burd & Co., and the Ching-chew Hong, as to who was to pay the 2100 dollars; and it was finally arranged between them that Fong Aming was actually to pay the money to Quantai, but that the Chin-chew Hong were to allow him out of the purchase-money for the lorcha the sum of 1000 dollars, being their contribution to the amount of the award, and that the balance of 1100 dollars was to be Fong Aming's contribution. This sum of 2100 dollars Mr. Block advanced for Fong Aming, and paid it to Messrs. Gaskell Brown, the proctors for Quantai, who acknowledged the receipt thereof from him on account of Lee-yeong-heen, the partner in the Chin-chew Hong, who had been made defendant in the suit. In the accounts between the Hong and Fong Aming, the sum of 1000 dollars was deducted from the total amount of the purchase-money for the lorcha. The ownership of the vessel was transferred to Fong Aming, and in his name she is registered. These are the simple facts connected with the purchase of the lorcha by a resident in this colony and her registry as a British vessel; and it is from these facts that the Imperial Commissioner Yeh has arrived at the erroneous conclusion expressed in this letter of the 12th ultimo, where he says, that a register was purchased for Soo Aching of the merchant Block for 1000 dollars—the fact being that Mr. Block interested himself in the matter solely for the purpose of extricating his comprador (Fong Aming) from the difficulty he had with the lorcha at this place. As an evidence of the truth of the above statement, the documents bearing reference to it have been placed in our hand, for the inspection of any person who may feel interested in the matter; and we are assured that Mr. Block received no remuneration whatsoever for his assistance, nor did he derive any profits, either directly or indirectly, nor had he any interest or share in the lorcha."

* One of the Chinese crew on board the *Arrow* described the incident of hauling down the flag as follows: "I heard the mandarin, who wore the crystal button, cry out, 'This is not a foreign lorcha, for there is no foreigner in command. Haul down her ensign!' Several of us assured the mandarin that we had an European captain. One of the soldiers hauled down the ensign, and flung it on the deck." This evidence was confirmed by that of the master, Thomas Kennedy, who returned on board the instant he perceived what had happened from the other lorcha, on which he was.—See depositions in Blue Book.

THE CHINESE CASE.

Arrow's crew, a junk thought to be in the Imperial service had been seized by the English commodore at Canton, and naval preparations were made to attack if necessary the forts near Whampoa and at the Bogue. The former operation was effected without loss to either side; and then Mr. Parkes directed another letter to Yeh, reminding him that "the matter which has compelled this menace still remains unsettled." Unless prompt reparation were made, it was already evident that the offensive measures directed against the Chinese authorities would have to go on.

If it was clear that the *Arrow* complication would, humanly speaking, never have arisen* had there been that regular diplomatic intercourse between the English Governor at Hongkong and the Chinese authorities in Canton which was provided for by the Treaty of Nankin and the arrangement with Keying, it is not less certain that the *Arrow* case would not have produced such serious results as it did but for the arrogance of Yeh. Throughout his replies to the numerous letters and despatches of the English officials there is not the least trace of any desire to offer an apology, or even to express regret for what had taken place. He repeated, even after the seizure of the Chinese junk, which he declared with ill-concealed gratification to be not a war-junk, although it carried eight or nine guns, that the English had no business to interfere in the matter, as the *Arrow* was a Chinese vessel. Moreover, he denied that the lorcha carried an English flag—a fact proved by several witnesses on the very day of the occurrence. There was consequently not the least ground for supposing that the Viceroy would make any concession in the direction of compliance with the demands presented on two separate occasions by Mr. Parkes, and any delay in the matter could only tend to encourage and prolong resistance. On the 22nd of October, therefore, the matter was placed in the hands of the Admiral on the

* Mr. Bonham had written, in April, 1849, the following prophetic words: "Let the Chinese Government well consider these things; and whatever may happen in future between the two countries that may be disagreeable to China, let the Chinese Government remember that the fault thereof will be upon them."—P. 102 Canton Blue Book, 1857.

station, Sir Michael Seymour; and on the following day the four forts known as those of the Barrier were attacked and taken without any loss to the English. When captured they were quickly dismantled and the guns in them were spiked.

It cannot therefore be alleged that the *Arrow* case came either unexpectedly or without warning. There had been a long series of insults and outrages which had shown that the Chinese did not respect treaties, and that the Government made but faint efforts to restrain the popular animosity that so frequently broke forth on the slightest pretexts. Those who have regarded the outrage of October, 1856, as if it were merely an untoward incident in the happy and friendly relations of two great Governments well disposed towards each other, should peruse the long and extensive official correspondence on the question of "Insults to foreigners in China," and if they do their only marvel will be that the hour of hostile collision should have been put off so long. At Canton itself the attack, in 1854, on Mr. Seth, a native of British India, was but the precursor of the grosser attack on two leading English merchants in 1856: It was only three months before the seizure of the *Arrow* crew that Mr. Bulkeley Johnson and Mr. Whittall had been stoned in the outskirts of Canton, and that, despite the urgent representations of Mr. Parkes, neither reparation for the outrage nor guarantee for greater protection in the future was vouchsafed. A placard calling upon the populace to attack and slay all foreigners was freely distributed throughout the city, and only withdrawn in consequence of the emphatic remonstrance of the English Consul. The arrest of an English missionary in Kwantung, the occurrence of a riot at Foochow during which an American gentleman lost his life, and the murder of a French missionary on the frontier of Tonquin, all showed that the question of foreign relationship was far indeed from being satisfactorily adjusted.

The last of these events promised to have more serious consequences than the other, for the French Government took up the brutal murder of M. Chapdelaine with great earnestness, and declared its determination to exact the fullest reparation for the offence and at all cost. Before the outrage on the *Arrow* had been committed, therefore, the question of foreign relations, not with England only, but with other countries, had reached so critical a pass as to afford but little hope of the continuation of peace, unless, of course, the Chinese authorities should consent at the eleventh hour to abandon what was an absolutely untenable position, and one that could only be preserved on the assumption that the Chinese Government was not to recognize in the European States its equals, and that that pretension was to be supported by superior power.

Those who persist in regarding the *Arrow* incident as being a matter to be judged by itself, and with complete indifference to the events that preceded and led up to it, may, of course, delude themselves into the belief that because its register as an English vessel had expired a few days it had forfeited its claim to protection under the English flag. But as a matter of fact it cannot be so separated, and the conviction becomes irresistible from the perusal of the documents of Yeh, the only spokesman of the Chinese Government, and the one enunciator of the national policy, that, if there had been no *Arrow* case at all, a hostile collision could not have been much longer averted. It is a mistaken view to consider that incident by itself. It furnished the crowning touch to the arrogance of Yeh, who believed that the forbearance of the English officials was inexhaustible, and that they were so loth to employ force that they might be defied and thwarted with impunity.

The proceedings of Sir Michael Seymour should have revealed how baseless were such hopes and speculations at the same time that they demonstrated the naval power of England. On the 23rd of October the English Admiral carried the Barrier Forts without any serious resistance, and, having made sure that they would prove as little hindrance to his retreat as they had been to his advance, he proceeded towards Canton, where, capturing the fort in the Macao passage on his way, he arrived the same afternoon. A further ultimatum was then presented to Yeh, informing him that unless he at once complied with every demand that had been made, the English Admiral would "proceed with the destruction of all the defences and public buildings of this city and of the Government vessels in the river." In fulfilment of this threat, as the only reply received from Yeh was a reiteration of his previous misstatements, Sir Michael Seymour dismantled the forts at Canton itself, and, having landed a body of marines for the protection of the factories, placed his war-ships opposite the city, as if he had the intention of bombarding it.

It is impossible to deny Yeh the credit of having the courage of his opinions, although in obstinacy alone lay his chance of personal safety. Seeing that his attitude had precipitated a quarrel which would be regarded with displeasure at Pekin, and knowing that the only way to avert his official ruin and disgrace was to obtain some success, Yeh, far from being cowed, showed greater confidence and assumed a higher tone after the capture of the forts than he had before. His defiance was expressed in the most emphatic terms, and the rage of the people who had suffered would, he said, speedily retrieve the injury inflicted on the Chinese. In these brave words no sign of yielding could be detected, and it was evident that the success which had up to this point attended the English had not been sufficient to ensure compliance with the terms demanded in reparation for the *Arrow* outrage. A still more significant proceeding was his placing the price of thirty dollars on the head of every Englishman brought to him, at the same time that he appealed to the patriotic to effect their extermination. In the face of this pronounced hostility there was nothing left save to renew operations of war against Canton itself.

On the 27th, and again on the 28th of October, the fire of the ships was directed first against Yeh's yamen and then on the city wall from guns placed on the Dutch Folly as well as from the fleet. The townspeople, warned of the approaching bombardment, abandoned those houses that were in the line of fire, and comparatively few lives were lost. The damage done to the walls was not as great as had been anticipated, and the Chinese troops took care to remain at a safe distance beyond shot and shell. However, after two days' bombardment, a breach was declared to be practicable, and a small body of marines planted the English flag on the walls. The Tsinghai gate was occupied, and Sir Michael Seymour and Mr. Parkes proceeded with a small force to the Viceroy's yamen, to which the English representatives had been rigidly refused the right of admission. It was found that no advantage would accrue from the retention of these posts, which were commanded by the guns of the fleet, and which were much exposed to attack by large parties of Chinese from the narrow streets and dark passages of Canton. That the possibility of a Chinese surprise proving dangerous was not chimerical was demonstrated by the comparatively severe loss suffered by the marines in attacking the wall. The events of the next few days were unimportant, being confined to a desultory bombardment on the part of the English to keep the breach open, and of many abortive attempts on that of the Chinese to close it up.

Active measures were renewed early in November, when, a fleet of war-junks having been collected outside the fort called the French Folly, it was decided to attack and disperse them, as they threatened to imperil the safety of the Admiral's communications. Sir Michael Seymour accordingly attacked them, and after a warm engagement the junks were destroyed and the French Folly fort captured. An attempt subsequently made to destroy the English fleet by fire-ships miscarried, although one of the vessels blew up almost under the bow of the steamer *Barracouta*. That the Viceroy had fully made up his mind to resist to the bitter end was shown by his proclamation of the 5th of November to the people of Canton, in which he said that he had "assembled a very large force and decided in his own mind as to the course he was to pursue;" and there was consequently no reason for further delaying the progress of the necessary measures. On the 9th of November a final ultimatum was presented, to the effect that unless reparation were granted within twenty-four hours active operations would be recommenced. To this the only reply given deserved remark for the skill in evading the points in dispute, as well as for the eloquent language expatiating on the growing indignation of the Chinese people.

On the 12th and 13th of November Sir Michael Seymour attacked the Bogue forts, mounting in all about four hundred guns, on both sides of the channel, and captured them after an ill-directed resistance with very trifling loss. With this success all the defences of the Chinese had fallen into the hands of the English, but at the same time that it seemed to crown their victory it had the disadvantage of leaving no further object of attack within their reach. If Yeh remained obdurate, and further operations should become necessary, it was clear that the small English force would be quite inadequate to carry them out with the same certainty of success as had hitherto attended all its efforts. That the bitterness of the official animosity rendered the continuance of military pressure necessary was foreshadowed in the attempt made to set fire to the ship *Niger* left off the factories, and which was only baffled by the vigilance of its officers. The indignation felt against the Chinese was becoming general among all the foreigners; and the squadron of the United States, in revenge for their flag having been fired upon, proceeded without any hesitation to bombard the forts and city walls, which had been re-armed after their capture and subsequent abandonment by Sir Michael Seymour.

The endurance of the Chinese in face of an enemy whom they could not defeat, and from whom they were suffering every day the most serious injuries, cannot fail to excite a feeling of admiration not unmixed with astonishment. Batteries and forts were disarmed and dismantled only to be re-armed and re-fortified the next week. The braves of the surrounding towns and villages came forward in their thousands to take the places of those who had fallen; and six weeks after Sir Michael Seymour had declared that the city of Canton was at his complete mercy, the Chinese did not hesitate to provoke the hostility of another great Power in the bitterness of their animosity against all foreigners. And in December, 1856, their hostility broke out to some purpose, for on the night of the 14th of that month a band of incendiaries succeeded in setting fire to the houses of the foreign settlement. The English factory alone escaped from the conflagration; and there Sir Michael Seymour proceeded to entrench himself in the garden of the factory, and in the church, which remained intact. He garrisoned this position with 300 men, composed equally of sailors, marines, and a detachment of a line regiment. The Dutch Folly fort was also held by a body of 140 blue jackets, and in this position the English admiral awaited the development of events. His plans were suddenly changed in consequence of the renewal of the conflagration within the limits of the English factory itself, and of the destruction of all the buildings which it had been proposed to defend. Sir Michael then determined to withdraw his troops and to conduct future operations from on board ship; but for a short time further he remained in occupation of the garden.

Having thus destroyed all vestiges of the foreign presence on land, the Chinese devoted their energies to the task of capturing such stray Europeans as it was possible to secure. On the 20th of December a party of Chinese, with singular skill, kidnapped a Mr. Cowper from on board his own house-boat at Whampoa, and carried him off. A few days later a still more daring outrage was perpetrated on board the postal steamer *Thistle*, plying between Canton and Hongkong. A party of seventeen soldiers and braves, concealing their weapons about their persons, took passage on board her; and when they had reached a safe or convenient spot they turned on the crew, killed the white passengers and officers, and, having guided the steamer up one of the creeks, set fire to her. They carried off the heads of their victims,* but left the rich cargo of the ship to be destroyed, a most unusual occurrence, and proving that they were not river pirates. Again, a few days later, a Bavarian boat-carer for an American doctor was murdered at Whampoa, and his head carried off for the purpose of procuring the reward for each white man killed, which had

* The victims were the captain, a Spanish passenger, an English soldier, two engineers, the crew of four Manilla men, and two others, one of whom was the Spanish passenger's servant, or eleven in all besides the mate, who jumped overboard and was drowned. The Spanish passenger happened to be a man of some importance, the Vice-Consul at Macao, named Don Diaz de Sobre Casas, and his death necessarily caused considerable diplomatic agitation.

been raised to as much as thirty pounds. To this pass had Yeh's frenzy brought the question; and the heads of Europeans treacherously seized and barbarously murdered were paraded throughout the villages of Kwantung in order to stimulate recruiting, and to raise national enthusiasm to a high pitch.

Although Sir Michael Seymour, after the burning of the greater portion of the foreign settlement, continued to hold the factory garden, and although, by means of his fleet, he was able to ensure the safety of the detachment left on shore, there was no longer any ground to question that the Chinese had succeeded for the moment in wearing out their opponent, and that a stronger expedition was needed from Europe before a definite result could be ensured. The Chinese also were never inactive, and their attempts to destroy the English war-vessels were so constant as to be productive of, at the least, continual alarm. There was almost daily apprehension of some desperate attempt to send fire-ships and rafts down the river, and stink-pots were constantly thrown from the city walls and forts, with the view of igniting the vessels at anchor. These incessant hostilities compelled the English admiral to sanction an attempt to destroy by fire the remaining suburbs between the city wall and the river, for it was here that the incendiaries found most shelter as well as the most convenient point for directing their efforts against the English fleet. The suburbs were accordingly destroyed by fire, but not without loss to the English. Then Sir Michael Seymour resolved to withdraw his small force from the land and the Dutch Folly fort, and to confine his line of defence to the broad stream of the river and the Macao fort opposite Honan. It had already become plain that with the small force at his disposal he had reached the limit of his power. Until fresh troops arrived from Europe there was, in short, no way of showing that Chinese endurance had not worn out English superiority in valour and military resources.

While Sir Michael Seymour sent home a request for 5000 troops to be sent to the Canton river from India, and while a few hundred men despatched from Singapore served to restore confidence at Hongkong,* Yeh was busily employed in strengthening the defences of Canton and in preparing to withstand whatever force the English barbarians might bring against him. For the moment Yeh was not dissatisfied with the result. He had sufficient facts to appeal to in order to persuade his own Government that his measures would ultimately be crowned with success. The people of Canton had enough confidence in their leader to see in the destruction of the foreign settlement, and in the gradual retirement of the English fleet, an earnest of their coming victory; and their hostility consequently became more unequivocal and pronounced in its implacability.

The confidence of the Chinese was raised to such a point by the withdrawal of the English from their position opposite the city, that they resumed their activity along the whole course of the Canton river, and not a day passed by without some attempt to destroy one or other of the vessels keeping open the navigation of the river. The junks grew more daring in their attacks from the sense of security they felt through the inability of the English vessels to pursue them up the shallow creeks of the river, and even ventured on more than one occasion to engage men-of-war. But it was in their fire-ships that they placed their main reliance, and many ingenious contrivances† were invented for the purpose of blowing up the foreign vessels. At the same time the work of destruction which had been commenced so successfully at Canton was continued at Whampoa, where the English and

* Several circumstances had alarmed the residents at Hongkong during this troubled period. Not only had there been official proclamations from the mainland ordering all Chinese subjects to leave the island, under pains and penalties of the harshest kind, but placards had been put up in the public streets offering "a handsome reward" for the heads of any Europeans. All these acts of hostility were cast into the shade by the attempt to poison the white men by putting arsenic in the bread sold by the chief baker of the town. Fortunately the would-be poisoner put too much arsenic into the bread, and the fact was discovered before any serious harm was done. Yeh repudiated at the time and afterwards all responsibility or complicity in the matter; and the truth was never ascertained.

† One of these was an explosive machine fixed in a saucepan, and so arranged as to burst on coming into contact with a ship's side.

American docks, factories, and residences were burnt towards the end of January, 1857. Not until several merchant vessels of light draught had been procured and armed was the English admiral able to cope on something like equal terms with the innumerable junks which always shunned a close encounter, and promptly sought safety in the creeks and estuaries of the Bocca Tigris. The rare occasions when they could be brought to action served to demonstrate over again the oft-proved valour and energy of the English sailor, although the incidents must remain here untold.

The peculiarity of the disturbances at Canton consisted in their being essentially the outcome of Yeh's personal policy and resentment. Elsewhere there were tranquillity, if not goodwill, and the expression of a desire for peace if not the friendly sentiment which rendered it a matter certain to follow. The Governor-Generals of the Two Kiang and of Fuhkien were forward in their protestations of a desire to maintain the cordial relations arranged for under the Treaty of Nankin, and threw upon Yeh the responsibility of his own actions. And even with regard to the Imperial Government itself the expression of opinion was, to say the least, ambiguous, although the young Emperor Hienfung was much impressed by the reports of many victories over the barbarian English, with which his lieutenant at Canton took care to keep him well supplied. While local zeal was roused to its highest pitch in order to give Yeh some chance of holding his ground and succeeding in his main object, not less energy had been evinced in recommending the Viceroy's proceedings to the central administration as expressing the best and most profitable policy for the Chinese ruler to pursue. There was much in that policy to commend itself to the favour of a proud and youthful prince; and could Yeh have only convinced Hienfung that his power was equal to his will, he would no doubt have obtained the hearty support of the Emperor. Even as it was, Hienfung was loth to discourage one whose views coincided so closely with his own private opinion, and whose main fault was his anxiety to uphold the claims of China to a place of superiority among the nations.

THE EMPEROR'S POLICY.

Hienfung's policy consisted in the wish that the quarrel should remain as far as possible a local one. In this way he thought to avoid any immediate danger to the central Government, at the same time that he believed his own dignity and security would not be compromised. In the event of any conspicuous success, he would thus derive all the benefit in a national sense from a victory over the Europeans. A document which purported to be an Imperial Edict gave Yeh the support to be derived from the expression of these views; but as he required definite assistance to hold his ground, it is doubtful if the announcement of what the Emperor wished and hoped to gain by his policy carried to his mind any sense of assurance or comfort. As Yeh had reported two victorious engagements in which the Chinese had inflicted a loss of 400 men, including an admiral, on the barbarians, it was not supposed that the victor in such an engagement could need any material support against an enemy whom he had so easily vanquished. However much concern, therefore, the central Government may have felt in these early disputes, which resulted in the military operations that have been described, their attitude continued to be one of strict abstention from any direct interference. The settled policy at Pekin was to cast all the responsibility upon Yeh. He was long versed in the ways of the Europeans. He had had many dealings with them; he must treat the question from his own experience, and at his personal risk. With him, in the event of success, would rest the credit of humbling and defeating the hated foreigner. With him also would lie the shame and the penalty of failure in a course essentially of his own seeking, and one wherein his action had been left untrammelled.

Only those who from want of application prefer to judge the bearing of a great question by some isolated occurrence or from a single incident, instead of by the light of all the events relating to the issues involved, will persist in regarding the *Arrow* case as the only, because the immediate, cause of the hostile collision between England and China. That outrage—for it was an outrage—was but the last of a long succession of acts showing the resolve of the ruling authorities at Canton to thwart and humiliate the English in every way, just as it was the precursor of many outrages unknown in the practice of fair warfare, and repugnant to human sentiment. Had there been no *Arrow* incident at all, we must repeat, the attacks on Europeans, the refusal to hold diplomatic intercourse on terms of equality, the whole tenor, in short, of Yeh's policy and attitude, rendered the outbreak of war sooner or later a matter that was inevitable. But even with regard to the *Arrow* case, which in the heat of Party warfare was made the mark of moral indignation at home, it is possible to declare that the more carefully the facts are examined, the more attentively the whole course of English relations with the Chinese at Canton is studied, the more evident does it become that no other policy was open to Sir John Bowring* and Mr. Parkes than that they pursued and recommended in 1856-7. The action of Sir John Davis ten years before, when his measures were much more summary and decisive, was far more open to adverse criticism, and was attended in the first place by a greater loss of human life. But the chief reason of all for insisting on the injustice of the sweeping and violent denunciations bestowed on the *Arrow* case is that the Chinese Viceroy had the command of peace and war in his own hands. At

* Sir John Bowring said, in his despatch of February 28th, 1857: "I have the comfort of believing that, notwithstanding the losses, privations, sufferings, and disquietudes which these events have produced, there exists an almost unanimity of opinion among Her Majesty's subjects in China as to the opportunity and necessity of the measures that have been taken, and a conviction that the crisis which has occurred was an inevitable one; while the councils of the Canton authorities were directed by such intolerable pride, presumption, faithlessness, and ignorance, as they have long exhibited. And it has greatly added to my gratification to know that the representatives of foreign Powers in China have generally concurred in approving of the course which has been pursued." When Sir John Bowring made the last statement, he had in his mind a recent despatch of Dr. Parker, the American Plenipotentiary to Yeh, in which the following lines occur: "The fountain of all difficulties between China and foreign nations is the unwillingness of China to acknowledge England, France, America, and other great nations of the West, as her equals and true friends, and to treat them accordingly. So far as respects this grave matter, the American Government is sensible that the English are in the right, and does choose to co-operate with them."

the time, and at any point during the following three months, he had only to say the word to ensure peace and the cessation of hostilities. That he did not say it must be attributed to his own blind obstinacy, while the presence of such a man in authority at Canton at so critical a moment must be reckoned among the many misfortunes which China has from time to time suffered since her foreign relations first became a matter of prime importance.

CHAPTER XII.

THE SECOND ENGLISH WAR.

IF there had ever been doubt in London as to the importance of the Chinese difficulty, it was dispelled when in 1856 Sir Michael Seymour sent home a request for 5000 troops. When it became known that he had called in all the reinforcements he could gather from the Straits Settlements, it was admitted that he must have felt the urgent necessity of neglecting no precaution to render his own position secure. The Chinese question then emerged from its position of comparative unimportance into one of almost national magnitude; and it was thought desirable to send an accredited ambassador of high rank to China, who was fully acquainted with the views of the Home Government, in order to convince the Pekin authorities that, while such acts as those of Yeh at Canton would not be tolerated, there was no desire to press with undue harshness on a country traditionally opposed to external intercourse. The choice fell upon the Earl of Elgin, a nobleman who added to broad statesmanlike views amiable qualities which generally served to smooth over the difficulties he encountered. Lord Elgin received his instructions * from Lord Clarendon on the 20th of April, 1857, and

---

* Those instructions were conveyed in two despatches of the same date, 20th April, 1857. (See Blue Book on Lord Elgin's Mission, 1857-9.) We quote the following as the more important passages: "The demands which you are instructed to make will be (1), for reparation of injuries to British subjects, and, if the French officers should co-operate with you, for those to French subjects also; (2) for the complete execution at Canton, as well as at the other ports, of the stipulations of the several Treaties; (3) compensation to British subjects, and persons entitled to

The Earl of Elgin and Kincardine.

within less than a week from that date he had set out for his destination.

At the same time that a high ambassador was sent to place matters on a satisfactory basis, preparations were made to meet Sir Michael Seymour's wish and to despatch an armed force to Hongkong. Fifteen hundred men were sent to Singapore from England, one regiment was ordered from Mauritius, a considerable detachment of native troops was to move from Madras; and such force as could be spared from Singapore had already been hurriedly despatched to Hongkong. General Ashburnham was appointed to the military command of the China Expedition, which was expected to rendezvous at Singapore in the latter portion of the summer. These vigorous measures could not have failed to effect a prompt settlement of the complication with China had they been carried out to their natural and expected conclusion. But at the very moment when there seemed every reason to hope that the prompt manifestation of English power would induce the Pekin Government to repudiate the acts of Yeh, and to conform its policy to the provisions of the treaty, an untoward event of the deepest significance interrupted these proceedings, diverted the attention of the British Government

British protection, for losses incurred in consequence of the late disturbances; (4) the assent of the Chinese Government to the residence at Pekin, or to the occasional visit to that capital, at the option of the British Government, of a Minister duly accredited by the Queen to the Emperor of China, and the recognition of the right of the British Plenipotentiary and chief Superintendent of Trade to communicate directly in writing with the high officers at the Chinese capital, and to send his communications by messengers of his own selection, such arrangements affording the best means of ensuring the due execution of the existing Treaties, and of preventing future misunderstanding; (5) a revision of the Treaties with China with a view to obtaining increased facilities for commerce, such as access to cities on the great rivers as well as to Chapoo and to other ports on the coast, and also permission for Chinese vessels to resort to Hongkong for purpose of trade from all ports of the Chinese Empire without distinction." These were the demands formulated by the English Government for the consent of China, and seven proposals were made as to how they were to be obtained should coercion become necessary. It was also stated that "it is not the intention of Her Majesty's Government to undertake any land operations in the interior of the country."

to a more critical matter, and by postponing rendered more difficult the attainment of that solution of the China question, which was as desirable in the interests of that country herself as it was in those of the Europeans.

On the 3rd of June, 1857, Lord Elgin arrived at Singapore, where he found an urgent letter from Lord Canning, the Governor-General of India, imploring him to alter the course of the China Expedition from Hongkong to Calcutta, as a military insurrection had broken out in the North-West Provinces, and every Englishman would be of untold value in weathering the storm that had suddenly beset the fortunes of the Paramount Power in Hindostan. In brief but pregnant sentences Lord Canning told the story of the early stages of the Indian Mutiny. The aid he asked for was not to proceed to the punishment of the mutineers in Delhi, but to prevent the further perpetration of outrages similar to those at Meerut and elsewhere in the valley of the Ganges, where "for a length of 750 miles there were barely 1000 European soldiers." To such an appeal there could be only one reply. The China Expedition was diverted to India, where the regiments that were to have chastised Commissioner Yeh rendered good service at Cawnpore and Lucknow, and Lord Elgin proceeded on his journey eastwards without that material force which always simplifies the process of diplomacy, but still hoping that tact and Sir Michael Seymour's squadron might suffice to enable him to effect the principal part of his commission.

Lord Elgin arrived at Hongkong in the first week of July, 1857; but before he reached the scene, events of considerable importance had occurred on the Canton river. The desultory engagements which had never wholly ceased during the winter months were followed by naval operations of a more definite, and, as it also proved, a more decisive character. Towards the end of May Sir Michael Seymour, having been reinforced in ships, and having also procured several merchant vessels of limited draught which he armed for the purpose of pursuing the junks up the creeks in which they were wont to seek shelter, resolved to assume the offensive against the large fleet of war-junks collected on the river above the city, with the intention of driving the barbarians back to the sea.

The first operation taken in hand was the destruction of a large number of junks, belonging to the Imperial service as well as to the loyal merchants of Canton, and collected in Escape Creek, one of those intervening between Hongkong and the Tiger Gates, or Bocca Tigris. The task of destroying this force was entrusted to Commodore Elliott, who accordingly proceeded on the 25th of May up the creek with such force as was available. The English expedition consisted of five gun-boats, with the manned galleys of three of the larger men-of-war. A short distance up the creek they found a number of junks drawn in a line across the stream, and as each of these vessels, forty-one in number, carried a gun of heavy calibre, in addition to many smaller pieces of artillery, the position of the Chinese force was far from being one that could be attacked without some consideration. However, the attack was made, and after some protracted firing the Chinese broke and fled. They were closely pursued, first by the gun-boats, and then, when those had grounded, by the row-boats. Twenty-seven junks were destroyed by either the English sailors or their own crews. Thirteen escaped, and of one the fate is not recorded.

The operations were renewed on the following days in the adjoining creeks, which were found to have intercommunication with each other;* and the pursuit was maintained with such energy that Commodore Elliott had the satisfaction of surprising the remaining junks at anchor off an island town called Tungkoon. The Chinese did not attempt to defend their boats against the impetuous onset of their assailants; but from the walls and houses of the town they opened a troublesome fire, which greatly annoyed the English and caused them some loss. There was after this a little street-fighting, and the Chinese made sufficient stand to show that there would be considerable difficulty in

---

* At this point, Mr. Wingrove Cook began his most graphic and interesting letters in his capacity of Special Correspondent for the *Times;* and during these two years they afford a most valuable and material aid towards the history of the time.

carrying off any of these junks as spoil of war and proof of victory. The largest junk was accidentally blown up, and the others were then burnt. The expedition returned to the main stream of the river, having inflicted an immense loss upon the Chinese navy, and a still ruder blow on the growing confidence and prestige of Yeh and his satellites.

The expedition to Escape Creek was the preliminary to a still more serious and dangerous undertaking. The town of Fatshan, west of Canton, from which in a straight line it is distant less than six miles, but by water more than twice that distance, had been made the principal centre of the warlike preparations by means of which Yeh counted on establishing the wisdom of his policy, and his own reputation as the national champion. Having learnt the complete success of Commodore Elliott's operation in his rear, Sir Michael Seymour resolved from his bases at the Macao Fort and in the Blenheim passage * upon making a forward movement into the upper reach of the river, known at the time as the Fatshan channel. On the 29th of May he hoisted his flag on the *Coromandel* steamer, a hired and quite insignificant vessel, which the Admiral had used on several occasions for his own convenience in personally directing the measures upon which he had decided. At the same time the gun-boats and larger ships were ordered to collect near the entrance to the Fatshan branch of the river. These numbered twenty vessels in all; but many of these, owing to their size, were useless for the projected attack.

At Macao Fort, where 250 marines held an inclosure surrounding a three-storied pagoda, the final arrangements were made for the attack on the Chinese position in the Fatshan channel. That position was unusually strong, and had been selected with considerable military judgment. An island, called after the hyacinth, lies in mid-stream, two miles from the entrance to this branch which joins the main course of the Sikiang a few miles above Fatshan. It is flat and presents no special feature for defence, but it enabled the

* The former is on Gough island, opposite Honan, south of Canton city. The latter is south of Haddington and Barrow islands, which again are south of Honan.

Chinese to draw up a line of junks across the two channels of the river, while a battery of six guns on the island itself served to connect the two divisions of war-ships with each other. The junks, to the number of seventy-two, were drawn up so that their stern-guns were pointed towards any boats proceeding up-stream, while their prows were conveniently placed for retreat to Fatshan, if flight became necessary. A steep hill on the left bank had been crowned with a battery of nineteen guns, and this position, strong at all points, being precipitous on one side, was deemed impregnable to attack. Other batteries had been erected along the shore; and when it is remembered that each junk carried, in addition to a large gun, several smaller cannon, it does not seem an exaggeration to say that there were more than 300 pieces of artillery and some 10,000 men engaged in holding a position which had been admirably chosen and carefully strengthened.

The attack on this formidable position began early in the morning of the 1st of June, not inappropriately, as that date was the anniversary of another famous victory in the naval annals of England. Sir Michael Seymour himself headed the advance in the *Coromandel*, having the boats in tow with 300 marines on board. He was followed by six gun-boats or small steamers, accompanied by the boats and crews of all the larger vessels of the fleet. Taken altogether the number of sailors and marines engaged exceeded two thousand. The Chinese look-out was good, and the approaching vessels were speedily detected. They were received with a tremendous fire from junks, batteries, and forts, under which the marines were landed, and ordered to attack and carry the battery on the hill. The guns therein had been so placed as to cover the river, and also the easy approaches which were considered the weak points of the position. The precipitous side had been left to its own strength and fancied security. Even the guns could not be depressed so as to be brought to bear on those who were climbing up by it. The resistance made by the Chinese is never very determined when they find that the weak point of a strong position has been detected, and that they are taken in flank. A few shot were rolled down on the climbers; some stink-pots were thrown;

and then the garrison slowly retired as the Englishmen streamed over the sides of their fortress. It was recorded by an eye-witness that the Chinese retired sulkily at a walk, and that the ill-directed volleys of the marines long failed to make them run. Who knows, but perhaps if their dash had been equal to their fortitude, or if they had had a leader to set the example, the result might have been different, or at least more stubbornly disputed?

But the chief events of the day were not with the marines on the hill, but with the sailors on the river. The tide was at low water, and the Chinese had barred the channel with a row of sunken junks, leaving a narrow passage between known only to themselves. The leading vessel struck on the hidden barrier, but the opening being discovered, other vessels got through. Others again, less fortunate, ran aground either against the same obstacle, or through the shallowness of the stream. However, the river soon rose rapidly, and the boats one after the other were carried over the barrier—only, however, to reach the stakes which the Chinese had placed to mark the range of the guns in their junks. Here the fire from the junks became so furious and so well-directed that it was matter of general astonishment how the boats escaped complete destruction; but the impetuous attack of the sailors was not to be denied. The line of junks was reached and pierced. Junk after junk was destroyed by fire. The patriotism of a whole province did not avail to guard the fleet which the zeal of the Viceroy and the treasure of the great commercial city of Canton had brought together.

The hero of the hour, by general assent, was Commodore Harry Keppel. He, at the head of his own galley and the boats of three of the larger vessels, mustering in all, perhaps, 500 cutlasses, had pierced the line of junks carrying out Nelson's principles. "Never wait, lads," was the spirit-stirring order Keppel shouted to his men, as he boarded the largest junk of the fleet. Nor let us deny their peculiar merit to the Chinese, attacked in an impetuous fashion unknown to their system of war, and always counting for more than mere numbers. If they abandoned their junk as the boarders clambered over the sides, it was in no pusillanimous panic.

They were resolved to baffle the victor of his anticipated prize: the junk was mined, and the English had scarcely left before it blew up. But the English officer had fixed on what he had to do. With his seven boats he hastened on, leaving the destruction of the junks to the rest of the fleet. In his own mind he had determined on the capture of Fatshan as the real way of discomfiting the enemy, and without any misgiving he hastened onwards to complete the work.

After four miles' hard rowing, the large island which lies immediately outside the town of Fatshan was reached, and here the Chinese had made preparations for defence scarcely less formidable than those at Hyacinth island, while the position presented greater natural difficulties to attack. The fire of the Chinese batteries was described as tremendous, at the short range of a quarter of a mile. Keppel's own galley was pierced by several successive shots, and reduced to a sinking condition. That leader had to abandon it, and some of his best officers, Kearney, Barker, and others, had fallen to rise no more.* Three of his boats were aground, one was sunk; there was no choice save to halt in the advance, if only for a breathing space. The gongs from the Chinese junks sounded the premonitory notes of triumph, but their rejoicings were premature. Thinking they had checked the attack, and becoming aware of the full extent of the disaster to their comrades lower down the river, the junks quitted their anchorage, and prepared to retire up the narrow channel to Fatshan. The movement was perceived in time, the English boats closed upon them once more, and the action was renewed. The firing on both sides continued furiously, another English boat was sunk, but the Chinese lost still more heavily. They sacrificed the chance of victory when they took to flight, and junk after junk was given to the flames, or, abandoned by its crew, became the prize of the conqueror. The men

---

* Major Kearney, the Assistant Quartermaster-General of the Expedition, was smashed to pieces by a round shot received full in the heart. Barker, a young middy, died of his wounds. A brother of the latter had been killed at Inkermann. Prince Victor of Hohenlohe, a flag-lieutenant, greatly distinguished himself on this occasion.

of Fatshan turned out along the banks to oppose the foe, and to prevent him carrying off the five junks which were his spoil. They fared no better than their kinsmen on the water; and Keppel returned reluctantly with his small and wearied, but still enthusiastic force, having the five junks in tow, to rejoin the Admiral. He had wished, no doubt, to hold Fatshan, and to put it to ransom; but Sir Michael Seymour prudently forbade the adventure. In these encounters thirteen men were killed and forty wounded,* a loss not heavy if the nature of the work accomplished is considered, but sufficient to remind the sceptical that the Chinese possess some fighting qualities.

When Lord Elgin reached Hongkong the first serious operation of the second war with China had been thus carried out. The Imperial fleet on the Canton river had been destroyed. There only remained to decide the important question, what was the best way to obtain the reopening of the Canton river and city to trade, and the surrender of some of its lofty pretensions by the Pekin Government. The English Plenipotentiary had arrived, but he had not brought with him the army which Sir Michael Seymour had stated to be necessary. It was evident that many months would elapse before other regiments could be supplied in the place of those diverted to India. Not merely was there much inconvenience to commerce from the delay in settling the question, but the Chinese were greatly encouraged by the evidence of the embarrassment in which the English were placed through the mutiny of the native troops in India. It was highly desirable that something should be attempted, but it was not clear what could be done. The garrison of Hongkong was less than 1500 men, and of these one-sixth were invalided. It was the hottest period of the year, and no European force could possibly take the field without the certainty of suffering severely from the climate. So much was plain, although many refused to recognize the hard logic of facts. This was the position of the case when Lord Elgin, having consulted the local

---

* Many of these were severely wounded, and some died. It was noticed that the Chinese shot inflicted cruel wounds.

authorities, felt compelled to decide upon the course of action he should pursue.

The opinion at Hongkong was unanimous among official and mercantile circles alike that the first step should be to take Canton and put an end to Yeh's power in that city. The merchants gave expression to this opinion in a memorial to Lord Elgin, Sir Michael Seymour held the same view on the subject, and Sir John Bowring did not conceal that in his mind he had come to the same conclusion. The boasts of the Chinese at Hongkong, the general belief in the impregnability of Canton, and the continued defiance of Yeh were all quoted or referred to as showing that the first step towards the solution of the China problem was to effect the arrangement of the Canton difficulty, which could only be accomplished by the capture of that city. The view was perfectly sound, but without the necessary force impossible of realization. Sir Michael Seymour said that 5000 soldiers were necessary to seize Canton and hold it against attack; General Ashburnham thought it might be done with 4000, provided they were all effectives, which was practically the same thing. The garrison of Hongkong, even by denuding the fleet, could not produce half that number. Obviously, therefore, an attack on Canton must be postponed until the arrival of fresh troops from Europe or India. The only question, as Lord Elgin said, was whether the wiser course was to do nothing, or to shift the scene of operations for a time to the mouth of the Peiho, where the naval forces of which he could dispose would enable him to address the Pekin Court with some of the authority justified by visible power.

Against a policy of inaction there are always strong objections. It is, indeed, only justifiable when it is not clear that the adversary can do anything, and when no other course seems open to be followed. But it is nearly always the proof of indecision, and indecision, perilous under all circumstances, is generally fatal in the East, where Europeans have to contend against superior numbers, and the irremovable antipathy of subject races, or of peoples who have felt the shame, if they have avoided the fate, of the vanquished. Lord

Elgin was not blind to this truth, and, resolving to do something, declared his intention to proceed with the fleet to the Peiho. He wrote home a long and able despatch on the subject, which received Lord Clarendon's approval, and the preparations were made for carrying the plan into execution.

But the scheme did not commend itself to the judgment of those who had been on the spot throughout the earlier stages of the difficulty. The quarrel with Yeh, they said, was one of a personal character. It should be dealt with and decided at Canton. Trade had continued undisturbed at the other Treaty Ports; but were the central Government drawn into the discussion, it would inevitably lead to the general suspension of intercourse. Already there were symptoms that the Emperor's sympathy was being gradually enlisted in Yeh's favour. The failure of any demonstration at the Peiho would result in the adoption of that official's policy at Pekin, unless he had been previously chastised in a most effectual manner. Lord Elgin could not help being swayed by these representations; he allowed himself to be so far moved by them as to give up the intention of proceeding to the north, almost at the very time that Lord Clarendon was expressing to him the approval of the Cabinet for having ignored the opinions of those on the spot and for having decided upon approaching Pekin direct. Instead of the expedition to the Peiho in the summer of 1857, Lord Elgin went to Calcutta to ascertain in person when Lord Canning would be able to spare those regiments which were to have constituted the China expedition. Excuses may be made for this change of plans, but the fact is undoubted that the Chinese were encouraged by this inaction and indecision. The very months that were to have witnessed the discomfiture of Yeh and the humiliation of the Chinese Government beheld instead the inaction of the English, and the arrival indeed of a High Ambassador from the Queen, but also his speedy departure. At Hongkong, such was the opposition to the projected expedition to the north, that the results of this indecision were approved of, even although Chinese confidence was raised by it to a higher point than ever.

LORD ELGIN'S JOURNEY.

It is unnecessary to follow Lord Elgin to Calcutta.* He returned to Hongkong on the 20th of September, and he found there matters very much the same as he had left them, with the exception that the total force at his disposal now barely sufficed to garrison that place. A blockade had been established of the Canton river, but it had not produced any important results or interesting incidents. The Russian envoy, Count Poutiatine, a man of great ability, who had been the first to predict the coming change in the attitude of the Japanese towards foreigners, had, however, made an experiment towards ascertaining the views of the Pekin authorities. He had been to the mouth of the Peiho, and had requested an interview. The Chinese officers would not allow him so much as to land. It was clear, therefore, that force would be quite as much needed to open the way to the capital as the gates of Canton.

Two months passed away in military preparations at Hongkong. A coolie corps of 750 natives, Chinese, Hakkas, and other races of inferior caste, had been organized by Captain Temple and Mr. Power. Fifteen hundred marines had arrived from England, others were at last on their way from India. The cooler weather had restored the health of the garrison, and emptied the hospitals of Hongkong. Captain Sherard Osborn had brought out a fleet of useful gun-boats, which were to undeceive the Chinese in their belief that the English could not follow their junks or navigate their smaller rivers. Still more, a French ambassador, Baron Gros, had arrived with instructions similar to Lord Elgin's, and he too could dispose of a small naval force to give effect to the

---

* He reached that city in the first week of August, bringing with him 1700 troops. The spread of the Mutiny had caused the diversion to India of two other regiments of the China Expedition. The crews of the *Shannon* and *Pearl* were then formed into that naval brigade which, under Captain William Peel, rendered such splendid service against the mutineers (see Colonel Malleson's "History of the Indian Mutiny," vol. ii.). If there was misfortune for those interested in the speedy adjustment of the China question in this alteration of the force's destination, it was also a merciful dispensation that in the great crisis the Governor-General was able to procure the assistance of these English troops and sailors.

wishes of his Government. The "absurd pretensions of China to superiority" were to be shown once and for all to be untenable. But the immediate question of the hour revolved round the coming attack on Canton rather than upon the exact form in which concessions were to be exacted from Pekin. General Ashburnham had left for India, and General van Straubenzee had assumed the command of the small land force left at Hongkong.

In November Sir Michael Seymour proposed to take some steps towards improving his position for the attack on the city. The principal of these was the occupation of the island of Honan; but in deference to Lord Elgin's wish that no measures should be taken until he had presented his ultimatum to Yeh, the plan was not carried out. On the 12th of December Lord Elgin sent Yeh a note informing him of his arrival in China as the representative with full powers of Queen Victoria. In this note, after dwelling on the generally amicable relations between England and China, he pointed out the repeated insults and injuries which had been inflicted upon foreigners, and on Englishmen in particular, by the authorities of the city of Canton, culminating in an insult to the English flag, and the repeated refusal to grant reparation. But even at the eleventh hour there was time to avert further evil and to stay the progress of hostile proceedings by making prompt and complete redress. The terms were plain and simple. The English demands were confined to two points—the complete execution at Canton of all treaty engagements, including the free admission of British subjects to the city, and compensation to British subjects and persons entitled to British protection for losses incurred in consequence of the late disturbances.

To this categorical demand Yeh made a lengthy reply, going over the whole ground of controversy, reasserting what he wished to believe were the facts, and curtly concluding that the trade intercourse might continue on the old conditions, and that each side should pay its own losses.* If

---

* This was probably his meaning; but his language might have the interpretation, Mr. Wade said, that the English Consul, Mr. Parkes, should bear all the cost himself!

this line of proceeding was intended as a joke, it was both a poor and a very dangerous one. In all probability he thought he was taking the most dignified course, and he may have trusted in the supposed strength of Canton and the military fervour of its population. At any rate, this was not the way to secure a peaceful solution of the question, and on the 15th of the month Sir Michael Seymour seized without opposition Honan point on the island of that name opposite the city. Another ten days were employed in bringing up the last of the troops from Hongkong, and perhaps still more in concerting a plan of action between the allies. But on Christmas Day, 1857, an ultimatum was presented, and forty-eight hours were allowed for the evacuation of the city. To this threat Yeh made no answer. It almost seemed as if he were incredulous to the end that the attack would be delivered, although more than 6000 men * had been at last assembled for the assault.

A preliminary reconnaissance had shown that the best line of attack was on the east side, where Lin's Fort, which could be carried at a rush, would afford a safe and strong position for ulterior operations. The distribution of the placards announcing the coming attack, which was made under great risk and in a most daring manner by Mr. Parkes and Captain Hall, had warned the people of what was going to happen,† and the inhabitants of the more exposed suburbs sought safety in timely flight. Early on the morning of the 28th December the cannonade from the ships showed that the bombardment had begun, and under cover of the fire, which was mainly directed against the city

* Composed as follows:—800 troops (59th, Engineers, etc.), 2500 marines, 1500 sailors, 900 French sailors and marines; together, 5700; with 987 coolie corps (Chinese and Malays); making a total of 6687.

† In this work they met with several adventures, one of which was of a ludicrous character. "They land a strongly-armed company suddenly in a suburb, and post up the proclamation or distribute it to the crowd which were assembled. In one of these rapid descents, Captain Hall caught a mandarin in his chair, not far from the outer gate. The captain pasted the mandarin up in his chair with the barbarian papers, pasted the chair all over with them, and started the bearers to carry this new advertising van into the city. The Chinese crowd, always alive to a practical joke, roared."—Wingrove Cook.

walls, the troops were landed in Kuper creek, opposite the island of the same name, and to the east of the city. The attack on Lin's Fort, where there were three guns in position, began the battle. After standing to their guns for half an hour the small garrison evacuated the position and escaped to the northern hills above Canton, where at Gough's Fort and along the neighbouring heights the Chinese had pitched their principal camps and made their definite plans of defence. This success was rendered of the less importance by the fact that the fort was destroyed soon afterwards by the accidental explosion of the magazine. The country round Lin's Fort consisted of wide undulating fields, which had been used as burial-grounds, and afforded excellent cover. The Chinese sought too late to avail themselves of this, but some skirmishing ensued before their braves were driven back to the camps on the hills. In this position the army passed the night of the 28th, in readiness to resume the more serious operations of the next day. While the infantry rested the bombardment was kept up during the hours of darkness with redoubled energy.

The order for assault at three different points in the eastern wall was given, and simultaneously the whole line rushed towards the wall, the ladders in front, under the command of Captain Bate, who was, however, one of the few men shot down by the desultory fire opened from the gingals. Until the men got close the fire was well sustained; but whether because these Chinese were not the best fighters of their kind, or that they were badly led, they abandoned their defences almost before the ladders were planted against the walls. But although they retired, their object was to make their way along the wide ramparts to the North Gate, where they would be in communication with their main body on Gough Hill. Here, reinforced by some Tartar troops, they endeavoured to restore the battle, and even charged up to the bayonets of the 59th. But they were driven back and out of the city to the large camps on the eminence already mentioned. At the same time the fort on Magazine Hill, the key of the city, and doubly important as commanding that on Gough Hill, was captured without

CAPTURE OF CANTON.

loss or resistance. In less than one hour and a half the attack had been crowned with complete success. The great city of Canton was in the hands of the English and their allies. The Chinese had shown inexplicable want of courage and resolution in defending their city, but the coolies on the side of the invaders had distinguished themselves by their remarkable coolness and pluck during the heat of the action.*

The victors established themselves in force on Magazine Hill, and made use of the walls as a road of communication with the ships. As yet they did not venture into the narrow streets of the city, where many of the late garrison remained concealed and maintained a desultory fire with the outposts at the gates or on the ramparts. The Chinese were compelled to evacuate the forts on Gough and the adjoining hills, as they were all commanded from the Magazine Hill, and their fortifications were in a few days blown up. So far as military success went, it was complete; but there was something strange in the fact that the greater part of the city still remained in possession of the natives and even of Yeh in person. The English troops held the northern heights and forts, as well as the wall in that direction, and thence along the eastern side to the river. The English fleet also commanded the whole course of the river; but the southern part of the town, including the Manchu quarter, continued in the hands of Yeh and his myrmidons. Even in the lowest stress of calamity that official had lost neither his fortitude nor his ferocity. He gave not the slightest symptom of surrender, and his very last act of authority was to order the execution of 400 citizens whom he considered traitors to their country, or perhaps enemies to his own interest. His tenure of power had now reached its close. The Chinese were increasing in boldness; their isolated attacks had become more frequent. From his yamen in the interior of the city Yeh still sent forth threats of defiance, and lavish promises of reward to those who would bring in

* The English loss was fourteen killed and eighty-three wounded, some of whom died subsequently. The French loss was thirty-four killed and wounded.—Official Return.

the heads of the barbarians. It became necessary to track this truculent and implacable enemy to his den. There could be no tranquillity in Canton while Yeh remained at large.

On the 5th of January, 1858, detachments from three different directions moved into the native city. Their object was the official quarter, where stood the public offices and the residences of Yeh and Pihkwei, the governor of the city. The Chinese were taken completely by surprise; and although there were many guards and servants about, no resistance was offered beyond the first few shots fired on penetrating into the narrow lanes that led to the heart of the town. Pihkwei was taken in his own house, the Treasury was carried at a rush, and the very considerable amount of silver stored there was safely removed with the assistance of the Chinese * themselves to the English camp. The French had the credit of capturing the Tartar general in his residence in the Manchu quarter—a vast stone-built suburb which had been long allowed to fall into decay, and the condition of which at once revealed the cause of Chinese defeat. The 7000 Manchu troops, who were supposed to be the mainstay of the Emperor's authority in the second city of his realm, had evidently ceased to exist as a military force for a considerable period. They had become gradually merged in the civil population; while the gloomy walled Manchu quarter remained deserted and desolate—the residence of bats and nauseous creatures.

But although much had been done, Yeh was still at large, and no one seemed to know where to seek him, as all the larger official buildings had been searched in vain. At this moment Mr. Parkes, whose indefatigable inquiries had been at last rewarded by a clue as to Yeh's whereabouts, appeared upon the scene, and, obtaining the assistance of Captain Key and a hundred sailors, proceeded in search of the great

* "But how to remove the heavy load of bullion? Crowds had assembled in front, and a happy thought occurred to one of the officers, 'A dollar's worth of cash to every coolie who will help to carry the silver to the English camp!' In a moment the crowd dispersed in search of their bamboo-poles, and in another moment there were a thousand volunteer Cantonese contending for the privilege of carrying for an enemy their own city's treasure."—Wingrove Cook.

mandarin. At the public library, where it had been said that he would be found, only one poor scholar remained poring, in the midst of the prevailing confusion, over one of the classics in a dark closet. To all questions he at first replied that he knew nothing; but at last he admitted that Yeh had been there some days before, and, more important, that he would now, in all probability, be found at a yamen in the south-west corner of the city. That information was confirmed by the Governor, and thither hastened Mr. Parkes, Captain Key, and the sailors. They arrived there just in time. All the preparations for a hurried flight were apparent. Coolies were packing up, mandarins were running about, Yeh himself was superintending the measures for departure. The sailors forced in the doors, and Captain Key had the pleasure of seizing Yeh when about to escape over the wall in the rear. One mandarin came forward with admirable devotion and proclaimed himself to be Yeh; but the imposture was detected. Captain Key's prisoner was identified by Mr. Parkes, and at once assured of his life, when his self-confidence, which had deserted him at the moment of capture, returned, and he resumed his wonted imperturbability.*

The capture of Yeh completed the victory of the foreigners. In some ways it was more important than the seizure of Canton. It deprived the chief enemy of the English, the man who had spared neither European captive † nor native

---

* Mr., now Lord, Loch says that "Yeh exhibited great self-possession, and remained perfectly quiet while his boxes, of which the room was full, were opened and examined for papers." But this was after Mr. Parkes had assured him that his life was safe. Captain Key, Yeh's capturer, it may be added, was the late Admiral Sir Astley Cooper Key.

† The capture of Mr. Cooper, at Whampoa, will be remembered. He was brutally treated and murdered, there was no moral doubt, by the order of Yeh and his War Committee. There were worse and less-known crimes still. Yeh revealed the fact that eighteen men had been taken, that they died, and that he had been at much trouble to have them properly buried. When asked for particulars, he replied, "How can I tell you who they were, and how can I remember when they were taken? You were fighting from October till January, when you were beaten off and expelled, and your ships ran away. It was during this time." This incident should give a fair idea of the innate arrogance of the Chinese officials. The only circumstance which seemed to bring home to Yeh his unpleasant predicament was when a party of the Coolie

opponent, of all means of showing his fierce resentment or of indulging his anti-barbarian predilections. Knowing what we did of his bitter and relentless hatred, of his falseness, of his breach of the simplest obligations of humanity, far too much consideration was shown towards him. But even the mistaken view of the English representatives as to his importance and the manner in which he should be treated could not save him from the punishment and disgrace which he had so thoroughly deserved. He was conveyed on board one of the ships, and thence, after a further interval, transported to Calcutta, where he died two years later.

Pihkwei was re-appointed Governor of Canton for the maintenance of order. A commission—a Frenchman and two Englishmen,* one of whom was Mr. Parkes—was nominated to assist him in the work of administration. European sailors and soldiers did the duty of policemen. The arms in the arsenals were surrendered and removed to a place of safety. A sense of security and of freedom filled the minds of the Cantonese such as they had perhaps never felt before; and the light-hearted but ever-industrious population turned with renewed energy to those pursuits on which their worldly happiness and prosperity depended. If the mandarins ever thought on the subject at all, there could hardly fail to have been, even to their minds, something suggestive in the order and absence of all cause of complaint visible under the rule of the barbarian conquerors.†

Corps, meeting him on his way to the ship, laid down their burdens and burst out laughing at him. Then he gnashed his teeth in helpless rage. The laughter of Hakkas at a high mandarin of the Empire gave the full point to English victory.

* Colonel Holloway and Captain Martineau des Chenez were the two other members.

† Among the most appalling incidents was the emptying of the prisons—loathsome dens where the victims of official tyranny underwent the most frightful suffering. The scenes witnessed of human misery and wretchedness defy description. Nor were the victims all Chinese. Two Portuguese were rescued; but in the prison set apart for Europeans, the story was unravelled piecemeal of six foreigners (four English and two Frenchmen) who had been most barbarously treated, and then poisoned. Mr. Wingrove Cook has given a moving description of the scenes he witnessed; but no revenge was taken.

AN IMPORTANT DESPATCH.

The difficulty at Canton having been thus settled for the time, it remained for Lord Elgin to undertake that more serious portion of his instructions which required him to place the diplomatic relations between England and China on a satisfactory basis by obtaining the right of direct communication with Pekin. On the 11th of February, 1858, Lord Elgin addressed the senior Secretary of State at the Chinese capital in a lengthy letter, stating what had occurred in the south, and enumerating the further points on which concessions would be required. The military occupation of Canton was to be continued; and the English Plenipotentiary and his French colleague would proceed to Shanghai, where they were prepared to enter into negotiations with the Chinese authorities. Perhaps the most significant sentence in this document was that stating that the English Ambassador would require the official appointed to discuss affairs with him to hold his commission direct from the Emperor of China. This despatch was entrusted to Mr. Oliphant, Lord Elgin's private secretary, for delivery through the Consul at Shanghai to the Viceroy of the Two Kiang for transmission to Pekin. A note in similar terms was sent in the same manner and at the same time by Baron Gros, the representative of France.

In the following month Lord Elgin left Hongkong* for Shanghai, having previously written to Sir Michael Seymour to say that it would be advisable, in view of possible contingencies, "to collect at Shanghai towards the end of March, or as soon after as may be convenient, as large a fleet, more especially of gun-boats drawing little water, as could be spared from service elsewhere."† Meanwhile Mr. Oliphant had succeeded in his mission. The Governor of Kiangsu, in the absence of the Governor-General of the double province of the Two Kiang, received the letter to the first Secretary of State, acknowledged its receipt in a note to Lord Elgin, and stated that he had duly forwarded it to Pekin. This was as

---

* Left March 3rd, reached Amoy on the 6th, Foochow on the 8th, and Ningpo on the 18th, and Shanghai before the 30th.

† Sir Michael Seymour replied that "one of the gun-boats and one gun-vessel have already sailed for Shanghai, and arrangements are in progress for others to follow."—P. 224 of Blue Book.

favourable a commencement for the negotiations as could be expected, for the great difficulty up to this point had been to obtain an admission from the provincial authorities that foreigners had the right to trouble the Pekin Government in any way ; and the merit of a mandarin was certainly enhanced in the eyes of the Emperor and his immediate advisers if he could prevent their being worried by the intrusiveness of the outer barbarians.

The reply of Yuching, Hienfung's chief minister, was not long delayed. When Lord Elgin reached Shanghai he found it awaiting him under cover of another letter from the Viceroy of the Two Kiang.* Yuching's letter was worthy of the great Yeh himself. In its language all the arrogance of the Chinese character stood revealed. There was an absolute refusal to recognize what seemed to the European mind the most obvious facts. Yuching spoke as the representative of a Government that admitted no equal. He seemed to be as blind to the meaning of the defeat at Canton as he was to

---

* The following is the text of Yuching's despatch : " I have perused the letter received, and have acquainted myself with all that it relates to. In the ninth moon of the year (1856) the English opened their guns on the provincial city (Canton), bombarding and burning buildings and dwellings, and attacked and stormed its forts. The gentry and people of both the city and the suburbs thronged the Court of Yeh, imploring him to make investigation and take order accordingly. These are facts of which all foreigners are alike aware. The seizure of a Minister, and occupation of a provincial city belonging to us, as on this occasion has been the case, are also (facts) without parallel in the history of the past. His Majesty the Emperor is magnanimous and considerate. He has been pleased by a decree, which we have had the honour to receive, to degrade Yeh from the Governor-Generalship of the Two Kwang for his maladministration, and to despatch his Excellency Hwang to Kwantung as Imperial Commissioner in his stead, to investigate and decide with impartiality; and it will of course behove the English Minister to wait in Kwantung, and there make his arrangements. No Imperial Commissioner ever conducts business at Shanghai. There being a particular sphere of duty allotted to every official on the establishment of the Celestial Empire, and the principle that between them and the foreigner there is no intercourse being one ever religiously adhered to by the servants of our Government of China, it would not be proper for me to reply in person to the letter of the English Minister. Let your Excellency, therefore, transmit to him all that I have said above, and his letter will in no way be left unanswered."

the pledges given in the Treaty of Nankin—that Treaty which was considered of such little importance at Pekin that the solemnly ratified copy was found in Yeh's yamen at Canton. It required but little knowledge to perceive that from a Government imbued with this high sense of its own dignity no concessions would be wrung save by force, and that even those that were obtained would be shirked and disregarded as frequently as its agents dared. Lord Elgin's reply to Yuching's indirect communication was to return the Viceroy's letter, to point out the infraction of the Treaty of Nankin, and to announce his intention of proceeding to the north, where he could place himself in closer communication with the high officers of the Imperial Government at the capital.

The foreign plenipotentiaries reached the Gulf of Pechihli in the middle of April, and the fleet had been instructed to collect there as speedily as possible from its different stations along the coast. When Lord Elgin appeared at the mouth of the Peiho he drafted a letter to Yuching in temperate language, stating that he had come as the representative of the Queen of England to the Peiho, and that he was willing to hold an interview with any minister duly appointed by the Emperor for the purpose of discussing and arranging together the several questions that had arisen. The letter concluded with a notice that if, after the expiry of six days, no minister should be so accredited, Lord Elgin would consider his pacific overtures to have been rejected, and that he would deem himself at liberty to adopt other measures to carry out his instructions. The appointment of three officials of moderate rank to act as Imperial Commissioners showed that there was a desire or at least the curiosity to know what the foreigners wished before proceeding to the extremity of refusing to hold all relations with them.

But it soon became clear that these Chinese officers had not received the full powers from their sovereign which Lord Elgin had stated to be necessary. They were only appointed to receive the foreign envoys and report what they wanted to the Throne. They had no authority to discuss and determine the various questions which pressed for decision;

and in consequence Lord Elgin declined to meet them. On the 6th of May he again addressed the Chinese representative to the effect that he could only negotiate with a minister having plenipotentiary powers, that the instances of Keying and Elepoo in 1842 formed a precedent for it, and that he would delay further proceedings for six days in order to allow time for the necessary authority to be received from Pekin. Five days later a reply was received, asserting that the powers of the officials appointed were as full as those of Keying had been, and that in any case they were quite ample for the adjustment of affairs.

To this distinct refusal there could only be one reply, and that was that the English Ambassador would proceed up the Peiho to place himself in nearer communication with the Pekin Government, and that the temporary possession of the forts at the mouth of that river would be requisite for the effectual execution of the measure. A delay of some days ensued in consequence of an informal representation by the Russian Envoy, Count Poutiatine, who had tried to play the part of a mutual friend throughout, that a settlement was not hopeless; but when that officer wrote that "the Chinese Emperor refused to admit foreign envoys to Pekin," it became impossible to doubt that the same violent remedies which had been employed in the south would have also to be used in the north.

The harmony of action which usually marks the relations of high English diplomatic officers and the military commanders with whom they may have to act in concert had been disturbed, a few weeks before the question with China had reached this crisis, by the feeling of disappointment which Lord Elgin experienced at what seemed to him the tardy arrival of the fleet in the Gulf of Pechihli. Unfortunately, as it must be considered, he gave expression to his sense of dissatisfaction in a long despatch to Lord Clarendon, which partook very much of the character of a charge against Sir Michael Seymour of supineness and inaction. It should be stated that that gallant admiral had said at Hongkong that he expected to reach Shanghai about the 16th of March, but he qualified that statement a few days later by saying that he could not leave Hongkong till the 15th of March; and that, therefore, he would not be in readiness to move from Shanghai with his force until the end of the first week of April. This delay at the outset might have suggested the idea that there was a possibility of the preparations requiring some longer time than had been supposed or allowed for. Be that as it may, Sir Michael Seymour was prevented leaving Hongkong until the 25th of March, and he did not reach the Gulf of Pechihli until the 24th of April, and the various vessels of the fleet arrived in the course of the following fortnight. Early in May twenty-five war-ships were drawn up opposite the forts which guarded the entrance to the Peiho, and the approach to Pekin from the sea.

Lord Elgin was not unnaturally annoyed at the delay which he termed "a most grievous disappointment," for he believed that if he had had ten or twelve gun-boats he would have been allowed by the forts to proceed unresisted to Tientsin, and that the Emperor's Government would have yielded at once everything that was demanded of them. It is certainly possible that the affair might have had that satisfactory issue; but hopes are a bad basis on which to found a charge against a gallant colleague, in connection with whom sluggishness was the last term that could be justly used. Of course it was intelligible that Lord Elgin and his diplomatic assistants should be disappointed at their month's delay off the Taku forts; but remembering the monsoon and the possibility of accident interfering with what was at the most an indefinite understanding, it is impossible to avoid the conclusion that greater caution would have been shown in staying at Shanghai till the naval force had been assembled than in hastening on to the Peiho, or, as that course was adopted, that a better and more generous feeling towards a colleague would have been evinced if the delay in the arrival of the ships had been attributed to circumstances coming under the category of the unavoidable.

On the 19th of May the allied fleet proceeded to the mouth of the river, and summoned the commandant to surrender his forts on the following morning. No reply being received to the summons, the gun-boats proceeded in-shore to make the attack. The Chinese fired the first shots, which were returned after the different vessels had arrived at short range. The bombardment continued for one hour and a quarter, when, all the gunners having been driven out of the batteries, the troops and sailors landed and seized the forts. Further resistance was encountered higher up the river, and a desperate attempt was made to let down a fleet of fire-ships among the foreign vessels. But the former was overcome, and the fire-junks drifted ashore instead of among the boats of Sir Michael Seymour and Admiral Rigault de Genouilly. The victors proceeded as far as the village or town of Taku, where they had established their advanced position while the forts in their rear were being dismantled. The resistance made by the Chinese, who included some of the best troops from the capital, was creditable without being obstinate. The forts had been renovated and armed with guns sent from Pekin and Tientsin. The *élite* of the Imperial Guard was stated to have held the entrenched camp in the rear of the batteries. But neither their courage nor their preparations availed them. Their commander, in despair at his defeat, committed suicide, and others imitated his example. The loss among the English was slight. The French suffered more heavily, partly from the accidental explosion of a magazine, partly from the unequal fortunes of battle.

The capture of the forts on the Peiho roused the Pekin Government to a sense of the imminent danger in which they stood. Their military resources had been devoted to their defence, and with their fall they were for the time exhausted. Tientsin could offer no resistance. The foreigners there commanded the entrance to the Grand Canal, and with it the route by which the capital was supplied with grain. No opposition could be made save at Pekin itself, and a siege of the capital might entail dangers far greater than were involved in the unconditional surrender of every claim advanced by the dreaded and still more hated Europeans. The fleet proceeded up the river to Tientsin, and Lord Elgin also hastened to that city, where he could count with some degree of confidence on the Chinese showing a more conciliatory demeanour. Before

OCCUPATION OF TIENTSIN.

he reached that place he had received another communication from the Imperial Commissioners, stating that they would repair in person to the Emperor and ascertain what arrangements he would sanction. At the same time they had the courage to declare that the ascent of the river by the English ships was highly improper. Their representations produced an immediate effect on the mind of the Emperor, as Kweiliang and Hwashana, both Manchus and dignitaries of the highest order, were instructed "to go by post route to the port of Tientsin for the investigation and despatch of business." The powers * conferred upon these officers were of the amplest kind, and greater even than those previously bestowed upon Keying.

It is a distinctive feature of the Chinese character that when the season has arrived for making concessions it can adapt itself to the necessities of the time, and show as broad and generous a spirit of toleration as those who have constantly in their mouths the assertion of human equality and mutual rights. These moments have, no doubt, been rare, but one of them had arrived when the English Ambassador reached Tientsin, and when it seemed as if the allied forces could make their way almost unresisted to the capital. Nothing could be more satisfactory than the proposals of

* The following is the text of the Imperial decree appointing them, dated 1st of June : " Tau having failed in his treatment of the questions regarding which the different nations had been earnestly preferring requests, we have specially commissioned Kweiliang and Hwashana to proceed to Tientsin and to devise means by which (these questions) may be satisfactorily discussed and decided. As, however, to judge from the communications written by the different nations, they are in doubt as to whether Kweiliang and his colleague are competent or not to act independently, we command Kweiliang and Hwashana, with affectionate earnestness, to set the right before them. If the matters (in question) be reasonable, the desire for a cessation of hostilities sincere, anything not injurious to China will certainly be granted them : there is no occasion for further doubt or suspicion. Kweiliang and his colleague have been specially chosen by us ; they will not fail (on the one hand) to be careful of the dignity of the State ; (on the other) to watch in silence the feelings of the people. In any conjunction requiring that the action taken be suited to the emergency, unless the case be in contravention of what is right and proper, their course is to deviate (from the beaten track) accordingly. Let them be zealous!"

the new Chinese representatives. They were most anxious to settle all matters without the least delay, and they had been invested with the fullest possible authority to arrange matters without reference to Pekin. Had the two Manchus been brought up in the school of Talleyrand and Metternich they could not have shown greater tact in managing the details of an important negotiation, or more eagerness to make as speedy an end as possible of an unpleasant business.

At this point in the negotiations there re-appeared upon the scene a man whose previous experience and high position entitled him to some consideration. Less than a week after Lord Elgin's preliminary interview with Kweiliang and Hwashana, he received a letter from Keying stating that he had come in obedience to the Emperor's commands to discuss and decide the foreign question. Keying acted separately from the other Commissioners; and his intervention promised to produce embarrassment and delay. It was not clear at first what he really wanted, or with what object he had sought an interview with Lord Elgin; but when he told Mr. Wade that the solution of the difficulty was the withdrawal of the fleet from the river, the motives of his visit and overtures became sufficiently evident. He had been sent in the expectation that from his special knowledge of the English he might succeed in inducing them to forego the great advantage of position which they had acquired by the possession of Tientsin.

The idea was probably his own, and he undertook the task in the hope of recovering the political power and rank of which he had been deprived eight years before. But it may have been that the Emperor Hienfung recollected the existence of the author of the Nankin Treaty, and thinking that he might be able to mislead the foreigners, or to obtain some concession from them, had commanded him to proceed to Tientsin. His fervour in the task he had accepted was increased by the knowledge that the penalty of failure would be death. Perhaps his efforts would have been not altogether unavailing, for Keying's reputation had been great among Europeans, if documents found in Yeh's yamen had not shown that he had played a double part throughout that old transaction, and that at heart he was as anti-foreign as the most Chauvinist of them all. Seeing that his plan was discovered, and that his wiles would be useless, Keying returned to Pekin. There he was at once arrested and brought before the Board of Punishment. Found guilty without delay, Prince Hwui Wang pressed for his immediate punishment, and it was ordered that, as he had acted "with stupidity and precipitancy," he should be strangled at once. As an act "of extreme grace and justice," the Emperor sent him, as a member of the Imperial Family, the order "to put an end to himself," and it was obeyed. Let it, however, be recorded to the credit of the aged minister that it was he who impressed upon the English representative the necessity of the Emperor's plenipotentiaries being provided with a seal or kwan fang, as without it no treaty or concession would be valid.

The discussion of the various points on which Lord Elgin insisted as the basis of a fresh treaty occupied several days; and more than one interview took place between Mr. H. N. Lay, one of Lord Elgin's Chinese Secretaries, and the Chinese Commissioners and their secretaries on the subject of these details. The matter to which the most serious objection was raised was that of allowing a Resident Minister at Pekin. This demand was opposed on general and on specific grounds. Such a thing had never been heard of, and was attended with peril both to the individual and to the Chinese Government. Then, changing their position, they asked would the minister wear the Chinese dress, would one minister suffice for all the Powers, would he make the kotow, or at least bend both knees to the Emperor? But every conversation ended with the declaration that these concessions were inadmissible and could never be granted.

On the 11th of June the Commissioners sent an important despatch, making the most of the concessions demanded, and suggesting, as a compromise on the main point, that the visit of an English Ambassador to Pekin might be postponed until a more favourable opportunity. The important admission was made that "there is properly no objection to the permanent residence of a Plenipotentiary Minister of Her Britannic Majesty;" and a later passage stated that the Emperor would select, after the conclusion of peace, an officer to proceed to convey his compliments to the Queen of England in token of amity. On the terms of this letter the Commissioners proceeded to draw up the regular treaty. Some further slight delays ensued, but on the 26th of June the treaty was formally signed, and on the 4th of July Lord Elgin received the ratification by Imperial Edict of the Treaty of Tientsin.*

There remained for settlement the scarcely less important revision of the tariff, which was to be undertaken by England alone, the other states contenting themselves with a most-favoured-nation clause which secured for them without trouble whatever privileges or advantages might be gained by the English. The discussion of this matter was resumed after Lord Elgin's return from Japan, where he had the satisfaction of promptly concluding a very favourable treaty. The Imperial Commissioners who had acted at Tientsin were re-appointed with several assistants, and with the Viceroy of the Two Kiang as a colleague, to proceed to Shanghai for the express purpose of arranging all commercial matters and placing them on the desired satisfactory footing. The arrangement of the details of the tariff was entrusted by Lord Elgin to Mr. Wade † and Mr. Oliphant. The general principle arrived at was that neither the import nor the export duties should exceed five per cent. *ad valorem;* but the principal clause, and the one of historical importance, was that legalizing the importation of opium on payment of a duty of thirty taels, or about ten pounds per chest, at the price then prevailing equivalent to 8 per cent.

It had long been evident that, apart from all consideration of the moral effect of the use of opium, the extensive

---

* The Treaty of Tientsin contained fifty-six articles, and one separate article with reference to the indemnity. The right to station an Ambassador at Pekin, "if Her Majesty the Queen see fit," was the most important concession.—See Appendix for this Treaty.

† Mr. Wade, in his despatch of October 1, 1858, expresses his indebtedness for assistance to Mr. Horatio Lay and Dr. Wells Williams.

smuggling of it into the country as a contraband article was attended with special dangers, and followed by distinct evil consequences of its own. Its exclusion did not prevent the Chinese obtaining the drug in any quantities they pleased, and only provided a cause of frequent strife along the coast at the same time that it resulted in defrauding the Government of a legitimate source of revenue. The representative of the United States, Mr. Reed, had been one of the first to perceive this, and it was greatly due to his arguments that Lord Elgin had taken up the position which he did on the subject, and which he was confirmed in maintaining by the ready acquiescence of the Chinese Commissioners in its wisdom and necessity.

The satisfactory arrangement of the tariff emboldened the Chinese representatives to assume a firmer tone with regard to the permanent residence of an English envoy at Pekin. On this point their language was always consistent. They deprecated the proposal not merely because it was novel, but because it promised to entail the gravest dangers for the strength and dignity of the Emperor's executive, at this moment hard pressed through the Taeping rebellion. These representations could not fail to produce some effect, especially as they were confirmed by the personal observation of the Europeans themselves. Obviously it was not to the interest of the Power which had just concluded a treaty with China that the Emperor's authority should be repudiated, and anything calculated to entail that result called for a distinct expression of disapproval. The attitude of the Chinese representatives on other points conciliated good will, and when their entreaties were added to their arguments it was found both advisable and politic to assure them informally, but none the less solemnly, that for the present the right should be waived, save in so far as it would be necessary to assert it in the following year for the purpose of the exchange of the Treaty ratifications at Pekin. That necessary act once performed, the English Plenipotentiary stated that his efforts would be to induce the Queen's Government to abstain from enforcing the extreme letter of its rights, at the price of embarrassing the Chinese Government. The practical settlement of the point was, therefore, to stand over until that occasion; but while there was much in the attitude of the Chinese ministers to justify the hope of a satisfactory issue, there was also evidence in the opposite and less agreeable direction. While Kweiliang and his colleagues were showing the greatest courtesy and zeal in arranging matters of detail in connection with a peace that was "to endure for ever," information not to be treated lightly declared that the Chinese were engaged in restoring and improving the fortifications on the Peiho, and in issuing secret edicts for the purpose of raising national effort to the point of staking everything on the expulsion of the foreigners. Which conduct better represented the national mind time alone could show.*

During these months of negotiation in the north, Canton had remained in the possession of the English forces, assisted by a small body of French, to show that the two great nations of the West held identical views on the subject of China's position with regard to Europeans. They had not been altogether uneventful. There had been alternate periods of confidence and tranquillity, of doubt and danger. Nowhere else did the population reveal so many elements of hostility, or so deep-rooted an antipathy towards foreigners. The teaching of such men as Lin and Yeh had evidently fallen upon fertile ground, and the Cantonese, instead of acquiring from their closer contact with foreigners a greater sympathy for them, seemed to discover a more intense and irremovable hatred. The occupation of the city by an English garrison, the proclamation of martial law to be administered by a foreign Commissioner and a native Governor, had been followed by such beneficial results that few of the respectable classes resident in the town were disposed to murmur at a rule which guaranteed absolute security. But in the surrounding villages and townlets it was different. There no advantage was obtained by the English occupation; and the gentry

* Lord Elgin left China in March, 1859, arriving in England on 19th of May. There will not be two opinions on the point that both in its features and its consequences Lord Elgin's Embassy to China was one of the most important missions ever sent from this country to the East.

of the province were incited by the natural impulse of patriotism, by the hope of office or notoriety, and even by a feeling of emulation, to arm their followers and employ their resources in raising bands of soldiers or braves to free the land of the strangers who had established themselves so easily and so securely in their chief city.

Soon after the first departure of Lord Elgin the garrison at Canton was reinforced by the arrival of two Bengal regiments;* and when the five forts on the northern hills had been all blown up the position in a military sense might be held to be secure, more especially as the Magazine Fort was to be, in extreme need, the rallying point. The danger which first presented itself was caused by attacks on detached parties venturing, either for amusement or reconnoitring purposes, beyond the limits of the town. The friendliness of the people of some of the nearer villages often encouraged these parties to go beyond safe limits, when they rarely failed to discover the presence of fortified camps and hostile villages. Collisions brought about in this manner frequently ensued; and if they fortunately did not entail any loss of life, they certainly increased the confidence and extended the influence of the hostile bands prowling about the neighbourhood. Although martial law prevailed in the city, proclamations were set up in different places offering rewards for European heads, and, what was still more significant, desperate and systematic attempts were made to earn them. Several of the followers of the native regiments were murdered, and more than one Englishman had reason to feel grateful for a narrow escape.

At first, Pihkwei was suspected of connivance in these outrages; and when the placards became more numerous and more hostile he was deposed and placed under arrest. Later information went far to exculpate him, and he was released.

---

* The 65th and 70th Native Infantry. A regrettable incident occurred soon after the arrival of the latter regiment. A party of sepoys, not looting, as Mr. Wingrove Cook reported, but employed in finding lodgings, were fired on by a French picket, and three men were killed or wounded. The circumstance made the more noise at the time, as French soldiers had not shown a very strict regard for the rights of property.—See Colonel Fisher's "Narrative of Three Years' Service in China."

It was then found that this manifestation of hostility emanated from the new Viceroy named Hwang, who had just been sent from Pekin to supersede Yeh, and also that he was strongly supported by the provincial gentry, who had formed themselves into patriotic committees. Prominent among these was that known as the Fayuen committee, which carried its zeal so far as to place a reward of 30,000 dollars on the head of Mr. Parkes. The principal result of this disturbed state of public feeling was that an order was sent from Downing Street, in October, 1858, to continue the occupation of Canton until further instructions.

Some natural hesitation was shown in attacking the hostile bands which had assembled in the neighbourhood, from a desire to afford no excuse for saying that the English were less scrupulous than they expected the Chinese to be in fulfilling the terms of the peace. This moderation was only misunderstood, and with the new year more vigorous proceedings were reluctantly sanctioned. The town of Shektsin, six miles north-west of Canton, had been turned into the principal camp and base of the loyal braves of Kwantung. The position was strong. Surrounded on three sides by a river sixty yards wide, the only approach to it was along a causeway completely commanded by the guns in the fortress. The Chinese had shown very considerable skill in constructing batteries on the opposite side of the river; and, in every way, Shektsin was a place not to be attacked without deliberation and extensive preparation. A strong force was directed against it by land, and the attack was made in two columns, while the gun-boats proceeded to bombard it from the river. For a time the garrison kept up a steady fire, but the gun-boats turned their position. The Chinese escaped with very trifling loss, and when the English and French stormers gained the interior they found the place abandoned.*

* Colonel Fisher, who was present, writes: "The enemy meanwhile had evaporated; no other term can describe the sudden breaking-up of what seemed a large body of men. A very few dead and wounded were found. Some labourers were here and there apparently busily employed in the fields, their scanty clothing suggesting the idea that their uniform was hidden in an adjoining hole, and that, by some mysterious process, their gingals had been transformed into hoes."

DOUBLE-FACED POLICY.

The effect produced by this expedition was excellent. Even the turbulent people of Fatshan received in a most respectful manner the officers and force which visited them a few weeks later. The agreeable change which had passed over the minds of even the patriotic gentry of Canton and the neighbourhood was finally demonstrated by the unopposed entry of the English general and troops into Fayuen itself. While the courtesy and hospitality of the authorities seemed to augur well for the future, the discovery of cannon, hastily concealed in the surrounding ponds, went to show how hollow and illusory these appearances and the expectations based on them were.

While, therefore, the Treaty of Tientsin and the events which accompanied and followed it justified some hope as to the future harmony of China's foreign relations, there were not wanting sinister reports to show that the Chinese Government was still far removed from the frame of mind necessary to admit the equality of the Western rulers and their right to depute resident ambassadors to Pekin. Nor was clearer evidence altogether wanting. Copies of secret decrees found at Shektsin went far towards proving that the Emperor had been insincere throughout the whole of the negotiations. His language in these documents, which cannot be suspected of fabrication, was very lofty, and could only bear the construction that he would not waive one iota of his rights and privileges, and that he intended to employ the whole force of his Empire in overthrowing the foreigners and in retrieving past disgrace and disaster.

Such language was more in accordance with what was known of Hienfung's character than the fair words and promises sent to Tientsin. He had come to the throne with the resolve to wipe out the stigma of Taoukwang's weakness and misfortune; but, instead of succeeding, he had incurred greater misery and disappointment. From his point of view he contended that Yeh had deceived and misled him, and that, taken at a disadvantage by the English admiral on the Peiho, he had been compelled to make a virtue of necessity, and to surrender privileges as deeply cherished as his life and honour. But his forces were gathering to his aid, and a little time would enable him to look to his defences. Should he yield his birthright without a struggle? These were unquestionably the thoughts that filled the mind of the young ruler; and there was to be no long interval before they were revealed. The question of a permanently resident ambassador at Pekin was to remain in abeyance, but in the course of a few months the representative of the English Queen would demand permission to proceed to the capital of China for the solemn exchange of the Treaty ratifications. What answer would he receive when he came?

CHAPTER XIII.

THE PEKIN CAMPAIGN.

THE matter that was to put the sincerity of the Chinese Government to the touch was the reception of the English officer entrusted with the duty of exchanging the ratified copies of the Treaty of Tientsin. Would that envoy be permitted to proceed to Pekin? If he were allowed to do so it would be a proof of good faith. Afterwards there would be room to allow that the objections of the Celestial authorities to residence in their capital were based on some valid reason, and not merely on a sentiment of blind hostility to foreigners. If they would only show on this one special occasion their anxiety to meet the English and other peoples on a footing of diplomatic equality, it would be possible to acquiesce in the reasonableness of their contention that so long as the Emperor's Government was encompassed by difficulties it would be politic not to enforce the right of permanent residence. The great object, after all, was to obtain some certain proof of the sincerity of the Government of Emperor Hienfung, and that was the point which Mr. Bruce's mission to Pckin was to test and decide.

By the most natural process of selection Mr. Frederick Bruce, who had been secretary to his brother's embassy, and who had returned to England with the copy of the Treaty of Tientsin, was appointed in the early part of 1859 to proceed to China as Her Majesty's representative for the purpose of exchanging the ratifications* of that treaty.

---

* See Lord Malmesbury's letter of 1st March, 1859. The exchange of ratifications had to be effected before the 26th June.

He was instructed to apprise the Chinese authorities that, while the English Government would not renounce the right of having a permanent ambassador at Pekin, it was prepared for the moment to waive it so far as to allow diplomatic relations to be for a time transacted at Shanghai. But with the resolve to insist on the ratification taking place at Pekin there existed also a fear that the Chinese would oppose that arrangement with all the means in their power. "All the arts at which the Chinese are such adepts will be put in practice to dissuade you from repairing to the capital," wrote the Foreign Secretary to Mr. Bruce; and the result only too fully confirmed the prescience of Lord Malmesbury. Any proposition to exchange the ratifications elsewhere than at Pekin was to be met with a simple and emphatic refusal. That point conceded, however, much should be yielded to the convenience or necessities of the Chinese.

Mr. Bruce arrived at Hongkong in April, and he found among the foreign community there ample confirmation of the fears of his own Government that the Chinese were entertaining the hope, even at the last moment, of averting the humiliation involved in the reception of the English Envoy at Pekin. Not only were rumours rife as to the extensive military preparations in progress on the Peiho, but the Chinese Commissioners, Kweiliang and Hwashana, had not quitted the neighbourhood of Shanghai, where they still seemed to contemplate being able to conclude the last offices in connection with the Treaty before returning to the capital with a claim on the gratitude of their master for having saved his dignity. The conflict between such expectations and the realities of the situation was precipitated by Mr. Bruce's formal letter to Kweiliang announcing his imminent departure for Tientsin, and his hope that safe conveyance to Pekin, and appropriate accommodation in that city, would be provided for himself and his suite.

But already it was apparent that the anti-foreign party, encouraged, as rumour had it, by Hienfung's own example, would make a desperate effort to thwart the British Envoy; and that, if Mr. Bruce was to succeed in his task, it would be necessary for him to be supported by as imposing a force as the British military commanders in the south could direct to the Peiho. What had been suspicion became conviction when the Imperial Commissioners presented a request to Mr. Bruce on his arrival at Shanghai to enter upon the discussion of some unsettled details, calmly ignoring that the ratification was stipulated to take place within a period of which only a limited number of days remained unexpired. Chinese policy has always relied upon procrastination as one of the strongest weapons at its disposal. It would have been in their eyes a legitimate device to have detained the English representative at Shanghai under various pretexts, and to have then taken full advantage of the expiration of the stipulated term to declare that the non-ratification of the Treaty invalidated its most important clauses.

Neither Mr. Bruce's instructions nor his own reading of the situation justified any delay in proceeding to the north. A land force was summoned from the garrison at Canton, the fleet was directed from the Canton river to the Peiho, and Admiral Hope, who had succeeded to the command of the China squadron, assumed the personal direction of the operations which were to ensure the safe and honourable reception of Mr. Bruce at Tientsin. The arrival of the fleet * preceded that of the envoy by a little more than two days, and Admiral Hope, in the execution of the plan agreed upon with Mr. Bruce, sent a notification to the officers at the mouth of the Peiho that the English Envoy was coming. The reception met with could not but be considered distinctly discouraging. Two boats were sent ashore in order to establish communications. The first unfavourable symptom observed was that the entrance to the river had been barred by a row of iron stakes, while a still more formidable line of inner defence, consisting of an admirably constructed boom, hindered the approach of any hostile force; and when the boats approached the shore they were warned not to attempt to land by an armed and angry crowd. In reply to the

---

* The fleet reached the Shalootien islands on the 16th of June. On the 17th it proceeded to the Peiho, and Mr. Bruce arrived on the 20th.

inquiries of the interpreter, it was said that these warlike preparations had been made against the rebels, that the garrison only comprised the local militia, and that no high official would be found nearer than Tientsin. In reply to a further demand, they were understood to promise that a sufficient passage for the English vessels would be made through the barriers in the course of a few days. On the occasion of a second visit the crowd became still more demonstrative, one man even drawing his sword on the interpreter; but the most unequivocal token of hostility was the closing up of the narrow passages through the stakes instead of their being widened, as had been promised.

In face of these proceedings, which could hardly be considered equivocal, there remained no alternative save to obtain by force that which was denied to friendship. The garrison declared themselves to be only the local militia acting in behalf of what they held to be their own rights, and without any reference to Pekin. There were reasons to doubt the correctness of this statement, but in the event of their defeat it simplified the position of Hienfung and his ministers. The latter could throw all the blame on the shoulders of the local officers, and deny their personal responsibility. There was, therefore, good reason to suppose that were a vigorous move made against the forts at the mouth of the river, the opposition of the Pekin Government would be as easily overcome as that of its soldiers. The result, of course, depended on the success of the attack; but no one anticipated that the forts would make a more effectual defence than they had the previous year, or that skill and enterprise would fail to obtain their usual rewards.

On the 25th of June, some preliminary matters having been arranged as to the disposal of the fleet, and as to how the marines and engineers told off to land were to be conveyed on shore, the attack on the forts began with the removal * of the iron stakes forming the outer barrier. This part of the operations was unopposed. A sufficient passage

* Performed by the *Opossum* steamer, which steamed up to them, fastened a hawser round each in turn, and then reversed engines.—Fisher.

was soon made, and the vessels proceeded towards the entrance of the river without a single shot having as yet been fired on the one side or the other. But when the ships reached and struck against the inner boom the forts immediately opened fire with a rapidity and precision which showed that the guns had been trained to bear on that very spot. Eleven vessels in all were engaged in the attack; four of these reached the inner boom and engaged the forts at comparatively close quarters. The severity of the fire was soon shown in the damaged condition of the ships. Two of the gun-boats were soon in a sinking state, and not one had escaped without severe injury. Many officers and men had been killed; and when, after a three hours' cannonade, the firing from the shore became less vigorous, either from want of ammunition or from loss of men, the English expedition had itself suffered too much to be able to take full advantage of the superiority which its artillery had demonstrated after so fierce a contest.

The doubtful fortune of the day might, it was hoped, be restored by an attack on land; and the marines and engineers, who had been sent from Hongkong, and who had been placed in junks, were brought up to attempt the capture of the forts by storm. The troops on landing had to cross for 500 yards a mud-bank, in which the men sank ankle deep; and as they were exposed all the time to a sustained and galling fire, they suffered considerable loss. Some of the marines, too, in their haste, rendered their guns useless by wetting their powder, or by jumping too quickly into the mud and getting them stuffed up with it. Before the attacking party reached the edge of the ditch it was clear that the chances were decidedly against a successful issue; the ladders and portable bridges had been all destroyed by the fire of the Chinese. An advance party got to within twenty yards of the works, but it could effect nothing. It was safely withdrawn under cover of the darkness, which very fortunately soon set in and shielded the retreat of the forlorn hope, and the Chinese were left in undisputed possession of the Taku forts and of the glory of the battle. The loss of three gun-boats, and of more than 300 men killed and wounded, was a very heavy price to pay; but the most serious of all the consequences of this disastrous attempt on the Taku forts consisted in its encouraging the Chinese to believe in their capacity to resist the English, and thus necessitated a fresh campaign. The engagement in the Fatshan channel had first shown Europeans of what a vigorous resistance Chinese troops were capable; but the defence of the Taku forts produced a wider and more profound impression. It was no longer wise or possible to treat the Chinese as adversaries of an utterly contemptible character.

The effect of this success on Chinese policy proved hardly less than it was on foreign opinion. The Chinese Government had up to that point been swayed by opposite counsels. The party in favour of peace and the ratification of the Treaty was hardly less able or active than that which demanded if not war at least an unyielding attitude towards foreigners. At the very moment that the garrison of the Taku forts was making its resolute and successful stand against Admiral Hope the former had gained the upper hand, and were causing a house to be prepared at Pekin for Mr. Bruce's use and reception. There is little doubt that had Admiral Hope's attack been successful the acts of the Chinese at the mouth of the Peiho would have been repudiated, and that the so-called peace party would have carried the day, much to their country's advantage. But if that was the probable result of an English success, the consequences of what happened were quite as unequivocally in favour of the war party. Sankolinsin, the Mongol prince who had first checked the Taeping rebels in their march on Tientsin, became the master of the situation, and declared that there was nothing to fear from an enemy who had been repulsed by the raw levies of Pechihli, while he held the flat country between Pekin and the Peiho with the flower of the Tartar Banners. The mind is most easily influenced by the recent event, and the successful defence of the Taku forts obliterated all remembrance of previous defeat. The ratification of the Treaty of Tientsin at Pekin became at once impossible, save at the point of the sword.*

* Mr. Bruce concluded his despatch home describing these events as

So distinct a repulse could not fail to be followed by a long delay in the resumption of military measures calculated to be decisive. Mr. Bruce returned to Shanghai, the land forces were sent back to Hongkong, and the vessels of the fleet were disposed so as to be of the best possible use in protecting the interests of English commerce. Beyond this nothing could be attempted until further instructions and reinforcements arrived from Europe. Nearly three months elapsed before the Cabinet in London had made up its mind as to the course it should pursue, but on the 26th of September, 1859, Lord John Russell wrote to say that military preparations had been authorized which would enable the objects of English policy to be obtained. While these preparations were in progress, and the new Cabinet of Lord Palmerston was somewhat reluctantly, if we are to judge from the delay, sanctioning the further employment of force, some events happened in China to show whither matters were tending.

The news of the victory at Taku was followed by a general ebullition of anti-foreign feeling in all the trading ports. At Shanghai a riot occurred, when an Englishman was killed, and Mr. Lay, an officer in the Chinese service, and several others, were wounded. The Russian minister, General Ignatieff, succeeded in reaching Pekin by the land route long open to Russia from Kiachta, and in obtaining the ratification of the Russian Treaty; but the details of his reception showed that the treatment accorded to him was not of a kind that would have satisfied what the English held to be the requirements of the occasion. The American Minister, Mr. Ward, also proceeded to Pekin, but not by the Peiho. The circumstances * of his visit would not have been held

follows:—"Whatever may be the ultimate decision of this Government with reference to the Treaty of Tientsin, I do not think that its provisions can be carried out until we recover our superiority in the eyes of the Chinese."

* The circumstances of this visit to Pekin were described as follows in the *North China Herald* of August 22nd, 1859:—" The mission was limited to twenty persons and landed at Pehtang. During residence in the capital, the Americans were confined to their quarters, and not allowed the use of horses. They were refused audience unless they made the kotow, and the exchange of the ratifications was effected not at Pekin,

satisfactory by either Mr. Bruce or the British Government. As Mr. Wade stated, the Government and people of China will hold ambassadors received in this manner at precisely the same value as a Loochooan or Siamese envoy.

The length of time required for communication between England and China entailed a delay which the impossibility of conducting naval operations in the Gulf of Pechihli during the winter further extended. But a demand arrived from London requiring the amplest apology to be promptly made for the attack on the ships by the Taku forts, and that if this were not forthcoming a heavy indemnity would be demanded and obtained by force as compensation for the insult and injury. In November, 1859, a plan of joint action was proposed and agreed upon between the Governments of France and England. An armed expedition was to be sent to the China Sea, and the island of Chusan was to be again occupied as a base for further operations in the Gulf of Pechihli. It was hoped that the expedition would have assembled at its rendezvous by the middle of April, 1860, and that decisive operations would have been begun before the end of that month. An ultimatum, with thirty days' grace, was presented by Mr. Bruce on the 8th of March, embodying certain terms with which the strictest compliance was stated to be necessary.*

but at Pehtang. An Imperial Decree of the 9th of August draws an unfavourable comparison to the English between the conduct of Mr. Bruce and Mr. Ward."

* The objects of the English Government were described in the official despatch of Lord John Russell dated the third of January, 1860, which were detailed by Mr. Bruce in his proclamation as follows :—
" The Emperor of China made, in June, 1858, a treaty of peace with my sovereign, the Queen of the United Kingdom of Great Britain and Ireland. The Emperor ordered, by special command, that this treaty should be signed by his ministers. It was provided and agreed to by the Emperor that the treaty should be ratified at Pekin within a year. But when, in pursuance of the orders of the Queen my sovereign, I attempted to go by the ordinary route of the Peiho to Tientsin, with a view to travel with my retinue from the mouth of the Peiho to Pekin, in the most friendly manner, I found the river blocked with stakes and rafts, and when the Queen's ships endeavoured to remove these obstacles they were fired upon, and many of the Queen's subjects were killed and wounded by the cannon of the Emperor of China. No notice had been given to me that

The troops which were to form the expedition were mainly drawn from India, and Sir Hope Grant,* who had not merely distinguished himself during the Mutiny, but who had served in the first English war with China during the operations round Canton, was appointed to the command of the army; while Admiral Hope, strongly reinforced in ships and with Admiral Jones appointed to assist him, retained the command of the naval forces. A force of five batteries of artillery, six regiments of infantry, two squadrons of cavalry, together with a body of horse and foot from the native army of India, amounting in all to about 10,000 men, was to be placed at the general's disposal in addition to the troops already in China. The French Government had agreed to send another army of about two-thirds this strength to co-operate on the Peiho, and General Montauban had been named to the command. The collection of this large expedition brought into prominence the necessity of employing as ambassador a diplomatist of higher rank than Mr. Bruce's; and accordingly in February Lord Elgin and Baron Gros were commissioned to again proceed to China for the purpose of securing the ratification of their own treaty. They were instructed to demand from the Chinese Government as compensation to both countries a sum equivalent to nearly five millions sterling.†

the way to Pekin by this the ordinary passage was to be prohibited, although a year had gone by since the signature of the treaty. The Queen has ordered me to ask for an apology for this injury, and to demand the ratification of the treaty. The Queen has asked that the Emperor should fulfil his solemn promise. This has been refused. It has been refused, also, to the Queen's august ally, the Emperor of the French. We go to seek redress for these wrongs and to require that the word of the Emperor should be observed, and that an indemnity should be paid for the loss of men and the heavy expense of obtaining redress. We wish to continue the friendly relations of commerce and peaceable communications with the people of China. We wish to carry on the war only against armed men, and the advisers of the Emperor of China who urge him to war. Rely upon our disposition to respect your property and your families. Peace may thus continue between our nations, and the Emperor be forced to do justice."

* Sir William Mansfield was first named for the command; but the Duke of Cambridge very justly insisted that, by right both of seniority and active experience, the command was the due of Sir Hope Grant.

† 60,000,000 francs to each, or £4,800,000 in all.

The impossibility of obtaining these concessions in any other way than by force was clearly shown in the reply sent by the minister Pang Wanching to the ultimatum of the English representative. In this document all his demands were categorically refused. No indemnity would be paid, no apology given. If the English went to Pehtang they might perhaps be allowed to proceed to Pekin; the route by Taku and the Peiho would never be open to them, and there was much more to the same effect expressed in language the reverse of courteous. To place their hostility in the most unequivocal light, the Grand Secretary Pang Wanching directed his reply to the Viceroy of the Two Kiang for transmission, thus openly ignoring that clause of the Tientsin Treaty which provided that there should be direct communication between the English representative and the ministers at the capital.

For a time the interest in the situation ceased to be diplomatic, and all attention centred in the military movements for curbing the pride of an arrogant Government. Sir Hope Grant reached Hongkong in March, and by his recommendation a stronger native contingent* was added, raising the English force in the field to more than 13,000 men. A lease, through the skilful negotiation of Mr. Parkes, was obtained in perpetuity, of Kowlun and Stonecutter island, where, from their salubrious position, it was proposed to place the troops on their arrival from India or England. Chusan was occupied the following month without opposition by an English brigade of 2000 men; but the effect produced by this move was practically none, and it may be doubted whether any end could be served by the temporary occupation of an island about the fate of which the Emperor cared nothing at all. The French commanders were opposed to it, and the views of the allies were already far from being completely in accord—the usual experience of all alliances.

The summer had commenced before the whole of the expedition assembled at Hongkong, whence it was moved

* One Sikh regiment, four Punjab regiments, two Bombay regiments, one Madras regiment of foot, and two irregular regiments of Sikh cavalry, known as Fane's and Probyn's Horse. Sir John Michel and Sir Robert Napier commanded divisions under Sir Hope Grant.

THE TAKU FORTS.

northwards to Shanghai about a year after the failure of the attack on the forts of the Peiho. A further delay was caused by the tardiness of the French, and July had begun before the expedition reached the Gulf of Pechihli. Then opposite opinions led to different suggestions, and while the English advocated proceeding to attack Pehtang, General Montauban drew up another plan of action. But the exigencies of the alliance compelled the English, who were ready, to wait for the French, who were not, in order that the assault might be made simultaneously. Before that time arrived the French commander had been brought round to the view that the proper plan of campaign was that suggested by the English commander; viz. to attack and capture Pehtang, whence the Taku forts might be taken in the rear. It is somewhat remarkable to observe that no one suggested a second time endeavouring to carry by a front attack these forts, which had in the interval since Admiral Hope's failure been rendered more formidable.

At Pehtang the Chinese had made few preparations for defence, and nothing of the same formidable character as at Taku. The forts on both sides of the river were neither extensive nor well armed. One contained thirteen guns, the other eleven. The garrison consisted largely of Tartar cavalry, more useful for watching the movements of the foreigners than for working artillery when exposed to the fire of the new Armstrong guns of the English. The attacking force landed in boats and by wading, Sir Hope Grant setting his men the example. No engagement took place on the night of disembarkation, and the advanced force slept on an elevated causeway bordered on both sides by the sea which had flooded a considerable extent of the country. When morning broke, a suspicious silence in the enemy's quarters strengthened the belief that Pehtang would not be defended; and Mr. Parkes, ever to the front when information was wanted, soon was able to confirm the impression. While the garrison had resolved not to resist an attack, they had contemplated causing their enemy as much loss as if he had been obliged to carry the place by storm, by placing shells in the magazine which would be exploded by the moving of some gunlocks put in a spot where they could not fail to be trodden upon. This plot, which was thoroughly in accordance with the practices of Chinese warfare, was fortunately divulged by a native more humane than patriotic, and Pehtang was captured and occupied without the loss of a single man.

This success at the commencement enabled the whole of the expedition to be landed without further delay or difficulty; but Pehtang was itself an inadequate base for so large a military force. The great merit of the movement was that it avoided a direct attack by the Peiho. The inconveniences of Pehtang as a station were so great that no longer halt would be made there than was inevitable, and three days after its capture reconnoitring parties were sent out to ascertain what the Chinese were doing, and whether they had made any preparations to oppose an advance towards Taku or Tientsin. Four miles from Pehtang the scouts came in sight of a strongly-entrenched camp, when several thousand men opened fire upon the reconnoitring parties with their gingals, and a dozen Europeans were wounded. The object being only to find out what the Celestial army was doing, and where it was, the Europeans withdrew on reaching the proximity of so strong a force. The great difficulty was to discover a way of getting from Pehtang on to some of the main roads leading to the Peiho; for the whole of the surrounding country had been under water, and was more or less impassable. In fact, the region round Pehtang consisted of nothing but mud, while the one road, an elevated causeway, was blocked by the fortified camp just mentioned as having been discovered by the reconnoitring party. A subsequent reconnaissance conducted by Colonel Wolseley* revealed the existence of a cart-track which might prove available for troops.

This track was turned to advantage for the purpose of taking the Chinese position in flank, and to Sir Robert Napier's division was assigned this, as it proved, difficult

---

* Now Lord Wolseley, then Deputy-Assistant Quartermaster-General to the Chinese Expedition, and the author of an excellent account of the campaign, published in 1862.

BATTLE OF SINHO.

operation.* When the manœuvre of outflanking had been satisfactorily accomplished, the attack was commenced in front. Here the Chinese stood to their position, but only for a brief time, as the fire from eighteen guns, including some 40-pounders, soon silenced their gingals, and they precipitately abandoned their entrenchments. While the engagement in front had reached this favourable termination Sir Robert Napier had been engaged on the right hand with a strong body of Tartar cavalry, which attacked with considerable valour, and with what seemed a possibility of success, until the guns opening upon them and the Sikh cavalry charging, their momentary dream of victory was dispelled. The prize of this battle was the village of Sinho with its line of earthworks, one mile north of the Peiho, and about seven miles in the rear of the Taku forts.

The next day was occupied in examining the Chinese position and in discovering, what was more difficult than its capture, how it might be approached. It was found that the village, which formed a fortified square protected by batteries, could be best assailed by the river-bank, for the only obstacle in this quarter was that represented by the fire of the guns of two junks, supported by a battery on the opposite side of the river. These, however, were soon silenced by the superior fire directed upon them, and the guns were spiked by Captain Willis and a few sailors who crossed the river for the purpose. The flank of the advance being thus protected, the attack on Tangku itself began with a cannonade from thirty-six pieces of the best artillery of that age. The Chinese fire was soon rendered innocuous, and their walls

* Sir Hope Grant described the march as follows :—" We encountered great difficulty in dragging the artillery along. The horses got bogged, the guns sank up to their axletrees, and the waggons stuck fast. At last we were compelled to leave the waggon bodies behind us, and to content ourselves with the gun and waggon limbers. At one time I really thought we should be obliged to give up the attempt; but Sir Robert Napier (afterwards Lord Napier of Magdala) was full of energy; the struggle was continued, and sound ground was reached." Mr. Robert Swinhoe, in his account of the North China Campaign, says: " It was a fearful trudge across that mud for the unfortunate troops. . . . The Punjaubees, finding their boots an impediment, preferred throwing them away, and, tucking up their trousers, pushed boldly on."

and forts were battered down. Even then, however, the garrison gave no signs of retreat, and it was not until the Armstrongs had been dragged to within a very short distance of the walls, and the foot-soldiers had absolutely effected an entrance, that the garrison thought of their personal safety and turned in flight.*

Some days before the battle and capture of Tangku, Lord Elgin had received several communications from Hang, the Governor-General of Pechihli, requesting a cessation of hostilities, and announcing the approach of two Imperial Commissioners appointed for the express purpose of ratifying the Treaty of Tientsin. But Lord Elgin very wisely perceived that it would be impossible to negotiate on fair terms unless the Taku forts were in his possession; and with the view of being in a position to discuss affairs with the Chinese at as early a date as possible, he wrote to Sir Hope Grant expressing his wish that there might be no unnecessary delay in reducing those forts, and in thus opening the way to Tientsin. The capture of Tangku placed the allied forces in the rear of the northern forts on the Peiho; and those forts once occupied, the others on the southern side would be practically untenable and obliged to surrender at discretion.

Several days were passed in preliminary observations and skirmishing. On the one side the whole of the Tartar cavalry was removed to the southern bank; on the other,

---

* Colonel Fisher gives a very graphic description of the attack on Tangku in his "Narrative of Three Years' Service in China." During the night preceding the attack Colonel Mann and he, with a party of engineers, constructed a trench at 500 paces from the wall—an operation which contributed not a little to the easy success on the following day. The following description of how the Chinese fought at a great disadvantage will be interesting :—"The Tartars really for a time fought nobly. I saw one man, stripped to his loins, fighting his gun singlehanded after every bit of parapet near him had been knocked away and our shot was crashing in all around him. . . . Having seen that one brave man, the survivor of all the gun detachment, working his gun alone, loading and firing among the corpses of his fellows, with no one near to applaud him nor witness his fall, working away, whatever his motive might be, until he fell like his comrades, I could not but picture to myself in all those grim groups of eight or ten perhaps at a gun, how one by one they had fallen and yet the survivors disdained to fly."

CAPTURE OF THE FORTS.

a bridge of boats was thrown aross the Peiho, and the approach to the northern fort carefully examined up to 600 yards from the wall. At this point again the views of the allied generals clashed. General Montauban wished to attack the southern forts. Sir Hope Grant was determined to begin by carrying the northern. The result furnished the most expressive commentary on the respective merits of the two plans. The attack * on the northern fort commenced on the morning of the 21st of August with a heavy cannonade; the Chinese, anticipating the plans of the English, were the first to fire. The Chinese fought their guns with extraordinary courage. A shell exploded their principal magazine, which blew up with a terrible report; but as soon as the smoke cleared off they recommenced their fire with fresh ardour. Although this fort, like the others, had not been constructed with the same strength in the rear as in the front, the resistance was most vigorous. A premature attempt to throw a pontoon across the ditch was defeated with the loss of sixteen men. The Coolie Corps here came to the front, and, rushing into the water, held up the pontoons while the French and some English troops dashed across. But all their efforts to scale the wall were baffled, and it seemed as if they had only gone to self-destruction. While the battle was thus doubtfully contested, Major Anson, who had shown the greatest intrepidity on several occasions, succeeded in cutting the ropes that held up a draw-bridge, and an entrance was soon effected within the body of the works. The Chinese still resisted nobly, and it was computed that out of a garrison of 500 men but 100 escaped.†

There still remained four more forts on the northern side of the river, and it seemed as if these would offer further resistance, as the garrisons uttered threats of defiance to a

---

* A division of 2500 English troops was alone engaged. Eleven heavy or siege guns, four batteries, and one rocket battery were employed in the cannonade. The French force consisted of 400 infantry and two field batteries.

† The English loss was 22 killed and 179, including 21 officers, wounded. Lord Napier of Magdala was hit in five places without being actually wounded. To these figures must be added the French loss.

summons to surrender. But appearances were deceptive, and for the good reason that all of these forts were only protected in the rear by a slight wall. The French rushed impetuously to the attack, only to find that the garrison had given up the defence, while a large number had actually retired. Two thousand prisoners * were made, and evidently no further resistance would be attempted. The fall of the forts on the northern bank was followed by an immediate summons to those on the southern to surrender; and as they were commanded by the guns in the former, they yielded with as good a grace as they could muster. The following day formal occupation was made, and the spoil included more than 600 cannon of various sizes and degrees of efficiency. On that day also the fleet, which had during these operations been riding at anchor off the mouth of the river, proceeded across the bar, removed the different obstacles that had been intended to hinder its approach, and Admiral Hope anchored in security off those very forts which had repulsed him in the previous year, and which would in all probability have continued to defy any direct attack from the sea. Let it not be said, therefore, that Sir Hope Grant's capture of the Taku forts reflected in any way on the courage or capacity of Admiral Hope for the failure in 1859. If it bore in any way on the earlier event, it went to show that the Chinese were capable of a skilful as well as a valiant defence.†

* Mr. Loch, in his "Narrative of Events in China," says : "In the inside there were upwards of two thousand men seated on the ground; they neither moved nor spoke as we approached. They had thrown away their arms and divested themselves of all uniform or distinctive badge that could distinguish them as being soldiers."

† It should be stated that after the capture of the northern forts Mr. Parkes, Mr. Loch, Major Anson, and three French officers crossed the river with a flag of truce, carried on the spear of a Sikh trooper, in order to arrange for the giving up of the southern forts. The undertaking was one of extreme danger and difficulty. The mandarins refused to make any sign, and as the small party passed below the walls of the forts they could see the gunners with their lighted matches through the embrasures. They made their way, however, unmolested to Hang's yamen at Taku, where the surrender of the other forts was soon agreed upon as the only way to obtain the cessation of hostilities. For a graphic description of the scene with Viceroy Hang, see Mr. (now Lord) Loch's narrative already mentioned.

TIENTSIN OCCUPIED.

By this decisive success, which fully justified the foresight of the English general, the road to Tientsin was opened both by land and by the river. The fleet of gun-boats, which had participated as far as they could without incurring any undue danger in the attack on the forts, was ordered up the Peiho; and the English ambassador, escorted by a strong naval and military force, proceeded to Tientsin, where it would be possible, without any loss of dignity, to resume negotiations with the Pekin Government, whose excessive pride made it seem false, but whose weakness had now been rendered painfully apparent. Up to this point the Chinese had never been altogether sincere in their peace overtures. They had not abandoned the hope of victory even when the large foreign army landed at Pehtang. The defeat at Sinho had somewhat shaken their confidence; but while the forts at the mouth of Peiho remained untaken the situation was not regarded as desperate. Papers found in the general's quarters at Sinho showed that, while Hang was expressing his own and his master's desire for peace, the military officers were requested to lose no occasion of achieving a military success. The one thing that was clear at Pekin was that only victory could save the national honour and avert the necessity of making those further concessions to foreigners which were incompatible with the dignified position claimed by the Emperor. The hope that Heaven might intervene in favour of the Celestial dynasty was never abandoned until Pekin itself had been reached; but after the capture of the Peiho forts it became clear that some terms must for the moment be arranged with the English, if only as a means of gaining time for the arrival of Sankolinsin's last levies from Mongolia.

The advanced gun-boats arrived at Tientsin on the 23rd of August, and three days later the greater portion of the expedition had entered that city. No resistance was attempted, although several batteries and entrenched camps were passed on the way. Precautions were at once taken to make the position of the troops as secure as possible in the midst of a very large and presumably hostile population. The people showed, according to the ideas of Europe, an extraordinary want of patriotic fervour, and were soon engaged, on the most amicable terms, in conducting a brisk trade with the invaders of their country; but there was never any doubt that on the first sign of a reverse they would have turned upon the foreign troops, and completed by all the means in their power their discomfiture. Several communications passed between the opposite camps during these days; and when Hang announced the withdrawal of all Chinese troops from Tientsin he expressed a wish that the English ambassador would not bring many vessels of war with him. But such requests were made more with the desire to save appearances than from any hope that they would be granted. The reality of their fears, and of their consequent desire to negotiate, was best shown by the appointment of Kweiliang, who had arranged the Treaty of Tientsin, as High Commissioner to provide for the necessary ceremonies in connection with its ratification.

Kweiliang apparently possessed powers of the most extensive character; and he hastened to inform Lord Elgin, who had taken up his residence in a beautiful yamen in Tientsin, that he had received the Emperor's authority to discuss and decide everything. In response to this notification the reply was sent that the three conditions of peace were an apology for the attack on the English flag at the Peiho, the payment of an indemnity, including the costs of the war, and, thirdly, the ratification and execution of the Treaty of Tientsin, including, of course, the reception at Pekin of the representative of the Queen of England on honourable terms adequate to the dignity of that great sovereign. To none of these was Kweiliang himself disposed to raise any objection. Only in connection with the details of the last-named point was there likely that any difference of opinion would arise; and that difference of opinion speedily revealed itself when it became known that the English insisted on the advance of their army to the town of Tungchow, only twelve miles distant from the walls of Pekin. To the Chinese ministers this simple precaution seemed like exacting the extreme rights of the conqueror, before, too, the act of conquest had been consummated; for already fresh troops were arriving from Mongolia and Manchuria, and the valour of Sankolinsin was beginning to revive.

That the Chinese Government had under the hard taskmaster, necessity, made great progress in its views on foreign matters was not to be denied, but somehow or other its movements always lagged behind the requirements of the hour, and the demands of the English were again ahead of what it was disposed to yield. Hienfung had at last been brought low enough to acquiesce in the reception of the English plenipotentiary in Pekin itself. No doubt both he and his ministers had anticipated being able to cover their retreat and discomfiture by a success snatched from the foreigners over some point of etiquette; but such hopes were rudely dispelled by the announcement that the English ambassador would not proceed to Pekin unless he were supported by the presence of that formidable army which had pierced the most efficient defences of the Empire and scattered the braves of Sankolinsin in mortal fray.

If the Chinese Government had promptly accepted the inevitable, and if Kweiliang had negotiated with as much decision as he pretended to be his mission, peace might have been concluded and the Chinese saved some further ignominy. But it soon became clear * that all the Chinese were thinking about was to gain time, and as the months available for active campaigning were rapidly disappearing it was imperative that not the least delay should be sanctioned. On the 8th of September Lord Elgin and Sir Hope Grant left Tientsin with an advanced force of about 1500 men; and marching by the high-road, reached the pretty village of Hosiwu, half-way between that town and the capital. A few days later this force was increased by the remainder of one division, while to Sir Robert Napier was left the task of guarding with the other Tientsin and the communications with the sea.

At Hosiwu negotiations were resumed by a nephew † of

---

* As the result of an interview between Messrs. Wade and Parkes on the one side and Hangki and ultimately Kweiliang also on the other. It was then discovered that the Commissioners had no express authority, and that consequently everything would have to be referred to the Emperor at Pekin. See Blue Book, pp. 156-8.

† Tsai, Prince of I.

the Emperor, who declared that he had received authority to conclude all arrangements; but he was curtly informed that no treaty could be concluded save at Tungchow, and the army resumed its advance beyond Hosiwu. The march was continued without molestation to a point beyond the village of Matow, but when Sir Hope Grant approached a place called Chan-chia-wan he found himself in presence of a large army. This was the first sign of any resolve to offer military opposition to the invaders since the capture of the Taku forts, and it came to a great extent in the manner of a surprise, for by a special agreement with Mr. Parkes the settlement of the difficulty was to be concluded at Chan-chia-wan in an amicable manner. Instead, however, of the Emperor's delegates, the English commander found Sankolinsin and the latest troops drawn from Pekin and beyond the Wall occupying in battle array the very ground which had been assigned for the English encampment.

The day before the English commander perceived that he was in face of a strong force Mr. Parkes and some other officers and civilians* had been sent ahead with an escort of Sikh cavalry to arrange the final preliminaries with the Imperial Commissioners at Tungchow, both as to where the camp was to be pitched and also as to the interviews between the respective plenipotentiaries of the opposing Powers. This party proceeded to Tungchow without encountering any opposition or perceiving any exceptional military precautions. Troops were indeed observed at several points, and officers in command of pickets demanded the nature of their business and where they were going, but the reply "To the Commissioners" at once satisfied all inquiries and opened every barrier. The one incident that happened was of happy augury

* The party consisted, besides Mr. Parkes, of Mr. Henry Loch, Mr. De Normann, and Mr. Bowlby, the Special Correspondent of the *Times*. The escort was composed of six English dragoons and twenty sowars of Fane's Horse under the command of Lieutenant Anderson. Colonel Walker and Mr. Thompson, of the Commissariat, also accompanied the party for a portion of the way (Loch's narrative). They were subsequently joined on their return by the French commissioner, Comte d'Escayrac de Lauture, who prepared an exhaustive memoir on the condition of the Chinese Empire, in six volumes.

for a satisfactory issue* if the result went to prove the fallaciousness of human expectations.

A change had in the meanwhile come over the minds of the Imperial Commissioners, whether in accordance with the working of a deep and long-arranged policy, or from the confidence created by the sight of the numerous warriors drawn from the cradle of the Manchu race for the defence of the capital and dynasty, can never be ascertained with any degree of certainty. Their tone suddenly assumed greater boldness and arrogance. To some of the Englishmen it appeared "almost offensive," and it was only after five hours' discussion between Mr. Parkes and the Commissioners at Tungchow that some sign was given of a more yielding disposition. The final arrangements were hastily concluded in the evening of the 17th of September for the arrival of the troops at the proposed camping-ground on the morrow, and for the interview that was to follow as soon afterwards as possible. While Mr. Parkes and some of his companions were to ride forward in the morning to apprise Sir Hope Grant of what had been agreed upon, and to point out the site for his camp, the others were to remain in Tungchow with the greater part of the Sikh escort.†

On their return towards the advancing English army in the early morning of the following day, Mr. Parkes and his party met with frequent signs of military movement in the country between Tungchow and Chan-chia-wan. Large bodies of infantry and gingal-men were seen marching from all quarters to the town. At Chan-chia-wan itself still more emphatic tokens were visible of a coming battle. Cavalry were drawn up in dense bodies, but under shelter. In a nullah one regiment of a thousand sabres was stationed with the men standing at their horses' heads ready for instant

---

* "A party of mandarins galloped up to us; one of them, evidently a man of high rank, asked which was Mr. Parkes. On his being told, he mentioned that he was the general who had commanded at the battle of Sinho. He said, 'It will be peace now, and I shall be glad to take by the hand those who fought me that day.'"—Loch's narrative.

† Mr. Parkes, Colonel Walker, Mr. Loch, Mr. Thompson, the Dragoons and three Sikhs formed the first party. De Normann, Bowlby, and Anderson remained at Tungchow with seventeen Sikhs.

action. At another point a number of men were busily engaged in constructing a battery, and in placing twelve guns in position. When the Englishmen gained the plain they found the proposed site of the English camp in the actual possession of a Chinese army, and a strong force of Tartar cavalry, alone reckoned to number six or seven thousand men, scouring the country. To all inquiries as to what these warlike arrangements betokened no reply was made by the soldiers, and when the whereabouts of the responsible general was asked there came the stereotyped answer that " he was many li away."

To the most obtuse mind these arrangements could convey but one meaning. They indicated that the Chinese Government had resolved to make another endeavour to avert the concessions demanded from them by the English and their allies, and to appeal once more to the God of Battles ere they accepted the inevitable. The first attitude of the Imperial Commissioners the day before had represented the true promptings of their hearts, and the subsequent change must be attributed to the desire to obtain a few more hours' grace for the completion of Sankolinsin's plans. When the whole truth flashed across the mind of Mr. Parkes, the army of Sir Hope Grant might be, and indeed was, marching into the trap prepared for it, with such military precautions indeed as a wise general never neglected, but still wholly unprepared for the extensive and well-arranged opposition planned for its reception by a numerous army established in a strong position of its own choosing. It became, therefore, a matter of the greatest importance to communicate the actual state of affairs to him, and to place at his disposal the invaluable information which the Englishmen returning from Tungchow had in their possession. But Mr. Parkes had still more to do. It was his duty to bring before the Chinese Imperial Commissioners at the earliest possible moment the knowledge of this flagrant breach of the convention he had concluded the day before, to demand an explanation, and to point out the grave consequences that must ensue from such treacherous hostility. In that supreme moment, as he had done on the many other critical occasions

SIR HARRY PARKES.

of his career in China—at Canton and Taku in particular—the one thought in the mind of Mr. Parkes was how best to perform his duty. He did not forget also that, while he was almost in a place of safety near the limits of the Chinese pickets, and not far distant from the advancing columns of Sir Hope Grant, there were other Englishmen in his rear possibly in imminent peril of their lives amid the Celestials at Tungchow.

Mr. Parkes rode back, therefore, to that town, and with him went one English dragoon, named Phipps, and one Sikh sowar carrying a flag of truce on his spear-point. We must leave them for the moment to follow the movements of the others. To Mr. Loch was entrusted the task of communicating with Sir Hope Grant; while the remainder of the party were to remain stationary, in order to show the Chinese that they did not suspect anything, and that they were full of confidence. Mr. Loch, accompanied by two Sikhs, rode at a hard canter away from the Chinese lines. He passed through one body of Tartar cavalry without opposition, and reached the advanced guard of the English force in safety. To tell his news was but the work of a minute. It confirmed the suspicions which General Grant had begun to feel at the movements of some bodies of cavalry on the flanks of his line of march. Mr. Loch had performed his share of the arrangement. He had warned Sir Hope Grant. But to the chivalrous mind duty is but half performed if aid is withheld from those engaged in fulfilling theirs. What he had done had proved unexpectedly easy; it remained for him to assist those whose share was more arduous and perilous. So Mr. Loch rode back to the Chinese lines, Captain Brabazon insisting on following him, again accompanied by two Sikhs,* but not the same who had ridden with him before. Sir Hope

---

* Sowars of Probyn's Horse. One was named Nal-sing, "for whom I shall always entertain an affectionate recollection" (Loch). Mr. Loch is the present Lord Loch. Captain Brabazon did not go, it should be stated, without an object, as the following extract from Sir Hope Grant's journal, edited by Captain Henry Knollys, will show:—"At first I refused this latter request, but Brigadier Crofton, commanding the Royal Artillery, pointed out how valuable would be the knowledge of the ground thus obtained, and I regret to say I yielded."—P. 109.

Grant had given him the assurance that unless absolutely forced to engage he would postpone the action for two hours.

This small party of four men rode without hesitation, and at a rapid pace, through the skirmishers of the Chinese army. The rapidity of their movements disconcerted the Chinese, who allowed them to pass without opposition and almost without notice. They rode through the streets of Chanchia-wan without meeting with any molestation, although they were crowded with the mustering men of the Imperial army. They gained Tungchow without let or hindrance, after having passed through probably not less than thirty thousand men about to do battle with the long hated and now feared foreigners. It may have been, as suggested, that they owed their safety to a belief that they were the bearers of their army's surrender! Arrived at Tungchow, Mr. Loch found the Sikh escort at the temple outside the gates unaware of any danger—all the Englishmen being absent in town, where they were shopping—and a letter left by Mr. Parkes warning them on return to prepare for instant flight, and saying he was off in search of Prince Tsai. In that search he was at last successful. He found the High Commissioner, he asked the meaning of the change that had taken place, and was told in curt and defiant tones that "there could be no peace, there must be war."

The last chance of averting hostilities was thus shown to be in vain. Prince Tsai endorsed the action of Sankolinsin. Mr. Parkes had only the personal satisfaction of knowing that he had done everything he could to prove that the English did not wish to press their military superiority over an antagonist whose knowledge of war was slight and out of date. He had done this at the greatest personal peril. It only remained to secure his own safety and that of his companions. By this time the whole party of Englishmen had re-assembled in the temple; and Mr. Loch, anxious for Mr. Parkes, had gone into the city and met him galloping away from the yamen of the Commissioner. There was no longer reason for delay. Not an Englishman had yet been touched, but between this small band and safety lay the road back through the ranks of Sankolinsin's warriors. From Tungchow to the advanced post of Sir Hope Grant's army was a ten-mile ride; and most of the two hours' grace had already expired. Could it be done?

By this time most of the Chinese troops had reached Chan-chia-wan, where they had been drawn up in battle array among the maize-fields and in the nullahs as already described. From Tungchow to that place the country was almost deserted; and the fugitives proceeded at "a sharp canter" and unmolested along the road till they reached that town. The streets were crowded partly with armed citizens and peasants, but chiefly with panic-stricken householders; and by this time the horses were blown, and some of them almost exhausted. Through this crowd the seven Englishmen and twenty Sikhs walked their horses, and met not the least opposition. They reached the eastern side without insult or injury, passed through the gates, and descending the declivity found themselves in the rear of the whole Chinese army. The dangers through which they had passed were as nothing compared with those they had now to encounter. A shell burst in the air at this moment, followed by the discharge of the batteries on both sides. The battle had begun. The promised two hours had expired. The fugitives were some ten minutes too late.

The position of this small band in the midst of an Asiatic army actually engaged in mortal combat with their kinsmen may be better imagined than described. They were riding down the road which passed through the centre of the Chinese position, and the banks on each side of them were lined with the matchlock-men among whom the shells of the English guns were already bursting. Parties of cavalry were not wanting here, but out in the plain where the Tartar horsemen swarmed in thousands the greatest danger of all awaited the Europeans. Their movements were slow, painfully slow, and the progress was delayed by the necessity of waiting for those who were the worse mounted.* In the accumulation of difficulties that stared them in the face not the least seemed to be that they were advancing in the teeth of their own

---

* Principally De Normann and Bowlby. But they were "all in the same boat, and, like Englishmen, would sink or swim together."

countrymen's fire, which was growing fiercer every minute. In this critical moment men turned to Mr. Parkes, and Captain Brabazon expressed the belief of those present in a cool brave man in arduous extremity when he cried out, " I vote Parkes decides what is to be done."

To follow the main road seemed to be certain destruction and death without the power of resisting ; for even assuming that some of them could have cut their way through the Tartar cavalry, and escaped from the English shell, they could scarcely have avoided being shot down by the long lines of matchlock-men who were ready to fire on them the instant they saw their backs. There was only one possible avenue of escape, and that was to gain the right flank of the army, and endeavour to make their way by a detour round to the English lines. Assuredly this was not a very promising mode of escape, but it seemed to have the greatest chances of success, if, indeed, it was not the only one feasible. But when the Chinese troops, who had up to this regarded their movements without interfering, saw this change in their course, they at once took measures to stop it. A military mandarin said if they persisted in their attempt they would be treated as enemies and fired upon ; but that he was willing to respect their flag of truce, and that if they would accompany him to the general's presence he would obtain a safe conduct for them. The offer was accepted, partly no doubt because it could not be refused, but still also on its own merits. Safe conducts during the heat of battle, even with civilized European peoples, are, however, not such easy things either to grant or to carry out.

Mr. Parkes accepted his offer, therefore, and he, Mr. Loch, and the Sikh trooper Nalsing, bearing a flag of truce, rode off with the mandarin in search of the general, while the five other Europeans and the Sikh escort remained on the road awaiting their return. They proceeded to the left, where it was understood that Sankolinsin commanded in person. They met with some adventures even on this short journey. Coming suddenly upon a large body of infantry, they were almost pulled from their horses, and would have been killed but for the mandarin rushing between them and shouting to the men "not to fire." A short distance beyond this they halted, when the approach of Sankolinsin was announced by loud shouts of his name from the soldiery. Mr. Parkes at once addressed him, saying that they had come under a flag of truce, and that they wished to regain their army. The Chinese commander replied to his remarks on the usages of war in true Tartar fashion—with laughter and abuse. The soldiers pressed round the unfortunate Englishmen and placed their matchlocks against their bodies. Escape was hopeless, and death seemed inevitable. But insult was more the object of the Mongol general than their death. They were dragged before him and forced to press the ground with their heads at the feet of Sankolinsin.* They were subjected to numerous other indignities, and at last, when it became evident that the battle was going against the Chinese, they were placed in one of the country carts and sent off to Pekin. While Mr. Parkes and Mr. Loch were thus ill-used, their comrades waiting on the road had fared no better. Shortly after their departure the Chinese soldiers began to hustle and jeer at the Englishmen and their native escort, and as the firing increased and some of the Chinese were hit, they grew more violent. When the news was received of what had happened to Mr. Parkes, and of how Sankolinsin had laughed to scorn their claim to protection, the soldiers could no longer be restrained. The Englishmen and the natives were dragged from their horses, cruelly bound, and hurried to the rear, whence they followed at no great distance their companions in misfortune.

While the greater portion of these events had been in progress, Colonel Walker, Mr. Thompson, and the men of the King's Dragoon Guards, had been steadily pacing up and down on the embankment as arranged, in order to show the Chinese that they suspected no treachery and had no fears. They continued doing this until a French officer

---

* Some of the Chinese officers did not share Sankolinsin's views. After this incident the prisoners were for a time placed in the tent of the second general in command, who treated them with civility, and told Mr. Parkes that "he deplored the failure of negotiations which, he said, the Chinese army had hoped would have brought the war to a happy conclusion."—Loch.

joined them, but on his getting into a dispute with some of the Chinese about his mule, he drew his pistol and fired it at them. He was immediately killed. There was then no longer the least hope of restraining the Chinese, so the whole of the party spurred their horses and escaped to the English army under a heavy but ineffectual fire from matchlocks and gingals.* It will be understood that this party was never in the same perilous position as the others. It had remained at the advanced post of the Chinese army, and when the disturbance came it was only a short gallop to a place of safety. But their flight was the signal for the commencement of the battle, although at that very moment, had they only known it, the chief party of Englishmen had gained the road east of Chan-chia-wan, and, if the battle had only been delayed a quarter of an hour, they might all have escaped.

But the two hours of grace were up, and Sir Hope Grant saw no further use in delay. General Montauban was still more impatient, and the men were eager to engage. They had to win their camping ground that night, and the day was already far advanced. The French occupied the right wing, that is the position opposite the spot where we have seen Sankolinsin commanding in person, and a squadron of Fane's Horse had been lent them to supply their want of cavalry. The battle began with the fire of their batteries, which galled the Chinese so much that the Tartar cavalry were ordered up to charge the guns, and right gallantly they did so. A battery was almost in their hands, its officers had to use their revolvers, when the Sikhs and a few French dragoons, led by Colonel Foley,† the English Commissioner with the French force, gallantly charged them in turn, and compelled them to withdraw. Neither side derived much advantage from this portion of the contest, but the repulse of the Tartar cavalry enabled the French guns to renew their fire with much effect on the line of Chinese infantry.

* Colonel Walker was wounded in the hand, Mr. Thompson in the back, and one of the dragoons in the leg. Sir Hope Grant speaks of there being one sowar and four dragoons only.
† The late General the Hon. Sir St. George Foley, K.C.B.

While the French were thus engaged on the right, the English troops had begun a vigorous attack from both their centre and left. The Chinese appeared in such dense masses, and maintained so vigorous, but fortunately so ill-directed a fire, that the English force made but little progress at either point. The action might have been indefinitely prolonged and left undecided, had not Sir Hope Grant suddenly resolved to reinforce his left with a portion of his centre, and to assail the enemy's right vigorously. This later part of the battle began with a charge of some squadrons of Probyn's Horse against the bodies of mounted Tartars moving in the plain, whom they, with their gallant leader * at their head, routed in the sight of the two armies. This overthrow of their chosen fighting-men greatly discouraged the rest of the Chinese soldiers, and when the infantry advanced with the Sikhs in front they slowly began to give ground. But even then there were none of the usual symptoms of a decisive victory. The French were so exhausted by their efforts that they had been compelled to halt, and General Montauban was obliged to curb his natural impetuosity, and to admit that he could take no part in the final attack on Chan-chia-wan. Sir Hope Grant, however, pressed on and occupied the town. He did not call in his men until they had seized without resistance a large camp about one mile west of the town, where they captured several guns. Thus ended the battle of Chan-chia-wan with the defeat and retreat of the strong army which Sankolinsin had raised in order to drive the barbarians into the sea, and which, as English witnesses stated, had occupied in the morning a position of very considerable strength in front of that town.

Although the battle was won, Sir Hope Grant, measuring the resistance with the eye of an experienced soldier, came to the conclusion that his force was not sufficiently strong to overawe so obstinate a foe; and accordingly ordered Sir Robert Napier to join him with as many troops as he could spare from the Tientsin garrison. Having thus provided for the arrival of reinforcements at an early date, he was willing to resume his onward march for Tungchow, where

* Colonel Probyn, the present General Sir Dighton Probyn.

it was hoped some tidings would be obtained of the missing officers and men. Two days intervened before any decisive move was made, but Mr. Wade was sent under a flag of truce into Tungchow to collect information. But he failed to learn anything more about Mr. Parkes, than that he had quitted the town in safety after his final interview with Prince Tsai. Lord Elgin now hastened up from Hosiwu to join the military head-quarters, and on the 21st of September, the French having been joined by another brigade, offensive operations were re-commenced. The delay had encouraged the Chinese to make another stand, and they had collected in considerable force for the defence of the Palikao bridge, which affords the means of crossing the Peiho west of Tungchow.

Here again the battle commenced with a cavalry charge which, despite an accident * that might have had more serious results, was completely successful. This achievement was followed up by the attack on several fortified positions which were not defended with any great amount of resolution, and while these matters were in progress on the side where the English were engaged, the French had carried the bridge with its twenty-five guns in position in very gallant style.† The capture of this bridge and the dispersion of the troops, including the Imperial Guard, which had been entrusted with its defence, completed the discomfiture of the Chinese. Pekin itself lay almost at the mercy of the invader, and, unless diplomacy could succeed better than arms, nothing would now prevent the hated foreigners violating its privacy not

---

* "The King's Dragoon Guards and Fane's Horse, with Probyn's regiment in support, now advanced to the charge; the first-named taking a bank and ditch on their way, and attacking the Tartars with the utmost vigour, instantly made them give way. Fane's men followed them in pursuit, and on reaching the margin of a road jumped into it over an interposing high bank and ditch. The first rank cleared it well; but the men in the rear, unable to see before them owing to the excessive dust, almost all rolled into the ditch. Nevertheless, the Tartars had but a poor chance, and suffered severely."—Sir Hope Grant's narrative.

† This success gave General Montauban his title of Comte de Palikao. Although a dashing soldier, he was not a skilful general. His advice in China was generally none of the most prudent, and in the Franco-Prussian war he was one of the earliest and most conspicuous failures.

merely with their presence, but in the most unpalatable guise of armed victors.

The day after the battle at the Palikao bridge came a letter from Prince Kung,* the Emperor's next brother, stating that Prince Tsai and his colleagues had not managed matters satisfactorily, and that he had been appointed with plenipotentiary powers for the discussion and decision of the peace question. But the prince went on to request a temporary suspension of hostilities—a demand with which no general or ambassador could have complied so long as officers were detained who had been seized in violation of the usages of war. Lord Elgin replied in the clearest terms that there could be no negotiations for peace until these prisoners were restored, and that if they were not sent back in safety the consequences would be most serious for the Chinese Government. But even at this supreme moment of doubt and danger, the subtlety of Chinese diplomacy would have free play. Prince Kung was young in years and experience, his finesse would have done credit to a grey-haired statesman. Unfortunately for him the question had got beyond the stage of discussion: the English ambassador had stated the one condition on which negotiations would be renewed, and until that had been complied with there was no need to give ear to the threats, promises, and entreaties even of Prince Kung.

Of course the Chinese diplomatist argued that the surrender of the prisoners would be one of the conditions of peace, and he had even the amazing temerity to ask that the English should withdraw their fleet from Taku. But he could not have expected to succeed in these efforts. He was only sounding the depths of English good temper and simplicity. But all his artifice failed in face of the simple sentence, "You must surrender Mr. Parkes and his companions." As the Prince gave no sign of yielding this point during the week's delay in bringing up the second division

* In 1859 he had been mentioned as being with Prince Hwuy, Hienfung's uncle, and another Manchu official, members of a board for managing the affairs of the barbarians. He had also taken part in the trial of Keying in 1858.

from Tientsin, Lord Elgin requested Sir Hope Grant to resume his march on Pekin, from which the advanced guard of the allied forces was distant little more than ten miles. The cavalry had reconnoitred almost up to the gates, and had returned with the report that the walls were strong and in good condition.* The danger to a small army of attempting to occupy a great city of the size and population of Pekin is almost obvious; and, moreover, the consistent policy of the English authorities had been to cause the Chinese people as little injury and suffering as possible. Should an attack on the city become unavoidable, it was decided, after the usual differences of opinion between the two commanders, that the point attacked should be the Tartar quarter, including the Palace, which occupies the northern half of the city. By this time it had become known that Parkes and Loch were living, that they were confined in the Kaou Meaou Temple, near the Tehshun Gate, and that latterly they had been fairly well treated. Communications had been received from them, and they had succeeded in baffling the designs of their captors, who wished to make their fears the means of contributing towards the attainment of the ends of Chinese diplomacy.

In execution of the plan of attack that had been agreed upon, the allied forces marched round Pekin to the northwest corner of the walls, having as their object the Summer Palace of the Emperor at Yuen Min Yuen, not quite four miles distant from the city. No enemy was encountered; the only difficulty that presented itself to the advance was from the number of brick-fields and houses, which rendered

* Every one was greatly impressed by the size and good condition of the walls of Pekin. Mr. Loch describes them as follows:—"The main wall of the city is almost sixty feet in height, the thickness at the top about fifty. The breadth at the base cannot be less than seventy to eighty feet; the height of the inner part of the wall above the city is in places from forty to fifty feet. There is a large building above the gate, which is used partly as a barrack and store. In some of the embrasures in this upper building wooden guns are mounted. The thickness of the semicircular wall is not so great as the main one, although very considerable. I doubt whether, if all our siege guns had fired at it for a week, they could have effected any practicable breach in a work of such solid construction."

THE EMPEROR'S FLIGHT.   343

marching very slow. Not only were the movements of the troops slow, but they proved to be very uncertain; for, whether by accident or design, the French force, which should have followed the English, got separated from it, and reached the Summer Palace first. When Sir Hope Grant arrived at that place he found it in General Montauban's possession. The peculiar feature in this event was that while the French had formed the rear, and were supposed to have missed their way, they arrived the first at the common destination. Scarcely any resistance had been made by the Imperial Guards, and the French troops were encamped in the spacious park which surrendered the central palace.*

On the approach of the foreign army, Hienfung fled in terror from his palace, and sought shelter at Jehol,† the hunting residence of the Emperors beyond the Wall. His flight was most precipitate; and the treasures of the Summer Palace were left at the mercy of the Western spoilers. The French soldiers had made the most of their start, and left comparatively little for their English comrades, who, moreover, were restrained by the bonds of a stricter discipline. But the amount of prize property that remained was still considerable, and, by agreement between the two generals, it was divided in equal shares between the armies. The capture and occupation of the Summer Palace completed the European triumph, and obliged Prince Kung to promptly acquiesce in Lord Elgin's demand for the immediate surrender of the prisoners if he wished to avoid the far greater calamity of a foreign occupation of the Tartar quarter of Pekin and the appropriation of its vaster and rarer collection of treasures.

* Sir Hope Grant wrote: "In different parts of the grounds were forty separate small palaces in beautiful situations. The park was carefully kept, the foot-paths and roads clean and in excellent order, and there were various pretty pieces of ornamental water. We found that the French had encamped near the entrance of the Great Audience Hall, and it was pitiful to see the way in which everything was being robbed."

† Jehol had been the favourite residence and hunting-place of the earlier Emperors; but in consequence of the death of Kiaking there it had fallen into disfavour, as it was esteemed a great misfortune to die away from home.

On the 6th of October Mr. Parkes wrote from his place of confinement that the French and English detained were to be returned on the 8th of the month, and that the Imperial commanders had been ordered at the same time to withdraw all their troops for a considerable distance from Pekin. These promises were carried out.* Prince Kung was at last resolved to make all the concessions requisite to ensure the speedy conclusion of peace. The restoration of the captives, who had been seized on the morning of the day which had witnessed Sankolinsin's discomfiture at Chan-chia-wan, removed what was thought to be the one obstacle to Lord Elgin's discussing the terms on which the respective Governments would resume diplomatic relations.

It was fortunate for China that the exact fate of the other prisoners was then unknown, and that Lord Elgin felt able, in consequence of the more friendly proceedings of Prince Kung, to overlook the earlier treatment of those now returned to him, for the narrative of Mr. Parkes and his fellow-prisoner was one that tended to heighten the feeling of indignation at the original breach of faith. To say that they were barbarously ill-used is to employ a phrase conveying a very inadequate idea of the numerous indignities and the cruel personal treatment to which they were subjected. Under these great trials neither of these intrepid Englishmen wavered in their refusal to furnish information or to make any concession compromising their country. Mr. Loch's part was in one sense the more easy, as his ignorance of the language prevented his replying, but in bodily suffering

* The prisoners returned were Mr. Parkes, Mr. Loch, and the trooper Nalsing, and of the French the Comte d'Escayrac de Lauture, author of the French official description of the expedition, and four soldiers. The fate of the rest was then unknown even to those who were released. Prince Kung supposed they had been carried off to the north with the retreating army, and assured Lord Elgin that they would of course be restored. Of the treatment they received after we last left them being hurried off in the rough carts of the country, both Mr. Loch and the French writer have given a full account in their published works. The greatest agony inflicted on them was during the drive into Pekin, when they were hurried in springless carts over the roughly paved roads into the capital. The Sikh trooper behaved with the admirable fortitude which was more natural in his English companions in misfortune.

he had to pay a proportionally greater penalty. The incidents of their imprisonment afford the most creditable testimony to the superiority which the pride of race as well as "the equal mind in arduous circumstance" gives weak humanity over physical suffering. They are never likely to pass out of the public memory; and those who remember the daring and the chivalry which had inspired Mr. Parkes and Mr. Loch on the day when Prince Tsai's treachery and Sankolinsin's mastery were revealed, will not be disposed to consider it exaggerated praise to say that, for an adventure so honourably conceived and so nobly carried out, where the risk was never reckoned and where the penalty was so patiently borne, the pages of history may be searched almost in vain for an event that, in the dramatic elements of courage and suffering, presents such a complete and consistent record of human gallantry and devotion as the capture and subsequent captivity of these English gentlemen and their Sikh companion.*

The further conditions as preliminary to the ratification of the Treaty of Tientsin were gradually if reluctantly complied with. On the 13th of October the north-east gate was handed over to the allied troops, but not before Sir Hope Grant had threatened to open fire on the walls. At the same time Prince Kung returned eight sowars of Fane's horse and one Frenchman, all the survivors, besides those already surrendered, of the small band which had ridden from Tungchow nearly a month before. The Chinese Prince stated in explanation that "a certain number were missing after the fight, or have died of their wounds or of sickness." But the narrative of the Sikhs was decisive as to the fate of the five Englishmen and their own comrades. They had been brutally bound with ropes which, although drawn as tight as human force could draw them, were tightened still more by cold water being poured upon the bands, and they had

* In the eyes of the Chinese Mr. Parkes was always a man of importance, at first to be more cruelly treated, then to be used more honourably. Mr. Loch was in comparison of no special interest. When the former was released and treated more favourably the latter would have been detained in his loathsome prison, but for Mr. Parkes refusing to accept any favour unless shared by Mr. Loch.

been maltreated in every form by a cruel enemy, and provided only with food of the most loathsome kind. Some of the prisoners were placed in cages. Lieutenant Anderson, a gallant young officer for whom future renown had been predicted, became delirious and died on the ninth day of his confinement. Mr. De Normann died a week later. What fate befell Captain Brabazon and his French companion the Abbé de Luc is uncertain, but the evidence on the subject inclines us to accept as accurate the statement that the Chinese commander in the fight at Palikao, enraged at his defeat, caused them to be executed on the bridge. The soldier Phipps endured for a longer time than Mr. Bowlby the taunts and ill-usage of their gaolers, but they at last shared the same fate, dying from the effects of their ill-treatment. The Chinese officials were more barbarous in their cruelty than even the worst scum among their malefactors; for the prisoners in the gaols, far from adding to the tortures of the unfortunate Europeans, did everything in their power to mitigate their sufferings, alleviate their pains, and supply their wants.*

The details of these cruel deeds raised a feeling of great horror in men's minds, and, although the desire to arrange the question of peace without delay was uppermost with Lord Elgin, still it was felt that some grave step was necessary to express the abhorrence with which England regarded this cruel and senseless outrage, and to bring home to the Chinese people and Government that Englishmen could not be murdered with impunity. Lord Elgin refused to hold any further intercourse with the Chinese Government until this great crime had been purged by some signal punishment. Sir Hope Grant and he had little difficulty in arriving at the decision that the best mode of expiation was to destroy the Summer Palace.† The French commander refused to

* The bodies of all the Englishmen, with the exception of Captain Brabazon, were restored, and of most of the Sikhs also.

† What was the Summer Palace like? may be asked. The following description from Mr. Swinhoe's work, already quoted, will give a fair idea:—" Behind the chief building came the summer park, the extent of wall surrounding the whole being about twelve miles. Pebbled paths led you through groves of magnificent trees, round lakes, into picturesque

participate in the act which carried a permanent lesson of political necessity to the heart of the Pekin Government, and which did more than any other incident of the campaign to show Hienfung that the hour had gone by for trifling. On the 18th of October the threat was carried into execution. The Summer Palace was destroyed by fire, and the sum of £100,000 was demanded and obtained from the Chinese as some compensation for the families of the murdered men. The palace of Yuen Min Yuen had been the scene of some of the worst sufferings of the English prisoners. From its apartments the high mandarins and the immediate courtiers of the Emperor had gloated over and enjoyed the spectacle of their foreign prisoners' agony. The whole of Pekin witnessed in return the destruction wrought on the sovereign's abode by the indignant English, and the clouds of smoke hung for days like a vast black pall over the city.

That act of severe but just vengeance consummated, the negotiations for the ratification of the treaty were resumed, and, not unexpectedly, proceeded with the greater despatch because of the more abundant testimony provided that the English were in earnest. Mr. Parkes and Mr. Loch were specially chosen to select an appropriate building within the city for the ratification of the treaty, and they rode through the streets at the head of an escort of English and Sikh cavalry. The same populace which a few weeks before had regarded their entry as the first symptom of a coming national triumph, now watched them with perhaps a closer scrutiny in anticipation of further barbarian exactions. The Hall of Ceremonies was selected as the place in which the ratifying act should be performed, while, as some punishment for the

summer-houses, over fantastic bridges. As you wandered along herds of deer would amble away from before you, tossing their antlered heads. Here a solitary building would rise fairy-like from the centre of a lake, reflecting its image on the limpid blue liquid in which it seemed to float, and there a sloping path would carry you into the heart of a mysterious cavern, artificially formed of rockery, and leading out on to a grotto in the bosom of another lake. The variety of the picturesque was endless, and charming in the extreme. The resources of the designer appear to have been unending, and no money spared to bring his work to perfection."

hostile part he had played, the palace of Prince Tsai was appropriated as the temporary official residence of Lord Elgin and Baron Gros. Both these buildings were situate in the Tartar quarter, but near the boundary wall of the Chinese city.*

The formal act of ratification was performed in this building on the 24th of October. Lord Elgin proceeded in a chair of state accompanied by his suite, and also by Sir Hope Grant with an escort of 100 officers and 500 troops, through the streets from the Anting or Eastern Gate to the Hall of Ceremonies. Prince Kung, attended by a large body of civil and military mandarins, was there in readiness to produce the Imperial edict authorizing him to attach the Emperor's seal to the treaty, and to accept the responsibility for his country of conforming with its terms and carrying out its stipulations. Some further delay was caused by the necessity of waiting until the edict should be received from the Emperor at Jehol authorizing the publication of the treaty, not the least important point in connection with its conclusion if the millions of China were to understand and perform what their rulers had promised for them. That closing act was successfully achieved, and more rapidly than had been expected. The Pekinese beheld English troops and officers in residence in their midst for the first time, and when the army was withdrawn and the Plenipotentiary, Lord Elgin, transferred to his brother, Mr. Frederick Bruce, the charge of affairs in China as Resident Minister, the ice had been broken in the relations between the officials of the two countries, and the greatest if not the last barrier of Chinese exclusiveness had been removed.†

* One of the most gratifying circumstances in connection with this war was the good understanding that prevailed between the foreign powers. General Ignatieff, the Russian ambassador, who knew the interior of Pekin well, supplied the English commander with an excellent map and much information about the chief buildings. Perhaps the kindest act of all was to afford the shelter of the Russian cemetery to the remains of those who had been murdered—an act in which we recognize some stronger feeling than international courtesy.

† The treaty as ratified contained two clauses more than the original convention of Tientsin—one legalizing emigration, the other ceding the peninsula of Kowlun in the rear of Hongkong to the English.

THE OBJECT OBTAINED.

The last of the allied troops turned their backs upon Pekin on the 9th of November, and the greater portion of the expedition departed for India and Europe just before the cold weather set in. A few days later the rivers were frozen and navigation had become impossible. Small garrisons were left at Tientsin and the Taku forts for the time being until relations had been arranged on what was to be their permanent basis; and Mr. Bruce took up his residence in the former town while a proper abode was being prepared for his reception at the capital. Lord Elgin's departure from China had been preceded by several interviews of a friendly character with Prince Kung, in which for the first time the conversation between the statesmen of the two countries turned upon the subjects in which they might mutually benefit each other, and upon the advantages that would accrue to China in particular from the adoption of the mechanical contrivances and inventions of Europe. Perhaps the most incontestable token of the change in the Imperial policy was afforded by the disgrace of the Tartar general, Sankolinsin, who had been mainly instrumental in urging Hienfung to continue the struggle, and whose personal feeling towards the foreigners had always been most bitter. With him fell also the high minister, Juilin, who, himself a Manchu, had always advocated resistance to the death, and supported in the Council the strongest measures of war.*

The object which the more far-seeing of the English residents had from the first hour of difficulty stated to be necessary for satisfactory relations—direct intercourse with the Pekin Government—was thus obtained after a keen and

---

This piece of land had been let to the English in perpetuity at a small rent. Mr. Loch gives a very graphic description of the scene of the ratification. Prince Kung was anxious and hesitating, but if he felt fear, Mr. Loch says, he concealed his apprehensions. Sir Hope Grant spoke of him as being "evidently overpowered with fear," which is not at all probable. As a matter of fact Prince Kung had a most trying task to perform, for which neither he nor any of his assistants had the least precedent. He passed through the ordeal with remarkable dignity and success for a young man of only twenty-eight years.

* The edict was thus expressed :—" Let Sang-ko-lin-sin be deprived of his nobility. Let Juilin be immediately deprived of his office; as a warning."—Mr. Wade's translation in Blue Book.

bitter struggle of thirty years. The first war, closing with the Treaty of Nankin, had contributed little more towards the solution of the question than to place a few additional facilities in the way of trade. The provisions which might perhaps have possessed greater importance were never enforced and were tacitly allowed to drop. A single disastrous war had not sufficed to bring the Pekin Government to reason or to wean it from traditions always remembered with feelings of pride.

The years following the signature of that treaty were not without their clouds and causes of anxiety. The refusal alone to open the gates of Canton was a most serious breach of treaty. It was followed, as we have seen, by many acts of hostility, and by a general line of policy quite incompatible with friendship. The appointment of Yeh was made for very much the same reasons as that of Lin had been—to humiliate the foreigner. It had been followed by an increased tension in the relations between the Canton yamen and the English authorities. The too-much-debated *Arrow* case came as the last of a long series of deeds in which all diplomatic courtesy was laid aside; and when once the English Government resorted to force, it was compelled to continue it until satisfactory results were produced and its objects attained. Success at first seemed to come for the asking. Sir Michael Seymour's victorious operations round Canton and at the mouth of the Peiho simplified the task of diplomacy; and Lord Elgin, despite the original disadvantage under which he laboured from the outbreak of the Indian Mutiny and the diversion of the China Expedition, was enabled by the success of the admiral to conclude a favourable treaty at Tientsin.

With the attempt twelve months later to obtain its ratification, the whole complication was suddenly re-opened. Admission to the Peiho was refused, and when an English squadron attempted to carry its way by force, it was repulsed with heavy loss. The defeat was the more important inasmuch as it was admittedly due, not to any mistake or rashness on the part of the admiral, but to the strength of the defences which the Chinese had erected in less than a year.

Another twelvemonth was employed in the fitting out and despatch of an expedition of 20,000 men in all, to bring the Court of Pekin to a more reasonable frame of mind, and Lord Elgin was again sent to China to complete the work he had half accomplished. We have seen how these purposes were effected, and how the superiority of European arms and discipline was again established over another brave but ill-prepared antagonist. Although vanquished, the Chinese may be said to have come out of this war with an increased military reputation. The dissension within the Empire—for, as we have yet to see, the revival of the foreign difficulty had led to increased activity on the part of the Taepings—prevented their utilizing the one great advantage they might have possessed of superior numbers; and had the other conditions of warfare been more equal, the steadiness and stubbornness of the Chinese whenever encountered between the sea and the ramparts of Pekin were such as to justify the belief that with proper arms, and under efficient leading, they would have successfully defended the approach to the capital.

The war closed with a treaty enforcing all the concessions made by its predecessor. The right to station an ambassador in Pekin signified that the great barrier of all had been broken down. The old school of politicians were put completely out of court, and a young and intelligent prince, closely connected with the Emperor, assumed the personal charge of the foreign relations of the country. As one who had seen with his own eyes the misfortunes of his countrymen, he was the more disposed to adhere to what he had promised to perform. Under his direction the ratified treaty of Tientsin became a bond of union instead of an element of discord between the cabinets of London and Pekin; and a termination was put, by an arrangement carried at the point of the sword, to the constant friction and recrimination which had been the prevailing characteristics of the intercourse for a whole generation. The Chinese had been subjected to a long and bitter lesson. They had at last learnt the virtue of submitting to necessity; but although they have profited to some extent both in peace and war by their experience, it requires some assurance to declare that they have even now accepted the inevitable. There is still greater reason to doubt if they have learnt the practical lesson of profiting by their own experience. That remains the problem of the future ; but in 1860 Prince Kung came to the sensible conclusion that for that period, and until China had recovered from her internal confusion, there was nothing to be gained and much to be lost by protracted resistance to the peoples of the West. Whatever could be retained by tact and finesse were to form part of the natural rights of China ; but the privileges only to be asserted in face of Armstrong guns and rifles were to be abandoned with as good a grace as the injured feeling of a nation can ever display.

CHAPTER XIV.

THE PROGRESS OF THE TAEPING REBELLION.

DURING these years of foreign war and difficulty the Taepings had not been inactive. Repulsed in their first attempts to subdue the provinces north of the Yangtsekiang, their leaders had returned to Nankin only to indulge their antipathies and to decide questions of rivalry by the sword. Had the Emperor's officers been prompt in mustering their forces in the year 1857, they would have found the Taepings a comparatively easy prey. But the Chinese have always preferred the slowest method in their proceedings, and it happened to be an occasion when no time should have been wasted. The favourable moment was permitted to pass by unutilized, and the main object with the officials was to conceal from Pekin the progress which the rebels were making in Central China. It was not until the end of the year 1860 that Prince Kung learnt from Mr. Bruce of the rapid successes of the Taepings, and that they had established their authority almost to the sea. Then the Emperor's immediate advisers realized for the first time that, having adjusted their disagreements with the foreigners, they would have to achieve the not less difficult task of asserting their authority in the most populous and productive region of the Empire. The undertaking to be seriously commenced in 1861 promised to be all the more difficult and protracted because of the delay that ensued after the first check inflicted upon the Taepings in 1857.

After the sanguinary events which occurred at Nankin in the year 1856, the E Wang or Assistant King left that city to oppose Tseng Kwofan, who, with the levies of Hoonan, was operating in Kiangsi. The departure of this leader had obliged Tien Wang to call to the front new men, and among the most capable of these was Li-su-Ching, who, for his valour and capacity around Nankin, had obtained the title of Chung Wang, or the Faithful King. During the operations of the year 1858 the Taepings fairly held their own in the valley of the Yangtsekiang, and, thanks to the great energy of Chung Wang, they forced the Imperialists to retire to a more respectful distance from Nankin, which they had actually beleaguered. The principal leaders on the Emperor's side were Tseng Kwofan and his brother, Tseng Kwo-tsiuen, Paochiaou, Tso Tsung Tang, and Li Hung Chang.

The Imperialists endeavoured to capture one of the principal posts of the Taepings at the town of Ganking, on the north bank of the Yangtse, and about 200 miles above Nankin. The advantage of this post was that it gave the latter the command of a second passage across the great river, and that it enabled them to check the advance of fresh troops down the river. The siege of Ganking was raised by Chung Wang; but a victory at Soosung won by General Paochiaou more than compensated for it. In 1858 the Imperialists, under Tseng on the one side, and Chang Kwoliang on the other, invested the Taeping capital for a second time, despite the efforts of Chung Wang to prevent it. As the town was well supplied with provisions, and as it was known that the Imperialists had no intention of delivering an assault, the Taepings were comparatively indifferent to the fact, and waited until their opponents should be tired out, or until the arrival of fresh troops from their own comrades in the other provinces would enable them to assume the offensive.

Although the Imperial commanders were lethargic, only one result could follow their operations if allowed to proceed without interruption. Nankin would have to yield in the end to starvation. In these straits Chung Wang proved the saviour of his party. The garrison was not large enough to attempt a sortie; and the other bodies of the Taepings scattered throughout the provinces did not possess any recognized leader from whom aid might be expected, or to whom an appeal for succour might be sent—now that E Wang had retired in disgust, and gone westwards to advance his own interests. The Imperialists had already invested the city upon three sides; only one remained open if the news of Tien Wang's sufferings were to reach his followers before it was too late. In such a moment of peril there was general reluctance to quit the besieged town; but unless some one did, and that promptly, the place was doomed. In this supreme moment Chung Wang offered to go himself. At first the proposal was received with a chorus of disapproval; but at last, when he went to the door of Tien Wang's palace and beat the gong which lay there for those who claimed justice, he succeeded in overcoming the opposition to his plan, and in impressing upon his audience the real gravity of the situation. His request was granted, and, having nominated trusty men to the command during his absence, he quitted the besieged city by the southern gate. A few days later, and Tseng's last levies had constructed their fortified camp in front of it.

Chung Wang reached in twenty-four hours Woohoo, where a cousin of his commanded a small body of Taeping troops. They concocted a plan of campaign, having as its principal object the worrying of the Imperial forces, with the view of making them relax their efforts against Nankin. In this they succeeded in an almost marvellous manner, considering the smallness of their force, the strength of the Imperialists in numbers and position, and the all-importance of the capture of Nankin.

Hienfung's generals long failed to realize that it was the possession of Nankin which alone made the Taepings formidable. Without that city in their power they would cease to be anything more than a band of brigands. So long as they held it they were able to claim the rights and privileges of a separate dynasty. Yet the capture of Nankin was put off until the last act of all, in order to effect the overthrow of the scattered armies of the rebels who would probably have dispersed immediately on its fall, and who would certainly have become the mark of popular resentment. The Imperial commanders had shown great apathy all through the crisis, but in 1858 they revealed more clearly than ever their utter inability to grasp the central fact in the position. Had they been able to do so, they would not have played the whole game into the hands of Chung Wang.

Chung Wang had escaped from Nankin towards the end of 1858. He collected some 5000 good men, and with these he at once began operations. The Imperialists were much too strong south of the river for him to attempt anything against them on that side. He therefore crossed to the northern bank and began his campaign by the capture of Hochow. He continued his advance, hoping to cut in two the more numerous army of General Tesinga who was opposed to him; but the enemy were too strong, particularly in cavalry, for him, and he was repulsed and obliged to retire. Even north of the river there did not seem much chance for the Taeping leader. The Imperialists gave him a short respite, during which he managed to drill his recruits; but on his making a second effort to reach Poukou, the small town opposite Nankin, he was defeated with the loss, as he admitted, of one thousand men. Chung Wang returned south of the river, held a hurried council at Tsinyang, recalled all the troops he could from Ganking, and, again returning to the northern bank, resumed his efforts to reach Poukou. There seemed, if possible, less chance than ever of success, for General Te had been reinforced, if only at the price of weakening the army round Nankin, and even Chang Kwo-liang had left his camp to see what was being done against Chung Wang. Things were in this state when the Taeping leader suddenly returned and resumed with all the energy of desperation his attempt to cut his way through the Imperial lines to Poukou. Whether the Imperialists were taken by surprise, or were so full of confidence from their recent success that they did not think it necessary to take precautions, they were beaten in one battle after another. The principal towns north of Nankin were occupied by the Taepings after little resistance, and in several encounters round Linchow the lieutenants of Hienfung were decidedly worsted.

But although the pressure on Nankin was relieved by these successes, the siege continued on the southern side, where the Imperial troops remained in excellent condition. The anxieties of Tien Wang were increased by a suspicion of Chung Wang's fidelity, and that there was some reason to believe him meditating desertion rested on apparently good foundation. The supplies of the rebels were falling short, and powder in particular was needed to enable them to carry on the struggle. The year 1859 was consequently one of little movement, partly from this cause, and partly also on account of the exhaustion of the combatants. The Imperialists, convinced that time was all in their favour, proceeded in the most leisurely manner, and were quite content to sustain a rigid blockade without risking their lives in unnecessary battles. They were the more reconciled to this deliberate plan of proceeding, because the Taepings had been gradually expelled from one town after another until all that was left in their possession were the places between Nankin and Ganking. It seemed as if nothing could then prevent the Taeping cause expiring from pure inanition.

Chung Wang's campaign north of the Yangtse had gained a respite for the Taepings; but, although the reverses of the Government troops were not few, superior numbers and resources had more than counterbalanced misfortune in the field. The environment of Nankin, weakened on the north by the capture of Poukou, was sustained with undiminished rigour on the southern side of the great river. In this extremity Chung Wang conceived a fresh plan for relieving the pressure on Nankin, if not of extricating the Heavenly ruler from his predicament. He resolved to get in the rear of the Imperial army and to operate along its base of supply. The idea was an extremely happy one, proving that Chung Wang possessed considerable natural capacity, at the same time that it showed that a desperate situation suggests remedies that would not, under ordinary circumstances, be deemed either prudent or possible.

In January, 1860, all Chung Wang's arrangements were completed. He had distributed considerable sums of money among his men in order to put them in a good humour, and he succeeded in eluding the vigilance of Chang Kwoliang, and in reaching Woohoo unobserved with the greater portion of his force. The Imperialists thought that the expedition was intended for the relief of Ganking, then closely pressed by Tseng Kwofan. Having assembled his forces at Woohoo, the leader left the Yangtse and marched inland to Nanliu, whence, turning eastwards, he gained Ningkoue, and then Kwante, towns on the borders of the provinces of Anhwui and Kiangsu. The full importance of this movement was not revealed until the siege of Hoochow, a large town in the silk district south of the Taho lake, and only fifty miles north of the important city of Hangchow. Leaving his cousin to besiege it, Chung Wang hastened on to attack Hangchow itself, the possession of which would confer immense prestige and material advantages on the cause of the rebels. Chung Wang had not more than 10,000 men with him, but he succeeded in capturing the greater portion of Hangchow, partly by a daring assault, partly through the treachery of some of its inhabitants. This was on the 19th of March, 1860, about ten weeks after he had set out from Nankin. The Tartar city held out, and was valiantly and successfully defended, until aid arrived from Chang Kwoliang at Nankin.

As soon as that commander heard of the movements in his rear, he at once realized the plan of campaign formed for the complete cutting off of his supplies. He then detached a considerable army from his main body under the command of his brother Chang Yuliang, for the express purpose of coming to an action with Chung Wang and preventing the realization of his schemes. The force besieging Hoochow was driven back on the main body at Hangchow, and on the 24th of March Chang Yuliang had the satisfaction of relieving Hangchow and of compelling Chung Wang to relinquish his hold on the town and to beat as precipitate a retreat as he could. For the moment it seemed that this Taeping army had been given over to destruction.

We will not deny to Chung Wang the admirable fortitude that is never so striking or laudable as when Fortune wears her darkest frown, and there seems no extrication from accumulated difficulties. Deprived of the prey which he already clutched, it looked for the moment as if Chung Wang would have every reason to regard himself as favoured if he succeeded in regaining such security as the towns on the

Yangtse could still afford. The celerity of his movements provided him, as it has greater commanders reduced to similar straits, with a safe issue from his perils. Long before Chang Yuliang had stifled the feelings of self-congratulation which he felt at the relief of Hangchow, Chung Wang had marched many miles back on the road to Nankin. In the height of his apprehension Chang Kwoliang had detached his best troops to pursue Chung Wang, so that when that chief outstripped his brother in his return march, the Imperial general found himself left with only an enfeebled force to defend the extensive lines before Nankin. Those lines were attacked with extraordinary vigour by the Taepings from without as well as from within. They were carried with a loss to the Imperialists of more than five thousand men, while the baffled generals, who had counted with such unconcealed confidence on the certain capture of Nankin in the course of a few months, were compelled to make an ignominious retreat, and to admit for once that pertinacity may prove unavailing if not allied with enterprise and audacity. The siege of Nankin was thus raised, and the forces which had been so long enclosed in that town were relieved for the moment from the presence of the foe who had so bitterly and persistently assailed them ever since their first arrival at Nankin, nearly seven years before.

The conduct of Tien Wang in face of this unexpected and undeserved deliverance was not of a kind to impress his friends with a belief in his fitness to raise a sinking cause or to deserve the favour of Heaven. He issued no proclamation to his followers on the occasion of this great victory, and he gave no rewards. His jealousy of Chung Wang increased, and he forbade his deliverer to re-enter the city. All that could be obtained from him was the behest that it would be well "to adhere to the precepts of Heaven," and the statement that "the surrounding aspect indicated signs of great peace." From such a leader it was clear that no material aid could be expected, and the Taepings looked more and more to Chung Wang as the only man capable of supporting their cause. Chung Wang was not allowed to remain long in idleness. He received the command, perhaps because he inspired the order, to go forth and capture the strong town of Soochow situated on the Grand Canal, and the nominal capital of Kiangsu.

The main body of the Imperialists had rallied at Changchow, some distance north of Soochow on the Grand Canal; and there Chang Kwoliang had at last been joined by his brother's army from Hangchow. A week after the relief of Nankin, Chung Wang resumed offensive operations, and when Chang Kwoliang attempted to check his forward march at Tayan, a battle ensued, in which, after some hours' fighting, the Imperialists were again defeated. Although their loss in men was very heavy, amounting, it was said, to as many as 10,000 killed and wounded, the most serious blow inflicted upon them was the death of Chang Kwoliang, whose energy almost atoned for his shortcomings as a commander. He was drowned in the canal during the heat of the engagement, and the spectacle of his fall so greatly discouraged his men that they at once gave way in all directions. The fate of the ex-Triad chief decided the day, and by this victory Chung Wang cleared the road to Soochow.

Two days later Chung Wang defeated Chang Yuliang at Changchow, thus to some extent compensating for the reverse he had experienced at his hands at Hangchow. Changchow surrendered on the 11th of May, but the Imperialist troops endeavoured to make a fresh stand at Wusieh, where a desperate battle was fought for twenty-four hours. The action was stubbornly contested, and for a moment it seemed as if the verdict would be in favour of the Imperialists; but Chung Wang's impetuosity again turned the day in his favour, and Wusieh became the prize of the victor. Upon its capture the Emperor's general, Hochun, who had taken a prominent part in the earlier siege of Nankin, committed suicide; and Hienfung was thus deprived of another officer who, despite many faults, had shown at least consistent zeal and courage in his service.

From these frequent actions Chang Yuliang had escaped, and with the remnant of his force he prepared to defend Soochow, a place at that time of greater size than strength. His intentions were baffled partly by the difficulty of his task, and partly by the discouragement of his troops. An attempt to destroy the suburbs by fire and thus make the place defensible was rendered abortive by the action of the people themselves, so that no resource was left save to abandon the town as promptly as possible. Chang Yuliang and his braves returned to Hangchow, where they remained in safety, while Ho Kweitsin, the governor-general of the provinces of the Two Kiang, implored aid from those very English who were on the point of proceeding to attack the capital of the Empire. The French, then as ever impelled by the restless feeling to participate in whatever warlike operations might be going on, turned a sympathizing ear to the complaints of the Chinese Viceroy, and promised that they would send a force of 1500 French troops if 500 English would combine with them, in order to reassert the Imperial authority, although those very troops owed their presence in China to the fact that they were there to wage war upon the Emperor. The caution of Mr. Bruce forbade the enterprise, but the application of Ho Kweitsin remains an incident almost unique in the annals of war of an officer of a Government appealing to a foreign enemy engaged in actual hostilities for aid against a national rebel. Although the English representative declined to comply with the request of the Chinese official, a proclamation (May 26th, 1860) was made in the joint names of the foreign representatives to the effect that they were fully resolved to prevent Shanghai from falling a second time into the hands of an insurgent force.

When Soochow passed into the possession of Chung Wang, the small towns around it also surrendered. By this means Quinsan, Tsingpu, Taitsan, and other places accepted Taeping garrisons without a blow, and a large part of the able-bodied population joined the standard of Chung Wang. Such attempts as Chang Yuliang made to recover the ground he had lost were all repulsed with loss, and he had to content himself with the defence of Hangchow. This unfortunate campaign proved fatal to Ho Kweitsin, who was degraded, summoned to Pekin, and after a short delay executed, although his advice had eventually to be adopted. The post of Viceroy of the Two Kiang was conferred upon Tseng

Kwofan, then at Kwante endeavouring to collect and reorganize some of the scattered forces. Chung Wang's success in Kiangsu encouraged the disaffected to bestir themselves in Chekiang; but although several towns were lost to the Emperor, the importance of the movement was never more than local, and the principal interest of the situation continued to centre in the attempts of the Taeping leader to acquire possession of the riches of Shanghai.

At Shanghai itself some preparations had been made to recover the neighbouring places, and the town of Tsingpu in particular had been fixed upon as the proper place to commence operations for the reassertion of Hienfung's authority. In this emergency the Shanghai officials had turned to the European residents, as their Governments had refused to be compromised; and the great Chinese merchants, forming themselves into a kind of association of patriotism, guaranteed the funds for fitting out and rewarding a small contingent force of foreigners. Two Americans, Ward and Burgevine, were easily tempted by the promise of good pay and by the possibility of distinction to raise a levy among the foreign and seafaring colony, and to place themselves at the disposal of this Shanghai committee. Of these two men, Ward was the recognized leader, and Burgevine acted as his quartermaster. The terms on which they were engaged was that in addition to high pay they were promised a large sum of money as a reward for the capture of certain positions. The place on which they were invited to make their first attempt, and as it were to prove their mettle, was Sunkiang, a large walled town nearly twenty miles south-west of Shanghai.

The first attack was made under Ward in July, 1860, when he had succeeded in collecting 100 Europeans and perhaps twice as many Manilla-men. It was repulsed, however, with some loss. Ward was a man of determination, and seeing the anticipated prize slipping away from him he resolved to make a further and more vigorous effort to capture the place. He succeeded in enlisting a further body of Manilla-men, and with these he renewed the attack. He seems to have resorted to a stratagem to effect his object, but, having gained possession of a gateway, he held it against every attack until the main body of the Imperialists joined him. The capture of Sunkiang brought home to the Chinese mind the valuable aid which a foreign contingent might render against the rebels. It also made Ward's force popular for the moment with the more adventurous portion of the European community; and while most joined for the sake of the high pay and plunder to be obtained, some entered it with the hope of seeing service and gaining military experience. Ward had been an officer in the American merchant service. He served as mate under Gough, another American, who commanded the fleet fitted out by Taotai Wou for operations on the Yangtse, and was thus brought into contact with the rich Chinese merchants of Shanghai. The capture of Sunkiang so far encouraged the officials at Shanghai that they requested Ward to proceed forthwith to attack Tsingpu, and in return for its capture they promised him a great reward.

Ward was nothing loth to undertake another enterprise that might prove of as profitable a character as the attack on Sunkiang had been. He returned to Shanghai to complete his arrangements, and soon had assembled in his camp at Sunkiang a force of twenty-five Europeans under a Swiss captain, 280 Manilla-men under Vincente, two Englishmen as officers, an English doctor, and lastly Burgevine in control of the stores. The force was very weak in artillery, which consisted of only two 6-pounders; and although a large Imperial army and flotilla were attached to the expedition, it was generally understood that the brunt of the fighting would fall upon Ward's force. The position of the Taepings at Tsingpu was one of considerable strength, as the walls were in a good state of repair, and the small field-pieces could make little or no impression upon them. There remained only the chance of carrying the place by assault; but even against this the Taepings had taken every precaution in their power, and their efforts had also been directed by an European, an Englishman named Savage. Savage had been a pilot on the coast; but, whether the war destroyed his profession or appealed to his secret instincts, he certainly quitted it with several of his comrades, and joined the Taepings, who seemed to those who only looked at the surface to be at last on the point of realizing the earlier objects of their enterprise.

Ward delivered his attack on Tsingpu during the night of the 2nd August, 1860; but although he reached the wall, he was driven back with very severe loss. All the Europeans except six were either killed or wounded, and Ward himself was wounded in the jaw. This first repulse, disastrous as it was, did not lead Ward to abandon the whole enterprise in despair, for he had set his heart on obtaining the large reward offered for its capture by Takee and his associates. He hastened off to Shanghai to enlist fresh volunteers, and to purchase heavier guns, on the want of which he threw the whole blame of his defeat. He succeeded in obtaining 150 recruits, chiefly Greeks and Italians, and also two 18-pounders. With this reinforcement he again proceeded, after an interval of three weeks, to attack Tsingpu. This time he hoped to carry it, not by an assault, but by a bombardment, and during seven days his guns fired continuously on the wall. It is not possible to say how much longer this cannonade might have continued, when Chung Wang, hearing that the garrison was pressed by the Imperialists, hastened from Soochow, and, taking Ward by surprise, drove him away in utter confusion. In addition to considerable loss in men, the American lost the guns and most of the military stores which he had just purchased. Chung Wang followed up his victory by capturing the positions of the Imperial commander Li Aidong, and by an attempt to recover Sunkiang. But he failed in the latter task, and his English colleague Savage was so seriously wounded that he died some weeks later from the effects at Nankin.

Baffled in his attempt at Sunkiang, Chung Wang, notwithstanding the previous warning that the allied powers would defend the city, resolved to attack Shanghai. The possession of Shanghai was, in a military sense, essential to him, as it was there that all the hostile measures made for the recovery of the places he had taken were being carried out. Hoping, therefore, to find the allies, whose armies he knew had proceeded to the north, unable to carry out their intentions, he and his colleague, the Kan Wang, marched on

Shanghai, burning and plundering all the villages on the road. During these operations several Christian seminaries were burnt down, although Kan Wang had been elected a member of a missionary society, and one French priest at least was murdered. The Imperial army occupied a fortified camp or stockade outside the western gate. This Chung Wang attacked and captured, the Imperialists retiring without offering much resistance. He had then to encounter a different foe. The walls of Shanghai were manned by the English and French troops forming the garrison, and when the Taepings attempted to enter the city with the fleeing Imperialists, they were received with a warm and destructive fire, which compelled them to retire. The attack was several times renewed at different points during the next four or five days; but each onset was repulsed with increasing loss to the assailants. The chief destruction caused was by the accidental conflagration which broke out in the southern and richest suburb of the town, and which only burnt itself out after several days. Chung Wang was obliged to retreat, but before doing so he sent in a message to say that he had come at the invitation of the French, that they were traitors, and that he could have taken the city but for the foreigners, as "there was no city which his men could not storm." Even the noblest of the Taepings had occasionally to descend to idle boasting.

Notwithstanding his repulse at Shanghai, Chung Wang marched past Sunkiang, which he could not take, and engaged the forces of Chang Yuliang, who, with Hangchow as his base, was still employed in some desultory operations against the places which the Taepings had seized south of that town. In these Chung Wang's promptitude again turned the scale against his old adversary, and after several disastrous skirmishes Chang Yuliang was compelled to retire upon Hangchow and wait until the departure of Chung Wang for a resumption of active operations. Chung Wang was soon recalled in all haste to Soochow, where the people were suffering intense misery. He relieved them as well as he could out of the spoil of the country he had overrun, and in their gratitude they erected to his honour an ornamental arch, which was destroyed on the recovery of that city. But there remained much work of a different character for the Faithful King to perform. His energy and promptitude carried all before them where he was present in person, but everywhere else the prospects of the Taepings and their heavenly dynasty were darkened. Ganking was in imminent danger of capture. The Imperialists were advancing to attack Nankin for the sixth time. Tseng Kwofan was at last entrusted with the sole command, and was burning to distinguish by some striking deed his elevation to the Viceroyalty of the two Kiang. Tien Wang, panic-stricken at the dangers near his person, sent in all haste for Chung Wang, the one man who sustained his tottering throne.

Chung Wang entrusted the command of the forces in Kiangsu to a chief who was granted the title of Hoo Wang, or Protecting King, while he went himself with much reluctance to Nankin. There he held several councils of war with Tien Wang and the other leaders; but he found them all given up to a life of indulgence, and indifferent to the events around them. Tien Wang's only panacea for the dangers springing up on all sides was to say that, as "the truly appointed Lord," he had only to command peace, in order for all difficulties and troubles to cease; and as for the other Wangs, they were intent upon amassing money. Chung Wang told them with much force that they would be wise to purchase rice, as in the probable event of a long siege they would find that far the more useful article. Even when in this respect they carried his recommendations into practice, the head Wangs, Tien Wang and his brother, Kan Wang, placed high taxes on the importation of rice, and amassed great wealth at the expense of their own followers. The necessary consequence followed, that the importation of rice was discontinued, and when the Imperialists resumed the investment of the city, Nankin was not as well provisioned as it would have been had Chung Wang's advice been promptly and properly carried out.

While the leading Wangs were engaged at Nankin in tardy preparations for the day of trouble, Chung Wang made a dash into the province of Kiangsi for the purpose of diverting Tseng Kwofan's attention. Although he succeeded in ravaging much of the region watered by the Kan river, and in obtaining the advantage in several skirmishes, this raid produced no decisive result, and in the one pitched battle the victory rested with the Tartar general Paochiaou. More serious operations were ordered for the relief of Ganking, then on the point of surrender, and for the recapture of Hankow. For these purposes four armies were placed in the field: two with instructions to operate on the northern side of the Yangtse, and two on the southern. All these armies were expected to concentrate at or near Hankow in the month of March, 1861. Their movements were not in accordance with the preconcerted plan. Chung Wang, in personal command of the principal force, was repulsed by Paochiaou, and compelled to withdraw into the province of Chekiang, where his brother had been already defeated with the loss of 10,000 men by Tso Tsung Tang. At this moment the whole course of this desultory struggle was altered by the conclusion of the foreign war. The English authorities being hardly less interested than the Chinese in the speedy establishment of peace, and the chances of any durable Taeping success being obviously hopeless, it followed that for the sake of humanity, not less than trade, the sooner an end was put to the struggle the better it would be for all parties.

At first the policy of the English towards the Taepings was based on some uncertainty except with regard to one point, viz. that Shanghai was to be considered outside the sphere of their operations. The open attack of Chung Wang had been resisted and repulsed by force; but from every point of view it was desirable that it should not be repeated. One clause of the Treaty of Tientsin provided for the opening of the Yangtse, and the Admiral, Sir James Hope, proceeded in person to carry out this stipulation. At Nankin he entered into direct communication with Tien Wang, and obtained from him a pledge not to allow any attack on Shanghai during the next twelve months. He also agreed that none of the Taeping forces should advance within a radius of thirty miles of that city. Sir James Hope's report of the state of the Taepings at Nankin, Ganking, and Kiukiang, effectually dispelled the few remaining hopes of resuscitating their cause.*

Mainly in consequence of this arrangement Ward, who was energetically employed in raising fresh troops, was arrested in May, 1861, as a disturber of the peace. He, however, repudiated American citizenship, declaring himself to be a Chinese subject and officer; and was in consequence released after brief detention. Some of his followers had remained with Burgevine before Tsingpu, and when that officer heard that the force was to be summarily disbanded he resolved to make one attempt to capture the place that had twice defied them before his men had been carried off. In his attack on the Taeping position he was repulsed with the loss of twenty-three men killed or wounded out of

* The following opinion of the Rev. J. Holmes, an American Baptist (who was murdered by the Nienfei robbers twenty-seven miles from Yeulai on the 6th October, 1861), writing in 1860, after a visit to Nankin, deserves record. He said: "I found, to my sorrow, nothing of Christianity but its name falsely applied, applied to a system of revolting idolatry; their idea of God is distorted until it is inferior, if possible, to that entertained by other Chinese idolaters. The idea they entertain of a saviour is low and sensual; and his honours are shared by another. The Eastern King is a saviour from disease as he is a saviour from sin." The Tien Wang issued an edict for the information of Mr. Holmes, and the junior lord or son of Tien Wang, a boy of twelve or fourteen years of age, issued two edicts to instruct foreigners at the same time. This "junior lord" is the temporal representative of his father, whose office is exclusively spiritual; he was proclaimed to be the adopted son of Jesus. (For these papers see Blue Book.) Mr. Holmes states that "we witnessed their worship. It occurred at the beginning of their Sabbath midnight of Friday at Ching Wang's private audience room. He was seated in the midst of his attendants; no females were present. They first sang or chanted, after which a written prayer was read and burned by an officer, upon which they rose and sang again, and then separated. The Ching Wang sent for me again before he left his seat, and asked me if I understood their worship. I replied that I had just seen it for the first time, and that I thought all departure from the rules laid down in Scripture was erroneous. He extenuated their change from these rules by stating that the Tien Wang had been to Heaven and had seen the Heavenly Father; our revelation of the Bible had been handed down for 1800 years, and that they had received a new revelation through the Tien Wang, and, upon this, they could adopt a different mode of worship."

THE EVER-VICTORIOUS ARMY.

the eighty men with whom he made the attempt. This disaster terminated the career of the foreign adventurers who served under the two Americans, as the force was at once disbanded and its originators compelled to remain inactive at Shanghai during the summer of 1861.

That period of inaction on the part of foreign adventurers was employed, on the whole, to the advantage of the Imperialists; for not only was Ganking at last captured, thus closing the Western Provinces to the rebels, but Ward and Burgevine, being compelled to desist from any further attempts to recruit Europeans, devoted their leisure to drilling the Chinese themselves, a change of proceeding destined to produce the most important results, for the men whom Ward thus disciplined formed the nucleus of the force which gained the proud title of the "Ever-Victorious Army." The name was given long before its claim to it had been justified; but the subsequent appropriateness has buried in oblivion the slender right it possessed at first to its assumption. While these preparations were being made on the resources of Shanghai for the recovery of what had been lost in Kiangsu, and while Tseng Kwofan and his lieutenants had obtained what seemed the earnest of coming triumph on the Yangtse, the year 1861 closed with two distinct reverses for the Emperor. The city of Ningpo, after several preliminary discussions between the Taeping leaders and the English officials, was occupied by the former without resistance on the 9th of December. The Imperial garrison, dubious as to the possibility of resistance, retreated without loss to a place of security.

Three weeks later the great city of Hangchow shared the same fate after an obstinate defence creditable in every way to the besieged. Chung Wang, after his retreat from Kiangsi, had marched through a portion of Chekiang, and, sitting down before Hangchow, devoted all his energies to the capture of that city. The garrison behaved very well under a valiant officer named Wang Yuling, but was too small to hold so extensive a position. The Chinese city was first captured, and on the 29th of December the Manchu quarter was carried by storm. Wang Yuling hung himself in his garden;

his officers, and most of the Tartar soldiers, blew themselves up in the powder-magazine. The Taeping victory, so far as it went, was decisive, although Hangchow was a city of little more than ruins inhabited by corpses. If the hope of triumph had long departed, the capacity of the Taepings for inflicting an enormous amount of injury had evidently not been destroyed. Chung Wang's energy alone sustained the Taeping cause, but the lovers of rapine and turbulence flocked in their thousands to his standard.

The Taepings, encouraged by these successes on the coast, renewed their attempt on Shanghai. It was said that Tien Wang had given special orders for its capture; but it seems more probable that Chung Wang undertook the task on his own responsibility, well knowing that its fall would entail the collapse of all the vigorous preparations being made for the resumption of the campaign, at the same time that it would effectually protect the most exposed flank of the Taeping armies. Notwithstanding the plain declarations of the English admiral that an attack on Shanghai would be resisted by the English forces, the Taepings hoped, from what had occurred at Ningpo, that no active opposition would be made to them could they promptly overcome the Imperialists and obtain possession of the town. The Taepings heralded their approach with a proclamation announcing that "the hour of the Manchus had come. Shanghai is a little place, and we have nothing to fear from it. We must take Shanghai to complete our dominions."

On the 14th of January, 1862, the Taepings had reached the immediate vicinity of the town and foreign settlement. The surrounding country was concealed by the smoke of the burning villages which they had ruthlessly destroyed. The foreign settlement was crowded with thousands of fugitives imploring the aid of the Europeans to save their houses and property. Their sufferings, which would at the best have been great, were aggravated by the exceptional severity of the winter. The English garrison of two native regiments and some artillery, even when supported by the volunteers, was far too weak to attempt more than the defence of the place; but this it was fortunately able to perform. The rebels, during the first week after their reappearance, plundered and burned in all directions, threatening even to make an attack on Woosung, the port at the mouth of the river. Here they were repulsed by the French, who were always much more pronounced in their favour of the Imperial cause, and who, whether for that reason or because of their natural temperament, were never loth to have a brush with the rebels. After this repulse other disasters speedily followed. Sir John Michel arrived at Shanghai with a small reinforcement of English troops, and Ward, having succeeded in disciplining two regiments of about one thousand strong in all, sallied forth from Sunkiang for the purpose of operating on the rear of the Taeping forces. Ward's capture of Quanfuling, with several hundred rebel boats which were frozen up in the river, should have warned the Taepings that it was nearly time for them to retire. However, they did not act as prudence would have dictated, and during the whole of February their raids continued round Shanghai. The suburbs suffered from their attacks, the foreign factories and boats were not secure, and several outrages on the persons of foreigners remained unatoned for. It became impossible to tolerate any longer their enormities. The English and French commanders therefore determined to attack the rebels, to enforce the original agreement with Tien Wang, and to clear the country round Shanghai of the presence of the Taepings for the space of thirty miles.

On the 21st of February, therefore, a joint force composed of 336 English sailors and marines, 160 French seamen, and 600 men from Ward's contingent, accompanied by their respective commanders, with Admiral Hope in chief command, advanced upon the village of Kachiaou, where the Taepings had strengthened their position, and placed guns on the walls. After a sharp engagement the place was stormed, Ward's men leading the attack with Burgevine at their head. The drilled Chinese behaved with great steadiness, and although much of their conduct was due to the example of the Europeans, they were admitted to have evinced gallantry at the same time that they acquired confidence in themselves. This success was followed by the release of a large number of villagers who had been kept in chains; and inspired the Imperial authorities with an increased belief in the eventual triumph of their cause.

The Taepings were not to be dismayed by a single defeat. They even resumed their attacks on the Europeans. On one occasion Admiral Hope himself was compelled to retire before their superior numbers, and to summon fresh troops to his assistance. They were to pay dear for this illusory success. The reinforcements consisted of 450 Europeans and 700 of Ward's force, besides seven howitzers. With these it was determined to attack Tseedong, a place of much strength surrounded by stone walls and ditches seven feet deep. The Taepings stood to their guns with great spirit, receiving the advancing troops with a very heavy fire. When, however, Ward's contingent, making a detour, appeared in the rear of the place, they hastily evacuated their positions; but they were too late. While they hesitated the English sailors had carried the walls, and, caught between the two fires, they offered a stubborn but futile resistance. More than 700 were killed and 300 were taken prisoners. The favourable opinion formed of "the Ever-Victorious Army" by the action at Kachiaou was confirmed by the more serious affair at Tseedong; and the English authorities at Shanghai took steps to assist Ward in the task of increasing his army, while Mr. Bruce at Pekin brought it under the favourable notice of Prince Kung and the Chinese Government. In consequence of this encouragement from the foreign authorities, special mention was made in an edict of the valiant conduct of the contingent known as the Ever-Victorious Army.

Having taken these hostile steps against the rebels, it necessarily followed that no advantage would accrue from any further hesitation with regard to allowing Europeans to enter the Imperial service for the purpose of opposing them. Ward was officially recognized, and allowed to purchase weapons and to engage officers. An Englishman contracted to convey 9000 of the troops who had stormed Ganking from the Yangtse to Shanghai. These men were Honan braves, who had seen considerable service in the interior of China, and it was proposed that they should garrison the towns of Kiangsu accordingly as they were taken from the rebels. The period of preparation about these matters was marked by several further raids on the part of the Taepings which led to no important event, and by an attempt to seize Chusan from Ningpo which was repulsed with loss. The arrival of General Staveley from Tientsin at the end of March with portions of two English regiments (the 31st and 67th) put a new face on affairs, and showed that the time was at hand when it would be possible to carry out the threat of clearing the country round Shanghai for the space of thirty miles.

The first place to be attacked towards the realization of this plan was the village of Wongkadza, about twelve miles west of Shanghai. Here the Taepings offered only a brief resistance, retiring to some stronger stockades four miles further west. General Staveley, considering that his men had done enough work for that day, halted them, intending to renew the attack the next morning. Unfortunately Ward was carried away by his impetuosity, and attacked this inner position with some 500 of his own men. Admiral Hope accompanied him. The Taepings met them with a tremendous fire, and after several attempts to scale the works they were repulsed with heavy loss. Admiral Hope was wounded in the leg, seven officers were wounded, and seventy men killed and wounded. The attack was repeated in force on the following day, and after some fighting the Taepings evacuated their stockades on finding that Ward's men had got in their rear, and were threatening their line of retreat.

The next place attacked was the village of Tsipoo; and notwithstanding their strong earthworks and three wide ditches, the rebels were driven out in a few hours. It was then determined to attack Kahding, Tsingpu, Nanjao, and Cholin, at which places the Taepings were known to have mustered in considerable strength. Kahding was the first attacked by General Staveley in person at the head of a very strong force. The stockades in front of it were carried with comparatively little loss, as the English commander resorted to the sure and safe principle in dealing with an Asiatic army of turning its flank. At Kahding itself, a strong walled city, the resistance was not as great as had been expected, the Taepings beginning to be seriously discouraged by the formidable enemies whose hostility they had aroused.

The capture of Kahding was followed by preparations for the attack on Tsingpu, which were hastened rather than delayed by a desperate attempt to set fire to Shanghai. The plot was fortunately discovered in time, and the culprits captured and summarily executed to the number of 200. Early in May a strong force was assembled at Sunkiang and proceeded by boat, on account of the difficulties of locomotion, to Tsingpu. The fire of the guns, in which the expedition was exceptionally strong, proved most destructive, and two breaches being pronounced practicable, the place was carried by assault. The rebels fought well and up to the last, on discovering flight to be impossible. The Chinese troops slew every man found in the place with arms in his hands. A few days later Nanjao was captured, but in the attack the French commander, Admiral Protet, a gallant officer who had been to the front during the whole of these operations, was shot dead. The rebels, disheartened by these successive defeats, rallied at Cholin, where they prepared to make a final stand. The allied force attacked Cholin on the 20th of May, and an English detachment carried it almost at the point of the bayonet. With this achievement the operations of the English troops came for the moment to an end, for a disaster to the Imperial arms in their rear necessitated their turning their attention to a different quarter.

The Chinese troops summoned from Ganking had at last arrived to the number of five or six thousand men ; and the Futai Sieh, who was on the point of being superseded to make room for Li Hung Chang, thought to employ them before his departure on some enterprise which should redound to his credit and restore his sinking fortunes. The operation was as hazardous as it was ambitious. The resolution he came to was to attack the city and forts of Taitsan, a place north-west of Shanghai, and not very distant from Chung

GREAT TAEPING VICTORY.

Wang's head-quarters at Soochow. The Imperialist force reached Taitsan on the 12th of May, but less than two days later Chung Wang arrived in person at the head of 10,000 chosen troops to relieve the garrison. A battle ensued on the day following, when, notwithstanding their great superiority in numbers, the Taepings failed to obtain any success. In this extremity Chung Wang resorted to a stratagem. Two thousand of his men shaved their heads and pretended to desert to the Imperialists. When the battle was renewed at sunrise on the following morning this band threw aside their assumed character and turned upon the Imperialists. A dreadful slaughter ensued. Of the seven thousand Honan braves, and the Tartars from Shanghai, five thousand fell on the field. The consequences of this disaster were to undo most of the good accomplished by General Staveley and his force. The Imperialists were for the moment dismayed, and the Taepings correspondingly encouraged. General Staveley's communications were threatened, one detachment was cut off, and the general had to abandon his intended plan and retrace his steps to Shanghai.

Desultory operations followed, but Kahding was abandoned to Chung Wang, who naturally claimed it as a decisive victory over "the foreign devils." After this success Chung Wang hastened to blockade both Tsingpu and Sunkiang, where Ward's contingent was in garrison. Almost at the same date as the defeat at Taitsan the Taepings had been expelled from Ningpo, after having offered many provocations to the English commanders. They made a desperate defence, several officers were killed in the attack, and the affair at Ningpo was described by one who had a right to express an opinion as altogether "the fiercest thing" during the course of our Chinese campaign.

Chung Wang laid regular siege to Sunkiang, where Ward was in person, and he very nearly succeeded in carrying the place by escalade. The attempt was fortunately discovered by an English sailor just in time, and repulsed with a loss to the rebels of 100 men. The Taepings continued to show great daring and activity before both Sunkiang and Tsingpu; and although the latter place was bravely defended, it became clear that the wisest course would be to evacuate it. A body of troops was therefore sent from Shanghai to form a junction with Ward at Sunkiang, and to effect the safe retreat of the Tsingpu garrison. The earlier proceedings were satisfactorily arranged, but the last act of all was grossly mismanaged and resulted in a catastrophe. Ward caused the place to be set on fire, when the Taepings, realizing what was being done, hastened into the town, and assailed the retiring garrison. A scene of great confusion followed; many lives were lost, and the commandant who had held it so courageously was taken prisoner. Chung Wang could therefore appeal to some facts to support his contention that he had got the better of both the Europeans and the Imperialists in the province of Kiangsu.

In the valley of the Yangtsekiang the cause of Tien Wang had not fared equally well. There one disaster had followed another. Not merely were the Imperialists successful in most of the open encounters, but they obtained, by a stratagem or act of treachery, possession of Ying Wang and some of the chief officials. An ex-rebel who had gone over to the Imperialists induced him to trust himself within the walls of Chuchow, where he and his followers were at once arrested and executed by Shingpao, the same officer who had commanded in the battle at the Palikao bridge, and who, it was confidently believed, had caused Captain Brabazon and the Abbé de Luc to be decapitated. The Taepings had also lost the position known as the Western Pillar, which is between Woohoo and Taeping. An army of 40,000 men under Tseng's brother encamped on the south-west side of the city. Tien Wang was smitten with panic by these dangers at his very door, and he sent off express messengers, three in one day, to Chung Wang to return to Nankin without a moment's waste of time. Chung Wang was highly displeased at being thus called away from the scene of his successes, but he had no choice save to obey. He left the command at Soochow to Mow Wang, and hastened back himself to Nankin.

By this time Ward's force had been raised to 5000 men, and another contingent known as the Franco-Chinese had been organized in Chekiang. Tso Tsung Tang had also resumed action in that province. He had recaptured the town of Yenchow, and had succeeded in drawing up a force of 40,000 men with which to oppose the chief Taeping leader in that part, the She Wang, or Attendant King. His operations were extremely deliberate, but he was steadily bringing up the fresh levies of Fuhkien and Chekiang for the purpose of driving the Taepings into a corner at Hangchow Bay. Chung Wang found himself reduced to inaction at Nankin from want of good troops, without which he did not dare attack the strong positions of the Imperialists. Tien Wang, as a sign of his displeasure and disappointment, deprived him of his title, and ordered him to proceed to the province of Anhui.

Meantime Ward and his force were showing increased activity. One attempt to recover Tsingpu was indeed repulsed with loss, but the second attack succeeded. Skirmishes were of daily occurrence, and when Ward proceeded to Ningpo to superintend the operations for the recovery of Tzeki, which had been lost, the fortune of war had again veered round to the side of the Government. Tzeki was retaken, but Ward was wounded in the attack, and died the following morning, September 22, 1862. Ward was only thirty-seven, and although not a skilful soldier, his energy and promptitude had made him a very efficient leader of an irregular force. He deserves to be specially remembered as the original organizer of the body to be known in history as "the Ever-Victorious Army." It was something significant of the difficulties of the commander of this force that Colonel Forrester, the second officer and the defender of Tsingpu who had been taken prisoner, and then ransomed, should decline it, which afforded Burgevine the opportunity of coming to the front.

The recapture of Kahding, specially ordered by the Home Government, was the first operation in which the disciplined Chinese served under their new commander, although the attack on Kahding was conducted by General Staveley in person, and there were more than 2000 British troops present. The place offered only slight resistance, and was recaptured with little loss and handed over to an Imperial garrison. After this the native force was augmented by a corps which had been specially trained by the English officers; and Captain Holland, of the Marine Infantry, was placed at Burgevine's disposal to act as his chief of the staff. The subsequent operations of the disciplined native force were for a time to be conducted under the supervision of Burgevine, whose base still remained at Sunkiang; while the new Futai, Li Hung Chang, with his lieutenant, General Ching, an ex-rebel who had come over to the Imperialists at Ganking, operated against the rebels from Shanghai. Mow Wang was worsted in more than one encounter, and his son was killed in battle by Ward's old lieutenant, Vincente. Unfortunately the progress of the campaign was greatly retarded by the feud which existed, and which soon broke out into acts, between Burgevine and Li, the Futai.

More than one circumstance contributed to embitter the quarrel. The Futai took all the credit of the successes over Mow Wang to his force, and ignored Burgevine's. General Ching was personally jealous of the Contingent, and hoped to secure a great military reputation from the overthrow of the rebels; and the chief obstacle in the way of the realization of his own wishes was "the Ever-Victorious Army." On the other hand, Burgevine was a man of high temper and strong passions, who was disposed to treat his Chinese colleagues with lofty superciliousness, and who met the wiles of the Futai with peremptory demands to recognize the claims of himself and his band. Nor was this all. Burgevine had designs of his own. Although the project had not taken definite form in his mind—for an unsubdued enemy was still in possession of the greater part of the province— the inclination was strong within him to play the part of military dictator with the Chinese; or, failing that, to found an independent authority on some convenient spot of Celestial territory. The Futai anticipated perhaps more than divined his wishes. In Burgevine he saw, very shortly after their coming into contact, not merely a man whom he disliked and distrusted, but one who, if allowed to pursue his plans unchecked, would in the end form a greater danger to the Imperial authority than even the Taepings. It is not possible to deny Li's shrewdness in reading the character of the man with whom he had to deal.

Although Burgevine had succeeded to Ward's command, he had not acquired the intimacy and confidence of the great Chinese merchant Takee and his colleagues at Shanghai, which had been the main cause of his predecessor's influence and position. In Ward they felt implicit faith; Burgevine was comparatively unknown, and where known only regarded with suspicion. The patriotism of the Shanghai merchants consisted in protecting their own possessions. Having succeeded in this, they began to consider whether it was necessary to expend any longer the large sums voluntarily raised for the support of the contingent. Whatever doubt they may have felt was sensibly strengthened by the representations of the officials, who declared that Li and Ching were quite able to hold the Taepings in check, and that Shanghai was perfectly secure. This argument had the excellent recommendation that it coincided with their wishes, and in a few weeks Burgevine at Sunkiang found that the liberal supplies accorded to his predecessor were beginning to fall away. As the immediate consequence of this step, the force was reduced to inaction with all its attendant evils, and the remaining months of the year 1862 passed without any resumption of military operations on their part.

Having thus succeeded in crippling the efficiency of the contingent, the Chinese officials determined to proceed still further for the confusion of Burgevine. At first, in order to test his obedience, it was proposed that he and his men should be sent round by sea to Nankin to take part in the siege of that city, about to be resumed. The ships were actually prepared for their despatch, and the Taotai Wou, who had first fitted out a fleet against the rebels, was in readiness to accompany Burgevine, when Li and his colleague, as suspicious of Burgevine's compliance as they would have been indignant at his refusal, changed their plans and countermanded the expedition. Instead of carrying out this project, therefore, they laid a number of formal complaints before General Staveley as to Burgevine's conduct, and requested the English Government to remove him from his command, and to appoint an English officer in his place. The charges against Burgevine did not at this time amount to more than a certain laxness in regard to the expenditure of the force, a disregard for the wishes and prejudices of the Chinese Government, and the want of tact, or of the desire to conciliate, in his personal relations with the Futai. There was an incompatibility between the Chinese and the foreign commanders in the field; that was all. Had Burgevine been an English officer there would have been an end of the difficulty at once, by his requesting to be relieved from an irksome position in which his actions were misunderstood and misrepresented.

But Burgevine, although a man of some birth and education, regarded the position from the standpoint of the adventurer who believes that his own interests form a supreme law and are the highest good. As commander of the Ever-Victorious Army he was a personage to be considered even by foreign Governments. He would not voluntarily surrender the position which alone preserved him from obscurity. Having come to this decision, it was clear that even the partial execution of his plans must draw him into many errors of judgment which could not but embitter the conflict, at the same time that it compromised the good name of Europeans.

The reply of the English commander was to the effect that personally he could not interfere, but that he would refer the matter to London as well as to Mr. Bruce at Pekin. In consequence of the delay thus caused the project of removing the force to Nankin was revived, and, the steamers having been chartered, Burgevine was requested to bring down his force from Sunkiang and to embark it at Shanghai. This he expressed his willingness to do on payment of his men, who were two months in arrear, and on the settlement of all outstanding claims. Burgevine was supported by his troops. Whatever his dislike to the proposed move, theirs was immeasurably greater. They refused to move without the payment of all arrears; and on the 2nd of January, 1863, they even went so far as to openly mutiny. Two days later

Burgevine went to Shanghai, and had an interview with Takee. The meeting was stormy. Burgevine used personal violence towards the Shanghai merchant, whose attitude was at first overbearing, and he returned to his exasperated troops with the money, which he had carried off by force. The Futai Li, on hearing of the assault on Takee, hastened to General Staveley to complain of Burgevine's gross insubordination in striking a mandarin, which by the law of China was punishable with death. Burgevine was dismissed the Chinese service, and the notice of this decree was forwarded by the English General, with a recommendation to him to give up his command without disturbance. This Burgevine did, for the advice of the English General was equivalent to a command, and on the 6th of January, 1863, Burgevine was back at Shanghai. Captain Holland was then placed in temporary command, while the answer of the Home Government was awaited to General Staveley's proposition to entrust the force to the command of a young captain of engineers named Charles Gordon.

The fortunes of the Ever-Victorious Army were not destined to be more favourable or less chequered under the leading of Captain Holland than they had been under his predecessors. Chung Wang, whose campaign in Anhui had produced such small results that he had even recommended Tien Wang to abandon Nankin and to seek his fortune elsewhere, had returned to Soochow, and in Kiangsu the cause of the Taepings again revived through his energy, although it languished elsewhere. In February a detachment of Holland's force attacked Fushan, but met with a check, when the news of a serious defeat at Taitsan, where the former Futai Sieh had been defeated, compelled its speedy retreat to Sunkiang. Li had had some reason to believe that Taitsan would surrender on the approach of the Imperialists, and he accordingly sent a large army, including 2500 of the contingent, to attack it. The affair was badly managed. The assaulting party was stopped by a wide ditch; neither boats nor ladders arrived. The Taepings fired furiously on the exposed party, several officers were killed, and the men broke into confusion. The heavy guns stuck in the soft ground and had to be abandoned ; and despite the good conduct of the contingent, the Taepings achieved a decisive success (February 13).

Chung Wang was able to feel that his old luck had not deserted him, and the Taepings of Kiangsu recovered all their former confidence in themselves and their leader. This disaster was a rude blow for Li Hung Chang ; and it was resolved that nothing should be attempted until the English officer, at last appointed, had assumed the active command. The campaign in Kiangsu had up to this point only contributed to increase the military reputation and experience of Chung Wang, whose energy more than counterbalanced the superior resources of the Imperialists and their European allies. A second attempt under Major Tapp to relieve Fushan had failed with loss. Several encounters had taken place round Ningpo, in which many officers were killed. A force had indeed been created claiming the brave boast of assured and endless victory ; but after more than two years' campaigning it had done little to justify its title. Perhaps intuitively it awaited the advent of its true leader. Although something had been accomplished since the conclusion of peace at Pekin towards restoring the Emperor's authority, there was no sign that the end of this protracted and sanguinary struggle was near. The energy of Chung Wang might have even justified a belief in its indefinite prolongation.

CHAPTER XV.

CHINESE GORDON'S CAMPAIGNS.

WHEN Captain Gordon assumed the command, on the 24th of March, 1863, the fortunes of the Imperialists had again sunk to a low point. The return of Chung Wang had been followed by a disaster to the forces of the Government, and the Taepings were further encouraged by it to believe in the superiority which they seldom failed to display under the leading of the Faithful King. It would have been unreasonable to suppose that the appointment of a young English engineer officer to the command of a force, which was considered more likely to disobey him than to accept him as its leader, would suffice to restore the doubtful fortune of a war that had already continued for two years under very similar conditions. Yet clearly the whole result depended on whether Gordon could succeed better than Ward, or Burgevine, or Holland, in vanquishing the more desperate and well-armed rebels, who were in actual possession of all the strong places in the province of Kiangsu, and whose detachments stretched from Hangchow to Nankin. There was also another danger. The disciplined Chinese contingent, now numbering five regiments with their foreign officers of all nationalities, adventurers unrestrained by any consideration of obedience to their own Governments, furnished the means of great mischief, should any leader present himself to exhort them to fight for their own hand and to carve out a dominion for themselves. The possibility was far from chimerical; it was fully realized and appreciated by the English authorities. A great responsibility, therefore, devolved upon Captain Gordon. He had not merely to beat a victorious enemy, and to restore the confidence and discipline of his defeated troops ; but he had also to advance the objects of the English Government, and to redeem the rights of a long-outraged people. Unlike his predecessors, he had no personal aims for himself, he did not wish to displace or weaken the authority of the Chinese officials, and his paramount thought was how to rescue the unfortunate inhabitants of Kiangsu from the calamities which had desolated their hearths, and driven whole towns and districts to the verge of destruction and despair.

On the 24th of March Gordon, now given the brevet rank of major, left Shanghai, reaching Sunkiang on the following day. There was some fear of an immediate outbreak after his arrival ; but the men had no leader, and Major Gordon established himself at head-quarters without opposition. An order issued on the following day to the effect that nothing would be done to injure their position served to quiet the officers and their men ; and the resumption of active operations fortunately diverted the current of their thoughts. The danger of keeping such a body of men inactive was obvious ; and the perilous condition of the garrison at Chanzu, which Major Tapp had failed to relieve a month before by his attack on Fushan, rendered a prompt movement on the part of the force absolutely necessary. Three days after his first appearance at Sunkiang, Major Gordon was back in Shanghai purchasing extra ammunition in preparation for his march northwards. On the last day of March the expedition, consisting of one regiment and some artillery, sailed in two steamers for Fushan, where they found the Imperial troops strongly encamped near the shore. Major Tapp had already joined them at the head of another portion of the contingent.

The rebels were in possession of two stockades some miles inland ; but although they were in great numbers, their position did not strike the English officer as being strong. The advanced posts of the Imperialists, consisting of Tapp's men, were within half a mile of these stockades. The old town of Fushan lay unoccupied on the left hand. Major Gordon at once seized it for the purpose of using the walls as a battery. A heavy gun was placed on the rampart, and four smaller ones in front, all of which began to fire on the rebel stockades on the 4th of March. The Taepings were not accustomed to such a vigorous fire, and soon retired. Their stockades were then carried, and on their attempting to recover them they were repulsed with loss. In consequence of this defeat the rebels withdrew in an unexpected and precipitate manner from before Chanzu, which was thus relieved without further bloodshed. The place had been most gallantly held by an ex-rebel chief, named Sute, and a Chinese mandarin Chu, aided by two Frenchmen. The relief of Chanzu was important, not merely as a military achievement, but also as affording practical proof of the safety with which rebels might abandon a hopeless cause and rally to the side of the Government. Major Gordon's command had, from every point of view, begun well.

Major Gordon returned to Sunkiang, where he employed himself in energetically restoring the discipline of his force, and in preparing for his next operation in the field, which Li Hung Chang wished should be the capture of Quinsan, a town half-way between Soochow and Taitsan, and the surrender of which would involve, as Li believed, the immediate fall of the last-named place. These preliminary measures occupied a fortnight, but the arrangements had barely been made for the advance on Taitsan, when Burgevine suddenly returned from Pekin and reappeared at Shanghai, accompanied by a Chinese official alleged to be instructed by Prince Kung and the Tsungli Yamen to reinstate him in the command of the Ever-Victorious Army. This circumstance was, to say the least, embarrassing, as he brought with him a formal statement on the part of both Sir Frederick Bruce and Mr. Burlinghame, the representative of the United States, that they had examined into the charges against him, found them to be untenable, and considered that he had been very harshly treated, and that he had a correspondingly strong claim on the consideration of the Chinese Government. His journey to Pekin had not been in vain.

On the 24th of April the force left Sunkiang for Quinsan, the infantry proceeding by land, the artillery by water with the steamer *Hyson*. On that very day Major Gordon had received a long communication from Li Hung Chang informing him of the proceedings in connection with Burgevine, but stating his final decision not to restore him to the command of the Ward force, a decision which reflected the greatest credit on Li's firmness and perspicuity. He also gave Major Gordon all the credit he deserved for what he had already done, stating that "the people and place were charmed with him," and that he had petitioned the Board at Pekin to confer upon him the rank of Tsungping or Brigadier-General. This despatch of the Futai was intended to undo and repair the mischief that would have been caused by the hasty and ill-considered resolve of the Ministers at Pekin, if carried into execution. General Brown, who had succeeded General Staveley in the command at Shanghai, fortunately took a correct view of the situation, and refused to recognize Burgevine unless the Futai reappointed him. Li was most careful to repudiate at the very earliest moment all intention of doing so, a decision which he had signified to Major Gordon in his letter of the 24th of April. The Tsungli Yamen had shown extraordinary favour towards foreigners, he said; but Li had only to consider the efficiency of the army and the welfare of the State. These demanded the retention of Gordon and the exclusion of Burgevine.

The force which had left Sunkiang with the intention of attacking Quinsan was compelled to suddenly alter its march by the news of an act of treachery at Taitsan which entailed the loss of 1500 Imperialists. The commandant had feigned a desire to surrender the place, and the Chinese, deceived by his representations, had allowed themselves to be entrapped into a false position, when the rebels, coming down in overwhelming strength, had slaughtered them to the number named. It became necessary to retrieve this disaster without delay, more especially as all hope of taking Quinsan had for the moment to be abandoned.

Major Gordon at once altered the direction of his march, and joining *en route* General Ching, who had, on the news, broken up his camp before Quinsan, hastened as rapidly as possible to Taitsan, where he arrived on the 29th of April. Bad weather obliged him to defer the attack until the 1st of May, when two stockades on the west side were carried, and their defenders compelled to flee, not into the town as they would have wished, but away from it towards Chanzu. On the following day, the attack was resumed on the north side, while the armed boats proceeded to assault the place from the creek. The firing continued from nine in the morning until five in the evening, when a breach seemed to be practicable, and two regiments were ordered to the assault. The rebels showed great courage and fortitude, swarming in the breach and pouring a heavy and well-directed fire upon the troops. The attack was momentarily checked; but while the stormers remained under such cover as they could find, the shells of two howitzers were playing over their heads and causing frightful havoc among the Taepings in the breach. But for these guns, Major Gordon did not think that the place would have been carried at all; but after some minutes of this firing at close quarters, the rebels began to show signs of wavering. A party of troops gained the wall, a fresh regiment advanced towards the breach, and the disappearance of the snake flags showed that the Taeping leaders had given up the fight. Taitsan was thus captured, and the three previous disasters before it retrieved.

On the 4th of May the victorious force appeared before Quinsan, a place of considerable strength and possessing a formidable artillery directed by an European. The town was evidently too strong to be carried by an immediate attack, and Major Gordon's movements were further hampered by the conduct of his own men, who, upon their arrival at Quinsan, hurried off in detachments to Sunkiang for the purpose of disposing of their spoil. Ammunition had also fallen short, and the commander was consequently obliged to return to refit and to rally his men. At Sunkiang worse confusion followed, for the men, or rather the officers, broke out into mutiny on the occasion of Major Gordon appointing an English officer with the rank of lieutenant-colonel to the control of the commissariat, which had been completely neglected. Those who had served with Ward and Burgevine objected to their being passed over, and openly refused to obey orders. Fortunately the stores and ammunition were collected, and Major Gordon announced that he would march in the following morning, whether with or without the mutineers mattered nothing to him. Those who did not answer to their names at the end of the first half-march would be dismissed, and he spoke with the authority of one in complete accord with the Chinese authorities themselves. The native soldiers obeyed him as a Chinese official, and the foreign officers feared to disobey him as they would have liked on account of his commanding the source whence they were paid. The mutineers fell in, and a force of nearly 3000 men, well-equipped and anxious for the fray, returned to Quinsan, where General Ching had, in the meanwhile, kept the rebels in close watch from a strong position defended by several stockades, and supported by the *Hyson*.

Immediately after his arrival, Major Gordon moved out his force to attack the stockades which the rebels had constructed on their right wing. These were strongly built; but as soon as the defenders perceived that the assailants had gained their flank they precipitately withdrew into Quinsan itself. General Ching wished the attack to be made on the Eastern Gate, opposite to which he had raised his own entrenchments, and by which he had announced his intention of forcing his way; but a brief inspection showed Major Gordon that that was the strongest point of the town, and that a direct attack upon it could only succeed, if at all, by a very considerable sacrifice of men. Like a prudent commander, Major Gordon determined to reconnoitre; and, after much grumbling on the part of General Ching, he decided that the most hopeful plan was to carry some stockades situated seven miles west of the town, and thence assail Quinsan on the Soochow side, which was weaker than the others. These stockades were at a village called Chumze. On the 30th of May the force detailed for this work proceeded to carry it out. The *Hyson* and fifty Imperial gun-boats conveyed the land force, which consisted of one regiment, some guns, and a large body of Imperialists. The rebels at Chumze offered hardly the least resistance, whether it was that they were dismayed at the sudden appearance of the enemy, or, as was stated at the time, because they considered themselves ill-treated by their comrades in Quinsan. The *Hyson* vigorously pursued those who fled towards Soochow, and completed the effect of this success by the capture of a very strong and well-built fort covering a bridge at Ta Edin. An Imperialist garrison was installed there, and the *Hyson* continued the pursuit to within a mile of Soochow itself.

While the late defenders of Chumze were thus driven in hopeless and irretrievable confusion along the narrow road to Soochow, those in Quinsan itself had been terribly alarmed at the cutting off of their communications. They saw themselves on the point of being surrounded, and they yielded to the uncontrollable impulse of panic. During the night, after having suffered severely from the *Hyson's* fire, the garrison evacuated the place, which might easily have held out; and General Ching had the personal satisfaction, on learning from some deserters of the flight of the garrison, of leading his men over the eastern walls which he had wished to assault. The importance of Quinsan was realized on its capture. Major Gordon pronounced it to be the key of Soochow, and at once resolved to establish his head-quarters there, partly because of its natural advantages, but also and not less on account of its enabling him to gradually destroy the evil associations which the men of his force had contracted at Sunkiang.

The change was not acceptable, however, to the force itself; and the artillery in particular refused to obey orders, and threatened to shoot their officers. Discipline was, however, promptly reasserted by the energy of the commander, who thus described the scene:—"The non-commissioned officers, as usual, all paraded, and were sent for by Major Gordon, who asked them the reason why the men did not fall in, and who wrote the proclamation. They, of course, did not know, and on Major Gordon telling them he would be obliged to shoot one in every five, they evinced their objection to this proceeding by a groan. The most prominent in this was a corporal, who was dragged out, and a couple of infantry who were standing by were ordered to load and directed to shoot the mutineer, which one did without the slightest hesitation." After this "the Ever-Victorious Army" became gradually reconciled to its new position at Quinsan. Major Gordon had difficulties with his Chinese colleague also; for General Ching wanted to take all the credit of the victory to himself, and, resentful at Gordon's not having attacked the East Gate, objected to his retaining the town, and said he ought to return to Sunkiang. However, his objections proved as unavailing as his secret disparagement of the English officer, who remained in Quinsan and who was fortunately relieved of the presence of many of the original members of the Ward force by their voluntarily returning to Sunkiang. He had no difficulty in supplying their places, and many of his recruits were the ex-Taeping soldiers who had been captured with Quinsan. General Ching proceeded in high dudgeon to Chumze and Ta Edin, where he placed his troops in quarters, while his large fleet of gun-boats ensured the safety of his communications and commanded the narrow paths or causeways on either side of the creek.

After the capture of Quinsan there was a cessation of active operations for nearly two months. It was the height of summer, and the new troops had to be drilled. The difficulty with Ching was arranged through the mediation of Dr. Macartney, who had just left the English army to become Li's right-hand man, and who was sent by that official from Shanghai for the express purpose. Dr. Halliday Macartney had been an assistant surgeon in the 99th, and went through the Pekin campaign in that capacity. At this time he was employed in a variety of capacities by the Futai. He "drilled troops, supervised the manufacture of shells, gave advice, brightened the Futai's intellect about foreigners, and made peace, in which last accomplishment his forte lay." How accurate that description was has been shown by Sir Halliday Macartney during his diplomatic career of more than twenty years.

Two other circumstances occurred to embarrass the young commander. There were rumours of some meditated movement on the part of Burgevine, and there was a further

ANOTHER MUTINY.

manifestation of insubordination in the force. The artillery had been cowed by Major Gordon's vigour, but its efficiency remained more doubtful than could be satisfactory to the general responsible for its condition, and one also relying upon it as the most potent arm of his force. He resolved to remove the old commander, and to appoint an English officer, Major Tapp, in his place. On carrying his determination into effect the officers sent in "a round robin," refusing to accept a new officer. This was on the 25th of July, and the expedition which had been decided upon against Wokong had consequently to set out the following morning without a single artillery officer. In face of the inflexible resolve of the leader, however, the officers repented, and appeared in a body at the camp begging to be taken back, and expressing their willingness to accept "Major Tapp or any one else" as their colonel.

With these troops, part of whom had only just returned to a proper sense of discipline, Gordon proceeded to attack Kahpoo, a place on the Grand Canal south of Soochow, where the rebels held two strongly-built stone forts. The force had been strengthened by the addition of another steamer, the *Firefly*, a sister-vessel to the *Hyson*. Major Gordon arrived before Kahpoo on the 27th of July; and the garrison, evidently taken by surprise, made scarcely the least resistance. The capture of Kahpoo placed Gordon's force between Soochow and Wokong, the next object of attack.

At Wokong the rebels were equally unprepared. The garrison at Kahpoo, thinking only of its own safety, had fled to Soochow, leaving their comrades at Wokong unwarned and to their fate. So heedless were the Taepings at this place of all danger from the north, that they had even neglected to occupy a strong stone fort situated on a creek of the Taho lake, and about 1000 yards north of the walls of Wokong. The Taepings attempted too late to repair their error, and the loss of this fort cost them that of the other stockades which they had constructed at different points. Several of these were without any garrison, either because their numbers were too few, or because they wished to husband their resources for the defence of Wokong itself. Their inaction entailed the defection of many of their adherents in the surrounding country, who went over to the Imperialists on Major Gordon's promise of their lives. A success obtained by General Ching and the Imperialists at Tungli entailed further discomfiture to the Taepings. Wokong itself was too weak to offer any effectual resistance; and the garrison on the eve of the assault ordered for the 29th of July sent out a request for quarter, which was granted, and the place surrendered without further fighting. A brother of Chung Wang had been in command there, but he had escaped by the Taho lake during the night before the attack. He had only received the title of Yang Wang a few days; but instead of preparing to signalize his promotion by some act of vigour, he had procured a theatrical company from Hangchow to amuse his hours of leisure. This portion of the campaign closed with the repulse of an attack on Kahpoo by some of the Soochow garrison led by Mow Wang in person, and with the preparations for the return of Major Gordon's force to its headquarters at Quinsan.

Meanwhile an event of far greater importance had happened than even the capture of these towns, although they formed the necessary preliminary to the investment of Soochow. Burgevine had come to the decision to join the Taepings. On his return from Pekin with the recommendations of Mr. Burlinghame and Sir Frederick Bruce in his pocket, and escorted by a delegate of the Tsungli Yamen, he had anticipated with more or less confidence his being promptly reinstated in the command of the Ever-Victorious Army, which, as he was careful to protest, he had never resigned. The firmness of Li Hung Chang baffled his project and disappointed his hopes. He had expected that the Governor of Kiangsu would at once defer to the wishes of the Ministers at Pekin, and would carry into execution Prince Kung's very friendly expressions. Li did nothing of the sort. He plainly declined to entrust Burgevine with any command, and the event amply justified the Futai's decision.

Disappointed in his main hope, Burgevine remained on at Shanghai, employing his time in watching the varying phases of a campaign in which he longed to take part, and of which he believed that it was only his due to have the direction, but still hesitating as to what decision it behoved him to take. His contempt for all Chinese officials became hatred of the bitterest kind of the Futai, by whom he had been not merely thwarted but over-reached, and predisposed him to regard with no unfavourable eye the idea of joining his fortunes to those of the rebel Taepings now that no opportunity presented itself for forming a third and independent party of his own. To him in this frame of mind came some of the dismissed officers and men of the Ward force, appealing to his vanity by declaring that his soldiers remembered him with affection, and that he had only to hoist his flag for most of his old followers to rally round him. There was little to marvel at if he also was not free from some feeling of jealousy at the success and growing fame of Major Gordon, for whom he simulated a warm friendship. The combination of motives proved altogether irresistible as soon as he found that several hundred European adventurers were ready to accompany him into the ranks of the Taepings, and to endeavour to do for them what they had failed to perform for the Imperialists, and what the opposition of the Futai and the discipline of Major Gordon prevented their attempting a second time.

On the 15th of July Dr. Macartney wrote to Major Gordon stating that he had positive information that Burgevine was enlisting men for some enterprise, that he had already collected about 300 Europeans, and that he had even gone so far as to chose a special flag, a white diamond on a red ground, and containing a black star in the centre of the diamond. On the 21st of the same month Burgevine wrote to Major Gordon saying that there would be many rumours about him, but that he was not to believe any of them, and that he would come and see him shortly. This letter was written as a blind, and, unfortunately, Major Gordon attached greater value to Burgevine's word than he did to the precise information of Dr. Macartney. He was too much disposed to think that, as the officer who had to a certain extent superseded Burgevine in the command, he was bound to take the most favourable view of all his actions, and to trust implicitly in his good faith. Although Beechy, Burgevine's agent, was arrested, the real conspirator himself remained at large, simply because Major Gordon, trusting to his word, had made himself personally responsible to the Chinese authorities for his good faith.

Burgevine's plans had been deeply laid. He had been long in correspondence with Mow Wang. His terms had been accepted, and he had finally made up his mind more than a fortnight before he wrote to Major Gordon declaring that he was coming to see him at Quinsan. On the 2nd of August Dr. Macartney left Shanghai in charge of a new steamer, the *Kajow*, and he reached Sunkiang in safety with his vessel; but during his absence to communicate with the town the *Kajow* was seized by "a party of thirty-two rowdies," who eventually proved to be Burgevine and his men. In this open manner did Burgevine first proclaim his adhesion to the rebel cause, and had he only possessed the natural capacity he might have inflicted an immense amount of injury on the Imperialists, reopened and extended all the old injuries, and prolonged the struggle for an indefinite period. Fortunately his capacity was not equal to his opportunites.

At this time Major Gordon came to the decision to resign, and he had hastened back to Shanghai in order to place his withdrawal from the force in the hands of the Futai. He arrived there on the very day that Burgevine seized the *Kajow* steamer at Sunkiang, and on hearing the news he at once withdrew his resignation, which had been made partly from irritation at the irregular payment of his men, and also on account of the cruelty of General Ching. Not merely did he withdraw his resignation, but he hastened back to Quinsan, into which he rode on the night of the very same day that had witnessed his departure. The immediate and most pressing danger was from the possible defection of the force to its old leader, when, with the large stores of artillery and ammunition at Quinsan in their possession, not even Shanghai with its very weak foreign garrison could be considered safe from attack. As a measure of precaution Major Gordon sent some of his heavy guns and stores back to Taitsan, where the English commander, General Brown, consented to guard them, while Gordon himself hastened off to Kahpoo, now threatened both by the Soochow force and by the foreign adventurers acting under Burgevine.

He arrived at a most critical moment. The garrison was hard pressed. General Ching had gone back to Shanghai, and only the presence of the *Hyson* prevented the rebels, who were well armed and possessed an efficient artillery, from carrying the fort by a rush. The arrival of Major Gordon with 150 men on board his third steamer, the *Cricket*, restored the confidence of the defenders, but there was no doubt that Burgevine had lost a most favourable opportunity. Instead of hastening with his prize from Sunkiang to take part in the operations against Kahpoo and Wokong, he made for the Taho lake, where he felt himself secure, and by which he proceeded to join his new ally, Mow Wang, at Soochow. Meantime that chief in person, assisted by a portion of the Europeans, had got a 12-pounder howitzer into position opposite the stockades at Kahpoo, which placed the rebels on a greater equality with Gordon's force, as even the steamers had to be careful of the shell fire. The fighting now became severe. The rebels fought with greater confidence, and it was evident to the young commander that each battle would be more and more stubbornly contested. But of the ultimate success of the Imperialists he never felt doubtful for a moment; and, after a week's continual engagement, he had the satisfaction of perceiving the whole Taeping force burn most of the villages in their possession and retire into Soochow. About the same time the present Sir Halliday Macartney took the towns of Fongching and Tseedong.

General Ching, who was a man of almost extraordinary energy and restlessness, resolved to signalize his return to the field by some striking act while Major Gordon was completing his preparations at Quinsan for a fresh effort. His headquarters were at the strong fort of Ta Edin, on the creek leading from Quinsan to Soochow, and, having the *Hyson* with him, he determined to make a dash to some point nearer the great rebel stronghold. On the 30th of August he had seized the position of Waiquaidong, where, in three days, he threw up stockades, admirably constructed, and which could not have been carried save by a great effort on the part of the whole of the Soochow garrison. Towards the end of September, Major Gordon, fearing lest the rebels, who had now the supposed advantage of Burgevine's presence and advice, might make some attempt to cut off General Ching's lengthy communications, moved forward to Waiquaidong to support him; but, when he arrived, he found that the impatient mandarin, encouraged either by the news of his approach or at the inaction of the Taepings in Soochow, had made a still further advance of two miles, so that he was only 1000 yards distant from the rebel stockades in front of the East Gate. Major Gordon had at this time been reinforced by the Franco-Chinese Corps, which had been well disciplined, under the command of Captain Bonnefoy, while the necessity of leaving any strong garrison at Quinsan had been obviated by the loan of 200 Belooches from General Brown's force.

The rebel position having been carefully reconnoitred, both on the east and on the south, Major Gordon determined that the first step necessary for its proper beleaguerment was to seize and fortify the village of Patachiaou, about one mile south of the city wall. The village, although strongly stockaded, was evacuated by the garrison after a feeble resistance, and an attempt to recover it a few hours later by Mow Wang in person resulted in a rude repulse chiefly on account of the effective fire of the *Hyson*. Burgevine, instead of fighting the battles of the failing cause he had adopted, was travelling about the country: at one moment in the capital interviewing Tien Wang and his ministers, at another going about in disguise even in the streets of Shanghai. But during the weeks when General Ching might have been taken at a disadvantage, and when it was quite possible to recover some of the places which had been lost, he was absent from the scene of military operations. After the capture of Patachiaou most of the troops and the steamers that had taken it were sent back to Waiquaidong, but Major Gordon remained there with a select body of his men and three howitzers.

The rebels had not resigned themselves to the loss of

Patachiaou, and on the 1st of October they made a regular attempt to recover it. They brought the *Kajow* into action, and, as it had found a daring commander in a man named Jones, its assistance proved very considerable. They had also a 32-pounder gun on board a junk, and this enabled them to overcome the fire of Gordon's howitzers and also of the *Hyson*, which arrived from Waiquaidong during the engagement. But notwithstanding the superiority of their artillery the rebels hesitated to come to close quarters, and when Major Gordon and Captain Bonnefoy led a sortie against them at the end of the day they retired precipitately. This action was followed by a suspension of arms and by the commencement of a correspondence and even of conversations between the Europeans who were brought by such a strange combination of circumstances into hostile camps on Chinese soil.

On the 3rd of October Burgevine wrote Major Gordon in terms of confidence on the success of the Taepings. Three days later Burgevine met Major Gordon at the front of the stockades, and expressed his wish to give in his surrender on the assurance that no proceedings would be taken against him or those who served under his flag. He attributed this sudden change in his plans to the state of his health; but there was never the least doubt that the true reasons of this altered view were dissatisfaction with his treatment by the Taeping leaders and a conviction of the impossibility of success. Inside Soochow, and at Nankin, it was possible to see with clearer eyes than at Shanghai that the Taeping cause was one that could not be resuscitated. But although Burgevine soon and very clearly saw the hopelessness of the Taeping movement, he had by no means made up his mind to go over to the Imperialists. With a considerable number of European followers at his beck and call, and with a profound and ineradicable contempt for the whole Chinese official world, he was loth to lose or surrender the position which gave him a certain importance. He vacillated between a number of suggestions, and the last he came to was the most remarkable, at the same time that it revealed more clearly than any other the vain and meretricious character of the man. In his second interview with Major Gordon he proposed that that officer should join him, and, combining the whole force of the Europeans and the disciplined Chinese, seize Soochow, and establish an independent authority of their own. It was the old filibustering idea, revived under the most unfavourable circumstances, of fighting for their own hand, dragging the European name in the dirt, and founding an independent authority of some vague, undefinable, and transitory character. Major Gordon listened to the unfolding of this scheme of miserable treachery, and only his strong sense of the utter impossibility, and indeed the ridiculousness of the project, prevented his contempt and indignation finding forcible expression. Burgevine, the traitor to the Imperial cause, the man whose health would not allow him to do his duty to his new masters in Soochow, thus revealed his plan for defying all parties, and for deciding the fate of the Dragon Throne. The only reply he received was the cold one that it would be better and wiser to confine his attention to the question of whether he intended to yield or not, instead of discussing idle schemes of "vaulting ambition."

Meantime, Chung Wang had come down from Nankin to superintend the defence of Soochow; and in face of a more capable opponent he still did not despair of success, or at the least of making a good fight of it. He formed the plan of assuming the offensive against Chanzu whilst General Ching was employed in erecting his stockades step by step nearer to the eastern wall at Soochow. In order to prevent the realization of this project, Major Gordon made several demonstrations on the western side of Soochow, which had the effect of inducing Chung Wang to defer his departure. At this conjuncture serious news arrived from the south. A large rebel force, assembled from Chekiang and the silk districts south of the Taho lake, had moved up the Grand Canal and held the garrison of Wokong in close leaguer. On the 10th of October the Imperialists stationed there made a sortie, but were driven back with the loss of several hundred men killed and wounded. Their provisions were almost exhausted, and it was evident that, unless relieved, they could not hold out many days longer. On the 12th of

October Major Gordon therefore hastened to their succour. The rebels held a position south of Wokong, and, as they felt sure of a safe retreat, they fought with great determination. The battle lasted three hours; the guns had to be brought up to within fifty yards of the stockade, and the whole affair is described as one of the hardest-fought actions of the war. On the return of the contingent to Patachiaou, about. thirty Europeans deserted the rebels, but Burgevine and one or two others were not with them.

Chung Wang had seized the opportunity of Gordon's departure for the relief of Wokong to carry out his scheme against Chanzu. Taking the *Kajow* with him, and a considerable number of the foreign adventurers, he reached Monding, where the Imperialists were strongly entrenched at the junction of the main creek from Chanzu with the canal. He attacked them, and a severely-contested struggle ensued, in which at first the Taepings carried everything before them. But the fortune of the day soon veered round. The *Kajow* was sunk by a lucky shot, great havoc was wrought by the explosion of a powder-boat, and the Imperialists remained masters of a hard-fought field. The defection of the Europeans placed Burgevine in serious peril, and only Major Gordon's urgent representations and acts of courtesy to the Mow Wang saved his life. The Taeping leader, struck by the gallantry and fair-dealing of the English officer, set Burgevine free; and on the very day that he wrote his second letter from Soochow he was permitted to leave that place—an act of generosity most creditable to Mow Wang. Burgevine came out of the whole complication with a reputation in every way diminished and sadly tarnished. He had not even the most common and brutal courage which would have impelled him to stay in Soochow and take the chances of the party to which he had elected to attach himself. Whatever his natural talents might have been, his vanity and weakness obscured them all. With the inclination to create an infinity of mischief, it must be considered fortunate that his ability was so small, for his opportunities were abundant. Gordon had shown him nothing but kindness, and Mr. Seward, Consul for the United States at

Shanghai, wrote officially and thanked Major Gordon for his great consideration to "misguided General Burgevine and his men." Burgevine was drowned in a Chinese river in June, 1865.

The conclusion of the Burgevine incident removed a weight from Major Gordon's mind. Established on the east and south of Soochow, he determined to secure a similar position on its western side, when he would be able to intercept the communications still held by the garrison across the Taho lake. In order to attain this object it was necessary, in the first place, to carry the stockades at Wuliungchow, a village two miles west of Patachiaou. The place was captured at the first attack and successfully held, notwithstanding a fierce attempt to recover it under the personal direction of Chung Wang, who returned for the express purpose. This success was followed by others. Another large body of rebels had come up from the south and assailed the garrison of Wokong. On the 26th of October one of Gordon's lieutenants, Major Kirkham, inflicted a severe defeat upon them, and vigorously pursued them for several miles. During this fight alone the rebels lost—in killed, wounded, and prisoners—nearly 3000 men.

The next operation undertaken was the capture of the village of Leeku, three miles north of Soochow, as the preliminary to investing the city on the north. Here Major Gordon resorted to his usual flanking tactics, and with conspicuous success. The rebels fought well; one officer was killed at Gordon's side, and the men in the stockade were cut down with the exception of about forty, who were made prisoners. Soochow was then assailed on the northern as well as on the other sides, but Chung Wang's army still served to keep open communications by means of the Grand Canal. That army had its principal quarters at Wusieh, where it was kept in check by a large Imperialist force under Santajin, Li's brother, who had advanced from Kongyin on the Yangtse. Major Gordon's main difficulty now arose from the insufficiency of his force to hold so wide an extent of country; and in order to procure a reinforcement from Santajin he agreed to assist that commander against his able opponent Chung Wang. With a view to accomplishing this, the Taeping position at Wanti, two miles north of Leeku, was attacked and carried with comparatively little loss from the rebels, although many of the assailants perished by the fire of their own comrades, owing to the European officers attacking without orders on two sides at the same moment.

At this stage of the campaign there were 13,500 men round Soochow, and of these, 8500 were fully occupied in the defence of the stockades, leaving the very small number of 5000 men available for active measures in the field. On the other hand, Santajin had not fewer than 20,000, and possibly as many as 30,000 men under his orders. But the Taepings still enjoyed the numerical superiority. They had 40,000 men in Soochow, 20,000 at Wusieh, and Chung Wang occupied a camp, halfway between these places, with 18,000 followers. The presence of Chung Wang was also estimated to be worth a corps of 5000 soldiers. Had Gordon been free to act, his plan of campaign would have been simple and decisive. He would have effected a junction of his forces with Santajin, he would have overwhelmed Chung Wang's 18,000 with his combined army of double that strength, and he would have appeared at the head of his victorious troops before the bewildered garrison of Wusieh. It would probably have terminated the campaign at a stroke. Even the decisive defeat of Chung Wang alone might have entailed the collapse of the cause now tottering to its fall. But Major Gordon had to consider not merely the military quality of his allies, but also their jealousies and differences. General Ching hated Santajin on private grounds as well as on public. He desired a monopoly of the profit and honour of the campaign. His own reputation would be made by the capture of Soochow. It would be diminished and cast into the shade were another Imperial commander to defeat Chung Wang and close the line of the Grand Canal. Were Gordon to detach himself from General Ching he could not feel sure what that jealous and impulsive commander would do. He would certainly not preserve the vigilant defensive before Soochow necessary to ensure the safety of the army operating to the north. The commander of the Ever-Victorious Army had consequently to abandon the tempting idea of crushing Chung Wang and of capturing the towns in the rear of Nankin, and to have recourse to safer but slower methods.

The loss of the steamer *Firefly*, which was carried off by a party of European and Chinese desperadoes from outside Li's camp at Shanghai, and the difficulty of operating in a country intersected in every direction by creeks and canals, compelled several changes of plan; but on the 19th of November Major Gordon had collected the whole of his available force to attack Fusaiquan, a place on the Grand Canal six miles north of Soochow. Here the rebels had barred the canal on three different points, while on the banks they occupied eight earthworks, which were fortunately in a very incomplete state. A desperate resistance was expected from the rebels at this advantageous spot, but they preferred their safety to their duty, and retreated to Wusieh with hardly the least loss. Not a man of the attacking force was hit, and only three of the rebels fell. The incapacity and cowardice of the Wang in command was conspicuous, and, as the victor said, if ever a Taeping leader deserved to lose his head, he did, for abandoning so strong and formidable a position. In consequence of this reverse Chung Wang withdrew his forces from his camp in face of Santajin, and concentrated his men at Monding and Wusieh for the defence of the Grand Canal.

The investment of Soochow being now as complete as the number of troops under the Imperial standard would allow of, Major Gordon returned to General Ching's stockades in front of that place, with the view of resuming the attack on the eastern gate. General Ching and Captain Bonnefoy had met with a slight repulse there on the 14th of October. The stockade in front of the east gate was known by the name of Low Mun, and had been strengthened to the best knowledge of the Taeping engineers. Their position was exceedingly formidable, consisting of a line of breastwork defended at intervals with circular stockades. Major Gordon decided upon making a night attack, and he arranged his plans from the information provided by the European and other deserters who had been inside. The Taepings were not without their spies and sympathizers also, and the

A FIRST DEFEAT.   403

intended attack was revealed to them. The attack was made at two in the morning of the 27th of November, but the rebels had mustered in force and received Major Gordon's men with tremendous volleys. Even then the disciplined troops would not give way, and encouraged by the example of their leader, who seemed to be at the front and at every point at the same moment, fairly held their own on the edge of the enemy's position. Unfortunately the troops in support behaved badly, and got confused from the heavy fire of the Taepings, which never slackened. Some of them absolutely retired, and others were landed at the wrong places. Major Gordon had to hasten to the rear to restore order, and during his absence the advanced guard were expelled from their position by a forward movement led by Mow Wang in person. The attack had failed, and there was nothing to do save to draw off the troops with as little further loss as possible. This was Major Gordon's first defeat, but it was so evidently due to the accidents inseparable from a night attempt, and to the fact that the surprise had been revealed, that it produced a less discouraging effect on officers and men than might have been deemed probable. Up to this day Major Gordon had obtained thirteen distinct victories besides the advantage in many minor skirmishes.

Undismayed by this reverse, Major Gordon collected all his troops and artillery from the other stockades, and resolved to attack the Low Mun position with his whole force. He also collected all his heavy guns and mortars and cannonaded the rebel stockade for some time; but on an advance being ordered the assailants were compelled to retire by the fire which the Taepings brought to bear on them from every available point. Chung Wang had hastened down from Wusieh to take part in the defence of what was rightly regarded as the key of the position at Soochow, and both he and Mow Wang superintended in person the defence of the Low Mun stockade. After a further cannonade the advance was again sounded, but this second attack would also have failed had not the officers and men boldly plunged into the moat or creek and swum across. The whole of the stockades and a stone fort were then carried, and the Imperial forces firmly established at a point only 900 yards from the inner wall of Soochow. Six officers and fifty men were killed, and three officers, five Europeans, and 128 men were wounded in this successful attack.

The capture of the Low Mun stockades meant practically the fall of Soochow. Chung Wang then left it to its fate, and all the other Wangs except Mow Wang were in favour of coming to terms with the Imperialists. Even before this defeat Lar Wang had entered into communications with General Ching for coming over, and as he had the majority of the troops at Soochow under his orders, Mow Wang was practically powerless, although resolute to defend the place to the last. Several interviews took place between the Wangs and General Ching and Li Hung Chang. Major Gordon also saw the former, and had one interview with Lar Wang in person. The English officer proposed as the most feasible plan that Lar Wang should surrender one of the gates. During all this period Major Gordon had impressed on both of his Chinese colleagues the imperative necessity there was, for reasons of policy and prudence, to deal leniently and honourably by the rebel chiefs. All seemed to be going well. General Ching took an oath of brotherhood with Lar Wang, Li Hung Chang agreed with everything that fell from Gordon's lips. The only one exempted from this tacit understanding was Mow Wang, always in favour of fighting it out and defending the town; and his name was not mentioned for the simple reason that he had nothing to do with the negotiations. For Mow Wang Major Gordon had formed the esteem due to a gallant enemy, and he resolved to spare no effort to save his life.

His benevolent intentions were thwarted by the events that had occurred within Soochow. Mow Wang had been murdered by the other Wangs, who feared that he might detect their plans and prevent their being carried out. The death of Mow Wang removed the only leader who was heartily opposed to the surrender of Soochow, and on the day after this chief's murder the Imperialists received possession of one of the gates. The inside of the city had been the scene of the most dreadful confusion. Mow Wang's men had sought to avenge their leader's death, and on the other hand the followers of Lar Wang had shaved their heads in token of their adhesion to the Imperialist cause. Some of the more prudent of the Wangs, not knowing what turn events might take amid the prevailing discord, secured their safety by a timely flight. Major Gordon kept his force well in hand, and refused to allow any of the men to enter the city, where they would certainly have exercised the privileges of a mercenary force in respect of pillage. Instead of this, Major Gordon endeavoured to obtain for them two months' pay from the Futai, which that official stated his inability to procure. Major Gordon thereupon resigned in disgust, and on succeeding in obtaining one month's pay for his men, he sent them back to Quinsan without a disturbance, although their indignation against Li Hung Chang personally was nearly kindled to a dangerous flame.

The departure of the Ever-Victorious Army for its headquarters was regarded by the Chinese officials with great satisfaction and for several reasons. In the flush of the success at Soochow both that force and its commander seemed in the way of the Futai, and to diminish the extent of his triumph. Neither Li nor Ching also had the least wish for any of the ex-rebel chiefs, men of ability and accustomed to command, to be taken into the service of the Government. Of men of that kind there were already enough. General Ching himself was a sufficiently formidable rival to the Futai, without any assistance and encouragement from Lar Wang and the others. Li had no wish to save them from the fate of rebels; and although he had promised and General Ching had sworn to their personal safety, he was bent on getting rid of them in one way or another. He feared Major Gordon, but he also thought that the time had arrived when he could dispense with him and the foreign-drilled legion in the same way as he had got rid of Sherard Osborn and his fleet. The departure of the Quinsan force left him free to follow his own inclination.

The Wangs were invited to an entertainment at the Futai's boat, and Major Gordon saw them both in the city and subsequently when on their way to Li Hung Chang. The exact circumstances of their fate were never known; but after searching the city and being detained in one of the Wang's houses during the night, and in the midst of many hundred armed Taepings, who would certainly have slain him had they known of their chiefs' murders, Major Gordon's lieutenant, Prince von Wittgenstein, discovered nine headless bodies on the opposite side of the creek, and not far distant from the Futai's quarters. It then became evident that Lar Wang and his fellow Wangs had been brutally murdered. It is impossible to apportion the blame for this treacherous act between Li Hung Chang and General Ching. The latter was morally the more guilty, but it seems as if Li Hung Chang were the real instigator of the crime.

The additional information recorded as to what took place during and immediately after the Soochow tragedy in the recently published "Life of Gordon" may here be summarized. It is not necessary to repeat the strictly personal passages between General Gordon and Sir Halliday Macartney on the subject of the latter's suggested succession to the command of the Ever-Victorious Army, or of the *amende* offered by the former to the latter for an injurious statement in an official report. The fresh matter, so far as the history of the main incident goes, is to the effect that General Ching assured Gordon that Lar Wang had broken the terms of the Convention at the very moment when he was already murdered, that Macartney went at Gordon's request and found that a tragedy had occurred, that Li Hung Chang took refuge in Macartney's camp and requested him to act as intermediary between himself and Gordon, and that in consequence Macartney hastened to Quinsan and had his dramatic interview with Gordon. The question of the responsibility for the murder or execution of the Wangs is set at rest for all historical purposes by the candid statement of Li Hung Chang, who said, "I accept myself the full and sole responsibility for what has been done. But also tell Gordon that this is China, not Europe. I wished to save the lives of the Wangs, and at first thought that I could do so, but they came with their heads unshaved, they used defiant language, and proposed a deviation from the Convention, and I saw that it would not be safe to show mercy to these rebels. Therefore what was done was inevitable." The original supposition put forward in this history is therefore fully confirmed, and the only justification advanced for the step is that it was taken in China, not in Europe.

Major Gordon was disposed to take the office of their avenger into his own hands, but the opportunity of doing so fortunately did not present itself. He hastened back to Quinsan, where he refused to act any longer with such false and dishonourable colleagues. The matter was reported to Pekin. Both the mandarins sought to clear themselves by accusing the other; and a special decree came from Pekin conferring on the English officer a very high order and the sum of 10,000 taels. Major Gordon returned the money, and expressed his regret at being unable to accept any token of honour from the Emperor in consequence of the Soochow affair. In this decisive way did Gordon express not merely his abhorrence of the deed, but the utter impossibility of an English officer co-operating with a Government and officials capable of perpetrating an act not to be justified on the ground of either morality or expediency.

A variety of reasons, all equally creditable to Major Gordon's judgment and single-mindedness, induced him after two months' retirement to abandon his inaction and to sink his difference with the Futai. He saw very clearly that the sluggishness of the Imperial commanders would result in the prolongation of the struggle with all its attendant evils, whereas, if he took the field, he would be able to bring it to a conclusion within two months. Moreover, the Quinsan force, never very amenable to discipline, shook off all restraint when in quarters, and promised to become as dangerous to the Government in whose pay it was as to the enemy against whom it was engaged to fight. Major Gordon, in view of these facts, came to the prompt decision that it was his duty, as well as the course most calculated to do good, to retake the field and strive as energetically as possible to expel the rebels from the small part of Kiangsu still remaining in their possession. On the 18th of February, 1864, he accordingly left Quinsan at the head of his men, who showed great satisfaction at the return to active campaigning.

Wusieh had been evacuated on the fall of Soochow, and Chung Wang's force retired to Changchow, while that chief himself returned to Nankin. A few weeks later General Ching had seized Pingwang, thus obtaining the command of another entrance into the Taho lake. Santajin established his force in a camp not far distant from Changchow, and engaged the rebels in almost daily skirmishes, during one of which the *Firefly* steamer was recaptured, and an Englishman named Smith mortally wounded. This was the position of affairs when Major Gordon took the field towards the end of February, and he at once resolved to carry the war into a new country by crossing the Taho lake and attacking the town of Yesing on its western shores. By seizing this and the adjoining towns he hoped to cut the rebellion in two, and to be able to attack Changchow in the rear. The operations at Yesing occupied two days; but at last the rebel stockades were carried with tremendous loss, not only to the defenders, but also to a relieving force sent from Liyang. Five thousand prisoners were also taken. Liyang itself was the next place to be attacked; but the intricacy of the country, which was intersected by creeks and canals, added to the fact that the whole region had been desolated by famine and that the rebels had broken all the bridges, rendered this undertaking one of great difficulty and some risk. However, Major Gordon's fortitude vanquished all obstacles, and when he appeared before Liyang he found that the rebel leaders in possession of the town had come to the decision to surrender. At this place Major Gordon came into communication with the general Paochiaou, who was covering the siege operations against Nankin which Tseng Kwofan was pressing with ever-increasing vigour. The surrender of Liyang proved the more important, as the fortifications were found to be admirably constructed, and seeing that it contained a garrison of 15,000 men and a plentiful supply of provisions.

From Liyang Major Gordon marched on Kintang, a town due north of Liyang and about halfway between Changchow

AN OMINOUS SILENCE.

and Nankin. When the troops appeared before it there were few signs of any vigorous defence; but, as Major Gordon surmised, the silence was ominous. The necessity of succeeding had been rendered all the greater by several repulses to the forces of Santajin and by the menacing position taken up by the Changchow garrison, which had made a forward movement against Wusieh on the one side and Fushan on the other. The capture of Kintang, by placing Gordon's force within striking distance of Changchow and its communications, would have compelled the rebels to suspend these operations and recall their forces. Unfortunately the attack on Kintang revealed unexpected difficulties. The garrison showed extraordinary determination; and, although the wall was breached by the heavy fire, two attempts to assault were repulsed with heavy loss, the more serious inasmuch as Major Gordon was himself wounded below the knee and compelled to retire to his boat. Two officers were killed and eleven wounded, while thirty-five men killed and eighty wounded raised the list of casualties to a formidable total. This was the second defeat Gordon had experienced.

In consequence of this reverse, which dashed the cup of success from Gordon's lips when he seemed on the point of bringing the campaign to a close in the most brilliant manner, the force had to retreat to Liyang, whence the commander hastened back with 1000 men to Wusieh. He reached Wusieh on the 25th of March, four days after the repulse at Kintang, and he there learnt that Fushan had been taken and that Chanzu was being closely attacked. The Imperialists had fared better in the south. General Ching had captured Kashingfoo, a strong place in Chekiang, and on the very same day as the repulse at Kintang Tso Tsung Tang had recovered Hangchow. Major Gordon, although still incapacitated by his wound from taking his usual foremost place in the battle, directed all operations from his boat. He succeeded, after numerous skirmishes, in compelling the Taepings to quit their position before Chanzu; but they drew up in force at the village of Waisso, where they offered him battle. Most unfortunately Major Gordon had to entrust the conduct of the attack to his lieutenants, Colonels Howard and Rhodes, while he superintended the advance of the gun-boats up the creek. Finding the banks were too high to admit of these being usefully employed, and failing to establish communications with the infantry, he discreetly returned to his camp, where he found everything in the most dreadful confusion, and that a terrible disaster had occurred. The infantry, in fact, had been outmanœuvred and routed with tremendous loss. Seven officers and 265 men had been killed, and one officer and sixty-two men wounded.

Such an overwhelming disaster would have crushed any ordinary commander, particularly when coming so soon after such a rude defeat as that of Kintang. It only roused Major Gordon to increased activity. He at once took energetic measures to retrieve this disaster. He sent his wounded to Quinsan, collected fresh troops, and, having allowed his own wound to recover by a week's rest, resumed in person the attack on Waisso. On the 10th of April Major Gordon pitched his camp within a mile of Waisso, and paid his men as the preliminary to the resumption of the offensive. The attack commenced on the following morning, and promised to prove of an arduous nature; but by a skilful flank movement Major Gordon carried two stockades in person, and rendered the whole place no longer tenable. The rebels evacuated their position and retreated, closely pursued by the Imperialists. The villagers who had suffered from their exactions rose upon them, and very few rebels escaped. The pursuit was continued for a week, and the lately victorious army of Waisso was practically annihilated. Two days after Waisso, General Ching died at Soochow of the effects of a wound received in the south. Gordon said of him, "He was a very brave and energetic leader, very apt in acquiring information, and the best general the Imperialists had."

The capture of Changchow was to be the next and crowning success of the campaign. For this enterprise the whole of the Ever-Victorious Army was concentrated, including the ex-rebel contingent of Liyang. On the 23rd of April Major Gordon carried the stockades near the west gate. In their capture the Liyang men, although led only by Chinese, showed conspicuous gallantry, thus justifying

THE LAST ACTION.

Major Gordon's belief that the Chinese would fight as well under their own countrymen as when led by foreigners. Batteries were then constructed for the bombardment of the town itself. Before these were completed the Imperialists assaulted, but were repulsed with loss. On the following day (April 27th) the batteries opened fire, and two pontoon bridges were thrown across, when Major Gordon led his men to the assault. The first attack was repulsed, and a second one, made in conjunction with the Imperialists, fared not less badly. The pontoons were lost, and the force suffered a greater loss than at any time during the war, with the exception of Waisso. The Taepings also lost heavily; but their valour could not alter the inevitable result. Changchow had consequently to be approached systematically by trenches, in the construction of which the Chinese showed themselves very adept. The loss of the pontoons compelled the formation of a cask-bridge; and during the extensive preparations for renewing the attack, several hundred of the garrison came over, reporting that it was only the Cantonese who wished to fight to the bitter end. On the 11th of May, the fourth anniversary of its capture by Chung Wang, Li requested Major Gordon to act in concert with him for carrying the place by storm. The attack was made in the middle of the day, to the intense surprise of the garrison, who made only a feeble resistance, and the town was at last carried with little loss. The commandant, Hoo Wang, was made prisoner and executed. This proved to be the last action of the Ever-Victorious Army, which then returned to Quinsan, and was quietly disbanded by its commander before the 1st of June.

To sum up the closing incidents of the Taeping war. Tayan was evacuated two days after the fall of Changchow, leaving Nankin alone in their hands. Inside that city there were the greatest misery and suffering. Tien Wang had refused to take any of the steps pressed on him by Chung Wang, and when he heard the people were suffering from want, all he said was, "Let them eat the sweet dew." Tseng Kwofan drew up his lines on all sides of the city, and gradually drove the despairing rebels behind the walls.

Chung Wang sent out the old women and children; and let it be recorded to the credit of Tseng Kwotsiuen that he did not drive them back, but charitably provided for their wants and despatched them to a place of shelter. In June Major Gordon visited Tseng's camp, and found his works covering twenty-four to thirty miles, and constructed in the most elaborate fashion. The Imperialists numbered 80,000 men, but were badly armed. Although their pay was very much in arrear, they were well fed, and had great confidence in their leader, Tseng Kwofan. On the 30th of June, Tien Wang, despairing of success, committed suicide by swallowing golden leaf. Thus died the Hungtsiuen who had erected the standard of revolt in Kwangsi thirteen years before. His son was proclaimed Tien Wang on his death becoming known, but his reign was brief.

The last act of all had now arrived. On the 19th of July the Imperialists had run a gallery under the wall of Nankin, and charged it with 40,000 pounds of powder. The explosion destroyed fifty yards of the walls, and the Imperialists attacking on all sides poured in through the breach. Chung Wang made a desperate resistance in the interior, holding his own and the Tien Wang's palace to the last. He made a further stand with a thousand men at the southern gate, but his band was overwhelmed, and he and the young Tien Wang fled into the surrounding country. In this supreme moment of danger Chung Wang thought more of the safety of his young chief than of himself, and he gave him an exceptionally good pony to escape on, while he himself took a very inferior animal. As the consequence Tien Wang escaped, while Chung Wang was captured in the hills a few days later. Chung Wang, who had certainly been the hero of the Taeping movement, was beheaded on the 7th of August, and the young Tien Wang was eventually captured, and executed also, by Shen Paochen. For this decisive victory, which extinguished the Taeping rebellion, Tseng Kwofan was made a Hou, or Marquis, and his brother Tseng Kwotsiuen an Earl. General Gordon thus described Tseng Kwofan, the elder of these brothers: "Tseng is the most powerful man in China out of Pekin. He is fifty-four years of age, short, rather fat, with a very Chinese face, and with black beard and moustache. He dressed in the poorest clothes, and keeps no state. He is generous, fair, and honest, and may be said to be patriotic. He is greatly liked by all Chinese."

The suppression of the Taeping rebellion was a relief to the Empire, and a mercy to the wretched and long-suffering people of Central China. It ensured the permanent fame of Major Gordon and the Ever-Victorious Army. The more critically this campaign is considered, the more remarkable does Chinese Gordon's success appear. Had he been an unscrupulous adventurer bent on personal aggrandisement, whether in the cause of the Pekin ruler or of the Nankin rebel, his achievements would have been the less surprising, as he would have had the members of his force heartily with him, and as he could have easily recruited it from the rowdy European population of Shanghai. But his victories were obtained in the cause of order and for the sake of a suffering people. Each of them was a blow levelled at the realization of the scheme that had passed through the brains of Burgevine and the other idlers of the treaty-ports. He fought not for himself, nor for any love of empty fame or reputation. He only saw that the opportunity was afforded him of doing a great and sterling service to humanity and to his own Government. He also realized the innate self-respect and many other virtues of the Chinese people. He perceived that their improvement must and would come from within, and not from without. His courage, his energy, his uprightness, all impressed the Chinese with a sense of the grandeur of his character, as they had never been impressed before by any other European, and as probably they never will be again. Even after his defeats at Waisso and Chang-chow their faith in him never wavered for an instant. Those defeats were accidents, which they never doubted would be promptly retrieved. Li Hung Chang had at first regarded him with suspicion. He saw in him a possible rival, a more capable executor of the policy which Burgevine had contemplated. Time was needed to reveal to him the consistent simplicity of a character which even to his own countrymen was almost unintelligible. With much of the temper and energy of Cromwell, Gordon has given the brightest example, in the annals of either his own country or of China, of what, to use the words of one of his lieutenants, the Christian soldier ought to be.*

* The following is the Imperial decree issued on his receiving the Yellow Jacket—an order, said Li Hung Chang, instituted by Kanghi for victorious generals on the occasion of the suppression of Wou Sankwei's revolt :—" On the representation of the assistance rendered by Gordon, Temporary Tsungping of Kiangsu, in the recapture of Changchow, we decreed him the rank of Titu (Field Marshal), Standards of Honour, and a Decoration as especial marks of distinction, and directed that Li should memorialize again when he had arranged the affairs of the Force. We have now received a memorial from Li that he has done this in a most admirable manner and requesting some further mark of our favour. It appears that last spring Gordon, conjointly with Imperial Forces, recaptured Fushan and relieved Chanzu, that he subsequently recaptured the Chow city of Taitsung, the district cities of Quinsan and Wukiang, and the provincial city of Soochow; that this year he has recaptured Thsing and Piaoyang, driven back the rebels who had broken out from Yanchow, and recaptured the Fu city of Changchow, for which services we have at various times decreed him honours. He has now arranged the affairs of the Ever-Victorious Force in an admirable manner. His services are of long standing, and the benefits arising from them are abiding; he has throughout behaved as a gallant soldier, and shown himself to have duly appreciated the importance of friendly relations between Chinese and foreigners, and we therefore decree that in addition to his present honours he be honoured with the Yellow Jacket and peacock's feathers, and that four Titu's full-dress uniforms be presented him as a mark of the affection and honour with which he is regarded. Respect this." In a letter written home at the time the recipient of these honours said characteristically : "Some of the buttons on the mandarin hats are very valuable. I am sorry for it, as they cannot afford it over well. It is, at any rate, very civil of them." During the campaign Gordon carried only a cane, called by the Chinese his "wand of victory."

CHAPTER XVI.

THE DEATH OF HIENFUNG AND THE ACCESSION OF TUNGCHE.

THE Emperor Hienfung did not long survive the establishment of formal intercourse with the foreign Governments. While his brother, Prince Kung, was engaged in the delicate task of arranging the affairs of the Tsungli Yamen, and the still more difficult operation of showing that China had abandoned all intention of lagging behind the rest of the world, the Emperor himself continued to remain at Jehol, whither he had fled in the first moment of alarm on the approach of the foreign armies to Yuen Min Yuen. He refused to so much as return to Pekin, and to witness the presence of those Europeans who detracted, as he considered, from his dignity. Had it been possible, there is no question that he would have sought a remedy for the evil by commanding the removal of the capital; but the transfer of the Imperial residence to any city in the south was not only at that particular moment impossible on account of the rebellion, but always to be deprecated on dynastic grounds as tending to destroy the individual character of the Tartar regime. For a moment there seemed an inclination to entertain the idea that Jehol itself might be transformed into a capital, but this hope, if it was ever seriously cherished, had to be abandoned as chimerical. Hienfung's absence affected the prosperity of the Pekinese; it could not deprive their city of its natural position as the northern metropolis.

The following facts should be recollected in connection with the first diplomatic relations of China with foreign

Powers. The Tsungli Yamen, or board of foreign affairs, was formed in January, 1861. On the 22nd of March in the same year Mr. Bruce left Tientsin to take up his residence at Pekin with Mr. Thomas Wade as Secretary of Legation. The quarters of the English ministry had been fixed at the palace of the Duke of Leang, a scion of the Imperial family (Leang-kung-foo). This building is let "in perpetuity" to the English authorities for 1500 taels a year. Soon after their instalment a staff of six student interpreters was brought out from England.

Hienfung showed his personal dislike to the new arrangement in more ways than by absenting himself from the capital. He collected round his person the most bigoted men of his court and family. He preferred those who had learnt nothing from recent events, and who, without even the courage of resistance, wished to claim undiminished privilege and superiority. Prominent among his closest friends was Tsai, Prince of I, who had taken so discreditable a part in the incidents that had culminated at Tungchow and Chanchiawan. With him were associated several members of the Imperial family, men of passion and prejudice. They undoubtedly meditated the recovery, at the earliest possible moment, of what they considered to be their right. No respect of treaties would restrain them from reasserting, as soon as they believed they had the power, claims which the Emperor had by treaty surrendered. The hopeful anticipation of the arrival of that time formed the one source of solace at Jehol, and the still youthful ruler easily allowed himself to forget, in the midst of his sycophants, the brother who was making such laudable efforts to maintain the dignity of the Empire in the eyes of the foreigners, and at the same time to restore domestic peace to his distracted country. The protracted residence of the Emperor at Jehol was a circumstance that could not have been permanently tolerated. It was deprecated as much by the numerous members of the Imperial family as by the citizens of Pekin. These enjoyed a regular allowance from the Palace. The continued absence of the Emperor interfered with its receipt, and reduced them to great want. It meant practically an abnegation of authority.

A COMET.

The conduct of official intercourse went on in the most amicable manner between Mr. Bruce and the other foreign representatives on the one hand, and Prince Kung, assisted by his able coadjutor the Manchu Wansiang, on the other. The utmost that Hienfung himself would do was to listen to all the information he could procure about the English and their country, but the study was so far calculated to increase his fear and distrust, for he rose from it with the one conviction impressed on his mind that "the English were always at war, or preparing to go to war with some one." While the relations at the capital were becoming more and more cordial, the Chinese ruler himself was disposed to brood over his injuries and to allow his suspicions to become intensified. In this he was encouraged by men like Prince Tsai, who could only hope for prominence by alienating the Emperor from the cause of progress as represented by Prince Kung. Their success was by no means inconsiderable, but the ill-health of Hienfung interfered with and ultimately thwarted their plans.

The English Minister had not been installed in his residence more than a fortnight when there came rumours of the serious illness of the Emperor. It was given out in a curious document that his doctors had declared his case to be hopeless, and that, even if he promptly abandoned some pernicious habits which he had contracted, he could not hope to live beyond a period of six months. All the available evidence went to show that, having moreover such little inducement to do so, he did not change his mode of life, but the greatest reticence was observed with regard to all his movements and his state of health. The summer months passed away without any decisive intelligence as to what was happening at Jehol, although rumours as to the gravity of Hienfung's complaint became so plentiful that a statement was even circulated and believed that his death had actually taken place. A comet appeared in the sky and was visible for several weeks, strengthening the belief of the superstitious in a coming change, and inclining men to believe more readily the statement that the great Emperor was about to go the long journey.

"When beggars die there are no comets seen,
　The heavens themselves blaze forth the death of princes."

In August Prince Kung hastened to Jehol, the object of his journey, and indeed the journey itself, being kept the closest secret. The members of the Tsungli Yamen were observed to be preoccupied, and even the genial Wansiang could not conceal that they were passing through a crisis. Not merely was Hienfung dying, but it had become known that he had left the governing authority during the minority of his son, a child of less than six years of age, to a Board of Regency composed of eight of the least intelligent and most arrogant and self-seeking members of the Imperial family, with Prince Tsai at their head. The Emperor died on the 22nd of August. A few hours later the Imperial Decree notifying the last wishes of the ruler as to the mode of government was promulgated. The Board of Regency assumed the nominal control of affairs, and Hienfung's son was proclaimed Emperor under the style of Chiseang ("the auspicious omen"). In all of these arrangements neither Prince Kung nor his brothers, nor the responsible ministers at the capital, had had the smallest part. It was an intrigue among certain members of the Imperial clan to possess themselves of the ruling power, and for a time it seemed as if their intrigue would be only too successful.

Nothing happened during the months of September and October to disturb their confidence, and at Pekin the routine of government continued to be performed by Prince Kung. That statesman and his colleagues employed the interval in arranging their own plan of action, and in making sure of the fidelity of a certain number of troops. Throughout these preparations Prince Kung was ably and energetically supported by his brother, Prince Chun, by his colleague, Wansiang, and by his aged father-in-law, the minister Kweiliang. When at the end of October it became known that the young Emperor was on the point of returning to Pekin, it was clear that the hour of conflict had arrived. At Jehol the Board of Regency could do little harm; but once its pretensions and legality were admitted at the capital, all the ministers would have to take their orders from it, and to resign the functions which they had retained. The issue clearly put was whether Prince Kung or Prince Tsai was to be supreme.

On the 1st of November the young Emperor entered his capital in state. He was driven through the streets in a carriage, with Tsi Thsi, the Empress Dowager, or the principal widow of Hienfung, and the Empress Tsi An, another of Hienfung's widows, occupying seats in the same carriage; but no European actually saw the cortège, because Prince Kung had asked Mr. Bruce and the other ministers as a favour to keep their suites at home until the procession reached the palace. A large number of soldiers, still dressed in their white mourning, accompanied their Sovereign from Jehol; but Shengpao's garrison was infinitely more numerous and thoroughly loyal to the cause of Prince Kung and order. The majority of the Regents had arrived with the reigning prince; those who had not yet come were on the road escorting the dead body of Hienfung towards its resting-place. If a blow was to be struck at all, it was necessary to do it quickly. The Regents had not merely placed themselves in the power of their opponents, but they had actually brought with them the young Emperor, without whose person Prince Kung could have accomplished little.

Prince Kung had spared no effort to secure, and had fortunately succeeded in obtaining, the assistance and co-operation of the Empress Dowager, Hienfung's principal widow. Her assent and that of her abler associate, the still living Empress Tsi An, had been obtained to the proposed plot before their arrival in Pekin, and it now only remained to carry it out. On the day following the entry into the capital Prince Kung hastened to the Palace, and, producing before the astonished Regents an Imperial Edict ordering their dismissal, he asked them whether they obeyed the decree of their Sovereign, or whether he must call in his soldiers to compel them. Prince Tsai and his companions had no choice save to signify their acquiescence; but on leaving the chamber in which this scene took place they hastened towards the Emperor's apartment in order to remonstrate against their dismissal, or to obtain from him some counter-edict reinstating them in their position. They were prevented from carrying out their purpose, but this proof of contumacy ensured their fate. They were at once arrested, and a second decree was issued ordering their degradation from their official and hereditary rank. To Prince Kung and his allies was entrusted the charge of trying and punishing the offenders.

The edict in which the assumption of governing power by the Empress was announced is so important and characteristic that it merits prominent reproduction :—

" The Princes, Nobles, and Officers of the Empire are hereby to learn that the disquiet of the sea-coast last year and the alarm of the capital were caused wholly by the vicious policy of the Princes and Ministers engaged in the matter. Tsai-yuen and his colleagues [Mu-yin] were in the next place (or more especially) unable to devote their attention to pacific counsels ; and, being without other device for the extinction of their responsibility, could propose nothing but that the English Envoys should be decoyed into their power and made prisoners, hence a breach of faith towards the foreign nations. Yet more, when Yuen-min-yuen and Hai-tien were spoiled and His late Majesty, our Emperor, in consequence, had taken a journey to Je-hol, the mind of the Sacred One was sore troubled that he was reduced to such extremity ; and when in due time the Prince and Ministers of the office, charged with the general administration of foreign affairs, had well arranged all foreign questions that required settlement, and its usual tranquillity was restored to the capital, within and without the walls, His Majesty again and again called on the Princes and Ministers [Tsai-yuen and his colleagues] to frame a decree announcing His return. Tsai-yuen, Twan-hwa, and Su-shuen, however, the one abetting the other in deceit, with all their strength kept from Him these facts, to which the opinion of all men bore testimony, ever alleging that foreign nations, both in sentiment and demeanour, were always shifting (*lit.* turning over and over). His late Majesty anxious and worn, [rested] neither by day nor by night. The cold, too, beyond the frontier was severe, and so the indisposition of the Sacred Person increased, until upon the 17th day of the 7th moon (22nd August), He ascended upon the Dragon to be a guest on high. Clasping the ground We cried to heaven ; within, We felt as though a fire were burning. Looking back We bethought us that the iniquity of Tsai-yuen and the others in their concealment of the truth, deserved not the bitter wrath of Ourself alone, but the bitter wrath of all the officers and people of the Empire ; and it was Our wish when first We ascended the throne to punish their guilt with severity. Still, remembering that they were Ministers appointed by His late Majesty in His last moments, We forebore awhile in expectation of their redeeming the past. Not so, however. On the 11th of the 8th moon (15th September), We called Tsai-yuen and the other members [of the Council] of eight to Our presence. The Censor Tung-yuan-chun, in a memorial respectfully setting forth his limited views, had prayed that the Empress Dowager should act as Regent for some years, and that when We should ourselves become competent to its administration, the government should be surrendered (or given back) to Us; also, that one or two of the Princes of the highest order should be chosen, and appointed to act as counsellors; also, that one or two of the high Officers of the Empire should be chosen and appointed to be Our preceptors—which three propositions were greatly to Our liking. There is no precedent, it is true, in the time of Our Dynasty, for the regency of an Empress Dowager; but could We have adhered tenaciously to standing rules, when, of the trusts committed to Us by His Majesty the departed Emperor, the most important was this, that We should think of nothing but the policy of the State, and welfare (or existence) of the people. This (the course suggested) is what is meant by the words, 'in business the first thing is the adoption of such changes as the occasion may require.' We accordingly gave Our special commands, in person, to Tsai-yuen and his colleagues to issue a Decree approving [the Censor's] prayer. When they came to make their reply, however, they so totally forgot their obligations as Our servants, as clamorously to raise objections [this in the first place]. In the second, when drawing up the Decree to be issued for Us, while professing in the light to obey, they in secret disobeyed Us, taking on themselves to make alterations [in the paper] which they then published as the declaration of Our will. What in very truth was their motive? when on every occasion, too, Tsai-yuen and his colleagues have been pretending that [this or that was impracticable, because] they dared not assume the supreme (or independent) authority; what was this act but an unmistakable (a true footprint of) assumption of the supreme authority?

"Though Our own youth and the imperfect acquaintance of the Empress Dowager with the business of the State might have put it in their power to practise imposition and concealment, so far as we were concerned, they could not, could they, impose upon the whole Empire as well? and were We now longer to forbear towards those who have proved so ungrateful for the great favour of His late Majesty, what answer, as with reverence we look upward, should We make to His spirit, now in heaven, or how should We satisfy the general feeling of the Empire?

"We command, then, that Tsai-yuen, Twan-hwa, and Su-shuen

be removed from their posts, and that King-shau, Mu-yin, Kwang-Yuen, Tu-Han, and Tsian-Yu-ying withdraw from the great Council; and We commission the Prince of Kung, in concert with the members of the Grand Secretariat, the Six Boards, the Nine High Courts, the Han-lin-Yuen, the Shen-sz'-Fu and the Censors, to consider impartially and to report to Us, the degree of punishment to which they are severally liable by law for their crimes.

"With reference to the forms under which Her Majesty the Empress Dowager is to administer the Government, We Command that [the same high Officers] do confer together and report to Us.

"A Decree extraordinary."

The bravest if not the ablest of the late Board of Regency, Sushuen, remained at large. He had been charged with the high and honourable duty of escorting the remains of Hienfung to the capital. It was most important that he should be seized before he became aware of the fate that had befallen his colleagues. Prince Chun, the father of the now reigning Emperor Kwangsu, volunteered to capture the last, and in a sense the most formidable, of the intriguers himself, and on the very day that these events happened at Pekin he rode out of the capital at the head of a body of Tartar cavalry. On the following night Prince Chun reached the spot where Sushuen was encamped, and, breaking into the house, arrested him whilst in bed. Sushuen did not restrain his indignation, and betrayed the ulterior plans he and his associates had entertained, by declaring that Prince Chun had been only just in time to prevent a similar fate befalling himself. He was at once placed on his trial with the other prisoners, and on the 10th of November the order was given in the Emperor's name for their execution. Sushuen was executed on the public ground set apart for that purpose; but to the others, as a special favour for their connection with the Imperial family, was sent the silken cord with which they were to put an end to their existence.

Another important step which had to be taken was the alteration of the style given to the young Emperor's reign. It was felt to be impolitic that the deposed ministers should retain any connection whatever in history with the young ruler. Were Hienfung's son to be handed down to posterity as Chiseang there would be no possibility of excluding their names and their brief and feverish ambition from the national annals. After due deliberation, therefore, the name of Tungche was substituted for that of Chiseang, and, meaning as it does "the union of law and order," it will be allowed that the name was not selected without proper regard for the circumstances of the occasion. Prince Kung was rewarded with many high offices and sounding titles in addition to the post of Chief Minister under the Two Empresses. He was made president of the Imperial Clan Court in the room of Tsai, Prince of I, and the title of Iching Wang, or Prince Minister, was conferred upon him. His staunch friends and supporters Wansiang, Paukwen, and Kweiliang were appointed to the Supreme Council. Prince Chun, to whose skill and bravery in arresting Sushuen Prince Kung felt very much indebted, was also rewarded. With these incidents closed what might have proved a grave and perilous complication for the Chinese Government. Had Prince Kung prematurely revealed his plans there is every reason to suppose that he would have alarmed and forewarned his rivals, and that they, with the person of the Emperor in their possession, would have obtained the advantage, if their own incapacity might have prevented their long retaining it. His patience during the two months of doubt and anxiety while the Emperor remained at Jehol was matched by the vigour and promptitude that he displayed on the eventful 2nd of November. That his success was beneficial to his country will not be disputed by any one, and Prince Kung's name must be permanently remembered both for having commenced, and for having ensured the continuance of, diplomatic relations with England and the other foreign Powers.

The increased intercourse with Europeans not merely led to greater diplomatic confidence and to the extension of trade, but it also induced many foreigners to offer their services and assistance to the Pekin Government during the embarrassment arising from internal dissension. At first these persons were, as has been seen, encouraged and employed more in consequence of local opinion in the treaty-ports than as a matter of State policy. But already the suggestion had been brought forward in more than one form for the employment of foreigners, with the view of increasing the resources of the Government by calling in the assistance of the very agency which had reduced them. A precedent had been established for this at an earlier period—before, in fact, the commencement of hostilities—by the appointment of Mr. Horatio N. Lay to direct and assist the local authorities in the collection of customs in the Shanghai district. Mr. Lay's experience had proved most useful in drawing up the tariff of the Treaty of Tientsin, and his assistance had been suitably acknowledged. In 1862, when the advantages to be derived from the military experience of foreigners had been practically recognized by the appointment of Europeans to command a portion of the army of China, it was thought desirable for many reasons that something should also be done to increase the naval resources of the Empire, and Mr. Lay, at Sir Robert Hart's suggestion, was entrusted with a commission for purchasing and collecting in Europe a fleet of gun-boats of small draught, which could be usefully employed for all the purposes of the Pekin Government on the rivers and shallow estuaries of the country. Mr. Lay said, "This force was intended for the protection of the treaty-ports, for the suppression of piracy then rife, and for the relief of this country from the burden of 'policing' the Chinese waters;" but its first use in the eyes of Prince Kung was to be employed against the rebels and their European allies.

Captain Sherard Osborn, a distinguished naval officer, was associated with Mr. Lay in the undertaking. An Order of Council was issued on the 30th of August, 1862, empowering both of these officers to act in the matter as delegates of the Chinese. Captain Osborn and Mr. Lay came to England to collect the vessels of this fleet, and the former afterwards returned with them to China in the capacity of their Commodore.

Difficulties arose on the threshold of the undertaking. Mr. Lay wrote in August, 1862, to say that he had chosen as the national ensign of the Chinese navy "a green flag, bearing a yellow diagonal cross," and he wrote again to request that an official notification should appear in the *Gazette*. Mr. Lay was informed that no notice could appear in the *London Gazette* except after the approval of the Pekin authorities; and Prince Kung wrote on the 22nd of October to say that the Chinese ensign would be of "yellow ground, and on it will be designed a dragon with his head toward the upper part of the flag." Mr. Lay preceded the vessels —seven gun-boats and one store-ship—and arrived at Pekin in May, 1863. At the capital he found two opinions prevailing, which did not promise to contribute to the harmony of the new arrangement. In the first place he found Sir Frederick Bruce resolved not to take any active part in the affair at all, without instructions to do so from his Government.

But if the attitude of Sir Frederick Bruce was embarrassing, that of the Chinese themselves was far more discouraging. Their fears had been already aroused as to the possibly independent attitude these foreign commanders might assume when affairs had settled down. The views of Prince Kung and Mr. Lay were distinctly opposed on the point of the position of the new ships as part of the external defences of China. The former considered that the fleet purchased in Europe out of Chinese treasure should form an integral portion of the warlike resources of the Empire, and be as subservient to the orders of the local authorities as if it were one of the old fleets of war-junks. Mr. Lay could not bring himself to take the same view. The fleet was to be virtually independent. Captain Sherard Osborn would, by his personal arrangement with Mr. Lay, act only upon "orders of the Emperor which may be conveyed direct to Lay," and, moreover, he refused to act on any orders conveyed through any different channel. To the unprejudiced observer it would seem that the proper persons to decide by whom the orders should be given were the Chinese themselves, and not their foreign officers and servants. When it is realized how much the originators of this scheme took the whole arrangement out of the hands of Prince Kung and his colleagues, there will not be much surprise at the scheme coming to the abortive and unfortunate end that it did.

Prince Kung had been most anxious for the speedy

arrival of the flotilla; and the doubtful fortune of the campaign in Kiangsu, where the gun-boats would have been invaluable, rendered him extremely desirous that they should commence active operations immediately on arrival. But he found, in the first place, that Mr. Lay was not prepared to accept the appointment of a Chinese official as joint-commander, and in the second place that he would not receive orders from any of the provincial authorities. Such a decision was manifestly attended with the greatest inconvenience to China; for only the provincial authorities knew what the interests of the state demanded, and where the fleet might co-operate with advantage in the attacks on the Taepings. Unless Captain Sherard Osborn were to act on the orders of Tseng Kwofan, and particularly of Li Hung Chang, it was difficult to see what possible use he or his flotilla could be to China. The founders of the new Chinese navy claimed practically all the privileges of an ally, and declined the duties devolving on them as directing a department of the Chinese administration. Of course it was more convenient and more dignified for the foreign officers to draw their instructions and their salaries direct from the fountain head; but if the flotilla was not to be of any practical use to China, it might just as well never have been created.

The fleet arrived in safety, but remained in inaction. The whole summer and autumn of 1863, with its critical state of affairs round Soochow, passed away without anything being done to show what a powerful auxiliary the new ships might be. The ultimate success of those operations without the smallest co-operation on the part of Captain Osborn or his flotilla virtually sealed its fate. In October, Wansiang, in the name of the Foreign Office, declared that the Chinese could not recognize or ratify the private arrangement between Mr. Lay and his naval officer, and that it was essential for Captain Osborn to submit to receive his instructions from the provincial authorities. In the following month Mr. Lay was summarily dismissed from the Chinese service, and it was determined, after some delay and various counter suggestions, to send back the ships to Europe, there to be disposed of. The miscarriage of the whole affair was, as Sir

Frederick Bruce said, probably due to Mr. Lay's taking upon himself the responsibility not merely of Inspector-General of Customs, but also of supreme adviser on all matters connected with foreign questions. His views were of the largest scope and most benevolent character so far as the progress of China was concerned. But then it was all to be attained under his own direction. The Chinese themselves were to take quite a subordinate position in their realization, and were to be treated, in short, as if they did not know how to manage their own affairs. Mr. Lay's dreams were suddenly dispelled, and his philanthropic schemes fell to the ground. Neither Prince Kung nor his colleagues had any intention to pave the way for their own effacement.

After Mr. Lay's departure the Maritime Customs were placed under the control of Mr. (now Sir) Robert Hart, who had acted during Mr. Lay's absence in Europe. This appointment was accompanied by the transfer of the official residence from Pekin to Shanghai, which was attended with much practical advantage. Already the customs revenue had risen to two millions, and trade was steadily expanding as the rebels were gradually driven back, and as the Yangtsekiang and the coasts became safer for navigation. Numerous schemes were suggested for the opening-up of China by railways and the telegraph; but they all very soon ended in nothing, for the simple reason that the Chinese did not want them. They were more sincere and energetic in their adoption of military improvements. English officers drilled Chinese troops in their permanent camp at Fungwang, and Sir Halliday Macartney constructed and organized a great arsenal at Soochow, which was afterwards removed to Nankin, as a town more conveniently situated. In 1866 the arsenal at the latter place was in full working order. Arrangements were also made to supply from America the places of the gun-boats which had returned to Europe, but the dilatoriness of the Chinese postponed the commencement of a fleet for ten years.

The anxieties of Prince Kung on the subject of the dynasty, and with regard to the undue pretensions and expectations of the foreign officials who looked on the

Chinese merely as the instruments of their self-aggrandisement, were further increased during this period by the depredations of the Nienfei rebels in the province of Shantung. During these operations Sankolinsin died, leaving Tseng Kwofan in undisputed possession of the first place among Chinese officials. Sankolinsin, when retreating after a reverse, was treacherously murdered by some villagers whose hospitality he had claimed. The career of the great Mongol prince, who had unsuccessfully opposed the allied forces during the Pekin campaign, terminated ignominiously; but his constant activity, when he was to a certain extent in disgrace, showed that he was unremitting in his fidelity to the Tartar ruler. The Nienfei rebellion continued to alarm and agitate the provinces on the northern bank of the Yellow river, and the task of suppressing them was rendered more difficult by the mutinous state of the soldiery. However, the Nienfei never became formidable in the sense of being a national danger; and although they continued for several years longer to be a source of trouble and disturbance, they owed their own safety as much to the celerity of their movements as to their military power.

The events of this introductory period may be appropriately concluded with the strange stroke of misfortune that befell Prince Kung in the spring of 1865, and seemed to show that he had indulged some views of personal ambition. The affair had probably a secret history, but if so, the truth is hardly likely to be ever known. The known facts were as follows: On the 2nd of April, 1865, there appeared an edict degrading the Prince in the name of the two Regent-Empresses, for Tsi An, the abler woman, had been associated with Tsi Thsi, the Empress of higher grade. The charge made against him was of having grown arrogant, and of assuming privileges to which he had no right. He was at first "diligent and circumspect," but he has now become disposed "to overrate his own importance." In consequence, he was deprived of all his appointments and dismissed from the scene of public affairs.

There was not much likelihood that a man, who had taken so decisive a share in arranging the accession of the ruling prince, and in the appointment of the Regents during his minority, would tamely acquiesce in being set on one side by the decree of two women. All his friends on the Imperial Council petitioned the Throne, representing in the plainest terms the great inconvenience that would be entailed by the withdrawal of Prince Kung from the control of public affairs. It was significantly observed in one of these memorials that "if the Imperial household be the first to begin misunderstandings" there was no telling where the excitement would not extend. These representations could scarcely fail to produce their due effect. Five weeks after his fall Prince Kung was reinstated on the 8th of May in all his offices, with the exception of that of President of the Council. This episode, which might have produced grave complications, closed with a return to almost the precise state of things previously existing. There was one important difference. The two Empresses had asserted their predominance. Prince Kung had hoped to be supreme, and to rule uncontrolled. From this time forth he was content to be their minister and adviser on terms similar to those that would have applied to any other official.

The year 1865, which witnessed this very interesting event in the history of the Chinese Government, beheld before its close the departure of Sir Frederick Bruce from Pekin, and the appointment of Sir Rutherford Alcock to fill the post of Resident Minister at Pekin. Sir Frederick Bruce left an example to his successors of how the dignity of the British Crown, in dealing with another great, if somewhat anomalous, Government was to be sustained. Sir Rutherford Alcock, who had represented his country in Japan during the trying years after the bombardment of Shimonoseki, then found the opportunity to put in practice some of the honourable sentiments to which he had given expression twenty years before at Shanghai. When Sir Rutherford left Yeddo for Pekin, the post of Minister in Japan was conferred on Sir Harry Parkes, who had been acting as Consul at Shanghai since the conclusion of the war. The relations between the countries were gradually settling down on a satisfactory basis, and the appointment of a Supreme Court for China and Japan at

Shanghai, with Sir Edmund Hornby as Chief Judge, promised to enforce obedience to the law among even the unsettled adventurers of different nationalities left by the conclusion of the Taeping rebellion and the cessation of piracy without a profitable pursuit. The Chinese were thus able to turn their attention from questions of foreign intercourse to the suppression with increasing vigour of the other insurrections which had been agitating the Empire.

CHAPTER XVII.

THE TWO MAHOMEDAN REBELLIONS.

WE have already described or noticed a sufficient number of human calamities, arising from disastrous foreign wars and a sanguinary civil rebellion, to have taxed the strength and imperilled the existence of the most powerful of Empires. But while the events which have been set forth and recorded were happening in the heart of China, along her coasts and at the capital, other misfortunes yet had befallen the executive, in the more remote quarters of the realm it is true, but still none the less resulting in the loss and ruin of provinces, and in the subversion of the Emperor's authority. Two great uprisings of the people occurred in opposite directions, both commencing while the Taeping rebellion was in full force, and continuing to disturb the country for many years after its suppression. The one had for its scene the great south-western province of Yunnan; the other the two provinces of the north-west, Shensi and Kansuh. They resembled each other in one point, and that was that they were instigated and sustained by the Mahomedan population alone. The Panthays and the Tungani were, as it may please the fancy, either indigenous tribes or foreign immigrants, who had adopted or imported the tenets of Islam. Their sympathies with the Pekin Government may never have been great, but they were impelled in both cases to revolt more by local tyranny than by any distinct desire to cast off the authority of the Chinese; but, of course, the obvious embarrassment of the central executive encouraged, by simplifying, the task of rebellion. The Panthay rising calls for description in the first place, because it began at an earlier period than the other, and also because the details have been preserved with greater fidelity.

Mahomedanism is believed to have been introduced into Yunnan in or about the year 1275, and it made most progress among the so-called aboriginal tribes, the Lolos and the Mantzu. The officials were mostly Chinese or Tartars, and, left practically free from control, they more often abused their power than sought to employ it for the benefit of the people they governed. In the very first year of Hienfung's reign (1851) a petition reached the capital from a Mahomedan land proprietor in Yunnan named Ma Wenchu, accusing the Emperor's officials of the gravest crimes, and praying that "a just and honest man" might be sent to redress the wrongs of an injured and long-suffering people. The petition was carefully read and favourably considered at the capital; but although a gracious answer was accorded, the Emperor was at the time powerless to apply a remedy.

Four years passed away without any open manifestation being given of the deep discontent smouldering below the surface. But in 1855 the Chinese and the Mahomedan labourers quarrelled in one of the principal mines of the province, which is covered with ancient mines of gold, iron, and copper. It seems that the greater success of the Mahomedans in the uncertain pursuit of mining had roused the displeasure of their Chinese colleagues. Disputes ensued, in which the Mussulmans added success in combat to success in mining; and the official appointed to superintend the mines, instead of remaining with a view to the restoration of order, sought his personal safety by precipitate flight to the town of Yunnan. During his absence the Chinese population raised a levy *en masse*, attacked the Mahomedans who had gained a momentary triumph, and compelled them by sheer weight of numbers to beat a hasty retreat to their own homes in a different part of the province. This success was the signal for a general outcry against the Mahomedans, who had long been the objects of the secret ill-will of the other inhabitants. Massacres

A PROJECTED MASSACRE.

took place in several parts of Yunnan, and the followers of the Prophet had to flee for their lives.

Among those who were slain during these popular disorders was a young chief named Ma Sucheng; and when the news of his murder reached his native village his younger brother, Ma Sien, who had just received a small military command, declared his intention to avenge him, and fled to join the Mahomedan fugitives in the mountains. In this secure retreat they rallied their forces, and, driven to desperation by the promptings of want, they left their fastnesses with the view of regaining what they had lost. In this they succeeded better than they could have hoped for. The Chinese population experienced in their turn the bitterness of defeat; and the mandarins had the less difficulty in concluding a temporary understanding between the exhausted combatants. Tranquillity was restored, and the miners resumed their occupations. But the peace was deceptive, and in a little time the struggle was renewed with increased fury.

In this emergency the idea occurred to the minds of some of the officials that an easy and efficacious remedy of the difficulty in which they found themselves placed would be by the massacre of the whole Mussulman population. In this plot the foremost part was taken by Hwang Chung, an official who bitterly hated the Mahomedans. He succeeded in obtaining the acquiescence of all his colleagues with the exception of the Viceroy of the province, who exposed the iniquity of the design, but who, destitute of all support, was powerless to prevent its execution. At the least he resolved to save his honour and reputation by committing suicide. His death simplified the execution of the project which his refusal might possibly have prevented. The 19th of May, 1856, was the date fixed for the celebration of this Chinese St. Bartholomew.

But the secret had not been well kept. The Mahomedans, whether warned or suspicious, distrusted the authorities and their neighbours, and stood vigilantly on their guard. At this time they looked chiefly to a high priest named Ma Tesing for guidance and instruction. But although on the alert, they were after all to some extent taken by surprise, and many of them were massacred after a more or less unavailing resistance. But if many of the Mussulmans were slain, the survivors were inspired with a desperation which the mandarins had never contemplated. From one end of Yunnan to the other the Mahomedans, in face of great personal peril, rose by a common and spontaneous impulse, and the Chinese population suffered in turn for their brutalities, and were compelled to take a hasty refuge in the towns. At Talifoo, where the Mahomedans formed a considerable portion of the population, the most desperate fighting occurred, and after three days' carnage the Mussulmans, under Tu Wensiu, were left in possession of the city. Their success inspired them with the hope of retaining the freedom they had won, and impressed with the conviction that nothing in their power to offer would atone for their acts of rebellion in the eyes of the Government, they had no choice save to exert themselves for the retention of their independence. They proceeded to fortify Talifoo, and to enlist in their service as many of the mountain tribes as would be tempted by the offer of good pay and the prospects of considerable booty. The rebels did not remain without leaders, whom they willingly recognized and obeyed; for the kwanshihs or chiefs, who had accepted titles of authority from the Chinese, cast off their allegiance and placed themselves at the head of the popular movement. The priest Ma Tesing, who had travelled much, including the pilgrimage to Mecca, was raised to the highest post of all as Dictator, but Tu Wensiu admitted no higher authority than his own within the walls of Talifoo.

While Ma Tesing exercised the supremacy due to his age and attainments, the young chief Ma Sien led the rebels in the field. His energy was most conspicuous, and in the year 1858 he thought he was sufficiently strong to make an attack upon the city of Yunnan itself. His hopes were baffled by the resolute defence of an officer named Lin Tzuchin, who had shown great courage as a partisan leader against the insurgents before he was entrusted with the defence of the provincial capital. According to some accounts Lin was one of the fierce intractable Miaotze race. Ma Sien

SIEGE OF YUNNAN. 435

was compelled to beat a retreat, and to devote himself to the organization of the many thousand Ijen or Lolos recruits who signified their attachment to his cause. For the successful defence of Yunnan Lin was made a Titu, and gradually collected into his own hands such authority as still remained to the Emperor's lieutenants. On both sides preparations were made for the renewal of the struggle, but before the year 1858 ended Ma Sien met with a second repulse at the town of Linan.

The year 1859 was not marked by any event of signal importance, although the balance of success inclined on the whole to the Mussulmans. But in the following year the Mahomedans drew up a large force, computed to exceed 50,000 men, round Yunnanfoo, to which they proceeded to vigorously lay siege. The Imperialists were taken at a disadvantage, and the large number of people who had fled for shelter into the town rendered the small stores of provisions less sufficient than ever for a protracted defence. Yunnanfoo was on the point of surrender when an event occurred which not merely relieved it from its predicament, but altered the whole complexion of the struggle. The garrison had made up its mind to yield. Even the brave Lin had accepted the inevitable and begun to negotiate with the two rebel leaders Ma Sien and the priest Ma Tesing. Those chiefs, with victory in their grasp, manifested an unexpected and surprising moderation. Instead of demanding from Lin a complete and unconditional surrender, they began to discuss with him what terms could be agreed upon for the cessation of the war and for the restoration of tranquillity to the province. At first it was thought that these propositions concealed some intended treachery, but their sincerity was placed beyond dispute by the suicide of the mandarin Hwang Chung, who had first instigated the people to massacre their Mahomedan brethren.

The terms of peace were promptly arranged, and a request was forwarded to Pekin for the ratification of a convention concluded under the pressure of necessity with some of the rebel leaders. The better to conceal the fact that this arrangement had been made with the principal leader of the disaffected, Ma Sien changed his name to Ma Julung, and received the rank of general in the Chinese service; while the high priest accepted as his share the not inconsiderable pension of two hundred taels a month. It is impossible to divine the true reasons which actuated these instigators of rebellion in their decision to go over to the side of the Government. They probably thought that they had done sufficient to secure all the practical advantages, and that any persistence in hostilities would only result in the increased misery and impoverishment of the province. They conceived no doubt that their kinsmen and followers would obtain justice and security; and, as for themselves, no moment would be more opportune for securing the largest possible personal advantage with the minimum of risk. But they were also influenced by other considerations. Powerful as they were, there were other Mahomedan leaders seeking to acquire the supreme position among their co-religionists; and foremost among these was Tu Wensiu, who had reduced the whole of Western Yunnan to his sway, and reigned at Talifoo. The Mahomedan cause, important as it was, did not afford scope for the ambitions of two such men as Ma Julung and Tu Wensiu. The former availed himself of the favourable opportunity to settle this difficulty in a practical and, as he shrewdly anticipated, the most profitable manner for himself personally, by giving in his adhesion to the Government, and by employing his talents for the settlement of his personal rivalry with his former associate, at the same time that they were given to support the tottering supremacy of the Pekin ruler.

This important defection did not bring in its train any certainty of tranquillity. Incited by the example of their leaders, every petty officer and chief thought himself deserving of the highest honours, and resolved to fight for his own hand. Ma Julung left Yunnanfoo for the purpose of seizing a neighbouring town which had revolted, and during his absence one of his lieutenants seized the capital, murdered the Viceroy, and threatened to plunder the inhabitants. Ma Julung was summoned to return in hot haste, and as a temporary expedient the priest Ma Tesing was elected Viceroy. When Ma

Julung returned with his army he had to lay siege to Yunnan-foo, and although he promptly effected an entrance into the city, it took five days' hard fighting in the streets before the force in occupation was expelled. The insurgent officer was captured, exposed to the public gaze for one month in an iron cage, and then executed in a cruel manner. Ma Tesing was deposed from the elevated position which he had held for so short a time, and a new Chinese Viceroy arrived from Kweichow.

The year 1863 opened with the first active operations against Tu Wensiu, who, during these years of disorder in central Yunnan, had been governing the western districts with some prudence. It would have been better if they had not been undertaken, for they only resulted in the defeat of the detachments sent by Ma Julung to engage the despot of Talifoo. Force having failed, they had recourse to diplomacy, and Ma Tesing was sent to sound Tu Wensiu as to whether he would not imitate their example and make his peace with the authorities. These overtures were rejected with disdain, and Tu Wensiu proclaimed his intention of holding out to the last, and refused to recognize the wisdom or the necessity of coming to terms with the Government.

The embarrassment of Ma Julung and the Yunnan officials, already sufficiently acute, was at this conjuncture further aggravated by an outbreak in their rear among the Miaotze and some other mountain tribes in the province of Kweichow. To the difficulty of coping with a strongly-placed enemy in front was thus added that of maintaining communications through a hostile and difficult region. A third independent party had also come into existence in Yunnan, where an ex-Chinese official named Liang Shihmei had set up his own authority at Linan, mainly, it was said, through jealousy of the Mahomedans taken into the service of the Government, and over whom he had gained some successes in the early stages of the war. The greatest difficulty of all was to reconcile the pretensions of the different commanders, for the Chinese officials and the Futai Tsen Yuying in particular regarded Ma Julung with no friendly eye.

With the year 1867, both sides having collected their

strength, more active operations were commenced, and Ma Julung proceeded in person, at the head of the best troops he could collect, to engage Tu Wensiu. It was at this time that the Imperialists adopted the red flag as their standard in contradistinction to the white flag of the insurgents. A desultory campaign ensued, but although Ma Julung evinced both courage and capacity, the result was on the whole unfavourable to him; and he had to retreat to the capital, where events of some importance had occurred during his absence in the field. The Viceroy, who had been staunchly attached to Ma Julung, died suddenly and under such circumstances as to suggest a suspicion of foul play; and Tsen Yuying had by virtue of his rank of Futai assumed the temporary discharge of his duties. The retreat of Ma Julung left the insurgents free to follow up their successes; and in the course of 1868 the authority of the Emperor had disappeared from every part of the province except the prefectural city of Yunnanfoo. This bad fortune led the Mussulmans who had followed the advice and fortunes of Ma Julung to consider whether it would not be wise to rejoin their co-religionists, and to at once finish the contest by the destruction of the Government. Had Ma Julung wavered in his fidelity for a moment they would all have joined the standard of Tu Wensiu, and the rule of the Sultan of Talifoo would have been established from one end of Yunnan to the other.

Tu Wensiu, having established the security of his communications with Burmah, whence he obtained supplies of arms and munitions of war, devoted his efforts to the capture of Yunnanfoo, which he completely invested. An amusing incident in the development of this struggle was that the besiegers supplied the besieged with salt, thus acquiring the money necessary to purchase their military equipment at Bhamo or Mandalay. The garrison was reduced to the lowest straits before Tsen Yuying resolved to come to the aid of his distressed colleague. The loss of the prefectural town would not merely entail serious consequences to the Imperialist cause, but he felt it would personally compromise him as the Futai at Pekin. In the early part of 1869, therefore, he threw himself into the town with three thousand men, and the forces of Tu Wensiu found themselves obliged to withdraw from the eastern side of the city. A long period of inaction followed, but during this time the most important events happened with regard to the ultimate result. Ma Julung employed all his artifice and arguments to show the rebel chiefs the utter hopelessness of their succeeding against the whole power of the Chinese Empire, which, from the suppression of the Taeping rebellion, would soon be able to be employed against them. They felt the force of his representations, and they were also oppressed by a sense of the slow progress they had made towards the capture of Yunnanfoo. Some months after Tsen Yuying's arrival, those of the rebels who were encamped to the north of the city hoisted the red flag and gave in their adhesion to the Government. Then Ma Julung resumed active operations against the other rebels, and obtained several small successes. A wound received during one of the skirmishes put an end to his activity, and the campaign resumed its desultory character. But Ma Julung's illness had other unfortunate consequences; for during it Tsen Yuying broke faith with those of the rebel leaders who had come over, and put them all to a cruel death. The natural consequence of this foolish and ferocious act was that the Mahomedans again reverted to their desperate resolve to stand firmly by the side of Tu Wensiu.

The war again passed into a more active phase. Ma Julung had recovered from his wounds. A new Viceroy, and a man of some energy, was sent from Pekin. Lin Yuchow had attracted the notice of Tseng Kwofan among those of his native province who had responded to his appeal to defend Hoonan against the Taepings sixteen years before; and shortly before the death of the last Viceroy of Yunnan, he had been made Governor of Kweichow. To the same patron at Pekin he now owed his elevation to the Viceroyalty. It is said that he had lost the energy which once characterized him; but he brought with him several thousand Hoonan braves, whose courage and military experience made them invaluable auxiliaries to the embarrassed authorities in Yunnan. A still more important circumstance as contributing towards the establishment of peace was the order sent from Pekin that the treasuries of six provinces should send to Yunnanfoo every month the total sum of 70,000 taels, until tranquillity had been restored. Although the whole of this amount was never received, still the officials in the south-west were thus provided with an invaluable source of revenue in which they were more deficient than in any other of the elements of war.

The details of the campaign that followed would fail to be instructive, and the mention of names that are not merely uncouth, but unpronounceable would only repel the reader. The result is the principal, or, indeed, the single fact worthy of our consideration. In the course of the year 1870 most of the towns in the south and the north of Yunnan were recovered, and communications were re-opened with Szchuen. As soon as the inhabitants perceived that the Government had regained its strength, they hastened to express their joy at the change by repudiating the white flag which Tu Wensiu had compelled them to adopt. The Imperialists, even to the last, increased the difficulty of their work of pacification by exhibiting a relentless cruelty. At Kunyang, after an eight months' siege, the chiefs on surrendering were invited to a banquet, and then executed to the number of three hundred. At the capture of Chengchiang, some months later, faith was deliberately broken by Tsen Yuying, and the town was sacked. The spoilers quarrelled among themselves, and their combats added to the confusion and slaughter. If the inhabitants thought to secure their safety by a speedy surrender, the Mussulmans were rendered more desperate in their resolve to resist. The chances of a Mahomedan success were steadily diminishing when Yang Yuko, a mandarin of some military capacity, who had begun his career in the most approved manner as a rebel, succeeded in capturing the whole of the salt-producing district which had been the main source of their strength.

In the year 1872 all the preliminary arrangements had been made for attacking Talifoo itself. A supply of rifles had been received from Canton or Shanghai, and a few pieces of artillery had also arrived. With these improved weapons the troops of Ma Julung and Tsen Yuying enjoyed a distinct advantage over the rebels of Talifoo. The horrors of war were at this point increased by those of pestilence, for the plague broke out at Puerh on the southern frontier, and before it disappeared devastated the whole of the province, completing the effect of the civil war, and ruining the few districts which had escaped from its ravages. The direct command of the siege operations at Talifoo was entrusted to Yang Yuko, who had obtained a reputation for invincibility; but when Tsen Yuying had completed his own operations by the death of Liang Shihmei, and the recovery of Linan and other places, he also proceeded to the camp before the Mahomedan capital for the purpose of taking part in the crowning operation of the war. General Yang was one of the most remarkable men in China. He was almost a hunchback, but so active that the people called him "the monkey." In the war, unlike most Chinese generals, who sit in their chairs in the rear, he was always on horseback, under fire, at the head of his men.

Tu Wensiu and the garrison of Talifoo, although driven to desperation, could not discover any issue from their difficulties. They were reduced to the last stage of destitution, and starvation stared them in the face. In this extremity Tu Wensiu, although there was every reason to believe that the Imperialists would not fulfil their pledges, and that surrender simply meant yielding to a cruel death, resolved to open negotiations with Yang Yuko for giving up the town. The Emperor's generals signified their desire for the speedy termination of the siege, at the same time expressing acquiescence in the general proposition of the town and garrison being admitted to terms. Although the Futai and Yang Yuko had promptly come to the mutual understanding to celebrate the fall of Talifoo by a wholesale massacre, they expressed their intention to spare the other rebels on the surrender of Tu Wensiu for execution, and on the payment of an indemnity. The terms were accepted, although the more experienced of the rebels warned their comrades that they would not be complied with. On the 15th of January, 1873, Tu Wensiu, the original of the mythical Sultan Suliman, the fame of whose power reached England, and who had been an object of the solicitude of the Indian Government, accepted the decision of his craven followers as expressing the will of Heaven, and gave himself up for execution.

He attired himself in his best and choicest garments, and seated himself in the yellow palanquin which he had adopted as one of the few marks of royal state that his opportunities allowed him to secure. Accompanied by the men who had negotiated the surrender, he drove through the streets, receiving for the last time the homage of his people, and out beyond the gates to Yang Yuko's camp. Those who saw the cortège marvelled at the calm indifference of the fallen despot. He seemed to have as little fear of his fate as consciousness of his surroundings. The truth soon became evident. He had baffled his enemies by taking slow poison. Before he reached the presence of the Futai, who had wished to gloat over the possession of his prisoner, the opium had done its work, and Tu Wensiu was no more. It seemed but an inadequate triumph to sever the head from the dead body, and to send it preserved in honey as the proof of victory to Pekin.

Four days after Tu Wensiu's death, the Imperialists were in complete possession of the town, and a week later they had taken all their measures for the execution of the fell plan upon which they had decided. A great feast was given for the celebration of the convention, and the most important of the Mahomedan commanders, including those who had negotiated the truce, were present. At a given signal they were attacked and murdered by soldiers concealed in the gallery for the purpose, while six cannon shots announced to the soldiery that the hour had arrived for them to break loose on the defenceless townspeople. The scenes that followed are stated to have surpassed description. Thousands were massacred. The unfortunate people who had received the Chinese soldiery with hospitality were butchered on their own hearths; and the work of slaughter, renewed at intervals in Tali and the surrounding villages, was only discontinued from fatigue. It was computed that 30,000 men alone perished after the fall of the old Panthay capital.

With the capture of Talifoo the great Mahomedan rebellion

in the south-west closed, after a desultory and most deplorable warfare during nearly eighteen years. The resources of the Government when once enlisted in the task had availed to restore peace and to crush the rebellious. The war was conducted with exceptional ferocity on both sides, and witnessed more than the usual amount of falseness and breach of faith common to Oriental struggles. Nobody benefited by the contest, and the prosperity of Yunnan, which at one time had been far from inconsiderable, sank to the lowest possible point. A new class of officials came to the front during this period of disorder, and fidelity was a sufficient passport to a certain rank. Ma Julung, the Marshal Ma of European travellers, gained a still higher station; and, notwithstanding the jealousy of his colleagues, acquired practical supremacy in the province. The high priest, Ma Tesing, who may be considered as the prime instigator of the movement, was executed or poisoned in 1874 at the instigation of some of the Chinese officials. Yang Yuko, the most successful of all the generals, only enjoyed a brief tenure of power. It was said that he was dissatisfied with his position as commander-in-chief, and aspired to a higher rank. He also was summoned to Pekin, but never got further than Shanghai, where he died, or was removed. But although quiet gradually descended upon this part of China, it was long before prosperity followed in its train. The young Emperor Tungche had, however, the satisfaction of witnessing the close of the Panthay* rebellion, as he had seen that of the Taeping eight years before.

About six years after the first mutterings of discontent

---

* "The word Panthay has received such complete recognition as the national name of the Mahomedan revolutionaries in Yunnan, that I fear it will be almost useless to assert that the term is utterly unknown in the country which was temporarily under the domination of Sultan Suliman. . . . The name Suliman is equally unknown."—Mr. Colborne Baber. As Colonel Yule has very clearly and sensibly pointed out, nobody supposed that the style Suliman was more than that used by the Hajjis anxious to spread his fame among Mahomedans west of Yunnan. The word Panthay was the name given by the Burmese to the Mahomedans of Yunnan. Although not a national name, it has a justifiable title to being perpetuated.

among the Mahomedans in the south-west, disturbances occurred in the north-west provinces of Shensi and Kansuh, where there had been many thousand followers of Islam since an early period of Chinese history. At most times they were obedient subjects and sedulous cultivators of the soil; but they were always liable to sudden ebullitions of fanaticism or of seditious turbulence, as, indeed, form the essence of their aggressive religion, and it was said that during the later years of his reign Keen Lung had meditated ordering a wholesale execution of the male population above the age of fifteen. The threat, if ever made, was never carried out, but it sufficed to show the extent to which danger was apprehended from the Tungan (a word signifying converts) population. The true origin of the great outbreak in 1862 in Shensi seems to have been a quarrel between the Chinese and Mahomedan militia as to their share of the spoil derived from the defeat and overthrow of a brigand leader named Lantachuen, who had been driven out of Szchuen and compelled to seek shelter elsewhere. Although the authority of the executive was triumphantly asserted over a rebel, the cause of order suffered from the incursion of Lantachuen by supplying the occasion of a grave conflict among the inhabitants themselves. After some bloodshed, two Imperial Commissioners named Mapeling and Chang Pe were sent from Pekin to restore order. The principal Mahomedan leader formed a plot to murder the Commissioners, and on their arrival he rushed into their presence and slew Chang Pe with his own hand. His co-religionists deplored the rash act, and voluntarily seized and surrendered him for the purpose of undergoing a cruel death. But although he was torn to pieces, that fact did not satisfy the outraged dignity of the Emperor. A command was issued in Tungche's name to the effect that all those who persisted in following the creed of Islam should perish by the sword.

From Shensi the outbreak spread into the adjoining province of Kansuh; and the local garrisons were vanquished in a pitched battle at Tara Ussu, beyond the regular frontier. The insurgents did not succeed, however, in taking any of the larger towns of Shensi, and after threatening with capture the once famous city of Singan, they were gradually expelled from that province, although their numbers made it clear that the complete pacification of the north-west would not be accomplished until the executive had been freed from some of its other troubles. The Mahomedan rebellion within the limits of China proper would not, however, have possessed more than local importance, but for the fact that it encouraged a similar outbreak in the country further west, and that it resulted in the severance of the Central Asian provinces from China for a period of many years.

The uprising of the Mahomedans in the frontier provinces appealed to the secret fears as well as to the longings of the Tungan settlers and soldiers in all the towns and military stations which marked the dreary route from Souchow to Kashgar. The sense of a common peril, more perhaps than the desire to attain the same object, led to revolts at Hami, Barkul, Urumtsi, and Turfan, towns which formed a group of industrious communities halfway between the prosperous districts of Kansuh on the one side and Kashgar on the other. The Tungani held the privileges which are never denied to those who maintain the fabric of a government in distant territories, but they may have felt that there could be no security for them after an edict had been issued forbidding the practice of their religion. The Tungani at the towns named, and at others in the same region, both on the southern and on the northern side of the Tian Shan range, revolted under the leading of their priests, and imitated the example of their co-religionists within the settled borders of China by murdering all who did not accept their tenets, or who seemed to possess the will and the power to dispute their supremacy. After a brief interval, which we may attribute to the greatness of the distance, to the vigilance of the Chinese garrison, or to the apathy of the population, the movement spread to the next three towns west of Turfan, Karashar, Kucha, and Aksu, where it came into contact with, and was stopped by, another insurrectionary movement under Mahomedan indeed but totally distinct auspices. West of Aksu the Tungan rebellion never extended south of the Tian Shan range.

The defection of the Tungani, who had formed a large

proportion, if not the majority, of the Chinese garrisons, paralyzed the strength of the Celestials in Central Asia. Both in the districts dependent on Ili, and in those ruled from Kashgar and Yarkand, the Chinese were beset by many great and permanent difficulties. They were with united strength a minority, and now that they were divided among themselves almost a hopeless minority. The peoples they governed were fanatical, false, and fickle. The ruler of Khokand and the refugees living on his bounty were always alert to take the most advantage of the least slip or act of weakness on the part of the governing classes. Their machinations had been hitherto baffled, but never before had so favourable an opportunity presented itself for attaining their wishes, as when it became known that the whole Mahomedan population was up in arms against the Emperor, and that communications were severed between Kashgar and Pekin.

We have described the attempts made at earlier periods on the part of the members of the old ruling family in Kashgar to regain their own by expelling the Chinese. In 1857 Wali Khan, one of the sons of Jehangir, had succeeded in gaining temporary possession of the city of Kashgar, and seemed for a moment to be likely to capture Yarkand also. He fell by his vices. The people soon detested the presence of the man to whom they had accorded a too hasty welcome. After a rule of four months, he fled the country, vanquished in the field by the Chinese garrison, and followed by the execrations of the population he had come to deliver. The invasion of Wali Khan further embittered the relations between the Chinese and their subjects; and a succession of governors bore heavily on the Mahomedans. Popular dissatisfaction and the apprehension in the minds of the governing officials that their lives might be forfeited at any moment to a popular outbreak added to the dangers of the situation in Kashgar itself, when the news arrived of the Tungan revolt and of the many other complications which hampered the action of the Pekin ruler.

It is not our purpose to narrate here the details of the rebellion in Kashgar. Neither space nor its direct influence on the history of China would sanction such close exactitude. But it may be said that in the year 1863 the Chinese officials had become so alarmed at their isolated position that they resolved to adopt the desperate expedient of massacring all the Mahomedans or Tungani in their own garrisons. The amban and his officers were divided in council and dilatory in execution. The Tungani heard of the plot while the governor was summoning the nerve to carry it out. They resolved to anticipate him. The Mahomedans at Yarkand, the largest and most important garrison in the country, rose in August, 1863, and massacred all the Buddhist Chinese. Seven thousand men are computed to have fallen. A small band fled to the citadel, which they held for a short time; but at length, overwhelmed by numbers, they preferred death to dishonour, and destroyed themselves by exploding the fort with the magazine.

The Tungani thus lost Kashgaria for the Chinese, as the other garrisons and towns promptly followed the example of Yarkand; but they could not keep it for themselves. The spectacle of this internal dissension proved irresistible for the adventurers of Khokand, and Buzurg, the last surviving son of Jehangir, resolved to make another bid for power and for the recovery of the position for which his father and kinsmen had striven in vain. The wish might possibly have been no more attained than theirs had he not secured the support of the most capable soldier in Khokand, Mahomed Yakoob, the defender of Ak Musjid. It was not until the early part of the year 1865 that this Khoja pretender, with his small body of Khokandian officers, and a considerable number of Kirghiz allies, appeared upon the scene. Then, however, their success was rapid. The Tungan revolt in Altyshahr resolved itself into a movement for the restoration of the Khoja dynasty. In a short time Buzurg was established as ruler, while his energetic lieutenant was employed in the task of crushing the few remaining Chinese garrisons, and also in cowing his Tungan allies, who already regarded their new ruler with a doubtful eye. By the month of September in the same year that witnessed the passage of the invading force through the Terek defile, the triumph of the Khoja's arms was assured. A few weeks later Mahomed Yakoob deposed his master, and caused himself to be proclaimed ruler in his stead. The voice of the people ratified the success of the man; and in 1866 Mahomed Yakoob or Yakoob Beg received at the hands of the Ameer of Bokhara the proud title of Athalik Ghazi, by which he was long known.

The Mahomedan rising spread still further within the limits of Chinese authority in Central Asia. While the events which have been briefly sketched were happening in the region south of the great Tian Shan range, others of not less importance had taken place in Ili or Kuldja, which, under Chinese rule, had enjoyed uninterrupted peace for a century. It was this fact which marked the essential difference between the Tungan rebellion and all the disturbances that had preceded it. The revolution in the metropolitan province of Ili was complicated by the presence of different races just as it had been in Kashgaria by the pretensions of the Khoja family. A large portion of the population consisted of those Tarantchis who were the descendants of the Kashgarians deported on more than one occasion by the Chinese from their own homes to the banks of the Ili; and they had inherited a legacy of ill-will against their rulers which only required the opportunity to display itself. The Tungan—or Dungan, as the Russians spell it—element was also very strong, and colonies of the Sobo and Solon tribes further added to the variety of the nationalities dwelling in this province. The Chinese population proper consisted also to a very large extent of convicts, or at the least of exiles banished from their own country to this remote quarter. The land of Ili, promising and flourishing oasis as it was in the barren regions of Asia, appeared in the eyes of the contented Chinamen as only endurable for the outcast.

It had been said with some truth that the Chinese ruled in this quarter of their dominions on the old principle of commanding by the division of the subjected; and it had been predicted that they would fall upon an evil day if ever any two of the dependent populations combined against them. There is little difficulty in showing that the misfortunes of the Chinese were due to their own faults. They neglected the plainest military precautions, and the mandarins thought only of enriching themselves. But the principal cause of the destruction of the fabric of their power was the cessation of the supplies which they were used to receive from Pekin. The government of these dependencies was only possible by the annual gift of a small portion of the Imperial treasure. When the funds placed at the disposal of the Ili authorities were diverted to other uses, it was no longer possible to maintain the old efficiency of the service. Discontent was provided with a stronger argument at the same time that the executive found itself embarrassed in grappling with it.

The news of the Mahomedan outbreak in China warned the Tungani in Ili that their opportunity had come. But although there were disturbances as early as January, 1863, these were suppressed, and the vigilance of the authorities sufficed to keep things quiet for another year. Their subsequent incapacity, or hesitation to strike a prompt blow, enabled the Mahomedans to husband their resources and to complete their plans. A temporary alliance was concluded between the Tungani and the Tarantchis, and they hastened to attack the Chinese troops and officials. The year 1865 was marked by the progress of a sanguinary struggle, during which the Chinese lost their principal towns, and some of their garrisons were ruthlessly slaughtered after surrender. The usual scenes of civil war followed. Populous cities were reduced to ruins and desolation. The surface of the country underwent a change. The population of the whole province fell off during the struggle to less than what the capital alone had contained in 1862. The ravages of disease and famine completed the destruction of what war had spared.

When the Chinese were completely vanquished and their garrisons exterminated, the victors, as might have been expected, quarrelled among themselves. The Tungani and the Tarantchis met in mortal encounter, and the former were vanquished, and their chief, Mayaghur Akhun, slain. When they renewed the contest, some months later, they were, after another sanguinary struggle, again overthrown. The Tarantchis then ruled the state by themselves, but the example they set of native rule was, to say the least, not encouraging. One chief after another was deposed and murdered. The same year witnessed no fewer than five leaders in the supreme place of power; and when Abul Oghlan assumed the title of Sultan the cup of their iniquities was already full. In the year 1871, an end was at last put to their enormities by the occupation of the province by a Russian force, and the installation of a Russian governor. Although it is probable that they were only induced to take this step by the fear that if they did not do so Yakoob Beg would, the fact remains that the Russian Government performed a laudable and beneficent act in the cause of order by interfering for the restoration of tranquillity in the Ili valley.

The Mahomedan outbreaks in South-Western and North-Western China resulted, therefore, in the gradual suppression of the Panthay rebellion, which was completed in the twelfth year of Tungche's reign, while the Tungan rising, so far as the Central Asia territories were concerned, remained unquelled for a longer period. The latter led to the establishment of an independent Tungan confederacy beyond Kansuh, and also of the kingdom of Kashgaria ruled by Yakoob Beg. The revolt in Ili, after several alterations of fortune, resulted in the brief independence of the Tarantchis, who were in turn displaced by the Russians under a pledge of restoring the province to the Chinese whenever they should return. Judged by the extent of territory involved, the Mahomedan rebellion might be said to be not less important than the Taeping; but the comparison on that ground alone would be really delusive, as the numerical inferiority of the Mahomedans rendered it always a question only of time for the central power to be restored, and for the majesty of the Emperor to be triumphantly reasserted.

CAHPTER XVIII.

THE REIGN OF TUNGCHE.

THE young Emperor Tungche, born 27th April, 1856, grew up amidst continual difficulties, although the successes of his principal lieutenants afforded good reason to believe that it was only a question of time before they would be finally removed. To the successes already described must be added the suppression of the Nienfei rebellion in the province of Shantung. It would have been unreasonable to suppose that the relations between the foreign merchants and residents and the Chinese would become, after the suspicion and dangers of generations, as cordial as those fortunately established in the diplomatic world at Pekin. The commercial and missionary bodies, into which the foreign community was naturally divided, had objects of trade or of religion to advance, which rendered them apt to take an unfavourable view of the progress made by the Chinese Government in the paths of civilization, and to be ever sceptical even of its good faith. Every one wished and expected the Chinese to throw themselves as impetuously as their neighbours the Japanese had done into the work of imitating the excellences, real or assumed, of Europe; and not the smallest consideration was paid to the prejudices of a proud people, or to the necessities of a Government charged with a task of peculiar and increasing difficulty. The main object with the foreign diplomatic representatives became not more to obtain justice for their countrymen than to restrain their eagerness, and to confine their pretensions to the rights conceded by the treaties.

A clear distinction had to be drawn between undue

coercion of the Government on the one hand, and the effectual compulsion of the people to evince respect towards foreigners and to comply with the obligations of the treaty on the other. Instances repeatedly occurred in reference to the latter matter when it would have been foolish to have shown weakness, especially as there was not the least room to suppose that the Government possessed at that time the power and the capacity to secure reparation for, or to prevent the repetition of, attacks on foreigners. Under this category came the riot at Yangchow in the year 1868, when some missionaries had their houses burnt down, and were otherwise maltreated. A similar outrage was perpetrated in Formosa; but the fullest redress was always tendered as soon as the Executive realized that the European representatives attached importance to the occurrence, and were in earnest in their demand for compensation.

The recurrence of these local dangers and disputes served to bring more clearly than ever before the minds of the Chinese Ministers the advisability of taking some step on their own part towards an understanding with European Governments and peoples. The proposal to depute a Chinese ambassador to the West could hardly be said to be new, seeing that it had been projected after the Treaty of Nankin, and that the minister Keying had manifested some desire to be the first mandarin to serve in the novel capacity. But when the Tsungli Yamen took up the question some years later, after the second peace and war, it was decided that in this as in other matters it would be expedient to avail themselves in the first place of foreign mediation. The favourable opportunity of doing so presented itself when Mr. Burlinghame retired from his post as Minister of the United States at Pekin. In the winter of 1867-68, Mr. Burlinghame accepted an appointment as accredited representative of the Chinese Government to eleven of the principal countries of the world, and two Chinese mandarins and a certain number of Chinese students were appointed to accompany him on his tour.

The importance of the Burlinghame Mission was certainly exaggerated at the time, and the speculations to which it gave rise as to the part China was about to take in the movement of the world, were no doubt based on erroneous data; but still it would be a mistake to say that it failed to produce none of the beneficial effect which had been expected. It was something for the outer world to learn, in those days when the Chinese presented to the mind of foreigners ideas only of weakness and falseness, that they had better characteristics, and that some day they might wield no inconsiderable power. Mr. Burlinghame was sanguine, and the expectations of his audiences, both in America and in Europe, overleapt all difficulties, and spanned at a step the growth of many years; but only the most shallow-minded observers will deny that Mr. Burlinghame's widest stretches of fancy were supported by an amount of truth which events are making clearer every year. Of course those who only looked on the surface, who saw the difficulties under which China staggered, and the dogged pride with which she refused the remedy forced upon her by foreigners, who had at least as much their own interests as hers in view, declared that Mr. Burlinghame's statements were "enthusiastic fictions." The Chinese themselves did not attach as much importance as they might have done to his efforts, and Mr. Burlinghame's mission will be remembered more as an educational process for foreign opinion than as signifying any decided change in Chinese policy. His death at St. Petersburg, in March, 1870, put a sudden and unexpected close to his tour, but it cannot be said that he could have done more towards the elucidation of Chinese questions than he had already accomplished, while his bold and optimistic statements, after arousing public attention, had already begun to produce the inevitable reaction.

Sir Rutherford Alcock's residence at Pekin, without being marked by any decisive matter similar to the incidents which had occurred during the critical years of the war, and the subsequent negotiations, witnessed many minor disturbances and differences which required his constant and unrelaxed attention. The outrages at Yangchow and in Formosa were followed by others at Swatow and Foochow. In all these cases redress was exacted in the promptest and most effectual manner by the nearest gun-boat. It was only when the populace broke out into anti-foreign fervour at a distance from the sea-coast that the means of redress were non-existent. Such was the case in Szchuen, where Père Rigaud and a large number of native Christians perished at the hands of a mob, without any possibility of obtaining immediate reparation. Sir Rutherford Alcock's principal work accomplished during this period was the revision of the Treaty of Tientsin. The new terms failed of course to satisfy everybody, but there is no reason to suppose that anything more favourable could have been procured at the time, or that any more vigorous action would have received the support of the British Government.

At Sir Rutherford's parting interview with Prince Kung, he said to the latter: "After all these discussions, now that we have entered into a convention regulating many points, I hope that, though I am going away, you will find other matters will settle themselves satisfactorily, and that there will be a gradual improvement in our relations, and in the progress of our commerce." Prince Kung replied very cordially: "Yes, we have had a great many discussions, but we know that you have always endeavoured to do justice, and if you could only relieve us of missionaries and opium there need be no more trouble in China." During Sir Rutherford's residence the Duke of Edinburgh visited Pekin.

In 1869 Sir Rutherford Alcock retired, and was succeeded in the difficult post of English representative in China by Mr. Thomas Wade, who had occupied a place inferior to none in the consideration of his Government as principal secretary and interpreter to our ministers and diplomatists during the whole of the trying period since the Treaty of Nankin. In the very first year of his exercise of the supreme direction of our diplomacy, an event occurred which eclipsed all the aggressive acts that had preceded it, and cast them into the shade. It may perhaps be surmised that this was the Tientsin massacre—an event which threatened to reopen the whole of the China question, and which brought France and China to the verge of war.

It was in June, 1870, on the eve of the outbreak of the Franco-Prussian war, that the foreign settlements were startled by the report of a great popular outbreak against foreigners

THE TIENTSIN MASSACRE.

in the important town of Tientsin. At that city there was a large and energetic colony of Roman Catholic priests, and their success in the task of conversion, small as it might be held, was still sufficient to excite the ire and fears of the literary and official classes. The origin of mob violence is ever difficult to discover, for a trifle suffices to set it in motion. But at Tientsin specific charges of the most horrible and, it need not be said, the most baseless character were spread about as to the cruelties and evil practices of those devoted to the service of religion. These rumours were diligently circulated, and it need not cause wonder if, when the mere cry of Fanquai sufficed to raise a disturbance, these allegations resulted in completely unhinging the public mind. The agitation against the missionaries had not been the production of a day, and it acquired increased force with continued impunity. It was well known beforehand that an attack on the missionaries would take place unless the authorities adopted very efficient measures of protection. The foreign residents and the consulates were warned of the coming outburst, and a very heavy responsibility will always rest on those who might, by the display of greater vigour, have prevented the unfortunate occurrences that ensued. At the same time, allowing for the prejudices of the Chinese, it must be allowed that not only must the efforts of all foreign missionaries be attended with the gravest peril, but that the acts of the French priests and nuns at Tientsin were, if not indiscreet, at least peculiarly calculated to arouse the anger and offend the superstitious predilections of the Chinese.

Dr. Wells Williams writes very soundly on this point in his "Middle Kingdom." He quotes the following important passage from the official despatch of the United States Minister, describing the originating causes of the outrage: "At many of the principal places in China open to foreign residence, the Sisters of Charity have established institutions, each of which appears to combine in itself a foundling hospital and orphan asylum. Finding that the Chinese were averse to placing children in their charge, the managers of these institutions offered a certain sum per head for all the children placed under their control given to them, it being understood that a child once in their asylum no parent, relative, or guardian could claim or exercise any control over it. It has for some time been asserted by the Chinese, and believed by most of the non-Catholic foreigners residing here, that the system of paying bounties induced the kidnapping of children for these institutions for the sake of the reward. It is also asserted that the priests or sisters, or both, have been in the habit of holding out inducements to have children brought to them in the last stages of illness for the purpose of being baptized *in articulo mortis*. In this way many children have been taken to these establishments in the last stages of disease, baptized there, and soon after taken away dead. All these acts, together with the secrecy and seclusion which appear to be a part and parcel of the regulations which govern institutions of this character everywhere, have created suspicions in the minds of the Chinese, and these suspicions have engendered an intense hatred against the sisters." The most unfortunate part of the incident was that "the day prior to the outbreak the district magistrate (chihien) called upon the French Consul, and stated that unless permission be given for a thorough examination of the sisters' establishment it was difficult to foretell the result. The Consul, construing the language into a threat, replied that the magistrate being inferior in rank to the Consul, no negotiation could take place between them for the purpose indicated or any other." Some of the foreign residents even went so far as to say that if the Consul had promptly acted in combination with the Chinese officials there would have been no massacre.

Had the officials in the town acted with promptitude and instituted an official inquiry with the view of demonstrating the falseness of the charges, it is probable that at the very last moment the outbreak might have been averted. Such a course had proved availing on equally critical occasions in some of the towns along the Yangtse; and the responsibility of not taking it rested in equal proportions between the Chinese officials and the French Consul. At that time Chung How, the Superintendent of Trade for the three

Northern Ports, was the principal official in Tientsin; but although some representations, not as forcible, however, as the occasion demanded, were made to him by M. Fontanier, the French Consul, on the 18th of June, three days before the massacre, no reply was given and no precautions were taken. On the 21st a large crowd assembled outside the Mission House. They very soon assumed an attitude of hostility, and it was clear that at any moment the attack might begin. M. Fontanier hastened off in person to Chung How, but his threats seem to have been as unavailing as his previous arguments. On his return he found the attack on the point of commencing. He made use of threats, and he fired a shot from his revolver, whether in self-defence or in the heat of indignation at some official treachery will never be known. The mob turned upon him, and he was murdered. The Chinese then hastened to complete the work they had begun. Chung How, like Surajah Dowlah, was not to be disturbed, and the attack on the Mission House and Consulate proceeded, while the officials responsible for order remained inactive. Twenty-one foreigners, including the French Consul, his secretary M. Simon, a member of the French legation at Pekin and his wife, a French storekeeper and his wife, three priests, ten Sisters of Charity, and a Russian merchant and his wife, were brutally murdered under circumstances of the greatest barbarity, while the number of native converts who fell at the same time can never be ascertained.

This event naturally produced a general feeling of horror and alarm. For the moment it was feared that the rioters would proceed to attack the rest of the foreign settlement. The mandarins still refrained from all intervention, and as there happened to be no gun-boat at Tientsin, the foreign residents were for the moment placed in an extremely dangerous predicament. They, of course, took all the measures they could to defend themselves, but it was said at the time that if the mob had only attacked at once they would probably have overcome such resistance as the Europeans could then have offered. They did not do so, however, chiefly because they distrusted or failed to realize their strength; and the massacre of Tientsin did not assume the larger proportions that were at one moment feared.

The Tientsin massacre was followed by a wave of anti-foreign feeling over the whole country; but although an official brought out a work entitled "Death-blow to Corrupt Doctrine" upon the subject, which obtained more than a passing notoriety, and notwithstanding that some members of the Imperial Family, and notably, as it was stated, Prince Chun, regarded the movement with favour, the arguments of Prince Kung and the more moderate ministers carried the day, and it was resolved to make every concession in the power of the Government in order to effect the pacific settlement of the dispute then created with France. The occurrence was one which made foreign opinion unanimously opposed to the Chinese. Let it be recorded in favour of Prince Kung's humanity, that on the very first receipt of the news he repudiated all sympathy with the acts of barbarity which had disgraced his fellow-countrymen. The outbreak of the war between France and Germany, while it contributed to a peaceful settlement of the question, rendered the process of diplomacy slow and dubious. The Tsungli Yamen, as soon as it realized that nothing short of the despatch of a mission of apology to Europe would salve the injured honour of France and convince her that the responsible ministers of the Emperor Tungche repudiated all connivance in the matter, determined that none other than Chung How himself should go to Paris to assure the French that the officials deplored the popular ebullition and had taken no part in it. The untoward result for France of the great war in Europe embarrassed her action in China. Chung How's assurances were accepted, the proffered compensation was received; but the Chinese were informed that, in recognition of France's moderation, and in return for the reception of their envoy by M. Thiers, the right of audience should be conceded to the French Minister resident at Pekin. The settlement of one difficulty served only to bring forward another, and to reveal a long vista of obstacles that had still to be overcome before the relations of China and the West were placed on a basis of enduring harmony.

THE AUDIENCE QUESTION.

The Audience Question naturally aroused the greatest interest at Pekin, where it agitated the official mind not merely because it signified another concession to force, but also because it promised to produce a disturbing effect on the minds of the people. The young Emperor was growing up, and might be expected to take a direct share in the administration at an early date. It was not an idle apprehension that filled the minds of his ministers lest he might lay the blame on them for having cast upon him the obligation of receiving ministers of foreign states in a manner such as they had never before been allowed to appear in the presence of the occupant of the Dragon Throne. The youth of the sovereign served to postpone the question for a short space of time, but it was no longer doubtful that the assumption of personal authority by the young Emperor Tungche would be accompanied by the reintroduction, and probably by the settlement, of the Audience Question. It was typical of the progress Chinese statesmen were making that none of them seemed to consider the possibility of distinctly refusing this privilege. Its concession was only postponed until after the celebration of the young Emperor's marriage.

It had been known for some time previous that the young ruler had fixed his affections on Ahluta, a Manchu lady of good family, and that the Empresses had decided that she was worthy of the high rank to which she was to be raised. The marriage ceremony was deferred on more than one plea until after the Emperor had reached his sixteenth birthday, but in October, 1872, there was thought to be no longer any excuse for postponement, and it was celebrated with great splendour on the 16th of that month. The arrangements were made in strict accordance with the precedent of the Emperor Kanghi's marriage in 1674, that ruler having also married when in occupation of the throne and before he had attained his majority. It was stated that the ceremonial was imposing, that the incidental expenses were enormous, and that the people were very favourably impressed by the demeanour of their young sovereign. But the event did not produce any immediate effect on the administration. An Act of general oblivion for civil offences was published, and the Court edicts declared that there was rejoicing throughout the land.

Four months after the celebration of his marriage, the formal act of conferring upon Tungche the personal control of his dominions was performed. In a special decree issued from the Board of Rites, the Emperor said that he had received "the commands of their Majesties the Two Empresses to assume the superintendence of business." This edict was directed to the Foreign Ministers, who in return presented a collective request to be received in audience. Prince Kung was requested "to take his Imperial Majesty's orders with reference to their reception." The question being thus brought to a crucial point in which it would be impossible to shelve it until finally settled one way or the other, it was not unnatural that the Chinese Ministers should make the most vigorous resistance they could to those details which seemed to and did encroach upon the prerogative of the Emperor as he had been accustomed to exercise it. For, in the first place, they were no longer free agents, and Tungche had himself to be considered in any arrangement for the reception of foreign envoys. The discussion of the question assumed a controversial character, in which stress was laid on the one side upon the necessity of the kotow even in a modified form, while on the other it was pointed out that the least concession was as objectionable as the greatest, and that China would benefit by the complete settlement of the question. It says a great deal for the fairness and moderation of Prince Kung and the ministers with him, that, although they knew that the Foreign Governments were not prepared to make the Audience Question one of war, or even of the suspension of diplomatic relations, they determined to settle the matter in the way most distasteful to themselves and most agreeable to foreigners. On the 29th of June, 1873, Tungche therefore received in audience the ministers of the principal Powers at Pekin, and thus gave completeness to the many rights and concessions obtained from his father and grandfather by the treaties of Tientsin and Nankin. The privilege thus secured caused lively gratification in the minds of all foreign residents, to whom it signified the great

DEATH OF TSENG KWOFAN.   461

surrender of the inherent right to superiority claimed by the Chinese Emperors. The long minority of Tungche's successor kept the practical importance of this right in the background, but the privilege of personal audience with the Chinese Emperor is one of the most cherished by the Foreign Powers, and is fully asserted by them all once a year.

The sudden death of Tseng Kwofan in the summer of 1872 removed unquestionably the foremost public man in China. After the fall of Nankin, he had occupied the highest posts in the Empire, both at that city and in the metropolis. He was not merely powerful from his own position, but from his having placed his friends and dependents in many of the principal offices throughout the Empire. It was said that more than half the Viceroys and Governors of China were his nominees. At first prejudiced against foreigners, he had gradually brought himself to recognize that there was merit in their system, and that some advantage might be gathered from adopting their knowledge. But the change came at too late a period to admit of his conferring any distinct benefit on his country from the more liberal policy he felt disposed to pursue with regard to the training of Chinese youths in the science and learning of the West. It was said that he was a typical Chinaman, and that had he been personally ambitious he might even have succeeded in displacing the Tartar *régime*. Be that as it may, the thought never assumed any practical shape in his mind, and to the end of his days Tseng Kwofan was satisfied to remain the steadfast supporter and adherent of the Manchus. In this also, as in other ways, he was closely imitated by his former lieutenant, Li Hung Chang, who succeeded to some of his dignities and much of his power.

On the close of the Taeping campaigns, Tso Tsung Tang had been raised from the Viceroyalty of Chekiang and Fuhkien to that of Shensi and Kansuh. The promotion was of the more doubtful value, seeing that both those provinces were in the actual possession of the rebels; but Tso threw himself into the task with energy, and within two years of his arrival he was able to report that he had cleared the province of Shensi of all insurgents. He then devoted his attention to the pacification of Kansuh; and after many desultory engagements proceeded to lay siege to the town of Souchow, on the extreme west of that province, where the Mahomedans had massed their strength. At the end of the year 1872 the Imperial army was drawn up in front of this place, but Tso did not consider himself strong enough to deliver an attack, and confined his operations to preventing the introduction of supplies and fresh troops into the town. Even in this he was only partially successful, as a considerable body of men made their way in, in January, 1873. In the following month he succeeded in capturing, by a night attack, a temple outside the walls, upon which the Mahomedans placed considerable value. The siege continued during the whole of the summer, and it was not until the month of October that the garrison was reduced to such extremities as to consider the expediency of surrender. When they yielded at last, it was said that the only supplies left in the place were some "seventy horses." The chiefs were hacked to pieces, and about four thousand men perished by the sword. The women, children, and old men were spared, and the spoil of the place was handed over to the soldiery. It was Tso's distinctive merit that, far from being carried away by these successes, he neglected no military precaution, and devoted his main efforts to the reorganization of the province. In that operation he may be left employed for the brief remainder of Tungche's reign. In 1874 it may be mentioned, however, that the campaign against Kashgaria had been fully decided upon. The *Pekin Gazette* contains many references to warlike preparations. A thousand Manchu cavalry were sent specially to Souchow; sheep-skins, horses, and ammunition in large quantities were also despatched to the far west, and lastly, General Kinshun, the Manchu general, was entrusted with the command of the army in the field.

The year 1874 witnessed more than one event in the foreign relations of China that claims notice. There never had been much good-will between China and her neighbours in Japan. The latter are too independent in their bearing to please the advocates of Chinese predominance, at the same time that their insular position has left them safe from the attack of the Pekin Government. Once the attempt had been made to subdue these islanders, but the result as described in the reign of the Mongol Kublai had been too discouraging to invite repetition. In Corea the pretensions of the ruler of Yeddo had been repelled, and for a time crushed; but wherever the sea intervened the advantage rested more or less decisively with him. The island of Formosa was dependent upon China, and the western districts were governed by officials duly appointed by the Viceroy of Fuhkien. But the eastern half of the island, separated from the cultivated districts by a range of mountains covered with dense if not impenetrable forests, is held by tribes who own no one's authority, and who act as they deem fit. In the year 1868 or 1869 a junk from Loochoo was wrecked on this coast, and the crew were murdered by the islanders. The civil war in Japan prevented any prompt claim for reparation, but in 1873 the affair was revived, and a demand made at Pekin for compensation. The demand was refused, whereupon the Japanese, taking the law into their own hands, sent an expedition to Formosa. China replied with a counter-demonstration, and war seemed inevitable. In this crisis Mr. Wade offered his good services in the interests of peace, and after considerable controversy he succeeded in bringing the disputants to reason, and in inducing them to agree to as equitable terms as could be obtained without having recourse to arms. The Chinese paid an indemnity, and the Japanese evacuated the island. Thanks to Mr. Wade's tact and timely intervention, a war that would have injured both parties and benefited nobody was for that occasion happily averted.

Although the development of foreign relations was proving more rapid and satisfactory than even hope had dared to anticipate, there were, of course, incidents every year that aroused apprehension for the moment, and that gave some reason to believe that an outbreak against the Fanquai might occur at any time if popular fanaticism were only aroused. None of these attained the same dimensions as the Tientsin massacre, although more than one missionary was murdered in the interior, and in more than one treaty-port the anger of the mob or the apathy of the officials entailed loss and danger to foreigners. From an early time the Canton river had been famed as the scene of piratical outrages, and one of the principal clauses of the Tientsin Treaty had bound the Chinese to take steps to put them down. A few gun-boats were purchased, entrusted to English and American commanders, and placed at the disposal of the Customs authorities. The new arrangements were known to have not produced perfect safety. The Bogue and the channels of the lower river were frequently the scene of attacks by water-thieves, but as Chinese subjects alone suffered, it was held to be a matter for the mandarins, and not for the consuls. Yet it was well known that the pirates would not be restrained by fear of their authorities from attacking the ships and persons of Europeans.

Those who live in the constant presence of danger acquire the habit of indifference, and long impunity encouraged the foreign residents at Canton to overlook the peril that attended their frequent journeys from that place to Hongkong or Macao. It so happened, however, that an English passenger had the misfortune to embark on board the ill-fated river steamer named the *Spark*, when she quitted Whampoa on her usual weekly journey to Macao, in the month of August, 1874. A number of pirates had taken passage on board her, while another band had obtained a junk to intercept her in her course and carry off the booty. At a convenient spot the pirates began the attack. The few officers were overpowered. The one English passenger, Mr. Walter Mundy, was seriously wounded and left for dead upon the deck. His assailants escaped, and, while some were captured and punished at a later period, the direct responsibility of the Chinese Government for having neglected to put down piracy in accordance with treaty obligation was never established. Mr. Mundy's prospects were destroyed, and he returned to England with blighted hopes and an enfeebled constitution. But Lord Derby declined to press his claim for compensation on the attention of the Pekin Government, and the Chinese were allowed to assume that the provisions against piracy could be enforced at their own will and convenience.

In all countries governed by an absolute sovereign it is as

interesting as it is difficult to obtain certain knowledge as to the real character of the autocrat. A most important change had been effected in the government of China, yet it is impossible to discover what its precise significance was, or to say how far it influenced the fortunes of the country. The Empresses had retired into private life. Prince Kung was only the minister of a young prince who had it in his power to guide affairs exactly as he might feel personally disposed. Prince Kung might be either the real governor of the state or only the courtier of his nephew. It depended solely on that prince's character. There were not wanting signs that Tungche had the consciousness, if not the capacity, of supreme power, and that he wished his will to be paramount. It is permissible to detect in his desire to get outside the palace, even in the night-time, the indication of a resolve to see things for himself, and to discover what was being done in the outside world. Such evidence as was obtainable agreed in stating that he was impatient of restraint, and that the prudent reflections of his uncle were not overmuch to his fancy. On the 10th of September the young ruler took the world into his confidence by announcing in a Vermilion Edict that he degraded Prince Kung and his son in their hereditary rank and as princes of the Empire for using "language in very many respects unbecoming." Whether Tungche took this very decided step in a moment of pique or because he perceived that there was a plan among his chief relatives to keep him in leading-strings, must remain a matter of opinion. At the least he must have refused to personally retract what he had done, for on the very following day (September 11th) a Decree appeared from the Two Empresses reinstating Prince Kung and his son in their hereditary rank and dignity. These ladies thus asserted a right of control over the Emperor's actions.

Not long after this disturbance in the interior of the palace, of which only the ripple reached the surface of publicity, there were rumours that the Emperor's health was in a precarious state, and in the month of December it was said that Tungche was seriously ill with an attack of a malignant nature. The disease seemed to be making satisfactory progress, for the doctors were rewarded; but on the 18th of December an edict appeared ordering or requesting the Empresses Dowager to assume the personal charge of the administration. Six days later another edict appeared which strengthened the impression that the Emperor was making good progress towards recovery. But appearances were deceptive, for, after several weeks' uncertainty, it became known that the Emperor's death was inevitable. On the 12th of January, 1875, Tungche "ascended upon the Dragon, to be a guest on high," without leaving any offspring to succeed him. There were rumours that his illness was only a plausible excuse, and that he was really the victim of foul play; but it is not likely that the truth on that point will ever be revealed, although time has strengthened the original doubts. Whether he was the victim of an intrigue similar to that which had marked his acession to power, or whether he only died from the neglect or incompetence of his medical attendants, the consequences were certainly favourable to the personal views of the two Empresses and Prince Kung. They resumed the exercise of that supreme authority which they had resigned little more than twelve months.

The most suspicious circumstance in connection with this event was the treatment of the young Empress Ahluta, who, it was well known, was pregnant at the time of her husband's death. Instead of waiting to decide as to the succession until it was seen whether Tungche's posthumous child would prove to be a son or a daughter, the Dowager Empresses hastened to make another selection and to place the young widow of the deceased sovereign in a state of honourable confinement. Their motive was plain. Had Ahluta's child happened to be a son, he would have been the legal Emperor, as well as the heir by direct descent, and she herself could not have been excluded from a prominent share in the Government. To the Dowager Empresses one child on the throne mattered no more than another; but it was a question of the first importance that Ahluta should be set on one side, ignored and forgotten. In such an atmosphere there is often grievous peril to the lives of inconvenient personages. Ahluta sickened and died. Her child was never born. The charitable gave her credit for having refused food through grief for her husband, Tungche. The sceptical listened to the details of her illness with scorn for the vain efforts to obscure the dark deeds of ambition.

In their extreme anxiety to realize their own designs and at the same time not to injure the constitution, the two Empresses had been obliged to resort to a plan that would only have been suggested by a desperate ambition. For the first time since the Manchu dynasty had been placed upon the throne, it was necessary to depart from the due line of succession, and to make the election of the sovereign a matter of individual fancy or favour instead of one of inheritance. The range of choice was limited; for the son of Prince Kung himself, who seemed to enjoy the prior right to the throne, was a young man of sufficient age to govern for himself; and moreover his promotion would have meant the compulsory retirement from public life of Prince Kung, for it is not proper in China for a father to serve under his son. The name of Prince Kung's son, if mentioned at all, was only brought forward to be dismissed. The choice of the Empresses fell upon Tsai Tien, the son of Prince Chun or the Seventh Prince, who on the 13th of January was proclaimed Emperor. Tungche died in the evening, and a family council was hurriedly assembled, and held in an adjoining chamber during the night. Tsai Tien was hastily sent for, "cross and sleepy as he was," and done homage to by his uncles. As he was of too tender an age (born 15th of August, 1871) to rule for himself, his nomination served the purposes of the two Empresses and their ally Prince Kung, who thus entered upon a second lease of undisputed power. The only notice taken of the possibility that Tungche might yet be provided with a son was that he should be proclaimed the next heir-apparent. Prince Chun retired from public life ostensibly on the ground of ill-health, and his son ascended the throne under the style of Kwangsu, or Illustrious Succession.

CHAPTER XIX.

THE REGENCY.

KWANGSU'S installation had been followed by a conflict of authority between the two Empresses and the Palace eunuchs. The latter appear to have come to the front during the brief reign of Tungche, but Tse An's vigorous measures soon shattered their power and destroyed their growing confidence.

The new ruler had scarcely been placed in the seat of power when a great catastrophe occurred in reference to the foreign relations of China. For the moment it threw every other matter into the shade, and seemed to render the outbreak of war between England and China a matter of almost complete certainty. In the year 1874 the Government of India, repenting of its brief infatuation for the Panthay cause, yet still reluctant to lose the advantages it had promised itself from the opening of Yunnan to trade, resolved upon sending a formal mission of explory under Colonel Horace Browne, an Anglo-Indian officer of distinction, through Burmah to that province. The difficulties in the way of the undertaking were comparatively few, as the King of Burmah was then friendly and seemed disposed at that time to accept his natural position as a dependent of Calcutta. The Pekin authorities, if not enthusiastic on the subject of frontier trade, were still outwardly not opposed to the journey; and if opposition were to be encountered anywhere, it would obviously be on the part of the local officials, which could only be ascertained by making the experiment.

It was thought desirable, with the view of preparing the officials and the public generally for the appearance of this foreign mission, as well as to better ensure the success of the undertaking, that a representative of the English embassy at Pekin, having a knowledge of the language and of the ceremonial etiquette of the country, should be deputed to proceed across China and meet Colonel Browne on the Burmese frontier. The officer selected for this delicate and difficult mission was Mr. Raymond Augustus Margary, who to the singular aptitude he had displayed in the study of Chinese added a buoyant spirit and a vigorous frame that peculiarly fitted him for the long and lonely journey he had undertaken across China. His reception throughout was encouraging. The orders of the Tsungli Yamen, specially drawn up by the Grand Secretary Wansiang, were explicit, and not to be lightly ignored. Mr. Margary performed his journey in safety; and, on the 26th January, 1875, only one fortnight after Kwangsu's accession, he joined Colonel Browne at Bhamo. Apparently—or perhaps, more strictly speaking, to those who thought that the Chinese would object as little to the arrival as to the departure of foreigners—there seemed no further obstacle to be overcome. Mr. Margary's arrangements promised to ensure a safe and honourable reception for the mission from the Government of India.

A delay of more than three weeks ensued at Bhamo, which, if inevitable, cannot be characterized otherwise than as unfortunate. Time was given for the circulation of rumours as to the approach of a foreign invader along a disturbed frontier held by tribes almost independent, whose predatory instincts were excited by the prospect of rich plunder at the same time that their leaders urged them to oppose a change which threatened to destroy their hold on the caravan route between Bhamo and Talifoo. Had it only afforded the opportunity for the collection of these tribes, this delay would have been attended with danger; and when on the 17th of February Colonel Browne and his companions—Dr. Anderson, Mr. Fforde, Messrs. Allen and Margary, 15 Sikhs, and 150 Burmese soldiers—approached the limits of Burmese territory, they found themselves in face of a totally different state of affairs from what had existed when Mr. Margary passed safely across the frontier three weeks before. The preparations for opposing the English had been made under the direct encouragement, and probably the personal direction of Lisitai, a man who had been a brigand and then a rebel, but who at this time held a military command on the frontier, in which he afterwards, despite his unconcealed guilt, attained a still higher rank.

When Colonel Browne renewed his preparations to advance, he was met with rumours of the opposition that awaited him. At first these were discredited, but on the renewed statements that a large Chinese force had been collected to bar the way, it was determined that Mr. Margary should ride forward and ascertain what truth there was in these rumours. The first town on this route within the Chinese border is Momein, which, under the name of Tengyue, was once a military station of importance, and some distance east of it again is another town, called Manwein. Mr. Margary set out on the 19th of February, and it was arranged that only in the event of his finding everything satisfactory at Momein was he to proceed to the latter place; and on the first suspicious occurrence he was to retreat at once to the main body.

We may discern the sanguine hopes of the intrepid explorer who sees himself within reach of a long-expected goal, yet we cannot make any charge of foolhardiness, in the confident tones of the letter which Mr. Margary addressed to Colonel Browne from Momein, reporting that all was quiet at that place, and that there were no signs whatever of any meditated resistance. The letter was the last news ever received from Mr. Margary. On the 19th of February he started from Momein, and the information subsequently obtained left no doubt that he was treacherously murdered on that or the following day at Manwein. An ominous silence followed, and Colonel Browne's party delayed its advance until some definite news should arrive as to what had occurred in front, although the silence was sufficient to justify the worst apprehensions. Three days later the rumour spread that Mr. Margary and his attendants had been murdered. In order to furnish some means of proving its accuracy, it was also stated that a Chinese army was advancing to attack the small English expedition; and on the 22nd of February a large Chinese force did make its appearance on the neighbouring heights. There was no longer any room to doubt that the worst had happened, and it only remained to secure the safety of the expedition. The Chinese numbered several thousand men under Lisitai in person, while to oppose them there were only four Europeans and fifteen Sikhs. Yet superior weapons and steadfastness carried the day against greater numbers. The Sikhs fought as they retired, and the Chinese, unable to make any impression on them, abandoned an attack which was both useless and full of peril.

The news of this outrage did not reach Pekin until a month later, when Mr. Wade at once took the most energetic measures to obtain the amplest reparation in the power of the Pekin Government to concede. The first and most necessary point in order to ensure not merely the punishment of the guilty, but also that the people of China should not have cause to suppose that their rulers secretly sympathized with the authors of the attack, was that no punitive measures should be undertaken, or, if undertaken, recognized, until a special Commission of Inquiry had been appointed to investigate the circumstances on the spot. Mr. Margary was both an accredited officer of the British Government, and he was also travelling under the special permission and protection of the Tsungli Yamen. The Chinese Government could not expect to receive consideration if it failed to enforce respect for its own commands, and the English Government had an obligation which it could not shirk in exacting reparation for the murder of its representative. The treacherous killing of Mr. Margary was evidently not an occurrence for which it could be considered a sufficient atonement that some miserable criminals under sentence of death, or some desperate individuals anxious to secure the worldly prosperity of their families, should undergo painful torture and public execution in order to shield official falseness and infamy.

Although no one ever suspected the Pekin Government of having directly instigated the outrage, the delays in instituting an impartial and searching inquiry into the affair strengthened an impression that it felt reluctant to inflict punishment on those who had committed the act of violence. Very probably this arose as much from the fear of stirring up the embers of discord among an unsettled people as from sympathy with the deed; but it certainly produced a feeling among the foreign community, partly of apprehension and partly of indignation, which did not augur well for harmonious relations, and which certainly increased the importance of the Yunnan affair. Nearly three months elapsed before any step was taken towards appointing a Chinese official to proceed to the scene of the outrage in company with the officers named by the English minister; but on the 19th of June an edict appeared in the *Pekin Gazette* ordering Li Han Chang, Governor-General of Houkwang, *i.e.* Hoonan and Hoopeh, to temporarily vacate his post, and "repair with all speed to Yunnan to investigate and deal with certain matters." Even then the matter dragged along but slowly. Li Han Chang, who, as the brother of Li Hung Chang, was an exceptionally well-qualified and highly-placed official for the task, and whose appointment was in itself some guarantee of sincerity, did not leave Hankow until August, and the English Commissioners, Messrs. Grosvenor, Davenport, and Colborne Baber, did not set out from the same place before the commencement of October. The intervening months had been employed by Mr. Wade in delicate and fluctuating negotiations with Li Hung Chang at Tientsin and with the Tsungli Yamen at Pekin. The end of the year was reached before the Commission to ascertain the fate of poor Mr. Margary had begun its active work on the spot.

The result was unexpectedly disappointing. The mandarins supported one another. The responsibility was thrown on several minor officials, and on the border-tribes or savages. Several of the latter were seized, and their lives were offered as atonement for an offence they had not committed. The furthest act of concession which the Chinese Commissioner gave was to temporarily suspend Tsen Yuying the Futai for remissness; but even this measure was never enforced with rigour. The English officers soon found that it was impossible to obtain any proper reparation on the spot, and the evidence acquired even as to the details of the murder was singularly meagre and conflicting. Sir Thomas Wade, who had received the well-earned honour of the Bath, refused to accept the lives of the men offered, whose complicity in the offence was known to be none at all, while its real instigators escaped without any punishment.

The new year, 1876, only opened, therefore, to reveal that the question was still unsettled, and that the solution which could not be discovered on the spot would have to be provided at the capital. Sir Thomas Wade again insisted in the most emphatic language that the Chinese would have to conform with the spirit and letter of their engagements, and that unless they proffered the full redress demanded for Mr. Margary's murder it would be impossible to continue diplomatic relations. To show that this was no meaningless expression, Sir Thomas Wade left Pekin, while a strong reinforcement of the English fleet demonstrated the resolve of the Government. In consequence of these steps, Li Hung Chang was, in August, 1876, or more than eighteen months after the outrage, entrusted with full powers for the arrangement of the difficulty ; and the small seaport of Chefoo was fixed upon as the scene for the forthcoming negotiations. Even then the Chinese sought to secure a sentimental advantage by requesting that Sir Thomas Wade would change the place of treaty to Tientsin, or at least consent to pay Li Hung Chang a visit there. This final effort to conceal the fact that the English demanded as an equal and not as a suppliant having been baffled, there was no further attempt at delay. The Chefoo Convention was signed, and signed in that town, to which the Viceroy proceeded from Tientsin. Li Hung Chang entertained the Foreign Ministers at a great banquet ; and the final arrangements were hurried forward for the departure of the Chinese Ambassador whose despatch had been decided upon in the previous year.

The most important passage in the Chefoo Convention was unquestionably that commanding the different viceroys and governors to respect, and afford every protection to, all foreigners provided with the necessary passport from the Tsungli Yamen, and warning them that they would be held responsible in the event of any of these travellers meeting with injury or maltreatment.

The next most important passage was that arranging for the despatch of an Embassy to London bearing a letter of regret for the murder of the English official. The official selected for this duty was Kwo Sungtao, a mandarin of high rank, long experience, and unexceptionable character. The letter was submitted to Sir Thomas Wade in order that its terms should be exactly in accordance with Chinese etiquette, and that no phrase should be used showing that the Chinese Government attached less importance to the mission than the occasion demanded. The Embassy, with Sir Halliday Macartney attached as secretary and interpreter, proceeded to Europe, and, whatever may be thought of its immediate effect, it must be allowed that it established a precedent of friendly intercourse with this country, which promises to prove an additional guarantee of peace.*

While the Yunnan complication was passing through these different phases, the capital had been almost as much exercised at the funeral obsequies of the late Emperor Tungche as at the possible outbreak of a foreign war. The young Empress Ahluta had died in March, but not until the month of October were all the arrangements completed for the removal of their bodies from their temporary resting-place in the Palace grounds to the permanent mausoleum among the members of the reigning family. Some attempt seems to have been made to induce the Two Empresses to abstain from accompanying the funeral party, but the champion of propriety met with a distinct rebuff. The State procession of mourners left the Palace on the 16th of October, and on the evening of the 25th the Court had returned to Pekin. In the attendant ceremonies the young Emperor, despite his tender age, took the most prominent part; and the whole event, as recorded in the pages of the *Pekin*

* One of the remaining clauses referred to the lekin or transit duties, but as the arrangement is practically inoperative it need not be detailed. Another stipulated for an English mission through Tibet, but this also was never carried out. Perhaps the most significant circumstance of all was that the Chefoo Convention was never ratified, and therefore, strictly speaking, all its unfulfilled clauses have lost their validity.

Gazette, is well worth attentive perusal as throwing light on the ways of a Court indisposed to admit the prying glances of inquisitive foreigners.

The Chinese are naturally inveterate gamblers, and in the gratification of their inclination they resort to the most puerile forms. Although the Board of Censors feels bound periodically to take notice of this national weakness whenever any catastrophe results from it, and to insist on the necessity of the Government adopting measures to put down the practice, the Chinese continued to indulge their favourite passion without fear of their rulers. No change took place in the ways of the people, and the action of the executive was not merely lax, but tolerant of the principal form of amusement prevalent among the masses. It is impossible to say how long this might have gone on, when the attention of the Pekin Government was attracted twenty-five years ago to this subject by a novel form of gambling, which not merely attained enormous dimensions, but which threatened to bring the system of public examination into disrepute. This latter fact created a profound impression at Pekin, and roused the mandarins to take unusually prompt measures.

Canton was the head-quarters of the gambling confederacy which established the lotteries known as the Weising, but its ramifications extended throughout the whole of the province of Kwantung. The Weising, or Examination sweepstakes, were based on the principle of drawing the names of the successful candidates at the official examinations. They appealed, therefore, to every poor villager, and every father of a family, as well as to the aspirants themselves. The subscribers to the Weising lists were numbered by hundreds of thousands. It became a matter of almost as much importance to draw a successful number or name in the lottery as to take the degree. The practice could not have been allowed to go on without introducing serious abuses into the system of public examination. The profits to the owners of the lottery were so enormous that they were able to pay not less than eight hundred thousand dollars as hush-money to the Viceroy and the other high officials of Canton. In order to shield his own participation in the profits, the Viceroy declared that he devoted this new source of revenue to the completion of the river defences of Canton.

The attention of the Pekin authorities had been directed to this matter in 1874, when the whole system was declared illegal, and severe penalties were passed against those aiding, or participating in any way in, the Weising company. The local officers did not enforce with any stringency these new laws, and the Weising fraternity enjoyed a further but brief period of increased activity under a different name. The fraud was soon detected, and in an Edict of 11th August, 1875, it was very rightly laid down that "the maintenance of the purity of Government demands that it be not allowed under any pretext to be re-established." But the most emphatic evidence of the anxiety of the Government to put down the evil was afforded by the disgrace and recall of the Viceroy Yinghan and several of the highest officials in Canton. By a subsequent Edict of 13th September in the same year they were all stripped of their official rank. In the following years more stringent Acts were passed against gambling of all kinds; but although they failed to eradicate the passions of the lower and idler orders in the great city of the south, they certainly availed to prevent the resuscitation in any form of the great popular fraud and imposition known as the Weising lotteries.

No Chinese official had attracted the same cordial sympathy among Englishmen as the Grand Secretary Wansiang. A Manchu of the most honourable Banner, he added to the uprightness and vigour of the Tartar all the polish and refinement of the Chinaman; while he possessed a naturally genial temper, which was still more agreeable and rare. Latterly, although hardly to be considered as oppressed by the weight of years, his health had been bad. In 1874 he had to petition the Throne for leave to retire from active work; and during the whole of the following year it was evident to his friends that he was not in a fit state to perform his onerous duties. He lingered on until May, 1876, when his death was recorded in a decree, summing up his virtues and services in language upon which it would be difficult to improve. He was described as a man "who shone by the purity and integrity of his character, no less than by the sedulous devotion of his intellect to the interests of the State. Loyal and stainless, far-seeing and straightforward, he was at once thorough in the earnestness that actuated his conduct, and inspired by sentiments of unselfish wisdom." In him Prince Kung lost a staunch ally and colleague, while the Foreign Ministers felt that they were deprived of a Chinese statesman with whom it was possible to transact business harmoniously and with despatch.

Great as had been the suffering from civil wars, there yet remained for China still greater suffering from the visitation of famine; and the year 1876 witnessed the commencement of a dearth in the two great provinces of Honan and Shansi which has probably never been surpassed as the cause of a vast amount of human suffering. Although the provinces named suffered the most from the prevalent drought, the suffering was general over the whole of Northern China, from Shantung and Pechihli to Honan, and the course of the Yellow River. At first the Government, if not apathetic, was disposed to say that the evil would be met by the grant of the usual allowance made by the Provincial Governors in the event of distress; but, when one province after another was absorbed within the famine area, it became no longer possible to treat the matter as one of such limited importance, and the high ministers felt obliged to bestir themselves in face of so grave a danger. Li Hung Chang, in particular, was most energetic, not merely in collecting and forwarding supplies of rice and grain, but also in inviting contributions of money from all those parts of the Empire which had not been affected by famine. Allowing for the general sluggishness of popular opinion in China, and for the absence of any great amount of currency, it must be allowed that these appeals met with a large and liberal response. The foreign residents also contributed their share, and even the charity of London found a vent in sending some thousands of pounds to the scene of the famine in Northern China. This evidence of foreign sympathy in the cause of a common humanity made more than a passing impression on the mind of the Chinese people, and in many parts of the country a distinct improvement in tone towards foreigners might be traced to this cause.

While the origin of the famine may be attributed to either the effects of drought or civil war, there is no doubt that its extension and the apparent inability of the authorities to grapple with it may be traced to the want of means of communication, which rendered it almost impossible to convey the needful succour into the famine districts. The evil ensuing from this want being so obvious, the hope was indulged that the Chinese would be disposed to take a step forward on their own initiative in the great and needed work by the introduction of railways and other mechanical appliances. This expectation was based upon a certain amount of fact, for, not without objection and delay, the Viceroy of the Two Kiang had given his assent to the construction of a short line between Shanghai and the port of Woosung. The great difficulty had always been to make a start; and now that a satisfactory commencement had been made, the foreigners were disposed in their eagerness to overlook all obstacles, and to imagine the Flowery Land traversed in all directions by the lines of their construction. The officials were still reluctant to admit that the inevitable hour had come for surrendering their roads to the contractors of Europe and America. Still the Woosung-Shanghai Railway became, at least in part, an accomplished fact. In the summer of 1876 half of it was finished and open for use, and during some weeks the excitement among the Chinese themselves was not less marked than their manifestations of approval.

The hopes based upon this satisfactory event were destined to be soon dispelled by the expression of animosity on the part of the officials. The Mandarins, determined to carry their object, announced their intention to resort to every means in their power to prevent the realization of the undertaking. The situation revealed such dangers of mob violence, that on the 24th of August Sir Thomas Wade felt compelled to request the Company to discontinue its operations, and the subject of the future of this little line became a matter of high diplomacy, carried on partly in the capital and partly at Nankin. It will be sufficient to summarize here the result. After some discussion, it was arranged that the Chinese should buy the line, and that after a stipulated period it should be placed under Chinese management. When that period had run out, the Chinese, instead of devoting themselves to the interests of the railway, and to the extension of its powers of utility, wilfully and persistently neglected it, with the express design of destroying it. At this juncture the Viceroy consented to allow the Governor of Fuhkien to remove the rails and plant to Formosa, where he was engaged in imparting some vigour to the Government. The fate of the Woosung railway destroyed the hopes created by its construction, and postponed to a later day the great event of the introduction of railways into China.

Notwithstanding such disappointments as this, and the ever-present difficulty of conducting relations with an unsympathetic people controlled by suspicious officials, there was yet observable a marked improvement in the relations of the different nations with the Chinese. Increased facilities of trade, such as the opening of new ports, far from extending the area of danger, served to promote mutual good-will and understanding. In 1876 a port—the capital Kiungchow—in the island of Hainan was made a treaty port, or rather the fact of its having been included in the treaty of Tientsin was practically accepted and recognized. In the following year four new ports were added to the list. One, Pakhoi, was intended to increase trade intercourse with Southern China. Two of the three others, Ichang and Wuhu, were selected as being favourably situated for commerce on the Yangtse and its affluents, while Wenchow was chosen for the benefit of the trade on the coast. Mr. Colborne Baber, who had taken part in the Yunnan commission, was despatched to Szchuen, to take up his residence at Chungking for the purpose of facilitating trade with that great province. The successful tour of Captain Gill, not merely through South-West China into Burmah, but among some of the wilder and more remote districts of Northern Szchuen, afforded reason to believe that henceforth travelling would be safer in China, and nothing that has since happened is calculated to weaken that impression.

The Chinese character is marked by a strange mixture of superstition and of the greatest scepticism. The former sentiment has sometimes led to the success of political impostors, who have flourished on the credulity of the people, and has rendered them more amenable to the influence of panic, of which all nations are on occasion susceptible. But perhaps the most extraordinary instance of that popular excitement which renders men capable of committing the greatest folly was afforded in the year 1876, on the occasion of what was known as the "Paper Man" mania. The province of Kiangsu was the principal scene of the disorders which followed from this agitation, but the movement extended into the neighbouring provinces. The exact meaning of this movement could never be fathomed. It was more grotesque than terrible. It was said that paper men were employed to go about the country cutting off the tails or queues of the people, and that those who lost their tails would certainly die within a short period. The whole affair deserves to be remembered only for its absurdity, but the terror it produced among the ignorant people was intense, and might have entailed serious consequences. The officials behaved with good sense, and after several months of feverish excitement the mania gradually calmed down, and the public mind regained its feeling of tranquillity.

When Kwangsu ascended the throne the preparations for the campaign against Kashgaria were far advanced towards completion, and Kinshun had struck the first of those blows which were to ensure the overthrow of the Tungani and of Yakoob Beg. The fall of Souchow had distinguished the closing weeks of the year 1873, and in 1874 Kinshun had begun, under the direction of Tso Tsung Tang, his march across the desert to the west. He appears to have followed a circuitous route, with the view of avoiding the strongly placed and garrisoned town of Hami. The exact route is not certain, but he seems to have gone as far north even as Uliassutai, where he was able to recruit some of the most faithful and warlike of the Mongol tribes. But early in 1875

THE CHINESE ADVANCE.   481

he arrived before the walls of Barkul, a town lying to the north-west of Hami. No resistance is stated to have been offered, and a few weeks later Hami shared the same fate, and admitted a Celestial garrison. The Tungani had retreated on the approach of the Chinese, and their main forces were assembled for the defence of the two towns of Urumtsi and Manas, which are situated on the northern side of the eastern spurs of the Tian Shan. Once Barkul and Hami were in the possession of the Chinese, it became necessary to reopen direct communications with Souchow. This task occupied the whole of the next twelve months, and was only successfully accomplished after many difficulties had been overcome, and when halting-stations had been established across Gobi. There is nothing improbable in the statement that during this period the Chinese planted and reaped the seed which enabled them, or those who followed in their train, to march in the following season.

With the year 1876 the really arduous portion of the campaign commenced. The natural difficulties to the commencement of the war from distance and desert had been all overcome. An army of about twenty-five thousand effective troops, besides a considerable number of Mongol and other tribal levies, had been placed in the field and within striking distance of the rebels. The enemies were face to face. The Tungani could retreat no further. Neither from Russia nor from Yakoob Beg could they expect a place of refuge. Both their numbers and the proximity of the Chinese rendered the adoption of any such course at the last extremity of doubtful wisdom and practicability. The Athalik Ghazi might help them to hold their own; he certainly would not welcome them within the limits of the six cities. The Tungani had, therefore, no alternative left save to make as resolute a stand as they could against those Celestials who had returned to revindicate their authority and to revenge their fellow-countrymen who had been slaughtered in their thousands twelve years before.

The town of Urumtsi, situated within a loop of the mountains, lies at a distance by road of more than 300 miles from Barkul. Kinshun, who had now been joined by Liu

Kintang, the taotai of the Sining district and a man of proved energy and capacity, resolved to concentrate all his efforts on its capture. He moved forward his army to Guchen, where he established a fortified camp and a powder-factory, and took steps to ascertain the strength and intentions of the enemy. Towards the end of July the Chinese army resumed its march. The difficulties of the country and in the collection of supplies were so great that the advanced guards of the opposing armies did not come into contact until the 10th of August. The Chinese general seems to have attempted on that date a night surprise; but although he gained some success in the encounter which ensued, the result must have been doubtful, seeing that he felt obliged to call off his men from the attack. It was only, however, to collect his forces for the delivery of a decisive blow. On the 13th of August a second battle was fought with a result favourable to the Chinese. Two days later the enemy, who held a fortified camp at Gumti, were bombarded out of it by the heavy artillery brought from the coasts of China for the purposes of the war, and after twenty-four hours' firing three breaches were declared to be practicable. The place was carried by storm at the close of four hours' fighting and slaughter, during which 6000 were stated to have been killed. Kinshun followed up his victory by a rapid march on Urumtsi. That place surrendered without a blow, and many hundred fugitives were cut down by the unsparing Manchu cavalry, which pursued them along the road to Manas, their last place of shelter.

As soon as the necessary measures had been taken for the military protection of Urumtsi, the Chinese army proceeded against Manas. Their activity, which was facilitated by the favourable season of the year, was also increased by the rumoured approach of Yakoob Beg with a large army to the assistance of the Tungani. At Manas the survivors of the Tungan movement proper had collected for final resistance, and all that desperation could suggest for holding the place had been done. The garrison were possibly cheered by the recollection that in February of the same year they had repulsed, with loss to their assailants, an ill-directed attempt to seize the town made by a body of Chinese troops from Chuguchak. They had now to deal with a more wary as well as a more energetic and better prepared antagonist. Kinshun appeared before Manas on the 2nd of September. On the 7th his batteries were completed, and he began a heavy fire upon the north-east angle of the wall. A breach of fourteen feet having been made, the order to assault was given, but the stormers were repulsed with the loss of 100 killed. The operations of the siege were renewed with great spirit on both sides. Several assaults were subsequently delivered; but although the Chinese always gained some advantage at the beginning, they never succeeded in retaining it. In one of these later attacks they admitted a loss of 200 killed alone. The Imperial army enjoyed the undisputed superiority in artillery, and the gaps in its ranks were more than filled by the constant flow of reinforcements from the rear.

The siege gradually assumed a less active character. The Chinese dug trenches and erected earthworks. They approached the walls by means of galleries in readiness to deliver the attack on any symptom of discouragement among the besieged. On the 16th of October a mine was sprung under the wall, making a wide breach; but although the best portion of the Chinese army made two assaults on separate occasions, they were both repulsed with loss. Twelve days later another mine was sprung, destroying a large portion of the wall; but when the Chinese stormers endeavoured to carry the remaining works, they were again driven back with heavy loss, including two generals killed in the breach. Although thus far repulsed, the Imperialists had inflicted very heavy losses on the besieged, who, seeing that the end of their resources was at hand, that there was no hope of succour, and that the besiegers were as energetic as ever, had at last arrived at the conclusion that they had no choice left save to surrender on the best terms they could obtain. On the 4th of November, after a two months' siege, Haiyen, as the Chinese named the Mahomedan leader, came out and offered to yield the town. His offer seems to have been partly accepted, and on the 6th of the month the survivors of the brave garrison, to the number of between two and three thousand men, sallied forth from the west gate. It was noticed as a ground of suspicion that all the men carried their weapons, and that they had placed their old men, women, and children in the centre of their phalanx, as if they contemplated rather a sortie than a tame and unresisting surrender.

The Chinese commanders were not indisposed to deal with the least suspicious circumstances as if they meant certain treachery. The Imperialists gradually gathered round the garrison. The Mahomedans made one bold effort to cut their way through. They failed in the attempt, and were practically annihilated on the ground. Those men who were taken by the cavalry were at once beheaded, whether in the city or among those who had gone forth, but the aged, the women and the children, were spared by Kinshun's express orders. All the leaders taken were tortured before execution as rebels, and even the bodies of the dead chiefs were exhumed in order that they might be subjected to indignity. The siege of Manas was interesting both for the stubbornness of the attack and defence, and also as marking the successful termination of the Chinese campaign against the Tungani. With its capture, those Mahomedans who might be said to be Chinese in ways and appearance ceased to possess any political importance. It would not be going much too far to say that they no longer existed. The movement of rebellion which began at Hochow in 1862 was thus repressed in 1876, after having involved during those fourteen years the north-western provinces of China, and much of the interior of Asia, in a struggle which for its bitter and sanguinary character has rarely been surpassed.

The successes of the Chinese gave their generals and army the confidence and prestige of victory, and the overthrow of the Tungani left them disengaged to deal with a more formidable antagonist. The siege of Manas had been vigorously prosecuted in order that the town might be taken before the army of Yakoob Beg should arrive. The Athalik Ghazi may have believed that Manas could hold out during the winter, for his movements in 1876 were leisurely, and betrayed a confidence that no decisive fighting would take place until the following spring. His hopes were shown to be delusive, but too late for practical remedy. Manas had fallen before he could move to its support. The Chinese had crushed the Tungani, and were in possession of the mountain passes. They were gathering their whole strength to fall upon him, and to drive him out of the state in which he had managed to set up a brief authority.

While the events recorded had been in progress Yakoob Beg had been ruling the state of Kashgaria with sufficient vigour and wisdom to attract the observation of his great neighbours the Governments of England and Russia. He had shown rare skill in adapting circumstances to suit his own ends. The people passively accepted the authority which he was prepared to assert with his Khokandian soldiery, and the independent state of Kashgaria might have continued to exist for a longer period had the Chinese not returned. But in 1875 the arrival of Kinshun at Barkul showed Yakoob Beg that he would have to defend his possessions against their lawful owners, while the overthrow of the Tungani and the capture of their strongholds in 1876 carried with them a melancholy foreboding of his own fate. The Athalik Ghazi made his preparations to take the field, but there was no certainty in his mind as to where he should make his stand or as to how he was to obtain the victory. With conflicting views in his brain he moved his army eastwards, establishing his camp first at Korla and then moving it on to Turfan, 900 miles distant from Kashgar.

The greatest efforts of this ruler only availed to place 15,000 men at the front, and the barrenness of the region compelled him to distribute them. The Ameer was at Turfan with 8500 men and twenty guns. His second son was at Toksoun, some miles in the rear, at the head of 6000 more and five guns. There were several smaller detachments between Korla and the front. Opposed to these was the main Chinese army under Kinshun at Urumtsi, while another force had been placed in the field at Hami by the energy of Tso, and entrusted to the direction of a general named Chang Yao. No fighting actually took place until the month of

March, 1877, and then the campaign began with a rapid advance by Chang Yao from Hami to Turfan. The Kashgarians were driven out of Pidjam, and compelled, after a battle, to evacuate Turfan. The Chinese records do not help us to unravel the events of the month of April. The campaign contained no more striking or important episodes, and yet the reports of the generals have been mislaid or consigned to oblivion. The Athalik Ghazi fought a second battle at Toksoun, where he rejoined his son's army, but with no better fortune. He was obliged to flee back to his former camp at Korla.

After the capture of Turfan the Chinese armies came to a halt. It was necessary to re-organize the vast territory which they had already recovered, and to do something to replenish their arsenals, and to restore commerce. During five months the Celestials stayed their further advance, while the cities were being re-peopled, and the roads rendered once more secure. Tso Tsung Tang would leave nothing to chance. He had accomplished two parts of the three, into which his commission might be naturally divided. He would make sure of his ground before attempting the third and the most difficult of all. And while the Chinese Viceroy had, for his own reasons, come to the very sensible conclusion to refresh his army after its arduous labours in the limited productive region situated between two deserts, the stars in their courses fought on his side.

Yakoob Beg had withdrawn only to Korla. He still cherished the futile scheme of defending the eastern limits of his dominion, but with his overthrow on the field of battle the magic power which he had exercised over his subjects had vanished. His camp became the scene of factious rivalry, and of plots to advance some individual pretension at the cost of the better interests, and even the security of the State. The exact details of the conspiracy will never be ascertained, partly from the remoteness of the scene, but also on account of the mention of persons of whom nothing was, or is ever likely to be, known. The single fact remains clear that Yakoob Beg died at Korla on the 1st of May, 1877, of fever according to one account, of poison administered by Hakim

Khan Torah according to another. Still the Chinese did not even then advance, and Yakoob's sons were left to contest with Hakim Khan Torah over the dismembered fragments of their father's realm.

A bitter and protracted civil war followed close upon the disappearance of the Athalik Ghazi. On the removal of his dead body for sepulture to Kashgar, his eldest son Kuli Beg murdered his younger brother over their father's bier. It was then that Hakim Khan came prominently forward as a rival to Kuli Beg, and that the Mahomedans, weak and numerically few as they were, divided themselves into two hostile parties. While the Chinese were recruiting their troops and repairing their losses, the enemy were exhausting themselves in vain and useless struggles. In June, 1877, Hakim Khan was signally defeated, and compelled to flee into Russian territory, whence on a later occasion he returned for a short time in a vain attempt to disturb the tranquillity of Chinese rule. When, therefore, the Chinese resumed their advance much of their work had been done for them. They had only to complete the overthrow of an enemy whom they had already vanquished, and who was now exhausted by his own disunion.

The Chinese army made no forward movement from Toksoun until the end of August, 1877. Liu Kintang, to whom the command of the advance had been given, did not leave until one month later; and when he arrayed his forces he found them to number about 15,000 men. It had been decided that the first advance should not be made in greater force, as the chief difficulty was to feed the army, not to defeat the enemy. The resistance encountered was very slight, and the country was found to be almost uninhabited. Both Karashar and Korla were occupied by a Chinese garrison, and the district around them was entrusted to the administration of a local chief. The information that the rebel force was stationed at the next town Kucha, which is as far beyond Korla as that place is from Toksoun, induced Liu Kintang to renew his march and to continue it still more rapidly. A battle was fought outside Kucha in which the Chinese were victorious, but not without stubborn resistance offered on more than one day. However, the Chinese success was complete, and with Kucha in their power they had simplified the process of attacking Kashgar itself. A further halt was made at this town to enable the men to recover from their fatigue, to allow fresh troops to come up, and measures to be taken for ensuring the security of communications with the places in their rear. At Kucha also the work of civil administration was entrusted to some of the local notables.

The deliberation of the Chinese movements, far from weakening their effect, invested their proceedings with the character of being irresistible. The advance was shortly resumed. Aksu, a once flourishing city within the limits of the old kingdom of Kashgar, surrendered at the end of October. Ush Turfan yielded a few days later. The Chinese had now got within striking distance of the capital of the state. They had only to provide the means of making the blow as fatal and decisive as possible. In December they seized Maralbashi, an important position on the Kashgar Darya, commanding the principal roads to both Yarkand and Kashgar. Yarkand was the principal object of attack. It surrendered without a blow on December 21st. A second Chinese army had been sent from Maralbashi to Kashgar, which was defended by a force of several thousand men. It had been besieged nine days, when Liu Kintang arrived with his troops from Yarkand. A battle ensued, in which the Mahomedans were vanquished, and the city with the citadel outside was captured. Several rebel leaders and some eleven hundred men were said to have been executed; but Kuli Beg escaped into Russian territory. The city of Kashgar was thus taken on the 26th of December, and one week later the town of Khoten, famous from a remote period for its jade ornaments, passed into the hands of the race who best appreciated their beauty and value.

The Chinese had thus brought to a triumphant conclusion the campaigns undertaken for the reassertion of their authority over the Mahomedan populations which had revolted. They had conquered in this war by the superiority of their weapons and their organization, and not by an overwhelming display

THE NEW DOMINION.   489

of numbers. Although large bodies of troops were stationed at many places, it does not seem that the army which seized the cities of Yarkand and Kashgar numbered more than twenty thousand men. Having vanquished their enemy in the field, the Celestials devoted all their attention to the reorganization of what was called the New Dominion. Their rule has been described by a Mussulman as being both very fair and very just.

Having conquered Eastern Turkestan, the Chinese next took steps for the recovery of Ili. Without the metropolitan province the undertaking of Tso Tsung Tang would lack completeness, while indeed many political and military dangers would attend the situation in Central Asia. But this was evidently a matter to be effected in the first place by negotiation, and not by violence and force of arms. Russia had always been a friendly and indeed a sympathetic neighbour. In this very matter of Ili, she had originally acted with the most considerate attention for China's rights, when it seemed that they had permanently lost all definite meaning. It was, therefore, by diplomatic representations on the part of the Tsungli Yamen to the Russian Minister at Pekin that the recovery of Ili was expected in the first place to be achieved. While Tso and his lieutenants were reorganizing the New Dominion and sending useless envoys to Tashkent, Prince Kung and the other grand secretaries were deciding on the course they ought to pursue. At about the same moment of time the Russian authorities at Tashkent came to the conclusion that the matter must rest with the Czar, and the Chinese official world perceived that they would have to depute a Minister Plenipotentiary to St. Petersburg.

The official selected for the difficult and, as it proved, dangerous task of negotiating at St. Petersburg, was that same Chung How who had been sent to Paris after the Tientsin massacre. He arrived at Pekin in August, 1878, and was received at several audiences by the Emperor while waiting for his full instructions from the Tsungli Yamen. He did not leave until October, about a month after the Marquis Tseng, son of Tseng Kwofan, set out from Pekin to take the place of Kwo Sungtao as Ambassador in London and Paris.

Chung How reached St. Petersburg in the early part of the following year, and the discussion of the various points in question, protracted by the constant removal of the Court to Livadia, occupied the whole of the summer months. At last it was announced that a treaty had been signed at Livadia, by which Russia surrendered the Kuldja valley, but retained that of the Tekes, which left in her hands the command of the passes through the Tian Shan range into Kashgar. There was never any good reason to suppose that the Chinese Government would accept as complete satisfaction the partial territorial concession obtained by Chung How. Chung How knew nothing about frontiers or military precautions, but he thought a great deal about money. He fought the question of an indemnity with ability, and got it fixed at five million roubles, or little more than half that at which it was placed by the later treaty.

The first greeting that met Chung How on his return told him what reception awaited him, at the same time that it revealed the sure fate of his treaty. He had committed the indiscretion of returning without waiting for the Edict authorizing his return, and as the consequence he had to accept suspension from all his offices, while his treaty was submitted to the tender mercies of the grand secretaries, the six presidents of boards, the nine chief ministers of state, and the members of the Hanlin. Three weeks later, Prince Chun was specially ordered to join the Committee of Deliberation. On the 27th of January, Chung How was formally cashiered and arrested, and handed over to the Board of Punishment for correction. The fate of the treaty itself was decided a fortnight later. Chung How was then declared to have "disobeyed his instructions and exceeded his powers." On the 3rd of March an Edict appeared, sentencing the unhappy envoy to "decapitation after incarceration."

At the same time that the Chinese resolved to refuse their ratification to Chung How's treaty, they expressed their desire for another pacific settlement, which would give them more complete satisfaction. The Marquis Tseng was accordingly instructed to take up the thread of negotiation, and to proceed to the Russian capital as Ambassador and Minister

Plenipotentiary. Some delay ensued, as it was held to be doubtful whether Russia would consent to the reopening of the question. But owing to the cautious and well-timed approaches of the Marquis Tseng, the St. Petersburg Foreign Office, propitiated by the voluntary pardon of Chung How at the special request of Queen Victoria, who telegraphed a request for mercy direct to the Empress Dowager, through Sir Thomas Wade, acquiesced in the recommencement of negotiations. After six months' discussion the Russian Government accepted the principle of the almost unqualified territorial concession for which the Chinese stood firm. On the 12th of February, 1881, these views were embodied in a treaty signed at St. Petersburg, and the ratification within six months showed how differently its provisions were regarded from those of its predecessor. With the Marquis Tseng's act of successful diplomacy the final result of the long war in Central Asia was achieved. The Chinese added Ili to Kashgar and the rest of the New Dominion, which at the end of 1880 was made into a High Commissionership and placed under the care of the dashing general Liu Kintang.

CHAPTER XX.

THE WAR BETWEEN FRANCE AND CHINA.

THE signature of the Treaty of St. Petersburg was the high-water mark of China's reputation in Europe. China, without any external support, without even looking for an ally, had resolutely faced a great Power, and insisted on the surrender to the very letter of her rights. She had stood firm, and Russia, of all Powers, had given way. The significance of such an incident might easily be, as we now know that it was, exaggerated. It did not mean that the strength of the Chinese Government was equal to a great war with the states of Europe, but that its diplomacy in Europe had been directed with such astuteness as to produce an impression of power that in reality had no existence. For this costless triumph China was indebted to the rare courage and skill of the Englishman who has been the true director of her diplomacy in the capitals of Europe since she made her appearance there, and whose portrait forms the frontispiece of this volume. I have said that Sir Halliday Macartney was the guide of her diplomacy, but it must not be supposed that he has had any part or share in the feeble policy favoured by the blind and weak-kneed rulers of China. Well would it have been for their unfortunate country if they had followed his advice, and stood firm at the right moment and given way when it was prudent and possible to abate with dignity antiquated and untenable pretensions. As they would not take advice they have had to suffer, and the twenty years of creditable effort and uniform success that culminated in the St. Petersburg Treaty have been followed by an equal period of discomfiture, defeat, and disaster, of which the termination is still far from being reached.

The Chinese very soon after the restitution by Russia of the province of Kuldja or Ili were brought into collision with France. The growth of French power in Indo-China had been predicted by that wise and apparently ill-appreciated English statesman in the East, Sir Stamford Raffles, long before the Emperor Napoleon planted the tricolour at the mouth of the Mekong. But thirty years went by without any important consequence ensuing from the occupation of Saigon, and the colony in Cochin China, that was to be the nucleus of the empire of which Dupleix dreamed, long wore a languid and depressed appearance. Yet thoughtful persons always saw in it the base of expansion in the future, and the remarkable explorations in Cambodia, Tonquin, and Yunnan of Garnier, Doudart de Lagrée, and Rocher afforded proof that French officers were not blind to the advantages of opening up that quarter of Asia. At a moment when the desire of the French nation to possess colonies threatens on so many scenes a return of the old rivalry between France and England, let the opinion be recorded that France is entitled to that fair field of expansion in Cambodia, Annam, and Tonquin which the events now to be described secured for her, and that in winning over to civilization and peace the millions dependent on the ancient dominion of Hué, she has undertaken a task that deserves our sympathy and admiration.

Great results seldom follow with rapidity the efforts of the explorers of unknown regions, and it was not until the first formation of a Colonial Party in Paris, under the auspices of the late M. Jules Ferry, that the French designs in Indo-China began to assume definite form. Towards the end of the year 1882 the French Government came to the decision to establish what it called a "definite protectorate" over Tonquin. Events had for some time been shaping themselves in this direction, and the colonial ambition of France naturally fixed itself on Indo-China as a promising field in which it might aggrandize itself with comparatively little risk and a wide margin of advantage. The weakness of Annam, which was displayed on many occasions during the history of the Chinese Empire, was never greater or more incontestably revealed than in the time of the youthful ruler Tuduc. It formed a strong, and in the result, an irresistible inducement to France to assert the protectorate which she had claimed in a vague and indefinite manner ever since the landing of a small naval force under Admiral de la Grandière at Hué had saved Tuduc's grandfather and averted a dynastic crisis. The reports of every explorer added to the attraction of the subject, and as the world began to attach increased importance to the opening out of the rich provinces of Yunnan and Szchuen, so did the value of the alleged route to this region by the Songcoi or Red river acquire more attractiveness in the eyes of the French authorities. These were the conditions that led to an extraordinary revival of French colonial activity, and the inexcusable apathy of England in her relations with both Burmah and Siam afforded an additional incentive to the French to act quickly. Their undertaking was in the first place given the modest character of an intention to render definite the proposed protectorate over Tonquin, and as the first step in the enterprise the occupation of the towns of Hanoi and Haiphong—the one the capital and the other the port of the Songcoi delta—was decided upon. The execution of this plan was attended with no difficulty, and before the end of the year 1882 a small French force was in occupation of these places and the conquest of Tonquin may be said to have commenced.

Among the neighbouring states of China, Tonquin, like the others, was ranked as a vassal of the Middle Kingdom. Many passages might be recalled from past history of China's interfering for the defence of Tonquin or for the settlement of internal domestic strife, and on some occasions Tonquin had been ruled as a Chinese province. The enforcement of the feudal tie was no doubt lax, and in the eyes of Europeans the rights of vassalage yielded to China by it and such states as Nepaul, Siam, and Burmah were too vague and meaningless to constitute a legal right or to command respect. Such as they were, they could only be made valid by an appeal to arms, and even in Chinese eyes many of them were not worth a struggle. Still, none the less the opinion was held at Pekin that the French seizure of Hanoi was an infraction of China's rights. At least such was the current report; but if so, they were careful not to show it, for the Chinese authorities took no steps to arrest the development of the French policy in Tonquin. That, indeed, could only have been done by proclaiming Tonquin a Chinese possession and by announcing the intention to defend it. If the Chinese had promptly taken this step at the moment that the diplomatic success at St. Petersburg was still fresh in all men's minds, there is no knowing but that France might have given way, and abandoned the enterprise.

But decision and the courage requisite to maintain strong resolutions were precisely the qualities in which the Chinese were lacking, and while Li Hung Chang and the other members of the Chinese Government were deliberating what course to pursue, the French were acting with great vigour in Tonquin and committing their military reputation to a task from which, once it was involved, their honour would not allow them to draw back. During the whole of the year 1883 they were engaged in military operations with the Black Flag irregulars, a force half piratical and half patriotic, who represented the national army of Tonquin. These men were not actually in the pay of the State. They fought, however, under regular chiefs, and were supplied with funds by public subscriptions. Their military training was very slight, but they were skilled in irregular warfare, the form of the country was in their favour, and they were as formidable on water as on land. Even when beaten they did not cease to be dangerous, and in the alternations of the struggle they often reappeared ready for the contest when they were thought to have been crushed.

The length and pertinacity of their resistance suggested the view that the Black Flags of Tonquin were paid and encouraged by the Chinese. Subsequent evidence established the fact that the Chinese did not take even an indirect part in the contest until a much later period. After the capture of Hanoi, the French were constantly engaged with the Black Flags, from whom they captured the important town of Sontay. The obstinacy of the defence suggested the idea that the place was held by Chinese Imperial troops, but after it was captured it was clearly seen that the statement was untrue. Up to that point the Chinese had carefully abstained from showing their hand, and indeed their councils were torn by conflicting views. While one faction was all in favour of asserting the extreme rights of China at every cost, another, and the more powerful in that it was led by Li Hung Chang, supported diplomatic measures, and dreaded the subjection of China's newly-acquired naval and military strength to the test of practical experience. Matters were in this state when the French arms experienced a severe reverse in the Tonquin delta.

The French fully believed that the conquest of Tonquin would be achieved without difficulty and without much cost. Even the Black Flags were regarded as little better than robbers, who, in the course of a little time, would all be shot down. The thought that they might be a formidable enemy never seems to have presented itself to any one. The French were entirely of this belief when a serious reverse obliged them to admit that the task was not so easy as they had imagined, and that it was not wholly free from risk. A considerable detachment under the command of Captain Henri Rivière, who was one of the most able and enterprising pioneers of French commerce and authority in the delta, was surprised near Hanoi. The French were defeated with considerable loss, Rivière himself was killed, and the fruits of previous success were lost. Under these circumstances it became necessary for France to make a great effort to retrieve the ground she had lost. The necessity for this was more clearly established when the French suffered a second reverse at Phukai. The Black Flags claimed this affair as a victory because the French were obliged to retreat. Under these circumstances it was inevitable that France should send out to the Far East troops and men-of-war to redeem the honour of her arms and attain the objects of her policy.

Up to this moment the operations of the French had been restricted to Tonquin, and the delta of the Songcoi. Having thoroughly coerced Tuduc, the young Emperor of Annam, the French felt secure against any diversion from that side,

ANNAM ANNEXED.

but very soon after the affairs at Sontay and Phukai this prince died, and the Annamese, encouraged perhaps by the occurrences in Tonquin and the delay in the arrival of reinforcements from Europe, openly proclaimed their hostility. It became necessary to extend the operations to Annam, and as the preliminary to a renewed attack on the Black Flags, Hué was occupied in August, 1883, a ruler of French proclivities was placed on the throne, and a French Resident installed. These conditions were set forth in a treaty which made Annam more clearly the tributary of France than it had ever been of China.

Some months elapsed before the French found themselves in sufficient force to resume operations in Tonquin, and it was not until December, 1883, that Admiral Courbet, to whom had been entrusted the command of the expedition, thought it would be safe to attack Sontay, which the Black Flags had reoccupied after the death of Henri Rivière and strongly fortified. Admiral Courbet attacked this place on the 11th December, and after a desperate resistance succeeded in driving out the Black Flags. The French suffered considerably, but they were to some extent recompensed by a very large quantity of spoil, including a considerable sum of money. Even after the fall of Sontay, the Black Flags did not disperse, and they engaged the French in repeated skirmishes. They took up a fresh position at Bacninh, which rumour declared they were making more formidable than Sontay, and owing to the slow progress made by the French force Admiral Courbet was superseded in the command by General Millot.

A new commander has always to justify his appointment, and General Millot determined to signalize his command with an attack on Bacninh. For this purpose he disposed of the very considerable force of 12,000 men, but General Millot was prudent as well as brave, and when he reconnoitred the strong position held by the Black Flags he declined to risk a front attack. He decided on threatening the rear and line of retreat of the enemy, well knowing that few or no Asiatics will stand under such circumstances. The circuitous march necessary to accomplish this object occupied four days, but complete success attended the manœuvre, for the Black Flags abandoned their formidable positions after little or no resistance. They were unable to remove the Krupp guns which were found in position, but this was the only spoil left in the hands of the victor. These guns were the first evidence that the Chinese had so far departed from their passive attitude as to assist the defenders of Tonquin. This was very far short of the open declaration of war which the Marquis Tseng had advised and threatened as the consequence of any attack on Sontay.

Bacninh was occupied in March, 1884, and then a lull followed on the scene of operations while diplomacy resumed in Paris and Pekin the task of concluding a pacific arrangement between France and China. The relations of the two States were still in name amicable. China had ostensibly done nothing, and in reality very little to invest her suzerain claims over Tonquin with reality. The party in power at Pekin showed that they did not attach any importance to those claims, that peace was their sole object, and that France might possess a free field for expansion in the Songcoi Valley. Whatever merit this course had on the score of putting off the evil day, it was certainly not the right policy to invest with actuality the shadowy pretensions of China in vassal states. These pretensions could only be maintained by the sword; as China did not intend to draw the sword, and as, moreover, its temper was brittle, they should have been promptly relegated to the receptacle for the abandoned claims of nations. The overthrow of the Black Flags at Sontay and Bacninh was quickly followed therefore by a treaty of peace negotiated by Commander Fournier with Li Hung Chang, who in this, as in many other similar matters of external policy, represented the Chinese Government. The treaty was signed on the 11th May, 1884, and while it waived all China's claims on the old Empire of Annam, it also assigned to France a larger part of Tonquin than she had absolutely acquired. The success of the French in establishing a definite protectorate over Tonquin seemed thus to have been attained with equal completeness and facility.

The Fournier treaty, instead of being a bond of union, was

to prove the cause of more serious discord. One of its chief provisions was the surrender of the position of Langson to the French. After their retirement from Bacninh the Black Flags had established themselves here and made it their stronghold. The peace convention stipulated that Langson was to be surrendered to the French, but in the draft published in China no date was specified for the event, and the Chinese no doubt assumed that they would be given the time to make the necessary arrangements and to bring the desirable pressure to bear on the Black Flags to induce them to retreat without resistance or compromising the Government. Slow in all their movements, time was needed to enable the Chinese to carry out their own promises, and unfortunately the draft of the convention contained specific dates and conditions for the fulfilment of the arrangement. Commander Fournier declared on his honour that the dates named in his draft were in the original convention, and no one can doubt that this was the real truth. When, however, the French troops advanced to take possession of Langson the matter took a new and serious turn, for the Black Flags, ignorant of or indifferent to what Chinese diplomatists had promised, resisted to the full extent of their power and skill, both of which were for the work to be done far from inconsiderable. The French detachment sent to occupy Langson, under the command of Colonel Dugenne, was attacked in an ambuscade at the Bacle pass, and compelled to retreat after some loss. The principal provision of the Fournier treaty was therefore rendered null and void, and France and China were brought into direct collision.

The Chinese disclaimed all responsibility in the matter on the ground that the French advance was premature in that the Fournier Convention mentioned no specific date. To that statement the French representative replied by declaring that his draft contained the dates, and the truth seems to have been that he had allowed himself to be circumvented by the more astute Chinese. However, France would not allow the Chinese Government to shake off its responsibility on this subterfuge. It demanded an instantaneous apology and an indemnity of ten millions sterling. The Chinese would have given the former, and paid a reasonable sum by way of compensation, but the amount asked was so excessive as to prevent its even being discussed. Stormy events followed, but before entering upon them it will be clearer for the reader to record that France eventually accepted £160,000 in lieu of the £10,000,000 claimed for the Bacle outrage.

After the Bacle affair, military operations were resumed not only in Tonquin but against China. The French Government would not openly declare war, because by so doing England would have had to proclaim her neutrality, and France would then have lost the advantages of Hongkong as a coaling station. She maintained the usual relations of friendly states, and at the same time she resorted to open violence; a position of an exceptionally favourable nature for attacking the Chinese at a disadvantage was thus obtained, and the French quickly turned it to account. Foochow, a Treaty port, is situated a little distance up the Min river or estuary, and the Chinese, alive to some if not all of the military defects of their situation, had strongly defended its approach from the sea. While the peace was thought to be assured, several French men-of-war had proceeded up the river and anchored off Foochow, or, in other words, above the defences of the port. How far it was fair to utilize that position of advantage secured under the assumption of peace for the purposes of war is a question of ethics that we need not stop to examine here. It will suffice to say that the French men-of-war, in accordance with instructions telegraphed from Paris to Foochow itself, attacked the Min forts in reverse, and, thanks to their favourable position, destroyed them with little or no loss. The destruction of the Min Forts was a complete set-off to the surprise at Bacle, and it was also the most complete success of the French throughout the struggle, but for the reason given it was not one in which the French can take undiluted pride.

The French continued also to derive all the advantage they could from the fact that there was still no formal declaration of war, and by using Hongkong as a coaling station they practically made England an ally in the operations against China. This situation would soon have become intolerable, and Sir Harry Parkes, who had succeeded Sir Thomas Wade in the post of British Minister at Pekin, in the autumn of 1883, wisely decided to clear it up by issuing a proclamation to the effect that as the hostilities in progress between France and China were tantamount to a state of war, the laws of neutrality must be strictly observed at Hongkong and by all British subjects. The French resented this step, and showed an intention to retaliate by instituting a right to search all coasting steamers for rice, but fortunately this pretension was not pushed to extremities, and the war closed before any grave international complications had arisen.

After the destruction of the Min forts, the war was carried on chiefly in the island of Formosa, whither the French sent a strong expedition. The port of Tamsui was occupied without much difficulty; but at Kelung the Chinese resisted with great determination, and, although Admiral Courbet succeeded in capturing one of the forts, the Chinese erected a line of entrenchments, and batteries that effectually prevented the French force making any advance. Nor did the fortune of war shine on the French in Tonquin, where a certain number of Chinese troops were sent to co-operate with the Black Flags at Langson, and from before which, in March, 1885, the French were compelled to beat a retreat. This reverse was not quite of the same magnitude as an absolute defeat, but it was a revelation of the difficulties of the task, and a warning not to tempt fortune too far. Very soon after the open declaration of war between France and China the French Government was brought face to face with this position, that its arms were making no progress in either Formosa or Tonquin, and that, to retain the fruits of the earlier success, a special effort was necessary. In these circumstances it became necessary to choose between the despatch of a large expedition to attack Pekin, and the resorting again to diplomacy to effect a pacific arrangement. The former was costly, uncertain, and affected by many extraneous considerations; it is not surprising that the French Government adopted the latter. On the 9th of June, 1885, a new treaty was signed by the respective plenipotentiaries, M. Patenotre and Li Hung Chang. It reiterated the terms of the Fournier agreement with the simple addition of a moderate indemnity for the attack on Colonel Dugenne in the Bacle defile.

The teaching of this war, the first in which China had engaged with an European antagonist since the march of the allies to Pekin, was inconclusive. On the one hand, the Chinese had shown no great military capacity, and their general conduct of the war had not been marked by any real grasp of military problems. On the other hand, their soldiers had shown admirable tenacity of purpose at both Langson and Kelung, while on no occasion did they absolutely disgrace themselves. The organization was bad, the policy of the Pekin Government was timid and uncertain, but the conduct of the army in the field seemed to justify the assumption that the day of tame submission in China was passed. We now know that this view of the case was too favourable, and that the faults and crimes of the Government and the ruling classes in China far outweigh and nullify the good qualities of the Chinese people. The time seems now remote, but it must inevitably come when the Chinese people, whether of their own volition or under foreign guidance, will secure a government adequate to their needs, and that will at the same time make itself respected by its neighbours.

But in one obvious particular the Franco-Chinese war marked an epoch in modern Chinese history, and it also marked it as a point of decline. The St. Petersburg Treaty with Russia had given back a long-lost possession. It had set the seal, as it were, to the contention that China never waived her rights, that she regarded her inherited pretensions as inalienable, and that what she had once possessed she reserved the right for ever to reclaim. Such was the proud and confident pretension to which the world was asked, in 1881, to pay heed. The war with France over Tonquin taught a different lesson. As a military experience it was far indeed from being a humiliating event for China, but too narrow a view must not be taken of such passages in the life of a nation or empire. The Chinese Government had taken up a very different position on the subject of Tonquin from that it had maintained in the case of Kuldja. Tonquin was undoubtedly a vassal state of China, for it was the dependency of the Annam ruler who sought investiture at the hands of the occupant of the Dragon Throne. It was also in close proximity to the thickly populated region of China dependent on Canton, whereas, on the other hand, Kuldja, although for a century an actual possession of the Empire, was situated by a distance of nearly two thousand miles from any centre of population in China. There was far more ground for China to stand firm in the matter of Tonquin than there was in that of Kuldja, and the excellent defence made by the Black Flags should have encouraged the Chinese to co-operate with them in holding what was known to be an avenue of approach to south-west China. But from the very beginning of the difficulty the authorities at Pekin and Li Hung Chang in particular, had let it be seen that they attached no value to the suzerain claim over Tonquin, and that they had no intention of fighting for it. The Marquis Tseng took, indeed, a higher tone, and would have struggled to achieve in France a similar diplomatic victory to that he had won in Russia, but his Government would not support him. The consequence was that, at the very moment when the view was beginning to prevail, through the complete recovery of Central Asia, that the Chinese were firm in their intentions, the clearest evidence was furnished by their own acts that they had no definite policy, and that their shadowy claims in many parts of Asia were not likely to be invested with substance by the timid and irresolute rulers at Pekin. What had happened with regard to Tonquin was obviously inevitable in the case of the other tributaries, as soon as they became objects coveted by other Powers.

CHAPTER XXI.

THE REIGN OF KWANGSU.

A FEW months after the signature of the treaty of St. Petersburg one of the two Regent Empresses died. This was the Empress Tsi Thsi, the principal widow of the Emperor Hienfung, and the nominal senior of the two ladies carrying on the government. Her illness was short and sudden, being due to heart disease; and when she died, on the 18th of April, 1881, she was only forty-five years of age. Her more capable and ambitious colleague, the Empress Tsi An, who was, however, only the concubine of the Emperor Hienfung, survived to carry on the administration; and she has been throughout, and still remains, the most powerful personage in China. Of her it will be simplest hereafter to speak as the Empress Dowager, and her form passes continually across the stage of Chinese affairs, even if shrouded in darkness, since the formal assumption of reigning authority by Kwangsu.

Closely associated with the Empresses since the death of Hienfung, and also more especially in the events following the nomination of Kwangsu, was Prince Kung, brother of the one and uncle of the other. He was a man of good sense and considerable ability, and of a patriotism beyond challenge. He was generally supposed to be the most powerful member of the administration, but how erroneous this supposition was was shown in a public and unmistakable manner by the following occurrence. Reference has already been made to a warning administered by the two Empresses to Prince Kung, in an early stage of their partnership; but on that occasion the reinstatement of the Prince within a very short period of his fall had pointed to the conclusion that he was the most powerful of the partners. This supposition was erroneous, and the mishap that befell the prince in July, 1884, furnished clear proof as to where the centre of power really lay. At the very moment of his greatest security, when, as President of the Tsungli Yamen, he posed as the virtual director of China's foreign policy, an imperial edict appeared, dismissing him from all his offices, and consigning him to a position of obscurity, in which he remained for eleven years. The causes of his fall were simply that he opposed the wishes of an autocratic lady who was determined to leave no one in doubt as to who was the ruler of the realm. He yielded the more rapidly, perhaps, because his more energetic brother Prince Chun, the father of the young Emperor, was ready and eager even to take his place. The Empress Dowager found in him and in Li Hung Chang allies willing and able to second her objects.

Prince Chun, whose name was mentioned at the time of the accession of Tungche, was a prince of considerable ardour and energy, anxious to play a great part, and not content with the ornamental position of father to the Emperor. He was also the recognized leader of the Chauvinist party; and, notwithstanding that it is forbidden by the fundamental laws of China for a father to serve under a son, he took an active part in the government, as President of the Board of National Defence, and as commander of the Pekin Field Force. There is no saying to what heights his ambition might not have led him, if his career had not been cut short by a sudden death in January, 1891. He possessed one rare quality among the directors of Chinese policy, a high courage, and in that way alone he might on important occasions have stiffened the purpose of his government.

The loss of Prince Chun was not the only one that befell China at this time. A few months earlier the Marquis Tseng, whose birth and European experience gave him an unique position among Chinese officials, died in the prime of his life, and at a moment when he seemed destined to be the regenerator of his country. He was closely allied with Prince Chun, and their combined influence would have been superior to that of Li Hung Chang, whose timidity deprived his counsel of most of its value. As the eldest son of Tseng Kwofan, the satrap who had triumphed over the Taepings, and who might have set up a new dynasty if he had been so disposed, the Marquis Tseng enjoyed an exceptional position in China. It was said at one time that all the viceroys and provincial governors of China were nominees of Tseng Kwofan, and among these were the well-known Li Hung Chang, Tso Tsung Tang, and his own brother Tseng Kwo Tsiuen. The Marquis had also seen with his own eyes the marvels of Europe, and he had made a considerable reputation as a diplomatist. He was specially impressed with the importance of a navy, and on his return to China he took a prominent part in the work of the Navy Board. Unfortunately for his country, his career was prematurely cut short in April, 1890. The death of these men did not produce the recall of Prince Kung, and facilitated the retention of supreme power by the Empress Dowager. It is said that there is a secret and sinister history for these events, and for the strangely accommodating manner in which one obstacle after another was removed from the path of this emulator of the Empresses Liuchi of the Hans and Kiachi of the Later Tsins.

The mention of the diplomatic services of the Marquis Tseng justifies the insertion here of the most important negotiation concluded in his time between England and China. We refer to the new arrangement on the subject of opium, with regard to the collection of lekin, made in 1885, while Lord Salisbury was in office. The levy of the lekin, or barrier tax, on opium had led to many exactions in the interior which were equally injurious to the foreign trade, and also to the Chinese Government, in that it never received the dues to which it was entitled. Its effective control over the customs dues did not go beyond the ports, and the local authorities pocketed or wasted the large sums they appropriated at the entrance of their respective jurisdictions. After the subject had been thoroughly discussed in all its bearings, a Convention was signed in London on the 19th of July, 1885, by which the lekin was fixed at eighty taels a chest, in addition to the customs duty of thirty taels; and also arranging that the whole of this sum should be paid in the Treaty Port before the opium was taken out of bond. The arrangement was greatly to the advantage of the Chinese Government, which came into possession of a large money revenue that had previously been frittered away in the provinces, and much of which had gone into the pockets of the officials. In connection with the customs of China it is impossible to pass on without a tribute to the services which Sir Robert Hart has rendered China during a period of forty years as Inspector-General. To his efforts the Pekin Government owes the large and increasing cash revenue which by more skilful management would have sufficed to firmly re-establish its power. The services Sir Robert Hart has rendered his own country during this long period have been scarcely less striking, and on the premature death of Sir Henry Parkes he was gazetted his successor in the post of British Minister Plenipotentiary at Pekin. For weighty reasons not unconnected with the development of Russian policy in China, he at once gave up his new post of Minister, and reverted to the old office of Inspector-General, which he still retains.

As the London Convention related to opium, it may be as well to make a parting reference to that much-debated article. This Convention, the text of which was drawn with such special care that it serves as a model for all Chinese drafts at the Foreign Office, was a further and final blow at the old theory that opium was forced upon the Chinese. Even Li Hung Chang, a master in the art of dissimulation, could no longer assert his old view that the opium traffic was iniquitous and the sole cause of disagreement between China and England. But the Convention did not stand alone as a piece of evidence on the subject of the true views of the Chinese Government about opium. In 1890 the Emperor of China issued an Edict legalizing the cultivation of opium in China, which, although practically carried on, and to such an extent in some provinces that it was the staple crop, was none the less an illegal practice punishable by severe penalties, including mutilation. The immediate consequence of this step was that the area under poppy cultivation in China largely increased. The great province or region of Manchuria now raises a crop not much less than that of Yunnan. So great is the quantity of native opium now raised throughout China that, despite some inferiority in quality, there is a prospect of Indian opium being practically driven out of the Chinese market as a practical revenge for the loss inflicted on China by the successful competition of Indian tea. But at least China is now clearly debarred from again posing as an injured party in the matter of the opium traffic.

For some years past, indeed as the natural consequence of the Chinese reappearance in Kashgaria, there has been a necessity for direct relations between India and China. This necessity was greatly increased by the British invasion of Burmah in 1885 and the annexation of that state in the following year. In this direction, as in Tonquin, China possessed shadowy tributary rights. They were good or they were bad just as much as China had the power to enforce them. They were invested with a value they did not possess by the exceptional good will and complaisance of the British Government. In order to exactly understand the terms of the first Burmah Convention, in 1886, it is necessary to describe the minor negotiations that led up to it.

The Chefoo Convention of 1876, closing the Yunnan incident, contained in a separate article a promise from the Chinese Government to allow an English mission to pass through Tibet. Years passed without any attempt to give effect to this stipulation; but at last, in 1884, Mr. Colman Macaulay, a member of the Indian Civil Service, obtained the assent of his Government to his making a request of the Chinese Government for the promised passports to visit Lhasa. He went to Pekin, and he came to London to interest the Marquis Tseng in his journey. He obtained the necessary permission and the promised passport from the Tsungli Yamen, and there is no doubt that if he had set off for Tibet with a small party he would have been honourably received and passed safely through Tibet to India. At least there is no doubt that the Chinese officials had made a very special effort to achieve this object. On the other hand, there is no doubt that such a journey, which might well have provided only a slight glimpse of Lhasa, would have been of little special importance. It might have been an interesting individual experience; it could not have been the international landmark it was to form in Mr. Macaulay's own mind.

This modest character for his long-cherished project did not suit Mr. Macaulay, and, unmindful of the adage that there may be a slip betwixt the cup and the lip, he not merely delayed the execution of his visit, but he made ostentatious preparations and he engaged many persons of scientific attainments to accompany him with the view of examining the mineral resources of Tibet. He had also altered his proposed journey through China into Tibet to one from India to Tibet. The Chinese themselves did not relish, and had never contemplated, such a mission; but their dissatisfaction was slight in comparison with the storm the rumours of this mission raised in Tibet itself. No doubt was possible that the Tibetans were prepared and resolved to oppose its admission by force of arms. The Chinese Government was thus brought face to face with a position in which it must either employ its military power to coerce the Tibetans, or tamely acquiesce in their refusal to pay respect to the passports of the Tsungli Yamen, and thus provoke a serious complication with this country. Such was the position of the Tibetan question when Burmah was annexed in January, 1886, and negotiations followed with China for the adjustment of her claims and the new frontier. Negotiations were carried on, first by Lord Salisbury and afterwards by Lord Rosebery, with the Chinese minister in London, and the draft of more than one convention was prepared. Among such contemplated arrangements were the despatch of a mission from Burmah to China, and of a return mission from China to place the Empires on an equality; the appointment of the head priest of Mandalay as the person by and through whom the mission should be sent, thus making it a purely native matter outside any participation by the British Government; and a third proposition was to cede territory in the Shan states and trade rights on the Irrawaddy as an equivalent for the surrender of the claim to tribute.

It is probable that one of these three arrangements would have been carried out, but that on certain points being referred to Pekin, the knowledge came to the ears of certain British officials that if the Tibetan mission were withdrawn the Chinese would be content with the formal admission of their claim to receive the tribute mission from Burmah without any specification as to how it was to be practically carried out. As both Governments wanted to bring about a speedy settlement of the question, the Chinese with the view of allaying the rising agitation in Tibet and getting rid of a troublesome question, and the English not less anxious to have the claims of China in Burmah defined in diplomatic language, the Convention which bears Mr. O'Conor's name was drawn up and signed with remarkable despatch. For the abandonment of the Macaulay Mission, and the mere recognition of their shadowy claim to tribute, the Chinese were quite willing to abandon the chance of more tangible possessions, such as a port on the Irrawaddy, which at one moment seemed within their reach. Diplomacy has since said a good deal more on this subject. The claim to any tribute at all has been waived, and in return China was given a very important and valuable slice of territory in the Shan states. The ceded territory was subsequently reduced, because China broke faith with England in the trans-Mekong territory of Kianghung by ceding part of it to France, and within the present year an Anglo-Chinese Delimitation Commission has been engaged in the task of defining with scrupulous exactitude the boundary of Burmah and Yunnan. Here, at least, the Chinese are showing an admirable ingenuity in securing the full letter of their rights and every yard to which they could lay claim, while Great Britain alone among the nations is ceding to the decrepit Pekin rulers the respect and the forbearance they might claim if they were strong, steadfast, and straightforward.

In the meanwhile the young Emperor Kwangsu, "the cross and sleepy child," placed on the throne at the midnight conclave in 1875, was growing up. The date on which he was to take possession of his own was looming in the distance, and, as a preliminary to his assumption of power, search had to be made for a suitable wife. In February, 1887—the month of the Chinese New Year—it was announced that his proposed marriage was postponed for two years in consequence of his tender age and delicate health. The postponement also had the considerable advantage of insuring for the Regent a further lease of power. About New Year's Day, 1889, when Kwangsu was well advanced in his eighteenth year, he was married to Yeh-ho-na-la, daughter of a Manchu general named Knei Hsiang. This lady had been carefully selected for the great honour of Empress of China out of many hundred candidates, and so far she has escaped the fate of the unfortunate Ahluta. The marriage was celebrated with the usual amount of state, and more than a million sterling was expended on the attendant ceremonies. At the same time the Empress Dowager made her resignation of power public in a farewell edict; but although she passed into a retreat, she still retained the substance of power, and ruled her adopted son, and, indeed, the whole of his court, with a rod of iron. If she had ruled them for her country's good, silence might have been extended to her machinations; but for the injuries that have befallen China her masterfulness has been largely responsible and much to blame.

The marriage and assumption of governing power by the Emperor Kwangsu brought to the front the very important question of the right of audience with the Chinese monarch by the foreign ministers resident at Pekin. This privilege had been conceded by China at the time of the Tientsin massacre, as part of the reparation made for that outrage, and on one occasion it had been put in force during the brief reign of Tungche. During the Regency it necessarily remained in abeyance; but the time had again arrived for putting it in effect, and after long discussions as to the place of audience and the forms to be observed, Kwangsu issued, in December, 1890, an Edict appointing a day soon after the commencement of the Chinese New Year for the audience, and also arranging that it should be repeated annually about the same date. In March, 1891, Kwangsu gave his first reception to the foreign representatives; but, after the interview was over, some dissatisfaction and legitimate criticism were aroused by the fact that the ceremony had been held in the Tse Kung Ko, or Hall of Tributary Nations. Since then some improvement has been effected in the arrangements, as this was one of the rare occasions on which foreigners were brought into direct contact with a Chinese ruler—the audience in Tungche's reign and Lord Macartney's interview with Keen Lung being the two most notable exceptions. The following description of the Emperor's personal appearance by one present at the audience is deserving of quotation:—

"Whatever the impression 'the Barbarians' made on him, the idea which they carried away of the Emperor Kwangsu was pleasing and almost pathetic. His air is one of exceeding intelligence and gentleness, somewhat frightened and melancholy-looking. His face is pale, and though it is distinguished by refinement and quiet dignity, it has none of the force of his martial ancestors, nothing commanding or imperial, but is altogether mild, delicate, sad, and kind. He is essentially Manchu in features, his skin is strangely pallid in hue, which is no doubt accounted for by the confinement of his life inside these forbidding walls and the absence of the ordinary pleasures and pursuits of youth, with the constant discharge of onerous, complicated, and difficult duties of state, which it must be remembered are, according to Imperial Chinese etiquette, mostly transacted between the hours of two and six in the morning. His face is oval-shaped, with a very long narrow chin and a sensitive mouth with thin nervous lips; his nose is well shaped and straight, his eyebrows regular and very arched, while the eyes are unusually large and sorrowful in expression. The forehead is well shaped and broad, and the head is large beyond the average."

Owing to the dissatisfaction felt at the place of audience which seemed to put the Treaty Powers on the same footing as tributary states, the foreign Ministers set themselves the task of exacting from the Tsungli Yamen the selection of a more suitable place in the Imperial city for the annual ceremony. The matter was no doubt referred to the Emperor

THE AUDIENCE QUESTION.

and the Court officials for consideration and decision, but as the European Powers were not in agreement as to the importance of the matter, no speedy solution was attained. The British Foreign Office attached great importance to the point, and when Sir Nicholas O'Conor was appointed Minister in succession to Sir John Walsham, an exception was made in his favour, and a place of superior importance to the Hall of Tributary Nations was selected for the ceremony of presenting his credentials. The Emperor agreed to receive him in the Cheng Kuan Tien palace, or pavilion, which forms part of the Imperial residence of Peace and Plenty within the Forbidden City. The British representative, accompanied by his secretaries and suite, in accordance with arrangement, proceeded to this palace on the 13th of December, 1892, and was received in a specially honourable manner at the principal or imperial entrance by the High Court officials. Such a mark of distinction was quite unprecedented, and it was noticed that the Emperor took a much greater interest in the ceremony than on preceding occasions, and followed with special attention the reading of the Queen's letter by Prince Ching, at the time President of the Tsungli Yamen. After this incident there was a permanent improvement in the reception every year of the Foreign diplomatists, and with the view of giving the more importance to the matter, the Tsungli Yamen adopted the practice of giving an annual dinner as a sort of compliment to the Imperial audience. The personal reception of Prince Henry of Prussia by the Emperor of China on 15th May, 1898, marked the final settlement of the Audience Question in favour of the right of foreign potentates to rank on an equality with the so-called Son of Heaven. It is impossible to suppress the reflection that if the policy of the British Government had been more skilfully directed this privilege would have been secured first by England, and not by Germany.

Although the Dowager Empress had ostentatiously retired from the administration and taken up her abode in a palace outside the walls, in the park of Haitien, near the old Summer Palace destroyed in 1860, evidence as to her power over the Government was forthcoming on numerous occasions. Li

Hung Chang in particular was her associate and ally, and after his temporary disgrace it was only her protection that prevented his losing his head. But the world was taken into the confidence of the ruling powers at Pekin when it was announced in 1894 that the Chinese Court had decided to celebrate the sixtieth birthday of the Empress Dowager in an extraordinary manner. The proposition was seriously made, and the arrangements were far completed towards executing it, that the sum of five millions sterling should be expended on this Jubilee. The reader need not discover in that extraordinary proposition proof of the excessive affection of the Emperor Kwangsu to one of the widows of his uncle, but the evidence it supplies as to the power of that lady is irrefutable. The Imperial lady's expectations were on this occasion doomed to disappointment. For over thirty years she had lorded things as she chose, but just as she was on the point of receiving the much-desired public tribute to her success and worth, the cup of anticipated triumph was dashed from her lips by the outbreak of the war with Japan. The millions had to be expended or wasted elsewhere, but they were not destined to obtain a triumph either in the streets of Pekin or in the field against the national enemy.

CHAPTER XXII.

THE WAR WITH JAPAN.

THE most striking passage in the modern history of China since the Taeping rebellion has now been reached; but in order to understand the events of the war with Japan it is necessary to describe the gradual development of the Corean question until it became the cause of strife between the two principal races of the Far East. The old struggles between China and Japan have been mentioned at different periods, but although the Japanese in the sixteenth century practically overran the peninsula, they retired, and Corea reverted to that position of dependence or vassalage under China which was the common condition of all her neighbours. The tie binding Corea to China was neither weaker nor stronger than that between China and Tonquin. In each case the essential point was whether China possessed the power to make good the letter of her rights. In Tonquin the result showed that she had not the power; but much had happened in the ten years intervening between the wars with France and with Japan to justify the opinion that China could make at least a good fight for her claims over Corea, and, moreover, Corea by its position was so far more important to China that it was felt she ought to make a special effort to maintain her hold on a country which had been called her "right arm of defence."

If these considerations pointed to the conclusion that the Chinese would fight hard for their rights in Corea, the weak and uncertain policy that preceded the outbreak of war shook faith in the wisdom and firmness of the Pekin Government long before the crisis arrived. The Chinese Government, and at that moment the phrase signified Li Hung Chang, was induced to believe, first, that something should be done to regulate the position in Corea, and, secondly, that this could only be effected by opening the country to the trade and influences of the outer world. Several disputes with foreign Powers, arising out of attacks on ships, missionaries, and travellers, had not merely raised an external interest in Corea, but had created some justification for interference in its affairs. Allowance must be made for the fact that while China was anxious to cling to her shadowy claim over Corea, and to invest it with substance, she was not anxious to accept the responsibility for every act committed by the truculent and quarrelsome Coreans.

In 1876 Japan began operations in Corea by securing the opening of Fushan to her trade as compensation for an outrage on some of her sailors. About the same time China annexed the so-called neutral territory on the frontier, and in 1880 Chemulpo was also opened to Japanese trade. The activity of the Japanese compelled the Chinese to act, and in 1881 a draft commercial treaty was drawn up, approved by the Chinese authorities and the representatives of the principal Powers at Pekin, and carried to the Court of Seoul for acceptance and signature by the American naval officer Commodore Schufeldt. The treaty was, of course, accepted by Corea, and all the Powers in turn became parties to it. The success of the Japanese had filled them with confidence, and when they saw the Chinese asserting their claims over Corea, and putting forward a pretension to control its destinies, they determined to advance their old right to have an equal voice with China in the peninsula. As the most effectual way of carrying out their plans they allied themselves with the so-called progressive party in Corea, which naturally took Japan as their model, while China, with equal appropriateness, was obliged or inclined to link her fortunes with the old and reactionary party in the state.

The plans of the Japanese met with much opposition, and in June, 1882, the Coreans attacked the Japanese Legation, murdered some of its inmates, and compelled the survivors to flee. Thereupon the Japanese sent a force to exact reparation, and the Chinese also sent a force to restore order. An arrangement was effected, but for two years a Chinese and Japanese force remained in proximity under the walls of Seoul. In December, 1884, a fresh collision occurred between the Japanese and the Coreans, aided this time by the Chinese. The former were again compelled to flee. This second outrage stirred the Japanese Government to take decided action, and while it obtained compensation from the Coreans for the outrage, it sent Count Ito to China to effect an arrangement with the Pekin Government. At that moment China occupied a stronger position in Corea than the Japanese. She was popular with the people, the old ties were undoubtedly strong, and the Treaty Powers were more disposed to work through her than Japan in extending trade influence through the peninsula. It now remains to show how completely the Government of China threw away these advantages by an agreement which tied her hands and placed her in a very different position from that she claimed, and had so long possessed.

Li Hung Chang was appointed Chinese plenipotentiary to negotiate with Count Ito, and a short but pregnant Convention was signed by them at Tientsin on the 18th of April, 1885. It consisted of only three articles: first, that both countries should withdraw their troops from Corea; secondly, that no more officers should be sent by either country to drill the Corean army; and thirdly, that if at any future time either country should send troops to Corea, it must inform the other country. By this Convention China admitted Japan's right to control Corea as being on an equality with her own. After that date it was impossible to talk of Corea as a vassal state of China, and all the advantages she possessed by tradition were surrendered by Li Hung Chang to the more astute representative of Japan.

For nine years after the Tientsin or Li-Ito Convention there was peace in Corea. In the spring of 1894 the assassination at Shanghai of Kim-Ok-Kiun, the leader of the Corean revolution in 1884 and a so-called reformer, drew attention to the affairs of the peninsula. Happening outside it, this event was still the originating cause of the important occurrences that followed during the summer of 1894 in Corea. Evidence was soon forthcoming that the murderer had been put up to commit the deed by the Corean authorities. On his return to Corea honours and rewards were bestowed upon him, while the body of Kim-Ok-Kiun was quartered as that of a traitor. At this moment the Tong Haks, a body of religious not political reformers, began to agitate for various concessions, and failing to obtain them, broke into open rebellion. At the end of May the Tong Haks obtained a considerable success over the Corean forces, three hundred of whom were slain. This defeat caused such consternation at Seoul that a request was at once sent to China to send a force to save the capital.

There was no reason why China should not comply with that request, and there were many reasons why she should. By the 10th of June 2000 Chinese troops were encamped at Asan, a port some distance south of Seoul, and its recognized port Chemulpo. A few Chinese men-of-war were also sent to the coast. Notification was made to Japan of the despatch of these forces to Corea under the terms of the Convention. The Japanese Government, having equal rights with China, determined to do the same, and, acting with extraordinary vigour and promptitude, they possessed within forty-eight hours of the arrival of the Chinese at Asan a far superior force of troops at Seoul and of ships at Chemulpo. They were also in complete possession of the capital and of the Court, which was wholly in sympathy with China and opposed to Japan.

In these circumstances China revived her pretensions to regard Corea as a vassal state. Japan refused to tolerate the pretensions on the ground, first, that she had never at any time admitted them, and secondly, that the Li-Ito Convention was clear in its tenor as to the equality of the rights of the two states. The Japanese made another very astute move. They called attention to the obvious evil consequences of misgovernment in Corea, and they proposed to China that she should join them in executing the needful reforms. China, hampered by her alliance with the reactionary party at Seoul, held back, and Japan, with the extraordinary promptitude that characterized all her proceedings, threw herself into the task alone. To do this with any prospect of success, it was necessary to secure the person of the King of Corea, and his palace was accordingly attacked by the Japanese, his guard dispersed, and the ruler of the peninsula secured as the tool or ally of his captors. The first document to which he was required to put his seal was one ordering the Chinese troops who had come at his invitation to leave the country. The Japanese acted nominally in the name of liberty and progress, but in truth it was only the great game of ambition, which they played remarkably well.

The seizure of the king's person on 23rd of July, 1894, was followed by two signal events. On the 25th the Japanese squadron attacked the transport *Kowshing* and its escort bringing fresh troops to Asan. In the engagement that followed, one Chinese man-of-war was sunk, one disabled, and 1200 troops were destroyed with the *Kowshing*. Here, again, the energy and success of the Japanese redeemed their reputation. The torpedoing of the unarmed *Kowshing* was a brutal act, not in accordance with the spirit of the age, and under different circumstances the firing on the British flag might have entailed serious consequences. On the same day as this fight General Oshima left Seoul with a small force to attack the Chinese camp at Asan. This the Chinese had abandoned for a better position at Song-hwan, which they strongly fortified. So formidable did it appear that the Japanese resorted to a night surprise as the safest mode of attack, and on the 29th of July they carried the place with a loss to the Chinese of 500 killed and wounded. Half the Chinese force, under their General Yeh, made a timely retreat on hearing of the loss of the *Kowshing*, and succeeded in reaching Pingyang, north of Seoul, on the main road to China. These preliminary encounters were followed by a mutual declaration of war between China and Japan on the 1st August.

The exciting events of July were followed by a period of tranquillity. The declaration of war produced a lull in hostilities. The interval was taken up by the preparations for the real fighting of the struggle. Japan poured her troops into Corea, while the Chinese fleet, missing its chances, hugged the harbours of Wei Hai Wei and Port Arthur in ignominious safety. It was not until the beginning of September that the Japanese army was in sufficient strength to detach a corps of 13,000 men in all to attack the Chinese position at Pingyang, a town of historic importance on the northern banks of the Taidong river. The chief command of the operations on the Japanese side was entrusted to General Nodzu. The Chinese were in considerable force, and held a naturally strong position, but the preliminary skirmishes indicated the radical ignorance of the Chinese in military knowledge.

The early morning of the 15th of September was the time fixed for the attack on Pingyang, and so well were the arrangements made, that all was in readiness to deliver the attack at the appointed signal, although one of the columns had marched across Corea from Gensan. The plan of the Japanese was simple. While their main force threatened Pingyang in front, the Gensan corps took up a position of attack on its east, and another corps a similar position on the west. Both these latter corps had crossed the Taidong river unknown to the Chinese. The passage of the river was difficult and slow, and the Chinese might easily have overwhelmed the Japanese; but instead of this result they allowed themselves to be lulled into a false sense of security, and to remain ignorant of even the fact that the river had been crossed by their enemy.

The battle began at sunrise on the 15th of September with an attack on the forts held by the Chinese on the left bank of the river commanding a bridge of boats across the Taidong. Here the Chinese fought well, and repulsed the Japanese with considerable loss; but this success had no influence on the result of the day, which was being decided on another part of the scene. The attack on the forts north of the river by the two flanking columns represented the serious part of the operation. Here five forts, more or less strong by nature, and by artifice, had to be captured, and for a time the Chinese made a most vigorous resistance. The Japanese were fortunately assisted by the artillery fire they were able to direct on the interior of the forts from a hill they had succeeded in capturing the night before. Aided by this advantage the Japanese succeeded in capturing the fort on Peony Hill, and the death of the Chinese general Tso-pao-kuei, who fought when wounded with a noble heroism to the last, shook the confidence of the whole Chinese army. It was then that the Japanese succeeded in capturing the Gemmu gate in the wall of Pingyang itself. When the day's struggle was over the Chinese had fully made up their mind to flee, and as soon as night set in the garrison began a disorderly retreat. As one of the Japanese divisions commanded the only line of retreat, the Chinese suffered heavily from the artillery and rifle-fire kept up on the disorderly crowd. Over 1500 Chinese were killed during this retreat, whereas in the battle itself they had only lost 500 killed in addition to wounded and prisoners.

The Japanese themselves lost 162 killed, 438 wounded, and 33 missing, who may fairly be added to the former total. At the moment when the Chinese began their flight from Pingyang they had made a respectable resistance, and if the other Chinese generals had been animated by anything like Tso's spirit, there is every reason to say that the first attack of the Japanese would have been repulsed, and that time would thus have been gained to make an orderly retreat. Much more than this would have been secured if the Chinese had shown the least knowledge of the military art. Then the Japanese would never have crossed the Taidong river, and the Gensan column would have been crushed before aid could have reached it. The battle of Pingyang was a great defeat for China, but some of the Chinese officers and men fought with great courage, and on the whole it was not the disgraceful military fiasco that has been alleged. It signified, however, the Chinese evacuation of Corea, for not a man paused until he had got the other side of the Yalu.

On the very day of the battle of Pingyang the Chinese fleet was engaged in the conveyance of troops to the mouth of the Yalu, where the Chinese were collecting a second army. The Chinese fleet, under the command of Admiral Ting, on its return from this task was encountered off the island of Hai Yang by the Japanese squadron, under Admiral Ito, on the 17th of September. The two fleets were of very equal strength. They each numbered ten fighting vessels, and if two of the Chinese ships were superior in strength, the Japanese were superior in steam power. The Chinese began to fire at a distance of four miles, while the Japanese reserved their fire until only two miles separated the adversaries. It was to quickness and manœuvring that the Japanese Admiral mainly trusted for victory, and his first attack consisted mainly in circling round the Chinese squadron. The weaker vessels on both sides were soon put out of action. The Chinese flagship, *Ting-yuen*, after a duel with the Japanese *Matsushima*, was severely damaged, and only saved from sinking by the intervention of her sister ship, the *Chen-yuen*. These two fine ships, thanks to their armour, succeeded in making their way out of the action with the torpedo boats, but four of the Chinese boats were sunk, and a fifth was destroyed. In men the Chinese lost 700 killed or drowned and 300 wounded, while the Japanese lost 115 killed and 150 wounded—one-third of these were on the Japanese flagship alone. The honours of the day rested with the Japanese, whose skilful manœuvring won the admiration of all interested in naval warfare. The direct consequences of this victory were considerable, for the Chinese fleet never afterwards attempted to contest the seas, and water communication with the Yalu was as effectually cut off as it had been in the first week of the war with Asan.

The Japanese army halted for more than a fortnight after the battle of Pingyang. By that time Marshal Yamagata had arrived with a considerable body of fresh troops, and he assumed the personal command in the field. The Japanese began their forward movement from Pingyang early in October, and on the 10th of the month their advanced guard reached the Yalu. A considerable Chinese army, under the command of General Sung, held the northern bank of the river, which was broad and difficult of passage. The neglect and military ignorance of the Chinese had allowed of the easy crossing of the Taidong, the same causes enabled the Japanese to cross the river boundary of China. General Sung's defence on the 25th and 26th October was contemptible, his large force withdrew from positions that could easily have been made impregnable, and despite the strength of their forts, which were admirably constructed, the Chinese officers and soldiers retreated after a merely nominal resistance. In the positions abandoned on the Yalu, the Japanese captured an enormous war *matériel*, including 74 cannons, over 4000 rifles, and more than 4,000,000 rounds of ammunition. The defeated Chinese army had retired to Feng-hwang, the border town of the old neutral zone, and for a moment it seemed as if they would make a stand there ; but on reaching it, on the 30th of the month, the Japanese found it evacuated, and rumour said that the Chinese army had dispersed in a senseless and irretrievable panic.

While Marshal Yamagata was forcing the passage of the Yalu, and beginning the invasion of China, another Japanese army under Marshal Oyama had landed on the Regent's Sword, or now more generally called the Leaoutung Peninsula, with the object of attacking the great Chinese naval station of Port Arthur. Port Arthur was not only very strongly defended by art, but its natural advantages were such that it only needed capacity and courage in its defence to be practically impregnable. In Chinese hands it was even formidable ; in those of the countrymen of Todleben it will be a second, and probably an inexpugnable Sebastopol. Over three hundred guns were in position, and the Chinese garrison numbered at least 10,000 men, while the attacking Japanese army did not exceed 13,000 men, although of course the co-operating Japanese fleet has to be added to the land forces. The Japanese landed at the mouth of the Hua-yuan river, nearly 100 miles north of Port Arthur. They then advanced south and captured the strongly fortified city of Chinchow without losing a single man. If this was surprising, what happened the next day at Ta-lien-wan bay was still more incredible. Here the Chinese had five batteries admirably constructed and heavily armed. The garrison was quite sufficient for an effective resistance, but on the approach of the Japanese it fled from its positions almost without firing a shot. In the forts, the victors found over 120 cannons,

2½ million rounds of cannon ammunition, and nearly 34 million rounds of rifle. This easy and bloodless capture of the outer defences of Port Arthur pointed to the early and inevitable fate of that fortress.

On the 20th November, 1894, the whole of the Japanese army was drawn up in front of Port Arthur while the fleet lay off the harbour. The preliminary reconnaissance showed the Japanese general that three forts on the northern side, known as Chair Hill, Table Hill, and Hope Terrace, practically commanded the others, and that their capture would probably entail the fall of the place. The Japanese began their attack early in the morning of 22nd November, and concentrated their efforts on the capture of the Chair Hill. Forty guns, of which half were siege guns, delivered their fire on this place, and in about one hour silenced its guns. The Japanese infantry then rushed to attack it, and with a loss of eighty killed and wounded they drove out the garrison. In consequence of this success, the Chinese soldiers abandoned the forts on Table Hill and Hope Terrace, which might easily have continued their defence. The panic-stricken troops from these positions were practically annihilated during their flight by the fire of a Japanese regiment which they met, and of the Japanese warships. The other forts fell in rapid succession. Only at the Dragon Hill forts did the Chinese offer any resistance worthy of the name, and then it was overcome by the impetuous gallantry of the Japanese attack. The remaining forts attempted no resistance, and thus in one day, for the insignificant loss of 18 men killed and 250 wounded, the Japanese captured the strongest position in China, and a naval fortress and arsenal on which six millions sterling had been expended.

The month of December was marked by the advance of the force under Marshal Yamagata into Manchuria, where a fresh Chinese army, under several commanders, of whom Ikotenga a Manchu was the most capable, had come down to defend the approaches to Moukden, the old Manchu capital and the home of the dynasty. The warfare partook of an irregular character, and skirmishes, rather than battles, characterized the progress of the campaign, which was

WEI HAI WEI.

rendered more difficult by the fact that winter had set in, and that the whole region was covered with snow. The Chinese fought in this part of the campaign with far greater courage than at any other, and in one fight at Kangwasai they inflicted a loss of 400 men on the Japanese. The capture of this village, hastily fortified, cost them far more than that of the strong fortress of Port Arthur, thus showing that the Chinese only lacked honest leading and some military experience to make a good fight. At the town of Kaiping the Chinese also offered a stout resistance, and although the Japanese carried the place, they had to confess a loss of over 300 killed and wounded. These instances of returning courage will be referred to when at some future date the Chinese have been turned into good soldiers.

There only remains now to be described the second most striking military episode of the war, viz. the capture of Wei Hai Wei, with the remainder of China's modern fleet, which had taken refuge in that harbour. It was not until the middle of January, 1895, when the Japanese found further campaigning in Manchuria slow and difficult, that they turned their energies in the direction of this place. Wei Hai Wei was called by the Emperor of Japan one of the leaves of the gate of China. It was strongly fortified, but neither by art nor by nature as strong as Port Arthur. On the 20th January, and following days, the Japanese troops were landed at Yungchang on the promontory of Shantung, a little west of the place to be attacked. On the 26th, the Japanese appeared at the gates of Wei Hai Wei. The land defences of this place consisted of a line of forts and batteries in the form of a semicircle round the range of hills commanding the bay and harbour. In the bay itself are two islands: one called Liukung is 500 feet high, and six miles in circumference, the other, Jih, is small, and covered by a fort. The defences of the place consist, therefore, of these two islands, besides the land forts, and the squadron under Admiral Ting furnished a powerful auxiliary, although its commander, whose courage was beyond dispute, did not deem it safe to venture out to engage the Japanese. The Chinese fleet comprised nine large vessels: six small gun-boats, seven large, and four small torpedo-boats. The entrance to the bay had also been protected by two strong booms, attached to which were torpedoes, and these seemed to preclude the possibility of the Japanese effecting an entrance. It should also be added that nearly half the garrison consisted of 4000 sailors on the fleet, and that these men had at least undergone some training, while in Admiral Ting they had a leader of proved courage and energy, whose spirit was not at all likely to fail.

The attack on the land side of Wei Hai Wei began on the 29th January, and continued throughout that and the following day. The Chinese resistance proved considerable, and at several points Admiral Ting's squadron intervened with such effect that the Japanese were repulsed. Jealousy between the naval and military leaders detracted from the vigour of the defence, as the generals refused Ting's offer to lend them the services of a number of men from the ships to work the guns in the forts properly. This refusal facilitated the capture of Wei Hai Wei. The Japanese had not been able to bring any guns with them, owing to the badness of the roads, but when they captured some of the forts they turned the guns in them on the others, and on Ting's fleet. When Ting realized that the Chinese soldiers in the forts would make no resistance, he sent landing-parties to the different batteries, and rendered all the guns in them useless. By this means he deprived the Japanese of the greater part of the artillery on which they counted for his destruction. The next day the Japanese occupied the remaining forts without resistance, for the whole of the land garrison had fled panic-stricken to Chefoo. For a time it seemed as if they had come to an end of their success, for Admiral Ting's squadron and the island forts continued to defy their assaults.

The Japanese could not afford to rest content with this half success, or to remain inactive. They therefore resorted to an attack by torpedo boats, and on the 5th of February this so far succeeded that the *Ting-yuen*, the great remaining vessel of the Chinese, was struck with two torpedoes, and sunk in a few hours. The Japanese had themselves suffered heavily, but on the following night they renewed the attack, and sank three Chinese vessels. This demoralized the

Chinese, and when the magazine on Jih island was blown up by an accidental shell the Chinese torpedo squadron attempted to escape to sea, but all the vessels were taken. On the 9th February, the *Ching-yuen* was sunk by a shell that struck her below the water-line, and with her the very last chance of victory disappeared. Still Admiral Ting would not give up the struggle, and it was only after receiving a telegram from Li Hung Chang that no help was possible, that he arranged to capitulate. When the terms were agreed on, Admiral Ting retired to his cabin and took a large dose of opium. Among those who fought on the Chinese side Admiral Ting was the most prominent officer to exhibit a high form of courage and some capacity. His name will be ever exempted from the charge of cowardice, and when all the details come to be told it will be known that he was not to blame for any shortcomings in the action of the Chinese fleet, from which so much was expected. Even under every disadvantage Ting held out at Wei Hai Wei for three weeks, whereas Port Arthur was lost in a day.

The war continued for a few weeks after the fall of Wei Hai Wei. The Japanese continued their advance in Manchuria, and captured the two places called Newchwang, thus securing a footing on the Gulf of Leaoutung, and menacing Pekin on the one side and Moukden on the other. At the moment when spring was about to render easy the prosecution of military operations in that northern region, the Japanese possessed an army of 100,000 men ready to advance on Pekin. There is no reason to believe that, however much the Chinese might have improved in courage and resolution for the defence of their capital, they could have offered a successful resistance to the Japanese advance. The prolongation of the war would therefore have signified only the further humiliation of China and the addition of the loss of Pekin to that of Port Arthur and Wei Hai Wei. Peace was, therefore, of the first necessity from the point of view of China's interests. Reserving for another chapter the consideration of the peace negotiations and terms, it will be appropriate to conclude this brief narrative of the war between China and Japan with a few general observations.

China entered on the war with a great and what seemed a growing reputation. She had done enough in the struggle with France to justify the opinion that she possessed considerable military power and a great capacity of endurance. On paper her navy was formidable. In Port Arthur she possessed a superior naval station to Hongkong, and Wei Hai Wei was scarcely in any way inferior. Her policy in Corea, it is true, had not been very skilful. It was directed to the attainment of opposite and incompatible objects, and with inexcusable inaptitude she tied her own hands and then advanced extreme and unattainable pretensions. The reforms of the Japanese were known to be more real and radical than those that had given a tinge to China's public existence. Opinions differed as to whether the Japanese fleet could cope with the Chinese, but every one allowed the superiority of the Japanese army. The balance of opinion inclined, therefore, to the view that the superior numbers and resources of the Chinese would supply their deficiencies and that the result would be indecisive.

The course of the campaign refuted these assumptions and destroyed one after another the preconceptions favourable to China. It was not merely that the Japanese generals and admirals, soldiers and sailors, exhibited an indisputable superiority over the Chinese, for that would have happened in any decisive war between equals, but the incidents of the struggle revealed in vivid colours that China had learnt nothing, and that her public men were destitute of spirit and honesty, and her soldiers of even the primitive attributes of patriotism. There were isolated instances of courage, but after the ignominious surrender of Port Arthur no foreign observer attempted to discover them. Even Admiral Ting's heroism excited incredulity, and the antiquated views of warfare held by Chinese military men, whose text-books went back for 2000 years, formed the theme of ridicule.

There is no doubt that the Chinese Government gave a deplorable exhibition of itself, and after what occurred it would be impossible to put faith in any military or naval changes carried out under the auspices of the Government then and still existing at Pekin. No military and naval reforms could command belief in their sincerity or efficacy until the ruling Government has been purged and has adopted new models. Of that no evidence has yet been afforded. But if, on the one hand, the downfall of China was complete and crushing, it would be folly for us to go to the other extreme and regard the Chinese nation as beneath contempt for all time as a fighting Power. To do so would be to play the game of our numerous adversaries. The collapse of the Chinese was due to clearly defined and ascertainable causes—the incapacity and shortsightedness of the Pekin authorities and the elaborate system of make-believe kept up by Li Hung Chang. When China has a different Government, inspired and directed, as it is now clear that it must be, by foreign influence and example, she will give a very different account of herself on the field of battle, and the Power that most successfully utilizes her toiling millions will possess the mastery of the world.

CHAPTER XXIII.

THE CONSEQUENCES OF DEFEAT.

The Chinese having been brought, by the fall of Wei Hai Wei and the advance of the Japanese army into Manchuria, to admit the necessity of peace, it only remained to secure the most favourable terms that could be obtained. To do this it was necessary, in the first place, to appoint a Plenipotentiary who should not only have full powers, but whose name would suffice to satisfy the Japanese Government that the Chinese were really in earnest in their request for peace, and that they would fulfil the conditions to which their representatives agreed. This was the more necessary because two months earlier the Chinese had sent a so-called peace mission under Chang Yin Huan, with inadequate powers to negotiate at Tokio, and the Japanese, on discovering the flaws in their credentials, had firmly and indignantly refused to do business.

For the purposes of the moment China possessed only two men of adequate rank and reputation. These were Prince Kung and Li Hung Chang. The former, in experience as well as in rank, was entitled to be considered the foremost man in China. In 1860, when Li Hung Chang was still an unknown official of no importance, Prince Kung had signed the Pekin Convention with Lord Elgin, and for a great many years he had practically controlled the foreign policy of China. But for ten years preceding the outbreak of the war with Japan he had been in disgrace, and the all-powerful Empress Dowager had decreed that for his opposition to her plans he should cease to have any part in the active administration. The misfortunes of the Japanese war, by lowering the reputation of those in power, had brought him back to office, but he wielded no great influence. Still, his nomination as Plenipotentiary would have been satisfactory to the Japanese; but, on the other hand, it was necessary for the Chinese representative, as coming from the defeated country, to proceed to Japan and to sue for peace. To that depth of concession a prince of the Imperial family, the uncle of the reigning Emperor, could not be brought. There remained, therefore, only the choice, practically speaking, of Li Hung Chang. Prince Kung was a patriotic and able prince, whose career his countrymen must hope has not yet finished. But on this occasion he could not and would not incur the personal ignominy of gracing by his presence the triumph of his country's enemy, as would have been signified by his proceeding to Shimonoseki.

In consequence of these considerations, which were not devoid of weight, Li Hung Chang remained the only possible representative for China in any peace negotiations that were at all likely to succeed. He was accordingly appointed Plenipotentiary with full powers, and reached Shimonoseki in that capacity on the 20th of March, 1895. Whatever opinion may be formed of Li Hung Chang as an able administrator or as a patriot, there can be no doubt of his skill in the art of diplomacy or at the game of chicane. If the Chinese could recover anything of all they had lost in war by skill of fence in the negotiations, no one was more qualified by character and experience than the ex-Viceroy to obtain it. The chances of the success of his mission, so far as success was possible, were greatly increased by an accidental occurrence which aroused a sentiment of pity for the aged statesman, and stirred the chivalrous ruler and people of Japan with an impulse to atone by some concession for a breach of the laws of hospitality.

Four days after his arrival, Li Hung Chang, while returning from the conference with Count Ito, the Japanese plenipotentiary, was shot in the cheek by a fanatic. The wound was not very serious, but the outrage roused great sympathy for Li Hung Chang, and China benefited by his suffering. The Emperor of Japan sent his own doctor to take care of the wounded minister, the Empress prepared the lint with her own hands. There was a general and unanimous chorus of sympathy and regret on the part of the Japanese people, and Li Hung Chang, a master of phrases, strengthened the feeling of sympathy by the happy phrase, "In truth the benevolence of Her Majesty the Empress of Japan is profound as the sea. When I return home and tell my Imperial mistress what has been done for me she will be very satisfied." In consequence of this occurrence, the Japanese at once granted an armistice, and the original terms they had put forward as the condition of peace were modified in several of their harshest conditions. On the 17th of April the Treaty of Shimonoseki was signed, and on the 8th of May— Li Hung Chang having returned to Pekin in the interim— the ratifications were exchanged at Chefoo.

The terms of the treaty come under three heads: the surrender of territory, the payment of an indemnity, and the concession of commercial facilities and rights, while the first article of all provided for the full and complete independence and autonomy of Corea. The surrender of territory was to comprise the islands of Formosa and the Pescadores and the southern part of the province of Shingking, including the Leaoutung or Regent's Sword Peninsula and the important naval harbour and fortress of Port Arthur. As indemnity, China was to pay 200 million Kuping taels in eight instalments with interest at the rate of 5 per cent. on the unpaid instalments. The commercial concessions included the admission of ships under the Japanese flag to the different rivers and lakes of China, and the appointment of consuls. The text of the treaty is given in the Appendix, and it is unnecessary to enlarge on its provisions.

The terms of peace imposed on China were certainly onerous, but considering the completeness of the Japanese triumph they could not be termed excessive. If they had not seriously disturbed the balance of power in the Far East they would no doubt have been allowed to stand, as no Government was disposed to take up the cause of China from disinterested motives. The British Government, with the largest commercial stake in the question, was by no means inclined to fetter the Japanese when they placed freedom of trade at the head of their programme. It wished China to be opened to external and beneficial influences, and that was exactly what the Japanese proposed to do. Moreover, Japan had shown throughout the war every wish to consider British views, and to respect their interests. Shanghai, in the first place, and the Yangtse Valley afterwards, were ruled outside the sphere of military operations. The identity of interests between England and Japan was clear to the most ordinary intelligence, and certainly the British Government was not the one that would seek to fetter the legitimate and beneficial expansion of the bold islanders of the Far East.

But other Powers did not regard the matter from the same point of view, and Russia saw in the appearance of the Japanese on the Pacific freeboard a spectre for the future. The Russian Government could not tolerate the presence of the Japanese on the mainland, and especially in a position which enabled them to command Pekin. They therefore resorted to a diplomatic move unprecedented in the East, and which furnished evidence of how closely European affairs were reacting on Asia. The then unwritten alliance between France and Russia was turned into a formal arrangement for the achievement of definite ends, and the powerful co-operation of Germany was secured for the attainment of the same object, viz. the arrest of Japan in her hour of triumph. This movement was destined to produce the most pregnant consequences, some of which are not yet revealed, but for the moment it signified that a Triple Alliance had superseded Great Britain in the leading *rôle* she had filled in the Far East since the Treaty of Nankin.

The ink was scarcely dry on the Treaty of Shimonoseki when Japan found herself confronted by the Three Powers, with a demand couched in polite language to waive that part of the Treaty which provided for the surrender of Port Arthur and the Leaoutung peninsula. The demand was clearly one that could not be rejected without war, and Japan could have no possible chance in coping with an alliance so formidable on land and sea. Japan gave way with a good grace, and negotiations followed which resulted in the resignation of her claim to the Leaoutung peninsula in return for an increase of the indemnity by the sum of six millions sterling. Wei Hai Wei was to be retained as bail, pending the payment of the indemnity; and the final payment in May, 1898, has released all Chinese territory on the mainland from the hands of the victors in the war of 1894–5. It will be seen that the question did not end here, but for the time being Japan's benefit from the war with China was a large indemnity, and the acquisition of the islands of Formosa and the Pescadores. The value of the latter possessions is, to say the least, doubtful, and time will have to establish it; but the indemnity has enabled Japan to purchase the new men-of-war and torpedo boats that will make her a Power at sea with which the strongest must reckon.

The Chinese rejoiced in the recovery of Leaoutung, which they represented, and perhaps believed, to be the disinterested act of the Three Powers. They thought nothing of the six millions they had paid away, and everything of the fact that the Japanese had been expelled from the position they had secured in the neighbourhood of their capital. For twelve months they seem to have indulged the hope that the assistance had been given out of disinterested motives, and that such concessions as Russia in particular might demand towards the construction of railways in Northern Asia, would fall very far short of the loss and injury inflicted by the continued presence of the Japanese in Leaoutung. For that period Russia was China's best friend, and France and Germany were content to wait on her convenience before presenting their little bills for payment àt Pekin. This brief respite soon expired, and the period of hope gave place to the reality that Governments, like individuals, are never altogether disinterested in their actions.

At the moment of the negotiations which resulted in the liberation of Leaoutung, Russia was represented at Pekin by Count Cassini, while the direction of her foreign policy was in the able hands of Prince Lobanow. The new and youthful

Emperor Nicholas had travelled in the Far East, and had come back with strong impressions on the subject of the importance of expanding his Empire in regions where trade and mineral wealth promised to reward his energy. Under his auspices the policy of Russia has taken an Eastern direction, and the events of the Chino-Japanese war were calculated to give it a specially rapid development. While the sovereign of Russia was personally keen on the extension of his power in the direction of the Pacific, it so happened that he possessed the very men most capable of advancing the objects he had at heart. On Count Cassini devolved in the first place the task of bringing the Chinese authorities round to the view that because Russia had recovered Leaoutung she was the only sincere friend China possessed, and that by her continued support alone could China hope to be preserved from the dangers by which she was surrounded.

The details of the secret negotiations and private understandings between Count Cassini and the Chinese officials with whom he did business are never likely to be known. It seems probable, however, that at the moment of signing the treaty of Shimonoseki, Li Hung Chang had some good grounds for believing that the clause relating to the Leaoutung promontory would never be enforced. If, as is probable, he knew that Russia had decided to intervene, he also knew that her intervention would not be gratuitous. The exact form of the payment was probably not decided, but that payment would have to be made in some form or other cannot have been a matter of doubt. The subject formed the one topic of discussion during the autumn and winter of 1895. It would have advanced more rapidly but for one circumstance, and that was the exclusion of Li Hung Chang from office, for the Emperor of China had steadily refused to restore him to the substantive posts he had held in the administration, and he was consequently without the authority to conclude any definite arrangements. The situation was therefore controlled by two separate but closely connected issues. The first was the return of Li Hung Chang to power, and the second the making of adequate concessions to Russia in return for her intervention.

When in the spring of 1896 it became necessary for China to nominate a special Ambassador to attend the Coronation of the Emperor at Moscow, the Chinese ruler nominated as his representative his Minister at the Russian capital, and what is still more noteworthy by the light of subsequent events, the Russian Government expressed its approbation of the appointment. When, however, the news reached Pekin, it was seen that if this arrangement were carried out, the return of Li Hung Chang to power might be regarded as indefinitely postponed. An unexpected turn was given to the question by the Russian Minister announcing that China would not be adequately represented at Moscow on such a memorable occasion as the Imperial Coronation, except by her most prominent and best-known official, Li Hung Chang. These representations, supported by the full weight of the Empress Dowager, produced their due effect, and Li Hung Chang was duly appointed Ambassador for the occasion. It soon became clear why this arrangement had been carried out. Before Li Hung Chang left China, he and Count Cassini had drawn up the heads of a Convention, and on his arrival at Moscow, he signed either there, or at St. Petersburg, a treaty which embodied the terms of payment to which Russia was entitled for her services. The statement as to the existence of this secret treaty has sometimes been traversed, but with every inducement to do so, and in the face of repeated challenges, no contradiction has ever been made with authority, and more recently such information has been obtained as to render any contradiction impossible.

The fact is therefore established that immediately after the rescue of Leaoutung, Russia took steps to obtain an equivalent from the embarrassed country she had rescued from her victorious adversary. She not only took the steps, but these, by the co-operation of Li Hung Chang, were crowned with success. The secret treaty gave Russia the control of that very Leaoutung peninsula which she had nominally saved at the cost to China of six millions sterling. In plain words, Russia had induced China to pay this money for the benefit of herself. We are too near the occurrence of these events to characterize them as they deserve without incurring a suspicion of partisanship, but at the right season history will know how to designate the course of Russia's so-called friendly policy towards China. It is unnecessary to lay stress on the other stipulations of the arrangements of 1895-6. They provided before everything, and in the first place, for the possession by Russia of Port Arthur and Talienwan. There is every reason to believe that Kiaochao was also to be assigned for the shelter of the Russian fleet, and the justification for these measures was, that the great ruler of Russia had taken China under his protection. A period of eighteen months elapsed before the full practical significance of these arrangements became evident, and in that period the evidence accumulated as to the need in which China stood of protection, and as to the continuance of the incapacity which had resulted in her downfall during the struggle with Japan.

Li Hung Chang came to Europe in the first place as Special Ambassador for the Imperial Coronation at Moscow; but his tour was extended, in a more or less accredited manner, to the other countries of the West. There was a prevalent and natural curiosity on the part of Europeans to see China's great man, the only visible embodiment of her rule, and this sentiment explained the demonstrativeness of the reception Li Hung Chang received in Berlin, Brussels, Paris, and London. The results of his tour were, however, none, because he had no authority to conduct, much less to conclude negotiations, and because all his efforts failed to obtain his restoration to the Viceroyship of Pechihli. On his return to China from Europe he found his position at Court, so far at least as his relations with the Emperor were concerned, no whit better than after his return from Shimonoseki. In order to obtain for him the requisite authority to fulfil the conditions of the arrangement with Russia, it was necessary to commence intrigues for the restitution of his rank and offices to Li Hung Chang, whose position was now confined to the honorary post of Grand Secretary. Despite the support of the Empress Dowager, whom Li Hung Chang regarded as "his Imperial Mistress," to the exclusion of the reigning sovereign, the success of these measures was not rapid. Li Hung Chang was restored to a seat on the Tsungli Yamen; but he was bitterly opposed by Prince Kung, the Emperor's uncle, and for twelve months it seemed as if his influence would never revive.

During this period of rather more than two years between the Treaty of Shimonoseki and the German occupation of Kiaochao, the Chinese did nothing to improve their position or to strengthen the defences of the country. A series of loans were issued to pay off the Japanese, and the balance left was used for the purchase of new ships and torpedo boats. The services of an English naval officer, Captain Dundas, have been engaged with the view of resuming the task that Captain Lang so admirably performed. It is said that Russia has supplied a certain number of officers for the training of the Manchurian garrison; but that measure, far from contributing towards the security of China, will only facilitate the process of absorption which Russia has begun. In Central and Southern China some tentative measures at military reform have been made, but the dismissal of the German officers employed at Nankin concluded those in the former region, while at Canton and on the southern frontier where Marshal Sou seems to have established cordial relations with his French neighbours, no steps whatever have yet been taken to introduce military discipline among the raw braves of the provincial garrisons. The same complete absence of result is apparent with regard to the civil and fiscal administration as is the case in the military. No reform whatever has been attempted, and to the very men who led China into disaster has been left the task of regenerating her. That simple fact explains why the last respite accorded China has proved so barren. In face of far graver perils than those that beset her in the short struggle with Japan, she finds herself with diminished fiscal resources, without an army or a navy, and, above all, without a clear policy or a leader, exposed to the attacks and encroachments of the greatest Powers and the most aggressive nations of the world. In her old age, with the remains of strength still evident and only awaiting the directing hand of a reformer, the picture the Chinese Empire presents would be piteous if all those who regard it were not engrossed in the designs prompted by self-interest. But for the moment China lies on the sea of time like a rudderless and mastless vessel awaiting the decree of Fate or the advent of a deliverer.

CHAPTER XXIV.

THE PARTING OF THE WAYS.

THE German occupation of Kiaochao, the important port and natural naval station on the southern side of the extreme promontory of the province of Shantung, marks the parting of the ways in China. It may be considered as commencing the dismemberment of China on the one hand, and as forming the termination of the policies previously followed by each of the Great Powers and trading nations on the other. Germany was the first to lay her hands on a portion of Chinese territory since the Japanese war, and it must be admitted that she acted with excellent judgment in that she secured probably the very finest position for a naval station and arsenal round the coast of China. Kiaochao was coveted by Russia, and in the Cassini Convention its name was mentioned as devolving on her at the right moment for occupation. Considering this fact and the close and cordial relations between the Courts of Berlin and St. Petersburg, it is impossible to arrive at any other conclusion than that Russia expressed her approbation of Germany's proceeding to effect the temporary occupation of the place to which she herself had established a prior claim. The supposition that Germany would attempt to do anything in the Far East displeasing to her neighbour on the Vistula is as impossible of belief as that Russia would acquiesce in the loss of a possession of which she had made sure. The assumption of an understanding between the German Emperor and the Russian Czar on the subject of China is the only theory on which the events of the winter of 1897-8 can be explained.

If that theory, and it is the only plausible theory that has yet been put forward, is adopted, a key is provided for the elucidation of recent events of which every person can at his own inclination make use. In the Far East we are then bound to recognize the working out of a concerted policy that was not adopted without thought, and that was set in motion for other than British or universal purposes. For the present juncture Russia and Germany are acting in concert, and as Russia signifies France as well, this means that the triple alliance which was formed against Japan has been revived for the ulterior ends of its component members.

In November, 1897, two German men-of-war entered the harbour of Kiaochao, and ordered the Commandant to evacuate the place in reparation for the murder of two German missionaries in the Province of Shantung. They gave him 48 hours within which to obey, and he telegraphed to Pekin for instructions. The Tsungli Yamen replied to the effect that he was to offer no resistance. The German seizure of Kiaochao was thus effected without loss or difficulty, and it was also remarkable for having been made without any preliminary notice or warning to the Chinese Government. Having taken possession of Kiaochao, the German Government then announced the terms on which it would consent to evacuate it. Four of the clauses related to the reparation demanded by the outrage on the missionaries, and were not open to exception; but the fifth claimed for Germany the right to construct all railways and to work any mines in the province of Shantung. The significance of this demand lay in the fact that it arbitrarily defined a sphere of influence for Germany in China on similar lines to those adopted in Africa. The Chinese, not wholly lost to a sense of their dignity if ignorant of their power, refused to discuss the matter until Kiaochao was evacuated, and Li Hung Chang appealed to the Russian representative at Pekin.

The German occupation of Kiaochao having reopened the question of the Far East, it is not surprising that Russia at once put forward her claim to compensation in a port free from ice on the Pacific. In December the Russian Government announced that the Chinese had given them permission to winter their fleet at Port Arthur, and in making this communication to Japan, the words used were that Port Arthur was lent "only temporarily as a winter anchorage." The Japanese reply was terse and dignified. They "credited" the statement and took note of it. In this manner Russia acquired the practical recognition of her hold on Port Arthur, but in the first instance she represented, as Germany did at Kiaochao, that her occupation was not final, and that she had only temporary objects in view. One month more gave a fresh turn to the question. Kiaochao was surrendered by China to Germany on a lease of ninety-nine years. Germany thus revealed her game. Russia carried hers one point further by adding Talienwan to Port Arthur, but in the first instance accompanying it by a declaration, to disarm hostile criticism, to the effect that "any port would be open to the ships of all the Great Powers, like other ports on the China mainland." Having made this promise, Russia proceeded to qualify and minimize it until practically nothing was left except the substantial fact of Russian possession. One month further of ambiguity and diplomatic fence followed, and then Russia announced that she must hold Port Arthur and Talienwan on the same terms as Germany held Kiaochao. The reason given for this demand was the curious one that their possession was essential to the proper defence of Manchuria against aggressive Powers, while in Europe no disguise was made in the matter of the fact that Russia had determined to secure these places as giving her the ice-free port to which she was entitled on the Pacific. On 27th March, 1898, a convention was signed at Pekin, giving the Russians the usufruct of Port Arthur and Talienwan. The use of the word "usufruct" gave the pundits an opportunity of displaying their knowledge, but its meaning in this instance was clear and simple. It signified that, whereas Germany had secured Kiaochao for ninety-nine years, Russia had obtained Port Arthur and Talienwan without conditions and for ever.

Germany and Russia having done so well at the expense of China, it followed that France would not be content to go away empty-handed, and she accordingly put forward her claim to compensation, and, by the aid of Russia's friendly co-operation, obtained possession of the port of Kwang-chau-fu, which is the best outlet to the sea of the southern province of Kwangsi. Some surprise was felt at the moderation of the French demand, as it was generally assumed that France had cast her eyes on Hainan, but perhaps her experience of island colonies was such as to deter her from embarking on a new venture like that of Madagascar. Of Hainan itself it may be said that, although its transfer from Chinese to European hands would not be difficult, its conquest from the aboriginal tribes might be attended with greater loss and trouble. At the same time that France obtained Kwang-chau-fu, she reiterated her claim, previously advanced by M. Gerard in 1895, to a prior right to control the future of the province of Yunnan. The claim in itself is neither more nor less natural than that put forward by Germany in Shantung, to which the British Government has so hastily expressed its compliance, but the legitimate development of British Burmah is incompatible with the pretensions that France has successfully advanced with the Tsungli Yamen.

When Germany, Russia, and France had made these successive moves, the British Government found itself compelled to take a corresponding step. It began by declaring that, whatever rights other Powers obtained in China, it should equally enjoy them by virtue of the most favoured nation clause in the Treaties with China. This was the principle of "the open door." Morally and theoretically it was perfectly sound and unassailable, but it could only have been vindicated on this occasion by the hazard and perhaps the certainty of war with Russia and France, and perhaps Germany as well. Perhaps the moment for taking that great risk in the Far East has not quite arrived, and it is only on that assumption that Lord Salisbury's policy will escape unanimous condemnation. It may at least be declared that at the moment of Russia's extreme action, Japan, our only probable ally, was not quite ready to embark on a great war. She had still to receive twelve millions of the war indemnity, and two years must elapse before she will obtain all the war vessels she has ordered to be constructed in foreign and principally British dockyards. If, then, we may assume that Japan desired the struggle for mastery in the Far East to be postponed until she was ready to take a more prominent part in it, then an excuse is available for the more lenient judgment of British policy. There is at least something to be said in favour of a course which met the wishes of an ally.

Having found the policy of maintaining the strict letter of treaty rights in China impossible, the British Government turned its attention to obtaining some similar right to that acquired by Russia and by Germany. Sir Claude Macdonald, British Minister at Pekin, discovered that the Chinese were not averse to letting us have Wei Hai Wei, and although the idea was repelled when first made, Lord Salisbury decided that its occupation was the only available means we possessed of answering Russia's seizure of Port Arthur. Accordingly Wei Hai Wei, the port on the northern coast of Shantung, was assigned to Great Britain on precisely the same terms as Port Arthur had been to Russia, and the date of occupation was fixed at the period when the Japanese should evacuate the place. Wei Hai Wei might undoubtedly be made a naval station of the first importance if a large sum were expended on its defences, but it would also require a large garrison, because the harbour and docks and island forts are completely commanded from the hills on the mainland. It will be remembered that during the siege Admiral Ting would have been compelled to make an immediate surrender if he had not landed and spiked the guns in the shore batteries. The occupation of Wei Hai Wei in itself is valueless, except as a demonstration that in the last resort a British Government may be driven to do something. At present it forms no part of the Government plan to spend two or three millions on a place which has no commercial value, and the British army cannot spare ten thousand men, or half that number, for a permanent garrison on the Gulf of Pechihli. The only possible use of Wei Hai Wei would be if we were to take in hand the training of a Chinese contingent, and to make Wei Hai Wei the base for such an interesting attempt. Then indeed might our occupation of Wei Hai Wei be made the starting-point of a serious and systematic attempt to save China.

THE JAPANESE.

There remains to describe briefly the part Japan has taken in the whole question. It has been marked by great reticence, reserve, and dignity. Japan has received the assurances of Russia without comment and with a brief declaration that she took note of them and believed them. She has secured the remainder of her money from China, and she will be able to complete her purchases in foreign dockyards. Her military reforms are also in progress, and the time is not remote when she will be able to place her half-million of trained soldiers on the continent of Asia. Japan has something to wait for. Every year sees her stronger and better able to assert her claims on the mainland. In the mean time she has obtained increased freedom of action in Corea. Russia, as far as she ever takes such a course, has waived her claims in that state. At the least Japan can count on being unfettered while she builds the railway from the port of Chemulpo to the capital of Seoul, and that may count for much in the future. While the European Powers have been very active in securing what they wanted and in defining their spheres of action, Japan has not, from a practical point of view, been indifferent. She is preparing for eventualities, not by useless protest or idle bluster, but by keeping her own counsel and developing her power.

Such is the existing position in the Far East. Russia, Germany, and France, acting on identical lines, have appropriated certain places and ports of China. They have each defined their positions without any reference to any outside authority, except perhaps to one another. Each has wrested from the helpless Government at Pekin privileges or monopolies for specific tasks. Russia has secured the outlet for her railway across Siberia, Mongolia, and Manchuria, and the naval station free of ice for her Pacific squadron. Germany has appropriated the mineral-bearing province of Shantung, and Great Britain has gone out of her way to say she will not interfere with her projects. France is laying the basis of an Imperial sway in Southern China, and threatening to bar the road of Anglo-India to the Yang-tse-kiang. Japan has momentarily retired from the scene, but only, it cannot be doubted, to husband and collect her energies for a fresh and greater effort.

Great Britain has secured an isolated position valueless without a large expenditure and an active policy. There is too little reason to suppose that either one or the other will be sanctioned or displayed. She has, on the other hand, obtained a promise that the post of Inspector-General of Customs, so long occupied with remarkable ability and address by Sir Robert Hart, shall always be held by an Englishman. The value of that promise depends on the life of the Pekin Government. It will obviously not possess much value when Pekin holds a Russian garrison, and when the occupant of the Dragon Throne is the vassal of St. Petersburg. To give it tangible significance it is necessary with as little delay as possible to obtain the removal of the Imperial Customs Department from Pekin to Shanghai, where it would be secure against arbitrary interference or perhaps even complete supersession. The reservation of the Yangtse valley as a sphere in which England will not tolerate interference is a matter that depends not on the pledges of Pekin, but on the naval power of this country.

The division of the Chinese Empire into what practically amounts to spheres of influence implies that it is moribund, and that the Manchu dynasty which has been in existence for 250 years approaches the term of its power. The assumption may prove correct, for it is difficult to discover in any section of Chinese society the public spirit and the patriotism needed to deliver a country from great perils and a nation from being conquered. If the Chinese realized their position there would be ground for hope; but so far as can be judged, there is not a public man in China who perceives that the State is on the verge of dissolution, and that nothing short of the most strenuous exertion will avail to save not the dynasty but the country from death.

The question which the British people more than their Government have to decide is whether they will stand aside and leave China to its fate, securing as best they can in the international scramble their material interests. They have at the present moment the choice of two courses. They can throw themselves with all their power and energy into the task of developing the Yangtse region, and of assisting the

Chinese to form a new administration and a new army at Nankin. If this course is followed the new China created by our efforts in the populous and wealthy provinces of the Middle Kingdom will be equal to the task of expelling the Russians, if need be, from the northern provinces. The Manchu dynasty, unworthy of its position, will have passed away, but the germs of a worthier administration will have been discovered. To carry out this project requires men and an approving Government. The former we have, but to secure a start the goodwill of the Foreign Office and of the Consular authorities is essential. Will it be forthcoming? The timid will tell us that it is only beginning the conquest of China ourselves in disguise, but if we recoil from the enterprise from fear of its magnitude we shall do nothing until the season for wise and profitable action has been lost, and we shall be outstripped in the race.

The other course open to us is to continue indefinitely the idle and useless warfare of diplomatic fence that has been exhibited during the winter of 1897–8. This system is the one favoured by senility and cowardice. It is marked by three regular periods. In the first, we lay down the most admirable and noble principles; in the second, we protest when we see them broken in the most flagrant and brazen manner; in the third, we accept meaningless and fleeting assurances, and imitate the very action that we began by censuring. A continuance in that path must end in the loss of our power, the destruction of our reputation, and the passing of "the great name of England" into a by-word among the nations.

THE END.

CHRONOLOGICAL TABLE.

Dynasty.	Emperor.	Year of Accession. B.C.	Year of Death, etc. B.C.	Length of Reign.
Semi-Mythical Period	Hwangti	2637	2577	60
	Chaohow	2577	2457	120
	Chwenhio	2457	2397	60
	Tikou	2397	2366	31
	Tichi	2366	2357	9
	Yao	2357	2257	100
	Chun, associated with Yao	2285		(reigned in all)
	Chun	2257	2208	77
	Yu, associated with Chun	2224		(in all)
The Hia	Yu	2208	2197	27
	Tiki	2197	2188	9
	Taikang	2188	2159	29
	Chungkang	2159	2118	41
	Siang	2146	2118	28
	Chaokang	2118	2057	61
	Chou	2057	2040	17
	Hoai	2040	2014	26
	Mang	2014	1996	18
	Lie	1996	1980	16
	Poukiang	1980	1921	59
	Kiung	1921	1900	21
	Kin	1900	1879	21
	Kungkia	1879	1848	31
	Kao	1848	1837	11
	Fa	1837	1818	19
	Kia	1818	1776	42
The Chang	Ching Tang	1776	1753	23
	Taikia	1753	1720	33
	Wouting	1720	1691	29
	Taikeng	1691	1666	25
	Siaokia	1666	1649	17
	Yungki	1649	1637	12
	Taiwou	1637	1562	75
	Chungting	1562	1549	13

THE HISTORY OF CHINA.

Dynasty.	Emperor.	Year of Accession. B.C.	Year of Death, etc. B.C.	Length of Reign.
The Chang	Waijen	1549	1534	15
	Hotankia	1534	1525	9
	Tsouy	1525	1506	19
	Tsousin	1506	1490	16
	Woukia	1490	1465	25
	Tsouting	1465	1433	32
	Nankeng	1433	1408	25
	Yangkia	1408	1401	7
	Pankeng	1401	1373	28
	Siaosin	1373	1352	21
	Siaoy	1352	1324	28
	Wouting	1324	1265	59
	Tsoukeng	1265	1258	7
	Tsoukia	1258	1225	33
	Linsin	1225	1219	6
	Kengting	1219	1198	21
	Wouy	1198	1194	4
	Taiting	1194	1191	3
	Tiy	1191	1154	37
	Chousin	1154	1122	32
The Chow	Wou Wang	1122	1115	7
	Ching Wang	1115	1078	37
	Kang Wang	1078	1052	26
	Chao Wang	1052	1001	51
	Mou Wang	1001	946	55
	Kung Wang	946	934	12
	Y Wang	934	909	25
	Hiao Wang	909	894	15
	I Wang	894	878	16
	Li Wang	878	827	51
	Siuan Wang	827	781	46
	Yeou Wang	781	770	11
	Ping Wang	770	719	51
	Hing Wang	719	696	23
	Chwang Wang	696	681	15
	Li Wang	681	676	5
	Hwei Wang	676	651	25
	Siang Wang	651	618	33
	King Wang	618	612	6
	Kwang Wang	612	606	6
	Ting Wang	606	585	21
	Kien Wang	585	571	14
	Ling Wang	571	544	27
	King Wang II.	544	519	25
	King Wang III.	519	475	44
	Youan Wang	475	468	7
	Chingting Wang	468	440	28
	Kao Wang	440	425	15

CHRONOLOGICAL TABLE.

Dynasty.	Emperor.	Year of Accession. B.C.	Year of Death, etc. B.C.	Length of Reign.
The Chow	Weili Wang	425	401	24
	Gan Wang	401	375	26
	Lie Wang	375	368	7
	Hien Wang	368	320	48
	Chintsen Wang	320	314	6
	Nan Wang	314	255	59
The Tsin	Chow Siang	255	250	5
	Hiao Wang	250	249	1
	Chwang Siang Wang	249	246	3
	Wang Ching	246	221	25
	Tsin Chi Hoangti	221	209	12
	Eulchi Hoangti	209	206	3
	Tsoupa Wang	206	202	4
The Han	Kaotsou	202	194	8
	Hiao Hweiti	194	187	7
	Kaohwang	187	179	8
	(Regency of Empress Liuchi.)			
	Wenti	179	156	23
	Kingti	156	140	16
	Vouti	140	86	54
	Chaoti	86	73	13
	Hiuenti	73	48	25
	Yuenti	48	32	16
	Chingti	32	6	26
			A.D.	
	Gaiti	6	1	7
		A.D.		
	Pingti	1	6	5
	Usurper, Wang Mang	6	23	17
	Ti Yuen	23	25	2
	Kwang Vouti	25	58	23
	Mingti	58	76	18
	Changti	76	89	13
	Hoti	89	106	17
	Changti II.	106	107	1
	Ganti	107	126	19
	Chunti	126	145	19
	Chungti	145	146	1
	Chiti	146	147	1
	Hiuenti	147	168	21
	Lingti	168	190	22
	Hienti	190	220	30
The Period of the Sankoue, or Three Kingdoms	Various minor Princes of Wei and the two Hans	from 220	to 265	45

THE HISTORY OF CHINA.

Dynasty.	Emperor.	Year of Accession. A.D.	Year of Death, etc. A.D.	Length of Reign.
The Later Tsin	Vouti	265	290	25
	Hweiti	290	307	17
	Hoaiti	307	313	6
	Mingti	313	317	4
	Yuanti	317	323	6
	Mingti	323	326	3
	Chingti	326	343	17
	Kangti	343	345	2
	Mouti	345	362	17
	Gaiti	362	366	4
	Tiy	366	371	5
	Kian Wenti	371	373	2
	Hiao Vouti	373	397	24
	Ganti	397	419	22
	Kungti	419	420	1
The Song	Vouti	420	423	3
	Ying Wang	423	424	1
	Wenti	424	454	30
	Vouti	454	465	11
	Mingti	465	473	8
	Gou Wang	473	477	4
	Chunti	477	479	2
The Tsi	Kaoti	479	483	4
	Vouti	483	494	11
	Mingti	494	499	5
	Paokwen	499	501	2
	Hoti	501	502	1
The Leang	Vouti	502	550	48
	Wenti	550	552	2
	Yuenti	552	555	3
	Kingti	555	556	1
The Chin	Vouti	556	564	8
	Wenti	564	567	3
	Petsong	567	569	2
	Suenti	569	580	11
The Soui	Wenti	580	601	21
	Vouti	601	605	4
	Yangti	605	617	12
	Kungti	617	618	1
The Tang	Kaotsou	618	627	9
	Taitsong	627	650	23
	Kaotsong	650	684	34
	Chungtsong	684	710	26
	Jouitsong	710	712	2
	Mingti	712	756	44
	Soutsung	756	763	7
	Taitsong II.	763	780	17
	Tetsong	780	805	25

CHRONOLOGICAL TABLE. 553

Dynasty.	Emperor.	Year of Accession. A.D.	Year of Death, etc. A.D.	Length of Reign.
The Tang	Chuntsong .	805	806	1
	Hientsung .	806	821	15
	Moutsung .	821	825	4
	Kingtsung .	825	827	2
	Wentsung .	827	841	14
	Woutsung .	841	847	6
	Hiuentsung	847	860	13
	Ytsong	860	874	14
	Hitsong .	874	889	15
	Chaotsung .	889	905	16
	Chao Hiuenti .	905	907	2
Five small Dynasties. {The Later Leangs (1)	Taitsou .	907	913	6
	Chouching .	913	915	2
	Ching .	915	923	8
The Later Tangs (2) .	Chwangtsong	923	926	3
	Mingtsong .	926	934	8
	Minti	934	934	a few months.
	Lou Wang .	934	936	2
The Later Tsin (3) .	Kaotsou .	936	943	7
	Tsi Wang .	943	947	4
The Later Han (4) .	Kaotsou .	947	948	1
	Ynti .	948	951	3
The Later Chow (5) .	Taitsou .	951	954	3
	Chitsong .	954	960	6
The Sung .	Taitsou .	960	976	16
	Taitsong .	976	998	22
	Chintsong I. .	998	1023	25
	Jintsong .	1023	1064	41
	Yngtsong .	1064	1068	4
	Chintsong II. .	1068	1086	18
	Chitsong .	1086	1101	15
	Hweitsong .	1101	1126	25
In 1115 the Kin Dynasty began to rule in Northern China concurrently with the Sung in Southern. For list of Rulers see further on.	Kingtsong .	1126	1127	1
	Kaotsong .	1127	1163	36
	Hiaotsong .	1163	1190	27
	Kwangtsong	1190	1195	5
	Ningtsong .	1195	1225	30
	Litsong	1225	1265	40
	Toutsong .	1265	1275	10
	Tihien .	1275	1276	1
	Touantsong .	1276	1278	2
	Tiping .	1278	1279	1
	Taitsou .	1115	1123	8
	Taitsong .	1123	1135	12
	Hitsong .	1135	1149	14
	Chuliang .	1149	1161	12

Dynasty.	Emperor.	Year of Accession. A.D.	Year of Death, etc. A.D.	Length of Reign.
The Kin	Chitsong	1161	1190	29
	Changtsong	1190	1209	19
	Choo Yungki	1209	1213	4
	Hiuentsong	1213	1224	11
	Gaitsong	1224	1234	10
The Mongol or Yuen	Chitsou (Kublai Khan)	1260	1295	35
	Chingtsong	1295	1308	13
	Woutsong	1308	1312	4
	Jintsong	1312	1321	9
	Yngtsong	1321	1324	3
	Taitingti	1324	1328	4
	Wentsong	1328	1333	5
	Chunti	1333	1368	35
The Ming	Hongwou	1368	1398	30
	Kien Wenti	1398	1403	5 [deposed
	Yonglo	1403	1425	22
	Gintsong	1425	1426	1
	Suentsong	1426	1435	9
	Yngtsong	1435	1450	15
	Chinwang or Kingti	1450	1458	8
	Yngtsong (restored)	1458	1465	7
	Hientsong	1465	1488	23
	Hiaotsong	1488	1506	18
	Woutsong	1506	1522	16
	Chitsong	1522	1567	45
	Moutsong	1567	1573	6
	Wanleh	1573	1620	47
	Kwantsong	1620	1621	1
	Chiti	1621	1624	3
	Hitsong	1624	1628	4
	Hoaitsong	1628	1644	16
The Manchu or Taitsing (still ruling)	Chuntche or Chitsou	1644	1661	17
	Kanghi	1661	1722	61
	Yung Ching	1722	1735	13
	Keen Lung	1735	{ 1796 abdctd. 1799 died. }	61
	Kiaking	1796	1821	25
	Taoukwang	1821	1850	29
	Hienfung	1850	1861	11
	Tungche	1861	1875	14
	Kwangsu	1875	still reigning.	

APPENDIX.

Treaty between Her Majesty and the Emperor of China, signed, in the English and Chinese Languages, at Nanking, August 29, 1842. (Ratifications exchanged at Hong Kong, June 26, 1843.)

HER Majesty the Queen of the United Kingdom of Great Britain and Ireland, and His Majesty the Emperor of China, being desirous of putting an end to the misunderstandings and consequent hostilities which have arisen between the two countries, have resolved to conclude a Treaty for that purpose, and have therefore named as their Plenipotentiaries, that is to say:

Her Majesty the Queen of Great Britain and Ireland, Sir Henry Pottinger, Bart., a Major-General in the employ of the East India Company, etc.;

And His Imperial Majesty the Emperor of China, the High Commissioners Keying, a Member of the Imperial House, a Guardian of the Crown Prince, and General of the garrison of Canton; and Elepoo, of the Imperial Kindred, graciously permitted to wear the insignia of the first rank, and the distinction of a peacock's feather, lately Minister and Governor-General, etc., and now Lieutenant-General commanding at Chapoo;*

Who, after having communicated to each other their respective full powers, and found them to be in good and due form, have agreed upon and concluded the following Articles:—

ARTICLE I.

There shall henceforward be Peace and Friendship between Her Majesty the Queen of the United Kingdom of Great Britain and Ireland and His Majesty the Emperor of China, and between their respective subjects, who shall enjoy full security and protection for their persons and property within the dominions of the other.

* Although only two Chinese Plenipotentiaries are here named, the Treaty was in fact signed by three.

Article II.

His Majesty the Emperor of China agrees, that British subjects, with their families and establishments, shall be allowed to reside, for the purpose of carrying on their mercantile pursuits, without molestation or restraint, at the cities and towns of Canton, Amoy, Foochow-foo, Ningpo, and Shanghai; and Her Majesty the Queen of Great Britain, etc., will appoint Superintendents, or Consular officers, to reside at each of the above-named cities or towns, to be the medium of communication between the Chinese authorities and the said merchants, and to see that the just duties and other dues of the Chinese Government, as hereafter provided for, are duly discharged by Her Britannic Majesty's subjects.

Article III.

It being obviously necessary and desirable that British subjects should have some port whereat they may careen and refit their ships when required, and keep stores for that purpose, His Majesty the Emperor of China cedes to Her Majesty the Queen of Great Britain, etc., the Island of Hong Kong, to be possessed in perpetuity by Her Britannic Majesty, her heirs and successors, and to be governed by such laws and regulations as Her Majesty the Queen of Great Britain, etc., shall see fit to direct.

Article IV.

The Emperor of China agrees to pay the sum of six millions of dollars, as the value of the opium which was delivered up at Canton in the month of March, 1839, as a ransom for the lives of Her Britannic Majesty's Superintendent and subjects, who had been imprisoned and threatened with death by the Chinese high officers.

Article V.

The Government of China having compelled the British merchants trading at Canton to deal exclusively with certain Chinese merchants, called Hong Merchants (or Co-Hong), who had been licensed by the Chinese Government for that purpose, the Emperor of China agrees to abolish that practice in future at all ports where British merchants may reside, and to permit them to carry on their mercantile transactions with whatever persons they please; and His Imperial Majesty further agrees to pay to the British Government the sum of three millions of dollars, on account of debts due to British subjects by some of the said Hong merchants, or Co-Hong, who have become insolvent, and who owe very large sums of money to subjects of Her Britannic Majesty.

Article VI.

The Government of Her Britannic Majesty having been obliged to send out an expedition to demand and obtain redress for the violent and unjust proceedings of the Chinese high authorities towards Her Britannic Majesty's Officer and subjects, the Emperor of China agrees to pay the sum of twelve millions of dollars, on account of the expenses incurred; and Her Britannic Majesty's Plenipotentiary voluntarily agrees, on behalf of Her Majesty, to deduct from the said amount of twelve millions of dollars, any sums which may have been received by Her Majesty's combined forces, as ransom for cities and towns in China, subsequent to the 1st day of August, 1841.

Article VII.

It is agreed, that the total amount of twenty-one millions of dollars, described in the three preceding Articles, shall be paid as follows:—

Six millions immediately.

Six millions in 1843; that is, three millions on or before the 30th of the month of June, and three millions on or before the 31st of December.

Five millions in 1844; that is, two millions and a half on or before the 30th of June, and two millions and a half on or before the 31st of December.

Four millions in 1845; that is, two millions on or before the 30th of June, and two millions on or before the 31st of December.

And it is further stipulated, that interest, at the rate of 5 per cent. per annum, shall be paid by the Government of China on any portion of the above sums that are not punctually discharged at the periods fixed.

Article VIII.

The Emperor of China agrees to release, unconditionally, all subjects of Her Britannic Majesty (whether natives of Europe or India), who may be in confinement at this moment in any part of the Chinese Empire.

Article IX.

The Emperor of China agrees to publish and promulgate, under His Imperial Sign Manual and Seal, a full and entire amnesty and act of indemnity to all subjects of China, on account of their having resided under, or having had dealings and intercourse with, or having entered the service of, Her Britannic Majesty, or of Her Majesty's officers; and His Imperial Majesty further engages to release all Chinese subjects who may be at this moment in confinement for similar reasons.

Article X.

His Majesty the Emperor of China agrees to establish at all the ports which are, by Article II. of this Treaty, to be thrown open for the resort of British merchants, a fair and regular tariff of export and import Customs and other dues, which Tariff shall be publicly notified and promulgated for general information; and the Emperor further engages, that when British merchandise shall have been once paid at any of the said ports the regulated customs and dues, agreeable to the Tariff to be hereafter fixed, such merchandise may be conveyed by Chinese merchants to any province or city in the interior of the Empire of China, on paying a further amount as transit duties, which shall not exceed *   per cent. on the tariff value of such goods.

Article XI.

It is agreed that Her Britannic Majesty's Chief High Officer in China shall correspond with the Chinese High Officers, both at the capital and in the Provinces, under the term "communication"; the subordinate British Officers and Chinese High Officers in the Provinces, under the terms "statement" on the part of the former, and on the part of the latter, "declaration"; and the subordinates of both countries on a footing of perfect equality; merchants and others not holding official situations, and therefore not included in the above, on both sides, to use the term "representation" in all papers addressed to, or intended for the notice of, the respective Governments.

Article XII.

On the assent of the Emperor of China to this Treaty being received, and the discharge of the first instalment of money, Her Britannic Majesty's forces will retire from Nanking and the Grand Canal, and will no longer molest or stop the trade of China. The military post at Chinhai will also be withdrawn; but the Islands of Koolangsoo, and that of Chusan, will continue to be held by Her Majesty's forces until the money payments, and the arrangements for opening the ports to British merchants, be completed.

---

* See Declaration on this subject, which follows the Treaty.

APPENDIX. 559

Article XIII.

The ratification of this Treaty by Her Majesty the Queen of Great Britain, etc., and His Majesty the Emperor of China, shall be exchanged as soon as the great distance which separates England from China will admit; but in the mean time, counterpart copies of it, signed and sealed by the Plenipotentiaries on behalf of their respective Sovereigns, shall be mutually delivered, and all its provisions and arrangements shall take effect.

Done at Nanking, and signed and sealed by the Plenipotentiaries on board Her Majesty's ship *Cornwallis* this twenty-ninth day of August, one thousand eight hundred and forty-two; corresponding with the Chinese date, twenty-fourth day of the seventh month, in the twenty-second year of Taoukwang.

(L.S.)   Henry Pottinger,
Her Majesty's Plenipotentiary.
Seal of the Chinese High Commissioner.
Signature of 3rd Chinese Plenipotentiary.
Signature of 2nd Chinese Plenipotentiary.
Signature of 1st Chinese Plenipotentiary.

Supplementary Treaty between Her Majesty and the Emperor of China, signed at Hoomun-Chae, October 8, 1843.

Whereas a Treaty of perpetual Peace and Friendship between Her Majesty the Queen of the United Kingdom of Great Britain and Ireland, and His Majesty the Emperor of China, was concluded at Nankin, and signed on board Her said Majesty's ship *Cornwallis* on the 29th day of August, A.D. 1842, corresponding with the Chinese date of the 24th day of the 7th month, of the 22nd year of Taoukwang, of which said Treaty of perpetual Peace and Friendship, the ratifications, under the respective Seals and Signs Manual of the Queen of Great Britain, etc., and the Emperor of China, were duly exchanged at Hong Kong on the 26th day of June, A D. 1843, corresponding with the Chinese date the 29th day of the 5th month, in the 23rd year of Taoukwang; and whereas in the said Treaty it was provided (amongst other things), that the five ports of Canton, Foo-chow-foo, Amoy, Ningpo, and Shanghai, should be thrown open for the resort and residence of British merchants, and that a fair and regular tariff of export and import duties, and other dues, should be established at such ports; and whereas various other matters of detail, connected with, and bearing relation to, the said Treaty of perpetual Peace and Friendship, have been since under the mutual discussion and consideration of the Plenipotentiary and accredited Commissioners of the High Contracting Parties; and the said tariff and details having been now finally examined into, adjusted, and agreed upon, it has been determined to arrange and record them in the form of a Supplementary Treaty of Articles, which Articles shall be held to be as binding, and of the same efficacy, as though they had been inserted in the original Treaty of perpetual Peace and Friendship.

Article I.

The Tariff of Export and Import Duties, which is hereunto attached, under the seals and signatures of the respective Plenipotentiary and Commissioners, shall henceforward be in force at the five ports of Canton, Foo-chow-foo, Amoy, Ningpo, and Shanghai.

Article II.

The General Regulations of Trade, which are hereunto attached, under the seals and signatures of the Respective Plenipotentiary and Commissioners, shall henceforward be in force at the five aforenamed ports.

Article III.

All penalties enforced or confiscations made under the third clause of the said General Regulations of Trade, shall belong and be appropriated to the public service of the Government of China.

Article IV.

After the five ports of Canton, Foo-chow, Amoy, Ningpo, and Shanghai, shall be thrown open, English merchants shall be allowed to trade only at those five ports. Neither shall they repair to any other ports or places, nor will the Chinese people at any other ports or places be permitted to trade with them. If English merchant-vessels shall, in contravention of this agreement, and of a Proclamation to the same purport, to be issued by the British Plenipotentiary, repair to any other ports or places, the Chinese Government officers shall be at liberty to seize and confiscate both vessels and cargoes; and should Chinese people be discovered clandestinely dealing with English merchants at any other ports or places, they shall be punished by the Chinese Government in such manner as the law may direct.

Article V.

The fourth clause of the General Regulations of Trade, on the subject of commercial dealings and debts between English and

Chinese merchants, is to be clearly understood to be applicable to both parties.

Article VI.

It is agreed that English merchants and others residing at, or resorting to, the five ports to be opened, shall not go into the surrounding country beyond certain short distances to be named by the local authorities, in concert with the British Consul, and on no pretence for purposes of traffic. Seamen and persons belonging to the ships shall only be allowed to land under authority and rules which will be fixed by the Consul, in communication with the local officers; and should any persons whatever infringe the stipulations of this Article, and wander away into the country, they shall be seized and handed over to the British Consul for suitable punishment.

Article VII.

The Treaty of perpetual Peace and Friendship provides for British subjects and their families residing at the cities and towns of Canton, Foo-chow, Amoy, Ningpo, and Shanghai, without molestation or restraint. It is accordingly determined that ground and houses, the rent or price of which is to be fairly and equitably arranged for, according to the rates prevailing amongst the people, without exaction on either side, shall be set apart by the local officers, in communication with the Consul, and the number of houses built, or rented, will be reported annually to the said local officers by the Consul, for the information of their respective Viceroys and Governors; but the number cannot be limited, seeing that it will be greater or less according to the resort of merchants.

Article VIII.

The Emperor of China having been graciously pleased to grant to all foreign countries whose subjects or citizens have hitherto traded at Canton, the privilege of resorting for purposes of trade to the other four ports of Foo-chow, Amoy, Ningpo, and Shanghai, on the same terms as the English, it is further agreed, that should the Emperor hereafter, from any cause whatever, be pleased to grant additional privileges or immunities to any of the subjects or citizens of such foreign countries, the same privileges and immunities will be extended to, and enjoyed by, British subjects; but it is to be understood that demands or requests are not on this plea to be unnecessarily brought forward.

Article IX.

If lawless natives of China, having committed crimes or offences against their own Government, shall flee to Hong Kong, or to the English ships of war, or English merchant ships, for refuge, they shall, if discovered by the English officers, be handed over at once to the Chinese officers for trial and punishment; or if, before such discovery be made by the English officers, it should be ascertained or suspected by the officers of the Government of China, whither such criminals and offenders have fled, a communication shall be made to the proper English officer, in order that the said criminals and offenders may be rigidly searched for, seized, and, on proof or admission of their guilt, delivered up. In like manner, if any soldier or sailor, or any other person, whatever his caste or country, who is a subject of the Crown of England, shall, from any cause or on any pretence, desert, fly, or escape into the Chinese territory, such soldier or sailor, or other person, shall be apprehended and confined by the Chinese authorities, and sent to the nearest British Consular or other Government officer. In neither case shall concealment or refuge be afforded.

Article X.

At each of the five ports to be opened to British merchants, one English cruiser will be stationed to enforce good order and discipline amongst the crews of merchant shipping, and to support the necessary authority of the Consul over British subjects. The crew of such ship of war will be carefully restrained by the officer commanding the vessel, and they will be subject to all the rules regarding going on shore, and straying into the country, that are already laid down for the crews of merchant-vessels. Whenever it may be necessary to relieve such ships of war by another, intimation of that intention will be communicated by the Consul, or by the British Superintendent of Trade, where circumstances will permit, to the local Chinese authorities, lest the appearance of an additional ship should excite misgivings amongst the people; and the Chinese cruisers are to offer no hindrance to such relieving ship, nor is she to be considered liable to any port-charges, or other rules laid down in the General Regulations of Trade, seeing that British ships of war never trade in any shape.

Article XI.

The post of Chusan and Koolangsoo will be withdrawn, as provided for in the Treaty of perpetual Peace and Friendship, the moment all the monies stipulated for in that Treaty shall be paid;

and the British Plenipotentiary distinctly and voluntarily agrees, that all dwelling-houses, store-houses, barracks, and other buildings that the British troops or people may have occupied, or intermediately built or repaired, shall be handed over, on the evacuation of the posts, exactly as they stand, to the Chinese Authorities, so as to prevent any pretence for delay, or the slightest occasion for discussion or dispute on those points.

Article XII.

A fair and regular Tariff of duties and other dues having now been established, it is to be hoped that the system of smuggling which has heretofore been carried on between English and Chinese merchants—in many cases with the open connivance and collusion of the Chinese Custom-house officers—will entirely cease; and the most peremptory Proclamation to all English merchants has been already issued on this subject by the British Plenipotentiary, who will also instruct the different Consuls to strictly watch over, and carefully scrutinize, the conduct of all persons, being British subjects, trading under his superintendence. In any positive instance of smuggling transactions coming to the Consul's knowledge, he will instantly apprise the Chinese Authorities of the fact, and they will proceed to seize and confiscate all goods, whatever their value or nature, that may have been so smuggled, and will also be at liberty, if they see fit, to prohibit the ship from which the smuggled goods were landed from trading further, and to send her away, as soon as her accounts are adjusted and paid. The Chinese Government officers will, at the same time, adopt whatever measures they may think fit with regard to the Chinese merchants and Custom-house officers who may be discovered to be concerned in smuggling.

Article XIII.

All persons, whether natives of China or otherwise, who may wish to convey goods from any one of the five ports of Canton, Foochow-foo, Amoy, Ningpo, and Shanghai, to Hong Kong, for sale or consumption, shall be at full and perfect liberty to do so, on paying the duties on such goods, and obtaining a pass, or post-clearance, from the Chinese Custom-house at one of the said ports. Should natives of China wish to repair to Hong Kong to purchase goods, they shall have free and full permission to do so; and should they required a Chinese vessel to carry away their purchases, they must obtain a pass, or port-clearance, for her at the Custom-house of the port whence the vessel may sail for Hong Kong. It is further settled, that in all cases these passes are to be returned to the officers of the Chinese Government, as soon as the trip for which they may be granted shall be completed.

Article XIV.

An English officer will be appointed at Hong Kong, one part of whose duty will be to examine the registers and passes of all Chinese vessels that may repair to that port to buy or sell goods; and should such officer at any time find that any Chinese merchant-vessel has not a pass, or register, from one of the five ports, she is to be considered as an unauthorized or smuggling vessel, and is not to be allowed to trade, whilst a report of the circumstance is to be made to the Chinese authorities. By this arrangement, it is to be hoped that piracy and illegal traffic will be effectually prevented.

Article XV.

Should natives of India who may repair to Hong Kong to trade, incur debts there, the recovery of such debts must be arranged for by the English Courts of Justice on the spot; but if the Chinese debtor shall abscond, and be known to have property, real or personal, within the Chinese territory, the rule laid down in the fourth clause of the General Regulations for Trade shall be applied to the case; and it will be the duty of the Chinese Authorities, on application by, and in concert with, the British Consuls, to do their utmost to see justice done between the parties. On the same principle, should a British merchant incur debts at any of the five ports, and fly to Hong Kong, the British authorities will, on receiving an application from the Chinese Government officers, accompanied by statements and full proofs of the debts, institute an investigation into the claims, and, when established, oblige the defaulter or debtor to settle them to the utmost of his means.

Article XVI.

It is agreed that the Custom-house officers at the five ports shall make a monthly return to Canton, of the passes granted to vessels proceeding to Hong Kong, together with the nature of their cargoes; and a copy of these returns will be embodied in one return, and communicated once a month to the proper English officer at Hong Kong. The said English officer will, on his part, make a similar return or communication to the Chinese authorities at Canton, showing the names of Chinese vessels arrived at Hong Kong, or departed from that port, with the nature of their cargoes; and the Canton authorities will apprise the Custom-houses at the five ports, in order that, by these arrangements and precautions, all clandestine and illegal trade, under the cover of passes, may be averted.

XVII., OR ADDITIONAL ARTICLE.
Relating to British Small Craft.

Various small vessels belonging to the English nation, called schooners, cutters, lorchas, etc., etc., have not hitherto been chargeable with tonnage dues. It is now agreed, in relation to this class of vessels, which ply between Hong Kong and the city, and the city and Macao, that if they only carry passengers, letters, and baggage, they shall, as heretofore, pay no tonnage dues; but if these small craft carry any dutiable articles, no matter how small the quantity may be, they ought, in principle, to pay their full tonnage dues. But this class of small craft are not like the large ships which are engaged in foreign trade; they are constantly coming and going; they make several trips a month, and are not like the large foreign ships, which, on entering the port, cast anchor at Whampoa. If we were to place them on the same footing as the large foreign ships, the charge would fall unequally; therefore, after this, the smallest of these craft shall be rated at 75 tons, and the largest not to exceed 150 tons; whenever they enter the port (or leave the port with cargo), they shall pay tonnage dues at the rate of one mace per ton register. If not so large as 75 tons, they shall still be considered and charged as of 75 tons; and if they exceed 150 tons, they shall be considered as large foreign ships, and, like them, charged tonnage dues, at the rate of five mace per register ton. Foo-chow and the other ports having none of this kind of intercourse, and none of this kind of small craft, it would be unnecessary to make any arrangement as regards them.

The following are the rules by which they are to be regulated:—

    1st. Every British schooner, cutter, lorcha, etc., shall have a sailing letter or register in Chinese and English, under the seal and signature of the Chief Superintendent of Trade, describing her appearance, burden, etc., etc.

    2nd. Every schooner, lorcha, and such vessel, shall report herself, as large vessels are required to do, at the Bocca Tigris; and when she carries cargo, she shall also report herself at Whampoa, and shall, on reaching Canton, deliver up her sailing letter or register to the British Consul, who will obtain permission from the Hoppo for her to discharge her cargo, which she is not to do without such permission, under the forfeiture of the penalties laid down in the 3rd clause of the General Regulations of Trade.

3rd. When the inward cargo is discharged, and an outward one (if intended) taken on board, and the duties on both arranged and paid, the Consul will restore the register or sailing letter, and allow the vessel to depart.

This Supplementary Treaty, to be attached to the original Treaty of Peace, consisting of sixteen Articles, and one Additional Article relating to small vessels, is now written out, forming, with its accompaniments, four pamphlets, and is formally signed and sealed by their Excellencies the British Plenipotentiary and the Chinese Imperial Commissioner, who, in the first instance, take two copies each, and exchange them, that their provisions may be immediately carried into effect. At the same time, each of these high functionaries, having taken his two copies, shall duly memorialize the Sovereign of his nation; but the two countries are differently situated as respects distance, so that the will of the one Sovereign can be known sooner than the will of the other. It is now therefore agreed, that on receiving the gracious assent of the Emperor in the Vermilion Pencil, the Imperial Commissioner will deliver the very document containing it into the hands of his Excellency Hwang, Judge of Canton, who will proceed to such place as the Plenipotentiary may appoint, and deliver it to the English Plenipotentiary to have and to hold. Afterwards, the Sign Manual of the Sovereign of England having been received at Hong Kong, likewise graciously assenting to and confirming the Treaty, the English Plenipotentiary will despatch a specially appointed officer to Canton, who will deliver the copy containing the Royal Sign Manual to his Excellency Hwang, who will forward it to the Imperial Commissioner, as a rule and a guide to both nations for ever, and as a solemn confirmation of our peace and friendship.

A most important Supplementary Treaty.

Signed and sealed at Hoomun-Chae, on the eighth day of October, 1843, corresponding with the Chinese date of the fifteenth day of the eighth moon, of the twenty-third year of Taoukwang.

(L.S.) HENRY POTTINGER.
Seal and Signature of the Chinese Plenipotentiary.

Convention signed at Bocca Tigris, April 4, 1846.

HER Majesty the Queen of the United Kingdom of Great Britain and Ireland, and His Majesty the Emperor of China, having, with a view to the settlement of all questions between the two

APPENDIX. 567

countries, and for the preservation of mutual harmony and good understanding, appointed as their Plenipotentiaries, that is to say, Her Majesty the Queen of Great Britain and Ireland, Sir John Francis Davis, a Baronet of the United Kingdom, Governor and Commander-in-chief of Her Majesty's Colony of Hong Kong, etc., and His Majesty the Emperor of China, the High Commissioner Keying, a Member of the Imperial House, a Cabinet Councillor, a Guardian of the Crown Prince, and Governor-General of the Two Kwang Provinces;

The said Plenipotentiaries respectively have, in pursuance of the above-mentioned ends, and after communicating to each other their respective full Powers, and finding them to be in good and due form, agreed upon and concluded the following Articles :—

1. His Majesty the Emperor of China having, on his own part, distinctly stated that when in the course of time mutual tranquillity shall have been insured, it will be safe and right to admit foreigners into the city of Canton, and the local authorities being for the present unable to coerce the people of that city, the Plenipotentiaries on either side mutually agree that the execution of the above measure shall be postponed to a more favourable period; but the claim of right is by no means yielded or abandoned on the part of Her Britannic Majesty.

2. British subjects shall in the meanwhile enjoy full liberty and protection in the neighbourhood, on the outside of the city of Canton, within certain limits fixed according to previous Treaty, comprising seventy localities of which the names were communicated by the district magistrates to the British Consul on the 21st of November, 1845. They may likewise make excursions on the two sides of the river where there are not numerous villages.

3. It is stipulated, on the part of His Majesty the Emperor of China, that on the evacuation of Chusan by Her Britannic Majesty's forces, the said island shall never be ceded to any other foreign Power.

4. Her Britannic Majesty consents, upon her part, in case of the attack of an invader, to protect Chusan and its dependencies, and to restore it to the possession of China as of old; but as this stipulation proceeds from the friendly alliance between the two nations, no pecuniary subsidies are to be due from China on this account.

5. Upon the receipt of the sign-manual of His Majesty the Emperor of China to these presents, it is agreed, on account of the distance which separates the two countries, that the Island of Chusan shall be immediately delivered over to the Chinese authorities;

and on the ratification of the present Convention by Her Britannic Majesty, it shall be mutually binding on the High Contracting Powers.

Done at Bocca Tigris, and signed and sealed by the Plenipotentiaries, this fourth day of April, 1846, corresponding with the Chinese date, Taoukwang twenty-sixth year, third moon, ninth day.

Inclosure in No. 181.

Treaty between Her Majesty and the Emperor of China. Signed, in the English and Chinese languages, at Tien-tsin, June 26, 1858.

HER Majesty the Queen of the United Kingdom of Great Britain and Ireland, and His Majesty the Emperor of China, being desirous to put an end to the existing misunderstanding between the two countries, and to place their relations on a more satisfactory footing in future, have resolved to proceed to a revision and improvement of the Treaties existing between them; and, for that purpose, have named as their Plenipotentiaries, that is to say :—

Her Majesty the Queen of Great Britain and Ireland, the Right Honourable the Earl of Elgin and Kincardine, a Peer of the United Kingdom, and Knight of the Most Ancient and Most Noble Order of the Thistle;

And His Majesty the Emperor of China, the High Commissioner Kweiliang, a Senior Chief Secretary of State, styled of the East Cabinet, Captain-General of the Plain White Banner of the Manchu Banner Force, Superintendent-General of the administration of Criminal Law; and Hwashana, one of His Imperial Majesty's Expositors of the Classics, Manchu President of the Office for the regulation of the Civil Establishment, Captain-General of the Bordered Blue Banner of the Chinese Banner Force, and Visitor of the Office of Interpretation;

Who, after having communicated to each other their respective full powers, and found them to be in good and due form, have agreed upon and concluded the following Articles :—

ARTICLE I.

The Treaty of Peace and Amity between the two nations, signed at Nankin on the twenty-ninth day of August, in the year one thousand eight hundred and forty-two, is hereby renewed and confirmed.

The Supplementary Treaty and General Regulations of Trade having been amended and improved, and the substance of their provisions having been incorporated in this Treaty, the said Supplementary Treaty and General Regulations of Trade are hereby abrogated.

ARTICLE II.

For the better preservation of harmony in future, Her Majesty the Queen of Great Britain and His Majesty the Emperor of China mutually agree that, in accordance with the universal practice of great and friendly nations, Her Majesty the Queen may, if She see fit, appoint Ambassadors, Ministers, or other Diplomatic Agents to the Court of Pekin; and His Majesty the Emperor of China may, in like manner, if He see fit, appoint Ambassadors, Ministers, or other Diplomatic Agents to the Court of St. James'.

ARTICLE III.

His Majesty the Emperor of China hereby agrees that the Ambassador, Minister, or other Diplomatic Agent, so appointed by Her Majesty the Queen of Great Britain, may reside, with his family and establishment, permanently at the capital, or may visit it occasionally, at the option of the British Government. He shall not be called upon to perform any ceremony derogatory to him as representing the Sovereign of an independent nation on a footing of equality with that of China. On the other hand, he shall use the same forms of ceremony and respect to His Majesty the Emperor as are employed by the Ambassadors, Ministers, or Diplomatic Agents of Her Majesty towards the Sovereigns of independent and equal European nations.

It is further agreed, that Her Majesty's Government may acquire at Pekin a site for building, or may hire houses for the accommodation of Her Majesty's Mission, and that the Chinese Government will assist it in so doing.

Her Majesty's Representative shall be at liberty to choose his own servants and attendants, who shall not be subjected to any kind of molestation whatever.

Any person guilty of disrespect or violence to Her Majesty's Representative, or to any member of his family or establishment, in deed or word, shall be severely punished.

ARTICLE IV.

It is further agreed, that no obstacle or difficulty shall be made to the free movements of Her Majesty's Representative, and that he, and the persons of his suite, may come and go, and travel at their pleasure. He shall, moreover, have full liberty to send and receive his correspondence, to and from any point on the sea-coast that he may select; and his letters and effects shall be held sacred and inviolable. He may employ, for their transmission, special couriers, who shall meet with the same protection and facilities for travelling as the persons employed in carrying despatches for the Imperial Government; and, generally, he shall enjoy the same privileges as are accorded to officers of the same rank by the usage and consent of Western nations.

All expenses attending the Diplomatic Mission of Great Britain shall be borne by the British Government.

Article V.

His Majesty the Emperor of China agrees to nominate one of the Secretaries of State, or a President of one of the Boards, as the high officer with whom the Ambassador, Minister, or other Diplomatic Agent of Her Majesty the Queen shall transact business, either personally or in writing, on a footing of perfect equality.

Article VI.

Her Majesty the Queen of Great Britain agrees that the privileges hereby secured shall be enjoyed in her dominions by the Ambassadors, Ministers, or Diplomatic Agents of the Emperor of China accredited to the Court of Her Majesty.

Article VII.

Her Majesty the Queen may appoint one or more Consuls in the dominions of the Emperor of China; and such Consul or Consuls shall be at liberty to reside in any of the open ports or cities of China, as Her Majesty the Queen may consider most expedient for the interests of British commerce. They shall be treated with due respect by the Chinese authorities, and enjoy the same privileges and immunities as the Consular Officers of the most favoured nation.

Consuls and Vice-Consuls in charge shall rank with Intendants of Circuits; Vice-Consuls, Acting Vice-Consuls, and Interpreters, with Prefects. They shall have access to the official residences of these officers, and communicate with them, either personally or in writing, on a footing of equality, as the interests of the public service may require.

Article VIII.

The Christian religion, as professed by Protestants or Roman Catholics, inculcates the practice of virtue, and teaches man to do as he would be done by. Persons teaching it or professing it,

APPENDIX. 571

therefore, shall alike be entitled to the protection of the Chinese authorities, nor shall any such, peaceably pursuing their calling, and not offending against the laws, be persecuted or interfered with.

Article IX.

British subjects are hereby authorized to travel, for their pleasure or for purposes of trade, to all parts of the interior, under passports which will be issued by their Consuls, and countersigned by the local authorities. These passports, if demanded, must be produced for examination in the localities passed through. If the passport be not irregular, the bearer will be allowed to proceed, and no opposition shall be offered to his hiring persons, or hiring vessels for the carriage of his baggage or merchandise. If he be without a passport, or if he commit any offence against the law, he shall be handed over to the nearest Consul for punishment, but he must not be subjected to any ill-usage in excess of necessary restraint. No passport need be applied for by persons going on excursions from the ports open to trade to a distance not exceeding 100 *li*, and for a period not exceeding five days.

The provisions of this Article do not apply to crews of ships, for the due restraint of whom regulations will be drawn up by the Consul and the local authorities.

To Nankin, and other cities disturbed by persons in arms against the Government, no pass shall be given, until they shall have been recaptured.

Article X.

British merchant-ships shall have authority to trade upon the Great River (Yang-tsz). The Upper and Lower Valley of the river being, however, disturbed by outlaws, no port shall be for the present opened to trade, with the exception of Chin-kiang, which shall be opened in a year from the date of the signing of this Treaty.

So soon as peace shall have been restored, British vessels shall also be admitted to trade at such ports as far as Han-kow, not exceeding three in number, as the British Minister, after consultation with the Chinese Secretary of State, may determine shall be ports of entry and discharge.

Article XI.

In addition to the towns and cities of Canton, Amoy, Foo-chow, Ningpo, and Shanghai, opened by the treaty of Nankin, it is agreed that British subjects may frequent the cities and ports of New-Chwang, Tang-chow, Tai-Wan (Formosa), Chau-Chow (Swatoa), and Kiung-Chow (Hainan).

They are permitted to carry on trade with whomsoever they please, and to proceed to and fro at pleasure with their vessels and merchandise.

They shall enjoy the same privileges, advantages, and immunities, at the said towns and ports, as they enjoy at the ports already opened to trade, including the right of residence, of buying or renting houses, of leasing land therein, and of building churches, hospitals, and cemeteries.

Article XII.

British subjects, whether at the ports or at other places, desiring to build or open houses, warehouses, churches, hospitals, or burial-grounds, shall make their agreement for the land or buildings they require, at the rates prevailing among the people, equitably, and without exaction on either side.

Article XIII.

The Chinese Government will place no restrictions whatever upon the employment, by British subjects, of Chinese subjects in any lawful capacity.

Article XIV.

British subjects may hire whatever boats they please for the transport of goods or passengers, and the sum to be paid for such boats shall be settled between the parties themselves, without the interference of the Chinese Government. The number of these boats shall not be limited, nor shall a monopoly in respect either of the boats, or of the porters or coolies engaged in carrying the goods, be granted to any parties. If any smuggling takes place in them, the offenders will, of course, be punished according to law.

Article XV.

All questions in regard to rights, whether of property or person, arising between British subjects, shall be subject to the jurisdiction of the British authorities.

Article XVI.

Chinese subjects who may be guilty of any criminal act towards British subjects, shall be arrested and punished by the Chinese authorities, according to the laws of China.

British subjects who may commit any crime in China shall be tried and punished by the Consul, or other public functionary authorized thereto, according to the laws of Great Britain.

APPENDIX. 573

Justice shall be equitably and impartially administered on both sides.

Article XVII.

A British subject having reason to complain of a Chinese must proceed to the Consulate, and state his grievance. The Consul will inquire into the merits of the case, and do his utmost to arrange it amicably. In like manner, if a Chinese have reason to complain of a British subject, the Consul shall no less listen to his complaint, and endeavour to settle it in a friendly manner. If disputes take place of such a nature that the Consul cannot arrange them amicably, then he shall request the assistance of the Chinese authorities, that they may together examine into the merits of the case, and decide it equitably.

Article XVIII.

The Chinese authorities shall, at all times, afford the fullest protection to the persons and property of British subjects, whenever these shall have been subjected to insult or violence. In all cases of incendiarism or robbery, the local authorities shall at once take the necessary steps for the recovery of the stolen property, the suppression of disorder, and the arrest of the guilty parties, whom they will punish according to law.

Article XIX.

If any British merchant-vessel, while within Chinese waters, be plundered by robbers or pirates, it shall be the duty of the Chinese authorities to use every endeavour to capture and punish the said robbers or pirates, and to recover the stolen property, that it may be handed over to the Consul for restoration to the owner.

Article XX.

If any British vessel be at any time wrecked or stranded on the coast of China, or be compelled to take refuge in any port within the dominions of the Emperor of China, the Chinese authorities, on being apprised of the fact, shall immediately adopt measures for its relief and security; the persons on board shall receive friendly treatment, and shall be furnished, if necessary, with the means of conveyance to the nearest Consular station.

Article XXI.

If criminals, subjects of China, shall take refuge in Hong Kong, or on board the British ships there, they shall, upon due requisition by the Chinese authorities, be searched for, and, on proof of their guilt, be delivered up.

In like manner, if Chinese offenders take refuge in the houses or on board the vessels of British subjects at the open ports, they shall not be harboured or concealed, but shall be delivered up, on due requisition by the Chinese authorities, addressed to the British Consul.

Article XXII.

Should any Chinese subject fail to discharge debts incurred to a British subject, or should he fraudulently abscond, the Chinese authorities will do their utmost to effect his arrest, and enforce recovery of the debts. The British authorities will likewise do their utmost to bring to justice any British subject fraudulently absconding or failing to discharge debts incurred by him to a Chinese subject.

Article XXIII.

Should natives of China who may repair to Hong Kong to trade incur debts there, the recovery of such debts must be arranged for by the English Courts of Justice on the spot; but should the Chinese debtor abscond, and be known to have property, real or personal, within the Chinese territory, it shall be the duty of the Chinese authorities, on application by, and in concert with, the British Consul, to do their utmost to see justice done between the parties.

Article XXIV.

It is agreed that British subjects shall pay, on all merchandise imported or exported by them, the duties prescribed by the Tariff; but in no case shall they be called upon to pay other or higher duties than are required of the subjects of any other foreign nation.

Article XXV.

Import duties shall be considered payable on the landing of the goods, and duties of export on the shipment of the same.

Article XXVI.

Whereas the Tariff fixed by Article X. of the Treaty of Nankin, and which was estimated so as to impose on imports and exports a duty at about the rate of five per cent. *ad valorem*, has been found, by reason of the fall in value of various articles of merchandise therein enumerated, to impose a duty upon these, considerably in excess of the rate originally assumed as above to be a fair rate, it is agreed that the said Tariff shall be revised, and that as soon as the Treaty shall have been signed, application shall be made to the Emperor of China to depute a high officer of the Board of Revenue to meet, at Shanghai, officers to be deputed on behalf of the British Government to consider its revision together, so that the Tariff, as revised, may come into operation immediately after the ratification of this Treaty.

Article XXVII.

It is agreed that either of the High Contracting Parties to this Treaty may demand a further revision of the Tariff, and of the Commercial Articles of this Treaty, at the end of ten years, but if no demand be made on either side within six months after the end of the first ten years, then the Tariff shall remain in force for ten years more, reckoned from the end of the preceding ten years; and so it shall be, at the end of each successive ten years.

Article XXVIII.

Whereas it is agreed in Article X. of the Treaty of Nankin, that British imports, having paid the tariff duties, should be conveyed into the interior free of all further charges, except a transit duty, the amount whereof was not to exceed a certain percentage on tariff value; and whereas no accurate information having been furnished of the amount of such duty, British merchants have constantly complained that charges are suddenly and arbitrarily imposed by the provincial authorities as transit duties upon produce on its way to the foreign market, and on imports on their way into the interior, to the detriment of trade; it is agreed that within four months from the signing of this Treaty, at all ports now open to British trade, and within a similar period at all ports that may hereafter be opened, the authority appointed to superintend the collection of duties shall be obliged, upon application of the Consul, to declare the amount of duties leviable on produce between the places of production and the port of shipment, and upon imports between the Consular port in question and the inland markets named by the Consul; and that a notification thereof shall be published in English and Chinese for general information.

But it shall be at the option of any British subject desiring to convey produce purchased inland to a port, or to convey imports from a port to an inland market, to clear his goods of all transit duties, by payment of a single charge. The amount of this charge shall be leviable on exports at the first barrier that they may have to pass, or, on imports, at the port at which they are landed; and, on payment thereof, a certificate shall be issued, which shall exempt the goods from all further inland charges whatsoever.

It is further agreed, that the amount of this charge shall be calculated as near as possible, at the rate of two-and-a-half per cent. *ad valorem*, and that it shall be fixed for each article at the Conference to be held at Shanghai for the revision of the Tariff.

It is distinctly understood that the payment of transit dues, by commutation or otherwise, shall in no way affect the tariff duties on imports or exports, which will continue to be levied separately and in full.

Article XXIX.

British merchant-vessels of more than one hundred and fifty tons burden shall be charged tonnage dues at the rate of four mace per ton; if of one hundred and fifty tons and under, they shall be charged at the rate of one mace per ton.

Any vessel clearing from any of the open ports of China for any other of the open ports or for Hong Kong, shall be entitled, on application of the master, to a special certificate from the Customs, on exhibition of which she shall be exempted from all further payment of tonnage-dues in any open port of China, for a period of four months, to be reckoned from the date of her port-clearance.

Article XXX.

The master of any British merchant-vessel may, within forty-eight hours after the arrival of his vessel, but not later, decide to depart without breaking bulk, in which he will not be subject to pay tonnage-dues. But tonnage-dues shall be held due after the expiration of the said forty-eight hours. No other fees or charges upon entry or departure shall be levied.

Article XXXI.

No tonnage-dues shall be payable on boats employed by British subjects in the conveyance of passengers, baggage, letters, articles of provision, or other articles not subject to duty, between any of the open ports. All cargo-boats, however, conveying merchandise subject to duty shall pay tonnage-dues, once in six months, at the rate of four mace per register ton.

Article XXXII.

The Consuls and Superintendents of Customs shall consult together regarding the erection of beacons or light-houses, and the distribution of buoys and light-ships, as occasion may demand.

APPENDIX. 577

Article XXXIII.

Duties shall be paid to the bankers authorized by the Chinese Government to receive the same in its behalf, either in sycee or in foreign money, according to the assay made at Canton, on the thirteenth of July, one thousand eight hundred and forty-three.

Article XXXIV.

Sets of standard weights and measures, prepared according to the standard issued to the Canton Custom-house by the Board of Revenue, shall be delivered by the Superintendent of Customs to the Consul at each port, to secure uniformity and prevent confusion.

Article XXXV.

Any British merchant-vessel arriving at one of the open ports shall be at liberty to engage the services of a pilot to take her into port. In like manner, after she has discharged all legal dues and duties, and is ready to take her departure, she shall be allowed to select a pilot to conduct her out of port.

Article XXXVI.

Whenever a British merchant-vessel shall arrive off one of the open ports, the Superintendent of Customs shall depute one or more Customs officers to guard the ship. They shall either live in a boat of their own, or stay on board the ship, as may best suit their convenience. Their food and expenses shall be supplied them from the Custom-house, and they shall not be entitled to any fees whatever from the master or consignee. Should they violate this regulation, they shall be punished proportionately to the amount exacted.

Article XXXVII.

Within twenty-four hours after arrival, the ship's papers, bills of lading, etc., shall be lodged in the hands of the Consul, who will, within a further period of twenty-four hours, report to the Superintendent of Customs the name of the ship, her register tonnage, and the nature of her cargo. If, owing to neglect on the part of the master, the above rule is not complied with within forty-eight hours after the ship's arrival, he shall be liable to a fine of fifty taels for every day's delay: the total amount of penalty, however, shall not exceed two hundred taels.

The master will be responsible for the correctness of the manifest, which shall contain a full and true account of the particulars of the cargo on board. For presenting a false manifest, he will subject himself to a fine of five hundred taels; but he will be allowed to correct, within twenty-four hours after delivery of it to the Customs officers, any mistake he may discover in his manifest, without incurring this penalty.

Article XXXVIII.

After receiving from the Consul the report in due form, the Superintendent of Customs shall grant the vessel a permit to open hatches. If the master shall open hatches and begin to discharge any goods without such permission, he shall be fined five hundred taels, and the goods discharged shall be confiscated wholly.

Article XXXIX.

Any British merchant who has cargo to land or ship, must apply to the Superintendent of Customs for a special permit. Cargo landed or shipped without such permit will be liable to confiscation.

Article XL.

No transhipment from one vessel to another can be made without special permission, under pain of confiscation of the goods so transhipped.

Article XLI.

When all dues and duties shall have been paid, the Superintendent of Customs shall give a port-clearance, and the Consul shall then return the ship's papers, so that she may depart on her voyage.

Article XLII.

With respect to articles subject, according to the Tariff, to an *ad valorem* duty, if the British merchant cannot agree with the Chinese officer in affixing a value, then each party shall call two or three merchants to look at the goods, and the highest price at which any of these merchants would be willing to purchase them shall be assumed as the value of the goods.

Article XLIII.

Duties shall be charged upon the net weight of each article, making a deduction for the tare weight of congee, etc. To fix the tare on any article, such as tea, if the British merchant cannot agree with the Custom-house officer, then each party shall choose so many chests out of every hundred, which being first weighed in gross, shall afterwards be tared, and the average tare upon these chests shall be assumed as the tare upon the whole, and upon this principle shall the tare be fixed upon all other goods and packages. If there should be any other points in dispute which cannot be settled, the British merchant may appeal to his consul, who will communicate the particulars of the case to the Superintendent of Customs, that it may be equitably arranged. But the appeal must be made within twenty-four hours, or it will not be attended to. While such points are still unsettled, the Superintendent of Customs shall postpone the insertion of the same in his books.

Article XLIV.

Upon all damaged goods a fair reduction of duty shall be allowed, proportionate to their deterioration. If any disputes arise, they shall be settled in the manner pointed out in the clause of this Treaty having reference to articles which pay duty *ad valorem*.

Article XLV.

British merchants who may have imported merchandise into any of the open ports and paid the duty thereon, if they desire to re-export the same, shall be entitled to make application to the Superintendent of Customs, who, in order to prevent fraud on the revenue, shall cause examination to be made by suitable officers, to see that the duties paid on such goods, as entered in the Custom-house books, correspond with the representation made, and that the goods remain with their original marks unchanged. He shall then make a memorandum on the port-clearance of the goods and of the amount of duties paid, and deliver the same to the merchant; and shall also certify the facts to the officers of Customs of the other ports. All which being done, on the arrival in port of the vessel in which the goods are laden, everything being found on examination there to correspond, she shall be permitted to break bulk, and land the said goods, without being subject to the payment of any additional duty thereon. But if, on such examination, the Superintendent of Customs shall detect any fraud on the revenue in the case, then the goods shall be subject to confiscation by the Chinese Government.

British merchants desiring to re-export duty-paid imports to a foreign country, shall be entitled, on complying with the same conditions as in the case of re-exportation to another port in China, to a drawback-certificate, which shall be a valid tender to the Customs in payment of import or export duties.

Foreign grain brought into any port of China in a British ship, if no part thereof has been landed, may be re-exported without hindrance.

Article XLVI.

The Chinese authorities at each port shall adopt the means they may judge most proper to prevent the revenue suffering from fraud or smuggling.

Article XLVII.

British merchant-vessels are not entitled to resort to other than the ports of trade declared open by this Treaty. They are not unlawfully to enter other ports in China, or to carry on clandestine trade along the coasts thereof. Any vessel violating this provision shall, with her cargo, be subject to confiscation by the Chinese Government.

Article XLVIII.

If any British merchant-vessel be concerned in smuggling, the goods, whatever their value or nature, shall be subject to confiscation by the Chinese authorities, and the ship may be prohibited from trading further and sent away, as soon as her accounts shall have been adjusted and paid.

Article XLIX.

All penalties enforced, or confiscations made, under this Treaty, shall belong and be appropriated to the public service of the Government of China.

Article L.

All official communications addressed by the Diplomatic and Consular Agents of Her Majesty the Queen to the Chinese authorities shall, henceforth, be written in English. They will for the present be accompanied by a Chinese version, but it is understood that, in the event of there being any difference of meaning between the English and Chinese text, the English Government will hold the sense as expressed in the English text to be the correct sense. This provision is to apply to the Treaty now negotiated, the Chinese text of which has been carefully corrected by the English original.

Article LI.

It is agreed, that henceforward the character "I" (barbarian) shall not be applied to the Government or subjects of Her Britannic Majesty, in any Chinese official document issued by the Chinese authorities, either in the capital or in the provinces.

Article LII.

British ships of war coming for no hostile purpose, or being engaged in the pursuit of pirates, shall be at liberty to visit all ports within the dominions of the Emperor of China, and shall receive every facility for the purchase of provisions, procuring water, and, if occasion require, for the making of repairs. The Commanders of such ship shall hold intercourse with the Chinese authorities on terms of equality and courtesy.

ARTICLE LIII.

In consideration of the injury sustained by native and foreign commerce from the prevalence of piracy in the seas of China, the High Contracting Parties agree to concert measures for its suppression.

ARTICLE LIV.

The British Government and its subjects are hereby confirmed in all privileges, immunities, and advantages conferred on them by previous Treaties; and it is hereby expressly stipulated that the British Government and its subjects will be allowed free and equal participation in all privileges, immunities, and advantages that may have been, or may be hereafter, granted by His Majesty the Emperor of China to the Government or subjects of any other nation.

ARTICLE LV.

In evidence of Her desire for the continuance of a friendly understanding, Her Majesty the Queen of Great Britain consents to include in a Separate Article, which shall be in every respect of equal validity with the Articles of this Treaty, the conditions affecting indemnity for expenses incurred and losses sustained in the matter of the Canton question.

ARTICLE LVI.

The ratifications of this Treaty, under the hand of Her Majesty the Queen of Great Britain and Ireland and His Majesty the Emperor of China, respectively, shall be exchanged at Peking, within a year from this day of signature.

In token whereof, the respective Plenipotentiaries have signed and sealed this Treaty.

Done at Tien-tsin, this twenty-sixth day of June, in the year of our Lord one thousand eight hundred and fifty-eight; corresponding with the Chinese date, the sixteenth day, fifth moon, of the eighth year of Hien Fung.

(L.S.)   ELGIN AND KINCARDINE.
Signature of First Chinese Plenipotentiary.
Signature of Second Chinese Plenipotentiary.
Seal of the Chinese Plenipotentiaries.

Separate Article annexed to the Treaty concluded between Great Britain and China, on the twenty-sixth day of June, in the year one thousand eight hundred and fifty-eight.

It is hereby agreed that a sum of two millions of taels, on account of the losses sustained by British subjects through the misconduct of the Chinese authorities at Canton; and a further sum of two millions of taels, on account of the military expenses of the expedition which Her Majesty the Queen has been compelled to send out for the purpose of obtaining redress, and of enforcing the due observance of Treaty provisions; shall be paid to Her Majesty's Representatives in China by the authorities of the Kwang-tung province.

The necessary arrangements with respect to the time and mode of effecting these payments shall be determined by Her Majesty's Representative, in concert with the Chinese authorities of Kwang-tung.

When the above amount shall have been discharged in full, the British forces will be withdrawn from the city of Canton.

Done at Tien-tsin, this twenty-sixth day of June, in the year of our Lord one thousand eight hundred and fifty-eight, corresponding with the Chinese date, the sixteenth day, fifth moon, of the eighth year of Hien Fung.

(L.S.)   Elgin and Kincardine.
Signature of First Chinese Plenipotentiary.
Signature of Second Chinese Plenipotentiary.
Seal of the Chinese Plenipotentiaries.

Convention of Peace between Her Majesty and the Emperor of China.

Signed at Peking, 24th October, 1860.

Her Majesty the Queen of Great Britain and Ireland, and His Imperial Majesty the Emperor of China, being alike desirous to bring to an end the misunderstanding at present existing between their respective Governments, and to secure their relations against further interruption, have for this purpose appointed Plenipotentiaries, that is to say:—

Her Majesty the Queen of Great Britain and Ireland, the Earl of Elgin and Kincardine; and His Imperial Majesty the Emperor of China, His Imperial Highness the Prince of Kung; who, having met and communicated to each other their full powers, and finding these to be in proper form, have agreed upon the following Convention, in Nine Articles:—

ART. I.—A breach of friendly relations have been occasioned by the act of the Garrison of Taku, which obstructed Her Britannic Majesty's Representative when on his way to Peking, for the purpose of exchanging the ratifications of the Treaty of Peace, concluded at Tientsin in the month of June, one thousand eight hundred and fifty-eight, His Imperial Majesty the Emperor of China expresses his deep regret at the misunderstanding so occasioned.

ART. II.—It is further expressly declared, that the arrangement entered into at Shanghai, in the month of October, one thousand eight hundred and fifty-eight, between Her Britannic Majesty's Ambassador the Earl of Elgin and Kincardine, and His Imperial Majesty's Commissioners Kweiliang and Hwashana, regarding the residence of Her Britannic Majesty's Representative in China, is hereby cancelled, and that, in accordance with Article III. of the Treaty of one thousand eight hundred and fifty-eight, Her Britannic Majesty's Representative will henceforward reside, permanently or occasionally, at Peking, as Her Britannic Majesty shall be pleased to decide.

ART. III.—It is agreed that the separate Article of the Treaty of one thousand eight hundred and fifty-eight is hereby annulled, and that in lieu of the amount of indemnity therein specified, His Imperial Majesty the Emperor of China shall pay the sum of eight millions of taels, in the following proportions or instalments, namely, —at Tientsin, on or before the 30th day of November, the sum of five hundred thousand taels; at Canton, on or before the first day of December, one thousand eight hundred and sixty, three hundred and thirty-three thousand and thirty-three taels, less the sum which shall have been advanced by the Canton authorities towards the completion of the British Factory site of Shameen; and the remainder at the ports open to foreign trade, in quarterly payments, which shall consist of one-fifth of the gross revenue from Customs there collected; the first of the said payments being due on the thirty-first day of December, one thousand eight hundred and sixty, for the quarter terminating on that day.

It is further agreed that these monies shall be paid into the hands of an officer whom Her Britannic Majesty's Representative shall specially appoint to receive them, and that the accuracy of the amounts shall, before payment, be duly ascertained by British and Chinese officers appointed to discharge this duty.

In order to prevent future discussion, it is moreover declared that of the eight millions of taels herein guaranteed, two millions will be appropriated to the indemnification of the British Mercantile Community at Canton, for losses sustained by them; and the remaining six millions to the liquidation of war expenses.

ART. IV.—It is agreed that on the day on which this Convention is signed, His Imperial Majesty the Emperor of China shall open the port of Tientsin to trade, and that it shall be thereafter competent to British subjects to reside and trade there, under the same conditions as at any other port of China, by Treaty open to trade.

ART. V.—As soon as the ratifications of the Treaty of one thousand eight hundred and fifty-eight shall have been exchanged, His Imperial Majesty the Emperor of China, will, by decree, command the high authorities of every province to proclaim throughout their jurisdictions, that Chinese, in choosing to take service in British Colonies or other parts beyond sea, are at perfect liberty to enter into engagements with British subjects for that purpose, and to ship themselves and their families on board any British vessels at the open ports of China; also that the high authorities aforesaid shall, in concert with Her Britannic Majesty's Representative in China, frame such regulations for the protection of Chinese emigrating as above, as the circumstances of the different open ports may demand.

ART. VI.—With a view to the maintenance of law and order in and about the harbour of Hongkong, His Imperial Majesty the Emperor of China agrees to cede to Her Majesty the Queen of Great Britain and Ireland, Her heirs and successors, to have and to hold as a dependency of Her Britannic Majesty's Colony of Hongkong, that portion of the township of Cowloon, in the province of Kwang-Tung, of which a lease was granted in perpetuity to Harry Smith Parkes, Esquire, Companion of the Bath, a Member of the Allied Commission at Canton, on behalf of Her Britannic Majesty's Government by Lau T'sung-kwang, Governor-General of the Two Kwang.

It is further declared that the lease in question is hereby cancelled, that the claims of any Chinese to property on the said portion of Cowloon shall be duly investigated by a mixed Commission of British and Chinese officers, and that compensation shall be awarded by the British Government to any Chinese whose claim shall be by that said Commission established, should his removal be deemed necessary by the British Government.

ART. VII.—It is agreed that the provisions of the Treaty of one thousand eight hundred and fifty-eight, except in so far as these are modified by the present Convention, shall without delay come into

APPENDIX. 585

operation as soon as the ratifications of the Treaty aforesaid shall have been exchanged. It is further agreed, that no separate ratification of the present Convention shall be necessary, but that it shall take effect from the date of its signature, and be equally binding with the Treaty above-mentioned on the high contracting parties.

ART. VIII.—It is agreed that, as soon as the ratifications of the Treaty of the year one thousand eight hundred and fifty-eight shall have been exchanged, His Imperial Majesty the Emperor of China shall, by decree, command the high authorities in the capital, and in the provinces, to print and publish the aforesaid Treaty and the present Convention, for general information.

ART. IX.—It is agreed that, as soon as the Convention shall have been signed, the ratification of the Treaty of the year one thousand eight hundred and fifty-eight shall have been exchanged, and an Imperial Decree respecting the publication of the said Convention and Treaty shall have been promulgated, as provided for by Article VIII. of this Convention, Chusan shall be evacuated by Her Britannic Majesty's troops there stationed, and Her Britannic Majesty's force now before Peking shall commence its march towards the city of Tientsin, the forts of Taku, the north coast of Shantung, and city of Canton, at each or all of which places it shall be at the option of Her Majesty the Queen of Great Britain and Ireland to retain a force, until the indemnity of eight millions of taels, guaranteed in Article III., shall have been paid.

Done at Peking, in the Court of the Board of Ceremonies, on the twenty-fourth day of October, in the year of our Lord one thousand eight hundred and sixty.

(L.S.) (Signed) ELGIN AND KINCARDINE.
Seal of Chinese Plenipotentiary.
Signature of Chinese Plenipotentiary.

AGREEMENT BETWEEN THE MINISTERS PLENIPOTENTIARY OF THE GOVERNMENTS OF GREAT BRITAIN AND CHINA.

Signed, in the English and Chinese Languages, at Chefoo, 13th September, 1876.

Ratified by the Emperor of China, 17th September, 1876.

AGREEMENT negotiated between Sir Thomas Wade, K.C.B., Her Britannic Majesty's Envoy Extraordinary and Minister Plenipotentiary at the Court of China, and Li, Minister Plenipotentiary of His Majesty the Emperor of China, Senior Grand Secretary,

Governor-General of the Province of Chih Li, of the First-Class of the Third Order of Nobility.

The negotiation between the Ministers above-named has its origin in a despatch received by Sir Thomas Wade, in the spring of the present year, from the Earl of Derby, Principal Secretary of State for Foreign Affairs, dated 1st January, 1876. This contained instructions regarding the disposal of three questions: first, a satisfactory settlement of the Yün Nan affair; secondly, a faithful fulfilment of engagements of last year respecting intercourse between the high officers of the two Governments; thirdly, the adoption of a uniform system in satisfaction of the understanding arrived at in the month of September, 1875 (8th moon of the 1st year of the reign Kwang Sü), on the subject of rectification of conditions of trade. It is to this despatch that Sir Thomas Wade has referred himself in discussions on these questions with the Tsung-li Yamên, farther reference to which is here omitted as superfluous. The conditions now agreed to between Sir Thomas Wade and the Grand Secretary are as follows:—

SECTION I.—*Settlement of the Yün Nan Case.*

(i.) A Memorial is to be presented to the Throne, whether by the Tsung-li Yamên or by the Grand Secretary Li is immaterial, in the sense of the memorandum prepared by Sir Thomas Wade. Before presentation, the Chinese text of the Memorial is to be shown to Sir Thomas Wade.

(ii.) The Memorial having been presented to the Throne, and the Imperial Decree in reply received, the Tsung-li Yamên will communicate copies of the Memorial and Imperial Decree to Sir Thomas Wade, together with a copy of a letter from the Tsung-li Yamên to the Provincial Governments, instructing them to issue a proclamation that shall embody at length the above Memorial and Decree. Sir Thomas Wade will thereon reply to the effect that for two years to come officers will be sent, by the British Minister, to different places in the provinces, to see that the proclamation is posted. On application from the British Minister, or the Consul of any port instructed by him to make application, the high officers of the provinces will depute competent officers to accompany those so sent to the places which they go to observe.

(iii.) In order to the framing of such regulations as will be needed for the conduct of the frontier trade between Burma and Yün Nan, the Memorial, submitting the proposed settlement of the Yün Nan affair, will contain a request that an Imperial Decree be issued, directing the Governor-General and Governor, whenever the

British Government shall send officers to Yün Nan, to select a competent officer of rank to confer with them and to conclude a satisfactory arrangement.

(iv.) The British Government will be free for five years, from the 1st of January next, being the 17th day of the 11th moon of the 2nd year of the reign Kwang Sü, to station officers at Ta-li Fu, or at some other suitable place in Yün Nan, to observe the conditions of trade; to the end that they may have information upon which to base the regulations of trade when these have to be discussed. For the consideration and adjustment of any matter affecting British officers or subjects, these officers will be free to address themselves to the authorities of the province. The opening of the trade may be proposed by the British Government, as it may find best, at any time within the term of five years, or upon expiry of the term of five years.

Passports having been obtained last year for a Mission from India into Yün Nan, it is open to the Viceroy of India to send such Mission at any time he may see fit.

(v.) The amount of indemnity to be paid on account of the families of the officers and others killed in Yün Nan; on account of the expenses which the Yün Nan case has occasioned; and on account of claims of British merchants arising out of the action of officers of the Chinese Government up to the commencement of the present year, Sir Thomas Wade takes upon himself to fix at Two Hundred Thousand Taels, payable on demand.

(vi.) When the case is closed, an Imperial Letter will be written, expressing regret for what has occurred in Yün Nan. The Mission bearing the Imperial Letter will proceed to England immediately. Sir Thomas Wade is to be informed of the constitution of this Mission, for the information of his Government. The text of the Imperial Letter is also to be communicated to Sir Thomas Wade by the Tsung-li Yamên.

SECTION II.—*Official Intercourse.*

Under this heading are included the conditions of intercourse between high officers in the capital and the provinces, and between Consular officers and Chinese officials at the ports; also the conduct of judicial proceedings in mixed cases.

(i.) In the Tsung-li Yamên's Memorial of the 28th September, 1875, the Prince of Kung and the Ministers stated that their object in presenting it had not been simply the transaction of business in which Chinese and Foreigners might be concerned; missions abroad and the questions of diplomatic intercourse lay equally within their prayer.

To the prevention of farther misunderstanding upon the subject of intercourse and correspondence, the present conditions of both having caused complaint in the capital and in the provinces, it is agreed that the Tsung-li Yamên shall address a circular to the Legations, inviting Foreign Representatives to consider with them a code of etiquette, to the end that foreign officials in China, whether at the ports or elsewhere, may be treated with the same regard as is shown them when serving abroad in other countries, and as would be shown to Chinese Agents so serving abroad.

The fact that China is about to establish Missions and Consulates abroad renders an understanding on these points essential.

(ii.) The British Treaty of 1858, Article XVI., lays down that "Chinese subjects who may be guilty of any criminal act towards British subjects shall be arrested and punished by Chinese authorities according to the laws of China.

"British subjects who may commit any crime in China shall be tried and punished by the Consul, or any other public functionary authorized thereto, according to the laws of Great Britain.

"Justice shall be equitably and impartially administered on both sides."

The words "functionary authorized thereto" are translated in the Chinese text "British Government."

In order to the fulfilment of its Treaty obligations, the British Government has established a Supreme Court at Shanghai, with a special code of rules, which it is now about to revise. The Chinese Government has established at Shanghai a Mixed Court; but the officer presiding over it, either from lack of power, or dread of unpopularity, constantly fails to enforce his judgments.

It is now understood that the Tsung-li Yamên will write a circular to the Legations, inviting Foreign Representatives at once to consider with the Tsung-li Yamên the measures needed for the more effective administration of justice at the ports open to trade.

(iii.) It is agreed that, whenever a crime is committed affecting the person or property of a British subject, whether in the interior or at the open ports, the British Minister shall be free to send officers to the spot to be present at the investigation.

To the prevention of misunderstanding on this point, Sir Thomas Wade will write a Note to the above effect, to which the Tsung-li Yamên will reply, affirming that this is the course of proceeding to be adhered to for the time to come.

It is farther understood that so long as the laws of the two countries differ from each other, there can be but one principle to guide judicial proceedings in mixed cases in China, namely, that the case is tried by the official of the defendant's nationality; the official of the plaintiff's nationality merely attending to watch the proceedings in the interests of justice. If the officer so attending be dissatisfied with the proceedings, it will be in his power to protest against them in detail. The law administered will be the law of the nationality of the officer trying the case. This is the meaning of the words *hui t'ung*, indicating combined action in judicial proceedings, in Article XVI. of the Treaty of Tientsin; and this is the course to be respectively followed by the officers of either nationality.

SECTION III.—*Trade.*

(i.) With reference to the area within which, according to the treaties in force, *likin* ought not to be collected on foreign goods at the open ports, Sir Thomas Wade agrees to move his Government to allow the ground rented by foreigners (the so-called Concessions) at the different ports, to be regarded as the area of exemption from *likin;* and the Government of China will thereupon allow I-ch'ang in the province of Hu-Pei, Wu-hu in An-Hui, Wên-chow in Che-Kiang, and Pei-hai (Pak-hoi) in Kwang-Tung, to be added to the number of ports open to trade, and to become Consular stations. The British Government will farther be free to send officers to reside at Ch'ung K'ing, to watch the conditions of British trade in Ssu-Ch'uen. British merchants will not be allowed to reside at Ch'ung K'ing, or to open establishments or warehouses there, so long as no steamers have access to the port. When steamers have succeeded in ascending the river so far, farther arrangements can be taken into consideration.

It is farther proposed as a measure of compromise that at certain points on the shore of the Great River, namely Ta-t'ung, and Ngan-Ching, in the province of An-Hui; Hu-K'ou, in Kiang-Si; Wu-suëh, Lu-chi-k'ou, and Sha-shih, in Hu Kuang; these being all places of trade in the interior, at which, as they are not open ports, foreign merchants are not legally authorized * to land or ship goods, steamers shall be allowed to touch for the purpose of landing or shipping passengers or goods; but in all instances by means of native boats only, and subject to the regulations in force affecting native trade.

Produce accompanied by a half-duty certificate may be shipped at such points by the steamers, but may not be landed by them for sale. And at all such points, except in the case of imports accom-

* N.B.—In the Chinese text, this sentence reads: ... are not authorize'd, *according to the Yangtsze Regulations,* to land and ship, etc.

panied by a transit duty certificate, or exports similarly certificated, which will be severally passed free of *likin* on exhibition of such certificates, *likin* will be duly collected on all goods whatever by the native authorities. Foreign merchants will not be authorized to reside or open houses of business or warehouses at the places enumerated as ports of call.

(ii.) At all ports opened to trade, whether by earlier or later agreement, at which no settlement area has been previously defined, it will be the duty of the British Consul, acting in concert with his colleagues, the Consuls of other Powers, to come to an understanding with the local authorities regarding the definition of the foreign settlement area.

(iii.) On opium, Sir Thomas Wade will move his Government to sanction an arrangement different from that affecting other imports. British merchants, when opium is brought into port, will be obliged to have it taken cognizance of by the Customs, and deposited in bond, either in a warehouse or a receiving hulk, until such time as there is a sale for it. The importer will then pay the tariff duty upon it, and the purchasers the *likin*; in order to the prevention of the evasion of the duty. The amount of *likin* to be collected will be decided by the different Provincial Governments, according to the circumstances of each.

(iv.) The Chinese Government agrees that Transit Duty certificates shall be framed under one rule at all ports, no difference being made in the conditions set forth therein; and that so far as imports are concerned, the nationality of the person possessing and carrying these is immaterial. Native produce carried from an Inland Centre to a Port of Shipment, if *bonâ fide* intended for shipment to a foreign port, may be, by treaty, certificated by the British subject interested, and exempted by payment of the half-duty from all charges demanded upon it *en route*. If produce be not the property of a British subject, or is being carried to a port not for exportation, it is not entitled to the exemption that would be secured it by the exhibition of a Transit Duty Certificate. The British Minister is prepared to agree with the Tsung-li Yamên upon rules that will secure the Chinese Government against abuse of the privilege as affecting produce.

The words *nei ti*, inland, in the clause of Article VII. of the Rules appended to the Tariff, regarding carriage of imports inland, and of native produce purchased inland, apply as much to places on the sea coasts and river shores, as to places in the interior not open to foreign trade; the Chinese Government having the right to make arrangements for the prevention of abuses thereat.

APPENDIX.

(v.) Article XLV. of the Treaty of 1858 prescribes no limit to the term within which a drawback may be claimed upon duty paid Imports. The British Minister agrees to a term of three years, after expiry of which no drawback shall be claimed.

(vi.) The foregoing stipulation, that certain ports are to be opened to foreign trade, and that landing and shipping of goods at six places on the Great River is to be sanctioned, shall be given effect to within six months after receipt of the Imperial Decree approving the Memorial of the Grand Secretary Li. The date for giving effect to the stipulations affecting exemption of imports from *likin* taxation within the foreign settlements, and the collection of *likin* upon opium by the Customs' Inspectorate at the same time as the Tariff duty upon it, will be fixed as soon as the British Government has arrived at an understanding on the subject with other foreign Governments.

(vii.) The Governor of Hongkong having long complained of the interference of the Canton Customs' Revenue Cruisers with the junk trade of that Colony, the Chinese Government agrees to the appointment of a Commission, to consist of a British Consul, an officer of the Hongkong Government, and a Chinese official of equal rank, in order to the establishment of some system that shall enable the Chinese Government to protect its revenue, without prejudice to the interests of the Colony.

SEPARATE ARTICLE.

Her Majesty's Government having it in contemplation to send a Mission of exploration next year by way of Peking through Kan-Su and Koko-Nor, or by way of Ssu-Ch'uen to Thibet, and thence to India, the Tsung-li Yamên, having due regard to the circumstances, will, when the time arrives, issue the necessary passports, and will address letters to the high provincial authorities, and to the Resident in Thibet. If the Mission should not be sent by these routes, but should be proceeding across the Indian frontier to Thibet, the Tsung-li Yamên, on receipt of a communication to the above effect from the British Minister, will write to the Chinese Resident in Thibet, and the Resident, with due regard to the circumstances, will send officers to take due care of the Mission; and passports for the Mission will be issued by the Tsung-li Yamên, that its passage be not obstructed.

Done at Chefoo, in the Province of Shan Tung, this thirteenth day of September, in the year of our Lord one thousand eight hundred and seventy-six.

(L.S.)   (Signed)   THOMAS FRANCIS WADE.
(L.S.)   (Signed)   CHINESE PLENIPOTENTIARY.

Treaty between Russia and China concerning the Re-establishment of the Authority of the Chinese Government in Ili.

His Majesty the Emperor and Autocrat of All the Russias and His Majesty the Emperor of China, being desirous of settling certain frontier questions concerning the interests of both Empires, and of drawing closer the friendly relations between the two countries, have named as their Plenipotentiaries, in order to arrive at an understanding on these questions :—

His Majesty the Emperor of All the Russias, his Secretary of State, Nicolas de Giers, Senator, Actual Privy Councillor, in charge of the Imperial Ministry for Foreign Affairs; and his Envoy Extraordinary and Minister Plenipotentiary at the Court of China, Eugene de Butzow, Actual Councillor of State ;

And His Majesty the Emperor of China, Tsêng, Marquis of Neyoung, Vice-President of the High Court of Justice, his Envoy Extraordinary and Minister Plenipotentiary at the Court of Russia, intrusted with special powers to sign the present Treaty as Ambassador Extraordinary.

The aforesaid Plenipotentiaries, intrusted with full powers, which have been found sufficient, have agreed to the following stipulations :—

Article I.

His Majesty the Emperor of All the Russias consents to the re-establishment of the Chinese Government in the country of Ili, which has been temporarily occupied, since 1871, by the Russian forces.

Russia remains in possession of the western part of that country, within the limits indicated by Article VII. of the present Treaty.

Article II.

His Majesty the Emperor of China undertakes to issue the necessary Decrees, in order that the inhabitants of Ili, to whatever race or religion they may belong, may be freed from all liability, whether as concerns their persons or their property, for acts committed during or after the disorders which have taken place in that country.

A Proclamation in conformity with this undertaking will be addressed by the Chinese authorities, in the name of His Majesty the Emperor of China, to the people of Ili, before that country is made over to the said authorities.

APPENDIX. 593

Article III.

The inhabitants of Ili will be at liberty to remain in the places where they at present reside as Chinese subjects, or to emigrate to Russia and to adopt Russian nationality. They will be called upon for a decision on the subject before Chinese authority is re-established in Ili, and a term of one year, to be reckoned from the date of the restoration of the country to the Chinese authorities, will be granted to those who express a wish to emigrate to Russia. The Chinese authorities will place no obstacles in the way of their emigration and of the removal of their personal property.

Article IV.

Russian subjects holding land in Ili will retain their rights of ownership, even after the re-establishment of the authority of the Chinese Government in that country.

This arrangement does not apply to those inhabitants of Ili who adopt Russian nationality at the time of the re-establishment of Chinese authority in that country.

Russian subjects whose lands are situated outside the areas assigned for Russian factories, in virtue of Article XIII. of the Kuldja Treaty of 1851, will pay the same taxes and contributions as Chinese subjects.

Article V.

The two Governments will send to Kuldja Commissioners, who will proceed on the one part to cede and on the other to resume the administration of the Province of Ili, and to whom will be confided, in general, the execution of the stipulations of the present Treaty which relate to the re-establishment in that country of the authority of the Chinese Government.

The said Commissioners will carry out their instructions in accordance with the understanding to be arrived at as to the manner of ceding on the one part, and of resuming on the other, the administration of Ili, between the Governor-General of Turkestan and the Governor-General of the Provinces of Chan-si* and Kan-sou, to whom the management of this business has been intrusted by the two Governments.

The transfer of the administration of Ili should be concluded within a term of three months or earlier, if possible, to date from the day of the arrival at Tashkend of the official delegated by the

---

* So printed in the Blue Book, but beyond question a mistake for Shensi. Kaŋsuh and Shensi form the same Viceroyalty.

Governor-General of Chan-si and Kan-sou to the Governor-General of Turkestan to notify to him the ratification and promulgation of the present Treaty by His Majesty the Emperor of China.

Article VI.

The Government of His Majesty the Emperor of China will pay to the Government of Russia the sum of 9,000,000 metallic roubles, to meet the expenses of the occupation of Ili by Russian troops since 1871, to satisfy all pecuniary claims which have been brought forward up to this date for losses of Russian subjects whose goods have been plundered in Chinese territory, and to assist the families of Russian subjects killed in armed attacks of which they have been the victims in Chinese territory.

The above-mentioned sum of 9,000,000 metallic roubles is to be paid within a term of two years from the date of the exchange of the ratifications of the present Treaty, in the order and in accordance with the conditions agreed to by the two Governments in the special Protocol annexed to the present Treaty.

Article VII.

The western part of Ili is incorporated with Russia, to serve as a place for the establishment of the inhabitants of that country who adopt Russian nationality, and who will therefore have had to abandon the lands they possessed.

The frontier between the Russian possessions and the Chinese Province of Ili, starting from the Bedjin-Taou Mountains, will follow the course of the Khorgos River as far as the spot where it falls into the River Ili, and, crossing this last river, will take a southerly direction, towards the Ouzontaou Mountains, leaving the village of Koldjat on the west. From this point it will follow in a southerly direction the line laid down by the Protocol signed at Tchougoutchak in 1864.

Article VIII.

A portion of the frontier-line to the east of Lake Zaïsan, as laid down by the Protocol signed at Tchougoutchak in 1864, having been found incorrect, the two Governments will nominate Commissioners who will jointly modify the former line, in such a manner as to correct the errors pointed out, and to establish a sufficient separation between the Kirghiz tribes subject to the two Empires.

The new line shall, as far as possible, take a direction intermediate between the old frontier and a straight line starting from the Kouïtoun Mountains towards the Saour Mountains, and crossing the Tcherni-Irtych.

Article IX.

The two Contracting Parties will name Commissioners for erecting boundary posts upon the line fixed by Articles VII. and VIII., as well as upon that portion of the frontier where no posts have been erected. The time and place of meeting of these Commissioners will be settled by an understanding between the two Governments.

The two Governments will also name Commissioners to examine the frontier and to erect boundary posts between the Russian Province of Ferganah and the western part of the Chinese Province of Kachgar. These Commissioners will take the present frontier as the basis of their labours.

Article X.

The recognized Treaty right of the Russian Government to appoint Consuls at Ili, at Tarbagataï, at Kachgar, and at Ourga is henceforward extended to the towns of Sou-Tcheou (Tsia-yu-kouan) and Tourfan. In the following towns: Kobdo, Ouliassoutaï, Khami, Ouroumtsi, and Goutchen, the Russian Government will establish Consulates accordingly as they are called for by the development of commerce, and after coming to an understanding with the Chinese Government.

The Consuls at Sou-Tcheou (Tsia-yu-kouan) and Tourfan will exercise Consular functions in the neighbouring districts, where the interests of Russian subjects may call for their presence.

The provisions of Articles V. and VI. of the Treaty concluded at Peking in 1860, relating to the concession of lands for Consular dwellings, for cemeteries, and for pasturage, will be in like manner applicable to the towns of Sou-Tcheou (Tsia-yu-kouan) and Tourfan. The local authorities will assist the Consuls in finding temporary residences until the Consular houses are built.

The Russian Consuls in Mongolia and the districts situated on the two slopes of the Tian-chan will, for travelling purposes and for forwarding their correspondence, make use of the Government postal establishments, according to the stipulations of Article XI. of the Treaty of Tien-tsin and Article XII. of the Treaty of Peking. The Chinese authorities, when called upon by them for this purpose, will afford them their aid and assistance.

The town of Tourfan not being a place open to foreign trade, the right of establishing a Consulate there shall not serve as a precedent upon which to rest a similar right with respect to the ports of China, to the internal provinces, and to Manchouria.

Article XI.

Russian Consuls in China will communicate on business matters, either with the local authorities of their place of residence or with the superior authorities of the district or province, accordingly as the nature of the interests respectively intrusted to them and the importance or urgency of the business to be transacted may require. The correspondence between them will take the shape of official letters. As to the rules of etiquette to be observed in their interviews, they will be based upon the consideration which the officers of friendly Powers owe to one another.

All questions arising on Chinese territory with regard to commercial or other matters between the dependents of the two States will be examined and settled by common consent by the Consuls and the Chinese authorities.

In disputes concerning commercial matters the parties may settle their differences amicably by means of arbitrators chosen by both sides. If by this course an understanding cannot be arrived at, the question will be examined and settled by the authorities of the two States.

Written engagements between Russian and Chinese subjects concerning orders for goods or their carriage, the hire of shops, houses, and other places, or relating to other similar transactions, may be presented for the legalization of the Consulates and of the higher local administrations whose duty it is to legalize documents presented to them. In case of the non-fulfilment of engagements contracted, the Consuls and the Chinese authorities will consider as to measures calculated to insure the execution of such obligations.

Article XII.

Russian subjects are authorized, as heretofore, to carry on trade free of duty in Chinese Mongolia, in those localities or aïmaks where there are Chinese authorities, as well as in those where there are none.

Russian subjects may likewise carry on trade free of duty in the towns and other localities of the Provinces of Ili, Tarbagataï, Kachgar, Ouroumtsi, and others, situated on the northern and southern slopes of the Tian-chan range, as far as the Great Wall. This privilege will be withdrawn when the development of trade necessitates the enactment of a Customs Tariff, in accordance with an understanding to be arrived at between the two Governments.

Russian subjects may import into and export from the aforesaid provinces of China, products of every kind, no matter what their origin may be. They may effect purchases and sales either for cash or by barter; they will be entitled to make payments in merchandise of all kinds.

ARTICLE XIII.

In the localities where the Russian Government is entitled to establish Consulates, as in the town of Kalgan, Russian subjects may construct houses, shops, store-houses, and other buildings on the land they may acquire by purchase, or which may be granted to them by the local authorities, in accordance with what is laid down for Ili and Tarbagataï by Article XIII. of the Kuldja Treaty of 1851.

Privileges granted to Russian subjects in the town of Kalgan, where there will be no Consulate, constitute an exception which cannot be extended to any other locality in the internal provinces.

ARTICLE XIV.

Russian merchants wishing to send from Russia by land goods for the inner provinces of China, may, as formerly, send them by the towns of Kalgan and Toun-Tcheou to the port of Tien-tsin, and thence to other ports and inner markets, and sell them in those different localities.

Merchants will use the same route to export to Russia goods purchased in the towns and ports above mentioned, or in the inner markets.

They will likewise be entitled to proceed on commercial business to Sou-Tcheou (Tsia-yu-kouan), the terminus of Russian caravans, and will there enjoy all the rights granted to Russian commerce at Tien-tsin.

ARTICLE XV.

Trade carried on by land by Russian subjects in the inner and outer provinces of China will be governed by the Regulations annexed to the present Treaty.

The commercial stipulations of the present Treaty, as well as the Regulations which serve as its complement, may be revised after the lapse of ten years, to date from the day of the exchange of the ratifications of the Treaty; but if, within the course of six months before that term expires, neither of the Contracting Parties should manifest a desire to proceed to its revision, the commercial stipulations, as well as the Regulations, will remain in force for a further term of ten years.

Trade by sea carried on by Russian subjects in China will come under the general Regulations established for foreign maritime commerce with China. Should it become necessary to modify these Regulations, the two Governments will come to an understanding on the subject.

Article XVI.

Should the development of Russian trade by land call for the enactment of a Customs Tariff applicable to goods exported from and imported into China, which shall harmonize better with the necessities of that trade than the existing Tariffs, the Governments of Russia and China will come to an understanding on the subject, taking as a basis for fixing the export and import duties an *ad valorem* rate of 5 per cent.

Pending the enactment of this Tariff, the export duties levied on certain kinds of teas of inferior quality, which are at present subject to the rates established ¡for teas of high quality, will be lowered in proportion to value. The settlement of those duties for each kind of tea will be sought for by means of an understanding between the Chinese Government and the Russian Envoy at Peking, within the term of one year, at the outside, from the date of the exchange of the ratifications of the present Treaty.

Article XVII.

Differences of opinion having heretofore arisen as to the application of Article X. of the Treaty concluded at Peking in 1860, it is hereby agreed that the stipulations of the aforesaid Article concerning the settlement of claims arising out of the theft or driving of cattle across the frontier will in future be interpreted to mean that parties found guilty of theft or driving astray will be condemned to pay the real value of the cattle not restored to the owners. It is understood that, in case of the insolvency of the guilty parties, the indemnity to be paid for the missing cattle shall not fall upon the local authorities.

The frontier authorities of both States will prosecute with the full rigour of the laws of their country parties guilty of driving astray or stealing cattle, and will take such measures as may lie in their power to restore to the rightful owners cattle which have been driven astray or which have crossed the frontier.

The tracks of cattle driven astray, or which have crossed the frontier, may be pointed out not only to the frontier guards, but also to the elders of the nearest villages.

Article XVIII.

The stipulations of the Treaty concluded at Aïgoun on the 16th May, 1858, concerning the rights of the subjects of the two Empires to navigate the Amour, the Soungari, and the Oussouri, and to trade with the inhabitants of riverain places, are and remain confirmed.

Both Governments will proceed to the establishment of an understanding concerning the mode of applying the said stipulations.

Article XIX.

The provisions of former Treaties between Russia and China, not modified by the present Treaty, remain in full force.

Article XX.

The present Treaty, after having been ratified by the two Emperors, will be promulgated in either Empire for the information and guidance of all persons concerned. The ratifications will be exchanged at St. Petersburg within six months from the date of the signature of the Treaty.

Having settled the aforesaid Articles, the Plenipotentiaries of the two Contracting Parties have signed and sealed two copies of the present Treaty in the Russian, Chinese, and French languages. Of the three texts duly collated and found to correspond, the French text shall be held to be authoritative for the interpretation of the present Treaty.

Done at St. Petersburg the 12th February, 1881.

(Signed) NICOLAS DE GIERS. (Signed) TSENG.
(L.S.) (L.S.)
(Signed) EUGÈNE BUTZOW.
(L.S.)

Protocol.

In virtue of the VIth Article of the Treaty signed this day by the Plenipotentiaries of the Russian and Chinese Governments, the Chinese Government will pay to the Russian Government the sum of 9,000,000 metallic roubles to meet the expenses of the occupation of Ili by Russian troops, and to satisfy divers pecuniary claims of Russian subjects. This sum is to be paid within a term of two years from the date of the exchange of the ratifications of the Treaty.

In order to fix the mode of payment of the aforesaid sum, the Undersigned have agreed as follows:—

The Chinese Government will pay the equivalent of the sum of 9,000,000 roubles in pounds sterling, viz. £1,431,664 2s., to

Messrs. Baring Brothers and Co., of London, in six equal parts of £238,610 13s. 8d. each, less the usual banking charges incurred by the transfer of these payments to London.

A space of four months shall intervene between the payments, the first being effected four months after the exchange of the ratifications of the Treaty signed this day, and the last after the completion of two years from the date of that exchange.

The present Protocol will have the same force and value as if it had been inserted word for word in the Treaty signed this day.

In token of which the Plenipotentiaries of the two Governments have signed the present Protocol and have affixed their seals to it.

Done at St. Petersburg the 12th February, 1881.

    (Signed) NICOLAS DE GIERS.   (Signed) TSENG.
            (L.S.)   (L.S.)
    (Signed) EUGÈNE BUTZOW.
            (L.S.)

English Text of Convention between great Britain and China relating to Burmah and Thibet. Signed at Peking, July 24, 1886.

WHEREAS Her Majesty the Queen of Great Britain and Ireland, Empress of India, and His Majesty the Emperor of China, being sincerely desirous to maintain and perpetuate the relations of friendship and good understanding which now exists between their respective Empires, and to promote and extend the commercial intercourse between their subjects and dominions, the following Convention has been agreed upon and concluded:—

On the part of Great Britain by Nicholas Roderick O'Conor, Esquire, Her Majesty's Secretary of Legation at Washington, and lately Her Majesty's Chargé d'Affaires in China, Companion of the Most Distinguished Order of St. Michael and St. George, duly empowered thereunto;

And on the part of China by his Highness Prince of Ch'ing, President of the Tsung-li Yamên, and his Excellency Sun, Minister of the Tsung-li Yamên, Senior Vice-President of the Board of Works.

ARTICLE I.

Inasmuch as it has been the practice of Burmah to send decennial Missions to present articles of local produce, England agrees that the highest authority of Burmah shall send the customary decennial Missions, the Members of the Missions to be of Burmese race.

APPENDIX.

Article II.

China agrees that, in all matters whatsoever appertaining to the authority and rule which England is now exercising in Burmah, England shall be free to do whatsoever she deems fit and proper.

Article III.

The frontier between Burmah and China to be marked by a Delimitation Commission, and the conditions of frontier trade to be settled by a Frontier Trade Convention, both countries agreeing to protect and encourage trade between China and Burmah.

Article IV.

Inasmuch as inquiry into the circumstances by the Chinese Government has shown the existence of many obstacles to the Mission to Thibet provided for in the Separate Article of the Chefoo Agreement, England consents to countermand the Mission forthwith.

With regard to the desire of the British Government to consider arrangements for frontier trade between India and Thibet, it will be the duty of the Chinese Government, after careful inquiry into the circumstances, to adopt measures to exhort and encourage the people with a view to the promotion and development of trade. Should it be practicable, the Chinese Government shall then proceed carefully to consider Trade Regulations; but if insuperable obstacles should be found to exist, the British Government will not press the matter unduly.

Article V.

The present Convention shall be ratified, and the ratifications shall be exchanged in London as soon as possible after the date of the signature thereof.

In witness whereof the respective negotiators have signed the same and affixed thereunto the seals of their arms.

Done in triplicate at Peking, this twenty-fourth day of July, in the year of our Lord one thousand eight hundred and eighty-six, corresponding with the Chinese date the twenty-third day of the sixth moon of the twelfth year of Kuang Hsu.

   (L.S.) Nicholas Roderick O'Conor.
         (L.S.)
  (Monogram) Ch'ing.
  (Monogram) Sun yu-wen.

Despatch from Her Majesty's Minister at Tôkiô, forwarding Copy of the Treaty of Peace concluded between China and Japan, April 17, 1895.

Presented to both Houses of Parliament by Command of Her Majesty. June, 1895.

Mr. Lowther to the Earl of Kimberley.—(*Received June* 18.)

Tôkiô, May 13, 1895.

My Lord,

The text of the Treaty of Shimonoseki was to-day published in the official *Gazette* accompanied by an Imperial Rescript explaining the course taken by Japan in view of the objections offered by certain of the Great Powers to the permanent occupation of the Liaotung Peninsula.

I have the honour to transmit herewith an official translation of the Treaty, and a translation of the Imperial Rescript.

I have, etc.

(Signed)   Gerald Lowther.

Inclosure 1.

Treaty between China and Japan, signed at Shimonoseki, April 17, 1895. (Translation.)

His Majesty the Emperor of Japan, and His Majesty the Emperor of China, desiring to restore the blessings of peace to their countries and subjects, and to remove all cause for future complications, have named as their Plenipotentiaries for the purpose of concluding a Treaty of Peace, that is to say:—

His Majesty the Emperor of Japan, Count Ito Hirobumi, Junii, Grand Cross of the Imperial Order of Paullownia, Minister-President of State, and Viscount Mutsu Munemitsu, Junii, First Class of the Imperial Order of the Sacred Treasure, Minister of State for Foreign Affairs;

And His Majesty the Emperor of China, Li Hung-chang, Senior Tutor to the Heir Apparent, Senior Grand Secretary of State, Minister Superintendent of Trade for the Northern Ports of China, Viceroy of the Province of Chihli, and Earl of the First Rank, and Li Ching-fong, ex-Minister of the Diplomatic Service, of the Second Official Rank;

Who, after having exchanged their full powers, which were found to be in good and proper form, have agreed to the following Articles:—

APPENDIX.

Article I.

China recognizes definitely the full and complete independence and autonomy of Corea, and, in consequence, the payment of tribute and the performance of ceremonies and formalities by Corea to China in derogation of such independence and autonomy shall wholly cease for the future.

Article II.

China cedes to Japan in perpetuity and full sovereignty the following territories, together with all fortifications, arsenals, and public property thereon :—

(*a.*) The southern portion of the province of Fêng-tien, within the following boundaries—

The line of demarcation begins at the mouth of the River Yalu, and ascends that stream to the mouth of the River An-ping; from thence the line runs to Fêng Huang; from thence to Haicheng; from thence to Ying Kow, forming a line which describes the southern portion of the territory. The places above-named are included in the ceded territory. When the line reaches the River Liao at Ying Kow it follows the course of that stream to its mouth, where it terminates. The mid-channel of the River Liao shall be taken as the line of demarcation.

This cession also includes all islands appertaining or belonging to the Province of Fêng Tien situated in the eastern portion of the Bay of Liao Tung, and in the northern part of the Yellow Sea.

(*b.*) The Island of Formosa, together with all islands appertaining or belonging to the said Island of Formosa.

(*c.*) The Pescadores Group, that is to say, all islands lying between the 119th and 120th degrees of longitude east of Greenwich and the 23rd and 24th degrees of north latitude.

Article III.

The alignments of the frontiers described in the preceding article, and shown on the annexed map, shall be subject to verification and demarcation on the spot by a Joint Commission of Delimitation, consisting of two or more Japanese and two or more Chinese delegates, to be appointed immediately after the exchange of the ratifications of this Act. In case the boundaries laid down in this Act are found to be defective at any point, either on account of topography or in consideration of good administration, it shall also be the duty of the Delimitation Commission to rectify the same.

The Delimitation Commission will enter upon its duties as soon as possible, and will bring its labours to a conclusion within the period of one year after appointment.

The alignments laid down in this Act shall, however, be maintained until the rectifications of the Delimitation Commission, if any are made, shall have received the approval of the Governments of Japan and China.

Article IV.

China agrees to pay to Japan as a war indemnity the sum of 200,000,000 Kuping taels. The said sum to be paid in eight instalments. The first instalment of 50,000,000 taels to be paid within six months, and the second instalment of 50,000,000 taels to be paid within twelve months after the exchange of the ratifications of this Act. The remaining sum to be paid in six equal annual instalments as follows: the first of such equal annual instalments to be paid within two years, the second within three years, the third within four years, the fourth within five years, the fifth within six years, and the sixth within seven years after the exchange of the ratifications of this Act. Interest at the rate of 5 per cent. per annum shall begin to run on all unpaid portions of the said indemnity from the date the first instalment falls due.

China shall, however, have the right to pay by anticipation at any time any or all of said instalments. In case the whole amount of the said indemnity is paid within three years after the exchange of the ratifications of the present Act, all interest shall be waived, and the interest for two years and a half, or for any less period, if then already paid, shall be included as a part of the principal amount of the indemnity.

Article V.

The inhabitants of the territories ceded to Japan who wish to take up their residence outside the ceded districts shall be at liberty to sell their real property and retire. For this purpose a period of two years from the date of the exchange of the ratifications of the present Act shall be granted. At the expiration of that period those of the inhabitants who shall not have left such territories shall, at the option of Japan, be deemed to be Japanese subjects.

Each of the two Governments shall, immediately upon the exchange of the ratifications of the present Act, send one or more Commissioners to Formosa to effect a final transfer of that province, and within the space of two months after the exchange of the ratifications of this Act such transfer shall be completed.

Article VI.

All Treaties between Japan and China having come to an end in consequence of war, China engages, immediately upon the exchange of the ratifications of this Act, to appoint Plenipotentiaries to conclude with the Japanese Plenipotentiaries a Treaty of Commerce and Navigation, and a Convention to regulate frontier intercourse and trade. The Treaties, Conventions, and Regulations now subsisting between China and European Powers shall serve as a basis for the said Treaty and Convention between Japan and China. From the date of the exchange of the ratifications of this Act until the said Treaty and Convention are brought into actual operation the Japanese Government, its officials, commerce, navigation, frontier intercourse and trade, industries, ships and subjects, shall in every respect be accorded by China most-favoured-nation treatment.

China makes, in addition, the following concessions, to take effect six months after the date of the present Act:—

1. The following cities, towns, and ports, in addition to those already opened, shall be opened to the trade, residence, industries, and manufactures of Japanese subjects under the same conditions, and with the same privileges and facilities as exist at the present open cities, towns, and ports of China.

(1.) Shashih, in the Province of Hupeh.
(2.) Chung King, in the Province of Szechuan.
(3.) Suchow, in the Province of Kiang Su.
(4.) Hangchow, in the Province of Chekiang.

The Japanese Government shall have the right to station Consuls at any or all of the above-named places.

2. Steam navigation for vessels under the Japanese flag for the conveyance of passengers and cargo shall be extended to the following places:—

(1.) On the Upper Yangtsze River, from Ichang to Chung King.
(2.) On the Woosung River and the Canal, from Shanghai to Suchow and Hangchow.

The Rules and Regulations which now govern the navigation of the inland waters of China by foreign vessels shall, so far as applicable, be enforced in respect of the above-named routes, until new Rules and Regulations are conjointly agreed to.

3. Japanese subjects purchasing goods or produce in the interior of China, or transporting imported merchandise into the interior of China, shall have the right temporarily to rent or hire warehouses for the storage of the articles so purchased or transported, without the payment of any taxes or exactions whatever.

4. Japanese subjects shall be free to engage in all kinds of manufacturing industries in all the open cities, towns, and ports of China, and shall be at liberty to import into China all kinds of machinery, paying only the stipulated import duties thereon.

All articles manufactured by Japanese subjects in China shall, in respect of inland transit and internal taxes, duties, charges, and exactions of all kinds, and also in respect of warehousing and storage facilities in the interior of China, stand upon the same footing and enjoy the same privileges and exemptions as merchandise imported by Japanese subjects into China.

In the event additional Rules and Regulations are necessary in connection with these concessions, they shall be embodied in the Treaty of Commerce and Navigation provided for by this Article.

Article VII.

Subject to the provisions of the next succeeding Article, the evacuation of China by the armies of Japan shall be completely effected within three months after the exchange of the ratifications of the present Act.

Article VIII.

As a guarantee of the faithful performance of the stipulations of this Act, China consents to the temporary occupation by the military forces of Japan, of Wei-hai-wei, in the Province of Shantung.

Upon the payment of the first two instalments of the war indemnity herein stipulated for and the exchange of the ratifications of the Treaty of Commerce and Navigation, the said place shall be evacuated by the Japanese forces, provided the Chinese Government consents to pledge, under suitable and sufficient arrangements, the Customs Revenue of China as security for the payment of the principal and interest of the remaining instalments of said indemnity. In the event no such arrangements are concluded, such evacuation shall only take place upon the payment of the final instalment of said indemnity.

It is, however, expressly understood that no such evacuation shall take place until after the exchange of the ratifications of the Treaty of Commerce and Navigation.

Article IX.

Immediately upon the exchange of the ratifications of this Act, all prisoners of war then held shall be restored, and China undertakes not to ill-treat or punish prisoners of war so restored to her by Japan. China also engages to at once release all Japanese subjects accused of being military spies or charged with any other military offences. China further engages not to punish in any manner, nor to allow to be punished, those Chinese subjects who have in any manner been compromised in their relations with the Japanese army during the war.

Article X.

All offensive military operations shall cease upon the exchange of the ratifications of this Act.

Article XI.

The present Act shall be ratified by their Majesties the Emperor of Japan and the Emperor of China, and the ratifications shall be exchanged at Chefoo on the 8th day of the 5th month of the 28th year of Meiji, corresponding to 14th day of the 4th month of the 21st year of Kuang Hsü.

In witness whereof, the respective Plenipotentiaries have signed the same and have affixed thereto the seal of their arms.

Done at Shimonoseki, in duplicate, this 17th day of the 4th month of the 28th year of Meiji, corresponding to 23rd day of the 3rd month of the 21st year of Kuang Hsü.

(L.S.) Count Ito Hirobumi, *Junii, Grand Cross of the Imperial Order of Paullownia, Minister-President of State, Plenipotentiary of His Majesty the Emperor of Japan.*

(L.S.) Viscount Mutsu Munemitsu, *Junii, First Class of the Imperial Order of the Sacred Treasure, Minister of State for Foreign Affairs, Plenipotentiary of His Majesty the Emperor of Japan.*

(L.S.) Li Hung-Chang, *Plenipotentiary of His Majesty the Emperor of China, Senior Tutor to the Heir Apparent, Senior Grand Secretary of State, Minister-Superintendent of Trade for the Northern Ports of China, Viceroy of the Province of Chihli, and Earl of the First Rank.*

(L.S.) Li Ching-Fong, *Plenipotentiary of His Majesty the Emperor of China, Ex-Minister of the Diplomatic Service, of the Second Official Rank.*

Separate Articles.

Article I.

The Japanese military forces which are, under Article VIII. of the Treaty of Peace signed this day, to temporarily occupy Wei-hai-wei shall not exceed one brigade, and from the date of the exchange of the ratifications of the said Treaty of Peace China shall pay annually one-fourth of the amount of the expenses of such temporary occupation, that is to say, at the rate of 500,000 Kuping taels per annum.

Article II.

The territory temporarily occupied at Wei-hai-wei shall comprise the Island of Liu Kung and a belt of land 5 Japanese *ri* wide along the entire coast-line of the Bay of Wei-hai-wei.

No Chinese troops shall be permitted to approach or occupy any places within a zone 5 Japanese *ri* wide beyond the boundaries of the occupied territory.

Article III.

The civil administration of the occupied territory shall remain in the hands of the Chinese authorities. But such authorities shall at all times be obliged to conform to the orders which the Commander of the Japanese army of occupation may deem it necessary to give in the interest of the health, maintenance, safety, distribution, or discipline of the troops.

All military offences committed within the occupied territory shall be subject to the jurisdiction of the Japanese military authorities.

The foregoing Separate Articles shall have the same force, value, and effect as if they had been word for word inserted in the Treaty of Peace signed this day.

In witness whereof the respective Plenipotentiaries have signed the same, and have affixed thereto the seal of their arms.

Done at Shimonoseki, in duplicate, this 17th day of the 4th month of the 28th year of Meji, corresponding to the 23rd day of the 3rd month of the 21st year of Kwang Hsü.

(L.S.)   Count Ito Hirobumi, *Junii, Grand Cross of the Imperial Order of Paullownia, Minister-President of State, Plenipotentiary of His Majesty the Emperor of Japan.*

(L.S.)   Viscount Mutsu Munemitsu, *Junii, First Class of the Imperial Order of the Sacred*

(L.S.) *Treasure, Minister of State for Foreign Affairs, Plenipotentiary of His Majesty the Emperor of Japan.*

Li Hung-Chang, *Plenipotentiary of His Majesty the Emperor of China, Senior Tutor to the Heir Apparent, Senior Grand Secretary of State, Minister-Superintendent of Trade for the Northern Ports of China, Viceroy of the Province of Chihli, and Earl of the First Rank.*

Li Ching-Fong, *Plenipotentiary of His Majesty the Emperor of China, Ex-Minister of the Diplomatic Service, of the Second Official Rank.*

Inclosure 2.

Imperial Proclamation, dated May 10, 1895.

(Translation.)

We recently, at the request of the Emperor of China, appointed Plenipotentiaries for the purpose of conferring with the Ambassadors sent by China, and of concluding with them a Treaty of Peace between the two Empires. Since then the Governments of the two Empires of Russia and Germany and of the French Republic, considering that the permanent possession of the ceded districts of the Feng-tien Peninsula by the Empire of Japan would be detrimental to the lasting peace of the Orient, have united in a simultaneous recommendation to our Government to refrain from holding those districts permanently.

Earnestly desirous as we always are for the maintenance of peace, nevertheless we were forced to commence hostilities against China for no other reason than our sincere desire to secure for the Orient an enduring peace. The Governments of the three Powers are, in offering their friendly recommendations, similarly actuated by the same desire, and we, out of our regard for peace, do not hesitate to accept their advice. Moreover, it is not our wish to cause suffering to our people, or to impede the progress of the national destiny by embroiling the Empire in new complications, and thereby imperilling the situation and retarding the restoration of peace.

China has already shown, by the conclusion of the Treaty of Peace, the sincerity of her repentance for her breach of faith with us, and has made manifest to the world our reasons and the object we had in view in waging war with that Empire.

Under these circumstances we do not consider that the honour and dignity of the Empire will be compromised by resorting to magnanimous measures, and by taking into consideration the general situation of affairs.

We have therefore accepted the advice of the friendly Powers, and have commanded our Government to reply to the Governments of the three Powers to that effect.

We have specially commanded our Government to negotiate with the Chinese Government respecting all arrangements for the return of the peninsular districts. The exchange of the ratifications of the Treaty of Peace has now been concluded, the friendly relations between the two Empires have been restored, and cordial relations with all other Powers have been strengthened.

We therefore command all our subjects to respect our will, to take into careful consideration the general situation, to be circumspect in all things, to avoid erroneous tendencies, and not to impair or thwart the high aspirations of our Empire.

(Imperial sign-manual.)

(Countersigned by all the Ministers of State.)

May 10, 1895.

INDEX OF SUBJECTS.

A

Abul Oghlan, ii. 504
Adams, J. Q., his opinion of the war, ii. 157 and *n.*
Ahluta, ii. 466
Aisin Gioro, 497
Aiyuli Palipata, 381, 382
Ak Musjid, ii. 447
Akoui, 696, 698
Akouta, 264-268
Aksakals, ii. 52
Aksu, ii. 445, 488
Albazin, 603
Alcock, Sir Rutherford, ii. 171, 185, 233, 239, 241, 429, 453, 454
Alihaya, 338, 342, 368
Alikouen, Count, 692
Allen, Mr., ii. 469
Alompra, 691
Alouhiya, 394
Altyshahr, *passim*
Amaral, Governor, ii. 193
Ama Wang, 550, 556, *passim*
Amazon-Guard, 137
Amherst, Lord, ii. 26-29
Amiot Père, quoted *passim*
Amour, 295
Amoy, *passim*
Amursana, 671 *et seq.*
Anderson, Dr., ii. 469
Anderson, Lieutenant, ii. 330 *n.*, 346
Annam, *passim*
"Annual Register," *passim*
Anshu, 185, 186
Anson, Major, ii. 325, 326 *n.*
Antchar, 311
Anting Gate, ii. 348
Apachi, 370
Apaoki, 266, 267
Apotsye, ii. 18
Arabs, 191
Argun, 320
Arikbuka, 327, 328, 357, 372
Arrow, the, attack on, ii. 258-265
Artchu, 342, 345, 348, 356
Asan, ii. 518

Ashburnham, Lieutenant-General, ii. 277
"Asiatic Researches," *passim*
Asiatic Society, transactions of, *passim*
Athalik Ghazi, ii. 448, 481
Attiret, 668
Audience, right of, ii. 460, 511, 512, 513
Australia, ii. 205
Avenger of Sorrow, ii. 245
Ayouka, 686, 687

B

Baber, Mr. Colborne, quoted *passim*
Bacle, ii. 499, 500
Bacninh, ii. 497, 498
Bactria, Greek kingdom of, 80
Baiji, 191
Baiju, 383, 384
Balfour, Captain G., ii. 162
Banners, the, 525 *n.*
"Barbarian Eye," a, ii. 67
Barhanuddin, ii. 52
Barhanuddin Khoja, 682, 683
Barker, a middy, ii. 283 and *n.*
Barkul, ii. 481
Bate, Captain, ii. 290
Batu, 320
Bayan (Hundred Eyes), 340-349, 355, 373-375, 378
Bayan (the second of name), 383
Beechy, ii. 394
Bell, English traveller, 51 *n.*
Belooches, ii. 396
Berkeley, Mr., ii. 112 *n.*
Bhamo, ii. 469
Bhatgaon, 703
Bisha, 184
"Black Crows," the, 217
Black Flags, ii. 495
Black Li, 464 *n.*
Blenheim Passage, ii. 280
Bocca Tigris, ii. 16, 272
Bogue, *passim*
Bogue Forts, ii. 96

INDEX OF SUBJECTS.

Bokhara, *passim*
Bonham, Mr. S. G., ii. 188, 250 and *n.*, 253, 263 *n.*
Bonnefoy, Captain, ii. 396, 402
Boojantai, 502
Books, burning of, 49
Bouvet, M., 643 *n.*
Bowlby, Mr., ii. 330, 333, 346
Bowring, Sir J., ii. 253 and *n.*, 254-259, 274
Brabazon, Captain, ii. 333 and *n.*, 346
Bremer, Sir G., ii. 91-94, 99
Bridges, Chinese, 54, 55
Brown, Colonel Horace, ii. 469, 470
Brown, General, ii. 395
Bruce, Sir F., ii. 311-313, 317, 319, 385, 416, 417, 425, 429
Budantsar, 290
Buddhism introduced into China, 104
Buddhists, persecution of, 148, 149
Burgevine, ii. 362, 363, 369, 377-381, 385, 387, 393-400
Burlinghame, Mr., ii. 452, 453
Burmah, 365-367, 689, 690 ; ii. 509
Burrell, Major-General, ii. 107 *n.*
Buzurg Khan, ii. 447, 448

C

Calcutta Review quoted, *passim*
California, Chinese emigration to, ii. 201, 206
Cambaluc, 357 and *n.*
Cambridge, H.R.H. Duke of, ii. 319 *n.*
Campbell, Col. Colin, ii. 127 *n.*, 128 *n.*
Canals, built by Yangti, 170 and *n.*
Canning, Lord, his letter, ii. 278
Cannons, mention of, 199
Canton, 352, 354 ; capture of, ii. 106 *et seq. passim*
Canton river, piracy on, ii. 463, 464
Capital moved from Singan to Honan, 96
Capuchin, 701
Cassim, Count, ii. 535 *et seq.*
Castiglione, 668
Cathay, 18 *n.*
Catherine of Russia, 722
Celestial Reason, ii. 11
Censors, Board of, ii. 5
Central Asia, affairs in, ii. 49-56, 173-177
Chahan Timour, 397
Chaho, 246
Chamen (probably Hainan), 237
Champa, 463
Chamuka, 292-295
Chan-chia-wan, ii. 338-340
Chandu, 357 *n.*

Chang dynasty, 8
Changai, 379
Changchi (1), Empress, 448, 449
Changchi (2), Empress, 469
Chang Chikia, 346-348, 352-355
Chang Ching Kong, 167
Changchow, 348 ; ii. 408-410
Changchun, his heroism, 336
Chang Chun Yuen, 639, *passim*
Changfoo, 443, 446
Chang Hienchong, 535
Chang Hofan, 353
Changju, 306
Chang Keen, his search for the Yuchi, 79, 80, 82
Changkiang, 348
Changki Pass, ii. 124
Changkua, 336-338
Chang Kwoliang, ii. 222-224, 238, 354, 356-360
Changnan, 73, 84, 89, 91. *See also* Singanfoo
Chang Pe, ii. 444
Changpelou, 106
Changsanchin, 412
Changsetao, 411
Changsha, ii. 223, 224
Changsse Ching, 397
Changsunchi, Empress, 180, 181
Changte, 122, 123
Changti, 5 *n.*
Changti (Han), 105
Changti, a child, 107
Changti, a general, 129
Changtsiun, 278
Changtu, 395
Changwen, 415
Chang Yao, ii. 485
Chang Yuchun, 413
Chang Yuliang, ii. 358-361, 365
Chankiang, ii. 127
Chantse, Prince, a minister, 23
Chanyang, Prince of, 117
Chanzu, ii. 384, 385
Chaochow, 351
Chaohien, 340
Chaohow, 5 ; arranges the official dress, *ibid.*
Chaoki, Prince of Twan, 262. *See* Hoeitsong (Sung)
Chao Maofa, 344 and *n.*, 345
Chaoti, 89, 90
Chaotsong, 218, 219
Chaotsou, 73
Chao Yuen, 253-255
Chapar, 383
Chapdelaine, M., ii. 264
Chapoo, ii. 125, 126
Chato, 217
Chayang, 341
Chechen, 457
Chefoo, ii. 473, 474 *n.*, 508

INDEX OF SUBJECTS.

Cheheng, 455
Chehou, 203
Chekiang, 215, *passim*
Cheking Tang, 229
Cheling Koan, 244
Chelun, 139
Chemen, battle of, 32
Chenching, 149
Chengchian, ii. 440
Chentsiei, 380, 381
Chentu, 112, 118, *passim*
Chepe Noyan, 300
Chepouching, 199
Chepsuntanpa, 611
Cherchen, 84
Chesin, 485, 487
Cheti, Han, 104
Chetsong Ming, 515
Chetsong (Sung), 261, 262
Chi, General, ii. 237
Chichi, 95
Chichow, 344
Chiking, National Ballads, translated by Dr. Legge, 14
China, reputation of, 16; origin of name, 17 *n*.
Chin-ah-Lin, ii. 244
Chincheng, Princess, 198
Chinchow, 363
Chinese, the, their antiquity, 1; their historical accuracy, 2; first settlers, 3; their early history, 15, 16; their religious beliefs, 19; their pride in Han dynasty, hence "sons of Han," 88; history one of Empire, not of people, 471, 472; superstition of, 655
Chinese Government, foreign policy of, ii. generally, Chapters I., II., IV., XI., XII., XIII., specially
Chinese language, ii. 153, 154
Chinese Repository, *passim*
Chinese Vitellius, a, 96
Ching Chelong, 555
Chingchi, Queen, 495
Ching Ching, able eunuch, 103
Ching, General, ii. 378, 379, 386, 388, 390, 395, 401, 405, 406, 408, 410
Chingkingchi, 158
Ching, Prince, ii. 513
Ching, principality, 132
Ching Tang, 8
Chingti (Han), 96
Ching Ting Wang (Chow), 30
Chingtse, princess of Tonquin, 98, 99
Chinhai, ii. 119
Chin Hongtsi, 211
Chinkiangfoo, ii. 126-128
Chinmao, 634
Chinnong, 3
Chinpasien, 166, 167
Chintang, 95
Chintien Pang, 442

Chintou, 3
Chintsong (Ming). *See* Wanleh
Chintsong (Sung), 248-251
Chintsong the Second (Sung), 258, 261
Chinwang, 452, 453
Chin Weiking, 487
Chinyong, 435
Chiseang, ii. 418, 423. *See* Tungche
Chitsong, 469-473
Choho, 412
Choki, 333. *See* Toutsong (Sung)
Cholin, ii. 373, 374
Chonghei, 300, 301
Chongli, 158, 159
Chongti (Han), 108
Chongtsong, 192, 193
Choo, principality, 43
Choo Yuen Chang, 391-397; expels Mongols, 398, 399. *See* Hongwou
Chouichow, 329
Chouihingkiukien, 170 *n*.
Choukin, the, 7, 9
Chousin, 9
Chouyang, 157
Chow Changling, ii. 183
Chow dynasty, 14, 36
Chowhing, 560
Chowhow (Prince), 83
Chowking, 562
Chowkow, 52
Chow Kwang Y., becomes Emperor Taitsong (Sung), 242
Chow Kwang Yn, 232-234, and *n*. *See* Taitsou (Sung)
Chowmodo, 616
Chow Pow, 114, 115
Chow Siang Wang, Prince of Tsin, 36, 38
Chowti (Song), 143, 144
Chow Wang, 65
Christians, 629; edict of 1692, 630-632, 656, 657
Christison, on opium, ii. 179 *n*.
Chu, ii. 385
Chu Changlo, 494, 495
Chuchow, 351; ii. 376
Chuen Gaisoowun, 184, 186
Chuenpee, ii. 82, 87
Chuguchak, ii. 483
Chukienchin, 455. *See* Hientsong (Ming)
Chukwang, 387
Chukwoko, 122, 123
Chukwoliang, 121
Chulahang, ii. 124
Chumze, ii. 388
Chun, 6, 7
Chun, Prince, ii. 200, 422, 423, 467, 505
Chung How, ii. 456-458, 489, 490, 491
Chungking, ii. 479

INDEX OF SUBJECTS.

Chungtsung, 519
Chungwan, 519-522, 526
Chung Wang, the hero of the Taepings, 237, 354-412
Chuning, Prince of. *See* Yesien
Chunking, 421
Chuntche, 549, 554 *et seq.*
Chuntche's widow, death of, 636
Chunti (Han), 109
Chunti (Mongol), 394 *et seq.*
Chuntsong, 208
Chunyuyue, 49
Chusan, ii. 92, 93, 171, 172 and *n.*, *passim*
Chutepala, 383, 384
Chutse, 207
Chuwen, 219-221
Chuwen, 431. *See* Kien Wenti
Chwang Siang Wang (Tsin), 38
Chwangtsong, 226. *See* Litsunhiu
Chwangtsou, 74
Clarendon, Lord, ii. 254, 255
Coleridge, 395
Comet, ii. 417
Confucius, his opinions of Laoutse, 20; his veneration for the past, 22; his disappointment and death, 23, 62; proclaimed King of Literature, 197; honour to him, 256, *passim*
Cook, Mr. Wingrove, ii. 279 *n.*, 307 *n.*
Coolie Corps, organization of, ii. 287, 325
Corea, 10, 183-185, 191, 265, 305, 331, 332, 363, 364, 484-489; ii. 515-519, 532
Cornwallis, the, ii. 142
Coromandel, steamer, ii. 280, 281
Courbet, Admiral, ii. 497
Cowper, Mr., kidnapped, ii. 269
Cow Tail, banner, 179
Cricket, the, ii. 395
"Crimson Eyebrows," the, 101 *n.*, 102-104
Crown of Chinese Emperors, 141 *n.*
Cushing, Mr. Caleb, ii. 163

D

D'Aguilar, Major-General, ii. 184
Dalai Lama, 599 *et seq.*
Dangan Pass, 525
Danyal, 665
Dardsha, 666, 667, 672
Datong, 486
Davatsi, 666, 667, 672, 674, 675
Davenport, Mr., ii. 472
David of Georgia, 321
Davis, Sir J., ii. 66, 135 *n.*, 153, 164, 171, 181, 184, 188
"Death-blow to Corrupt Doctrine," ii. 458

Degarchi, 704
Delamarre, history of Mings quoted *passim*
Dent, Mr., ii. 81
Derby, Lord, ii. 464
D'Herbelot, *passim*
Dilun Boldak, 292
Dolonor, 609
Doonghai, 503
Dorgun, Prince, 566. *See* Ama Wang
Douglas, Professor, quoted, 17 *n.*, *passim*
Drury, Admiral, ii. 21, 22
Dugenne, Colonel, ii. 499
Du Halde quoted, 51 *n.*, *passim*
Dutch, the, *passim*
Dutch Folly (fort), ii. 100, 266
Duvaleur, M., 719

E

East India Company, ii. 14, 15 *passim*, 65
Edkins, Dr., *passim*
Eleang, ii. 99, 102, 256 and *n.*
Elepoo, ii., 42, 134-136, 138, 139, 146
Eleuths, *passim*
Elgin, Earl of, ii. 276 and *n.*; negotiates Treaty of Tientsin, 278-310; returns to China, 319 *et seq.*
Elixir of Immortality, 87 *n.*
Ellenborough, Lord, ii. 124
Elliot, Admiral, ii. 96 *n.*
Elliot, Captain, ii. 72, 74, 75, 81, 83, 89 and *n.*, 110
Elliott, Commodore, ii. 279, 280
Ellis, Mr. Henry, ii. 28 *n.*
Empresses Dowager, the two, ii. 419 *et seq.*
Empress mother (Taoukwang), ii. 195
England, *passim*
English, the, 492 *n.*, 709 *passim*
English Government, only choices left for, ii. 546, 547
Erchu Jong, 163, 164
Escape Creek, affairs in, ii. 279
Eulchi, 52
Eunuchs, 115, *passim*
Europeans first to reach Canton, 468 *n.*, 490
Ever-Victorious Army, the, ii. 369, *passim*
E Wang, ii. 222 *n.*, 353

F

Famines, *passim*
Fanching, 338
Fanchong, 99, 100
Fane's Horse, ii. 338, 340 *n.*
Fang Chung Yen, 256, 257
Fangkua Chin, 388, 393, 394

INDEX OF SUBJECTS. 615

Fanguki, 42
Fanwenhu, 336
Fashiba (Japanese ruler), 483, 489
Fatshan, attack on foreigners at, ii. 180, 181
Fatshan channel, ii. 280-284
Fayuen, ii. 308, 309
Feast of Lanterns, *passim*
Feihou, 246
Ferry, M. Jules, ii. 493
Feyanku, 611-613, 616-618
Firefly the, ii. 391
First Regulo, 635, 636
Fishbourne, Captain, ii. 240
Fisher, Colonel, his "Narrative of Three Years' Service," ii. 307 *n*.
Fleming, Mr. G., English traveller, 51 *n*.
Fo, or Buddha, 104
Fohi, 3
Foley, Col. St. G., ii. 338 and *n*.
Fongching, 423, 428
Fongsian, 311
Fongtsiang, 409, 410
Fongy, skilful general, 100
Fontanier, M., ii. 457
Foochow, 351; ii. 206, 500
Fooshan, 484, 485
Fooshun, 506
Foreign merchants, surrender opium, ii. 81
Formosa, 595; ii. 143, 463, 501, 532
Forrester, Colonel, ii. 377
Fortune, Mr. R., ii. 180
Fou Kangan, 713
Foukien, a ruler, 138
Fouleang, 368
Fournier, M., 498
Fouta, 680-682, 692 *n*.
Fou Wang, Prince, 494, 495
Fou Wang, 548, 549
Fouyue, 9
France, ii. 287 *et seq.*; war with China, Chapter XX., 542, 543
Franco-Chinese, the, ii. 396
French Folly, fort, ii. 267
Fuhkien, 80, *passim*
Fung Shui, ii. 167
Fusaiquan, ii. 402
Fushan, ii. 381, 382
Fushan (Corea), ii. 516
Fuyuta, 423, 425, 426

G

Gabet, M., 709 *n*.; ii. 179
Gaiourcheritala, 416
Gaiti (Han), 96, 97
Galdan, 598-616; death of, 617
Galdan Chereng, 659 *n*., 664, 665
Ganhoa, Prince of, 470
Gankiai, a general, 145, 146

Ganking, ii. 225
Ganlo, 340
Ganlochan, 200-202
Ganpangyen, 516, 517
Ganti, Han, 105
Gan Wang, Chow, 30
Garnier, ii. 493
Gaubil, Père, 7, *passim*
Genghis Khan, his birth and birthplace, 292; meaning of name, 296; his wisdom, 297-308; death of, 309, 310
Genouilly, Admiral Rigault de, ii. 300
Gerard, M., ii. 543
Gerbillon, *passim*
Germany, ii., Chapter XXIV.
Gewgen, 139
Gibbon, his decline and fall, *passim*
Gill, Captain, quoted *passim*
Ginching, 157
Gingall, ii. 110
Gintekin, 286
Gintsong (Ming), 443
Ginyang Sieou, 256, 257
Gleig, "Life of Lord Auckland," ii. 120 *n*.
Golden Dragon, the, ii. 59, 61
Golden Mirror, the, 186
Golden River, 695 *et seq.*
Goloyken, Count, ii. 23
Goolo, 502
Goorkhas, 703-707
Gordon, General, ii., MS. account of Taeping rebellion, 220 *n*.; the new information in the "Life of Gordon," 406; in command of the Ever-Victorious Army, 383-414
Gough, Sir H., ii. 100-133
Gough's fort, ii. 290
Gou Wang, 152
Grandière, Admiral de la, ii. 494
Grant, Sir Hope, 319 and *n*., 319-352
Granville, Lord, ii. 253
Great Wall, the, 50, 51, *passim*
Green Water-lily, ii. 172
Grey, Lord, ii. 184
Gribble, Mr., ii. 87
Gros, Baron, ii. 287, 319
Grosvenor, Mr., ii. 472
Guchen, ii. 482
Guignes, de, the critic, opinion of, 15 *n*., *passim*
Guizot, M., 167
Gumti, ii. 482
Gunner, poor, case of, ii. 17
Gurkhan, 281
Gutzlaff, Mr., quoted *passim*
Gyalpo, 701

H

Hada, 502
Hadfield, Lieutenant, ii. 112

INDEX OF SUBJECTS.

Hahema, 462
Haichan, 382, 383
Haidsu, 527
Hailing, 291
Hailing, a general, ii. 130
Hainan, 237, 464 *n.*; ii. 56
Haiphong, ii. 494
Haiyen, ii. 483
Hakim Khan Torah, ii. 487
Hakkas, the, ii. 216 and *n.*
Hall, Captain, ii. 289 and *n.*
Hall of Ceremonies at Pekin, ii. 348
Hama, 389
Hami, 50, *passim*
Han Dynasty, 54 *et seq.*
Hanchen, 462, 463
Hanchong, 568
Hanchong Yen, 263
Hangchow, 348, 349; ii. 365, 369
Hanghai, 374
Hanki, 258
Hankow, ii. 224
Hanlin College, 200, 405
Hanoi, ii. 494
Hanpou, 264
Hansin, 56, 64
Hantan, 42
Hanyang, ii. 224
Harikari, 29
Hart, Sir R., ii. 427, 507, 546
Hay, Captain, ii. 192
Heang Yung, General, ii. 227
Hengan, ii. 42, 61
Hengchin, 569
Henkiang, 126
Heouchow, 119
Heouchu, 162
Herbert, Sir T., ii. 97
Hereditary Succession, first established in China, 8
Hermes, the, ii. 234
Hia Dynasty, 7
Hia, *passim*
Hiakoue, 345, 346
Hiangma, rebels, 467
Hiaohoei, 63
Hiaokong, Prince of Tsin, 32, 33
Hiaotsong, 283-285
Hiaotsong (Ming), 461
Hiao Wenti (Han), 68-70
Hienfung, Emperor, ii. 199-352, 415-418
Hienping, 301
Hienti (Han), 115, 116
Hientsong (Ming), 456-461
Hientsong (Tang), 209-211
Hien Wang (Chow), 32
Hienyang, 45
Hikin, a general, 143-145
Hingchang, 485
Hingking, 507
Hingteh, ii. 218

Hiongnou, or Huns, 40, 58, 77-82, 85, 92, 93, 95
Historians, Chinese, 2
Hitsong (Tang), 216, 217
Hitsong (Ming). *See* Tienki, 511
Hiuchi, 93
Hiuho, 215
Hiung Tingbi, 510, 511
Hiuy, siege of, 150
Hoaiho, river, 159
Hoai Yang, 99
Ho Aluk, ii. 245
Hoangfoukoue, 160
Hoangho, 5, 9; great overflow, 75; course of, 408 *n.*, *passim*
Hochau, 326, 327
Hochi, Empress, 112
Hochila, 383, 384
Hochow, 714
Hochun, ii. 237, 360
Hochung, 312
Hoeiti (Han), 63, 65
Hoeitsong, 262, 263, 265-270
Hohenlohe, Prince Victor, ii. 283 *n.*
Hohien, her intrigue, 93, 94
Hoki, 679
Hokiuping, 81, 82
Ho Koong Yay, ii. 28, 29
Hokwan, ii. 3, 4
Ho Kwang, 89, 91, 93, 94
Ho Kweitsin, ii. 361
Hola, 279, 280
Holland, Capt., ii. 381
Honan, 311
Honanta, 382
Hong, the, ii. 67
Hongchang, 414
Hongkong, ii. 87, 104, *passim*
Hongwou, 401-430
Hoochow, ii. 358
Hoorha, 503
Hootoo river, ii. 229
Hootooala, 497
Hoo Wang, ii. 366, 411
Hope, Admiral, ii. 313-316, 321, 326, 367, 373
Hoppo, ii. 4, *passim*
Hornby, Sir E., ii. 430
Horni, 606
Horses, rare in China, 11
Hosiwu, ii. 330
Hoti (Han), 100, 101
Hoti, last of Tsis, 154
Hotsin, 115
Houanti, 112, 113
Houcha, 301
Houchi, 161-163
Houlao, 144
Houliei, 127
Houlieoupi, 226
Hourhoei, 606, 607
Howard, Col., ii. 409

INDEX OF SUBJECTS.

Howorth, Sir H., quoted *passim*
Howqua's Folly, ii. 100
Hoyan, 391
Huart, M. Imbault, ii. 120 *n.*
Huc, Abbé, quoted, ii. 179, *passim*
Hué, ii. 13
Huen, 497, 498
Hung-tsiuen, Taeping leader, ii. 216 *et seq.*
Hushahu, 291, 302, 304
Hwaiking, ii. 229
Hwaiti, 133-135
Hwang Chung, ii. 433
Hwangti, 5 *n.*
Hwangti, 3; his vigour and beneficence, 4; divides Empire into provinces, 4; regulates calendar, builds roads and ships, 5
Hwanhiuen, 140
Hwan Wen, 138
Hwashana, ii. 301, 302, 312
Hweiti, 131-133
Hwei Wen Wang, 33, 35
Hwen Hu, 154
Hwifa, 502
Hwui Wang, ii. 303
Hwunho, 508
Hwuy Wang, ii. 37, 58, 341 *n.*
Hyacinth island, ii. 283
Hyson, ii. 388, 389, *passim*

I

Ides, 637 *n.*
Ignatieff, General, ii. 317; offers Russian cemetery, 348 *n.*
Ili, 680, 682, 685 *n.*; ii. 31, 449, 489-491
India, embassies from, 192, *passim*
Indian Mutiny, outbreak of, ii. 278
Ing Wang, last of the Tsins, 52
Irkutsk, ii. 30
Isdegard, 192
Ismaloff, M., 637, 638
Ito, Count, ii. 517

J

James, H. E. M., 51 *n.*
Jancigny, Col. de, ii. 120
Japan, 190, 360, 361; defeats Mongols, 362-364; in Formosa, ii. 463; war with China, 515-534; future policy, 545
Java, 372
Jehangir, ii. 52 *et seq.*
Jehol, 725, *passim*
Jesuits, *passim*
Jiaho, 497
Jiefan, 508

Jihchin, 204
Jinfou, 255
Jintsong (Sung), 252-257
Johnson, Mr. B., ii. 264
Jones, Admiral, ii. 319
Jones, ii. 397
Joui Song, 196
Juilin, ii. 349, and *n.*
Juji, 139. *See* Gewgen.
Julien, M. Stanislas, quoted *passim*
Jungaria, 598, *passim*
Juriats, 292
Jutse Yng, 95

K

Kabul Khan, 290, 291
Kachiaou, ii. 371
Kahding, ii. 373
Kahpoo, ii. 391
Kaidu, 347, 352
Kaifong, 249, 269, 270, 312, *passim*
Kaimow, 184
Kaiyuen, 509
Kajow, the, ii. 394, 399
Kalgan, ii. 31
Kamul. *See* Hami.
Kanchang, ii. 231
Kanchow, 560
Kanghi, 585-645
Kangti (Later Tsin), 137
Kang Wang, Prince, 271-273. *See* Kaotsong (Sung).
Kankiang, 343
Kanmala, 374
Kansuh, *passim*
Kanta, 303
Kan Wang, ii. 365
Kaochi (Tonquin), 99
Kaochun, 249, 253
Kaohin, 445, 446
Kao Hwan, 159
Kaoki, 304
Kaokia, 319
Kaoleang, battle of, 245
Kaoli. *See* Corea
Kaopien, 216
Kaotsong (Sung), 274-283
Kaotsong (Tang), 188-192
Kaotsou, 173-176
Kaou Meaou Temple, ii. 342
Kaoutson (Han). *See* Lieou Pang
Kao Wang (Chow), 30
Kaoyuen, 168
Karai, 697
Kara Khitay, 281
Karakoram, 320, *passim*
Karashar, 182, *passim*
Kashgar, 182; ii. 54, 446
Kashingfoo, ii. 409
Kearney, Major, ii. 283 and *n.*

INDEX OF SUBJECTS.

Keen Lung, 661-734
Kelung, ii. 502
Keng Kang, great general, 99
Keo, General, ii. 118 *n*.
Keppel, Commodore, his gallantry at Fatshan, ii. 282-285
Keraits, 293, 294, *passim*
Kerulon, 289, *passim*
Keshen, ii. 42, 43, 94-96; his treasure, 101 *n*., 207
Key, Captain, ii. 293
Keying, ii. 42, 136, 137, 150 *et seq*., 302, 303
Khakhan, 139
Khalkas, 597 *et seq*.
Khatmandu, 703, 704, *passim*
Khitans, 200, 225; end of, 268, *passim*
Khitay, 18 *n*.
Khoits, 666
Khojas, ii. 52, 53, 177
Khokand, 685; ii. 52
Khoten, 182; ii. 488
Khudayar Khan, ii. 175
Khulagu, 320
Ki, Empress, 399
Kiachi, Empress, 131
Kiahing, 349
Kiaking, ii. 1-36
Kiang, the two, ii. 84
Kianghung, ii. 510
Kiangnan, a province, forms kingdom of Wou, 25
Kiangping, 469
Kiangtsai, 580-584
Kianling, 129
Kiaochao, ii. 540-542
Kiaochi, 325
Kiassetao, 335, 339, 342, 343, 347
Kia Yu Koan, 415
Kichow, 525
Kiei Kiasse, 215
Kienkang, 136. *See* Nankin
Kien Moankiang, 368
Kiennie, 127
Kienning, 560
Kien Wang (Chow), 25
Kien Wenti (Ming), 431-440
Kikieou Koan, 246
Kilin, or pavilion, 88
Kim dynasty, 274-288, 299-315
Kim-Ok-Kiun, ii. 517
Kinchin Hoan, 559
Kincsay, 363
Kingchow, 532 *n*.
King's Dragoon Guards, ii. 340 *n*.
Kingti (Han), 72, 73
Kingti, last of the Leangs, 166
Kingti (Ming), 453
Kingtsong, 212
King Wang (Chow), 15
King Wang II. (Chow), 26
Kingyang, 413

Kinkou, 42
Kinling, 249
Kinlong, 564
Kinshun, General, ii. 480-482, 485
Kinsing, 426
Kintang, ii. 409
Kintsong (Sung), 269, 270
Kioachi. *See* Tonquin
Kipin, 96
Kipou, 56
Kirghiz, ii. 52, 176
Kirkham, Major, ii. 400
Kirong, 704
Kisiang, 474
Kiteouchan, 422
Kitse, King of Corea, 10
Kiuchessa, 554, 565
Kiukiang, ii. 225, 343
Kiukiu, Prince, 607
Kiunchin, 72
Kiungchow, ii. 481
Kiusiu, 363
Knei Hsiang, ii. 511
Koan-kia-tong, 410
Kobdo, 616, *passim*
Koeen, 426
Koko, 380
Kok Robat, ii. 177
Kolikisse, 379
Kolo, 515
Kongchang, 411
Kongsunyang, 32, 33
Kongsunyuen, 121
Kongti, last of the later Tsins, 141
Kongti (Soui), 171, 172
Kongti (Later Chow), 232
Kongtse Niang, 33
Kongtsong (Sung), 350
Kongyin, ii. 400
Kongyuta, 529
Kongyuta, 569
Korla, ii. 483
Kortsin tribe, 523, *passim*
Koshinga, 557 *et seq*.
Koukou, 397
Koutuktoo, 604
Kowlun, ii. 320
Kowshingha, ii. 519
Kowtsin, Prince of Yue, 29
Krusenstern, ii. 25
Kuava, 372
Kublai Khan, 321-335, 352, 355, 356-377
Kucha, 182, *passim*
Kuchu, 319
Kueiling, 559
Kukukoto, 613
Kuku Timour, 408
Kulangsu, ii. 117, 162
Kuli Beg, ii. 486-488
Kulitchi, 441
Kuneng, 435

INDEX OF SUBJECTS. 619

Kung, Prince, ii. 200, 341, 343, 345, 348, 349, 353, 385, 415, 418, 419, 422, 423, 425, 465, 467, 504, 505, 531
Kuriltai, 296 and *n*.
Kutan, 319
Kutang, 421
Kutula, 291
Kuyuk, 320, 321
Kwan fang, ii. 303
Kwang, Admiral, ii. 87
Kwangchaufu, ii. 543
Kwangsi, province, ii. 211, *passim*
Kwangsu (Emperor), ii. 510–512
Kwang Vouti, 96–100
Kwang Wang (Chow), 23
Kwang Wang, 351
Kwantsong (Sung), 287
Kwantung, 241, *passim*
Kweichow, *passim*
Kweiliang, ii. 301, 302, 312, 418
Kweiling, ii. 218
Kwei Wang, 558 *et seq.*
Kweiyang, 517
Kweyang, ii. 223
Kwo Sungtao, sent to Europe, ii. 474
Kwo Tsey, 201–206
Kwo Wei, 231

L

Ladrones, ii. 18 *et seq.*
Lagrenée, M. de, ii. 167, 168
Laguerre, Admiral, ii. 242, 243
Laichow, 529
Lange, M. de, 637 and *n*.
Langson, ii. 499
Lanho, 544
Lantachuen, ii. 444
Lantao, ii. 20
Lanyu, 428
Lao Chang, 71, 72
Laos, 381
Laoutse, the first religious reformer, 14, 15 ; his life, 20, 21
Lar Wang, ii. 406–408
Latsan Khan, 624
Lauture, Comte d'Escayrac de, quoted *passim*
Lay, Mr. G. T., ii. 162 *n*.
Lay, Mr. H. N., ii. 303, 424, 425
Leangki, 112, 113
Leang Kungfoo, ii. 416
Leaous. *See* Khitans
Leaousi, 532
Leaoutung, *passim*
Leeku, ii. 400, 401
Legaspi, 490 *n*.
Legge, Dr., tribute to, 14
Lessihin, 648
"Lettres Edifiantes," quoted *passim*

Lhasa, 625 ; *passim* ii.
Li Aidong, ii. 364
Liang Shihmei, ii. 437
Libraries, 406 *n*.
Lichimin, 174–176. *See* Taitsong
Lichingki, 196
Lichingkien, 183
Li Chingliang, 500
Li Ching Tong, 560
Li Chitsao, 493
Lichitsi, 184, 185
Li Chongsin, 236, 237
Li Chungwei, 426 and *n*.
Lieouchao, 150
Lieouchi, 70, 71
Lieouchi, 161, 162
Lieouchin, 124
Lieouchi Yuen, 231
Lieou Chun or Chunti, 152
Lieou Foutong, 392
Lieou Hiei, 115
Lieou Hiouen, 97, 98
Lieouho, 90, 91
Lieouju, 256
Lieoukangkong, 24
Lieouki, 69
Lieou Kichou, 219
Lieou Kieou. *See* Loo Choo
Lieouki Yuen, 244
Lieou Koukia, 381
Lieou Pang, Han, 52–64
Lieou Penti, 98
Lieoupi, 119–121
Lieou Pien. *See* Pienti
Lieou Pou Wei, 41
Lieousan, 136
Lieou Sieou, 96. *See* Kwang Vouti
Lieousiuen, 370
Lieousiun, 150
Lieousong, 133–136
Lieoutan, 89, 90
Lieoutsenie, 151
Lieouwen Hoan, 334–339 and *n*., 341
Lieouyao, 136
Lieouyong, 73
Lieouyu, 139–143
Lieouyuen, 133, 134
Lihan, Prince, 212
Li Han Chang, ii. 472
Li Hung Chang, ii. 354, 378 *et seq.* ; responsibility for Wangs, 406, 407, 473, 517, 529, 531, 535
Likang, 275
Likeyong, 217–221, 223, 224
Likin, ii. 506, *passim*
Li Kwangli, 84–86, 90
Likwangpi, 202, 203
Li Kweiching, 541
Liling, 90
Lilongki, 196
Limou, 41
Lin, Commissioner, ii. 79 *et seq.*, 203

INDEX OF SUBJECTS.

Lin's fort, ii. 289
Lingan, 342
Ling Hai Wang, 167
Lingkong, Prince of Chin, 24
Lingti (Han), 114
Ling Wang (Chow), 2, 25
Lin Limming pass, ii. 229
Lintin, ii. 20
Lin Tzuchin, ii. 434
Lin Weihe, ii. 85
Lin Yuchow, ii. 461
Liouy, 419
Lisin, a general, 43
Lisitai, ii. 471
Lisseh, 40, 41, 44, 46, 48, 49
Lissetao, 210
Lisseyuen, 228
Litan, Prince, 332
Literati, the great struggle with, 47–49
Litingchi, 336, 337, 351
Li Tseching, 534, 535, 544–547
Litsong, 318, 321
Litsongkou, 229
Litsunhiu, 224–227
Little Tibet, 199
Liuche, 279
Liuchi, Empress, a Chinese Lucretia Borgia, 65–68
Liukiang, 329
Liukin, 465
Liu Kintang, ii. 487, 488
Liusiun, 225
Liutsi, 467
Liuyen, 489
Livadia, treaty of, ii. 490
Li Wang, 11, 12
Li Wang (Chow), 31, 32
Liyang, 408, 409
Liyuen, Prince of Tang, 171–173. *See* Kaotsou (Tang)
Lob Nor, 624
Lobsang Kalsang, 700
Loch, Sir Henry (now Lord), ii. 293, 326 *n*., 330 *n*., 333 *et seq*.
Lockhart, Dr., ii. 186 *n*.
Loo, Prince of, 556
Loochow, 224
Lorcha, ii. 258 *n*.
Lou Chong Hien, 285
Loukai, 127
Loukang, 129
Loukia, 62
Loungsi, 182
Lousionfoo, 353
Lousun, 120
Low Mun, ii. 402, 403
Loyang, 14, 54, *passim*
Luc, Abbé de, ii. 346
Luwenti, 326
Ly Wenchong, 416

M

Macartney, Lord, 721; his family, 722; ambassador to Russia, *ibid*.; governor of Madras, 724; Hyder Ali's opinion of, 724; received by Emperor, 725
Macartney, Sir Halliday, of family of Earl Macartney, 722, ii. 390, 393; captures towns, 395; relations with Gordon, 406, 407; comes to Europe, 474; services to China, 492, 493
Macaulay, Mr. C., ii. 508 *n*.
Machi, 104
Madacou, 287, 288
Magay, ii. 240
Magelhaens, A., 656
Mahomed Ali, ii. 54, 175
Mahomedans, 714, *passim*
Mailla, Père, quoted, *passim*
Maitilipala, 424
Ma Julung, ii. 439 *et seq*.
Malin, 508
Malleson, Colonel, his "History of the Indian Mutiny" quoted, ii. 287 *n*.
Malmesbury, Lord, ii. 253
Mamien, 110
Manas, ii. 482 *et seq*.
Manchu family, princes of, ii. 32
Manchuria, *passim*
Manchus, 496 *et seq*.
Mangu, 321, 327
Manilla, 490, 491
Manning, Mr. T., 709 *n*., ii. 25 *n*.
Mansfield, Sir Wm., ii. 319 *n*.
Mansour, 470
Mansu, 457
Mantzu, ii. 432
Manwein, ii. 470
Maotetso, 144
Mapor, 383
Margary, Mr. R. A., ii. 469–472
Markham, Sir Clements, *passim*
Martineau des Chenez, Captain, ii. 294 *n*.
Ma Sien, ii. 437 *et seq*.
Ma Suchang, ii. 433
Mateng, 313
Ma Tesing, ii. 439 *et seq*.
Matsi, 591
Mawenchin, 462, 463
Ma Wenchu, his prayer, ii. 432
Mayaghur Akhun, ii. 449
Maye, 59
Mayuen, 102, 103
Meadows, Mr. T., *passim*
Medhurst, Dr., ii. 154, *passim*
Meenning, Prince, ii. 10. *See* Taoukwang
Mehe (or Mete), 58–61, 66, 71
Mekong, ii. 371
Mencius, 33, 34

INDEX OF SUBJECTS.

Metcho, 194
Metello, Don A., 656
Miaotze, 481, 693-698; ii. 58 *et seq.*
Michie, English traveller, 51 *n.*
Mien, Burmah, 365, *passim*
Millot, General, ii. 496
Min, river, ii. 500
Minchen, 421
Mines, in Yunnan, ii. 432
Mingan, 304
Mingti (Han), 102, 103, 228 *n.*
Mingti (Later Tsin), 135
Mingti (Song), 152
Mingtsong, 228 and *n.*
Mingyuchin, 397
Missionaries, *passim*
Momein, ii. 470
Monding, ii. 400
Mongchang, 493
Mongchi, Empress, 263
Mongchi, her valour, 158
Mongching, 135
Mongkong, 313, 317, 321
Mongkwan, eunuch-general, 132
Mongols, the, 289 *et seq.*
Mongtsin, 128
Montauban, General, ii. 319 *et seq.*
Morrison, Dr., ii. 153
Morrison, Mr. J. R., ii. 153 *n.*
Moti, 224, 225
Moti (later Tsin), 137
Moukden, 512, *passim*
Moungtien, 50; commits suicide, 52
Mounsey, Mr., quoted, 488 *n.*
Mouteng Yong, 473
Moutsong, 211
Moutsong, 478, 479
Mou Wang, 10, 11
Mouye, battle of, 9
Mow Wang, ii. 378 *et seq.*
Muchangah, ii. 201 and *n.*
Muhule, 305-307
Mundy, Mr. Walter, ii. 464

N

Nagel, General, ii. 30
Nahachu, 419, 428
Naimans, 294, 295
Nalsing, the brave Sikh, ii. 333 *n.*
Nanchao, 200
Nangan, 573
Nanhai, 62
Nanhiong, 573
Nankin, 136; capture of by Bayan, 345, 392; ii. 135, 136 *n., passim*
Nan Wang, 34, 36
Nanyang, 536
Nanyong, 351
Nanyuei, 69, 75
Napier, Lord, ii. 66 *et seq.*

Napier, Lord, of Magdala, ii. 320 *n.*, 325 *n.*, 339
Nasiuddin, 366
Nayakot, 707
Nayan, 373
Nepaul, 703 *et seq.*
Neuchang, 510
Newar, 703
New Dominion, ii. 489, 491
Nienfei, ii. 451
Nikan Wailan, 498, 499
Ninghia, 412, *passim*
Ningpo, ii. 95 *et seq.*
Ningtsong (Sung), 287, 288
Ningyuen, 518, 519
Ninkiassu, 312-314
Nipchu, treaty of, 636
Niuche, 264, *passim*
Niu Kien, ii. 138
Niutchin, Tartar tribe, 237
Niyamoho, 276, 277, 279
Nodzu, General, ii. 520
Noorhachu (Manchu), 496-522
Normann, Mr. de, ii. 330 *n.*, 335 *n.*, 346
Nouvelles des Missions Orientales, *passim*

O

Observatory, Imperial, 493
Ochterlony, Sir D., ii. 26
O'Conor, Sir N., ii. 510, 513
Official corruption, extent of, ii. 209, 210
Ogelen Eke, 292
Ogotai, 311
Oliphant, Mr., ii. 295
Olito, 276
Onon, 289
Opium, ii. 73 *et seq.* See Chapter V., 305
Ordus, the, 470 and *n.*, 474
Osborn, Captain Sherard, ii. 424, 425
Osborn-Lay flotilla, history of, ii. 424-426
Oshima, General, ii. 519
Ouchin, trains army of Wou, 25
Oufan, 426
Ouki, 31, 39
Oukimai, 278, 279
Oulan Poutong, 607
Oulo, 282-287
Ourga, 294, *passim*
Ousselou, 85
Ousun, 82 and *n.*, 91
Ouwei, 80

P

Pakba Lama, 358
Palikao, 546; ii. 340

INDEX OF SUBJECTS.

Palisades, the, 524
Palmerston, Lord, ii. 249 et seq.
Panchow, 102-104
Pandects of Yunglo, 405
Pang Wanching, ii. 320
Pankeng, 9
Panmei, 241, 246
Panpiao, 129
Panthays, ii. 443 n.
Panti, 675, 676
Paochiaou, ii. 354
Paokwen, 154
Paoting, 546
Paper-man mania, ii. 480
Papesifu, 380, 381
Parennin, P., 643 n.
Parker, Sir Wm., ii. 114 et seq.
Parkes, Sir Harry S., ii. 162 n.; 171, 258, 259 et seq.; 321 et seq.; 330 et seq.; 429, 501
Parliamentary Papers quoted, passim
Parthians, 107
Patachiaou, outside Soochow, ii. 396
Patan, 710
Patenotre, M., 501
Pauthier, M., quoted, 51 n.
Pawang, 53
Pears, Captain, ii. 128
Pearson, Dr., introduces vaccination, ii. 13
Peel, Captain W., ii. 287 n.
Pehan, 242, 245
Pehtang, ii. 321 et seq.
Peiho, ii. 299, 300, 315, 325
Pei Wang, ii. 222 n., 238, 239
Pekin, 357, 541; ii. 342 n., passim
Pekin Gazette, origin of, 228 n., quoted passim
Pe-leen-keaou, ii. 7
Pereira, 602
Perestralo, Raphael, 468 n.
Persia, 192
Pescadore islands, 596
Peter the Great, 637 and n.
Pet-pin, 409
Petsong, 167
Philippines, 491, 633
Phipps, Trooper, ii. 333, 346
Pidjam, ii. 486
Pienchow, 249
Pienkiao, treaty of, 178
Pienti, 115
Pigtail, the, origin of, 514 n.
Pihkwei, ii. 292, 294
Pingching, 60, 61
Pingki, 88, 89
Pingleang, 145
Pingti (Han), 90
Pingtseuen, battle of, ii. 60
Ping Wang, 13, 14
Pingwang, ii. 408
Pingyang, 135, 485

Pintiei, 264
Pirates. See Ladrones
Poki, 647
Polo, Marco, 349 n., 357 n., 360
Polo Timour, 396
Ponghu, 596
Popai, 481
Porcelain tower at Nankin, ii. 143
Porshu, 297
Port Arthur, ii. 520, 523, 533, 542
Portuguese, the, 490, 512 n., 513; ii. 5, passim
Pottinger, Sir H., ii. 114 n., 114-160, 179 n.
Poulin, 199
Poutiatine, Count, ii. 287
Pouyen Timour, 400
Power, Mr., ii. 287
Poyang, Lake, 343; ii. 225
Printing introduced, 228 n.
Prithi Narayan, 703
Probyn's Horse, ii. 339 and n.
Protet, Admiral, ii. 374

Q

Quanfuling, ii. 371
Quincey, De, 688 n.
Quinsan, ii. 361, 385 et seq.

R

Raffles, Sir Stamford, ii. 493
Red caps, 622
Reed, Mr., ii. 305
Remusat, M. de, his memoir on Laoutse, 21, passim
Rhodes, Colonel, ii. 409
Ricci, 492
Richards, Captain, ii. 128
Rigaud, Père, ii. 454
"Rising Sun." See Japan
Rivière, Captain, ii. 496
Rocher, M. E., ii. 493
Roger, Michel, 492
Roman Empire, or Great Thsin, 106
Rosebery, Lord, ii. 508
Ross, Rev. W., quoted passim
Russell, Lord J., ii. 317
Russia, 636-638, 717, 718; ii. 44, 45, 489-491, 533-537, 542, 544

S

Saghalien. See Amour
Sakya Muni, 104
Saichangah, ii. 207
St. Petersburg, treaty of, ii. 490
Salisbury, Lord, ii. 509
Saltoun, Lord, ii. 128

INDEX OF SUBJECTS. 623

Samarcand, 93
Samuka, 304, 305
Sanchuen, battle of, 254
Sankocheli, 410
Sankolinsin, ii. 231, 316, 336, 337, 338, 349 and *n.*
Sankoue, 118
Sanpou, a title, 182, 189, 190, 191, 204
Sanpu, the river, 181
Sansu, 195
Santajin, ii. 400 *et seq.*
Sarhoo Hill, 508
Sarimsak, 684 ; ii. 52
Satchar, 597
Savage, ii. 363
Schaal, Adam, 493
Schoedde, Major-General, ii. 128
Schufeldt, ii. 516
Scourges of God, 310
Scythians, 80. *See* Yuchi
Secret Societies, ii. 7 *et seq., passim*
Sembuen, 692
Senhouse, Sir Le F., ii. 110 *n.*
Serra, Padre, ii. 15, *passim*
Sesostris, 9
Sessaka, 647
Seven Khojas, the, ii. 177
Seward, Mr., ii. 399
Seymour, Sir M., ii. 264 *et seq.*
Shachow, 78
Shadwell, General, his "Life of Lord Clyde," *passim*
Shanghai, ii. 126 *et seq., passim*
Shanhaikwan, 519 and *n.*
Shansi, *passim*
Shantung, *passim*
Shapuntsai, ii. 191, 192
Shektsin, ii. 308, 309
Shengpao, ii. 376
Shen Paochen, ii. 412
Shensi, *passim*
She Wang, ii. 377
Shimonoseki, ii. 532 *et seq.*
Shiwei, 289
Shu Kofa, 550, 552
Siam, ii. 20, *passim*
Siangkong, Prince of Tsin, 13, 14
Siangtan, 562
Sianyang, siege of, 335-339
Siaoho, a strategist, 56, 58, 64
Siaolun, 154
Siaopaoyong, 154
Siaotaoching, 152, 153
Siaotse, or Vouti, 153
Siaoy, 154, 166
Siaoyen, 154, 156, 164, 165
Siberia, 615
Sichow. *See* Turfan
Sieh, futai, ii. 374, 375
Sienpi, 113, *passim*
Sikhs, ii. 345, 471
Sikiang, ii. 211

Simon, M., ii. 457
Sinchang, 483
Sinching, 122, 123
Singanfoo, 54, *passim*
Singtur, 367
Sinhing, 341
Sinho, ii. 323
Sining, 625
Sinlo, 183, 191
Sioochow, 552
Sioua, 266, 267
Sirikul, 684
Siuchow Hoei, 389
Siuenchow, 351
Siuenti, 91-94
Siuen Wang, 12
Siukan, 110
Si Wang, a human monster, 567-569
Sobo, ii. 448
Solon, ii. 448
Songari, 496
Songkoi, 371
Songlontsi, 380, 381
"Son of Heaven," a title of the Emperor, *passim*
Sonom, 696, 697
Sontay, ii. 497
Sony, 585
Soochow (Kiangsu), ii. 360 *et seq.*, 406, 407
Soodsu, 497
Soosung, ii. 354
Sopouomo, 81
Sosan, Prince, 602
Sotou, 367, 368
Souchow (Kansuh), ii. 480
Soui, Prince of, 167
Souou, 90, 93
Sourniama, 648, 649
Souting Fang, 191
Soutsin, 34
Soutsong, 201-203
Spaniards, the, 490, 491
Spark, the, ii. 464
Ssechaoy, 203
Ssemachangming, 138
Ssemachi, 123, 133
Ssemachong, 131
Ssemachow, 123, 124
Ssemachuen, 135
Ssemakwang, 256, 257
Ssematoan, 135
Ssematsien, historian, 86
Ssemay, 121
Ssemaye, 135
Ssemayen, 125
Sseseming, 202, 203
Stanton, Mr. V., ii. 93, 96
Staunton, Sir G., 721 *n.* ; ii. 27
Staveley, General, ii. 373 *et seq.*
Straubenzee, General van, ii. 288
Su, Viceroy, ii. 200 *et seq.*

Subutai, 312, 313
Sucama, 586
Suenti (Chin), 167
Suentsong, 214
Suentsong (Ming), 445-447
Su Hongju, 517
Suliman, Sultan, ii. 443 *n.*
Summer Palace, ii. 346 and *n.*, 347
Sund Fo, 704-707, 721
Sunghen, a pirate, 139, 140
Sungs, war with Mongols. See Chapter XXII.
Sung Tajin, ii. 21, 30, 31, 39
Sunhouchin, 346
Sunhow, 129, 130
Sunkiang, ii. 384, *passim*
Sunkiuen, 119-122
Supreme Court, established at Shanghai, ii. 429
Suranchi Beg, ii. 53
Sushuen, ii. 422
Suta, 398, 401, 408-414, 416, 425 *n.*
Sute, ii. 385
Su Weitsou, 438
Swinhoe, Mr. R., ii. 323 *n.*
Szchuen, 421 ; ii. 200, *passim*

T

Ta Chereng, 666
Ta Edin, ii. 389, 390
Taepings, meaning of name, ii. 221 *n.*, 211 *et seq.*
Tai, prince of, becomes Hiao Wenti, 68
Tai, 352
Taichow, 476
Taijuts, 292, 293
Taikia, 8
Taikok, ii. 97
Taipe, reputed progenitor of Japanese emperors, 29
Taitong, 538, 567 *passim*
Taitsan, ii. 374, 375 *passim*
Taitsong (Sung), 242-247
Taitsong (Manchu), 522-532
Taitsong the Great, 176-187
Taitsong the Second (Tang), 203, 204
Taitsou (Sung), 235-242
Taivou, 8
Taiwan. See Formosa, 241
Taiyuen, 202, 244, 538
Takee, ii. 379 *et seq.*
Taku forts, ii. 300, 315, 321
Talifoo, 323 ; ii. 434 *et seq.*
Taltanga, 678, 679
Tan, Prince, 42, 43
Tanchu, 6
Tang dynasty, 173 *et seq.*
Tang, prince of, 241
Tangku, ii. 324

Tangut. See Hia
Tang Wang, 556 *et seq.*
Tantaotsi, 144
Taou, 21
Taoukwang, Emperor, ii. 37-198
Taoutihking, the Bible of Taouism, 21
Tao Wang, Prince of Tsi, 66
Taoyenchi, 142
Tapp, Colonel, ii. 382, *et seq.*
Tarantchis, ii. 55, 174, 449
Tara Ussu, ii. 444
Tartars, the, 13, 24, *passim*. See Hiongnou
Tasutumor, 399
Tatakhun, 297
Tatungah, ii. 218
Tau, ii. 301
Tawan, 84
Tayan, ii. 360
Tchaohoei, 680-684 *n.*
Techow, 435
Tehshun Gate, ii. 342
Tekwang, 229
Temple, Captain, ii. 287
Temudar, 383
Temujin, a chief, killed, 292
Temujin, 292-295 ; becomes Genghis Khan, 296. See Genghis
Tengai, 124
Tenghien, 517
Tengri Maidan, 706
Teouman, 58
Teshu Lama, 704
Teshu Lumbo, 704, 706
Tesinga, ii. 356
Tetsong, 205-208
Texeiro, G. de, 512 *n.*
Thangho, 420 *et seq.*
Thiers, M., ii. 458
Thistle, outrage on, ii. 269 and *n.*
Thom, Mr. T., ii. 162 *n.*
Thompson, Mr., ii. 330 *n.*
Ti, or Emperor, meaning of, 5
Tianchow, India, 109
Tian Shan, *passim*
Tibet, first embassy to China, 181, 182, 189, 190, 194, 198, 199, 204, 385, 622 *et seq.*, 704 *et seq.* ; ii. 510
Ticounai, 280-284
Tiechi, 384
Tienki, 511 *et seq.*
Tientsin, treaty of, ii. 303 *et seq.*, 456-458, *passim*
Tien Wang, ii. 216-412
Tien Wang (the son), ii. 412
Tiki, 7
Timkowski, M., ii. 44
Timour, Mongol, 378-381
Timour Pouhoa, 398
Timour (Tamerlane), 399
Ting, Admiral, ii. 525-528
Tingan, 435

INDEX OF SUBJECTS.

Tinghai, ii. 93
Ting Wang (Chow), 23, 24
Tipa, 623
Tiping, 351, 353
Toanyng, 113
Togan, 365
Tohan Timour, 386; becomes Chunti, 387–389
Toksoun, ii. 485, 487
Tongchang, 435
Tongchi, Empress, 115
Tongcho, 115, 116
Tongchow, 577
Tonghou, 58, 59
Tong Kwekang, 602
Tong Wen Ping, 329
Tonquin, 371, 443
Topa, Prince of Wei, 140
Topasse of Wei, 143, 144
Topatao, 144–150
Topaze, attack on, ii. 46
Toto, 389
Toufachukineng, 127
Toufan, or Toupo, 181. *See* Tibet
Touho river, 231
Toukinei, or Turks, 168
Toula, 452
Toumon, 451, 452
Tourguts, 687
Tousong, 507, 508
Tou Timour, 385, 386
Toutsong, 333, 339, 340
Touyu, 128, 129
Triads, ii. 8, 212 and *n*., *passim*
Tronson, Captain, ii. 239
Troughton, case of, ii. 71
Tsai, Prince of I., ii. 334, *et seq*.
Tsaichau, 313
Tsai Tien, ii. 467
Tsangchi, 150
Tsaokingsong, 160
Tsaotsan, 66
Tsechow, 236
Tseedong, ii. 372
Tsekinghoan, 434
Tseng Kwofan, ii. 223 *et seq*.; death of, 461
Tseng Kwo-tsiuen, ii. 354 *et seq*.
Tseng, Marquis, ii. 490, 491, 498, 505, 506
Tsenka, 599
Tsen Yuying, ii. 437 *et seq*.
Tsetong, 161
Tse Wang Rabdan, 615, 619 *et seq*.
Tsi An, ii. 419, 423, 429, 466, 467, 491, 513, 514, *passim*
Tsi, Empress, 62
Tsi, Prince of, 33
Tsi, Princess, 65
Tsien Tang, river, 557
Tsiho, 147
Tsikikwang, 477

VOL. II.

Tsiking, 392
Tsin Chi Hwangti, 39–51
Tsin dynasty, 37 *et seq*.
Tsin, Prince of, 34, 35
Tsinchow, 411
Tsinghai gate, ii. 267
Tsingho, Prince of, 110, 503
Tsingpu, ii. 185, *passim*
Tsingzeyuen, 319
Tsinleang, 516
Tsin Vouti, 125–128, 130, 131
Tsinyang, 58
Tsinyuen, 409
Tsipoo, ii. 373
Tsi Thsi, Empress, ii. 419, 423, 429, 504
Tsiunpouy, 89
Tsiusima, 362
Tsi Wang, 230, 231
Tsongching, 523, 539–541
Tsongtse, 275, 276
Tso-pao-kuei, ii. 521
Tso Tsung Tang, ii. 354, 461, 480 *et seq*.
Tsowfang, 121
Tsowjoui, 120
Tsowmow, 123, 124
Tsowpi, 119–121
Tsowpin, 242
Tsow Tsow, 116, 117
Tsungli Yamen, ii. 415, *passim*
Tuduc, King, ii. 193, 494
Tula, 614
Tuli, 311, 312
Tungani, ii. 444, 449, *passim*
Tungche, 451–467
Tungchow, ii. 328, 329, 332–334
Tung Jungkwei, 514
Tung Wang, ii. 222 *n*., 236
Tunkwan, a strong fortress, 201, 310
Tunting, lake, 347
Turakina, 320 *n*.
Turfan, ii. 485, 487
Turner, Mr., ii. 18
Tutuka, 374
Tu Wensiu, ii. 437 *et seq*.
Twan Keng, General, 113, 114
Ty, Prince of Yen, 431 *et seq*.

U

United States, *passim*
Uriangkadai, 323–326, 331, 332, 365
Urmston, Mr., ii. 46
Urumtsi, ii. 481, 482
Ush Turfan, ii. 488
Usien, 313
Usuri, 496
Utubu, 302–307

2 S

INDEX OF SUBJECTS.

V

Vassal States, ii. 494
Verbiest, 493
Victoria, Queen, accession of, ii. 76 *n.*, 92 *n.*; 103, 104 *n.*; saves Chunghow, 491
Vincente, ii. 363
Voltaire, 719
Vouti (Han), 73-85; his death, 86, 87
Vouti Second (later Tsin), 131
Vouti (Song), 150, 151
Vouting, 9
Voutsong, 213, 214
Vox populi vox Dei, a Chinese saying for, 7

W

Wade, Sir T., ii. 162 *n.*, 304, 454 *et seq.*
Waiquaidong, ii. 395, 396
Waisso, ii. 409, 410
Wali Khan, ii. 446
Walipou, 269-271
Walker, Col., ii. 331 *n.*, 337
Walsham, Sir J., ii. 513
Wanganchi, 259; a Socialist, 260
Wangchin, 448-452
Wangchinou, 140
Wang Jwan, 396
Wangki, 123
Wangkien, 326
Wang Khan (Kerait), 294, 295
Wang Kua, 76-78
Wang Leangchin, 347
Wang Mang, 90-92, 94
Wang Pen, a general, 42-44
Wang Sanchen, 517
Wangs, the Taeping, ii. 406, 407
Wangsiun, 127, 130
Wangtien, 332 *n.*
Wangtong, North, ii. 100
Wang Tsien, his good advice, 43, 44
Wangyen, 264
Wang Yeouchi, 281
Wang Yuling, ii. 369
Wanlan, 698
Wanleh (Ming), 480-495
Wansiang, ii. 476, 477
Wanti, ii. 401
Ward, ii. 362 *et seq.*
Ward, Mr., ii. 317 and *n.*
Water-lily, the, ii. 7 *et seq.*
Weddell, Capt., 492 *n.*
Wei, *passim*
Weichan, 488
Wei Ching, 176
Weichoui, 178
Weichun, 104
Weigao, Prince, 104

Wei Hai Wei, ii. 520, 525, 544
Weiho, 138
Weijoui, 159, 160
Weiki, 285
Weili Wang (Chow), 30
Weising lottery, ii. 475
Wei Tsing, 80, 81
Wei Wang, Prince of Tsi, 31
Wencheng, princess, 182
Wenchow, 350
Wenti (Chin), 167
Wenti (Chow), 144, 146-148
Wen Tien Sang, 369
Wenti (Leang), 165
Wentsong, 212, 213
West river, ii. 211
Whampoa, 719; ii. 82, *passim*
Whittall, Mr., ii. 264
Williams, Dr. Wells, ii. 455, *passim*
Williamson, traveller, quoted, 51 *n.*, *passim*
Willis, Capt., ii. 323
Wittgenstein, Prince von, ii. 406
Wochow, 329
Wokong, ii. 395
Wolseley, Col. (now Lord), ii. 324 *n.*
Women rulers, 190, *passim*
Wongkadza, ii. 373
Woohoo, ii. 356
Woola, 502
Woosuen, ii. 221
Woosung, ii. 127, 478
Wou, ii. 241 *et seq.*
Wou, a great empress, 188-195
Wou, prince of, 26
Wou, state, family flee to Japan, 29
Wouchang, ii. 224, *passim*
Wou Sankweii, ii. 542-546, 550, 560, 586, 588, 593
Wou Shufan, 593
Wou Siang, ii. 543, 544
Woutsong, 465-468
Wou Wang, 9, 10
Wou Wang, of Tsin, 35
Wuchow, ii. 221
Wuhlahai, 297
Wurantai, ii. 219 and *n.*, 221
Wusieh, ii. 409, *passim*

X

Xanadu, 395. *See* Changtu
Xavier, Francis, 477 *n.*

Y

Yaik, 688
Yakoob Beg, ii. 448, 485, 486
Yaloo river, 185, 485; battle of, ii. 522
Yalookiang, 501

INDEX OF SUBJECTS. 627

Yamagata, Marshal, ii. 524
Yangabad, ii. 54
Yangchi, 132
Yangchow, 351
Yanghou, 130
Yang Inglong, 489
Yangkao, 506, 507
Yang Kien, 167–169
Yangsiun, 131
Yangti, 170, 171
Yangtsekiang, *passim*
Yangyeh, 245
Yang Yuko, ii. 441
Yankwang, 170. *See* Yangti
Yao, 5, 6
Yaochu, 322 *et seq.*
Yaoujin, ii. 61. *See* Miaotze
Yarkand, ii. 446, 488
Yaroslaf of Russia, 321
Yeh, Commissioner, ii. 254 *et seq.*
Yeh, General, ii. 519
Yeh-ho-na-la, Empress, ii. 511
Yeho, 510 *passim*
Yeliu Apaoki, 223, 225, 227
Yeliu Chutsai, 320, 322
Yeliu Hiuco, 247
Yeliu Liuko, 305
Yellow Bonnets, revolt of, 115
Yellow Caps, 622
Yellow Girdles, ii. 32
Yellow Jacket, origin of the, ii. 414 *n.*
Yen, 42, *passim*
Yenan, 534
Yenchow, 212, 556
Yenking, 303, 304
Yensong, 475
Yenta, 473 *et seq.*
Yeou Wang, 12, 13
Yesien, 450–453
Yesun Timcur, 384
Yihchoo. *See* Hienfung
Yih-hoh. *See* Prince Chun
Yih-hwui, ii. 200
Yihshan, ii. 113, *passim*
Yihsu. *See* Prince Kung
Yih-tah, ii. 200
Yissugei, father of Genghis, 291, 292
Ylawoua, 283
Ynchow, 312
Yngchang, 416

Yngtsong (Ming), 448, 449, 452, 454, 455
Yngtsong (Sung), 257
Ynti, 231, 232
Yochow, ii. 224
Yongchi, 344
Yongkiu, 201
Yonglo, 441–443
Younghusband, Captain, 51 *n.*
Ytsong, 215, 216
Yu, 6–8
Yu mountain, battle of, 312
Yuchen, 76
Yuchi, 79, 80; identified with Scythians, 80
Yuching, his despatch, ii. 296
Yue, Prince of, 29
Yuei, 74–76
Yueichow, 278
Yuen, 28
Yuen dynasty, 356
Yuen Chow, 115, 116
Yuenhiu, 161
Yuenkio, 161
Yuen Min Yuen, ii. 346, 347, *passim*
Yuenti, 94, 95
Yuenti (later Tsin), 167
Yueny, 162
Yuen Yingtai, 512
Yuenyng, 159
Yueti, 79. *See* Yuchi
Yukwang, 414
Yule, Colonel, quoted or referred to, 17 *n.*, *passim*
Yu Ngao, 559
Yungchang, 365
Yungching, 646–660
Yungping, 545
Yunnan, 84, 427 ; ii. 431 *et seq.*
Yunnanfoo, ii. 434 *et seq.*
Yusuf, ii. 53, 55
Yu Tsing Wang, 607
Ywang, 350

Z

Zaylon, 363
Zuhuruddin, ii. 177
Zeren Donduk, 624

RENEWALS: 691-4574

DATE DUE

MAY - 5			

GAYLORD PRINTED IN U.S.A.